Mozley and Whiteley's Law Dictionary

Herbert Newman Mozley, George Crispe Whiteley

MOZLEY AND WHITELEY'S

LAW DICTIONARY.

Second Edition

BY

LEONARD H. WEST, LL.D.,

OF THE UNIVERSITY OF LONDON; LATE TUTOR TO THE LAW SOCIETY; SOLICITOR;

AND

F. G. NEAVE, LL.D.,

OF THE UNIVERSITY OF LONDON; GOLD MEDALLIST; SOLICITOR.

LONDON:

BUTTERWORTH & CO., 12, BELL YARD, TEMPLE BAR, W.C.

Law Publishers.

TORONTO: THE CANADA LAW BOOK CO.

1904.

BRADBURY, AGNEW, & CO. LD., PRINTERS,
LONDON AND TONBRIDGE.

Rec. Oct. 17, 1904

PREFACE TO SECOND EDITION.

THIS Edition has been thoroughly revised and the work in part re-written. Since the publication of the First Edition a large number of Statutes of first-rate importance have been enacted. The provisions of these Statutes and the effect of numerous important judicial decisions have necessitated many alterations in the text.

It has been the object of the Editors to produce a Law Dictionary suitable for students and practitioners. Many Titles relating to obsolete subjects have been omitted; the matter relating to others has been compressed; Scotch and Indian words, for the most part, have been omitted. On the other hand, many new Titles have been introduced, and translations of Latin maxims and phrases have been added.

It is hoped that these alterations will render the book more practically useful.

LEONARD H. WEST.

F. G. NEAVE.

LONDON,
April, 1904.

EXTRACT FROM AUTHORS' PREFACE
TO FIRST EDITION.

THE primary object of this Work is to give an exposition of legal terms and phrases of past and present use. But, as the mere exposition of a word or phrase would often be barren and unsatisfactory, we have in many cases, especially when dealing with the legal terms of the present day, added an exposition of the law bearing upon the subject-matter of the Title.

To many of the Titles which have reference to the historical portions of the law, we have appended the law-Latin or Norman-French words which were used as their equivalents by the mediæval lawyers when writing (as they often did) in one or other of those languages respectively.

There is a difference in the practice of lexicographers as to the order of Titles consisting of more than one word. Some place the order according to the letters of the Title considered as a whole; others regulate the order by the letters of the first word. This being so, it may be as well to state that we have adopted the latter principle. Thus, " Writ of Right " has precedence over " Writer to the Signet," because " Writ " would precede " Writer " if the words stood alone, notwithstanding that " e " (the fifth letter in " writer ") precedes in the alphabet " o " (the first letter of " of ").

We append to this Preface a list of the abbreviations used in the course of the Book. We do not in this list include authorities which are referred to in full, nor any series of Legal Reports. A catalogue of all the Reports, with the abbreviations generally used to denote them, will be found under the Title " Reports," pp. 264—277. Moreover, the names of the principal current series are included in the Titles of the Dictionary.

LIST OF ABBREVIATIONS.

[*As to* REPORTS, *see pp.* 264—277.]

Arch. Crim. Plead. ....Archbold's Pleading Evidence and Practice in Criminal Cases.
Arnould, Mar. Ins. ....Arnould's Marine Insurance.
Aust. Jur. ....Austin on Jurisprudence.
Bell............................Scotch Dictionary, by Professor Robert Bell.
Bell, Wm. ....Scotch Dictionary, by William Bell.
Bl. ....Sir Wm. Blackstone's Commentaries.
Bouvier ....Bouvier's Law Dictionary.
Chit. Stat. ....Chitty's Statutes.
Coote, Eccl. Pract. ....Coote's Ecclesiastical Practice.
Coote, Prob. Pract. ....Coote's Probate Practice.
Cowel ....Cowel's Interpreter.
Cox & Saunders' Cr. Law ...Cox and Saunders on the Criminal Law Consolidation Acts.
Crump, Mar. Ins. ....Crump on Marine Insurance.
Dan. Ch. Pr. ....Daniell's Chancery Practice.
Encycl. Brit. ....Encyclopædia Britannica.
Eng. Encycl. ....English Encyclopædia.
Fawcett, L. & T. ....Fawcett's Law of Landlord and Tenant.
Hall Int. Law ....Hall's International Law.
Hallam, Const. Hist. ....Hallam's Constitutional History.
Haydn, Dict. Dates............Haydn's Dictionary of Dates.
Haynes' Eq. ....Haynes' Outlines of Equity.
Kerr's Act, Law ....Kerr's Action at Law.
May's Parl. Pract. ....May's Parliamentary Practice.
Oke's Mag. Syn. ....Oke's Magisterial Synopsis.
Paterson ....Paterson's Compendium.
Phillimore's Int. Law ....Phillimore's International Law.
Powell, Ev. ....Powell on Evidence.
Reg. Orig. ....Register of Original Writs.
Robson, Bkcy. ....Robson on Bankruptcy.
R. S. C. ....Rules of the Supreme Court.
Sm. Man. Eq. ....Smith's Manual of Equity.
Sm. Merc. Law ....Smith's Mercantile Law.
Snell ....Snell's Principles of Equity.
Steph. Com. ....Stephen's Commentaries.
Steph. Plead....................Stephen on Pleading.
Taylor on Evid..................Taylor's Law of Evidence.
T. L. ....Termes de la Ley, or Terms of the Law.
Toml. ....Tomlins' Law Dictionary.
Wh. Int..........................Wheaton's Elements of International Law.
Wms. Exors. ....Sir E. V. Williams on Executors.
Wms. P. P........................Joshua Williams on Personal Property.
Wms. R. P. ....Joshua Williams on Real Property.
Woodfall, L. & T...............Woodfall's Landlord and Tenant.
Yearly Practice..................The Yearly Supreme Court Practice.

A

CONCISE LAW DICTIONARY.

A 1. In shipping phraseology, this denotes a first-class vessel.

A and B lists. [See CONTRIBUTORY.]

A FORTIORI (from a stronger [reason]), all the more.

A MENSA ET THORO (from table and bed). [DIVORCE.]

A POSTERIORI. [A PRIORI.]

A PRIORI. An argument derived from considerations of an abstract character, or which have but a remote and possibly indirect (though none the less real) bearing upon the point under discussion, is called an argument *à priori;* whereas an argument derived from actual observation or other direct consideration is called an argument *à posteriori.*

A VERBIS LEGIS NON RECEDENDUM EST (from the words of the law there should not be any departure). A rule to be applied in the interpretation of Acts of parliament whereby the words of the statute are to be the primary guide for the court rather than the intention of the legislature.

A VINCULO MATRIMONII (from the bond of matrimony). [DIVORCE.]

AB ANTIQUO (from ancient time).

AB INITIO (from the beginning), specially in relation to trespass. If a man abuse an authority given him by the law, he becomes, by the common law, a trespasser *ab initio,* so that the legality of his first proceedings is vitiated by his subsequent illegal acts. See *Six Carpenters' Case,* 1 *Smith's Leading Cases.*

AB INTESTATO (from an intestate). Succession *ab intestato* means the succession to the property of a person dying intestate, *i.e.,* without a will.

ABACTORS (Lat. *Abactores;* from *ab* and *agere,* to lead away). Drivers away, or stealers of cattle not by one and one, but in great numbers at once.

ABANDONMENT. In marine insurance, abandonment is the act of cession, by which, in cases of the constructive total loss of a vessel or goods in the progress of a voyage, the owners give up to the insurers or underwriters what remains of the vessel or goods on condition of receiving the whole amount of insurance. Notice of such abandonment must be given to the underwriters within reasonable time after the loss. 2 *Steph. Com.* ; *Arnould's Marine Insurance.* [TOTAL LOSS.]

ABATEMENT sometimes signifies the act of the abator, and sometimes the result of the act to the thing abated.

1. *In commerce* it means a deduction made from payments due, and it is also used to denote the allowance sometimes made at the custom-house for damages received by goods in warehousing or during importation.

2. *Abatement amongst Creditors* takes place where the assets of a debtor are not sufficient to pay his creditors in full, so that they are compelled to share the assets in proportion to their debts.

3. *Abatement amongst Legatees* in like manner is enforced where there are not sufficient assets to pay the legacies in full. But pecuniary or general legacies abate proportionately before specific legacies and before demonstrative legacies until the fund out of

ABATEMENT—*continued.*

which the latter are payable is exhausted ; and in addition a legacy may be expressly preferred to another of the same class.

4. *Abatement of an Action or Suit* takes place when, from some supervenient cause, one of the parties thereto is no longer before the court ; so that, unless his place be supplied, there is no one to proceed therein.

Now by R. S. C., 1883 (Ord. XVII.), in case any devolution of the estate or title of any party to an action occurs during the action, the action shall not abate, but an order may be made for the successor in interest to be made a party to the action.

Of course this order can only be obtained provided the right of action itself survives.

5. *Abatement of Freehold* is where a person dies seised of an inheritance, and before the heir or devisee enters, a stranger, who has no right, makes entry and gets possession of the freehold : this entry is called an abatement, and he an abator. 3 *Steph. Com.* [DISSEISIN ; INTRUSION ; OUSTER.]

6. *Abatement, Pleas in,* are those which show ground for quashing the proceedings. They do not dispute the cause of action, but only point out an error, unconnected with the merits of the case, *e.g.,* misnaming or misdescription of parties, which unless remedied is fatal to the suit. Now almost entirely obsolete owing to the large powers of amendment given in civil proceedings by the Judicature Acts (see Ord. XXI. r. 20), and in criminal proceedings by 7 Geo. 4, c. 64 ; 14 & 15 Vict. c. 100, s. 1.

7. *Abatement of Nuisances, i.e.,* their removal. A self-remedy allowed to one injured by a nuisance. The abatement must be done peaceably and without causing unnecessary damage.

ABBREVIATURE. A short draft.

ABDUCTION. The leading away of any person. More strictly the taking away of a wife from her husband, a child from its parent, a ward from her guardian and a female servant from her master. In some cases the act is criminal, and in others a civil action will lie against the aggressor ; and see 24 & 25 Vict. c. 100, and Criminal Law Amendment Act, 1885, as to girls under the ages of 16 and 21 years respectively. 4 *Steph. Com.* [HEIRESS.]

ABEARANCE. Behaviour. [GOOD BEHAVIOUR.]

ABET (Fr. *Bouter ;* Lat. *Impellere, Excitare*). To encourage or set on. Thus an abettor of a crime is one who, being present either actually or constructively, aids in the commission of the offence. 4 *Steph. Com.* [ACCESSORY.]

ABEYANCE (probably from the Fr. *Bayer,* to expect). An estate is said to be in *abeyance* when there is no person *in esse* in whom it can vest ; though the law considers it as always potentially existing, and ready to vest whenever a proper owner appears. This estate has also been called *in nubibus* (in the clouds), and *in gremio legis* (in the bosom of the law). The fee simple of the glebe of a parson is said to be in abeyance. 1 *Steph. Com.*

ABJURATION, OATH OF. The oath formerly required to be taken by every person holding any office in the state ; and whereby the person taking it *abjured* any allegiance to the Pretender. Abolished. See 31 & 32 Vict. c. 72, and 34 & 35 *Vict.* c. 48 ; 2 *Steph. Com.*

ABJURATION OF THE REALM. [SANCTUARY.]

ABORTION. A miscarriage, or the premature expulsion of the contents of the womb before the term of gestation is completed. To procure abortion is a felony. See 24 & 25 *Vict.* c. 100, s. 58.

ABRIDGMENT. A short comprehensive treatise or digest of the law, *e.g.,* the works of Fitzherbert, Brooke and Rolle, Viner, Comyns and Bacon. 1 *Steph. Com.*

ABROGATE. To annul or repeal.

ABSCOND. To go out of the jurisdiction of the courts, or to conceal oneself to avoid legal process. It is an act of bankruptcy (*q.v.*).

ABSCONDING DEBTOR. See 32 & 33 Vict. c. 62, and MESNE PROCESS.

ABSENCE. 1. Non-appearance of a party to an action.

2. Beyond seas of party entitled to sue, now no longer a disability ; but such absence of party liable to be sued generally gives party entitled an extension of time for suing.

3. Unheard of for seven years, a presumption of death ; absence of husband or wife for seven years is under certain circumstances a defence to an indictment for bigamy.

ABSOLUTE. Complete, unconditional. A rule or order absolute is one which is complete and can be put into force at once, in contradistinction to a rule or order *nisi*, which is made on the application of one party only (*ex parte*) to be made absolute unless the other party appear and show cause why it should not be made absolute. Such applications can no longer be made except in certain cases. See *R. S. C.* 1883, *Ord. LII. r.* 2.

ABSQUE IMPETITIONE VASTI. [WITHOUT IMPEACHMENT OF WASTE.]

ABSTRACT OF TITLE. A summary or abridgment of the deeds constituting the title to an estate, furnished by a vendor or mortgagor to an intending purchaser or mortgagee. This is usually perused by the purchaser's or mortgagee's solicitor and verified by an examination of the original deeds. This is followed by requisitions on title (*q.v.*). *Greenwood's Manual of Conveyancing.*

An *Abstract-in-Chief* is one made direct from a document and not from a mere recital of it.

ABUSE OF PROCESS is the malicious and improper use of some regular legal proceeding to obtain some advantage over an opponent.

ABUTTALS, or **ABBUTTALS** (Fr. *Abutter*). The buttings or boundings of lands, showing to what other lands, highways or places they belong, or are abutting.

AC ETIAM (and also). A clause giving the real cause of action and following a fictitious allegation which was introduced for the purpose of giving to the Court of Queen's Bench a civil jurisdiction which did not properly belong to it. 3 *Steph. Com.* [BILL OF MIDDLESEX.]

ACCEDAS AD CURIAM (that you go to court). A writ that lay for one who had received a false judgment in a court-baron or hundred-court, and issued out of Chancery to the sheriff, who was thereby directed to make a record of the judgment and return it to the King's Bench or Common Pleas, that its validity in point of law might be there inquired into. 3 *Steph. Com.*

ACCELERATION. The hastening of the vesting in possession of a reversion or remainder by the determination of the prior particular estate by surrender, etc., before its natural termination.

ACCEPTANCE. "A thing in good part, and as it were a kind of agreeing to some act done before, which might have been undone and avoided if such acceptance had not been." *Cowel.*

1. If, for instance, a lease for more than three years be made verbally, acceptance of rent from the lessee if he obtain possession will create a tenancy from year to year binding upon the lessor; and on the same principle, acceptance of rent may confirm a lease, which has been put an end to by notice, the acceptance here operating as a withdrawal, waiver or abandonment of the notice.

2. As to what is a sufficient acceptance of goods under a contract of sale of goods of the value of ten pounds or upwards, see Sale of Goods Act, 1893, s. 4 (3).

ACCEPTANCE OF A BILL is an engagement by the drawee (*i.e.*, the person on whom the bill is drawn) to pay the bill according to the tenor of his acceptance. After the acceptance the drawee is called the *acceptor.* The acceptance must be in writing, and it is usually made by the acceptor's writing the word "accepted" across the bill and signing his name. See *Bills of Exch. Act,* 1882, *s.* 17; 2 *Steph. Com.*

ACCEPTANCE SUPRA PROTEST, or an *acceptance for honour,* is an acceptance of a bill for the honour of the drawer or an indorser, when the drawee refuses to accept. It is made by some friend of the drawer or indorser to prevent the bill being sent back upon him as unpaid, after a protest (*supra protest*) has been drawn up declaratory of its dishonour by the drawee. This operates not as an engagement to pay absolutely, but only to pay in the event of its being presented to, and dishonoured by, the drawee when it arrives at maturity, on its then being protested for non-payment, and afterwards duly presented for payment to the "acceptor for honour." The latter then becomes absolutely liable to the holder, but, on the other hand, has a right of recourse against the party for whose honour he accepted it, or any party who may be antecedent to him in the series of names. 2 *Steph. Com.* See *Bills of Exch. Act,* 1882, *ss.* 65—8.

ACCEPTING SERVICE is where the solicitor for a defendant on his behalf accepts service of a writ or other process of a court, and undertakes to

ACCEPTING SERVICE—*continued.*
appear, so as to avoid the necessity of such writ or process being served on his client. [SERVICE, 3.] This undertaking the courts will enforce, if necessary, by attachment. [ATTACHMENT.]

ACCEPTOR. A person who accepts a bill of exchange. [ACCEPTANCE OF A BILL; BILL OF EXCHANGE.]

ACCESS, approach, or the means of approaching. The presumption of a child's legitimacy is rebutted if it be shown that the husband had not access to his wife within such a period of time before the birth as admits of his having been the father; but neither husband nor wife may give evidence to prove non-access.

ACCESSION. 1. A mode of acquiring property by right of occupancy, founded on the civil law; whereby the original owner of anything which receives an accession by natural or artificial means, as by the growth of vegetables, etc., the pregnancy of animals, etc., is entitled to it under such its state of improvement: but if the thing itself, by such operation, is changed into a different species, as by making wine, oil, or bread, out of another's grapes, olives, or wheat, it belongs to the new operator; who is only to make a satisfaction to the former proprietor for the materials which he has so converted. 2 *Bl.* 404; 2 *Steph. Com.*

2. In international law, accession is occasionally used as a technical expression denoting the absolute or conditional acceptance, by one or several states, of a treaty already concluded between other sovereignties. *Calvo.*

3. The word means also the coming of a king or queen to the throne on the death of the prior occupant thereof.

ACCESSORY is he who is not the chief actor in an offence, nor present at its performance, but is some way concerned therein, either *before* or *after* the fact committed. An accessory *before* the fact is one who being absent at the time of the crime committed, doth yet procure, counsel, or command another to commit a crime. An accessory *after* the fact is he that receives, favours, aids, assists, or comforts any man that hath done any murder or felony, whereof he hath knowledge; as by furnishing means of escape or concealment, or assisting to rescue or protect him. 4 *Steph. Com.*; *Arch. Crim. Pleading.*

ACCESSORY TO ADULTERY. The Divorce Court cannot decree a divorce, if the petitioner has been accessory to, or connived at, the adultery; 20 & 21 *Vict. c.* 85, *ss.* 29, 31. The word "accessory" was introduced into this statute for the purpose of noticing a more positive and actual aid in the adultery than is included in the word "connivance." 2 *Steph. Com.* [COLLUSION; CONNIVANCE.]

ACCIDENT. As a ground for seeking the assistance of a court of equity, accident means not merely inevitable casualty, or the act of God, or, as it is called, *vis major*, but also such unforeseen events, misfortunes, losses, acts, or omissions as are not the result of negligence or misconduct.

Against the consequences arising from the accidental loss, or destruction, of a deed, the courts will grant relief. In the case of the loss of a negotiable instrument, see Bills of Exch. Act, 1882, ss. 69, 70. *Ashburner's Equity.*

ACCOMMODATION BILL. A bill to which a person has put his name, whether as drawer, acceptor, or indorser, without consideration, for the purpose of accommodating some other party who desires to raise money on it. The accommodation party thus becoming liable upon it, may, if compelled to pay, have his remedy over against the person accommodated. [ACCEPTANCE OF A BILL; BILL OF EXCHANGE.]

ACCOMMODATION LAND. Land bought by a builder or speculator who erects houses thereon and then leases portions thereof upon an improved ground rent.

ACCOMMODATION WORKS. Works such as gates, bridges, etc., which a railway company is required to make and maintain for the accommodation of the owners and occupiers of land adjoining the railway. 8 *Vict. c.* 20, *s.* 68.

ACCORD. An agreement between the party injuring and the party injured, by reason of any trespass or breach of contract; which when performed is a bar to all actions on account of the injury, the party injured having thereby received satisfaction for, or redress of, the injury. [SATISFACTION.]

ACCOUNT, or **ACCOMPT.** 1. Open, or current: Where the balance is not struck or is not accepted by all the parties.

ACCOUNT, or ACCOMPT—*continued.*

Formerly an "action of account" lay to obtain a statement, but now recourse is usually had to the Chancery Division where the account may be obtained summarily under Ord. XV.

2. Stated : An account no longer open or current, but closed by the statement, agreed to by both the parties, of a balance due to the one or other of them. Action will usually be brought thereon in the King's Bench Division and the writ specially endorsed enabling the plaintiff in case of defendant appearing to take summary proceedings by summons under Ord. XIV.

3. Settled : Where discharged.

ACCOUNT DUTY. Similar to probate duty but payable in respect of property given during lifetime, *e.g., donatio mortis causa,* or gift *inter vivos* within twelve months before death. Now superseded by estate duty (*q.v.*).

ACCOUNTABLE RECEIPT. A written acknowledgment of the receipt of money or goods to be accounted for by the receiver.

ACCOUNTANT - GENERAL. [PAY-MASTER-GENERAL.]

ACCRETION. Generally synonymous with accruer. [ACCRUE.] But the word is specially used to denote an accession to an owner of land on the sea shore, or fresh land recovered from the sea by alluvion or dereliction. 1 *Steph. Com.* [ALLUVION ; DERELICTION.]

ACCROACH, or ACCROCHE (Fr. *accrocher,* to fix or hook), means attempting to exercise royal power. 4 *Steph. Com.*

ACCRUE. *Lit.* to grow to, as interest accrues to principal. It also means to arise, as when a cause of action is said not to have accrued to the plaintiff within six years, *actio non accrevit infra sex annos.*

ACCUMULATION. When the interest of a fund, instead of being paid over to some person or persons, is itself invested as often as it accrues, so as to be reserved for the benefit of some person or persons in the future, the income is said to be accumulated. Restrictions are imposed upon accumulation, partly by the rules against perpetuities [PERPETUITY], and partly by Thellusson Act (39 & 40 Geo. 3, c. 98) and Accumulations Act, 1892. 1 *Steph. Com.*; 2 *Steph. Com.* [THELLUSSON ACT.]

ACCUMULATIVE JUDGMENT OR SENTENCE. A sentence passed on a person already under sentence for a crime ; the second sentence to commence after the expiration of the first and not to run concurrently.

ACKNOWLEDGMENT. 1. Of debt, if in writing signed by debtor or his agent, will prevent Statutes of Limitation from running : 9 Geo. 4, c. 14, s. 1, and 19 & 20 Vict. c. 97, s. 13.

2. Of signature to a will by testator. If the signature be not made in the presence of two witnesses its subsequent acknowledgment in their presence will satisfy the Wills Act, 1837.

ACKNOWLEDGMENT OF DEEDS, BY MARRIED WOMEN. The method provided by 3 & 4 Will. 4, c. 74, as amended by the Conveyancing Act, 1882, for ascertaining and verifying the consent of a married woman to a conveyance of her real property if it is not her separate property : to give validity to which instruments, the wife must be examined separately and apart from her husband by a judge or a commissioner appointed for the purpose, touching her knowledge of the contents of the deed, and her consent thereto, and must declare the same to have been freely and voluntarily executed by her, a memorandum thereof being endorsed on the deed. 1 *Steph. Com.*

ACKNOWLEDGMENT OF RIGHT TO PRODUCTION OF DEEDS, introduced by Conveyancing Act, 1881, s. 9, in place of former covenants, where title deeds related to properties held or conveyed to different owners. If a vendor retains any portion of the property to which the deeds relate he is entitled to retain the deeds, and will give to the purchaser an acknowledgment of right to production and to copies, and an undertaking for safe custody. If the whole property is disposed of but to two or more separate purchasers, the largest purchaser will take the deeds and give acknowledgment and undertaking. 1 *Steph. Com.*

ACQUIESCENCE. Consent either express or implied. A means by which a right may be lost, though the party entitled thereto might have asserted it successfully had he presented his claim in due time.

ACQUISITIVE PRESCRIPTION. Prescription whereby a right is acquired, otherwise called positive prescription. [PRESCRIPTION.]

ACQUITTAL (Fr. *Acquitter*; Lat. *Acquietare*, to discharge, or keep in quiet). 1. A deliverance, and setting free from the suspicion or guilt of an offence. Thus he that is discharged of a criminal offence by judgment, on its merits, if subsequently charged with the same, or legally the same offence, he may plead *autrefois acquit*, or, as more usual, raise the defence under the general plea of " not guilty." 4 *Steph. Com.*
2. To be free from entries and molestations by a superior lord for services issuing out of lands.

ACQUITTANCE. A discharge in writing of a sum of money, or other duty which ought to be paid or done. If under seal, it is called a release.

ACT IN PAIS (Fr. *Pais*, or *Pays*, country). An act done " in the country," *e.g.*, an ordinary conveyance, as distinguished from an act done in court, which is a matter of record. 1 *Steph. Com.* [MATTER IN PAIS.]

ACT OF ATTAINDER. An Act of parliament passed for attainting a person, or rendering a person liable to the consequences of attainder. [ATTAINDER.]

ACT OF BANKRUPTCY. An act or event done or suffered by a person, which would be available within three months as the ground for a petition by a creditor or creditors to the amount of 50*l.*, for a receiving order against the debtor's estate. Enumerated in Bankruptcy Act, 1883 (46 & 47 Vict. c. 52), and Bankruptcy Act, 1890 (53 & 54 Vict. c. 71). 2 *Steph. Com.; Robson Bkcy.* [ADJUDICATION; BANKRUPT.]

ACT OF GOD. A phrase used to define those occurrences which man has no power to foresee or prevent : a destructive storm, for instance, or a sudden and unforeseen death [*cf.* VIS MAJOR].

ACT OF GRACE. An Act of parliament proceeding from the Crown in the first instance instead of receiving royal assent after passing through parliament, *e.g.*, an Act at the commencement of a reign granting pardons. 2 *Steph. Com.* In Scotland an Act so termed was passed in 1696 for providing maintenance for debtors imprisoned by their creditors.

ACT OF INDEMNITY. A statute passed for the protection of those who have committed some illegal act, subjecting them to penalties. An annual Indemnity Act used to pass for the protection of those who had acted in certain capacities without the necessary qualification ; as justices, for instance, without taking the oaths. Indemnity Acts have also been passed after a suspension of the Habeas Corpus Acts (57 Geo. 3, cc. 3, 55 ; 58 Geo. 3, c. 6), and to protect a ministry who have issued an order in council not justifiable in law. 2 *Steph. Com.; Dicey's Law of the Constitution.*

ACT OF LAW. An event happening otherwise than by act of party. Specially title so acquired. Thus the eldest son of an intestate succeeds to his father's real estate by act of law. Also remedy given by law, viz., retainer by executor, or remitter (*q.r.*).

ACT OF PARLIAMENT. A statute ; a law made by the legislature, the king, lords, and commons in parliament assembled.
Acts of parliament are of three kinds :
 1. " Public."
 2. " Local or special."
 3. " Private or personal."

ACT OF SETTLEMENT (12 & 13 Will. 3, c. 2), by which the crown was settled (on the death of Queen Anne) upon Sophia, Electress of Hanover, and the heirs of her body being Protestants. 2 *Steph. Com.*

ACT OF SUPREMACY (1 Eliz. c. 1), by which the supremacy of the Crown in matters ecclesiastical was established. 2 *Steph. Com.*

ACT OF UNIFORMITY (14 Chas. 2, c. 14). An Act regulating public worship. See also 35 & 36 Vict. c. 37, and Public Worship Regulation Act, 1874 (37 & 38 Vict. c. 85). 2 *Steph. Com.*

ACTIO PERSONALIS MORITUR CUM PERSONA. [ACTIONS PERSONAL.]

ACTION (Lat. *Actio*). The lawful demand of one's right. It is defined by Justinian, *jus prosequendi in judicio quod alicui debetur;* a right of prosecuting, in a judicial proceeding, that which is due to any one. Now generally used to denote the actual pursuit of this right, or the means of its exercise. In this view, *i.e.*, with reference to the right enforced or redress obtained, actions are divided into *civil* and *penal*, and also into *real, personal, and mixed.* 3 *Steph. Com.* [ACTIONS CIVIL AND PENAL ; ACTIONS MIXED ; ACTIONS REAL AND PERSONAL.]

ACTION OF THE WRIT. A phrase used when the defendant pleaded some matter by which he showed that the plaintiff had no cause to have the writ he brought, though it might well be that he might have another writ or action for the same matter. Now obsolete.

ACTION ON THE CASE (Lat. *Actio super casum*). A remedy, given by statute Westminster the Second, c. 24, for wrongs and injuries committed without immediate violence, and so called because commenced by newly-framed writs in which the plaintiff's whole case or cause of complaint was set forth at length. 3 *Steph. Com.* [CASE.]

ACTIONES NOMINATÆ (named actions). Forms of action previous to the statute 13 Edw. 1 (West. 2nd), c. 24, prescribed for redressing those wrongs which most usually occurred, as opposed to actions on the case. [ACTION ON THE CASE.]

ACTIONS ANCESTRAL, POSSESSORY AND DROITURAL, were actions for the recovery of land, distinguished with reference to the title relied upon by the plaintiff or demandant ; as in an action *ancestral*, the seisin or possession of his ancestor ; in a *possessory* action, his own possession or seisin.

An action possessory is sometimes distinguished from an action droitural, inasmuch as (in theory, at least) the object of the former is to ascertain the right of possession ; and that of the latter the right of property. 3 *Steph. Com.* [ACTIONS REAL AND PERSONAL.]

ACTIONS CIVIL AND PENAL. A *civil* action is brought to enforce a civil right merely, as if a man seek to recover a sum of money formerly lent, etc. A *penal* action aims at some penalty or punishment in the party sued, be it corporal or pecuniary ; specially an action brought for recovery of the penalties given by statute. [QUI TAM ACTION.] *Criminal* actions, usually styled prosecutions, are of a public nature, in the name of the king, against one or more individuals accused of a crime. [ACTION.]

ACTIONS MIXED partook of the nature both of real and personal actions, for therein real property was demanded and also personal damages for a wrong sustained. These suits are all abolished.

Arrears of rent may be recovered by the landlord by ordinary action, in which the possession of the property may also be recovered. 3 *Steph. Com.* [ACTIONS REAL AND PERSONAL.]

ACTIONS PERSONAL. 1. An action for a purely personal right (as for a bodily injury, or injury to the reputation), which must be brought, if at all, by the party injured, and is not transmissible to his representatives, according to the maxim, *Actio personalis moritur cum personâ,* "a personal action dies with the person." But this maxim must not be understood to apply in cases of breach of contract causing damage to a man's estate through the medium of a personal injury, as by incapacitating him from work, or depriving his family of his support. And see exceptions by 4 Edw. 3, c. 7 ; 3 & 4 Will. 4, c. 42 ; and 9 & 10 Vict. c. 42. 3 *Steph. Com.* [LORD CAMPBELL'S or FATAL ACCIDENTS ACT.]

2. As opposed to real action. [PERSONAL RIGHTS.] See also ACTIONS REAL AND PERSONAL.

ACTIONS POPULAR. [QUI TAM ACTIONS.]

ACTIONS REAL AND PERSONAL. 1. Real actions were the old feudal actions brought for the recovery of land or any freehold interest therein. 3 *Steph. Com. ; Wms. R. P. Introduction.* By 3 & 4 Will. 4, c. 27, s. 36, all the real and mixed actions then in existence were abolished, with four exceptions therein specified. And, of these four, one (the action of "ejectment") was entirely remodelled by the Common Law Procedure Act of 1852, and by the Judicature Act and rules thereunder, is superseded by an ordinary action for recovery of land ; and the three others (writ of dower, writ of right of dower, and *quare impedit*), by the Common Law Procedure Act of 1860, are assimilated in their procedure to personal actions.

2. *Actions personal,* as opposed to actions real, are such whereby a man claims a debt, or personal duty, or damages in lieu thereof ; and likewise whereby a man claims a satisfaction or damages for some injury done to his person or property. The former are said to be founded on contracts, or to arise *ex contractu vel quasi ex contractu ;* the latter upon torts or wrongs, or to

ACTIONS REAL AND PERSONAL—*contd.*
arise *ex delicto vel quasi ex delicto.* Of the former nature are all actions for debts, and claims of that nature, non-delivery of goods, and non-performance of agreements ; of the latter, all actions for trespasses, assaults, defamatory words, and the like. 3 *Steph. Com.*

ACTIVE TRUST. A trust requiring active duties on the part of the trustee. The Statute of Uses does not apply to these. 1 *Steph. Com.* [TRUST ; BARE TRUSTEE.]

ACTOR. The proctor or advocate in civil courts or causes. *Actor* is also a plaintiff, as contrasted with *reus,* a defendant. *Cowel ;* 3 *Steph. Com.*

ACTS OF COURT. Legal memoranda in the nature of pleadings used in the Admiralty Courts. *Bouvier.*

ACTS OF SEDERUNT are ordinances of the Court of Session in Scotland, corresponding to General Rules and Orders in England and Ireland.

ACTS OF UNION. With Wales, 27 Hen. 8, c. 26, and 34 & 35 Hen. 8, c. 6 ; with Scotland, 5 Anne, c. 8, and 6 Anne, cc. 6 and 23 ; with Ireland, 39 & 40 Geo. 3, c. 67.

ACTUARY (Lat. *Actuarius*). 1. A clerk or scribe that registers the canons and constitutions of the convocation.
2. Now usually a person who calculates the risks and premiums for fire, life, and other insurances.

ACTUS DEI NEMINI NOCET (or *facit injuriam*). The act of God does injury to no one. [ACT OF GOD.]

ACTUS NON FACIT REUM NISI MENS SIT REA. An act does not make a man guilty unless there be guilty intention. As a general rule of our law a guilty mind is an essential ingredient of crime, and this ought to be borne in mind in construing all penal statutes. *Broom's Legal Maxims.*

AD IDEM. Tallying in the essential point. Must be *consensus ad idem* in contract.

AD JURA REGIS. A writ that lay for one holding a crown living against him that sought to eject him, to the prejudice of the king's title in right of his crown.

AD LITEM (for the suit). A guardian appointed by the court to defend a suit on behalf of an infant is called a guardian *ad litem.* 2 *Steph. Com.* [GUARDIAN ; INFANT.]

AD LONGAM. At length.

AD OSTIUM ECCLESIÆ (at the door of the church). One of the five species of dower formerly recognised. After Edward IV. it fell into total disuse, and was abolished by 3 & 4 Will. 4, c. 105, s. 13. 1 *Steph. Com.*

AD QUOD DAMNUM. 1. A writ which, at common law, ought to be sued out before the Crown grants certain liberties, as a fair, market, or such like, which may be prejudicial to others.
2. A writ to be sued out whenever it was proposed to alter the course of a common highway, for the purpose of inquiring whether the change might in any way be prejudicial to the public. 3 *Steph. Com.*
3. A similar writ was given by stat. 27 Edw. 1, st. 2, preliminary to a licence being granted by the Crown to alienate in mortmain. 1 *Steph. Com.* But all of them are now obsolete.

AD SECTAM (at the suit of). Used, generally, in its abbreviated forms *ads.* and *ats.,* in the designation of the title of an action when the defendant's name is placed first. Thus, the suit *Brown* v. *Smith* may also be described Smith *ats.* Brown.

AD TERMINUM QUI PRÆTERIT. A writ of entry which formerly lay for the lessor or his heirs after the term granted had expired, and the lands were withheld. Other remedies are now provided by 4 Geo. 2, c. 28, and 11 Geo. 2, c. 19 ; and the writ itself is abolished by 3 & 4 Will. 4, c. 27, s. 36. [DOUBLE RENT ; DOUBLE VALUE.]

AD VALOREM (according to the value). A duty, the amount of which depends upon the value of the property taxed, is called an *ad valorem* duty.

AD VENTREM INSPICIENDUM, or *de ventre inspiciendo.* 1. A writ formerly issued where a widow was suspected to feign herself with child, in order to produce a supposititious heir to an estate, to examine whether she were with child or not. Now obsolete. 2 *Steph. Com.*

AD VENTREM INSPICIENDUM—*contd.*

2. The phrase is also used sometimes to designate the order of a court (before whom a woman is capitally convicted, and pleads in stay of execution that she is quick with child), directing a jury of matrons to inquire into the fact. [JURY OF MATRONS.]

AD VITAM AUT CULPAM (for life or until misbehaviour). [QUAMDIU BENE SE GESSERIT.]

ADDITION. A title given to a man besides his proper name and surname; that is to say, of what estate, degree, or mystery he is, and of what town, hamlet, or country.

ADDRESS FOR SERVICE. Address given by one party to an action or proceedings for service of notices, etc., by other. As to address to be given by plaintiff, see R. S. C., Ord. 18.

ADEMPTION OF A LEGACY is the implied revocation of a bequest in a will by some subsequent act of the testator; as when a specific chattel is bequeathed, and the testator afterwards sells it; or when a parent bequeaths a legacy to his child, and afterwards makes a provision for the child in satisfaction thereof.

ADHERENCE. The action by which, in Scotland, the mutual obligation of marriage may be enforced by either party. *Bell.* It corresponds to the English action for the restitution of conjugal rights.

ADHERENT. Being *adherent* to the king's enemies, as by giving them aid. intelligence, or the like, constitutes high treason, by 25 Edw. 3, c. 2. *4 Steph. Com.*

ADJOURN. To put off the hearing of a case to a future day or *sine die.* Usually in discretion of the court.

ADJOURNED SUMMONS. A summons taken out in the chambers of a judge of the Chancery Division may be "adjourned" from the master to the judge in chambers, or if of sufficient importance direct into open court to be argued by counsel.

ADJUDICATION. 1. The giving of judgment; a sentence or decree. Thus we say, it was adjudged for the plaintiff, etc.

2. An adjudication of bankruptcy, or that A. B. was adjudicated a bankrupt following the making of a receiving order if no composition is accepted. [BANKRUPT.]

3. By Commissioners of Inland Revenue as to amount of stamp duty chargeable upon a document where in case of doubt application has been made to them under s. 12 of the Stamp Act, 1891. A stamp indicating their decision is impressed or affixed. There is an appeal to the High Court.

ADJURATION. A swearing or binding upon oath.

ADJUSTMENT, in marine insurance, is the settling of the amount of the loss, and of the indemnity which the assured is entitled to receive, and, in the case of several underwriters, of the proportion which each underwriter is liable to pay in respect thereof. Average (*q.v.*) may be the subject of adjustment. *Arnould's Marine Insurance.*

ADMEASUREMENT OF DOWER (Lat. *Admensuratio dotis*). A writ, now abolished, which lay for the heir against a widow, who held from the heir or his guardian more land as dower than she was by law entitled to. 1 *Steph. Com.* [DOWER.]

ADMEASUREMENT OF PASTURE (Lat. *Admensuratio pasturæ*). An old writ which lay for surcharge of pasture. 3 *Steph. Com.* [SURCHARGE OF COMMON.]

ADMINISTRATION has several significations. The king's ministers, or collectively the ministry, is not unfrequently called the *Administration*, as charged with the administration, or management of public affairs. 2 *Steph. Com.* The administration of justice by judges, magistrates, etc.

The affairs of a lunatic may be said to be *administered* by his committee; the affairs of a bankrupt, by his trustee; and the affairs of an absent person, by his agent, factor, or attorney, etc. But the word is specially used in reference to the following cases:—

1. The administration of a deceased's estate; that is, getting in the debts due to the deceased, and paying his creditors to the extent of his assets, and otherwise distributing his estate to the persons who are by law entitled thereto. The person charged with this duty is

ADMINISTRATION—*continued.*

spoken of as "executor" or "administrator," according as he has been appointed by the deceased in his will, or by the Probate Division. [ADMINISTRATION SUIT; ADMINISTRATOR; EXECUTOR.]

2. The administration of a convict's estate under ss. 9—20 of the Forfeitures Abolition Act, 1870.

ADMINISTRATION SUIT. A suit instituted in Chancery for the administration of a deceased's estate. This suit may be instituted by an executor or administrator, or any person interested in the deceased's estate as creditor, legatee, next of kin, etc. Where, however, there is no doubt as to the solvency of a deceased's estate, the proper course for a creditor is not to institute an administration suit, but to sue the deceased's representative at law. Administration proceedings are now usually taken by originating summons (*q.v.*).

It may be for general administration or for the furnishing of particulars, accounts, or certain other limited purposes. *R. S. C., Ord. LV.*

ADMINISTRATOR (SIMPLE) is one to whom the administration of the estate of a deceased is committed by letters of administration from the Probate Division of the High Court of Justice, in cases where the deceased left no will. If the administrator die, his executors are not administrators, but a new administration may be granted, of such of the goods as remain to be administered, to some person, who is then called an administrator *de bonis non.* So administration may be granted *durante absentia*, when the executor acting under a will is out of the realm; or *pendente lite*, where the validity of the will itself is questioned; or *cum testamento annexo*, where the testator has left a will and has not appointed an executor, or has appointed an executor who is either unable or unwilling to act. If a stranger, that is not administrator nor executor, take the goods of the deceased, and administer of his own wrong, he shall be charged and sued not as an administrator, but as an executor *de son tort.* [EXECUTOR DE SON TORT.] There is also another sort of administrator, where one makes his will, and makes an infant his executor. Here administration will be committed to some friend during the minority of the executor, *durante*

minore ætate. And this administration ceases when the infant comes of age. 2 *Steph. Com.* Also administration *ad colligenda bona*, for temporary purposes in case of perishables, etc. The word "administrator" is also used to designate the officer appointed by the Crown to administer the property of a person convicted of treason or felony. [ADMINISTRATION, 2.]

ADMINISTRATRIX. A woman to whom administration is granted. [ADMINISTRATION; ADMINISTRATOR.]

ADMIRAL, or Lord High Admiral, has been defined to be a high officer that has the government of the navy, and the hearing and determining of all causes, as well civil as criminal, belonging to the sea: and for that purpose had a court called the Admiralty. His functions in the government of the navy, however, are committed to the Lords, or Lords Commissioners, of the Admiralty, who are appointed by letters patent to perform them, and of whom one is First Lord. The judicial duties of the admiral were performed by his deputy, who was called the Judge of the Admiralty, and now by judges of the High Court. [ADMIRALTY.]

ADMIRALTY. The Probate, Divorce and Admiralty Division of the High Court of Justice, created by the Judicature Act, 1873, so far as regards admiralty, succeeded to the civil jurisdiction of the High Court of Admiralty. It has jurisdiction over claims for salvage, damage arising by collision or otherwise on the high seas and other maritime causes. The jurisdiction over questions concerning booty of war, formerly determined in a separate court, called the *Prize Court*, is now also vested in the Admiralty Division of the High Court. 3 *Steph. Com.* The criminal jurisdiction of the old Court of Admiralty over offences committed on the sea, or upon the coasts out of the body of any county, is now exercised by the Central Criminal Court, or the judges of assize. Certain county courts also have admiralty jurisdiction. 4 *Steph. Com.*

ADMISSION is when the patron presents to a vacant benefice, and the bishop, upon examination, admits the clerk. In the same sense a man is said to be admitted to a corporation, or to the freedom of a city, on having complied with the preliminary conditions. The

ADMISSION—*continued.*

admission of a solicitor is, when, having served his articles and been examined, he is, on conforming to certain regulations, admitted to the privileges of his profession. Personal attendance before the Master of the Rolls is not now necessary.

ADMISSIONS, in *evidence*, are the testimony which the party admitting bears to the truth of a fact against himself. In practice these are usually made in writing by the solicitors in an action, in order to save the expense of formal proof. *R. S. C., Ord. XXXII.* [NOTICE TO ADMIT.] By the Judicature Act all allegations in pleadings not specifically denied are taken to be admitted.

ADMITTANCE. The admission, either on a surrender or on descent, of the tenant by the lord of the manor into the possession of a copyhold estate; whereby the tenant's title to his estate is said to be perfected. 1 *Steph. Com.* [SURRENDER, 3.]

ADMITTENDO CLERICO. A writ, now practically obsolete, which lay after judgment in action of *quare impedit*, and was directed to the bishop requiring him to admit his, the patron's, clerk. [QUARE IMPEDIT.]

ADMONITION. A judicial reprimand to an accused person on being discharged from further prosecution. Specially in ecclesiastical proceedings—the lightest punishment.

ADMORTIZATION. [AMORTIZATION.]

ADOPTION. An act by which a person appoints as his heir the child of another. There is no law of adoption in this country.

ADULTERATION. The mixing an inferior or deleterious substance with another substance with the intent that the mixture may be sold as pure or genuine. Punished by Food and Drugs Acts, 1875 and 1899, Public Health Acts and others. *Stone's Justices' Manual.*

ADULTERY. Sexual intercourse between two married persons not being husband and wife, or between two persons one of whom is married.

By a husband it is a ground for judicial separation, and when combined with other offences, for dissolution. By a wife, it is a ground for either judicial separation or dissolution, and for a claim for damages against the adulterer. [DIVORCE.]

ADVANCE ON FREIGHT. A sum paid in advance by the charterer of a ship or his agent on account of freight to become due. [FREIGHT.]

ADVANCEMENT. That which is given to a child by a father, or other person standing *in loco parentis*, in anticipation of what the child might inherit. 2 *Steph. Com.* [SATISFACTION ; PORTION.]

ADVANCEMENT CLAUSE. Frequently inserted in wills or settlements authorising the trustees to realise a portion (say one-half) of a beneficiary's share for his advancement, *e.g.*, purchase of a business. The maintenance clause formerly inserted, dealt only with the *income* of the share, and is now covered by the Conveyancing Act, 1881, s. 42.

ADVENTURE. The sending to sea of a ship or goods at the risk of the sender. Almost obsolete term. [See CONSIGNMENT.]

ADVENTURE, BILL OF. A writing signed by a merchant stating that the property in goods shipped in his name, belongs to another at whose risk the goods are and covenanting to account for the produce.

ADVERSE POSSESSION. Where one person is in possession of property under any title, and another person claims to be the rightful owner of the property under a different title, the possession of the former is said to be an "adverse possession" with reference to the latter. A rightful owner neglecting to assert his claim within a given period (defined, according to the circumstances of the case, by various Acts of parliament called Statutes of Limitation) is henceforth barred of his right thereto. [LIMITATION ; OCCUPANCY.] This is to be distinguished from Prescription (*q.v.*).

ADVICE, LETTER OF. A notification by one person to another in respect of a business transaction in which they are mutually engaged, *e.g.*, by consignor to consignee, of goods having been forwarded to him ; or by one merchant to another of the drawing of bills upon him.

ADVOCATE. A person privileged to plead for another in court. Formerly with us confined to those who practised in the Ecclesiastical and Admiralty Courts, but now that these courts have been thrown open to all barristers-at-law, the title has lost its distinctive meaning. 3 *Steph. Com.* [BARRISTER; SOLICITOR.]

ADVOCATE, KING'S. A member of the College of Advocates, appointed by letters patent, who has to advise the Crown in questions involving ecclesiastical and international law. 3 *Steph. Com.*

ADVOCATE, LORD. The principal Crown lawyer in Scotland. [*Cf.* ATTORNEY-GENERAL FOR ENGLAND.]

ADVOCATES, FACULTY OF. In Scotland the barristers practising before the Supreme Court are called *advocates.* The Faculty of Advocates is a corporate body, consisting of the members of the bar in Edinburgh, founded in 1532, the members of which are entitled to plead in every court in Scotland, and in the House of Lords.

ADVOW, or **AVOW** (Lat. *Advocare;* Fr. *Avouer*). To justify or maintain an act formerly done. 3 *Steph. Com.* [REPLEVIN.]

ADVOWEE, or **AVOWEE** (Lat. *Advocatus*), is he that hath right to present to a benefice. So *advowee paramount* is, by the Statute of Provisors, 25 Edw. 3, taken for the king, the highest patron.

ADVOWSON (Lat. *Advocatio*). The right to present to a benefice (*Stat. West.* 2, c. 5), the *jus patronatûs* of the Canon Law. Advowsons are either *appendant* or *in gross*, or partly the one and partly the other. An advowson is *appendant* when it is annexed to the possession of a manor and passes with it; *in gross*, belonging to the person of its owner. Or if a partial right of presentation be granted to a stranger, the advowson may be *appendant* for the term of the lord, and *in gross* for the term of the stranger. Advowsons are also said to be *presentative* or *collative.* An advowson is *presentative* when the patron has the right to present his clerk to the bishop, and to demand his institution if he be qualified; *collative* when the bishop and patron are one and the same person, so that the bishop performs by one act (*collation*),

the separate acts of presentation and institution. There was formerly a third species, viz., *donative,* when the patron by a *donation* could place the clerk into possession without presentation, institution, or induction; but all *donative* benefices are converted into *presentative* by the Benefices Act, 1898 (61 & 62 Vict. c. 48). 2 *Steph. Com.* [APPROPRIATION; IMPROPRIATION.]

ADVOWTRY. Adultery.

AFFECTUM, CHALLENGE PROPTER. [CHALLENGE.]

AFFEERORS, appointed in courts leet, to set the fines on such as have committed faults arbitrarily punishable, and for which no express penalty is appointed by statute. 4 *Steph. Com.*

AFFIDAVIT (Lat. *Affido*). Statement in writing and on oath, sworn before some one who has authority to administer it. 2 *Steph. Com.*

AFFIDAVIT OF DOCUMENTS. [DISCOVERY.]

AFFIDAVIT OF INCREASE. An affidavit filed for the purposes of taxation of costs, verifying such payments, *e.g.,* counsels' and witnesses' fees, which do not appear on the face of the proceedings. This affidavit is ordinarily only required in practice where the opposite party disputes any of the alleged payments or the taxing officer specially requires it.

AFFIDAVIT OF SCRIPTS. [SCRIPTS.]

AFFIDAVIT TO HOLD TO BAIL. Filed on an application under the Debtors Act, 1869, by a plaintiff for the arrest of the debtor showing debt of 50*l.*, and that debtor's leaving the kingdom would prejudice the prosecution of the action.

AFFILIATION. The process by which a single woman or married woman living apart from her husband applies to a magistrate charging a person by name as the father of a child born to her. The magistrate then issues a summons to the person so charged, to appear before two or more justices in petty session, who are to hear the evidence on both sides. If the woman's evidence is corroborated in some material particular by other testimony, to the satisfaction of the justices, they may adjudge the

AFFILIATION—*continued.*
man to be the *putative father* of the child in question, and make an order on him for the payment to the mother of a weekly sum of money not exceeding 5*s.* for its maintenance up to 13 or 16 years of age. 2 *Steph. Com.* Commonly called a bastardy order. *Saunders' Affiliation and Bastardy* and *Stone's Justices' Manual.* [BASTARD.]

AFFINITY. The relationship resulting from marriage, between the husband and the blood relations of the wife ; and also between the wife and the blood relations of the husband. 2 *Steph. Com.* [CONSANGUINITY.]

AFFIRM. To ratify or confirm a former law or judgment. Hence a court of appeal is said to affirm the judgment of the court below. To *affirm* also means to make a solemn declaration, equivalent to a statement upon oath. [AFFIRMATION.]

AFFIRMATION. The testimony given either in open court, or in writing, of those who are permitted to give their evidence without having an oath administered to them, as all persons objecting to take an oath are now enabled by law to do. Oaths Act, 1888 (51 & 52 Vict. c. 46). 2 *Steph. Com.*

AFFIRMATIVE, THE (as opposed to the negative), is some positive fact or circumstance which is alleged to be or have been, and which is generally therefore to be proved, according to the rule of law "that the affirmative of the issue must be proved." [RIGHT TO BEGIN.]

AFFOREST. To turn ground into forest.

AFFRAY (Fr. *Effrayer*, to affright or scare). The fighting of two or more persons in some public place, to the terror of his majesty's subjects ; for, if the fighting be in private, it is no affray but an *assault.* 4 *Steph. Com.*

AFFREIGHTMENT (Lat. *Affretamentum*). The freight of a ship. The contract of affreightment is either by Charterparty or Bill of Lading (*q.v.*). [FREIGHT.]

AFORETHOUGHT. A word used to define the premeditation, which generally distinguishes murder from manslaughter. It matters not in law for how short a time this premeditation may have been conceived in the mind. [MALICE.]

AFTER-MATH. The second crop of grass : or the right to have the last crop of grass or pasturage.

AGAINST THE FORM OF THE STATUTE. A phrase used to indicate that the matter complained of, whether in an action or an indictment, was prohibited by statute. Now, although the words are still commonly used, they are not of essential importance. 4 *Steph. Com.*

AGE. The periods of life when men and women are enabled by law to do that which before, for want of age and consequently of judgment, they could not legally do. 2 *Steph. Com.* [DOLI CAPAX ; FULL AGE ; INFANT.]

AGENCY, DEED OF. A revocable and voluntary trust for payment of settlor's debts.

AGENT. A person authorised, expressedly or impliedly, to act for another, who is thence called the principal, and who is, in consequence of, and to the extent of, the authority delegated by him, bound by the acts of his agent. 2 *Steph. Com.* This term includes most kinds of agents, such as factors and brokers, and the stewards of landowners. It is also usually applied to designate the London solicitor acting on the instructions of the solicitor in the country. Agents may be either *general*, who can bind their principals in all matters of a class, or *special*, in a particular transaction only. The agent is not usually personally liable. [DEL CREDERE COMMISSION.]

AGGRAVATION, or *matter of aggravation*, is that which is introduced into the pleading for the purpose of increasing the amount of damages, but which does not affect the right of action itself. [ALIA ENORMIA.]

AGIST (Fr. *Giste*, a bed or resting-place ; Lat. *Stabulari*). Agistment now generally means the taking in by any one (not as formerly by officers of the king's forests only) of other men's cattle to graze in his ground at a certain rate per week, or the payment made for so doing. See s. 45 of Agricultural Holdings Act, 1883, as to privilege of agisted cattle from distraint. There is also an *agistment* of sea-banks, viz., where lands are charged to keep up the sea-banks, and are hence termed *terræ agistatæ.* 2 *Steph. Com.*

AGNATES (Lat. *Agnati*), in Scotch law, are relations on the father's side ; as cognates (*cognati*) are relations through the mother. A distinction derived from the Roman law, according to which the *agnati* were the legal relations, and the *cognati* the natural relations.

AGREEMENT (said to be from the Latin *Aggregatio mentium*) is the consent or joining together of two minds in respect of anything done or to be done ; also the written evidence of such consent. An agreement, or *contract*, exists either where a promise is made on one side, and assented to on the other ; or where two or more persons enter into an engagement with each other, by a promise on either side. 2 *Steph. Com. ; Anson on Contracts ; Pollock on Contract*. [CONTRACT.]

AGRICULTURAL HOLDINGS ACT, 1883 (46 & 47 Vict. c. 61), regulates rights of tenants of agricultural land, giving compensation for unexhausted improvements, etc. [TENANT-RIGHT.]

AID (Fr. *Aide* ; Lat. *Auxilium*). Sometimes signifies a *subsidy* (14 *Edw.* 3, *st.* 2, *c.* 1), but more usually a service or payment due from tenants to their lords. This *aid* was demanded for three purposes, viz., to ransom the lord's person, if taken prisoner ; to make the lord's eldest son a knight ; and to give a marriage portion to the lord's eldest daughter. This imposition, a relic of the old feudal laws, was abolished by 12 Car. 2, c. 24. Parliamentary grants in aid are frequently made, *e.g.*, to local authorities in aid of local taxation. 1 *Steph. Com.*

AIDER BY VERDICT is where a defect or error in any pleading in an action, which might in the first instance have been objected to by the opposite party, is, after verdict, no longer open to objection ; or, in other words, is *cured by the verdict*. 4 *Steph. Com.*

AIR. The enjoyment of air free and unpolluted is a natural right, and interference with such right is actionable, unless such interference is by virtue of an easement. See *Gale on Easements.* 1 *Steph. Com.*

AIRWAY, a passage for the admission of air into a mine. To maliciously fill up or obstruct the same is felony. 24 & 25 *Vict. c.* 97, *s.* 28.

ALBA FIRMA, or White Rents. A rent, payable in white or silver money, and so-called to distinguish it from the *reditus nigri*, or black-mail, which was payable in work, grain and the like. Also called Blanch-firmes. 1 *Steph. Com.*

ALDERMAN (Sax. *Ealdorman*, signifying literally, elder man). An officer who formerly presided with the bishop in the *schyregemote*, taking cognizance of civil questions, while the latter attended to disputes of a spiritual nature. He was *ex officio* a member of the *witanagemote*. His importance declined when the bishop left the shiremote, and the trial of causes was gradually transferred to the superior courts. There were anciently aldermen of the county, and aldermen of the hundred, etc., etc. ; and one officer indeed had the title of *aldermannus totius Angliæ*. By the Local Government Act, 1888, this title, which had become confined to the persons associated with the mayor in the government of a city or town corporate, was revived for a proportion of the members of the county councils created by the same Act. 3 *Steph. Com.*

ALEATORY CONTRACT. One the effect of which depends on an uncertain event.

ALIA ENORMIA (other wrongs). The plaintiff's declaration in an action of trespass sometimes concludes by way of summary, "and *other wrongs* to the plaintiff then and there did against the peace, etc." This brings in evidence various "matters of aggravation," and is called in pleading an allegation of *alia enormia.* [AGGRAVATION.]

ALIAS (else, otherwise). [ALIAS DICTUS.] An *alias* writ is a second writ, issued after a former writ has been sued out, in the same cause or matter, to no effect. Abolished by 15 & 16 Vict. c. 76, s. 10.

ALIAS (DICTUS) (otherwise called). A second or other name applied to a person where it is doubtful which of two or more names is his real name.

ALIBI (elsewhere). When an accused person, in order to show that he could not have committed the offence with which he is charged, sets up as his defence that he was *elsewhere* at the time when the crime is alleged to have taken place, this defence is called an *alibi.*

ALIEN (Lat. *Alienus*). Generally a person born outside the dominions of the Crown of England, that is, out of the allegiance of the king. But to this rule there are some exceptions. Thus, the children of the sovereign, and the heirs of the Crown, wherever born, have always been held natural born subjects; and the same rule applies to the children of our ambassadors born abroad. And by various statutes extending from 25 Edw. 3, st. 2, down to 33 & 34 Vict. c. 14, the restrictions of the common law have been gradually relaxed, so that many, who would formerly have come under the definition of an alien, may now be regarded as natural born subjects to all intents and purposes. For the rights and disabilities of aliens, see 2 *Steph. Com.*, and 33 & 34 Vict. c. 14. By this last-mentioned statute a British-born subject may under certain circumstances expatriate himself and become an alien. [NATURALISATION ; NATURAL-BORN SUBJECTS.]

ALIEN AMI. An alien born in, or the subject of, a friendly state.

ALIEN ENEMY. An alien born in, or the subject of, a hostile state.

ALIENATION. A transferring of property, or the voluntary resignation of an estate by one man, and its acceptance by another. 1 *Steph. Com.*

ALIENE TO (Fr. *Aliener*, Lat. *Alienare*, to alienate, to put away from one's self). To transfer property to another. Generally used of landed property. 1 *Steph. Com.*

ALIENI JURIS (of another's right). An expression applicable to those who are in the keeping or subject to the authority of another, and have not full control of their person and property. In English law there are generally reckoned three classes of such persons; infants (*i.e.* minors), married women (in some cases) and lunatics. [SUI JURIS.]

ALIMONY (Lat. *Alimonia*). An allowance for the support of a wife judicially separated from her husband, settled at the discretion of the judge on consideration of all the circumstances of the case, and usually proportioned to the rank and quality of the parties. This is called permanent alimony. In causes between husband and wife the husband may be ordered to allow his wife alimony during the suit: called alimony *pendente lite. Oakley on Divorce.*

ALIO INTUITU. With another intention, that is, with a purpose other than the ostensible one.

ALITER (otherwise). A phrase used for the sake of brevity in pointing out a distinction.

ALIUNDE (from another source, from another place, in another way). Thus if, when a case is not made out in the method anticipated, it may be proved *aliunde*, that is, by other and different evidence.

ALL FOURS. A phrase, often used in our courts of justice, to signify that a case or a decision agrees in all its circumstances with some other case or decision.

ALLEGATION. The assertion or statement of a party to a suit or other proceeding (civil or criminal) which he undertakes to prove. Especially is the word used in ecclesiastical suits, in which if a defendant has any circumstances to offer in his defence, he must do so by way of " defensive allegation." 3 *Steph. Com.*

ALLEGIANCE. " The tie which binds the subject to the sovereign, in return for that protection which the sovereign affords the subject." *Bl.* Allegiance is either *natural* and perpetual, or *local* and temporary ; the former being such as is due from all men born within the sovereign's dominions immediately upon their birth ; the latter, such as is due from an alien, or stranger born, during the time that he continues within the king's dominion and protection. 2 *Steph. Com. ; Westlake Private International Law.* [ALIEN ; NATURAL-BORN SUBJECTS.]

ALLOCATION (Lat. *Allocatio*). Properly a placing or adding to ; in law an allowance made upon an account in the Exchequer.

ALLOCATUR (it is allowed). The certificate of the master, or taxing officer of a court, after a solicitor's bill has been *taxed* by him, that the amount certified by him is allowed as costs, or, as they are then called, " taxed costs." [TAXATION OF COSTS.]

ALLODIUM. Free lands, which pay no fines or services, and are not holden of any superior. Opposed to *feuds*. English land is rather in nature of feuds, being in theory held of Crown or lord with right of escheat. 1 *Steph. Com.*

ALLONGE. A slip of paper applied to a bill of exchange, upon which indorsements are written where there is no room for them on the bill itself. *Bills of Exchange Act*, 1882, *s.* 32 (1).

ALLOTMENT. Share of land assigned on partition or under an enclosure award. As to provision of allotment gardens, etc., for labourers and others, see Acts of 1882, 1887, 1890, 1894 (45 & 46 Vict. c. 80 ; 50 & 51 Vict. c. 48 ; 53 & 54 Vict. c. 65 ; and 56 & 57 Vict. c. 73).

ALLOTMENT LETTER, of shares in a joint stock company concluding the contract to take shares. Must be stamped.

ALLOTMENT NOTE. A writing by a seaman, whereby he makes an assignment of part of his wages in favour of his wife, father or mother, grandfather or grandmother, brother or sister. Every allotment note must be in a form sanctioned by the Board of Trade. The allottee, that is, the person in whose favour it is made, may recover the amount before justices of the peace.

ALLUVION. Land that is gained from the sea by the washing up of sand and earth, so as in time to make *terra firma*. 1 *Steph. Com.* [DERELICTION.]

ALMONER, or **ALMNER.** An officer of the king's house whose duties are now considered fully performed by an attendance at the distribution of royal alms on Maundy Thursday ; that is, the Thursday before Easter.

ALNAGER. [AULNAGER.]

ALODIUM. [ALLODIUM.]

ALTERATION in deeds or other documents generally vitiates the instrument if made in a material part after execution. In deeds presumed to have been made before or at time of execution ; in wills, after execution ; and see Wills Act (7 Will. 4 & 1 Vict. c. 26), s. 21. As to bills of exchange, see 45 & 46 Vict. c. 61, s. 64.

AMALGAMATION. In company law the union by merger of two or more companies (Companies Act, 1862, s. 161 ; Life Assurance Companies Act, 1870, ss. 14, 15).

AMBASSADOR. A representative sent by one sovereign power to another, with authority conferred on him by letters of credence to treat on affairs of state : the highest rank among diplomatic officials. His person is protected from civil arrest, and his goods from seizure under distress or execution, by 7 Anne, c. 12. 2 *Steph. Com.; Hall's International Law.*

AMBIDEXTER. Properly a man that can equally use both his hands ; but in a legal sense a juror who takes bribes from both the parties to an action to promote their respective interests. [EMBRACERY.]

AMBIGUITY. Uncertainty of meaning in the words of a written instrument. Where the doubt arises upon the face of the instrument itself, as where a blank is left for a name, the ambiguity is said to be *patent*, as distinguished from a *latent* ambiguity, where the doubt is introduced by collateral circumstances or extrinsic matter, the meaning of the words alone being *primâ facie* sufficiently clear and intelligible. A *patent* ambiguity in a deed cannot, according to law, be explained by parol evidence, and this defect renders the instrument, as far as it extends, inoperative. Latent ambiguities may, however, be explained by parol evidence ; since the doubt having been produced by circumstances extraneous to the deed, the explanation must of necessity be sought for through the same medium. 1 *Steph. Com. Pleadings* must not be ambiguous or doubtful in meaning ; and when two different meanings present themselves, that construction shall be adopted which is most unfavourable to the party pleading.

AMBULATORY. Changeable, revocable ; as when we say that a man's will is ambulatory in his lifetime.

AMENDMENT. A correction of any errors in writ or pleadings in actions or prosecutions. Large powers of amendment have been given by modern statutes. For amendment in civil proceedings, see R. S. C. 1883, Ord. XXVIII., and County Court Rules ; and in criminal proceedings, see 11 & 12 Vict. c. 46, s. 4 ; 12 & 13 Vict. c. 45, s. 10 ; and 14 & 15 Vict. c. 100, ss. 1 and 2. Leave of court is usually necessary for amendment of writ in civil proceedings,

AMENDMENT—*continued.*
but there are large powers of amendment of claim or counterclaim without leave. 3 *Steph. Com.* 552 ; *Arch. Crim. Pleadings.*

AMENDS, TENDER OF.

AMERCIAMENT, or **AMERCEMENT**. A punishment in the nature of a fine ; but in old times a fine was a penalty certain, imposed under some statute by a court of record ; an amerciament was imposed by a jury at their discretion, whereby the offending party stood *at the mercy* of the lord. 3 *Steph. Com.*

AMICUS CURIÆ (a friend of the court). A bystander, usually a barrister, who informs a judge in court on a point of law or fact on which the judge is doubtful or mistaken.

AMNESTY. An act of pardon by which crimes against the Government up to a certain date are so condoned that they can never be brought into charge. It originates with the Crown, and may be general, to all concerned, or particular.

AMORTIZATION (Fr. *Amortissement*) is (1) an alienation of lands and tenements in mortmain [MORTMAIN], (2) the redemption of stock by a sinking fund.

AMORTIZE. To alienate lands in mortmain.

AMOVE. To remove.

AMOVEAS MANUS, or **OUSTER LE MAIN.** [MONSTRANS DE DROIT.]

AMPLIATION (Lat. *Ampliatio*). An enlargement ; but, in a legal sense, a deferring of judgment, until the cause be further examined.

AMY (Lat. *Amicus* ; Fr. *Ami*). [NEXT FRIEND.]

AN, JOUR ET WASTE. [YEAR, DAY, AND WASTE.]

ANCESTOR (Lat. *Antecessor*), in a legal sense, is not exclusively applied to the *ancestor* of a family ; but extends to any person from whom an estate is inherited. 1 *Steph. Com.*

ANCESTRAL ACTIONS. [ACTIONS ANCESTRAL, POSSESSORY, AND DROITURAL.]

ANCHORAGE. A duty paid by the owners of ships for the use of the haven where they cast anchor.

ANCIENT DEMESNE, or **ANTIENT DEMESNE.** A tenure existing in certain manors, which were in the hands of the Crown at the time of Edward the Confessor, or William the Conqueror. Some of the tenants in these crown manors were for a long time pure and absolute villeins, dependent on the will of the lord. Others were in a great measure enfranchised by the royal favour, and had many immunities and privileges granted to them.

Tenants in antient demesne differed from copyholders in so far as their services were fixed and determinate. 1 *Steph. Com.* ; and see *Scriven on Copyholds.*

ANCIENT LIGHTS. Light, through windows which have remained in the same place and condition, and have been enjoyed for twenty years. *Stat. 2 & 3 Will. 4, c.* 71 ; 1 *Steph. Com.* ; *Goddard on Easements.*

ANCIENT WRITINGS. Deeds and other documents which are more than thirty years old. These when put in evidence "prove themselves," that is, they do not ordinarily require proof of their execution when coming from the proper custody.

ANCILLARY (Lat. *Ancilla*, a slave). Auxiliary, or subordinate.

ANCIPITIS USUS (of doubtful use). A phrase used, especially with reference to the law of contraband, of articles of doubtful use, *i.e.*, which might be contraband or not according to circumstances.

ANIMALS either (1) *domitæ naturæ*, by nature tame, which are the subject of absolute ownership, considered personal property and may be the subject of larceny ; or (2) *feræ naturæ*, by nature wild and in which a merely qualified ownership may be acquired while they are alive, which pass with the land on which they are, and cannot at common law be the subject of larceny. Such qualified ownership may be acquired in them either *per industriam*, by taming or keeping them under control, *propter impotentiam*, by their being too weak to get away, or *propter privilegium*, by franchise from the Crown, *e.g.*, in warren. See as to larceny of animals, 24 & 25 Vict. c. 96 ; malicious injuries, 24 & 25 Vict. c. 97, ss. 40, 41 ; cruelty, 12 & 13 Vict. c. 92, and 17 & 18 Vict. c. 60 ; 63 & 64 Vict. c. 33 ; there are also statutory provisions as to vivisection, contagious diseases, etc.

ANIMUS CANCELLANDI. ANIMUS RE-VOCANDI. The intention of cancelling. The intention of revoking, specially in relation to will.

ANIMUS FURANDI. The intention of stealing—at common law it must be present at time of taking.

ANIMUS MANENDI. The intention of remaining, which is material for the purpose of ascertaining a person's *domicile.* [DOMICILE.]

ANIMUS REVERTENDI. The intention of returning.

ANNATS (*Annates*). [FIRST FRUITS.]

ANNI NUBILES. The marriageable age of a woman, *i.e.*, in English law, twelve, but consent of parents or guardians should be obtained up to twenty-one, though the marriage is not void without it.

ANNIENTED (Fr. *Anéantir*; Lat. *Abjicere*). Frustrated; brought to nought.

ANNOISANCE. A nuisance. 22 *Hen.* 8, *c.* 5. [NUISANCE.]

ANNUITY. A yearly sum payable. If charged upon real estate it is more properly called a rent charge. And see 44 & 45 Vict. c. 41, s. 44. Even if chargeable only upon the person of the grantor it may be made descendible to a man and his heirs, while personalty in general can devolve only upon the executors or administrators. 1 *Steph. Com.*

Annuities are often granted by Government, or by the Commissioners for the Reduction of the National Debt, to depositors in savings banks, under certain Acts of parliament. 3 *Steph. Com.*

ANNULLING AN ADJUDICATION IN BANKRUPTCY. This may be (1) where a composition has been subsequently accepted (see s. 23 of Act of 1883), (2) where court is of opinion debtor ought not to have been adjudged, or (3) where the debts are paid in full (see ss. 35, 36). The effect is not to render everything done under the bankruptcy null and void *ab initio;* but merely to stop all further proceedings in the bankruptcy, generally leaving everything done under it, up to the annulling, in full force and operation. There are also provisions for annulment of receiving order and of a composition or scheme of arrangement. 2 *Steph. Com.*

ANNUS LUCTUS (the year of grief). The year after a husband's death, within which his widow was, by the civil law, not permitted to marry. 2 *Steph. Com.*

ANSWER. By the Judicature Acts a "statement of defence" takes the place of defendant's "answer" under the old system of pleading.

In Divorce.—The defence of a respondent or co-respondent in the Divorce Court is called an answer. Also in *civil* suits in ecclesiastical matters, and generally an answer to an accusation means the defence of the accused person thereto.

ANTE LITEM MOTAM. Before a suit is put in motion.

ANTE-DATE. To date a document before the day of its signature or execution. As to bills of exchange, etc., see 45 & 46 Vict. c. 61, s. 13 (2).

ANTENATI. Born before a certain period. Specially before marriage.

ANTE-NUPTIAL. Before marriage.

ANTICIPATION. Specially in relation to the separate property of a married woman. She may be restrained either by will or settlement from alienating by way of anticipation such property, and may thus be protected against the influence or coercion of her husband. The court can now remove the restraint with her consent and for her benefit (Conveyancing Act, 1881, s. 39). Also see Married Women's Property Act, 1893, s. 2, and Trustee Act, 1893, s. 45.

ANTIGRAPHY. A copy or counterpart of a deed.

ANTINOMY. Conflict between two laws or the provisions of a law.

ANTIQUA (or **VETERA) STATUTA** (ancient statutes). The Acts of parliament from Richard I. to Edward III.

APOGRAPH. A copy, an inventory.

APOLOGY in actions for libel may operate as a defence, or in mitigation of damages. See 6 & 7 *Vict. c.* 96, *ss.* 1, 2 ; and see *R.S.C., Ord. XXXVI., r.* 37.

APPARATOR, or **APPARITOR.** A messenger who cites offenders to appear in the spiritual courts, and serves the process thereof.

APPARENT HEIR, or **HEIR APPARENT.** One whose right of inheritance is indefeasible, provided he outlive his ancestor. 1 *Steph. Com.*

APPEAL. 1. A complaint to a superior court of an injustice done by an inferior one. The party complaining is styled the appellant, the other party the respondent. In *civil* causes, appeals from the county court lie to a divisional court of the High Court of Justice; from the Chancery, King's Bench, and Probate, Divorce and Admiralty Divisions of the High Court, to the Court of Appeal; from the Court of Appeal, to the House of Lords. The Judicial Committee of the Privy Council is also the ultimate court of appeal in ecclesiastical matters, and from the Colonial courts. Appeal from a master or district registrar lies to judge in chambers, and thence to divisional court, or, in some cases (*e.g.,* on practice or procedure, or in the Chancery Division), to the Court of Appeal. Leave is in many cases necessary for appeal, *e.g.,* usually from interlocutory orders, and the rules as to time for appeal and notice must be complied with. In *criminal* causes there is in certain cases a right of appeal from decision of magistrates in petty sessions to quarter sessions, but there is no appeal proper from trial or indictment. See, however, RESERVATION OF A CASE FOR COURT FOR CROWN CASES RESERVED; SPECIAL CASE TO DIVISIONAL COURT; MOTION IN ARREST OF JUDGMENT; COURT OF ERROR; CERTIORARI AND NEW TRIAL, if misdemeanor tried on information in King's Bench.

2. An accusation by a private subject (appellor) against another (appellee) for some heinous crime, demanding punishment on account of the particular injury suffered, rather than for the offence against the public. Now obsolete. 4 *Steph. Com.*

APPEARANCE. As regards the defendant in an action, appearance is entered by his delivering to the proper officer of the court a memorandum importing either that he appears to defend the action in person, or that some solicitor, whose name is given, appears on his behalf. This must usually be done within eight days from the service of the writ or summons. Provision is also made in the case of persons under disability for appearance by guardian, committee, etc. In county court no appearance is entered, but in case of default summons (for a certain sum) notice of intention to defend must be given within eight days, otherwise judgment may be obtained by default. In the High Court, failure of defendant to appear will in some cases (*e.g.,* liquidated claims) give plaintiff right to final judgment; in others (*e.g.,* claims for damages), interlocutory judgment; in others (*e.g.,* Chancery actions), the action must still proceed. 3 *Steph. Com.*

APPELLANT. [APPEAL.]

APPELLATE JURISDICTION. The jurisdiction exercised by a court of justice in appeals.

APPELLEE. [APPEAL, 2; APPROVER.]

APPELLOR. [APPEAL, 2; APPROVER.]

APPENDANT. Annexed to, or belonging to, some principal thing or corporeal hereditament. Thus we have advowsons and commons *appendant* to a manor, and common of fishing *appendant* to a freehold; and *appendants* are naturally and originally annexed to the principal, as distinguished from *appurtenances,* which may be created at any time, and either by express grant or prescription. 1 *Steph. Com.*

APPOINTEE. A person to whom or in whose favour what is technically termed " a power of appointment " is exercised. [APPOINTMENT; POWER.]

APPOINTMENT. Besides its ordinary meaning, this word is specially used of the appointment, under a *power of appointment,* limiting the *use* in lands or other property for the benefit of some person or persons. [POWER.]

APPORTIONMENT. The dividing of a legal right into its proportionate parts, according to the interests of the parties concerned. The word is generally used with reference to the adjustment of rights between two persons having successive interests in the same property, such as a tenant for life and the reversioner. By the common law, if the interest of a person in the rents and profits of land ceased between one day of payment and another (as by the death of a tenant for life), the sum which had accrued since the last day of payment was lost to him or his representatives, and went to the person entitled to the reversion. By the Apportionment Act, 1870 (33 & 34 Vict.

APPORTIONMENT—*continued.*
c. 35), it is provided that all rents, annuities, dividends, and other periodical payments in the nature of income, shall be considered as accruing from day to day, and shall be apportionable in respect of time accordingly. 1 *Steph. Com.*; and see Conveyancing Act, 1881, s. 12.

APPRAISEMENT. Valuation. A commission of appraisement to value treasure-trove, waifs, and estrays, seized by the king's officer, was issued after the filing of an information in the King's Exchequer (now Bench), and a proclamation for the owner (if any) to come in and claim the effects. After the return of the commission, a second proclamation was made ; and, if no claimant appeared, the goods were condemned to the use of the Crown. 3 *Steph. Com.* Appraisement of goods seized by way of distress for rent, etc., was formerly necessary before the goods could be sold, but this is not now so unless the tenant requires it.

APPRENTICE (Fr. *Apprendre*, to learn). One who is bound by deed indented, or indentures, to serve his master and be maintained and instructed by him. 2 *Steph. Com.*

APPROBATE AND REPROBATE. To take advantage of the beneficial parts of a deed, and reject the rest. This the law does not in general admit of. [ELECTION.]

APPROPRIATION. 1. The perpetual annexation of an ecclesiastical benefice to the use of some spiritual corporation, sole or aggregate, being the patron of the living. The patrons retained the tithes and glebe in their own hands, without presenting any clerk, they themselves undertaking to provide for the service of the church. [VICAR.] When the monasteries and religious houses were dissolved, the appropriations belonging to them became vested in the Crown, and many of these were afterwards granted out to subjects, and are now in the hands of lay persons, called by way of distinction *lay impropriators.*
2. The application of a particular payment for the purpose of paying a particular debt. The debtor at the time of paying has the first right of appropriation, but, as a general rule, the creditor may apply the payment if the debtor does not ; if neither does so the law usually appropriates earliest payment to earliest debt (*Clayton's case*).

APPROVE (Lat. *Approbare*). To improve ; especially of land. 1 *Steph. Com.*

APPROVEMENT. 1. The improvement or partial inclosure of a common. Consent of Board of Agriculture now necessary (56 & 57 Vict. c. 57).
2. The profits arising from land approved. [APPROVE.]
3. The act of an approver. [APPROVER.]

APPROVER (Lat. *Approbator*). A person, formerly called an *appellor*, who, when indicted of treason or felony, and arraigned for the same, did confess the fact before plea pleaded, and appeal or accuse others, his accomplices, of the same crime, in order to obtain his pardon. This could only be done in capital offences. If the accused, or, as he was called, the *appellee*, were found guilty, he suffered the judgment of the law, and the approver had his pardon *ex debito justitiæ ;* but if the jury acquitted the appellee, the approver received judgment to be hanged, upon his own confession of the indictment. 4 *Steph. Com.* [KING'S EVIDENCE.]

APPURTENANCES, or THINGS APPURTENANT (Lat. *Pertinentia*). Things both corporeal and incorporeal belonging to another thing as the principal, but which have not been naturally or originally so annexed, but have become so by grant or prescription, such as hamlets to a manor, common of pasture, turbary, piscary, and the like. 1 *Steph. Com.* [APPENDANT.]
Common appurtenant may arise not only from long usage but from grant, and it may extend to beasts not generally commonable, thus differing in some degree from *common appendant.* 1 *Steph. Com.*

ARBITRATION is where two or more parties submit all matters in dispute to the judgment of *arbitrators*, who are to decide the controversy ; and if they do not agree, it is usual to add, that another person be called in as *umpire*, to whose sole judgment it is then referred : or frequently there is only one arbitrator originally appointed. The decision, in any of these cases, is called an *award ;* but sometimes, when the umpire gives the decision, it is termed *umpirage.* The Arbitration Act, 1889 (52 & 53 Vict. c. 49), contains many important provisions with respect to arbitration. 3 *Steph. Com.*

ARCHBISHOP. The chief of all the clergy in his province. He has the inspection of the bishops of that province, as well as of the inferior clergy ; or, as the law expresses it, the power to *visit* them. There are two archbishops for England : Canterbury, styled Primate of all England ; and York, Primate of England. 2 *Steph. Com.*

ARCHDEACON. An ecclesiastical officer subordinate to the bishop throughout the whole of a diocese or in some particular part of it. He is usually appointed by the bishop, and has a kind of episcopal authority. He *visits* the clergy, and has his separate court for punishment of offenders by spiritual censures, and for hearing all other causes of ecclesiastical cognizance. As a general rule, the jurisdictions of the archdeacon and the bishop are concurrent, but with appeal from former to latter. He also examines for ordination, induction, etc. 2 *Steph. Com.*

ARCHES, COURT OF, is a court of appeal belonging to the Archbishop of Canterbury, whereof the judge, who sits as deputy to the archbishop, is called the *Dean of the Arches,* because he anciently held his court in the church of St. Mary-le-Bow (*Sancta Maria de Arcubus*). This court was afterwards held in the hall at Doctors' Commons, and subsequently at Westminster. Its proper jurisdiction is only over the thirteen peculiar parishes belonging to the archbishop in London ; but, the office of Dean of the Arches having been for a long time united with that of the archbishop's principal official, he now, in right of the last-mentioned office (as does also the official principal of the Archbishop of York, who since the Public Worship Regulation Act, 1874, is the same judge as for Canterbury), receives and determines appeals from the sentences of all inferior ecclesiastical courts within the province. Many original suits are also brought before him, in respect of which the inferior judge has waived his jurisdiction. [LETTERS OF REQUEST.]

From the Court of Arches and from the parallel court of appeal in the province of York, an appeal lies to the Judicial Committee of the Privy Council. 3 *Steph. Com.*

ARGUMENT. The process of drawing inferences. The discussion of legal or other points by counsel.

ARGUMENTATIVE PLEA. A plea not direct and positive, and liable to be struck out as being embarrassing.

ARMS AND ARMOUR, in legal language, is extended to anything that a man, in his anger or fury, takes into his hand to cast at, or strike, another. In all actions of trespass as opposed to trespass on the case, it was formerly necessary, and in certain indictments it is still necessary, to allege that the acts complained of were done *vi et armis,* " with force and arms," the force being the gist of the complaint. 3 *Steph. Com.* ; 4 *Steph. Com.*

ARRAIGN, ARRAIGNMENT (Lat. *Ad rationem ponere,* to call to account). To arraign is to call a prisoner to the bar of the court, to answer the matter charged upon him in the indictment. The prisoner is to be called to the bar by his name ; the indictment is to be read to him distinctly in the English tongue, after which, it is to be demanded of him, whether he be guilty of the crime whereof he stands indicted, or not guilty. He may then either confess, plead not guilty, or stand mute. 4 *Steph. Com.* [MUTE ; PEINE FORTE ET DURE.]

ARRAIGNS, CLERK OF THE. A person who assists the clerk of assize, more particularly in taking the *arraignments.* [ARRAIGN.]

ARRANGEMENTS between debtors and creditors outside the law of bankruptcy must be in accordance with the Act of 1887. [COMPOSITION, 2.] As to arrangements within the bankruptcy law, see s. 3 of the Act of 1890.

ARRAY is the setting forth in order of a jury of men that are impanelled upon a cause, whence comes the verb *to array* a panel, that is, to set forth in order the men that are impanelled. Hence we say to "challenge the array," and to "quash the array." [CHALLENGE.]

ARREARS. Money owing after time for payment, *e.g.,* interest, rent.

ARRENTATION (Spanish, *Arrendar*). The licensing an owner of lands in the forest to enclose them with a low hedge and little ditch, according to the assize of the forest, under a yearly rent. *Saving the arrentations* is reserving the power to grant such licences. *Cowel.*

ARREST. A restraint of a man's person, obliging him to be obedient to the law. An arrest is the beginning of imprisonment, whereby a man is first taken, and restrained of his liberty, by power or colour of a lawful warrant ; also it signifies the decree of a court, by which a person is arrested.

One person may, without warrant, arrest another on reasonable suspicion of felony, and will be protected in doing so—

1. If the person arresting be a peace officer ; *or*

2. If he can prove that the felony was committed by some one ; *or*

3. If the arrest be made in joining in a "hue and cry." 4 *Steph. Com.*

Arrest without warrant also allowed in certain other criminal cases.

A warrant of arrest may also be obtained in Admiralty proceedings to detain the ship or other *res* the subject of the action.

ARREST OF JUDGMENT. A staying or withholding of judgment, although there has been a verdict in the case, on the ground that there is some error on the face of the record, from which it appears that the plaintiff has at law no right to recover in the action, or that prisoner should not be sentenced. 3 *Steph. Com.*; 4 *Steph. Com.*

ARRESTMENT. The Scotch term for the arrest of a person or the seizure of his effects, analogous to the English attachment.

ARRESTO FACTO SUPER BONIS MERCATORUM ALIENIGENARUM. A writ that lay for a denizen against the goods of an alien found within the kingdom, as a recompense for goods taken from him in a foreign country, after restitution had been denied. *Reg. Orig.* 129.

ARRETTED is he that is convened before any judge, and charged with a crime. *Cowel.*

ARRHÆ. Earnest, evidence of a completed bargain.

ARSON. The malicious and wilful burning of a house or other building. Extended by 24 & 25 Vict. c. 97, to crops, mines, and other subjects. 4 *Steph. Com.*

ART AND PART means where a person is guilty of aiding and abetting a criminal in the perpetration of a crime.

ART UNIONS. Voluntary associations for the purchase of paintings and other works of art to be distributed by chance or otherwise amongst the members. Excepted from the law against lotteries if complying with 9 & 10 Vict. c. 48, thereon.

ARTICLED CLERK. A person bound by articles to serve with some practising solicitor, previously to being admitted himself as a solicitor. The period of service under articles is in general five years ; but in certain cases it is only four or three years. 3 *Steph. Com.*; 6 & 7 *Vict. c.* 73 ; 23 & 24 *Vict. c.* 127 ; 37 & 38 *Vict. c.* 68 ; 40 & 41 *Vict. c.* 25 ; 51 & 52 *Vict. c.* 65.

ARTICLES. A word used in various senses.

1. Agreements between different persons expressed in writing, sealed or unsealed, are often spoken of as "articles." A contract made in contemplation of marriage is in general spoken of as "marriage articles," if it contemplate a further instrument, *i.e.*, settlement, to carry out the intention of the parties. So also "articles of partnership," "articles of association," etc. The use of the term is somewhat capricious. [See also ARTICLED CLERK.]

2. Rules are sometimes spoken of as "articles" ; as when we speak of "articles of war," "articles of the navy," "articles of a constitution," "articles of religion," the thirty-nine articles drawn up by Convention in 1562, which must be subscribed to on taking holy orders.

3. The complaint of the promoter in an ecclesiastical cause is called "articles." So, an impeachment by the House of Commons is expressed in what are called "articles of impeachment." See 2 *Steph. Com.*; 3 *Steph. Com.* ; 4 *Steph. Com.*

ARTICLES OF ASSOCIATION. Regulations governing the mode of conducting the business of a joint stock company and its internal organisation. These must usually accompany the Memorandum of Association, which sets out the objects and capital, etc., of the company. In the case of a company limited by shares, Table A of the Companies Act, 1862, may be taken as the articles of the company.

ARTICLES OF THE PEACE. A form of complaint by a person who fears that another may do him some bodily hurt.

ARTICLES OF THE PEACE—*continued.* Articles of peace may be exhibited in the King's Bench, Assize Court, or Sessions Court; and upon the articles being sworn to by the complainant, sureties of the peace are taken on the part of the party complained against. And the court may require bail for such time as they shall think necessary for the preservation of the peace. 4 *Steph. Com.* [KEEPING THE PEACE.]

ARTICULI CLERI (Articles of the Clergy). Statutes made touching persons and causes ecclesiastical, such as 9 Edw. 2, stat. 2; 14 Edw. 3, stat. 3.

ARTIFICIAL PERSONS. [NATURAL PERSONS.]

AS AGAINST. An expression indicating a partial effect or influence. Thus an action may be dismissed as against certain parties to it, who have been wrongfully made parties, while maintained against others.

AS OF. A judgment *as of* Trinity Sittings is a judgment not delivered in Trinity Sittings, but having the same legal effect.

ASPORTATION. [ASPORTAVIT.]

ASPORTAVIT (he carried away). The technical words in indictments for larceny, when indictments were in Latin, were *felonice cepit et asportavit:* "he feloniously took and carried away": the carrying away, or asportation, being an essential part of the crime, though the slightest removal is sufficient. 4 *Steph. Com.*

ASSACH, or **ASSATH**. A kind of excuse or purgation, formerly a custom in Wales, by which an accused person cleared himself by the oaths of 300 men. Abolished by 1 Hen. 5, c. 6. *T. L.*

ASSART (Lat. *Assartum;* Fr. *Assartir,* to make plain). An offence committed in the forest, by pulling up by the roots the woods that are thickets and covert for the deer, and by making them plain as arable land.

ASSAULT (fr. Fr. *Assailler*) is defined by Blackstone "to be an attempt or offer to beat another, without touching him": and though no actual suffering is proved, yet the party injured may have redress by action for damages as a compensation for the injury, or nominally by criminal prosecution. A *battery* is the unlawful beating of another, and includes the least touching of another's person wilfully or in anger. Practically, however, the word assault is used to include the battery. 3 *Steph. Com.*; 4 *Steph. Com.*

ASSAY (Fr. *Essay*). A proof, a trial. Thus the *assay* of weights and measures is the examination of them by officials.

ASSEMBLY, UNLAWFUL. [UNLAWFUL ASSEMBLY.]

ASSENT. Consent. The executor's assent to a bequest is essential to perfect a legatee's title. Since Land Transfer Act, 1897, the legal estate in realty may be transferred to the devisee, by assent by personal representative.

ASSESSED TAXES. Assessed or charged in respect of particular subjects, *e.g.*, male servants, horses, carriages, dogs.

ASSESSORS. Persons who assess the public rates or taxes, also persons who assist a judge with their special knowledge of the subject which he has to decide: thus we speak of "legal assessors," "nautical assessors," "mercantile assessors." By s. 56 of the Judicature Act, 1873, the High Court or Court of Appeal may call in the aid of one or more assessors specially qualified, and may try and hear the matter in question with their assistance. Largely employed in the Admiralty Division. See also County Court Admiralty Jurisdiction Act, 1868, s. 14. In the House of Lords, 54 & 55 Vict. c. 53, s. 3; and before the Judicial Committee of the Privy Council in ecclesiastical matters, 39 & 40 Vict. c. 59, s. 14. 3 *Steph. Com.*

ASSETS (Fr. *Assez,* enough). By *assets* is meant such property as is available for the payment of the debts of an insolvent individual or company, or of a person deceased.

Assets of a deceased person are divided into *real assets,* consisting of what is called *real estate,* and *personal assets,* consisting of what is called *personal estate,* which are administered according to different rules.

Assets of a deceased person are also divided into *legal,* such as a creditor of the deceased might make available in an action at law for the payment of his debt; and equitable assets such as could be made available to a creditor in a court of equity only. They include such real assets as the testator has left expressly for the payment of his debts.

ASSETS—*continued.*

The importance of the distinction has now ceased to exist, as, since 1870, specialty and simple contract creditors rank *pari passu* against legal as well as equitable assets, and by the Land Transfer Act, 1897, s. 2, the executor or administrator may sell lands for any lawful purpose of administration, though there be no charge for payment of debts. [MARSHALLING ASSETS.]

ASSIGN, TO (Lat. *Assignare*), has two significations : (1) to make over a right or interest to another ; (2) to point out, or set forth. In the former sense we speak of the assignment of a lease, or of a debt or *chose in action* (*q.v.*) ; in the latter sense we have—to assign error, to assign perjury, to assign waste, etc. 1 *Steph. Com.*

Assign, as a substantive, is used in the sense of assignee. 1 *Steph. Com.* [ASSIGNEE.]

ASSIGNEE, or ASSIGN. One who is appointed by another to do any act in his own right, or who takes the rights or title of another by assignment, as distinguished from a *deputy* who acts in the right of another. Such an assignee may be either *by deed*, *i.e.*, by act of party, as when a lessee assigns his lease to another ; or *in law*, he whom the law so makes, without any appointment of the person, as an administrator who is the assignee in law to the intestate. An assignee of land is not at common law bound by or entitled to the benefit of covenants which do not run with the land.

Assignees *in bankruptcy* were those in whom the property of a bankrupt became vested for the benefit of the creditors. They are now, by the Bankruptcy Act, 1883, called *official receivers and trustees. Robson, Bkcy.*

ASSIGNMENT OF DOWER. The act by which the share of a widow in her deceased husband's real estate was ascertained and set apart to her. 1 *Steph. Com.*

ASSIGNMENT OF ERRORS. The statement of the case of the plaintiff in error, setting forth the errors complained of. [ERROR.]

ASSIGNOR. One who transfers or assigns property to another. [ASSIGNEE.]

ASSISA CADERE. To be non-suited.

ASSISA CONTINUANDA. A writ directed to the justices of assize, for the continuance (*i.e.*, the adjournment) of a cause, where certain records alleged cannot be procured in time by the party desiring to use them.

ASSITHMENT was a weregeld or compensation for murder, by a pecuniary mulct, due to the heirs of the person murdered.

ASSIZE (Lat. *Assideo*, to sit together) signifies, originally, the jury who are summoned by virtue of a writ of assize, who try the cause and "sit together" for that purpose. By a figure it was made to signify the court of jurisdiction, which summoned this jury together by a commission of assize, or *ad assisas capiendas ;* and hence the judicial assemblies held by the Queen's commission in every county to deliver the gaols, and to try causes at *nisi prius*, are termed in common speech the *assizes.* See now the Judicature Act, 1873, ss. 11, 16, 29, 37, 77, 93, and 99. The holding of Winter and Spring Assizes is regulated by orders in council issued under the Winter Assizes Acts, 1876 and 1877, and the Spring Assizes Act, 1879 (39 & 40 Vict. c. 57 ; 40 & 41 Vict. c. 46 ; and 42 Vict. c. 1).

It is also an *ordinance* or *statute*, as the " Assize of Bread and Ale," the " Assize of Clarendon," and " Assize of Arms " ; and is sometimes used to denote generally anything reduced to a certainty in respect to number, quantity, quality, weight or measure.

ASSIZE, COURTS OF, are composed of two or more commissioners, called judges of assize, who are sent by special commission from the Crown, on *circuits* all round the kingdom, to try such matters as are then under dispute. These judges of assize are the successors of the ancient "justices in eyre," *justiciarii in itinere.* They sit by virtue of four several authorities : (1) Commission of *Oyer and Terminer*, which gives them power to deal with treasons, murders, felonies, etc., and this is their largest commission ; (2) of *gaol delivery*, which requires them to try every prisoner in gaol, for whatsoever offence he be there ; (3) of *Nisi Prius*, which empowers them to try, by a jury of twelve men of the county in which the venue is laid, all civil causes in which issue has been joined in one of the divisions of the High Court of Justice ; and (4) *Commission of peace* in every county of their

ASSIZE, COURTS OF—*continued.*

circuit, by which all justices of the peace, having no lawful impediment, are bound to be present at the assizes, to attend the judges. If any make default, the judges may set a fine upon him at their pleasure and discretion. The sheriff of every shire is also to attend in person, or by sufficient deputy. There was formerly a fifth commission, that *of assize*, but the abolition of assize and other real actions has thrown this commission out of force. 3 *Steph. Com.* [ASSIZE, WRIT OF ; CIRCUIT ; NISI PRIUS.]

ASSIZE OF DARREIN PRESENTMENT (or last presentation). A writ directed to the sheriff to summon an assize or jury, to inquire who was the last patron that presented to a church then vacant, of which the plaintiff complained that he was deforced (*i.e.*, unlawfully deprived) by the defendant ; and according as the assize determined that question, a writ issued to the bishop, to institute the clerk of that patron in whose favour the determination was made. 3 *Steph. Com.* It was abolished by stat. 3 & 4 Will. 4, c. 27, s. 36, and the action of *quare impedit* was substituted. But since the C. L. P. Act, 1860, s. 26, no *quare impedit* can be brought, but an action may be commenced in the King's Bench (formerly Common Pleas) Division of the High Court.

ASSIZE OF MORT D'ANCESTOR. [MORT D'ANCESTOR.]

ASSIZE OF NOVEL DISSEISIN. A writ which lay to recover possession of lands, of which the claimant had been lately disseised (that is, dispossessed). Abolished by stat. 3 & 4 Will. 4, c. 27, s. 36. 3 *Steph. Com.*

ASSIZE, RENTS OF, are either chief rents or quit rents. 1 *Steph. Com.* [CHIEF RENTS ; QUIT RENTS.]

ASSIZE, WRIT OF. A real action, now abolished, used for the purpose of regaining *possession* of lands whereof the demandant or his ancestors had been unjustly deprived by the tenant or possessor of the freehold, or those under whom he claimed. It proved the title of the demandant by showing his or his ancestor's possession, and it was not necessary (as it was in a writ of entry) to show the unlawful commencement of the tenant's possession. 3 *Steph. Com.* [ENTRY, WRIT OF.]

ASSIZES RELIEF ACT, 1890 (52 & 53 Vict. c. 12). To relieve the court of assize from the trial of persons charged with offences triable at quarter sessions.

ASSOCIATE. 1. An officer in each of the superior courts of common law, whose duty is to keep the records and documents of the court to which he is attached, to attend its *Nisi Prius* sittings, and in each case to enter the verdict and to make up the postea or formal entry of the verdict, and deliver the record to the party entitled thereto. *Stat.* 15 & 16 *Vict. c.* 73, *ss.* 1—6. By the Judicature Act, 1873, s. 77, associates are now officers of the Supreme Court of Judicature, and, by the Judicature (Officers) Act, 1879, are styled "Masters of the Supreme Court."

2. A person associated with the judges and clerk of assize in the commission of general gaol delivery.

ASSOCIATION. A commission granted either by writ or patent to the justices of assize, to have other persons associated to them to take the assizes, that a sufficient supply of commissioners may never be wanting. It usually takes place when, from the illness of a judge, the press of business, or some other cause, additional help is required.

ASSOCIATION, ARTICLES OF. [ARTICLES OF ASSOCIATION.]

ASSOCIATION, MEMORANDUM OF. [MEMORANDUM OF ASSOCIATION.]

ASSOIL (Lat. *Absolvere*) signifies to deliver or discharge a man of an excommunication.

ASSUMPSIT (he has undertaken). A voluntary promise, by which a man, for a consideration, *assumes* and takes upon him to perform or pay anything to another.

This word now is chiefly applied to the action which lay where a party claimed *damages* for breach of *simple contract*, *i.e.*, a promise not under seal. 3 *Steph. Com.* [COVENANT ; DEBT.]

ASSURANCE. 1. The legal evidences of the transfer of property are called the *common assurances* of the kingdom. They are also called *conveyances*, and are in general effected by an instrument called a *deed.* 1 *Steph. Com.*

2. Insurance. [INSURANCE.]

ASYLUM. 1. A place in which offenders could find refuge.

2. An institution for the retention and treatment of lunatics. Either public or private, but all are now subject to Government regulation.

AT ARM'S LENGTH. When a person is not, or having been, ceases to be, under the influence or control of another, he is said to be " at arm's length " with him, *e.g.*, *cestui que trust* and trustee.

ATIA. [DE ODIO ET ATIA.]

ATS. [AD SECTAM.]

ATTACHIAMENTA BONORUM. A distress levied upon the goods or chattels of any one sued for a personal debt by the legal *attachiatores*, or bailiffs, as a security to answer the action. *Cowel.*

ATTACHIAMENTA DE SPINIS ET BOSCO. The privilege granted to the officers of the forest to take thorns, bush, or windfall within the precincts or liberties committed to their charge. *Cowel.*

ATTACHMENT. 1. The taking into the custody of the law the person or property of one already before the court, or of one whom it is sought to bring before it. This is done by means of a judicial writ, called a *writ of attachment*. An attachment differs from an *arrest* or *capias*, as it may extend to a man's goods as well as to his person; and from a *distress*, as it may extend to his person as well as his goods. The process of attachment is the method which has always been used by the superior courts of justice for the punishment of all " contempts of court." 3 *Steph. Com.*

2. Attachment of debts. [GARNISHEE.]

ATTACHMENT, FOREIGN. The attachment of the goods of foreigners, *i.e.*, persons out of the jurisdiction of the court, found within any liberty or city for a debt due. Now superseded by garnishee proceedings. See 3 *Steph. Com.* [GARNISHEE.]

ATTAINDER. When a person convicted of treason or felony was sentenced to death for the same, or when judgment of outlawry for treason or felony was pronounced against any one, he was said to be *attainted*, and the fact was called an *attainder*. His property was forfeited and his blood was said to be corrupted. This result was abolished by 33 & 34 Vict. c. 23, s. 1; except that nothing therein is to affect the law of forfeiture consequent upon outlawry. 4 *Steph. Com.* [BILL OF ATTAINDER; CORRUPTION OF BLOOD; FORFEITURE.]

ATTAINT, WRIT OF. A writ, now abolished, which was in the nature of an appeal, and was the principal remedy for the reversal of an improper verdict. The practice of setting aside verdicts upon motion and granting *new trials* superseded the use of attaints, and the writ itself is now abolished by stat. 6 Geo. 4, c. 50, s. 60. 3 *Steph. Com.*

ATTEMPT to commit a crime. One of the series of acts necessary to the commission of the crime, and directly approximating thereto. Generally punishable as a misdemeanor.

ATTENDANT TERM. A term held " upon trust to attend an inheritance "; that is, an estate for years in land held in trust for the party entitled to the inheritance thereof on the expiration of the term of years; thus giving protection to him against any unknown incumbrance created *since* the creation of the term, but before the party became entitled to the inheritance. See now Satisfied Terms Act, 1845 (8 & 9 Vict. c. 112). [OUTSTANDING TERM.]

ATTERMINING. The purchasing or gaining longer time for the payment of a debt. *Cowel.*

ATTESTATION. The subscription by a person of his name to a deed, will, or other document executed by another, for the purpose of testifying to its genuineness.

1. Deed or document *inter vivos*. A deed ought to be duly attested, that is, show that it was executed by the party in the presence of a witness or witnesses: in most cases this is rather for preserving the evidence, than for constituting the essence, of the deed, but attestation is essential for the validity of bills of sale (41 & 42 Vict. c. 31; 45 & 46 Vict. c. 43), and for deeds executing powers of appointment (22 & 23 Vict. c. 35, s. 12), and in a few other cases. 1 *Steph. Com.*

2. Will. Every will must now, by the Wills Act of 1837, be made in the presence of two or more witnesses present at the same time, such witnesses *attesting* and subscribing the will in the

ATTESTATION—*continued.*
presence of the testator, though not necessarily in the presence of each other. 1 *Steph. Com.* Before this Act three witnesses were necessary for a will of real property, but none for a will of personal property.

ATTESTATION CLAUSE. The clause wherein a witness to a deed, will, or other document certifies to its genuineness. It is not legally essential, even for a will (1 Vict. c. 26, s. 8), but is the simplest evidence of due execution. [ATTESTATION.]

ATTESTED COPY. A copy of a document verified as correct.

ATTORN. 1. In feudal times a lord could not alien or transfer the fealty he claimed from a vassal without the consent of the latter. In giving this consent, the vassal was said to *attorn* (or *turn* over his fealty to the new lord), and the proceeding was called an *attornment.* 1 *Steph. Com.* This doctrine of attornment was extended to all lessees for life or years, and became very troublesome, until, by 4 & 5 Anne, c. 16, s. 9, attornments were made no longer necessary. 1 *Steph. Com.*
2. To *turn over* or intrust business to another; hence the word *attorney* is used to signify a person intrusted with the transaction of another's business. [POWER OF ATTORNEY.]

ATTORNEY. One appointed by another man to do something in his stead. [ATTORN; ATTORNEY-AT-LAW; POWER OF ATTORNEY.]

ATTORNEY-AT-LAW is one who is put in the place, stead or *turn* of another, to manage his matters of law. Formerly every suitor was obliged to appear in person, but later it was permitted in general that attorneys might be made to prosecute or defend any action in the absence of the parties to the suit. Attorneys were officers of the Superior Courts of Law at Westminster, and corresponded to the solicitors of the Court of Chancery and the proctors of the Admiralty and Ecclesiastical Courts. Since the Judicature Act, 1873 (s. 87), all are styled solicitors of the Supreme Court. [SOLICITORS.]

ATTORNEY-GENERAL. The principal law officer of the Crown, and the head of the bar of England. It is his duty, among other things, to prosecute on behalf of the Crown, to file, *ex officio,* informations in the name of the Crown. 3 *Steph. Com.* [INFORMATION.]

ATTORNEY OF THE DUCHY COURT OF LANCASTER (now styled "attorney-general"). The second officer of that court, who, for his skill in law, is placed as assessor to the Chancellor of the Duchy, the Chancellor being for the most part some honourable person, chosen rather for some special trust reposed in him, than for any great learning.

AUCTIONEERS, licensed agents to sell property and conduct sales or auctions. He is deemed the agent of both parties, and can bind both by his memorandum of sale under the Statute of Frauds. The duties of excise on sale by auction were repealed by 8 & 9 Vict. c. 15, and a new duty of 10*l.* annually on auctioneers' licences imposed. 2 *Steph. Com.* [SALE BY AUCTION ACT.]

AUDI ALTERAM PARTEM (hear the other side). Both sides should be heard before a decision is given.

AUDIENCE COURT (*Curia audientiæ Cantuariensis*) is a court belonging to the Archbishop of Canterbury, of equal authority with the Arches Court, though inferior both in dignity and antiquity. The Archbishop of York has also an audience court. But these courts, as separate courts, have long since been disused.

AUDIENDO ET TERMINANDO. A writ or commission, directed to certain persons, when any riotous assembly, insurrection, or heinous misdemeanor or trespass, is committed for the appeasing and punishment thereof. [OYER AND TERMINER.]

AUDITA QUERELA. A writ that lay for the defendant against whom judgment was given, and who was therefore in danger of execution, or was perhaps actually in execution; but who was entitled to be relieved upon some matter of discharge which had happened since the judgment. The indulgence shown by the court in granting relief *upon motion* had almost superseded the remedy by *auditâ querelâ,* and it was abolished by Ord. XLII., r. 22, of the Rules of Court under the Judicature Acts. 3 *Steph. Com.*

AUDITOR is defined to be an officer of the king, or some other great person, who, by yearly examining the accounts of all under officers accountable, makes up a general book that shows the difference between their receipts or charges and their payments or allowances. *Stat.* 33 *Hen.* 8, *c.* 33.

The name has in modern times been assumed by persons employed to check the accounts of corporations, companies and partnerships.

AULA REGIA (or *Aula Regis*). A court established by William the Conqueror in his own hall. This court was composed of the king's great officers of state resident in his palace, and usually attendant on his person, assisted by persons learned in the laws, who were called the king's justiciars or justices, and by the greater barons of parliament, all of whom had a seat in the *aula regia*, and formed a kind of Court of Appeal, or rather of advice, in matters of great moment and difficulty. This court was at first bound to follow the king's household in all his progresses and expeditions, whereby the trial of common causes was found very burdensome to the subjects. By the eleventh chapter of *Magna Charta*, it was enacted that thenceforth, " *Communia placita non sequantur curiam regis, sed teneantur in aliquo certo loco.*" (Common pleas should not follow the king's court, but be held in some certain place.) This " certain place" was established in Westminster Hall, where it continued until the Judicature Act, section 26 of which Act empowers the High Court and the Court of Appeal to sit at any place. 3 *Steph. Com.* [SUPREME COURT OF JUDICATURE.]

AULNAGER. The king's officer, whose duty it was to measure all cloths made for sale, and levy the duty thereon. 2 *Steph. Com.*

AURUM REGINÆ (queen's gold). A royal revenue which belonged to every queen consort. It was due from every person who made a voluntary offering or fine to the king amounting to ten marks or upwards, for and in consideration of any privileges, or other matter of royal favour conferred upon him by the king. 2 *Steph. Com.*

AUTHENTIC ACT. An act or document certified by a notary or public authority.

AUTHENTICATION. A certificate of an act being in due form of law, given by proper authority.

AUTHORITY. (1) Power given by one person to another enabling the latter to do some act. As to authority given by trustees to solicitors or bankers, see Trustee Act, 1893, s. 17 ; (2) a governing body, *e.g.*, county council or other local authority ; (3) grounds for some legal proposition, *e.g.*, judicial decisions, or opinions of authors of standing.

AUTRE DROIT, IN. In right of another. A person may hold property in his own right or in right of another, *e.g.*, trustee in right of *cestui que trust*, or an executor or administrator in right of the deceased and his legatees, devisees, next of kin, or heir at law.

AUTRE VIE. The life of another ; thus an estate *pur autre vie* is an estate for the life of another. 1 *Steph. Com.*

AUTREFOIS ACQUIT (beforetime acquitted). By this plea a prisoner charged with an offence pleads that he has been tried before and acquitted of the same offence. The plea, however, is only good in reference to a verdict of *acquittal* by a *petty jury* ; and, therefore, if a man be committed for trial, and no bill be found against him, or if the petty jury having him in charge be discharged by the judge before verdict, he is still liable to be indicted for the same crime. The first indictment must have been such that he could have been lawfully convicted upon it, and the true test whether such a plea is a sufficient bar in any particular case is, whether the evidence necessary to support the second indictment would have been sufficient to procure a legal conviction on the first. 14 *&* 15 *Vict. c.* 100, *s.* 28, and *c.* 99, *s.* 13 ; 4 *Steph. Com.*

AUTREFOIS ATTAINT. A plea by an accused person that he has formerly been attainted for the same crime. Before the statute 7 & 8 Geo. 4, c. 28, this plea might have been pleaded where a man, after being attainted of one felony, was afterwards indicted for *another* offence : for, the prisoner being dead in law by the first attainder, it was deemed superfluous to endeavour to attaint him a second time. But, by sect. 4 of that statute, no plea setting forth any attainder shall be pleaded in bar of any indictment, unless the attainder be for the same offence as that charged in the indictment. 4 *Steph. Com.*

Attainders are now abolished, and the plea of *autrefois convict* supersedes this. *Ibid.; stat.* 33 & 34 *Vict. c.* 23.

AUTREFOIS CONVICT. A plea by an accused person that he has been previously convicted of the same crime of which he is accused. This plea is a good plea in bar to an indictment. It depends upon the same principle, and is governed by the same rules as *autrefois acquit (q.v.).* As to the form of the plea, see 14 & 15 *Vict. c.* 100, s. 28. 4 *Steph. Com.*

AUXILIUM. An aid or service paid by a tenant to his lord. [AID.]

AUXILIUM FACERE ALICUI IN CURIA REGIS. To be another's friend and solicitor in the king's court. *Cowel.*

AUXILIUM VICECOMITI (aid to the sheriff). The aid or customary dues formerly paid to the sheriff for the better support of his office.

AVENAGE (Lat. *Avena*, oats). A certain quantity of oats paid to a landlord in lieu of some other duties, or as a rent from the tenant.

AVENTURE. [ADVENTURE; MISADVENTURE.]

AVERAGE. 1. That service which the tenant owes the lord, to be done by the beasts of the tenant.

2. Stubble or short standing straw in cornfields after harvest.

3. *General Average* is the contribution which the proprietors, in general, of a ship, cargo, and freight, make towards the loss sustained by any individual of their number, whose property has been sacrificed for the common safety. The proportion which the value of the property so sacrificed bears to the entire value of the whole ship, cargo, and freight, including what has been sacrificed, is first ascertained; and then the property of each owner contributes in the proportion so found. Under the usual maritime policies the underwriters are liable for these payments made by the assured. 2 *Steph. Com.*

4. *Particular Average,* as distinguished from General Average, is a loss upon the ship, cargo or freight, severally, to be borne by the owner of the particular property on which it happens; and, in cases where the loss is not total, it is called *average* or *partial* loss. In every case of partial loss the underwriter is liable to pay such proportion of the sum he has subscribed as the damage sustained by the subject of insurance bears to the whole value at the time of insurance.

5. *Petty Arerage* consists of small charges paid by the master for the benefit of the ship and cargo, such as pilotage, towage, etc.

6. A small duty which merchants who send goods in another man's ship pay the master for his care, over and above the freight. [*Cf.* PRIMAGE.]

AVERIA CARUCÆ. Beasts of the plough. 3 *Steph. Com.*

AVERIUM. An heriot, consisting of the best live beast the tenant dies possessed of. [HERIOT.]

AVERMENT (Lat. *Verificatio*) has different meanings. 1. A positive statement of facts as opposed to an argumentative or inferential one. 2. The offer of a defendant to make good or justify his plea, either a *general* averment or a *particular* one, where a special method of verification was mentioned. 3. The technical name (in pleading) for allegations, such as occur in declarations on contracts, of the due performance of all the conditions precedent, which the form and effect of each contract show to be necessary. For rules of pleading, see now R. S. C., Ord. XIX.

AVOIDANCE. 1. A vacancy; especially of the vacancy of a living by the death of the incumbent.

2. Making void or null; especially of a plea by a defendant in *confession and avoidance* of the plaintiff's declaration. [CONFESSION AND AVOIDANCE.]

3. Destroying the effect of a written instrument, or of any disposition therein,

(1) By revocation on the part of any person entitled to revoke the same.

(2) By establishing its invalidity in a court of justice. 2 *Bl.;* 1 *Steph. Com.*

AVOWRY. [ADVOW; REPLEVIN.]

AVOWTERER. An adulterer.

AVOWTRY. Adultery.

AVULSION. The sudden removal of soil from the land of one man, and its deposit upon the land of another, by the action of water. The soil in such case belongs to the owner from whose land it is removed.

AWARD. The decision of an arbitrator. [ARBITRATION.]

AWAY-GOING CROP. A crop sown during the last year of a tenancy, but not ripe till after its expiration. The out-going tenant is generally entitled to take the crop either by the express terms of his contract or by the custom of the county. Under modern farming agreements a claim for compensation is usually substituted. [EMBLEMENTS.]

AYANT CAUSE, in France, is one to whom the rights of another in an action are transferred by legacy, gift, sale, exchange, etc.

BACKADATION, or **BACKWARDATION.** A premium given to obtain the loan of stock against its value in money, when stock is more in demand than money. *Stutfield's Stock Exchange.*

BACKBERIND THIEF. A thief taken carrying those things that he hath stolen in a bundle or fardel on his back.

BACK-BOND. A deed which qualifies or attaches a condition to an absolute disposition and in conjunction with it constitutes a trust.

BACKING A WARRANT. The indorsement by a justice of the peace, in one county or jurisdiction, of a warrant issued in another. 4 *Steph. Com.* ; *Stone's Justices' Manual.*

BACKSIDE. Formerly used to denote a yard at the back of a house, and belonging thereto.

BAD (in substance). The technical word for an unsound plea.

BADGER. One who buys corn or victuals in one place and takes them to another to sell ; formerly required a licence.

BAIL (Fr. *Bailler*, to deliver). The freeing or setting at liberty one arrested or imprisoned, upon others becoming sureties by recognizance for his appearance at a day and place certainly assigned, he also entering into his own recognizance. The party is delivered (or *bailed*) into the hands of the sureties, and is accounted by law to be in their custody ; they may, if they will, surrender him to the court before the date assigned and free themselves from further responsibility. By Bail Act, 1898, justices are empowered to dispense with sureties if of opinion that it will not defeat the ends of justice. [*Cf.* MAINPRISE,] Also, the sureties in such case are commonly said to become bail. [COMMON BAIL ; SPECIAL BAIL.]

BAIL BOND. A bond taken by a sheriff after arrest for the appearance of a defendant, generally with two sureties. Also used in certain civil proceedings, *e.g.,* under Debtors Act, 1869, to hold a defendant to bail.

BAIL COURT. A branch of the Court of King's Bench, sometimes called the Practice Court, which sat for the purpose of taking new bail in addition to, or substitution for, existing bail, and for ascertaining the sufficiency of persons offering themselves as bail, and otherwise disposing of applications of ordinary occurrence in practice, and for other purposes.

BAILABLE OFFENCE. An offence for which justices may or are bound to take bail. 4 *Steph. Com.* ; *Stone's Justices' Manual.*

BAILEE. A person to whom goods are entrusted by way of bailment. [BAILMENT.]

BAILIE, or **BAILLIE,** in Scotch Law signifies a magistrate of a borough.

BAILIFF (Lat. *Ballivus.*) A subordinate officer, appointed to execute writs and processes, and do other ministerial acts. Thus, there are *bound* (or bum) bailiffs, employed by the sheriffs, and *bound* annually to the sheriff, with sureties, for the due execution of their office ; *special* bailiffs, bailiffs of manors, hundreds, liberties, and bailiffs of county and inferior courts. 2 *Steph. Com.*

BAILIFF-ERRANT. A bailiff's deputy.

BAILIWICK. The county or area over which a sheriff exercises jurisdiction ; also that liberty which is exempted from the sheriff of the county, over which the lord of the liberty appointeth a bailiff, with such powers within his precinct as the under-sheriff exercises under the sheriff of the county.

BAILMENT. A delivery of goods from one person, called the *bailor*, to another person, called the *bailee*, for some purpose, upon a contract, express or implied, that, after the purpose has been fulfilled, they shall be re-delivered to the bailor, or otherwise dealt with according to his directions, or kept till he reclaims them. 2 *Steph. Com.; Story on Bailments.*

Bailments are of three kinds :—

1. Those for the exclusive benefit of the *bailor*, as, if A. leaves plate with B. to keep safely and securely without reward. He, the bailee, is only responsible in respect of gross negligence.

2. Those for the mutual benefit of *bailor* and *bailee;* as, if C. lets a horse to D. for so much per hour ; or if E. gives F. (a tailor) clothes to repair, in the course of his trade, etc. The bailee must exercise ordinary care.

3. Those for the exclusive benefit of the *bailee;* as, if G. lends H. a book to read, without reward. The bailee is responsible for even slight negligence.

If the bailee fraudulently appropriates the goods, he is guilty of larceny. *Stat. 24 & 25 Vict. c. 96, s. 3.*

BAILPIECE. The slip of parchment on which the recognizance entered into by parties becoming bail is transmitted to the court.

BAIRMAN. A bankrupt or debtor left bare or naked.

BALANCE ORDER. A special order served upon a contributory to a company, after default made, to pay within four days the balance of a call due from him.

BALIVO AMOVENDO. A writ to remove a bailiff out of his office for want of sufficient living in his bailiwick. *Cowel.*

BALLASTAGE. A toll paid for the privilege of taking ballast from the bottom of a port or harbour.

BALLOT, VOTE BY. A method of secret voting. By the Ballot Act, 1872, this method of voting was introduced at parliamentary and municipal elections. Does not apply to the universities.

BANC, or BANCO, SITTINGS IN. Formerly sittings of one of the superior courts of Westminster, for the purposes of determining matters of law and transacting judicial business other than the trial of actions. Sittings *in banco* are opposed to sittings at *nisi prius*, in which a judge sits to try a case, with or without a jury. The business of the courts sitting *in banco* is transferred to divisional courts of the High Court of Justice by ss. 40, 41, of the Judicature Act, 1873. See 3 *Steph. Com.* [See DIVISIONAL COURT.]

BANDIT. A man outlawed, put under the ban of the law.

BANERET, or KNIGHT BANNERET (Lat. *Miles vexillarius*). A knight made in the field, with the ceremony of cutting off the point of his standard, and making it, as it were, a banner ; and accounted so honourable that if created in the king's presence he ranked next to a baron and before a baronet. 2 *Steph. Com.*

BANISHMENT. Expulsion from the realm ; only permissible under special Acts of parliament. [TRANSPORTATION.]

BANK HOLIDAYS. Days made holidays by statute for banks, customs, inland revenue offices, bonding warehouses, docks, and most Government offices, viz., Easter Monday, Whit Monday, first Monday in August, day following Christmas Day, and any other day specially proclaimed by the Crown. 34 & 35 *Vict. c.* 17 ; 38 & 39 *Vict. c.* 13 ; 45 & 46 *Vict. c.* 61 ; *R. S. C., Ord. LXIV.* 2 *Steph. Com.*

BANK RATE. The minimum rate of discount charged for the time being by the Bank of England for discounting, *i.e.,* cashing before due, the bills of the first mercantile houses. The fluctuations in the Bank Rate are notified from time to time to the public.

BANK-CREDIT. Accommodation allowed to a person on security given to a bank to draw upon the bank up to a certain amount agreed upon.

BANKER'S BOOKS EVIDENCE ACT, 1879, makes a copy of an entry in a banker's book *primâ facie* evidence of such entry upon proof that the copy has been checked by comparison with the original entry.

BANK-NOTE. A promissory note issued by a bank, undertaking to pay to bearer on demand the amount of the note.

BANKRUPT. A debtor who, by reason of some act or circumstance indicating a failure to meet his liabilities, and called an "act of bankruptcy," has been adjudicated a "bankrupt" by the High Court of Justice or by a county court exercising bankruptcy jurisdiction. With a few exceptions, anyone, whether in trade or not, may be made a bankrupt, and proceedings are commenced by a petition for a receiving order either by a creditor or by the debtor himself, and upon such order the whole of the debtor's property, with a few minor exceptions, vests in an official receiver, and subsequently, if appointed, in a trustee, and becomes distributable among all the creditors in proportion to their debts, subject to certain preferential payments for rates, taxes, wages, etc. On obtaining his discharge from the court the debtor is (with a few exceptions) freed from all debts existing at the time of his bankruptcy. *Bankruptcy Acts,* 1883, 1890, 46 & 47 *Vict. c.* 52 ; 53 & 54 *Vict. c.* 71 ; *and rules thereunder. Robson's Bankruptcy.* [ACT OF BANKRUPTCY ; ADJUDICATION.]

BANNIMUS. The form of expulsion of any member from the University of Oxford, by affixing the sentence in some public place, as a denunciation or promulgation of it.

BANNITUS. An outlaw, a banished man.

BANNS, BANS, or **BAN.** A public notice given of anything. In England we use this word "banns" especially in the publishing of matrimonial contracts in the church before marriage. 2 *Steph. Com.*

BANNUM, or **BANLEUGA.** The utmost bounds of a manor or town.

BAR. A term used in several senses.
1. Of the place where prisoners stand to be tried ; hence the expression "prisoner at the bar."
2. Of the place where barristers stand in court to speak for their clients ; hence the term *barristers.*
3. Of the profession of a barrister, and the persons who practise it.
4. Of an impediment : thus we speak of uses or limitations in a deed "in bar of dower," because they are intended to prevent a wife becoming entitled to dower out of the lands comprised in the deed. [DOWER.] Also of "barring," or destroying, an entail.
5. Of *pleas in bar,* which are pleas which go to the root of a plaintiff's action, and, if allowed, destroy it entirely.
6. A trial at bar is a trial by jury before two or more judges of the Supreme Court for matters of great importance, or where the Crown is concerned. 3 *Steph. Com.*

BAR FEE. A fee of twenty pence which every prisoner acquitted of felony anciently paid to the gaoler.

BAR OF THE HOUSE. The place at which witnesses before either house of parliament are examined, and to which persons guilty of a breach of privilege are brought to receive judgment. *May's Parl. Pract.*

BARE TRUSTEE is a trustee who has no duty to perform other than, on request, to convey the estate to his *cestui que trust* or according to the latter's direction.

BARGAIN AND SALE is properly a contract for sale of lands or goods, transferring the property from the bargainor to the bargainee, but it is used specially to describe a form of conveyance of lands. Prior to the Statute of Uses (27 Hen. 8, c. 10) the effect of a bargain and sale was, that the bargainor stood seised of the land to the use of the bargainee, to the extent to which it was affected by the transaction ; *i.e.,* though the bargainor's estate was still good *at law,* yet a court of *equity* considered the estate as belonging to the bargainee, who had paid the money. But the Statute of Uses had the effect of transferring the bargainee's interest into a *legal estate.* To secure publicity in the transfer of legal estates it was provided by 27 Hen. 8, c. 16, that a bargain and sale of freehold estate must be by deed indented, sealed, and enrolled, either in the county where the lands lie, or in one of the King's Courts of Record at Westminster, within six months after the date of the deed. 1 *Steph. Com.* ; *Wms. R. P.*

BARLEYCORN. (1) The third of an inch : (2) a nominal rent or consideration.

BARMOTE, BERGHMOTH, or **BERGHMOTE COURTS** are two courts, called the Great and Small Barmote Courts, having jurisdiction under s. 16 of the High Peak Mining Customs and Mineral

BARMOTE COURTS—*continued.*

Courts Act, 1851 (14 & 15 Vict. c. 94), over the parts of the hundred of High Peak in Derbyshire, in which the king in right of the Duchy of Lancaster, is entitled to the mineral duties. Both courts are courts of record under s. 15 of the Act. They are presided over by a judge, called " the steward," the executive officer being called the barmaster or berghmaster. See 3 *Steph. Com.*

BARON has the following meanings :—

1. A degree of nobility next to a viscount. Barons hold (*a*) by prescription, (*b*) by patent. Not by tenure (*Berkeley Peerage Case*, 1861).

2. A judge of the Court of Exchequer. These judges were superseded by justices of the High Court, King's Bench Division, by Judicature Acts.

3. Baron is the word used formerly of a husband in relation to his wife.

4. The chief magistrates of London were also anciently called barons before they had a lord mayor, as appears by several ancient charters. 2 *Steph. Com.*

BARONET (Lat. *Baronettus*) is a dignity or degree of honour created by letters patent and descendible to issue male, and hath precedency before banerets, knights of the bath, and knights bachelors, excepting only such banerets as are made *sub vexillis regis in aperto bello, et ipso rege personaliter præsente.* [BANERET.]

This order was created by King James I. in 1611. 2 *Steph. Com.*

BARONY. The honour and territory that gives title to a baron. Also a tract of land in Ireland.

BARRATOR, or **BARRETOR**. 1. A deceiver, a vile knave or unthrift.

2. A person guilty of barratry. [BARRATRY.]

BARRATRY. 1. Any wilfully wrongful or fraudulent act committed by the master of a ship or the mariners, causing damage to the ship or cargo, to which the owner is not a consenting party. 9 *Steph. Com.*

2. *Common barratry* is the offence of *frequently* inciting and stirring up suits and quarrels between his majesty's subjects, either at law or otherwise. 2 *Steph. Com.*

3. In Scotland the offence committed by a judge who is induced by a bribe to pronounce judgment.

4. It is also applied to the simony of clergymen going abroad to purchase benefices from the see of Rome.

BARRISTER. A person called to the bar by the benchers of the Inns of Court giving exclusive right of audience in the Supreme Court except in Bankruptcy. A barrister cannot sue for fees, but is not liable for negligence. See 3 *Steph. Com.* and *Chit. Stat. Vol. VI.*

BARTON, BERTON, or **BURTON,** is a term used in Devonshire and other parts for the demesne lands of a manor ; sometimes for the manor-house itself ; and in some places for outhouses and foldyards. [DEMESNE.]

BAS CHEVALIERS. Low or inferior knights holding by base tenure : simple knights are called knights bachelors or base-chevaliers.

BASE COURT. An inferior court, not of record, as the court baron.

BASE ESTATE. The estate which base tenants have in their land ; base tenants being those who hold at the will of their lord. Pure copyholders are reckoned among base tenants. [COPYHOLD.]

BASE FEE. 1. The estate created by a tenant in tail, not in possession, who bars the entail without the consent of the protector of the settlement. He thus bars his own issue but not any remainder or reversion and creates a base fee determinable on the failure of his issue in tail.

2. An estate descendible to heirs general, but terminable on an uncertain event. So long, however, as it lasts, it differs in nothing from a fee simple.

Thus if land be granted to the use of A. and his heirs until B. returns from Rome, and then to the use of B. and his heirs, A.'s estate, so long as it lasts, is a base fee.

3. An estate held at the will of the lord. 1 *Steph. Com.*

BASILICA. A body of law framed A.D. 880 by the Emperor Basilius.

BASTARD, in English law, is one that is born of parents not legally married. 1 *Steph. Com.*

In the Scotch and other systems derived from the Roman civil law, one born a bastard may be legitimated by the subsequent marriage of the parents.

BASTARD EIGNÉ. When a man has a bastard son and after marries the mother, and by her has a legitimate son, the eldest son is *bastard eigné* (*eigné* being from the French *aisné* or *ainé*), and the younger son is *mulier puisné*. 1 *Steph. Com.*

BASTARDY ORDER. [AFFILIATION.]

BATH, KNIGHT OF THE. [KNIGHT OF THE BATH.]

BATTEL. [WAGER OF BATTEL.]

BATTERY. A violent striking or beating of any man : in law this includes any touching or laying hold of another, however slight. 3 & 4 *Steph. Com.*

BAWDY HOUSE. [BROTHEL.]

BEACONAGE (*Beconagium*). Money paid towards the maintenance of a beacon. 3 *Steph. Com.*

BEADLE. [BEDEL.]

BEAR, on the Stock Exchange, is a seller of stock which he cannot deliver ; *i.e.*, one who speculates for the fall in price of stock which he does not possess, thus enabling him to subsequently buy it for less than he has previously sold it for. [BULL, 2.]

BEARER. 1. He who bears down or oppresses others. 4 *Edw.* 3, c. 11. [MAINTENANCE.]
2. Money payable under a cheque or security may be expressed to be payable to a certain person or bearer, in which case anyone who presents the security may claim payment, and in case of transfer endorsement will not be necessary.

BECAUSE OF VICINAGE. [COMMON, I.3.]

BEDEL (Fr. *Bedeau*) signifies a messenger or apparator of a court that cites men to appear and answer ; also an inferior officer of a parish or liberty, to give notice of vestry meetings, etc.

BEDFORD LEVEL REGISTRY. An office for the registration of conveyances of lands forming part of the great level of the fens, in order that the grantees may obtain the privileges conferred by 13 Car. 2, c. 17, and subsequent Acts thereon.

BEERHOUSE. A house licensed for the sale of beer for consumption either on or off the premises, as opposed to beershop for sale off only. [ALEHOUSE.]

BENCH. A word often used with reference to judges and magistrates ; thus we speak of "judges on the bench," "the judicial bench," "a bench of magistrates." Also the bishops of the Episcopal bench.

BENCH WARRANT. A warrant issued by the presiding judicial officer at assizes or sessions for the apprehension of an offender ; so called in opposition to a justice's warrant, issued by an ordinary justice of the peace or police magistrate. 4 *Steph. Com.*

BENCHERS. Principal officers of each inn of court, in whom the government of the inn is vested. 1 *Steph. Com.*

BENEFICE. An ecclesiastical living, or care of souls of a parish ; see 61 & 62 Vict. c. 48. Anciently used of the interest of a grantee of lands under a feudal grant ; a feud. 1 *Steph. Com.* ; 4 *Steph. Com.*

BENEFICIAL INTEREST. This expression is used to indicate a right of substantial enjoyment or equitable interest, in opposition to merely nominal ownership or legal interest. Thus, if A. holds lands in trust for B., A. is said to have the legal estate, and B. is said to have the beneficial interest, or to be the beneficiary or *cestui que trust*.

BENEFICIARY. 1. The person in possession of a benefice (*q.v.*).
2. One who has the beneficial interest.

BENEFICIO PRIMO ECCLESIASTICO HABENDO. An old writ directed from the king to the chancellor or lord keeper, to bestow the benefice that first shall fall in the king's gift, above or under such a value, upon this or that man.

BENEFIT BUILDING SOCIETY. A society established to raise a subscription fund, by advances from which the members shall be enabled to build or purchase dwelling-houses, or to purchase land, such advances being secured to the society by mortgage of the premises so built and purchased. 3 *Steph. Com.* ; *Wurtzburg's Building Societies.*

BENEFIT OF CLERGY (Lat. *Privilegium clericale*), or, as it is more shortly expressed, "clergy," originally consisted in the privilege allowed to a clerk in orders, when prosecuted in the

BENEFIT OF CLERGY—*continued.*

temporal court, of being discharged from thence, and handed over to the Court Christian in order to make canonical purgation, that is, to clear himself on his own oath and that of twelve persons as his compurgators. In England this was extended to all who could read, and so were capable of becoming clerks, and ultimately allowed by stat. 5 Ann. c. 6, without reference to the ability to read. The privilege of benefit of clergy was entirely abolished in 1827 by stat. 7 & 8 Geo. 4, c. 28, s. 6.

Benefit of clergy had no application except in capital felonies; and from several of these it had been taken away by various statutes, constituting the offences to which they respectively applied "felony without benefit of clergy." 4 *Steph. Com.*

BENEVOLENCE. Nominally a voluntary gratuity given by subjects to the king, but which was in reality a forced loan or tax. It was made an article in the Petition of Right, 3 Car. 1, that no man shall be compelled to yield any gift, loan or benevolence, tax, or such like charge, without common consent by Act of parliament. 1 *Steph. Com.; Hall. Const. Hist.*

BENEVOLENT SOCIETY. [FRIENDLY SOCIETY.]

BEQUEATH. To dispose of personal property by will. In reference to real property the word "devise" is generally used.

BEQUEST. A disposition by will of personal property; a legacy.

BERBIAGE. A rent paid for the depasturing of sheep. *Cowel.*

BERCARIA. A sheepfold or other inclosure for sheep.

BERGHMOTH, or **BERGHMOTE.** See BARMOTE COURTS.

BERTON. See BARTON.

BESAIEL, BESAILE, or **BESAYLE,** *great-grandfather.*

BESTIALITY. The crime of men having carnal intercourse with beasts.

BETACHES. Laymen using glebe lands.

BETTER EQUITY. Where A. has, in the contemplation of a court of equity, a superior claim to land or other property than B. has, he is said to have a *better*

equity. Thus, a second mortgagee, advancing his money without knowledge of a prior mortgage, has a better equity than the first mortgagee who has not secured for himself the possession of the title deeds, or has parted with them, so as to enable the mortgagor to secure the second advance as upon an unincumbered estate.

BETTING HOUSES, the Act for the suppression of (16 & 17 Vict. c. 119). Betting in public places is prohibited by 30 & 31 Vict. c. 134, s. 23. See *Powell* v. *Kempton Park Racecourse Co.*, 1899, A. C. 143, as to meaning of "place" for betting.

BEVERCHES. Customary services done at the bidding of the lord by his inferior tenants.

BEYOND SEAS. An expression to indicate that a person is outside of the United Kingdom, the Channel Islands, and the Isle of Man. Plaintiff's absence beyond the seas does not now give him further time to sue, 19 & 20 Vict. c. 97, s. 12, and 37 & 38 Vict. c. 57, but defendant's absence suspends operation of Statutes of Limitation. 3 *Steph. Com.* [ABSENCE.]

BID. To offer a price for a thing which is being sold. May be withdrawn before acceptance except where under seal. [PROFFER.]

BIGAMY (*Bigamia*). The offence of marrying a second time, by one who has a former husband or wife still living and not divorced. 4 *Steph. Com.; Russell on Crimes.*

BILANCIIS DEFERENDIS. A writ, now obsolete, directed to a corporation for the carrying of weights to any haven, there to weigh the wool that persons by our ancient laws were l,censed to transport.

BILATERAL CONTRACT. One in which the parties are under obligations reciprocally towards each other, *e.g.*, sale where one becomes bound to deliver the thing sold and the other to pay the price.

BILBOES. A punishment at sea, answering to the stocks.

BILINGUIS (two-tongued). In a legal sense is used for a jury *de medietate linguæ*, of which part were Englishmen and part strangers. [DE MEDIETATE LINGUÆ.]

BILL. This word has several significations :—

1. An account delivered by a creditor to his debtor in respect of goods supplied or work done. Thus, a *bill of costs* is a bill furnished by a solicitor to his client, as to which see 6 & 7 Vict. c. 73, s. 37 ; 33 & 34 Vict. c. 38 ; and 44 & 45 Vict. c. 44, and general order thereunder.

2. A bill in equity or chancery was the written statement whereby the plaintiff in a chancery suit complained of the wrong upon which the suit was based, and sought the appropriate redress. Its place has been taken by a writ and statement of claim since the Judicature Acts.

3. A bill of indictment against a prisoner is the presentment charging his offence, and submitted to the grand jury, and to this they either return " a true bill " or " ignore the bill." 4 *Steph. Com.*

4. Bill in parliament. A measure submitted to either house of parliament for the purpose of being passed into law. When a measure has been actually passed into law, it is called an " Act."

Bills are divided into public and private bills. It may be laid down generally (though not without exception) that bills for the particular interest or benefit of any person or persons, of a public company or corporation, a parish, a city, a county, or other locality, are treated as *private bills*, to be distinguished from measures of public policy in which the whole community are interested, which are called *public bills*.

A public bill must be introduced by a member of the house. In the House of Lords, any peer is at liberty to present a bill, and have it laid upon the table ; but, in the Commons, a member must first move for and obtain permission from the house, before he can bring in a bill. *May's Parl. Pract. ; Anson's Law of the Constitution, Part I.*

5. See also the titles following.

BILL OF ADVENTURE. [ADVENTURE, BILL OF.]

BILL OF ATTAINDER. A bill brought into parliament for attainting any person or persons. [ATTAINDER.]

BILL OF COMPLAINT. Same as BILL, 2.

BILL OF CONFORMITY. A bill filed by an executor or administrator when the affairs of the testator or intestate were so much involved that he could not safely administer the estate except under the direction of the court of chancery. Now superseded by action or summons for administration. See *R. S. C., Ord. LV.*

BILL OF COSTS. See BILL, 1.

BILL OF DEBT, or **BILL OBLIGATORY.** A written acknowledgment of a debt by a merchant, setting out the amount, the date, and the place of payment. It may be under seal or not.

BILL OF ENTRY. An account of the goods entered at the custom house both inwards and outwards. It must state the name of the merchant, the quantity and species of the goods, etc.

BILL OF EXCEPTIONS. If, during a civil trial, a judge, in his directions to the jury, or his decision, mistook the law, counsel on either side might require him publicly to seal a *bill of exceptions*, which was a statement in writing of the point wherein he was supposed to err, so that the point might be settled by a court of error. Bills of exceptions were abolished by the Judicature Acts and Rules, and the present mode of proceeding is by motion for a new trial. 3 *Steph. Com.*

BILL OF EXCHANGE. Defined by the Bills of Exchange Act, 1882, as an unconditional order in writing, addressed by one person (the drawer) to another (the drawee, and afterwards acceptor), signed by the person giving it, requiring the person to whom it is addressed to pay on demand, or at a fixed or determinable future time, a sum certain in money to, or to the order of, a specified person, or to bearer (the payee). *Chalmers' Bills of Exchange ; 2 Steph. Com.*

BILL OF HEALTH. A certificate, signed by a consul and given to the ship's master on leaving a port, showing the sanitary condition of the port at the time the ship sailed. It may be *clean*, suspected (or touched), or foul.

BILL OF INDEMNITY. An Act of parliament passed every session (until rendered unnecessary by the passing of the Promissory Oaths Act, 1868) for the relief of those who had neglected to take the necessary oaths, etc., required for the purpose of qualifying them to hold their respective offices.

BILL OF LADING. A mode of authenticating the transfer of property in goods sent by ship. It is, in form, a receipt from the captain to the shipper or consignor, undertaking to deliver the goods, on payment of freight, to some person whose name is therein expressed, or endorsed thereon by the consignor. The delivery of this instrument will transfer to the party so named (usually called the consignee), or to any other person whose name he may think fit to endorse thereon, the property in such goods. It is thus used both as a contract for carriage and a document of title. 3 *Steph. Com.; Scrutton's Charter Parties and Bills of Lading.*

BILL OF MIDDLESEX was a fictitious mode of giving the Court of King's Bench jurisdiction in personal actions by arresting a defendant for a supposed trespass. Abolished by 2 Will. 4, c. 39; and since 1 & 2 Vict. c. 110, all personal actions in the superior courts are commenced by writ of summons. 3 *Steph. Com.* [AC ETIAM; LATITAT.]

BILL OF PAINS AND PENALTIES. A bill introduced into parliament for affecting any person or persons with pains and penalties short of death without the usual criminal proceedings.

BILL OF PARCELS. Invoices (*q.v.*).

BILL OF PARTICULARS. A specific statement by a plaintiff to a defendant of what he seeks to recover by his action, or of a defendant's set-off. [PARTICULARS OF CLAIM OR DEFENCE.]

BILL OF PEACE. A bill formerly filed in chancery for quieting litigation by a person threatened with a multiplicity of actions, all involving the same point. It determined the point in issue, if not already sufficiently determined, and then granted an injunction against further litigation thereon. Now superseded by an action in the nature of a bill of peace, which is not confined to the Chancery Division. Where there are several existing actions involving the same question, a *consolidation* order may be obtained. [CONSOLIDATION ORDER.]

BILL OF REVIEW. [REVIEW, BILL OF; BILL OF REVIVOR; REVIVOR.]

BILL OF RIGHTS. A declaration delivered by the Lords and Commons to the Prince and Princess of Orange, 13th February, 1688-9, and afterwards enacted in parliament, when they became king and queen, by 1 W. & M. st. 2, c. 2. It declared illegal certain acts of the late king, and insisted on the rights and liberties asserted therein as being the "true, ancient, and indubitable rights of the people of this kingdom." 2 *Steph. Com.; May's Parl. Pract.*

BILL OF SALE. An assignment under seal of chattels personal. 2 *Steph. Com.* Provision was first made by the Bills of Sale Act, 1854, for the registration of bills of sale within twenty-one days from the making thereof. The Act of 1878 applies now only to absolute bills of sale, *i.e.*, given otherwise than by way of mortgage, *e.g.*, a gift where donor remains in possession. The Act of 1882 applies to every bill of sale by way of mortgage. Both classes must be registered within seven days and re-registered every five years, and those under the Act of 1882 must set forth the consideration for which made, and must not be for less than 30*l.* or they will be void. The Act of 1882 also makes void every bill of sale unless it be made in a form scheduled to the Act. *Robson, Bkcy.; Reed, Bills of Sale.*

BILL OF SIGHT. A document furnished to the customs officer by an importer of goods, who, being ignorant of their precise quality and quantity, describes the same to the best of his knowledge and information. *Customs Consolidation Act*, 1876.

BILL OF SUFFERANCE. A licence granted at the custom-house to a merchant, to suffer him to trade from one English port to another without paying custom.

BILLA VERA. A true bill found by a grand jury. 4 *Steph. Com.* [BILL, 3; GRAND JURY.]

BILLETING SOLDIERS. Soldiers are said to be "billeted" when they are dispersed among the several innkeepers and victuallers throughout the kingdom. Regulated now by the Army Act, 1881. 2 *Steph. Com.*

BILLIARDS. Every house where a public billiard table is kept (other than a house licensed for the sale of intoxicating liquors for consumption on the premises) must be licensed by justices of the peace (8 & 9 Vict. c. 109, ss. 10, 14).

BILLS OF MORTALITY are returns of the deaths which occur within a particular district.

In the metropolis the cities of London and Westminster, the borough of Southwark, and thirty-four out-parishes in Middlesex and Surrey, used to be said to be " within the bills of mortality." The system from which the phrase was derived is now practically superseded by the system of civil registration of deaths established in 1836 (6 & 7 Will. 4, c. 86).

BI-PARTITE. Of two parts.

BIRDS. Domesticated birds (*domitæ naturæ*) may be the subject of larceny at common law, and any birds ordinarily kept in a state of confinement or for any domestic purposes are subjects of larceny by ss. 21—23 of the Larceny Act, 1861. Wild birds and the eggs thereof are or may be protected during certain seasons by the Wild Birds Protection Acts, 1880, 1881, 1894, and 1896. And see Wild Animals in Captivity Protection Act, 1900.

BIRETTUM. The cap or coif of a judge or serjeant-at-law.

BISHOP. The principal officer of the Church in each diocese. He is elected by the sovereign's *conge d'élire (q.v.).* A *suffragan* bishop is a deputy or assistant bishop in spiritual matters, a *coadjutor* in temporal matters. 1 *Bl.* 155, 156 ; 2 *Steph. Com.*

BISHOP'S COURT. The consistory court in each diocese, held, under the authority of the bishop, by his chancellor. 2 *Steph. Com.* ; 3 *Steph. Com.*

BISSEXTILE, vulgarly called Leap-year, every fourth year. It is called bissextile, because formerly, in each such year, the *sixth* day before the calends of March was *twice* reckoned, viz., on the 24th and 25th of February. These days were, in each leap-year, by 21 Hen. 3, to be accounted but one day, and the supernumerary day in leap-years is now added to the end of February and called the 29th. 1 *Steph. Com.*

BLACK CAP. The full head dress of a judge, which is worn when sentence of death is passed upon an offender.

BLACK MAIL denoted, in the northern counties, a certain rate of money, or other consideration, paid to persons near the borders, allied with robbers, for protection and safety from the danger of such. These robbers were called moss-troopers.

Also rents paid in grain or baser money were called *reditus nigri,* or *black mail,* as opposed to *reditus albi,* or *white rents,* which were payable in silver. 1 *Steph. Com.* [ALBA FIRMA.]

BLACK ROD is the usher belonging to the most noble order of the Garter ; so called because of the black rod he carries in his hand. He is also usher of the House of Lords. He is also called the *gentleman usher,* as opposed to his deputy, who is called the *yeoman usher.* He is appointed by letters patent from the Crown. He executes the orders of the house for the commitment of parties guilty of breaches of privilege and of contempt, and assists at the introduction of peers, and other ceremonies. *May's Parl. Pract.*

BLACKSTONE. Sir William Blackstone was a judge of the Court of Common Pleas from 1770 to 1780. He was born July 10, 1723, and in the years from 1765 to 1769 published the four volumes of his famous Commentaries on English Law. He died Feb. 14, 1780.

BLANCH-FIRMES. [ALBA FIRMA.]

BLANCH-HOLDING. One of the ancient tenures of the law of Scotland, the duty payable being nominal, *e.g.,* a peppercorn if demanded. It corresponds nearly to free and common socage in England.

BLANK ACCEPTANCE. An acceptance written on blank stamped paper, and acting as a *primâ facie* authority by the acceptor to complete the bill for any amount the stamp will cover. See *s.* 20 of *Bills of Exchange Act,* 1882.

BLANK BAR (also called *common bar*) was a plea which a defendant sometimes pleaded in an action of trespass, when he wished the plaintiff to point

BLANK BAR—*continued.*
out with greater particularity the place where the trespass was committed.

BLANK INDORSEMENT. [INDORSE-MENT.]

BLANKS. A kind of white money (value 8*d.*) coined by Henry V. for his French possessions ; forbidden to be current in this realm by 2 Hen. 6, c. 9.

BLASPHEMY. The offence, punishable with fine and imprisonment, of denying the being or providence of the Almighty, or contumelious reproaches of our Saviour Christ; also all profane scoffing at the Holy Scripture, or exposing it to contempt and ridicule. 4 *Steph. Com.*

BLOCKADE. An operation of war by which one of the belligerents is able so to apply his force to one of the enemy's ports or coast lines as to render it dangerous to attempt to enter or leave. A blockade to be binding must be effective ; and a party violating it must be proved to have been aware of its existence. Any attempt on the part of a neutral ship to enter or leave a blockaded place with goods or forbidden information is deemed a breach of blockade, and exposes the vessel to seizure and confiscation. *Hall's Int. Law ; Phillimore's Int. Law ; Twiss's Law of Nations.* [DECLARATION OF PARIS.]

BLOOD. That relationship without which none shall claim to succeed as heir by descent to the purchaser. *Co. Litt.* 12 *a.* [HALF BLOOD ; WHOLE BLOOD.]

BLOODWIT. An amerciament for blood shed.

BOARD. A body of persons having delegated to them certain powers of the central government, as the Board of Trade, the Board of Admiralty ; or elected for the purposes of local government, as a board of guardians under the Poor Law Acts, or elected as directors by the shareholders in public companies.

BOARD OF AGRICULTURE. By Act of 1889 constituted to take over the powers and duties of the Inclosures commissioners, Land commissioners, Copyhold commissioners, and certain others.

BOARD OF CONTROL. A board of commissioners for the affairs of India, appointed in 1784, to operate as a check upon the directors of the East India Company. Abolished 1858, when the powers and rights vested in the East India Company in trust for her then Majesty ceased, and became vested in her and exercised in her name. 1 *Steph. Com.*

BOARD OF GREEN CLOTH. A board composed of the lord steward and treasurer of the royal household, comptroller and other officers, having the management of the royal household ; so called from the green cloth on the table.

BOARD OF TRADE. A committee of the Privy Council, charged with the consideration of matters relating to trade and foreign plantations, the supervision of railways and merchant shipping, and other matters of a miscellaneous character. 2 *Steph. Com.*

BOC (Ang.-Sax.). A charter.

BOCK-HORD, or **BOOKHOARD**, is a hoard for books, that is, a place where books, writings or evidences are kept.

BOCLAND, or **BOOKLAND**, also called charter-land, was land held by deed under certain rents and free services, and in effect differed nothing from free-socage land.

BODY OF AN INSTRUMENT signifies the main and operative part, as opposed to the recitals, etc., in a deed, to the title and jurat in an affidavit.

BONA. In the civil law includes all sorts of property, movable and immovable.

BONÂ FIDE. In good faith, without fraud or deceit. *Bonâ fide* holder of a bill of exchange or other security—one without knowledge of any defect in title. See now s. 29 of Bills of Exchange Act, 1882.

BONA NOTABILIA are such goods as a party dying hath in another diocese than that wherein he dies, amounting to 5*l.* at least, which whoso hath, his will must be proved before the archbishop of the province. Now that the granting of probates and letters of administration is transferred, by stat. 20 & 21 Vict. c. 77, and the Judicature Act, 1873, to the Probate Division of the High Court, the law as to *bona notabilia* has become obsolete. 2 *Steph. Com. ; 3 Steph. Com.*

BONA VACANTIA. Goods found without any apparent owner. They belong to the first occupant or finder, unless they be royal fish, shipwrecks, treasure trove, waifs and estrays which belong to the Crown. *2 Steph. Com.*

BONA WAVIATA. Such goods stolen as are waived (or thrown away) by a thief in his flight, for fear of being apprehended. *2 Steph. Com.* [WAIFS.]

BOND. An instrument under seal, whereby a person binds himself to do or not to do certain things; this is a *single bond.* The person so binding himself is called the *obligor;* the person to whom he is bound, who is entitled to enforce the bond, is called the *obligee.* In some cases the obligor binds himself to pay a certain sum, called a *penal sum* or *penalty,* to which a condition is added, that, if he does or does not do a particular act (that is, if he complies with the conditions which the bond is intended to secure), the bond shall be void, otherwise it is to be of full force and effect. This is a *double* bond. The obligee, however, cannot recover the whole penalty, but only the actual loss proved to have been suffered. *2 Steph. Com.*

Bonds are frequently issued by governments and companies as security for money borrowed by them.

BOND CREDITOR. A creditor whose debt is secured by a bond.

BOND NOTE. A written description of goods intended to be shipped, delivered by the exporter or his agent to the officer of customs. *Stat. 16 & 17 Vict. c. 107, s. 120.*

BOND TENANTS. A name sometimes given to copyholders and customary tenants.

BONDED GOODS. Imported goods deposited in a government warehouse until duty is paid.

BONDSMAN. A surety.

BONIS ASPORTATIS. Writ of trespass in respect of goods wrongfully taken otherwise than under distress.

BONIS NON AMOVENDIS is an old writ directed to the sheriffs of London, etc., to charge them, that one condemned by judgment in an action, and prosecuting a writ of error, be not suffered to remove his goods, until the error be tried.

BONO ET MALO. Special writs of gaol delivery, which it was anciently the practice to issue for each particular prisoner, were termed writs *de bono et malo.* *4 Steph. Com.*

BONUS. Premium or advantage; an occasional extra dividend paid by a company either out of profits or capital, and to be treated accordingly as between tenant for life and remainderman.

BOOK OF COMMON PRAYER. The book prescribed by the Act of Uniformity, constituting the standard of faith, worship and discipline in the Church of England. *2 Steph. Com.*

BOOKLAND. [BOCLAND.]

BOOTY OF WAR. Prize of war on land, as opposed to prize at sea. It belongs by right to the Crown, but is usually given to the captors. Jurisdiction on matters of booty of war is in the Admiralty Division (3 & 4 Vict. c. 65, s. 22). *3 Steph. Com.*

BORDER WARRANT, in Scotch law, is a warrant granted by a judge ordinary on the border between England and Scotland, on the application of a creditor, for arresting the person or effects of a debtor residing on the English side, until he finds security *judicio sisti. Bell.* [JUDICIO SISTI.]

BOROUGH is defined by Cowel as "a corporate town which is not a city." As used in the Reform Act, 1832, it means a town entitled to send a member to parliament, or "parliamentary borough," and in the Municipal Corporations Act, 1882, a town incorporated for the purposes of internal government, or "municipal borough." See MUNICIPAL CORPORATION.

BOROUGH COUNCIL. [MUNICIPAL CORPORATION.]

BOROUGH COURT. The court of record for a borough, generally presided over by the recorder. *3 Steph. Com.*

BOROUGH ENGLISH. A customary descent of lands or tenements, of Saxon origin, whereby, in all places where the custom holds, lands and tenements descend to the youngest son; or, if the owner of the land have no issue, then to the youngest brother. *1 Steph. Com.*

BOROUGH FUND. The revenues of a municipal borough derived from the rents and profits of the land, houses, etc., belonging to the borough in its corporate capacity and supplemented where necessary by a borough rate. See *ss.* 138—144, *Municipal Corporations Act*, 1882.

BOROUGH SESSIONS. The sessions held quarterly, or oftener, in a borough, before the recorder, where there is one, on a day appointed by him.

BOTE. Compensation. Thus manbote, that is, compensation or amends for a man slain. It is also synonymous with *estorers* (*q.v.*). Thus house-bote is word for repairs or burning in the house; plough-bote, wood for making and repairing instruments of husbandry. 1 *Steph. Com.*

BOTTOMRY, BOTTOMRY BOND, or **BUM-MAREE.** A maritime bond in the nature of a mortgage of a ship, when the owner borrows money to enable him to carry on his voyage, and pledges the keel or bottom of the ship as a security for the repayment. In which case it is understood that, if the ship be lost, the lender loses his whole money; but, if it returns in safety, then he shall receive back his principal, and also the premium or interest agreed upon. 2 *Steph. Com.*

BOUGHT AND SOLD NOTES are copies of entries and memoranda made by brokers of their transactions in buying and selling stock, or shares, or other personal property, and delivered to the vendors and purchasers for whom they act. The copy of any such entry, delivered to the purchaser, is called the *bought* note: the copy delivered to the vendor is called the *sold* note.

BOUND BAILIFFS. [BAILIFF.]

BOUNTY. A premium paid by Government to producers, exporters or importers in order to encourage certain industries.

BOVILL'S ACT. 1. To amend the law relating to petitions of right (23 & 24 Vict. c. 34).
2. Relating to partnerships (28 & 29 Vict. c. 86); repealed, but substantially re-enacted by the Partnership Act, 1890.

BRACTON. A famous lawyer of the reign of Henry III., renowned for his knowledge both of the common and civil laws. He wrote a celebrated book, *De Legibus*

et Consuetudinibus Angliæ (Concerning the Laws and Customs of England). 1 *Steph. Com.*

BRAWLING. Quarrelling or chiding, or creating a disturbance, in a church or churchyard. 4 *Steph. Com.*

BREACH. An invasion of a right or violation of a duty. The word is specially used in the following expressions :—
1. *Breach of Close.* Unlawfully entering upon another person's land. 3 *Steph. Com.*
2. *Breach of Covenant or Contract.* A non-fulfilment of a covenant or contract, whether by commission or omission.
3. *Breach of the Peace.* A disturbance of the public peace. 4 *Steph. Com.*
4. *Breach of Pound.* Taking by force, out of a pound, things lawfully impounded. 3 *Steph. Com.*
5. *Breach of Prison.* The escape from arrest of a person lawfully arrested for a crime. 4 *Steph. Com.*
6. *Breach of Privilege.* An act or default in violation of the privilege of either house of parliament, as, for instance, by false swearing before a committee of the house, or by resisting the officers thereof in the execution of their duty. *May's Parl. Pract.*
7. *Breach of Promise.* A phrase used especially with reference to the non-fulfilment of a promise to marry.
8. *Breach of Trust.* A violation by a trustee of the duty imposed upon him by the instrument creating the trust.

BREAKING A CLOSE. An unlawful entry on another's land. [BREACH, 1.]

BREAKING BULK signifies opening a box or parcel of goods; a phrase used especially with reference to fraudulent conduct by a bailee. The Larceny Act of 1861 (24 & 25 Vict. c. 96, s. 3), provided that a bailee fraudulently converting to his own use goods entrusted to him shall be guilty of larceny, although he shall not break bulk. Also in respect of sale of goods, the making use of the goods, which may take away any right to return them. [BAILMENT.]

BREAKING OF ARRESTMENT in Scotch law is where a debtor, whose debt has been arrested in favour of some person other than his creditor by reason of a debt due from the creditor to such other person, disregards the arrestment, and pays the debt to his creditor, in contempt of the law, as if the arrestment had not been made. [ARRESTMENT.]

BREHON. An unwritten and customary law formerly in force in Ireland ; so called from the judges, who were denominated Brehons. Abolished by 40 Edw. 3. 1 *Bl.* ; 1 *Steph. Com.*

BRETOISE, or **BRETOYSE.** The law of the Welsh Marches observed by the ancient Britons.

BREVE. A writ.

BREVET, or **BREVET RANK,** is where an officer is given a degree of rank in the *army at large* above that which he is entitled to hold *in his particular regiment;* without, however, increased pay.

BREVET D'INVENTION. In French law, a patent for an invention.

BREVIA MAGISTRALIA. Writs framed by the Masters in Chancery to meet new injuries where the old forms of action were inapplicable.

BREVIA TESTATA. Written memoranda, of which our modern deeds are nothing more than amplifications, introduced by our feudal ancestors to perpetuate the tenors of the various conveyances and investitures, when grants by parol had become the foundation of frequent dispute and uncertainty. 1 *Steph. Com.*

BREVIBUS ET ROTULIS LIBERANDIS. A writ or mandate directed to an outgoing sheriff to deliver to his successor the county, with the appurtenances, *una cum rotulis, brevibus, etc., i.e.,* with the rolls, writs, and all other things belonging to that office.

BRIBERY. The taking or giving of money for the performance or non-performance of a public duty. See *Corrupt and Illegal Practices Prevention Acts,* 1883 and 1884.

BRIDEWELL. A house of correction.

BRIEF. An abridgment of a client's case written out by the solicitor for the instruction of counsel in a civil or criminal proceeding. It will be followed by the witnesses' evidence either by affidavit or oral.

BRIGBOTE, or **BRUGBOTE.** Contribution to the repair of bridges. It signifies also freedom from giving aid to the repair of bridges.

BRITTON. A famous treatise of the reign of Edward I., at whose command it was apparently written ; founded on Bracton and Fleta. 4 *Steph. Com.*

BROAD ARROW. The mark on government stores, indicating that they belong to the Crown. 4 *Steph. Com.*

BROCAGE, or **BROKERAGE.** The wages or hire of a *broker.* Brokerage for procuring a marriage is contrary to public policy, and not recoverable.

BROKER (from the French word *Broieur*). A grinder or breaker into small pieces ; because he that is of that trade draws the bargain into particulars. Now usually an agent between the contracting parties in mercantile transactions, paid by a commission, or brokerage. There is another sort of brokers, commonly called *pawnbrokers,* who have a shop, and let out money at interest to people upon pawns or pledge. See *Pawnbrokers Act,* 1892. See now 63 & 64 Vict. c. 51, by which any money-lender other than a pawnbroker acting under the above Act, and certain other excepted parties, must register at Somerset House as money-lenders, and comply with other requirements. 2 *Steph. Com.*

BROTHEL. A place resorted to by persons of both sexes for prostitution, not a house occupied by one woman where she receives a number of men. To keep such a place is an offence at common law. See *Criminal Law Amendment Act,* 1885.

BUDGET. The financial statement of the national revenue and expenditure for each year, submitted to parliament by the Chancellor of the Exchequer. *May's Parl. Pract.*

BUGGERY. An abominable crime committed with mankind or animals, and rendering a person liable to penal servitude for life.

BUILDING LEASE. A lease of land for a long term, usually ninety-nine years, at a rent called a ground rent, the lessee covenanting to build thereon.

BUILDING SOCIETY. See BENEFIT BUILDING SOCIETY.

BULL. 1. An instrument granted by the Pope of Rome, and sealed with a seal of lead, containing in it his decrees, commandments or other acts, according to the nature of the instrument. 4 *Steph. Com.*

2. A *bull,* on the Stock Exchange, is one who *buys* stock for settlement at a future date, without intending to take delivery, but with a view to gain by a rise in price in the interval. [BEAR.]

BULLION. The ore or metal whereof gold is made. It signifies with us gold or silver in mass or billet.

BUM-BAILIFF. See BAILIFF.

BURDEN OF PROOF (or *onus probandi*). The duty of proving one's case. It is a rule of evidence that the point in issue is to be proved by the party who asserts the affirmative, according to the maxim, *ei incumbit probatio qui dicit, non qui negat.*

Thus, in general, the burden of proof lies upon the plaintiff or prosecutor: but he may adduce evidence sufficient to establish a *primâ facie* case, and the burden of proof is then said to be *shifted* on to the other side.

BURG, or BURGH. [BOROUGH.]

BURGAGE TENURE. A tenure whereby burgesses, citizens, or townsmen hold their lands or tenements of the king or other lord, for a certain yearly rent. It is a species of free socage. Borough English is the most important burgage custom. 1 *Steph. Com.*

BURGAGE-HOLDING. A tenure by which lands in royal boroughs in Scotland are held of the sovereign.

BURGBOTE. A tribute or contribution towards the building or repairing of castles or walls of a borough or city. [BOTE.]

BURGESSES were said to be the inhabitants of a borough or town, driving a trade there. But in particular: 1. Those who serve in parliament for any such borough or corporation. 2. Under the Municipal Corporations Act, 1882, those persons who are entitled to vote on an election of the council. 2 *Steph. Com.*

BURGHMOTE. A court of a borough or city.

BURGLARY (Lat. *Burgi latrocinium*) is the crime of house-breaking by night, *i.e.*, between 9 p.m. and 6 a.m., and it consists either (1) in breaking and entering a dwelling-house by night, with intent to rob or do some other felony ; or (2) in breaking out of a house by night, after having committed a felony therein, or after having entered with intent to commit a felony. 4 *Steph. Com.* ; 24 & 25 *Vict. c.* 96. [HOUSEBREAKING ; NIGHT.]

BURIAL in some part of the parish churchyard is a common law right of all parishioners (and a moral right of strangers, *Kempe* v. *Wickes,* 3 Phil. 265, 274), and will be enforced by *mandamus.* Under the Burial Acts, burial boards are appointed to provide additional graveyards where necessary.

BUTLERAGE OF WINES. 2 *Steph. Com.* [PRISAGE.]

BY-LAWS, or BYE-LAWS. Laws made by councils, boards, corporations, and companies, under powers conferred by Acts of parliament, for the government of their members and the management of their business. And, independently of statutory powers, bye-laws made by a corporation aggregate are binding on its members, unless contrary to the laws of the land, or contrary to and inconsistent with their charter, or manifestly unreasonable. 3 *Steph. Com.*

C. A. V. [CUR ADV. VULT.]

C. I. F. Cost, insurance, and freight. A price quoted " c.i.f." at a certain place usually includes everything up to delivery at port or place of destination. *Cf.* F.O.B.

C. L. P. A., or more frequently C. L. Proc. Acts. Abbreviations for Common Law Procedure Acts.

CA. SA. [CAPIAS AD SATISFACIENDUM.]

CABINET. Those privy councillors who, under the name of cabinet ministers or cabinet council, actually transact the immediate business of the government, and assemble for that purpose from time to time as the public exigencies require. The " cabinet council " is a body unknown to the law ; it was first established by Charles I. 2 *Steph. Com.*

CADIT QUÆSTIO. There's an end to the argument.

CADUCIARY RIGHT, in Scotch law, is the Crown's right of escheat to the estate of a deceased person on failure of heirs ; caduca in Roman law meaning the lapse of a testamentary disposition.

CÆSARIAN OPERATION. A surgical operation. If a child is saved in this way after the mother's death the husband cannot take as tenant by the curtesy : if before, *secus.*

CÆTERORUM. Administration *cæter-orum* is administration granted to the residue of an estate, after a *limited* power of administration, already given as to part of the estate, has been exhausted. *Wms. Exors.* [ADMINISTRATION, 1 ; ADMINISTRATOR.]

CAIRNS' ACT. 21 & 22 Vict. c. 27, by which the Court of Chancery was empowered to give damages in certain cases ; also to summon a jury for the trial of issues of fact. 3 *Steph. Com.*

CALENDAR. 1. A list of prisoners' names at a quarter sessions or assizes.

2. See MONTH.

CALL. 1. Instalments whereby the capital in public companies is gradually paid up by the shareholders. See *Companies Acts.*

2. The conferring on students of the degree of barrister-at-law.

3. The right to demand the allotment or transfer of shares at or before a given date at a given price.

CALL OF THE HOUSE. The calling over the names of members in either house of parliament, pursuant to a resolution of the house ordering the attendance of the members thereof, which order may be enforced by fine and imprisonment. *May's Parl. Pract.*

CALLING THE JURY. This consists in successively drawing out of a box, into which they have been previously put, the names of the jurors on the panels annexed to the *nisi prius* record, and calling them over in the order in which they are so drawn ; and the twelve persons whose names are first called, and who appear, are sworn as the jury ; unless some just cause of challenge or excuse, with respect to any of them, shall be brought forward. 3 *Steph. Com.*

CALLING THE PLAINTIFF. The old method of non-suiting a plaintiff who did not appear when called by the crier. [NON-SUIT.]

CALLING UPON A PRISONER. When a prisoner has been found guilty upon an indictment, the clerk of the court calls upon him to say why judgment should not be passed upon him.

CALLS ON CONTRIBUTORIES. Demands made by a joint stock company, or its official liquidator, upon persons liable to contribute to its assets. 3 *Steph, Com.*

CAMERA. The judge's private room behind the court, where he sometimes hears suits for nullity of marriage on physical grounds, etc.

CAMERA STELLATA. The Star Chamber. [STAR CHAMBER.]

CAMPBELL'S ACTS. [LORD CAMPBELL'S ACTS.]

CANCELLATION. The striking out or revocation of the contents of an instrument by drawing lines (*cancelli*) across it. Mere cancellation does not now revoke a will.

CANCELLI. Lattice-work placed before a window, a doorway, the tribunal of a judge, or any other place. See CANCELLATION.

CANDLEMAS DAY. The feast of the Purification of the Blessed Virgin Mary (February 2), one of the Scotch quarter days.

CANON. 1. A cathedral dignitary, appointed sometimes by the Crown and sometimes by the bishop. 2 *Steph. Com.* The benefice attached to it is called a *canonry.* [CHAPTER.]

2. A law or ordinance of the Church.

3. In civil law a rule, *e.g.*, the canons of inheritance.

CANON LAW. A body of Roman ecclesiastical law, compiled in the twelfth, thirteenth, and fourteenth centuries, from the opinions of the ancient Latin fathers, the decrees of General Councils, and the decretal epistles and bulls of the Holy See, and first codified by Gratianus in 1139. 1 *Steph. Com.*

In the year 1603 certain canons were enacted by the clergy under James I. But, as they were never confirmed in parliament, it has been held that, where they are not merely declaratory of the ancient canon law, but are introductory of new regulations, they do not bind the laity ; whatever regard the clergy may think proper to pay them. They were revised again in 1865. 1 *Steph. Com.*

CANONS OF INHERITANCE. See DESCENT.

CANTRED, or **KANTRESS,** is as much in Wales as a hundred in England ; for *cantre* in the British tongue signified *centum* (a hundred). 28 *Hen.* 8, c. 3.

CAP OF MAINTENANCE. One of the regalia or ornaments of state belonging to the sovereign ; also used by the mayors of several cities in England.

CAPAX DOLI. [DOLI CAPAX.]

CAPE. A judicial writ formerly used in the old real actions for the recovery of land. It was of two kinds, the *cape magnum*, or *grand cape*, and the *cape parvum*, or *petit cape*.

Cape magnum was a writ which issued where the tenant or defendant made default at the day appointed for his appearance.

Cape parvum was a writ of the same kind, which issued when the tenant or defendant, *having appeared* at the day assigned, *afterwards* made default.

But the proceedings in real actions are now abolished by 3 & 4 Will. 4, c. 27, s. 36, and 23 &¡24¡Vict. c. 126, s. 26. See 3 *Steph. Com.* [ACTIONS REAL AND PERSONAL.]

CAPE AD VALENTIAM. A species of *cape magnum*. [CAPE.]

CAPIAS. A writ, usually addressed to the sheriff, by which process is issued against an accused person after indictment found, where the accused is not in custody, in cases not otherwise provided for by statute. 4 *Steph. Com.* For other kinds of *capias*, see the following titles and mesne process. [MESNE.]

CAPIAS AD AUDIENDUM JUDICIUM. A writ issued in cases where a defendant has, in his absence, been found guilty of misdemeanor, to bring him in to receive judgment. 4 *Steph. Com.*

CAPIAS AD RESPONDENDUM. 1. A writ under which an absconding defendant in a civil action was formerly arrested or obliged to give special bail. 3 *Steph. Com.*

2. A writ issued against a defendant in misdemeanor against whom an indictment has been found to compel him to appear for arraignment.

CAPIAS AD SATISFACIENDUM (generally called a *ca. sa.*). A writ by which, on a judgment for an amount exceeding 20*l.*, execution might issue against the person of the debtor, who might be arrested and imprisoned thereunder. This writ has been practically abolished by sect. 4 of the Debtors Act, 1869 (32 & 33 Vict. c. 62). 3 *Steph. Com.* ; *Robson, Bkcy.*

CAPIAS IN WITHERNAM (that you take by way of reprisal.) A writ in the nature of a reprisal, formerly issuing in two cases :—

1. For the arrest of a person, who, having had another in his custody, and being ordered to release him on security being given to the sheriff for his appearance, caused him instead to be "eloigned," or taken out of the sheriff's jurisdiction.

2. For taking the goods of a person, who, having "distrained" goods and being ordered to deliver them up on a proper security being given, caused them instead to be "eloigned," or taken out of the sheriff's jurisdiction, or to places to him unknown. 3 *Steph. Com.* [REPLEVIN.]

CAPIAS PRO FINE was a writ which formerly issued upon judgment given for the plaintiff in an action, directing that the defendant be taken up (*capiatur*) till he paid a fine to the king for the public misdemeanor, coupled with the private injury in cases of force, falsehood in denying his own deed, or unjustly claiming property in replevin, or of contempt by disobeying the command of the king's writ, or the express prohibition of some statute. If, on the other hand, the verdict was for the defendant, the plaintiff was adjudged to be amerced for his false claim. Abolished by 5 & 6 Will. & M. c. 12.

CAPIAS UTLAGATUM (that you take the outlaw). A writ of execution which is either *general* against the person only, or special against the person, lands, and goods : but outlawry is abolished now in civil cases. 4 *Steph. Com.*

CAPITA, DISTRIBUTION PER. A distribution of an intestate's personal estate, wherein each claimant has a share in his own right as in equal degree of kindred to the deceased, and not as representing another person, *i.e.*, distribution *per stirpes.* 2 *Steph. Com.* [STIRPES, DISTRIBUTION PER.]

CAPITAL. The nett amount of property belonging to a merchant, after deducting the debts he is owing. This term, however, is more strictly applied, either to the sum of money which he has embarked in his business at first, or to the available sum he may afterwards have at command for carrying it on.

CAPITAL PUNISHMENT. Death by hanging. It can now only be awarded for murder, treason, piracy with violence, or setting fire to ships, etc., in port of London.

CAPITATION TAX, FEE, GRANT, etc., is one raised or paid on each individual or according to the *heads*, *e.g.*, for each child in a school.

CAPITE. Tenants *in capite* were those who held land *immediately* from the sovereign either in right of his Crown or of some honour or manor. 1 *Steph. Com.* [FEUDAL SYSTEM.]

CAPITULARY. A code of laws.

CAPTION. That part of a legal instrument, *e.g.*, of an indictment, which shows where, when, and by what authority it is taken, found, or executed.

CAPTURE. A seizure ; a word especially used of the seizure of a ship or cargo, etc., at sea by a belligerent in time of war. See 2 *Steph. Com.*

CARCEL-AGE. Prison fees.

CARGO. Goods and merchandises shipped for carriage by water.

CAROOME. A licence by the Lord Mayor of London to keep a cart.

CARRIER. A person that carries goods for another for hire.

A *common carrier* is one who exercises the business of carrying as a public employment, and undertakes to carry goods for all persons indiscriminately. The law casts upon the common carrier a duty (1) to carry for everyone who offers to pay his hire, which no one else is bound to do, except upon agreement; (2) to answer for all things carried as insurers : this liability, however, is restricted by the Carriers Acts, 1830 and 1865. 2 *Steph. Com.*

CARRYING COSTS. A verdict is said to " carry costs" in those cases where by law it *primâ facie* involves the payment of costs by the unsuccessful party to the party in whose favour the verdict is given. In trials by jury costs follow the event unless otherwise ordered for good cause. 3 *Steph. Com.*

CARTE BLANCHE. A white sheet of paper ; a phrase used especially to signify a paper given by one man to another with nothing on it but the signature of the former, so that the latter may fill it up at his discretion. Hence the figurative expression, " to give any one *carte blanche*," that is, unlimited authority.

CARTEL, or **CHARTEL**. An instrument executed between two belligerent powers for settling the exchange of prisoners of war and other like matters. *Twiss's Law of Nations ; Phillimore's International Law ; Wheaton's International Law ; Hall's International Law.* Also a challenge to a duel to decide legal controversy.

CARTEL SHIP. A ship employed in effecting the exchange of prisoners of war.

CARUCATE, or **CARVE OF LAND**, or **CARVAGE**. A plough land, from *caruca*, a plough. It is a certain quantity of land, varying from 60 to 120 acres, by which the subjects have been sometimes taxed, and is supposed to be that quantity which can be tilled by one plough in a year and a day. The tribute levied upon a carue or plough of land is called *carucagium*.

CASE. A form of action which lay for damages for wrongs or injuries not accompanied with immediate violence, *i.e.*, where *covenant* or *trespass* did not apply. 3 *Steph. Com.* See TRESPASS ON THE CASE.

CASE RESERVED. [RESERVING POINTS OF LAW.]

CASE, SPECIAL. [SPECIAL CASE.]

CASE STATED. A statement of facts prepared by one court for the opinion of another on a point of law. Thus it was formerly the practice of the Court of Chancery to refer difficult questions of law, which might arise in the course of a suit, to one of the common law courts, in the form of a "case stated" for the opinion of the common law court. 3 *Bl.* This was abolished by s. 61 of the Chancery Jurisdiction Act, 1852 (15 & 16 Vict. c. 86). Now by stat. 22 & 23 Vict. c. 63, a case may be stated by an English court for the opinion of a Scotch court, in a matter involving Scotch law, etc.

We also speak of a "case stated" by justices of the peace under stat. 20 & 21 Vict. c 43, for the opinion of a superior court in a matter of law.

A counsel who opens a case before a jury is also said to "state the case" to the jury. 3 *Steph. Com.*

CASSETUR BREVE, or BILLA (let the writ or bill be quashed). The name of a judgment quashing or making void a writ of summons in an action or an entry on the record that the plaintiff withdraws his bill, on a plea in abatement by the defendant. Abolished. See DISCONTINUANCE.

CAST. Defeated at law, condemned in costs or damages.

CASTIGATORY FOR SCOLDS. [SCOLD.]

CASTING AN ESSOIGN. See ESSOIGN.

CASTLE WARD, or GUARD, or GARD. An imposition laid upon such of the king's subjects as dwell within a certain compass of any castle, towards the maintenance of such as watch and ward the castle.

CASU PROVISO and CASU CONSIMILI. The first was a writ of entry given by the Statute of Gloucester, 6 Edw. 1, c. 7, to a reversioner of land which a dowress (or tenant in dower) of the land had disposed of in fee, or for other greater estate than that which she held in the land. It could be brought in the lifetime of the dowress, and in this respect it differed from the writ *ad communem legem.* The writ *casu consimili* was given in a like case where a tenant for life or limited owner other than a dowress had disposed of the land. Abolished by stat. 3 & 4 Will. 4, c. 27, s. 36.

CASUAL EJECTOR. The fictitious tenant (generally called Richard Roe) nominal defendant in the old action of ejectment. [EJECTMENT.]

CASUAL PAUPER. A person who applies for relief in a parish in which he is not settled. 3 *Steph. Com.*

CASUS BELLI. An occurrence giving rise to or justifying war.

CASUS FŒDERIS. A case stipulated by treaty, or which comes within the terms of a contract.

CASUS OMISSUS. A case inadvertently left unprovided for by statute.

CATALLA. Chattels. [CHATTELS.]

CATCHING BARGAIN. A purchase from an expectant heir, for an inadequate consideration. See EXPECTANT HEIR.

CATCHLAND. Land in Norfolk, so called because it is not known to what parish it belongs, and the minister who first seizes the tithes of it enjoys them for that year.

CATCHPOLE. A name formerly given to a sheriff's deputy, or to a constable, or other officer whose duty it is to arrest persons.

CATHEDRAL. The principal church of a diocese. 2 *Steph. Com.*

CATTLEGATE. Common for one beast.

CAUSA CAUSANS. The immediate cause, the *causa proxima*, the last link in the chain of causation.

CAUSA JACTITATIONIS MATRIMONII (a cause of boasting of marriage). [JACTITATION.]

CAUSA MORTIS. [DONATIO MORTIS CAUSA.]

CAUSE. 1. A suit or action at law.
2. That which produces or effects a result.

CAUSE OF ACTION. The ground on which an action can be maintained; but often extended to any claim on which a given action is in fact grounded, whether or not legally maintainable.

CAUSE-LIST. The printed list of causes made out for each day during the sittings of the courts; the causes being tried in the order of their entry.

CAUTION (1.) in ecclesiastical, admiralty, and Scotch law, signifies *surety* or *security*. It is also called *cautionary*.
2. Under s. 53 of the Land Transfer Act, 1875, a caution may be issued by any person interested to prevent dealings with the land without notice to the cautioner.

CAVEAT (let him beware). An intimation made to the proper officer of a court of justice to prevent the taking of any step, *e.g.*, grant of probate, without intimation to the party interested (caveator) to appear. *Bell.* See also 2 *Steph. Com.*

CAVEAT EMPTOR (let the buyer beware). A maxim implying that the buyer must be cautious, as the risk is his and not that of the seller. The rule of law as to the sale of goods is, that if a person

CAVEAT EMPTOR—*continued.*
sells them as his own, and the price be paid, and the *title* prove deficient, the seller may be compelled to refund the money. But as to the *soundness* of the wares, the vendor is not usually bound to answer; but there are several exceptions now embodied in the Sales of Goods Act, 1893 (56 & 57 Vict. c. 71, ss. 13—15). 2 *Steph. Com.*

CAVEAT VIATOR (let the traveller beware). Where a person has gratuitous permission to pass over private land he is a bare licensee and must take the risk of accident, no obligation being thrown on the owner to exercise any care to secure his safe passage.

CEAP. A bargain, anything for sale; chattel; also cattle as being the usual medium of barter (ceap-gild).

CEDE. To assign or transfer.

CEDENT (Sc.). An assignor.

CENSURE. 1. A custom in certain manors in Devon and Cornwall, where all persons above the age of 16 years are cited to swear fealty to the lord, to pay 11*d.* per poll and 1*d.* ever after (censores).
2. A condemnatory judgment, or, more particularly, a reprimand from a superior.

CENSUS. A numbering of the people. First taken in 1801 in England, and now taken every 10 years.

CENTRAL CRIMINAL COURT. The court established by stat. 4 & 5 Will. 4, c. 36, for trial of offences committed in London, Middlesex, and certain parts of Essex, Kent, and Surrey. The court sits at least twelve times in the year. Practically, those who preside for the trial of offences there are one or more judges of the High Court, the Recorder of London, and the Common Serjeant of the City of London, though the Lord Mayor, Lord Chancellor, and others are nominally judges of the court. It has generally the same criminal jurisdiction as the assizes.

CENTRAL OFFICE OF THE SUPREME COURT. Established by Judicature Act, 1879, to consolidate the offices of the masters of the divisions of the High Court.

CORPUS (I have taken the body). sheriff's return to a *capias* or other writ requiring him to seize the body of a party, indicating that he has complied with the writ. [CAPIAS.]

CERTIFICATE is used for a writing made in any court, to give notice to another court of anything done therein. *Cowel.*

CERTIFICATE OF CONFORMITY. A certificate formerly granted to a bankrupt, indicating that he had conformed in all points to the directions of the law. An order of discharge is now substituted for the certificate of conformity. *Robson, Bkcy.*

CERTIFICATE OF MASTER. The written statement of a master in Chancery, embodying the result of inquiries and accounts in a chancery action taken before the master, in accordance with the judgment or order made by the judge. [CHIEF CLERK.]

CERTIFICATE OF SHARES. A document declaring its owner entitled to shares or stock in a joint stock company.

CERTIFICATE, TRIAL BY. A form of trial in which the evidence of the person certifying was the only proper criterion of the point in dispute. Now practically obsolete. 3 *Steph. Com.*

CERTIFICATION. A writ formerly granted for a review or re-trial of a matter decided in an action; now entirely superseded by the remedy afforded by means of a new trial.

CERTIFIED COPY. One signed and certified as true by the official in whose custody the original is; as to when admissible in evidence, see *Taylor on Evidence.*

CERTIORARI (to be more fully informed of). A writ commanding an inferior court *to certify* an indictment or other proceeding to a superior court, with the view to its removal thither for trial. Thus:—
1. An indictment against a peer for felony is removed into parliament, or into the court of the Lord High Steward, by writ of *certiorari.*
2. An indictment may be removed from an inferior court to the Court of King's Bench by writ of *certiorari.* 4 *Bl.*; 3 *Steph. Com.*; 4 *Steph. Com.*
In many cases of summary conviction the right to *certiorari* has been taken away by statute.

CERT-MONEY. Head money paid yearly by the residents of several manors to the lords thereof for the certain keeping of the leet : called *certum letæ.*

CERTUM EST QUOD CERTUM REDDI POTEST (that is certain which can be rendered certain). It is a rule that rent must be certain, in order to support a distress. If, however, it is definitely ascertainable, that is enough to satisfy the rule.

CESS, or **CESSE.** An assessment or tax.

CESSANTE RATIONE LEGIS, CESSAT IPSA LEX (the reason of the law ceasing, the law itself ceases).

CESSAVIT. A writ that formerly lay in default of distress to recover land against a tenant who had for two years neglected to perform due service, or to pay rent.

CESSER. 1. The ceasing or termination. 2. *Proviso for Cesser.* Where terms for years were raised by settlements it was usual to introduce a proviso that they should cease when the trusts were at an end. Now, however, by 8 & 9 Vict. c. 112, every term ceases *ipso facto* when the trusts for which it was created are satisfied.

CESSET EXECUTIO (let execution be stayed). Thus, on a judgment in favour of a party in respect of a reversion claimed by him at the expiry of a lease, there must be a *cesset executio* during the continuance of the lease.

CESSET PROCESSUS (let process be stayed). An order to stay proceedings in an action. See STET PROCESSUS.

CESSIO BONORUM (the yielding up of goods). The cession, or yielding up, by a debtor, of his goods to his creditors. Under the Roman law this only operated to discharge the debtor *pro tanto* but exonerated him from imprisonment. This was the foundation of the modern law of bankruptcy, and the French and Scottish law conform to the Roman in its leading outlines.

CESSIO IN JURE. (Roman law.) A fictitious suit in which the person who was to acquire the thing claimed it as his own, and the person who was to transfer it acknowledged the justice of the claim, and the magistrate thereupon pronounced it to be the property of the claimant.

CESSION is the name given to the vacancy created by an incumbent of a living in taking another benefice, whereby the first is adjudged void according to stat. 1 & 2 Vict. c. 106, and others. *Cowel* ; 1 *Bl.* ; 2 *Steph. Com.* [PLURALITY.]

CESSOR. A tenant of land who neglects the duties to which he is bound by his tenure. *Cowel.* [CESSAVIT.]

CESTUI QUE TRUST. The person for whose benefit a trust is created ; the person entitled to the equitable, as opposed to the legal, estate. Thus, if land be granted unto and to the use of A. in trust for B., B. is *cestui que trust,* A. is trustee. 1 *Steph. Com.* ; *Wms. R. P.* ; *Lewin on Trusts.*

CESTUI QUE USE. The person for whose benefit a use is created. His rights are the same as those of *cestui que trust,* the latter expression not being employed till after the Statute of Uses. 1 *Steph. Com.* ; *Wms. R. P.*

CESTUI QUE VIE. He for whose life any land or tenement is granted. Thus, if A. be tenant of lands for the life of B., B. is called the *cestui que vie.* 1 *Steph. Com.* ; *Wms. R. P.*

CHAFEWAX, or **CHAFFWAX.** An officer in Chancery that fitteth the wax for the sealing of the writs, and such other instruments as are there to be made out. Abolished by 15 & 16 Vict. c. 87, s. 23.

CHALLENGE. An objection taken against jurors.

Challenges to a jury are of two kinds. (A.) For cause, viz :—

1. *Challenges to the array,* by which a party excepts to the whole panel of the jurors, by reason of the partiality of the sheriff or his under officer who arrayed the panel : either *principal,* in case of direct partiality, or *for favour,* inferred partiality. This is unusual.

2. *Challenges to the separate polls,* by which a party excepts to individual jurors. These may be made (1) *propter honoris respectum* (by reason of honour), as if a lord of parliament be empanelled on a jury ; (2) *propter defectum:* as if a man have not estate sufficient to qualify him for being a juror ; (3) *propter affectum,* for suspicion of bias or partiality ; (4) *propter delictum,* for some crime or misdemeanor that affects

CHALLENGE—*continued*.

the juror's credit and renders him infamous.

(B.) Peremptory. Challenges to the number of twenty may, on trials for felony, be made by a prisoner without assigning cause. The Crown may also challenge jurors in the first instance without assigning cause, until all the panel is gone through and it is found that there cannot be a full jury without the persons so challenged. 3 *Steph. Com.*; 4 *Steph. Com.*

Challenges *propter affectum* are also divided into *principal challenges*, and *challenges to the favour*. See FAVOUR, CHALLENGE TO.

CHALLENGES TO FIGHT. Sending or bearing by word or letter is a misdemeanor punishable by fine and imprisonment.

CHAMBERLAIN. This word is variously used in our chronicles, laws, and statutes, as—

1. The Lord Great Chamberlain of England, to whose office belongs the government of the palace at Westminster and of the House of Lords during session.

2. The Lord Chamberlain of the King's House, the King's Chamberlain, to whose office it especially appertaineth to look to the king's chamber and wardrobe, and to govern the under servants belonging to the same. He has also authority to license theatres within the metropolis, and within those places where the sovereign shall usually reside; also to license plays intended to be acted for hire at any theatre in Great Britain. 6 & 7 *Vict. c.* 68; 3 *Steph. Com.*

3. The Chamberlain of London is the receiver of the rents and revenues belonging to the city.

CHAMBERS. The offices of a judge in which a large part of the business of the Superior Courts is transacted by a judge or a master. Applications by way of summons, and inquiries incidental to a suit, are made in chambers.

CHAMBERS OF THE KING (*Regiæ cameræ*). The havens or ports of the kingdom are so called in our ancient records. *Cowel*.

CHAMPARTY, or **CHAMPERTY** (Lat. *Campi partitio*, a dividing of the land). A maintenance of any man in an action or suit, upon condition to have part of the things (be it lands or goods) when it is recovered. *Cowel*. It is an offence against public justice. 4 *Bl.*; 4 *Steph. Com.*

CHAMPION OF THE KING. An officer whose duty it is, at the coronation of our kings, when the king is at dinner, to ride armed into Westminster Hall, and, by a herald, make a challenge that, if any person shall deny the king's title to the Crown, he is there ready to defend it; which done, the king drinks to him, and sends him a gilt cup with a cover full of wine, which he hath for his fee. *Cowel*.

CHANCEL. That part of a church where the communion table stands. The rector or impropriator is bound to repair it.

CHANCELLOR. A word used in several senses.

1. The Lord High Chancellor, who is the highest judicial functionary in the kingdom, and prolocutor or Speaker of the House of Lords by prescription. He is a privy councillor and cabinet minister by virtue of his office, and usually (though not necessarily) a peer of the realm. He goes out of office with the ministry. He may not be a Roman Catholic. 2 *Steph. Com.*; 3 *Steph. Com.*

2. The Chancellor of the Duchy of Lancaster, who presides over the court of the duchy; this court has a concurrent jurisdiction with the Court of Chancery in matters relating to the duchy. *Cowel*; 3 *Bl.*; 3 *Steph. Com.*

3. The Chancellor of the Exchequer is an officer who formerly sat in the Court of Exchequer, but he is now known as the minister of state who has control over the national revenue and expenditure. See 2 *Steph. Com.*

4. The Chancellor of a University, who is the principal officer of the university. His office is for the most part honorary. The Chancellor's Court of Oxford or Cambridge has a jurisdiction over the members of the university, and the judge of the court is the vice-chancellor or his deputy. 3 *Bl.*; 3 *Steph. Com.*; 1 *Steph. Com.*; 4 *Steph. Com.*

5. The Chancellor of a Diocese is the officer appointed to assist a bishop in matters of law, and to hold his consistory courts for him. 1 *Bl.*; 2 *Steph. Com.*

6. The Chancellor of the Order of the Garter and other military orders is an officer who seals the commissions and keeps a register of proceedings, etc.

CHANCE-MEDLEY, or casual affray, is a phrase properly applied to such killing as happens in self-defence upon a sudden *rencontre*. It is sometimes erroneously applied to any manner of manslaughter by misadventure. *Cowel ; 4 Bl. ; 4 Steph. Com.*

CHANCERY, COURT OF. 1. Since the Judicature Act, 1873, superseded by the Chancery Division of the High Court of Justice. There were formerly two distinct tribunals in the Court of Chancery, the one *ordinary*, being a court of common law, the other *extraordinary*, being a court of equity. The so-called "extraordinary" jurisdiction of the court is now the *ordinary* jurisdiction of the Chancery Division, consisting of such matters as the execution of trusts, redemption and foreclosure of mortgages, partnership disputes, specific performance of contracts relating to land. *3 Steph. Com.*

2. *Chancery Court of the Duchy of Lancaster.* See CHANCELLOR, 2.

3. *Chancery Court of York.* Court of the Archbishop of York, for ecclesiastical matters in the province. See ARCHES COURT, and 37 & 38 *Vict. c.* 85.

CHANGER. An officer belonging to the king's mint, whose business was chiefly to exchange coin for bullion, brought in by merchants or others. *Cowel.*

CHANGING OF SOLICITOR. Before 1883 no solicitor in an action could be changed without the order of a judge, but by R. S. C. 1883, Ord. VII. r. 3, it may be done by filing a notice.

CHAPEL is of two sorts, either adjoining to a church as a parcel of the same (as in the case of a lady chapel), or else separate from the mother church, where the parish is wide, and commonly called a chapel of ease, because it is built for the ease of one or more parishioners that dwell too far from the church. *Cowel.*

CHAPERON. A hood or bonnet anciently worn by knights of the Garter ; in heraldry, a little escutcheon fixed in the forehead of the horses that draw a hearse. *Cowel.*

CHAPTER (*Capitulum*) consists of certain dignitaries called canons, appointed sometimes by the Crown, sometimes by the bishop, and sometimes by each other, attached to a cathedral church and presided over by a dean. This body constitutes the council of the bishop in both spiritual and temporal affairs of the see. *2 Steph. Com.*

CHARGE. A word used in various senses.
1. Of the address delivered by the presiding judicial officer to the grand jury or petty jury, at assizes or sessions, instructing them in their duties. *4 Steph. Com.*
2. Of the bishop's address to his clergy at a visitation.
3. Of a criminal accusation against any one.
4. Of an incumbrance on land or on a fund, *e.g.*, by way of equitable mortgage, for duty, for improvements.
5. A commission.
6. Expenses or costs.

CHARGE D'AFFAIRES. A resident minister of an inferior grade accredited by the government of one state to the minister of foreign affairs of another. He may be either originally sent and accredited by his government, or merely temporarily substituted in the place of the public minister of his nation during his absence. *Wh. Int. Law ; Phillimore's Int. Law.*

CHARGE SHEET. The paper on which are entered the charges intended to be brought before a magistrate.

CHARGING ORDER. An order obtained by a judgment creditor who has obtained a judgment for a sum of money in a suit or action against another, under stat. 1 & 2 *Vict. c.* 110, that the property of the judgment debtor in government stock, or in the stock of any public company in England, shall stand *charged* with the payment of the amount for which judgment shall have been recovered, with interest. *3 Steph. Com. ; R. S. C. 1883, Ord. XLVI. r. 1.*

CHARITABLE USES. Uses for the maintenance of schools, hospitals, etc. An enumeration of such uses is given in the preamble of stat. 43 *Eliz. c.* 4, passed in 1601. *3 Steph. Com.* [MORTMAIN.]

CHARITY COMMISSIONERS. A body of commissioners for England and Wales, appointed by the Crown under the Charitable Trusts Acts. They have power to examine into all charities, and to prosecute all necessary inquiries by certain officers called assistant commissioners ;

CHARITY COMMISSIONERS—*continued.*
to require trustees and other persons to render written accounts and statements, or to attend and be examined on oath, in relation to any charity or its property ; to authorise suits concerning the same, and to sanction building leases, etc. 3 *Steph. Com.*

CHARTA. A charter, for the holding an estate ; also a statute. *Toml.*

CHARTA MAGNA. [MAGNA CHARTA.]

CHARTEL. [CARTEL.]

CHARTER is taken in our law for written evidence of things done between man and man.
    1. Royal charters either to persons, *e.g.*, letters patent for title, or to corporations, *e.g.*, to a company, giving sovereign rights, as to British North Borneo Company, Royal Niger Company, British South Africa Company.
    2. Charters of private persons are deeds and instruments under seal for the conveyance of lands, etc. 1 *Steph. Com.*

CHARTERER. 1. One who "charters" or hires a ship under a charter-party ; also called "freighter." [CHARTER-PARTY.]
2. An owner of freehold land in Cheshire.

CHARTER-LAND. Land held by deed under certain rents and free services ; in effect free-socage lands. Otherwise called bookland.

CHARTER-PARTY (Lat. *Charta partita,* a writing divided). A mercantile instrument, by which one who would export goods from this country, or import them from abroad, engages for hire usually an *entire* vessel for the purpose, at a freight or reward thereby agreed for. 2 *Steph. Com.* [BILL OF LADING.]

CHASE signifies—
    1. The driving of cattle to or from any place. Also droveway.
    2. A place for receiving deer, etc. It was commonly less than a forest, and larger and better stored with keepers and game than a park. Also a chase differs from a park in not being enclosed. Also chacea.
    3. A right of keeping and hunting beasts of chase, or royal game, either in one's own ground, or in that of another. 1 *Steph. Com.*

CHATTELS (Lat. *Catalla*). The name given to things which in law are deemed personal property. Chattels are divided into *chattels real* and *chattels personal ;* chattels real being interests less than freehold in land which devolve after the manner of personal estate, as leaseholds. As opposed to freeholds, they are regarded as personal estate. But as being interests in real estate, they are called *chattels real* to distinguish them from movables, which are called *chattels personal.* 1 *Steph. Com.* ; 2 *Steph. Com.* ; *Wms. R. P. & P. P.*

CHAUD-MEDLEY. The killing of a man in an affray in the *heat* of blood or passion ; a word often erroneously used as synonymous with chance-medley. 4 *Steph. Com.*

CHEAT. To defraud another of his rights or property by means of some deceitful practice, *e.g.*, using false weights and measures.
    Cheating at play is punishable in like manner as obtaining money under false pretences. See 8 & 9 *Vict. c.* 109, *s.* 17.

CHEATORS. [ESCHEATORS.]

CHECK - WEIGHER. A person elected under the Coal Mines Regulation Act, 1887, by ballot of the miners employed in a mine, to check the weight of the output from the mine.

CHEQUE. A written order addressed by a person (the drawer) to a banker to pay money, generally to some third party (the payee) ; it is defined by 45 & 46 Vict. c. 61, s. 73, as a bill of exchange drawn on a banker payable on demand.
    A cheque may be drawn in favour of a specified person, or payable to his order, in which cases it requires endorsement for transfer, or payable to bearer, when it is transferable by mere delivery. The law of cheques is codified in the above-mentioned Act.
    A *crossed* cheque is a cheque crossed with two lines, between which are *either* the name of a bank *or* the words "and company" in full or abbreviated. In the former case the banker on whom it is drawn must not pay the money for the cheque to any other than the banker named ; in the latter case he must not pay it to any other than a banker. 2 *Steph. Com.*

CHEVAGE (*Chevagium*). A sum of money paid by villeins to their lords in acknowledgment of their villenage. *Cowel.*

CHIEF BARON. The title given to the judge who presided in the Court of Exchequer. Now superseded by Lord Chief Justice of England.

CHIEF CLERK. The officers formerly called chief clerks are now called masters. They are officers of the Chancery Division. They are appointed by and attached to the chambers of the judges of that division. They hear summonses and dispose of the less important matters thereon, and prepare others for the judge. They also take accounts and institute inquiries under judgment or order of court, and embody the result in a "certificate" to be dealt with by the judge on the "further consideration" of the action. [CERTIFICATE OF MASTER; FURTHER CONSIDERATION.]

CHIEF CONSTABLE. 1. Used by Sir Edward Coke as synonymous with *high constable*. 2 *Steph. Com.*
2. Now a person at the head of a constabulary force. This officer is appointed in counties by the standing joint committee of quarter sessions and county council; in towns usually by the town council. 2 *Steph. Com.* [CONSTABLE.]

CHIEF, EXAMINATION IN, is the examination of a witness by the party who produces him.

CHIEF JUSTICE. The title given to the heads of the Courts of King's Bench and Common Pleas. Now superseded by the Lord Chief Justice of England (*q.v.*). 3 *Steph. Com.* 377.

CHIEF, TENANTS IN. Those who hold land immediately of the king; otherwise called tenants *in capite*. [CAPITE.]

CHIEF-RENTS. 1. Rents fixed by custom payable to the lord of a manor by the freeholders thereof. 1 *Steph. Com.* 620.
2. A rent-charge payable by the purchaser of land to the seller as consideration for the sale. *Copinger and Monro's Rents.* [ASSIZE, RENTS OF.]

CHIEVANCE. Usury.

CHILTERN HUNDREDS. His majesty's hundreds of Stoke, Desborough, and Bonenham. The office of steward or bailiff of these hundreds is ordinarily given by the Treasury to any member of the House of Commons who wishes to retire from the house; it being a settled principle of parliamentary law that a member, after he is duly chosen, cannot relinquish his seat; and, in order to evade this restriction, a member who wishes to retire accepts office under the Crown, which legally vacates his seat, and obliges the house to order a new writ. *May's Parl. Pract.*

CHIMIN (Fr. *Chemin*). A way. Either the king's highway or a private way. *Cowel.*

CHIMINAGE. A toll for wayfarage through a forest. *Cowel.*

CHIMNEY MONEY was a tax formerly payable upon every chimney in a house. It was abolished by 1 W. & M. st. 1, c. 10.

CHIROGRAPH (handwriting). A public instrument or gift of conveyance, written on two parts of the same piece of parchment with some words or letters of the alphabet between them; through which the parchment was cut, either in a straight or indented line. This practice was observed in the case of fines of land until their abolition in 1833; but in all other cases it has long since been disused. 1 *Steph. Com.* [DEED; FINE, 1.]

CHIVALRY (*Servitium militare*), from French *chevalier*; in our common law a tenure of land by knight-service. *Cowel*; 2.*Bl.*; 1 *Steph. Com.* [KNIGHT-SERVICE; COURT OF CHIVALRY.]

CHOSE. A thing. *Choses* are of two kinds—*choses in action*, and *choses in possession*. A *chose in action* is a thing of which a man has not the present enjoyment, but merely a right to recover it (if withheld) by action. Thus money at a bank, or money due on a bond, is a *chose in action*. This may now be assigned by writing, signed by the assignor, absolute in terms and notice in writing being given to the debtor (Judicature Act, 1873, s. 25). A *chose in possession* is a thing of which the owner is in the actual enjoyment. *Cowel*; 2 *Bl.*; 2 *Steph. Com.*

CHOSE LOCAL and **CHOSE TRANSITORY.** A *chose in possession* may be a *chose local*, annexed to a place, as a mill; or a *chose transitory*, which is movable, and may be carried from place to place. But these expressions are now obsolete.

CHURCH DISCIPLINE ACT. 3 & 4 Vict. c. 86. [CLERGY DISCIPLINE ACT.]

CHURCH-RATES. The rates by which the expenses of the church are defrayed. Since the stat. 31 & 32 Vict. c. 109, they are not compulsory on the persons rated, and the only consequence of refusing to pay them is a disqualification from interfering with the monies arising from the rate. 1 *Bl.*; 3 *Bl.*; 2 *Steph. Com.*; 3 *Steph. Com.* [EASTER DUES AND OFFERINGS.]

CHURCHESSET. Corn paid to the Church.

CHURCHWARDENS, or **CHURCH REVES.** The guardians or keepers of the church, and representatives of the body of the parish. In general the minister chooses one, and the parishioners another. They are chosen yearly in Easter week. They have the care and management of the goods belonging to the church, such as the organ, bells, Bible, and parish books. *Cowel*; 1 *Bl.*; 2 *Steph. Com.*

CHURL (*Churle, Ceorle, Carl*) was in the Saxon times a tenant at will, of free condition, who held land of the Thanes, on condition of rents and services.

CINQUE PORTS. The five ports of Hastings, Romney, Hythe, Dover and Sandwich; to which Winchelsea and Rye have since been added. They have an especial governor or keeper, called by his office the Lord Warden of the Cinque Ports, and divers privileges granted unto them. The jurisdiction of the Lord Warden in civil suits is now taken away by 18 & 19 Vict. c. 48, but they still possess a peculiar maritime jurisdiction. 2 *Steph. Com.*

CIRCUIT. A division of the kingdom (now seven in number), each comprising several counties. Into each of these circuits usually two commissioners, called judges of assize, are sent by special commission from the Crown, four times a year. Under s. 23 of the Judicature Act, 1875, the King in Council has full power over circuits, counties, and assize towns to alter them in any way. By an Order in Council of the 28th July, 1893, continuous common law sittings in town and continuous circuits are provided as and from 1st October, 1893. See *Annual Practice, Vol. II.*; 3 *Steph. Com.*

The kingdom is also divided into circuits for the purposes of the county courts. To each of these circuits is assigned a judge, chosen by the Lord Chancellor. 3 *Steph. Com.*

CIRCUITY OF ACTION is a longer course of proceeding than is necessary to effect any result.

Now all counter-claims may be raised in the defence to an action to avoid circuity. *Judicature Act*, 1873, *s.* 24 (3). [COUNTER-CLAIM.]

CIRCULAR NOTES are instruments in the nature of letters of credit, drawn by bankers upon their foreign correspondents in favour of persons travelling abroad. [LETTERS OF CREDIT.]

CIRCUMSPECTE AGATIS (that ye act circumspectly) is the title of a statute or writ made 13 Edw. 1, st. 4, relating to prohibitions and other Church matters. 3 *Steph. Com.*; *Oke's Mag. Syn.*

CIRCUMSTANTIAL EVIDENCE. Proof of circumstances from which, according to the ordinary course of human affairs, the existence of some fact may reasonably be presumed. 3 *Steph. Com.* It is thus opposed to direct or positive evidence of the fact itself.

CIRCUMSTANTIBUS (by - standers). [TALES.]

CITATION. A summons to a party to appear; applied particularly to process in the Scotch courts, and in the ecclesiastical courts. *Bell.* And also to the commencement of proceedings in Probate and Divorce. 3 *Steph. Com.*

The word is also frequently applied to the quoting of legal cases and authorities in courts of law.

CITY is defined by Cowel as being such a town-corporate as hath a bishop and a cathedral church; by Blackstone, as a town incorporated, which is or hath been the see of a bishop. 1 *Bl.* There seems, however, to be no necessary connection between a city and a see. 1 *Steph. Com.*

CITY OF LONDON COURT. A court in the City of London, formerly called the Sheriff's Court, which is now, by s. 185 of the County Courts Act, 1888 (51 & 52 Vict. c. 43), classed among the county courts, so far as regards the administration of justice. 3 *Steph. Com.* But the privileges of the corporation, in the appointment of the judge and other officers of the court, are not affected by that Act.

CITY OF LONDON POLICE. [CONSTABLE, 3.]

CIVIL stands for the opposite of criminal, of ecclesiastical, of military, or of political. 1 *Mill's Log.*

CIVIL BILL COURTS. The local courts of civil jurisdiction in Ireland, analogous to English county courts.

CIVIL DEATH. This expression was formerly used to indicate—
1. That a man had entered a monastery, and being *professed* in religion, became *dead* in law.
2. That a man had become outlawed.
3. That a man had become attainted of treason or felony.
The old doctrine of civil death is now obsolete ; but a person who has been absent and not heard of for a period of seven years is, for many purposes, presumed to be dead.

CIVIL LAW is defined in Justinian's Institutes as " that law which every people has established for itself " ; in other words, the law of any given state. But this law is now distinguished by the term *municipal law :* the term *civil law* being applied to the Roman civil law. [CORPUS JURIS CIVILIS.]

CIVIL LIST. An annual sum granted by parliament at the commencement of each reign in lieu of revenue of Crown lands, for the expense of the royal household and establishment, as distinguished from the general exigencies of the state. 2 *Steph. Com.*

CIVIL RESPONSIBILITY. To be *civilly* responsible for any act of omission means to be liable in an action or other proceeding at the suit of a private person or corporation, or (in certain cases) at the suit of the Crown suing as for a private wrong. This is opposed to criminal responsibility, which means liability to answer in a criminal court. The action, etc., is styled civil remedy, in opposition to prosecution, which is brought by the Crown.

CIVIL SIDE. The side of a court devoted to civil causes.

CLAIM (Lat. *Clameum*). A challenge of interest in anything that is in the possession of another, or at least out of the possession of the claimant. *Cowel.* [CONTINUAL CLAIM ; FINE, 1 ; STATEMENT OF CLAIM.]

CLAIM OF LIBERTY. A suit or petition to the sovereign in the Court of Exchequer to have liberties and franchises confirmed there by the Attorney-General.

CLAUSUM FREGIT (" he broke the close," that is, committed an unwarrantable entry upon another's soil). These words are generally used in reference to an action of trespass in entering another's land. 3 *Bl. ;* 3 *Steph. Com.*

CLAVES INSULÆ. The House of Keys of the Isle of Man. [KEYS.]

CLEAN HANDS are required from a plaintiff, *i.e.*, he must be free from reproach, or taint of fraud, etc., in his conduct *in respect of the subject matter of his claim ;* everything else is immaterial.

CLEAR DAYS. A phrase used to indicate the calculation of days from one day to another, excluding both the first and last day.

CLEARANCE. A certificate, given by the collector of a port, that a ship has paid dues and been cleared at the customs house and may sail ; and *clearance* has therefore been properly defined as *a permission to sail.*

CLEARING HOUSE. The place where the operation termed " clearing " is carried on ; " clearing " being a method adopted by London banks for exchanging the drafts of each other's houses and settling the difference. *McLeod on Banking.*

CLERGY, besides its ordinary sense, signifies " benefit of clergy." [BENEFIT OF CLERGY.]

CLERK OF ARRAIGNS. An assistant to the clerk of assize (*q.v.*).

CLERK OF ASSIZE. An officer in each circuit, who records all judicial proceedings done by the justices of assize, and acts generally as the clerk of the assize court. He is assisted sometimes by a deputy clerk of assize, and an officer called the clerk of arraigns.

CLERK OF RECORDS AND WRITS. An officer of the Court of Chancery. Their duties are now transferred to the masters of the Supreme Court and their office abolished. See *Jud. Act,* 1879.

CLERK OF THE CROWN IN CHANCERY.
A public officer whose duty it is to issue
writs for elections on receiving the Lord
Chancellor's warrant ; and to deliver to
the clerk of the House of Commons the
list of members returned to serve in
parliament ; to certify the election of
representative peers for Scotland and
Ireland, etc. *2 Steph. Com.; May's
Parl. Pract.* Provision was made by
stat. 2 & 3 Will. 4, c. 111, for the abolition of this office when it should become
vacant. The office has, however, been
continued by 15 & 16 Vict. s. 87, s. 23,
and 37 & 38 Vict. c. 81, s. 8, by which
the duties formerly performed by the
Keeper or Clerk of His Majesty's
Hanaper are now performed by the
Clerk of the Crown in Chancery.

CLERK OF THE HOUSE OF COMMONS.
One of the officers of the House of
Commons, appointed by the Crown for
life, by letters patent, in which he is
styled " Under Clerk of the Parliaments, to attend upon the Commons."
See *May's Parl. Pract.*

CLERK OF THE PARLIAMENTS. The
chief officer of the House of Lords,
appointed by the Crown, by letters
patent. *May's Parl. Pract.*

CLERK OF THE PEACE. An officer who
acts as clerk to the court of quarter
sessions, and records all their proceedings. He is also clerk to the county
council and is appointed and remov-
able by the standing joint committee
of the county council and justices. See
Local Government Act, 1888 ; *4 Steph.
Com.*

He has various other duties under
different Acts of parliament. As to
appointment etc. in quarter sessions
boroughs, see Municipal Corporation
Act, 1882, s. 164.

CLIENT. A person who consults a solicitor. A solicitor, also, in reference to
the counsel he instructs, is spoken of as
a *client*. It has also become common
of late to use the word in reference to
other professions.

CLOSE. A word most frequently used
for a person's land. *3 Bl.; 3 Steph.
Com.* [CLAUSUM FREGIT.]

CLOSE COPY. The copy of a document
made by a solicitor acting as agent for
the use of his solicitor client.

CLOSE ROLLS, or **CLAUSE ROLLS.**
[CLOSE WRITS.]

CLOSE WRITS. Grants of the king, sealed
with his great seal, but directed to particular persons, and for particular purposes—and which, therefore, not being
proper for public inspection, are closed
up and sealed on the outside—are called
writs close, *litteræ clausæ*, or *letters
close*, and are recorded in the *close rolls*;
in the same manner as letters patent,
literæ patentes, are in the *patent rolls*.
1 *Steph. Com.*

CLOUGH. 1. A valley, as used in Domesday Book. *Cowel.*
2. Also an allowance of 2 lb. per cwt. on
buying goods wholesale by weight.

CLUB. A voluntary association, for social
or other purposes, of a number of persons
who subscribe a certain sum either to a
common fund for the benefit of the
members or to a particular individual ;
in the former case it is a " members "
club and in the latter a " proprietary "
club. In a proprietary club the expense
and risk are borne by a contractor who
takes all profits. A members club is
usually managed by a steward under
the superintendence of a committee,
and the members, merely as such, are
not liable for debts incurred by the
committee or for goods supplied to the
club. A club as a body has no position
recognised in law : it is not a partnership, nor a company, nor a society subject to statutory rules, except under the
Licensing Act, 1902 (2 Ed. 7, c. 28).

COADJUTOR BISHOP. A bishop appointed under stat. 32 & 33 Vict.
c. 111, s. 4, in aid of a bishop
incapacitated by permanent mental
infirmity from the due performance of
his episcopal duties. *2 Steph. Com.*
[SUFFRAGAN.]

COAL must be sold by weight only.
Weights and Measures Act, 1889.

COAL MINES. See *Coal Mines Regulation Acts*, 1887, 1896.

COAST GUARD. A body of officers and
men raised and equipped by the Commissioners of the Admiralty, for the
defence of the coasts of the realm, and
for the more ready manning of the navy
in case of war or sudden emergency, as
well as for the protection of the revenue
against smugglers. *19 & 20 Vict.
c. 83.*

COCKPIT. A name which used to be given
to the Judicial Committee of the Privy
Council, the room where it sat being
built on the site of the old cockpit in
Whitehall Place.

CODE. A system or collection of laws.

CODE NAPOLEON, otherwise called the *Code Civil*, is a code composed of thirty-six laws, the first of which was passed in 1803 and the last in 1804, which were united in one body under the name of *Code Civil des Français*. *Bouvier*.

Sometimes, however, the name is extended to the whole of Napoleon's legislation.

CODICIL. A schedule or supplement to a will, when the testator desires to add, explain, alter, or retract anything; it must be executed with the same formalities as a will under Wills Act (1 Vict. c. 26). 1 *Steph. Com.*; 2 *Steph. Com.*

COGNATI. Relations on the mother's side. [AGNATES.]

COGNITION AND SALE. A process before the Court of Session for obtaining a warrant to sell a ward's estate. *Bell.*

COGNIZANCE, or **CONUSANCE.** 1. The hearing of a thing judicially.
2. An acknowledgment of a fine. [FINE, 1.]
3. A cognizance is also a form of defence in the action of replevin, by which the defendant insists that the goods were lawfully taken as a distress. It differs from an *avowry* in that by an *avowry* the defendant asserts he took the goods in his own right; by a *cognizance* he asserts that he took them as servant for another. 3 *Bl.*; 3 *Steph. Com.*

COGNIZANCE (*Judicial*). Knowledge upon which a judge is bound to act without having it proved in evidence; as the public statutes of the realm, the several seals of the sovereign, etc. A judge is not bound to take cognizance of current events, however notorious, nor of the law of other countries.

COGNIZANCE OF PLEAS. An exclusive right to try causes within a limited jurisdiction. 2 *Bl.* 38.

COGNIZOR and **COGNIZEE OF A FINE.** The cognizor is he who passed or acknowledged a fine of lands, etc. to another, called the cognizee. 32 *Hen.* 8, c. 5; 1 *Steph. Com.* [FINE.]

COGNOVIT ACTIONEM. An instrument in writing whereby a defendant in an action confesses a plaintiff's demand to be just. 3 *Bl.* 397.

Under the Debtors Act, 1869 (32 & 33 Vict. c. 62), ss. 24, 25, 26, such an instrument is invalid unless attested by a solicitor attending at the request of the party executing it, and subscribed by such solicitor, and also filed in the Court of King's Bench within twenty-one days after the execution thereof. 3 *Steph. Com.*; *Robson, Bkcy.*

CO-HEIR. One of several to whom an inheritance descends.

COIF. A title given to serjeants-at-law, who were called serjeants of the coif, from the coif they wore on their heads. 3 *Steph. Com.*

COIN. The coining of money is in all states the prerogative of the sovereign power. 24 & 25 Vict. c. 99 makes it felony to counterfeit coin. See also 33 & 34 Vict. c. 10.

COKE, SIR EDWARD. Lord Chief Justice of the King's Bench in the time of James I. He compiled reports, and was the author of four volumes of "Institutes" on the subject of the common law, and of an edition of Littleton's Treatise on Tenures. 1 *Bl.*; 1 *Steph. Com.*

COLIBERTS. Tenants in socage.

COLLATE. To bestow a living by *collation*. [ADVOWSON; COLLATION TO A BENEFICE.]

COLLATERAL. That which hangeth by the side. An assurance collateral to a deed is one which is made, over and besides the deed itself. Thus if a man covenant with another, and enter into a bond for the performance of his covenant, the bond is called a collateral assurance. *Cowel.*

COLLATERAL CONSANGUINITY. The relationship between persons who descend from a common ancestor, but neither of whom descends from the other. 2 *Bl.*

COLLATERAL ISSUE on a criminal charge is an issue arising out of a plea which does not bear on the guilt or innocence of the accused. 4 *Bl.*; 4 *Steph. Com.*

COLLATERAL SECURITY. An additional security, for the better safety of a mortgagee.

COLLATIO BONORUM, in the Roman law, was where a portion advanced by a parent in his lifetime to a son or daughter was upon his death reckoned as part of his estate, or, as English lawyers would say, "brought into hotchpot" (*q.v.*). 2 *Bl.*; 2 *Steph. Com.*

COLLATION. The comparison of a copy with the original document, in order to ascertain its correctness.

COLLATION TO A BENEFICE. When the ordinary is also the patron, and *confers* the living, the presentation and institution are one and the same act, and are called a collation to a benefice. *Cowel ; 1 Bl. ; 2 Steph. Com.*

COLLATIVE ADVOWSON. [ADVOWSON ; COLLATION TO A BENEFICE.]

COLLEGIATE CHURCH. A church consisting of a body corporate of dean and ·canons, such as Westminster, Windsor, etc., independently of any cathedral. *2 Steph. Com.*

COLLIGENDUM BONA DEFUNCTI (LETTERS AD). Letters granted, formerly by the ordinary, and now by the Court of Probate, to such discreet person as the Court of Probate shall think fit, authorising him to keep the goods of a deceased person in his safe custody, and to do other acts for the benefit of such as are entitled to the property of the deceased. These letters differ from letters of administration in so far as they do not make the grantee the legal representative of the deceased. They are granted in the event of the person who is legally entitled to take out probate or letters of administration refusing to do so. *2 Bl. ; 2 Steph. Com.*

COLLISTRIGIUM. A pillory.

COLLUSION. A deceitful agreement between two or more persons, to defraud another person or other persons of their right, or to frustrate some rule of public policy. The word is generally, though not necessarily, used with reference to collusive legal proceedings, and specially divorce. *20 & 21 Vict. c. 85.* The judgment obtained by such collusion is a nullity.

COLONIES. The distant possessions or dependencies of the British Crown in various quarters of the globe. Colonies are no part of the mother country, but distinct, though dependent dominions. In general they are either gained from other states by conquest or treaty, or else they are acquired by right of occupancy only. *1 Steph. Com.*

COLONUS. A husbandman or villager, who was bound to pay yearly a certain tribute, or at certain times in the year

to plough some part of the lord's land ; and from hence comes the word *clown*. *Cowel.*

COLOUR, in pleading, signifies an *apparent* or *primâ facie* right ; and the meaning of the old rule that pleadings in *confession and avoidance* [CONFESSION AND AVOIDANCE] should give colour is, that they should *confess* the matter adversely alleged, to such an extent at least as to admit some apparent right in the opposite party, which requires to be encountered and *avoided* by the allegation of new matter. Colour was either express, *i.e.*, inserted in the pleading, or implied.

Abolished by ss. 49 and 64 of the Common Law Procedure Act, 1852. *3 Steph. Com.*

COLOURABLE. Not real, the reverse of *bonâ fide, e.g.,* an alteration made only for the purpose of evading the law of copyright.

COMBAT. [WAGER OF BATTEL.]

COMBINATION, UNLAWFUL. An assembly of workmen or others met to perpetrate unlawful acts. See *Conspiracy and Protection of Property Act,* 1875 ; *4 Steph. Com.*

COMES. A count or sheriff or superior officer of a county or comitatus.

COMITATU COMMISSO. A writ whereby a sheriff was authorised to take upon himself the command of a county. *Cowel.*

COMITATU ET CASTRO COMMISSO. A writ whereby the charge of a county, together with the keeping of a castle, was committed to the sheriff. *Cowel.*

COMITATUS. A county.

COMITY OF NATIONS. This expression is generally used to indicate the practice adopted by the courts of justice in one country of giving effect (within certain limits) to the laws of another country, and the judgments given by its courts.

COMMANDITE, in French law, is a partnership of several persons, of which some contribute their money, and others their talents or industry. *Ferrière.*

COMMENDAM, or **ECCLESIA COMMENDATA**. A benefice that, being void, is commended to the care of some sufficient clerk to be supplied, till it may be conveniently provided with a pastor. Also, when a beneficed parson is made a bishop, and the king gives him power to retain his benefice, he is said to hold it *in commendam. Cowel;* 1 *Bl.;* 2 *Steph. Com.; Hall. Const. Hist. ch.* 6. The holding of livings *in commendam* is for the future abolished by 6 & 7 Will. 4, c. 77, s. 18. 2 *Steph. Com.*

COMMISSARY. One who is sent to execute some office or duty for a superior. In ecclesiastical law, an officer of the bishop who exercises spiritual jurisdiction in distant parts of the diocese.

COMMISSION. The warrant, or letters patent, that all men, exercising jurisdiction, either ordinary or extraordinary, have for their power to hear and determine any cause or action. *Cowel.*

The word is also used in numerous other ways. It is used of the bailment called *mandatum;* of instructions given to an agent; of a broker's remuneration, etc. For certain special instances of its use, see the following titles.

COMMISSION, ASSENT TO BILLS BY. This is when, under 33 Hen. 8, c. 21, the sovereign gives his assent by letters patent under the great seal, signed with his hand, and notified in his absence to both houses assembled together in the upper house. 1 *Bl.;* 2 *Steph. Com.; May's Parl. Pract.*

COMMISSION DAY. The opening day of an assize; so called because the judges' commissions are then opened and read. [ASSIZE, COURTS OF.]

COMMISSION DEL CREDERE. [DEL CREDERE.]

COMMISSION OF ARRAY. [ARRAY, COMMISSIONS OF.]

COMMISSION OF ASSIZE. [ASSIZE, COURTS OF.]

COMMISSION OF ASSOCIATION. [ASSOCIATION.]

COMMISSION OF DELEGATES. A commission under the great seal to certain persons, usually lords, bishops and judges of the law, to sit upon an appeal to the King in the Court of Chancery in ecclesiastical and admiralty suits. The Commission or Court of Delegates is now abolished by 2 & 3 Will. 4, c. 92, and its functions transferred to the Judicial Committee of the Privy Council.

COMMISSION OF GAOL DELIVERY. [ASSIZE, COURTS OF.]

COMMISSION OF LUNACY. A commission granted by the Lord Chancellor to inquire into the state of mind of an alleged lunatic. [LUNACY.]

COMMISSION OF NISI PRIUS. [ASSIZE, COURTS OF.]

COMMISSION OF OYER AND TERMINER. A commission granted to judges and others to *hear and determine* treasons, felonies, etc. *Cowel.*

Under this commission, persons may be tried, whether they are in gaol or at large; but the judges can only proceed upon an indictment found at the same assizes. 4 *Bl.* 270; 4 *Steph. Com.* [ASSIZE, COURTS OF.]

COMMISSION OF THE PEACE. A commission under the great seal, constituting one or more persons justice or justices of the peace. 2 *Steph. Com.;* 3 *Steph. Com.* [JUSTICE OF THE PEACE.]

COMMISSION TO EXAMINE WITNESSES. By this is meant a commission issued to a foreign country, or other place out of the jurisdiction of a court in which a suit is instituted, for the purpose of obtaining such evidence of witnesses residing in such foreign country or other place, as may be material to the question before the court. 3 *Bl.;* 3 *Steph. Com.*

COMMISSIONERS, ECCLESIASTICAL. [ECCLESIASTICAL COMMISSIONERS.]

COMMISSIONERS FOR OATHS are solicitors appointed by the Lord Chancellor to administer oaths to persons making affidavits to be used in law suits, etc. See *Commissioners for Oaths Act,* 1889 and 1891.

COMMISSIONERS OF SEWERS. [COURT OF COMMISSIONERS OF SEWERS.]

COMMITMENT. The sending of a person to prison. The word is also used of the document or warrant by which a commitment is directed.

COMMITTEE, JUDICIAL. [JUDICIAL COMMITTEE.]

COMMITTEE OF COUNCIL ON EDUCATION. The committee of the Privy Council charged to consider applications for aid from the money granted by parliament for the purpose of education. *2 Steph. Com.*

COMMITTEE OF INSPECTION. A committee, not exceeding five in number, nor less than three, appointed by the general body of creditors of a bankrupt, for the purpose of superintending the administration by the trustee of the bankrupt's property. *Bankruptcy Act, 1883 ; 2 Steph. Com.*

COMMITTEE OF LUNATIC. A person to whom the maintenance of a lunatic, or the management of his estate, is committed. *2 Steph. Com.* In the former case the committee is called a committee of the *person* of the lunatic ; in the latter case he is called a committee of his *estate. 1 Bl. ; 2 Steph. Com.*

COMMITTEE OF SUPPLY. A committee into which the House of Commons resolves itself for considering the amount of supply to be granted to his Majesty. *May's Parl. Pract.*

COMMITTEE OF THE WHOLE HOUSE. A parliamentary committee, composed of every member of the house. To form it in the Commons, the speaker quits the chair, another member being appointed chairman. In the Lords, the chair is taken by the chairman of committees. In these committees a bill is debated clause by clause, amendments made, blanks filled up, and sometimes the bill is entirely re-modelled. *1 Bl. ; 2 Steph. Com.; May's Parl. Pract.*

COMMITTEE OF WAYS AND MEANS. A committee into which the House of Commons resolves itself, for the purpose of considering the ways and means of raising a supply which has been already voted. *2 Steph. Com.; May's Parl. Pract.*

COMMODATUM. A gratuitous loan of a specific chattel. It is a species of bailment. [BAILMENT.]

COMMON, or **RIGHT OF COMMON,** is a profit which a man hath in the land of another, as to pasture beasts therein, to catch fish, to dig turf, to cut wood, or the like. It is chiefly of five kinds : common of *pasture*, of *piscary*, of *turbary*, of *estovers*, and *in the soil.*

I. Common of *pasture* is the right of feeding one's beasts on another's land. This kind of common is either *appendant, appurtenant, because of vicinage,* or *in gross.*

1. *Common appendant* is a right belonging to the owners or occupiers of arable land, under the lord of a manor, to put commonable beasts upon the lord's waste, and upon the lands of other persons within the same manor. Commonable beasts are either beasts of the plough, or such as manure the ground.

2. *Common appurtenant* ariseth from no connection of tenure, but may be annexed to lands in other lordships ; or may extend to such beasts as hogs, goats, or the like, which neither plough nor manure the ground. This kind of common can be claimed only by special grant or prescription.

3. *Common because of vicinage* is where the inhabitants of two townships, which lie contiguous to each other, have usually intercommoned with one another ; the beasts of the one straying mutually into the other's fields, without any molestation from either. This is only a permissive right ; and therefore either township may inclose and bar out the other, though they have intercommoned time out of mind.

4. *Common in gross,* or at large, is such as is neither appendant nor appurtenant to the land, but is annexed to a man's person, being granted to him and his heirs by deed, or claimed by prescriptive right.

II. Common of *piscary* is a liberty of fishing in another man's water.

III. Common of *turbary* is a liberty of digging turf upon another's ground.

IV. Common of *estovers* or *estouviers*—that is, necessaries ; from *estoffer*, to furnish—is a liberty of taking necessary wood, for the use of furniture of a house or farm, from off another's estate.

V. Common *in the soil* consists of the right of digging for coals, minerals, stones, and the like.

2 Bl. ; 1 Steph. Com. ; Wms. R. P.
The inclosure of commons is regulated now by the Inclosure Acts and the Commons Act, 1899. *2 Steph. Com.*

COMMON ASSAULT. An assault unaccompanied with circumstances of aggravation.

COMMON ASSURANCES. [ASSURANCE, 1.]

COMMON BAIL. Especially applied to the two fictitious persons John Doe and Richard Roe, in their capacity as sureties put in by the defendant in an action, upon entering an appearance, for his future attendance and obedience. [BAIL.]

COMMON BAR. [BLANK BAR.]

COMMON BENCH. A name sometimes given to the Court of Common Pleas. 3 *Steph. Com.*

COMMON CARRIER. [CARRIER.]

COMMON COUNTS. Counts in a plaintiff's declaration which state the most ordinary causes of action, as for money lent ; money received by the defendant for the use of the plaintiff ; work and labour ; goods sold and delivered, etc. As technical forms of pleading they are now superseded by the Jud. Acts, 1873, 1876.

COMMON FINE. A small sum of money, otherwise called *head silver*, which the persons resident within the jurisdiction of certain courts-leet paid to the lord.

COMMON FORM, PROOF OF WILL IN. This was the proof of a will by an executor on his own oath before the ordinary, or his surrogate, as opposed to proof in more solemn form, *per testes* (by witnesses), when the validity of the will was disputed. 2 *Steph. Com.*

COMMON INFORMER. An informer who sues on a penal statute which entitles *any* one to sue to recover the penalty imposed. 3 *Bl.;* 3 *Steph. Com.*

COMMON INTENDMENT, or **COMMON INTENT.** Ordinary meaning.

COMMON JURY. A jury consisting of persons who possess only the ordinary qualification of property. 3 *Steph. Com.* See 3 *Bl.* [JURY.]

COMMON LAW. The ancient unwritten law of this kingdom. 1 *Bl.*

The term "Common Law" is used in various ways :—

1. Of the ancient law above mentioned embodied in judicial decisions, as opposed to statute law, or the law enacted by parliament.

2. Of the original and proper law of England, administered in the Common Law Courts, that is, the Superior Courts of Westminster, and the Nisi Prius Courts, as opposed to the system called *Equity*, which was administered in the Court of Chancery. Since the Judicature Act all courts administer law and equity concurrently.

3. Of the municipal law of England as opposed to the Roman civil law, or other foreign law.

COMMON PLEAS. [COURT OF COMMON PLEAS.]

COMMON PRAYER. [BOOK OF COMMON PRAYER.]

COMMON RECOVERY. [RECOVERY.]

COMMON SCOLD (Lat. *Communis rixatrix*). [SCOLD.]

COMMON SEAL. An expression used of the seal of a corporation.

COMMON SERJEANT OF LONDON. A judicial officer of the City of London, next to the recorder. He is *ex officio* one of the judges of the Central Criminal Court. 4 *Steph. Com.*

COMMON, TENANCY IN. A tenancy in common is where two or more hold the *same* land (1) under different titles : or (2) accruing under the same title, other than *descent*, but at different periods ; or (3) under the same written instrument, but by words importing that the grantees are to take in distinct shares. This tenancy therefore happens where there is a unity of possession merely ; but there may be an entire disunion of interest, of title, and of time. 1 *Steph. Com.* [CO-PARCENARY ; JOINT TENANCY.]

Tenancy in common may also exist in movable property. 2 *Steph. Com.*

COMMON, TENANTS IN, are such as occupy the same land under a tenancy in common. See preceding title.

COMMON VOUCHEE. The person who was commonly "vouched to warranty" in the fictitious proceeding called a *common recovery*. The crier of the court was generally employed for this purpose. 1 *Steph. Com.; Wms. R. P.* [RECOVERY ; VOUCHING TO WARRANTY.]

COMMONABLE. 1. Held in common.

2. Allowed to pasture on common land. Commonable beasts are either beasts of the plough or such as manure the ground. *Blackstone.*

COMMONALTY. Persons who are not the nobility or peerage. 1 *Bl.* ; 2 *Steph. Com.*

COMMONWEALTH. A word which properly signifies the common weal or public policy ; sometimes it is used to designate a republican form of government : and especially the period of English history from the execution of Charles I. in 1649 to the restoration of the monarchy under Charles II. in 1660.

COMMORANCY. The residence together of several persons within a district. See 4 *Bl.*

COMMORIENTES. Persons dying by the same accident or on the same occasion. In English law there is no presumption of survivorship.

COMMUNEM LEGEM. See CASU PROVISO and CASU CONSIMILI.

COMMUTATION OF TITHES. The substitution of a rent-charge adjusted according to the average price of corn, for the payment of tithes in kind. 2 *Steph. Com.*

COMMUTATIVE CONTRACT. One in which each of the contracting parties gives and receives an equivalent.

COMPANY. A body of persons associated together for the purposes of trade or business ; sometimes called a joint stock company. Companies are formed (1) by charter, (2) by special Act of parliament, (3) by registration at Somerset House.

Companies are regulated chiefly by the Companies Clauses Consolidation Act, 1845, and the Companies Acts, 1862 to 1900.

The liability of members of companies is usually limited, either by the charter, Act of parliament, or memorandum of association.

COMPASSING. Contriving or imagining.

COMPENSATION. 1. An allowance for the apprehension of criminals.
2. The money paid by a railway company or other parties taking land under an Act of parliament, for the purchase of the interest in the land of the parties entitled thereto.
3. Money paid for damage caused by any wrong or breach of contract, or, under the Felony Act, 1870 (33 & 34 Vict. c. 23), to persons defrauded or injured by any felony.
4. A set-off (Sc.). [SET-OFF.]

COMPLAINANT. One who commences a prosecution against another.

COMPOS MENTIS. Of sound mind.

COMPOSITION. 1. A *real composition*. This is when an agreement is made between the owner of lands and the incumbent, with the consent of the ordinary and the patron, that the lands shall, for the future, be discharged from payment of tithes, by reason of some land or other *real* recompense given in lieu and satisfaction thereof. 2 *Steph. Com.*
2. A sum of money agreed to be accepted by the creditors of a debtor in satisfaction of the debts due to them from the debtor. A composition may be a private one effected by deed and registered under the Deeds of Arrangement Act, 1887, when only creditors assenting to it will be bound ; or a composition in bankruptcy proceedings, when, if passed by the requisite majority of creditors and approved by the court, it will bind all creditors entitled to prove, and of course no registration under the Act of 1887 is necessary.

COMPOUND HOUSEHOLDER. Modern statutes having enabled the owners of small houses to pay the rates for the occupiers and receive a composition for so doing, in order to prevent the occupiers being disfranchised it was further enacted that the occupiers might claim to be rated themselves, and persons so claiming became commonly known as compound householders. See 14 & 15 *Vict. c.* 14, and *Rogers' Elections*, *Vol. I.*

COMPOUNDING. 1. Arranging, coming to terms.
2. Compounding a felony is where a party robbed or otherwise injured by a felony takes a reward from the felon, or in case of theft takes back the stolen goods upon agreement not to prosecute ; this is called *theftbole*, and is punishable with fine and imprisonment. 4 *Steph. Com.* It is no offence to compound a misdemeanor unless the offence is virtually an offence against the public.
3. Compounding for a debt. See COMPOSITION.

COMPRINT. A surreptitious printing by a man of another's books. See COPYRIGHT.

COMPROMISE. An adjustment of claims in dispute by mutual concession, either without resort to legal proceedings, or on the condition of abandoning such proceedings if already commenced.

COMPTROLLER. 1. One who observes and examines the accounts of the collectors of public money. 2 *Steph. Com.*

2. The *comptroller in bankruptcy* was an officer appointed under the repealed Bankruptcy Act, 1869 ; the trustee in any bankruptcy being required to forward the statement of his accounts, after they had been audited by the committee of inspection. 2 *Steph. Com.*

3. An officer of the royal household.

4. The *comptroller of the hanaper* was an officer of the Court of Chancery, whose office was abolished in 1842 by 5 & 6 Vict. c. 103, s. 1.

COMPULSORY PILOT. [PILOTAGE AUTHORITIES.]

COMPURGATORS. The twelve persons who, when a parson was tried and made oath of his own innocence, were called upon to swear that they believed he spoke the truth. Supposed to be the origin of trial by jury. 4 *Steph. Com.* [BENEFIT OF CLERGY.]

COMPUTO. An ancient writ to compel a bailiff, receiver or accountant to yield up his accounts. Also lay against guardians.

CONCEALERS. Persons who were used to find out lands which were kept privily from the king by persons having no title thereto.

CONCEALMENT, *i.e.*, (1) *suppressio veri* to the injury or prejudice of another : if active and fraudulent it is ground for rescinding a contract. (2) Of birth is a misdemeanor. See 24 & 25 *Vict. c.* 100, *s.* 60. (3) Of documents of title to lands or testamentary instruments is felony. See 24 & 25 *Vict. c.* 96, *ss.* 28, 29, and 25 & 26 *Vict. c.* 67, *s.* 44.

CONCESSIT SOLVERE (he granted and agreed to pay). An action of debt upon a simple contract. It lies by custom in the Mayor's Court, London, and the Bristol City Court.

CONCILIATION. A settling of disputes without litigation. See *Conciliation Act,* 1896, 59 & 60 *Vict. c.* 30.

CONCLUDED is often used in the same sense as *estopped*. [CONCLUSION ; ESTOPPEL.]

CONCLUSION is when a man, by his own act upon record, hath charged himself with a duty, or other thing. In this sense it is tantamount to *estoppel*. [ESTOPPEL.] And this word *conclusion* is taken in another sense, as for the end or later part of any declaration, plea in bar, replication, conveyance, etc. *Cowel.*

CONCORD. 1. Part of the process by which a fine of lands was levied, prior to the abolition of fines by 3 & 4 Will. 4, c. 74. It was the agreement by which the pretended defendant acknowledged that the lands in question were the right of the complainant. 2 *Bl.* ; 1 *Steph. Com.* [FINE, 1.]

2. A compromise

CONCURRENT JURISDICTIONS. The jurisdiction of several different tribunals authorised to deal with the same subject-matter at the choice of the suitor.

CONCURRENT WRITS. Duplicate originals, or several writs running at the same time for the same purpose, for service on a person, when it is not known where he is to be found ; or for service on several persons, as when there are several defendants in an action. *R. S. C.* 1883, *Ord. VI.*

CONDITION. A restraint annexed to a thing so that by the non-performance the party to it shall receive prejudice and loss, and by the performance commodity or advantage : it is also defined to be what is referred to an uncertain chance which may or may not happen. The following are the most important kinds of condition : (1) A condition in a deed, or express : a condition in law or implied. (2) Precedent or subsequent. 1 *Steph. Com.*

CONDITIONAL FEE, otherwise called a fee simple conditional, properly comprises every estate in fee simple granted upon condition ; but the term is usually understood to refer to that particular species called a " conditional fee " at the common law, which is an estate restrained in its form of donation to *some particular heirs* (exclusive of others) : as, to the heirs of a man's body, or to the heirs male of his body ; which the judges of former days construed, not as an estate descendible

CONDITIONAL FEE—*continued.*
to some particular heirs, but an estate upon condition that the land was to revert to the donor, if the donee had no heirs of his body. This construction of gifts of lands was put a stop to by c. 1 of the Statute of Westminster the Second, commonly called the statute *De donis conditionalibus*, in the year 1285, which provided that henceforth the will of the donor should be observed *secundum formam in cartâ doni expressam* (according to the form expressed in the charter of gift). 2 *Bl.*; 1 *Steph. Com.* [DE DONIS; ESTATE.]

CONDITIONAL LIMITATION is a phrase used specially in the two following ways :—
1. Of an estate or interest in land so expressly defined and limited by the words of its creation that it cannot endure for any longer time than till a particular contingency happens. 1 *Steph. Com.* That is, a *present* interest, to be divested on a *future* contingency.
2. Of a future use or interest limited to take effect upon a given contingency, in derogation of a preceding estate or interest. This is likewise called a *shifting* or *secondary* use, and also an *executory interest*. It is a future estate to come into possession upon a given contingency. 1 *Steph. Com.* [ESTATE; EXECUTORY INTEREST.]
Thus, if land be granted to the use of A. and his heirs until B. returns from Rome, and then to the use of B. and his heirs, A.'s estate is a conditional limitation of the first sort, and B.'s estate is a conditional limitation of the second sort above mentioned.

CONDITIONS OF SALE. The terms stated in writing, upon which an estate or interest is to be sold by public auction. The Conveyancing Act, 1881, applies certain conditions of sale to all contracts, unless otherwise expressly stated.

CONDITIONS PRECEDENT AND SUBSEQUENT. A condition *precedent*, in a conveyance or disposition of an estate, is a condition which must happen or be performed before the estate or interest can vest. A condition *subsequent* is a condition of the failure or non-performance of which an estate already vested may be defeated. 2 *Bl.*; 1 *Steph. Com.*

CONDONATION. A pardoning or remission, especially of conjugal offence.

The immediate effect of *condonation* is to bar the party condoning of his or her remedy for the offence in question. 2 *Steph. Com.*

CONDUCT MONEY. Money for the payment of the reasonable expenses of a witness at a trial.

CONDUCTIO. (Roman law.) A hiring (*q.v.*).

CONEY. A rabbit. See GAME.

CONFEDERACY. A combination of two or more persons to commit some unlawful act or to do some damage or injury to another. [CONSPIRACY.]

CONFERENCE. 1. In parliamentary practice, is a mode of communicating important matters by one house of parliament to the other by means of deputations of their own members. *May's Parl. Pract*; 2 *Steph. Com.*
2. A meeting between a counsel and solicitor to advise on their client's cause.

CONFESSING ERROR. The consent by a party in whose favour judgment has been given that such judgment shall be reversed, on allegation by the opposite party of "error" in fact or in law. [ERROR.]

CONFESSION AND AVOIDANCE is a plea in bar whereby a party *confesses* the facts as stated by his adversary, but alleges some new matter by way of *avoiding* the legal effect claimed for them. As, if a man be sued for an assault, he may admit the assault, but plead that he committed it in self-defence. 3 *Steph. Com.*

CONFESSION BY CRIMINAL may be in open court when called upon to plead to the indictment or elsewhere. [VOLUNTARY CONFESSION.]

CONFESSION, JUDGMENT BY. See COGNOVIT ACTIONEM.

CONFESSION OF DEFENCE. Where defendant alleges a ground of defence arising since the commencement of the action, the plaintiff may deliver confession of such defence and sign judgment for his costs up to the time of such pleading unless otherwise ordered. *R. S. C.* 1883, *Ord. XXIV. r.* 3.

CONFESSION OF PLEA. Same as CONFESSION OF DEFENCE (*q.v.*).

CONFESSO, BILL TAKEN PRO. [PRO CONFESSO.]

CONFIDENTIAL COMMUNICATION. [PRIVILEGED COMMUNICATION.]

CONFIRMATIO CHARTARUM (confirmation of the charters). A statute enacted 25 Edw. 1, A.D. 1297, confirming and making some additions to Magna Charta (*q.v.*). 1 *Steph. Com.*; 2 *Steph. Com.*

CONFIRMATION. 1. A conveyance of an estate or right, whereby a voidable estate is made sure and unavoidable or a particular estate is increased. 1 *Steph. Com.*
2. The ratification by the archbishop of the election of a bishop by dean and chapter.
3. Confirmation is also the Scotch term corresponding to *probate* and *letters of administration* in England.

CONFISCATE. To appropriate to the revenue of the Crown.

CONFLICT OF LAWS. The discordance between the laws of one country and another, as applied to the same subject-matter; as, for instance, in the case of a contract made in one country and intended to be executed in another. See *Story's Conflict of Laws; Westlake's Private International Law; Dicey's Conflict of Laws.*

CONFORMITY, BILL OF. A bill filed by an executor or administrator against the creditors of the deceased, for the adjustment of their claims, where the affairs of the testator or intestate are found to be so much involved that it would not be safe to administer the estate, except under the direction of the Court of Chancery: a final decree was then issued by the court, to which all parties were bound to *conform.*

CONFUSION. A word in Scotch and French law, signifying the merger or extinguishment of a debt by the debtor succeeding to the property of his creditor, or *vice versâ*. *Bell.*

CONFUSION OF GOODS is where the goods of two persons are so intermixed that the several portions can be no longer distinguished; as if the money, corn or hay of one man be intermixed with that of another. If the intermixture be by consent, it is supposed the proprietors have an interest in common in proportion to their shares, but if one

man wilfully intermixes his property with another's without his consent, the law gives the entire property to him whose right is invaded and endeavoured to be rendered uncertain without his consent. 2 *Bl.*; 2 *Steph. Com.*

CONGE D'ACCORDER signifies leave to accord or agree for the purpose of levying a fine, prescribed by stat. 18 Edw. 1. *Cowel*; 2 *Bl.*; 1 *Steph. Com.* [CONCORD; FINE, 1.]

CONGÉ D'ÉLIRE. The king's permission to a dean and chapter to choose a bishop. The dean and chapter are bound to elect such person as the Crown shall recommend (whose name is given in the letter missive which accompanies the *congé d'élire*), on pain of incurring the penalties of a *præmunire.* 1 *Bl.*; 2 *Steph. Com.*

CONGEABLE. A thing lawfully done, or done with leave. *Cowel.*

CONJOINTS. Persons married to each other.

CONJUGAL RIGHTS, SUIT FOR RESTITUTION OF, is a suit by a husband to compel his wife to live with him, or by a wife to compel the husband to take her back. 2 *Steph. Com.*

CONJURATION. A plot or compact made by men to do any public harm. In our common law it is specially used for such as have personal conference with the devil, or evil spirits, to know any secret, or to effect any purpose. 5 *Eliz. c.* 16; *Cowel.* The laws against conjuration and witchcraft were repealed in 1736, by 9 Geo. 2, c. 5. 4 *Bl.*; 4 *Steph. Com.*

CONNIVANCE signifies shutting of the eye. It is used especially with reference to a husband tacitly encouraging his wife to commit adultery, in order that he may obtain a divorce. Such connivance, if established, will deprive the husband of his remedy. 2 *Steph. Com.*; 20 & 21 *Vict. c.* 85.

CONSANGUINEUS FRATER. A brother by the father's side, in contradistinction to *frater uterinus*, the son of the same mother.

CONSANGUINITY. Relationship by blood, as opposed to *affinity*, which is relationship by marriage. 2 *Steph. Com.* AFFINITY.]

CONSCIENCE, COURTS OF. Local courts for the recovery of small debts, formed before the passing of the County Courts Act, 1846 (9 & 10 Vict. c. 95), in various parts of the kingdom, by special Acts passed for that purpose. They are by that Act for the most part abolished. 3 *Steph. Com.*

CONSENT presupposes a physical power, a mental power and a free and serious use of them, and if it be obtained by any fraud or undue influence it is not binding.

CONSEQUENTIAL DAMAGE OR INJURY is damage or injury arising by *consequence* or *collaterally* to one man, from the culpable act or omission of another. 3 *Steph. Com.*

CONSERVATOR OF THE PEACE is he that hath an especial charge, by virtue of his office, to see the king's peace kept. Some conservators of the peace are so *virtute officii*, some are specially appointed, and are now called justices of the peace. 2 *Steph. Com.*

CONSIDERATION. A compensation, matter of inducement, or *quid pro quo*, for something promised or done. Valuable consideration is necessary to make binding every contract not under seal. It need not be adequate but must be of some value in the eye of the law and must be legal : it must also be present or future, it must not be past. 2 *Steph. Com.*

There is also a consideration called the consideration of "blood ;" that is, natural love and affection for a near relation. This is, for some purposes, deemed a *good* consideration ; but it is not held to be a *valuable* consideration, so as to support an action on a simple contract. It is sometimes called *meritorious* consideration. 2 *Steph. Com.; Anson on Contracts.*

CONSIDERATUM EST PER CURIAM (it is considered and adjudged by the court). The formal and ordinary commencement of a judgment.

CONSIGNATION, in Roman and Scottish law, is the payment of money by a debtor into the hands of a party other than the creditor, either because the creditor refuses to accept it, or by prior special agreements between debtor and creditor. It includes the depositing of money with a stakeholder. *Bell; Paterson.*

CONSIGNMENT. The act of delivering goods ; also the goods themselves so delivered. He who consigns the goods is called the consignor, and the person to whom they are sent is called the consignee. 2 *Steph. Com.*

CONSISTORY COURTS. Courts held by diocesan bishops within their several cathedrals, for the trial of ecclesiastical causes arising within their respective dioceses. The bishop's chancellor, or his commissary, is the judge : and from his sentence an appeal lies to the archbishop. *Cowel ; 3 Bl.; 3 Steph. Com.*

CONSOLATO DEL MARE. An ancient collection of the customs of the sea, including points relating to maritime warfare. It was probably compiled in the latter part of the fourteenth century, and seems to have been first published at Barcelona. *Twiss' Law of Nations.*

CONSOLIDATED FUND. A fund formed by the union, in 1787, of three public funds, then known as the *Aggregate* Fund, the *General* Fund, and the *South Sea* Fund. This Consolidated Fund has since been combined with that of Ireland, and forms the *Consolidated Fund of the United Kingdom*. It constitutes almost the whole of the ordinary public income of the United Kingdom of Great Britain and Ireland, and is pledged for the payment of the whole of the interest of the National Debt, and is also liable to several other specific charges imposed upon it from time to time by Act of parliament. 2 *Steph. Com.*

CONSOLIDATING ACTIONS. [CONSOLIDATION ORDER.]

CONSOLIDATION. 1. The uniting of two benefices into one. *Cowel.*

2. The word is also used with reference to the consolidation of two or more parishes into one union, for the purpose of the relief and management of the poor. 3 *Steph. Com.*

3. Also, in Scotland, the merging of the estate of a proprietor of land with that of his superior, by the latter taking an "infeftment" or formal assignment of the interest of his inferior. *Bell ; 37 & 38 Vict. c. 94, s. 6.*

CONSOLIDATION OF MORTGAGES. A mortgagee, whether original or by assignment, who held more than one mortgage by the same mortgagor, had a right in equity to compel the mortgagor to redeem all the mortgages if he sought to redeem one of them. See as to consolidation of mortgages, section 17 of the Conveyancing Act, 1881.

CONSOLIDATION ORDER. A rule for consolidating actions, invented by Lord Mansfield, the effect of which is to bind the plaintiffs or defendants in several actions by the verdict in one, where the questions in dispute, and the evidence to be adduced, are the same in all. The application for such a rule is most frequently made in actions against underwriters upon policies of insurance. *Order XLIX.*, *r. 8*, *R.S.C.*, 1883 ; and *Libel Act*, 1888 (51 & 52 *Vict. c.* 64), *s.* 5.

CONSOLS. The Consolidated Fund of the United Kingdom. [CONSOLIDATED FUND.]

CONSPIRACY. A combination or agreement between two or more persons to carry into effect a purpose hurtful to some individual, or to particular classes of the community, or to the public at large. See also Conspiracy and Protection of Property Act, 1875. 4 *Steph. Com.*

CONSTABLE. An inferior officer to whom the service of maintaining the peace, and bringing to justice those by whom it is infringed, is more immediately committed.

1. *High and Petty Constables.*

High constables may be appointed at the courts leet of the franchise or hundred over which they preside, or, in default of that, by the justices at their special sessions. The proper duty of the high constable seems to be to keep the peace within the *hundred*, as the petty constable did within the *parish* or *township*. And see 32 & 33 Vict. c. 47.

Petty constables were inferior officers in every town and parish, subordinate to the high constable. Their principal duty was the preservation of the peace, though they also had other particular duties assigned to them by Act of parliament, particularly the service of the summonses and the execution of the warrants of the justices of the peace, relative to the apprehension and commitment of offenders. The county and borough police have now superseded them, and (unless under exceptional circumstances) they have not been appointed since 24th of March, 1873. 2 *Steph. Com.*

2. *Metropolitan Police.*

The Metropolitan Police Force is a body of men established in 1829, by stat. 10 Geo. 4, c. 44, and is under the immediate orders of an officer called the Commissioner of Police of the Metropolis, and two assistant commissioners.

The Metropolitan Police District does not include the City of London, but otherwise it extends to a radius of about fifteen miles from Charing Cross.

The Metropolitan Police Force is under the general control of the Home Secretary.

3. *The City of London Police.*

The City of London Police Force was established in 1839, by stat. 2 & 3 Vict. c. 94. The management of the City Police is placed in the hands of a commissioner, appointed by the Lord Mayor, aldermen, and commons of the City, with the approval of his Majesty.

4. *Borough Police or Constabulary.*

In boroughs incorporated under the Municipal Corporations Act (5 & 6 Will. 4, c. 76), a police or constabulary force is maintained for the preservation of the peace therein ; and this is appointed by, and is under the superintendence of, the *watch committee* of the borough, but see as to certain small boroughs 51 & 52 Vict. c. 41, s. 39. 2 *Steph. Com.*

5. *County Constabulary.*

In each county there is now also established a *county constabulary*, under the superintendence of a *chief constable* (*q.v.*).

6. *Special Constables.*

These are appointed by the magistrates to execute warrants on particular occasions, or to act in aid of the preservation of the peace on special emergencies. This office, in the absence of volunteers, is compulsory. 2 *Steph. Com.*

CONSTABLEWICK. The place within which lie the duties of a constable.

CONSTAT. A certificate of what appears (constat) upon the record touching the matter in question. An exemplification of the enrolment of letters patent under the great seal is called a *constat.*

CONSTITUENT. 1. One who appoints an agent ; particularly,
2. One who by his vote constitutes or elects a member of parliament.

CONSTITUTION is a word generally used to indicate the form of the supreme government in a state. Where this is established by a written instrument, as in the United States, the written instrument is called the Constitution. The word is also used of the enactments of the Roman emperors.

CONSTITUTIONAL. In countries having a written constitution, such as Switzerland and the United States, the word *constitutional* means " in conformity with the constitution," and the word *unconstitutional* means " in violation of the constitution " ; the constitution, in all such countries, being the supreme law of the state. But, as applied to the legislation of the British parliament, the words in question are words of vague and indefinite import ; they are often used as signifying merely approval or aversion, as the case may be. Sometimes they are used with greater precision, to indicate conformity with, or variation from, some traditional maxim of legislation, especially in reference to the *constitution* of the supreme legislative body.

CONSTRUCTION. Interpretation.

CONSTRUCTIVE is an adjective, nearly synonymous with " implied " ; meaning that the act or thing to which it refers does not exist, though it is convenient, for certain legal purposes, to assume that it does. See the following titles.

CONSTRUCTIVE MURDER is said to be committed where a person in the course of committing some *felony*, the natural and probable consequence of which is not to cause the death of a human being, does in fact cause such a death. Considerable doubt has in recent years been thrown upon the view that this is murder. See *Stephen, J.* in *Reg.* v. *Serné*, 16 Cox, 311.

CONSTRUCTIVE NOTICE. Notice imputed by construction of law. Whatever is sufficient to put any person of ordinary prudence on inquiry, is constructive notice of everything to which that inquiry might have led. See *Conveyancing Act*, 1882, *s.* 3.

CONSTRUCTIVE TOTAL LOSS. [TOTAL LOSS.]

CONSTRUCTIVE TREASON. An act raised by forced and arbitrary construction to the crime of treason ; as the accroaching, or attempting to exercise, royal power, was in the 21 Edw. 3, held to be treason in a knight of Hertfordshire, who forcibly assaulted and detained one of the king's subjects until he paid him 90l. 4 *Bl.* ; 4 *Steph. Com.*

CONSTRUCTIVE TRUST is a trust which is raised by construction of a court of equity, in order to satisfy the demands of justice, *without reference to the presumable intention of any party.* Thus, for instance, a constructive trust may arise where a person, who is only joint owner, permanently benefits an estate by repairs or improvements ; for, a lien or trust may arise in his favour, in respect of the sum he has expended in such repairs or improvements. And it thus differs from an *implied* trust, which arises from the *implied* or presumed intention of a party. *Sm. Man. Eq.*

CONSUETUDINARIUS. A ritual or book, containing the rites and forms of divine offices, or the customs of abbeys and monasteries. *Cowel.*

CONSUETUDINIBUS ET SERVITIIS (customs and services). An old writ which lay against a tenant who "deforced" (or deprived) his lord of the rent or service due to him. *Cowel.*
Abolished by stat. 3 & 4 Will. 4, c. 27. s. 36.

CONSUETUDO EST ALTERA LEX (custom is another law).

CONSUETUDO LOCI OBSERVANDA EST (the custom of a place is to be observed).

CONSUL. An agent appointed by a state to reside in a city belonging to another state, for the purpose of watching over the commercial interests of the subjects of the state from which he has received his commission. He is not clothed with the diplomatic character. His appointment is communicated to the government of the state wherein he is appointed to reside, and its permission is required to enable him to enter upon his functions. This permission is given by an instrument called an *exequatur*. *Twiss' Law of Nations, Pt. I. s.* 206 ; *Phillimore's Int. Law, Pt. VII.*

CONSULTARY RESPONSE. The opinion of a court of law upon a special case.

CONSULTATION. 1. A writ whereby a cause, being formerly removed by prohibition, from the Ecclesiastical Court, or Court Christian, to the King's Court, is returned thither again ; for the judges of the King's Court, finding the cause to be wrongfully called from the Court Christian, upon this *consultation* or deliberation, decree it to be returned again. *Cowel* ; 3 *Bl.* It is analogous to the writ of *procedendo*. [PROCEDENDO.]
2. A meeting of two or more counsel and the solicitor instructing them for deliberating or advising.

CONSUMMATE TENANT BY CURTESY.
The estate or interest of a husband as
tenant by the curtesy is said to be
consummate on the death of his wife, as
opposed to the *initiate* tenancy which
arises on the birth of a child capable of
inheriting the estate. 1 *Steph. Com.*
[CURTESY.]

CONSUMMATION. The completion of a
thing, especially of a marriage by
cohabitation.

CONTAGIOUS DISEASES ACTS. 1.
Animals : For the prevention of the
spread of certain diseases (see the Acts
of 1878, 1890, and 1894).
2. Persons (see 29 Vict. c. 35, and 32 &
33 Vict. c. 96). These Acts aimed at the
prevention of venereal diseases, including gonorrhœa, and applied to
certain naval and military stations
only. They were repealed by 49 Vict.
c. 10.

CONTANGO. The sum paid per share or
per cent. on a settling day of the Stock
Exchange, for continuing a " Bull "
account to the next settlement. *Fenn's
Compendium.* [BULL.]

CONTEMPT OF COURT. Anything which
plainly tends to create a disregard of the
authority of courts of justice ; as the
open insult or resistance to the judges
who preside there, or disobedience to
their orders. Contempt of court is
punishable by the immediate imprisonment of the offender. 4 *Steph. Com.*

Anything which is a breach of the
privileges of either house of parliament,
according to the law and usage of parliament, is a 'contempt of the High
Court of Parliament, and punishable by
the house by committal. *May's Parl.
Pract. ; Hallam's Const. Hist. ch.* 16.

CONTENEMENT seemeth to be the freehold land which lieth to a man's
tenement or dwelling-house that is in
his own occupation. Some, however,
take it to signify that which is
necessary for the support of a man
according to his condition of life.
Others understand by it the credit or
reputation which a man hath by reason
of his freehold. *Cowel.*

CONTENTIOUS BUSINESS. Legal business where there is a contest, as opposed
to non-contentious business where there
is no such contest : the term is most
frequently used in connection with
obtaining probate or administration.

CONTENTIOUS JURISDICTION. That
part of the jurisdiction of a court which
is over matters in dispute, as opposed
to its *voluntary* jurisdiction, which is
merely concerned in doing what no one
opposes. 3 *Bl.*

CONTINGENCY WITH DOUBLE ASPECT.
An expression sometimes used to denote
the express limitation of one contingent
remainder in substitution for another
contingent remainder. As if land be
given to A. for life, and if he have a
son, then to that son in fee ; and if he
have no son, then to B. in fee. 1 *Steph.
Com.* [CONTINGENT REMAINDER.]

CONTINGENT REMAINDER is an estate
in remainder upon a prior estate,
limited (*i.e.*, marked out in a deed or
other written instrument) to take
effect, either to a dubious and uncertain person, or upon a dubious and
uncertain event. 1 *Steph. Com.*

Thus, if land be given A., a bachelor,
for life, and after his death to his
eldest son ; this remainder to the
eldest son of A. is *contingent*, as it is
not certain whether A. will have any
son. So, if land be given to A. for life,
and after his death to B., in case C.
shall then have returned from Rome ;
B.'s interest during A.'s life, until C.
shall have returned from Rome, is a
contingent remainder.

A contingent remainder is defined
by Fearne as a remainder limited to
depend on an event or condition, which
may never happen or be performed, or
which may not happen or be performed
till after the determination of the preceding estate. *Fearne on Contingent
Remainders.*

A contingent remainder (1) cannot
take effect until the " prior particular
estates " (*i.e.*, the interests for life, or
otherwise, appointed to take effect
before it) have come to an end ; also
(2) it cannot take effect unless the
requisite contingency has happened.
In the former respect it resembles a
vested remainder, and differs from an
executory interest. In the latter, it
differs from a *vested remainder*, and
resembles an *executory interest.* It has
the weakness of both these estates, and
the strength of neither. See, however,
the Contingent Remainders Act, 1877.
[EXECUTORY INTEREST ; REMAINDER ;
VESTED REMAINDER.]

In many cases which may be conceived, the distinction between a
vested and a contingent remainder is
one of extreme technicality.

CONTINUANCE. An adjournment of the proceedings in an action; or, more strictly, the entry on the record expressing the ground of the adjournment, and appointing the parties to reappear at a given day. Hence, a plea *puis darrein continuance* signifies an allegation of new matter of defence which has arisen *since the last adjournment* or *continuance*. Continuances are not now entered on the record or otherwise. 3 *Steph. Com.*

CONTINUANCE, NOTICE OF. Where a plaintiff could not be ready for trial on a day for which notice had been given, he might give notice of *continuance* and *continue* his notice to any future sitting. It is now obsolete; notice of trial not being given now for any particular sittings.

CONTINUANDO. In actions for trespasses of a permanent nature, where the injury is continually renewed, the plaintiff's declaration may allege the injury to have been committed *by continuation* from one given day to another, which is called laying the action with a *continuando*, and the plaintiff shall not be compelled to bring separate actions for every day's separate offence.

CONTINUATION CLAUSE in a marine insurance means a clause whereby the period covered by a policy is extended beyond 12 months, in cases where the vessel insured is at sea at the expiration of such 12 months. See *s.* 11 of *Finance Act,* 1901.

CONTRA BONOS MORES (against good morals).

CONTRA FORMAM COLLATIONIS (against the form of the gift) was an old writ which lay where a man gave lands to a religious house, for the perpetual performance of some divine service, and the abbot or his successor wrongfully alienated the lands; then the donor or his heirs had this writ to recover the lands.

CONTRA FORMAM FEOFFAMENTI (against the form of the feoffment). An old writ that lay for the heir of a tenant who, having entered into possession of certain lands or tenements, under a charter of "feoffment" from his lord, on the condition of performing certain services, was afterwards "distrained" (*i.e.*, had his goods seized) for the non-performance of services *not* required by the charter of feoffment. [FEOFFMENT.]

CONTRA FORMAM STATUTI. [AGAINST THE FORM OF THE STATUTE.]

CONTRA PACEM. "Against the peace of our lord the king, his crown and dignity"; a form formerly necessary in indictments for offences against the common law; the form is still usual but the omission of these words does not now render an indictment bad. 14 & 15 *Vict. c.* 100, *s.* 24 ; 4 *Steph. Com.*

CONTRABAND, in its primary sense, denotes something prohibited by *ban* or *edict,* and indicates a prohibited trade.

But the most usual application of the term is to such articles as are contraband of war ; that is, munitions and such other articles of merchandise carried in a neutral vessel in time of war as may be made directly available for hostile purposes by one belligerent against the other.

The latter belligerent is entitled to seize such articles *in transitu,* and in certain cases even to confiscate the ship in which they are carried. All belligerents have the right of visitation and search to prevent the conveyance of contraband goods to an enemy.

The definition of contraband articles has varied at different times, and on several occasions has been settled by treaties between states. *Twiss' Law of Nations,* Pt. II. ch. 7 ; *Phillimore's Int. Law,* Pt. X. ch. 1.

CONTRACT. A *contract* has been variously defined. Thus it is said to be "an agreement between competent persons, upon a legal consideration, to do or abstain from doing some act"; or more shortly as "an agreement enforceable at law." The agreement may be by *parol,* that is, by word of mouth, or writing not under seal; or it may be by specialty (*i.e.,* by writing under seal), in which case it is more properly termed a *covenant.* And where a contract is not by speciality, it is called a *parol* or *simple contract,* to distinguish it from a contract by specialty. A simple contract may be either *written* or *verbal.* A simple contract must be made upon a *consideration,* in order that an action may be founded upon it. [CONSIDERATION.] And, in certain cases, defined by the

CONTRACT—*continued.*

Statute of Frauds (29 Car. 2, c. 3) and the Sale of Goods Act, 1893, the contract, or some note or memorandum thereof, must be made in writing and signed by the party to be charged therewith. 2 *Steph. Com.;* see also *Addison, Anson, Chitty, Leake, and Pollock, on Contracts.*

CONTRACT, ACTION OF. An action of contract, or *ex contractu,* is an action in which the wrong complained of is a *breach of contract,* and is opposed to an action of *tort,* which is brought for a wrong *independent of contract.* 3 *Steph. Com.*

CONTRACT-NOTE. The note sent by a broker or agent to his principal advising him of the sale or purchase of any stock or marketable security. See *Stamp Act,* 1891, *s.* 52.

CONTRIBUTION, SUIT FOR. A suit in equity, brought by one of several parties who has discharged a liability common to all, to compel the others to contribute thereto proportionably. See next title.

CONTRIBUTIONE FACIENDA. An old writ that lay where more were bound to one thing, and yet one was put to the whole burden. The writ was to compel the others to contribute thereto. *Cowel.* Now superseded by the suit for contribution mentioned in the previous title.

CONTRIBUTORY. A person liable to contribute to the assets of a company which is being wound up, as being a member or (in some cases) a past member thereof. Two lists of contributories are made out. The " A " list contains the names of those who were shareholders at the time of the winding-up order, who are primarily liable. The " B " list contains the names of those who have ceased to be shareholders within the 12 months preceding. These latter are liable in a secondary degree. 3 *Steph. Com.*

CONTRIBUTORY NEGLIGENCE. Culpable negligence, by which a man contributes to the happening of an accident to himself, for which others are partially, or even mainly, responsible. The injured person will not be entitled to recover damages for the injury if it can be shown that, but for his negligence, the accident would not have happened.

CONTROLLER. [COMPTROLLER.]

CONTUMACE CAPIENDO (of taking the contumacious person). A writ for the purpose of enforcing obedience to the decree of an ecclesiastical court, under the provisions of 53 Geo. 3, c. 127. By that Act it is provided that, where a lawful citation or sentence of the ecclesiastical court has not been obeyed, or where a contempt in face of the court has been committed, the judge shall have power to pronounce the offender " contumacious and in contempt " ; and, after a certain period, to signify the same to the sovereign in Chancery ; whereupon a writ *de contumace capiendo* shall issue, for the arrest of the party. 3 *Steph. Com.*

CONUSANCE. [COGNIZANCE.]

CONUSANT. Knowing or understanding.

CONUSOR. [COGNIZOR OF A FINE.]

CONVENTICLE ACTS. The statutes 16 Car. 2, c. 4, and 22 Car. 2, c. 1, by which all meetings, consisting of five persons or more (exclusive of the family), assembled for the exercise of religion in any manner other than according to the liturgy and practice of the Church of England, were prohibited, and those taking part in them subjected to penalties ; also justices of the peace and officers of militia were empowered to disperse by force all such unlawful meetings, and to break open houses for the purpose. These provisions were, however, mitigated by the Toleration Act, and other subsequent enactments, and repealed by 52 Geo. 3, c. 155. *Hallam's Const. Hist.;* 2 *Steph. Com.*

CONVENT O. A covenant.

CONVENTION. 1. The name of an old writ that lay for the breach of a covenant.

2. A name given to such meetings of the Houses of Lords and Commons as take place by their own authority, without being summoned by the king. This can only take place at great national crises. Thus, in the year 1660, the Convention Parliament met, which restored King Charles the Second ; and in 1688, the Lords and Commons met to dispose of the crown and kingdom in favour of the Prince of Orange. 2 *Steph. Com.*

3. A treaty with a foreign power.

CONVENTIONAL ESTATES are *estates* (*i.e.*, interests in land) expressly created by the acts of parties, as opposed to estates created by construction or operation of law. 1 *Steph. Com.*

CONVERSION. 1. The converting by a man to his own use of the goods of another. This will be a ground for an action by the latter (formerly known as an action for *trover* and *conversion*), or for a prosecution for *larceny* or *embezzlement*, according to circumstances. 3 *Steph. Com.*; 4 *Steph. Com.*; *Oke's Mag. Syn.*

2. That change in the nature of property by which, for certain purposes, real estate is considered as personal, and personal estate as real, and transmissible and descendible as such. Thus money directed to be employed in the purchase of land, and land directed to be sold and turned into money, are to be considered as that species of property into which they are directed to be *converted*.

CONVEYANCE. The transfer of the ownership of property, especially landed property, from one person to another; or the written instrument whereby such transfer is effected.

CONVEYANCER. He who draws conveyances; especially a barrister who confines himself to drawing conveyances, and other chamber practice.

CONVEYANCING. The practice of drawing conveyances and legal documents, which is a branch of the study and practice of the law.

CONVEYANCING ACTS, 1881, 1882, and 1892, passed with the object of simplifying the documents used on the transfer of land (see 44 & 45 Vict. c. 41, 45 & 46 Vict. c. 39, and 55 & 56 Vict. c. 13).

CONVEYANCING COUNSEL are certain counsel (in actual practice as conveyancers, of not less than ten years' standing) not less than six in number, appointed by the Lord Chancellor, for the purpose of assisting the court in the investigation of the title to any estate, and upon whose opinion the court or any judge thereof may act under the 40th section of 15 & 16 Vict. c. 80. No special provision is made for these counsel by the Judicature Acts except in so far as they can retain their offices as officers of the Supreme Court (Jud. Act, 1873, ss. 77 *et seq.*).

CONVICT is he that is found guilty of an offence by the verdict of a jury, or else appeareth and confesseth. *Cowel.*

The term, however, is, by s. 6 of the Felony Act, 1870 (33 & 34 Vict. c. 23), restricted in that Act to mean any person against whom, after the passing of that Act, judgment of death, or of penal servitude, shall have been pronounced or recorded by any court of competent jurisdiction in England, Wales, or Ireland, upon any charge of treason or felony. The same Act enables the Crown to appoint administrators of the property of convicts. *Oke's Mag. Syn.*

CONVICTION is where a man, being indicted for a crime, confesses it, or, having pleaded not guilty, is found guilty by the verdict of a jury. A summary conviction is where a man is found guilty of an offence on summary proceeding before a police magistrate or bench of justices. See *Summary Jurisdiction Acts* of 1848 and 1879, and the *Summary Jurisdiction Rules* of 1886; 4 *Steph. Com.*; *Oke's Mag. Syn.*

CONVOCATION. The general assembly of the clergy, to consult of ecclesiastical matters in time of parliament.

There are two convocations, the one for the province of Canterbury, the other for that of York; and there are two distinct houses of either convocation, of which the archbishop and bishops form the upper house, and the lower consists of deans, archdeacons, the proctors for (*i.e.*, representatives of) the chapters, and the proctors for the parochial clergy. 2 *Steph. Com.*

CONVOY. A ship of war, or ships of war, appointed to protect merchantmen against hostile inspection and seizure. *Abbott on Shipping*, Pt. 3, c. iii.

COPARCENARY is where lands descend from an ancestor to two or more persons possessing an equal title to it. It arises by common law or particular custom. By common law, as where a landowner dies intestate, leaving two daughters, who inherit equally: by particular custom, as where lands descend by the custom of gavelkind to all the males in equal degree.

An estate in *coparcenary* is distinguished from an estate held in *common*, in that the former always arises from descent *ab intestato*: the latter arises from a deed or will, or the destruction of an estate in joint tenancy or coparcenary. 1 *Steph. Com.*

COPARCENERS. Those who hold an estate in coparcenary. [COPARCENARY.]

COPARTNERSHIP. The same as partnership.

COPE. 1. A mineral duty payable to his Majesty out of the mines within the jurisdiction of the Barmote Courts. [BARMOTE COURTS.]
2. A hill.
3. The roof or covering of a house.
. A church vestment.

COPYHOLD signifies tenure by copy of court roll at the will of the lord of a manor according to the custom thereof. It is in *manors* only that copyholds are to be found; and it is by the immemorial *custom* of the particular manor that the copyholder's interest must be regulated. Copyholders were originally villeins or slaves, permitted by the lord, as an act of pure grace or favour, to enjoy the lands at *his* pleasure; being in general bound to the performance of certain services. By the time of Edw. 3, the will of the lord came to be controlled by the custom of the manor. Most of the statutes dealing with this tenure, its conversion into freehold commutation, etc., are now embodied in the Copyhold Act, 1894 (57 & 58 Vict. c. 46). 1 *Steph. Com.*; *Wms. R. P.*

COPYRIGHT. The right of an author to print and publish his own original work, exclusively of all other persons. The law of copyright is now regulated by the stat. 5 & 6 Vict. c. 45, passed in the year 1842, which provides that the copyright of every book published in the life of the author shall endure for his natural life, and for seven years longer; or if the seven years shall expire before the end of forty-two years from the first publication, the copyright shall then endure for such period of forty-two years; and that when the work is posthumous, the copyright shall endure for forty-two years from the first publication, and belong to the proprietor of the author's manuscript. Copyrights in sculptures and designs have also been protected by various Acts of parliament, of which the most recent are the Copyright of Designs Act, 1858 (21 & 22 Vict. c. 70), and the Patents, Designs and Trade Marks Act, 1883, Part III. (46 & 47 Vict. c. 57), for the protection of designs for articles of ornament and utility, and the Act of 1862 (25 & 26 Vict. c. 68), for the protection of paintings, drawings, and photographs. As to international copyright see the International Copyright Act, 1886 (49 & 50 Vict. c. 33); as to colonial copyright see 10 & 11 Vict. c. 95, and (Canada) 38 & 39 Vict. c. 53. 2 *Steph. Com.*; *Coppinger; Shortt; Scrutton.*

CORAM NOBIS (before us). A phrase put into the mouth of the sovereign in speaking of proceedings in the King's Bench.

CORAM NON JUDICE (before one who is not a judge). When a cause is brought and determined in a court whereof the judges have not any jurisdiction, then it is said to be *coram non judice*, and the judgment is void.

CORAM PARIBUS (before his peers).

CO-RESPONDENT is properly any person made respondent to, or called upon to answer, a petition, or other proceeding, jointly with another. But, since the passing of the Divorce Act, 1857, the word has become very much confined and is applied almost exclusively to a person charged by a husband, suing for a divorce, with adultery with the wife, and made, jointly with her, a respondent to the suit.

CORNAGE. A tenure binding the tenant to wind a horn when the Scots or other enemies entered the land, in order to warn the king's subjects. It was a species of grand serjeanty. 1 *Steph. Com.*

CORODY signifies, in the common law, a sum of money, or allowance of meat, drink and clothing, due to the king from an abbey or other house of religion, whereof he is the founder, towards the reasonable sustenance of such one of his servants as he thinketh good to bestow it on.

The word was also used for the right (now disused) in the king to send one of his chaplains to be maintained out of a bishopric, or to have a pension allowed him till the bishop promoted him to a benefice. 1 *Bl.*; 2 *Steph. Com.*

CORONATION OATH. The oath administered to every king or queen who succeeds to the imperial crown of these realms, whereby the king or queen swears to govern the kingdom of England, and the dominions thereto belonging, according to the statutes in parliament agreed on, and the laws and customs of the same, and to maintain the Protestant reformed religion established by law. The form of the oath is prescribed by 1 W M. c. 6. 2 *Steph. Com.*

CORONATORE ELIGENDO. A writ, whereby the sheriff was commanded to call the freeholders of a county together for the election of a coroner. This mode of election was continued by the Coroners Act, 1887 (50 & 51, Vict. c. 71), but by the Local Government Act, 1888, the writ is now to be directed to the county council, and they are made the electors. In boroughs the coroner is appointed by the borough council under ss. 171-174 of the Municipal Corporations Act, 1882. *2 Steph. Com.*

CORONATORE EXONERANDO (for relieving a coroner). A writ for the removal of a coroner, or relieving him of his duties, for a cause to be therein assigned. See the *Coroners Act*, 1887, *s.* 8 ; *2 Steph. Com.* [CORONER.]

CORONER. An ancient officer of the land, so called because he dealeth wholly for the king and crown.

The Lord Chief Justice of the King's Bench is the sovereign coroner of the whole realm, that is, wherever he remaineth. *Cowel.*

The coroner was formerly chosen by the freeholders, at a county court held for that purpose. For this purpose there was a writ *de coronatore eligendo.* [CORONATORE ELIGENDO.] The principal duty of a coroner is to inquire concerning the manner of the death of any person who is slain, or dies suddenly, or in prison. Another branch of his office was to inquire concerning shipwrecks, and certify whether wreck or not, and who was in possession of the goods, but he is now relieved of these duties and also some others by section 44 ;of the Coroners Act, 1887. Concerning treasure trove, he is also to inquire who were the finders, and where it is. The coroner is also a conservator of the king's peace, and becomes a magistrate by virtue of his appointment. *2 Steph. Com.*

He may be removed by the Lord Chancellor for extortion, neglect, inability, or misbehaviour in his office, or by the court convicting him of such misbehaviour under the Coroners Act, 1887, s. 8, or by the writ *de coronatore exonerando.* [CORONATORE EXONERANDO.] *2 Steph. Com.*

CORPORATION. A number of persons united and consolidated together so as to be considered as one person in law, possessing the character of perpetuity, its existence being constantly maintained by the succession of new individuals in the place of those who die, or are removed. Corporations are either *aggregate* or *sole.* Corporations aggregate consist of many persons, several of whom are contemporaneously members thereof, as the mayor and commonalty of a city, or the dean and chapter of a cathedral. Corporations sole are such as consist, at any given time, of one person only, as the king or queen, a bishop, a vicar, etc. A corporation must sue, or be sued, by its corporate name. 1 *Steph. Com.* ; 3 *Steph. Com.* [MUNICIPAL CORPORATION.]

CORPOREAL PROPERTY. Such as affects the senses, and may be seen and handled by the body, as opposed to *incorporeal property*, which cannot be seen or handled, and exists only in contemplation. Thus a house is corporeal, but the annual rent payable for its occupation is incorporeal. Corporeal property is, if movable, capable of manual transfer : if immovable, possession of it may be delivered up. But incorporeal property cannot be so transferred, but some other means must be adopted for its transfer, of which the most usual is an instrument in writing. 1 *Steph. Com.; Wms. R. P. Introd.*

CORPUS. The capital of a fund, as opposed to the income.

CORPUS CUM CAUSA. A writ formerly issuing out of the Chancery to remove "both the body and the record" (*i.e.,* to remove a person imprisoned for debt, together with the record of the cause) into the King's Bench.

CORPUS JURIS CANONICI. The body of the Roman canon law. 1 *Steph. Com.* [CANON LAW.]

CORPUS JURIS CIVILIS. The body of the Roman civil law, published in the time of Justinian, containing :—1. The Institutes or Elements of Roman Law, in five books. 2. The Digest or Pandects, in fifty books, containing the opinions and writings of eminent lawyers. 3. A new Code, or collection of Imperial Constitutions, in twelve books. 4. The Novels, or New Constitutions, posterior in time to the other books, and amounting to a supplement to the Code. 1 *Steph. Com.*

CORRECTION, HOUSE OF. [HOUSE OF CORRECTION.]

CORROBORATION. Evidence in support of principal evidence. Required in actions for breach of promise, bastardy proceedings, and some other cases.

CORRUPT PRACTICES. Treating, undue influence, bribery, and personation are corrupt practices at elections. See *Corrupt and Illegal Practices Prevention Act*, 1883 (46 & 47 *Vict. c.* 51); *Municipal Elections Corrupt and Illegal Practices Act*, 1884 (47 & 48 *Vict. c.* 70) ; and the *Public Bodies Corrupt Practices Act*, 1889 (52 & 53 *Vict. c.* 69).

CORRUPTION OF BLOOD was one of the consequences of an attainder for treason or felony, whereby an attainted person could neither inherit lands or other hereditaments from his ancestors, nor retain those he was already in possession of, nor transmit them by descent to any heir ; but the same escheated to the lord of the fee, subject to the king's superior right of forfeiture ; and the person attainted also obstructed all descents to his posterity, whereon they were obliged to derive a title through him to a remoter ancestor. [ESCHEAT.]

Corruption of blood is now abolished by stats. 3 & 4 Will. 4, c. 106, s. 10, and 33 & 34 Vict. c. 23, s. 1. 1 *Steph. Com.; 4 Steph. Com.; Wms. R. P.*

CORSEPRESENT. An offering made to the church when a corpse came to be buried. Generally the body of the best beast was, according to the law or custom, offered or presented to the priest. *Cowel*; 2 *Bl.*; 2 *Steph. Com.* [MORTUARY.]

CORSNED. A kind of superstitious trial used among the Saxons, to purge themselves of any accusation, by taking a piece of cheese or bread, of about an ounce in weight, called *corsned* or *corsned bread*, and eating it with solemn oaths and execrations, that it might prove poison, or their last morsel, if what they said was not strictly true. 4 *Steph. Com.*

CORTES. The name of the legislative assemblies of Spain and Portugal.

COSENAGE. [COSINAGE.]

COSENING. Cheating, defrauding.

COSHERING. An ancient privilege claimed by lords to lie and feast themselves and their followers at their tenants' houses.

COSINAGE (*Cognatione, Consanguineo*). One of the old writs available for an heir against an "abator," that is, a person who, on the death of the deceased, entered upon the land to the prejudice of the heir. This particular writ lay where the deceased stood to the heir in the relation of great-great-grandfather or cousin, or more distant relation, either lineally or collaterally. If the deceased stood in the relation of great-great-grandfather to the heir, the writ was also called a writ of *tresaiel* or *tresayle*. This and similar writs, having been long obsolete, were abolished in 1833, by stat. 3 & 4 Will. 4, c. 27, s. 36.

COST-BOOK MINING COMPANIES. Partnerships for working mines. An agent, usually called a purser, is appointed by the partners. It is his duty to manage the affairs of the mine and to enter in a book, called the cost-book, the minutes of their proceedings, the names of all the partners or shareholders, and the number of shares held by each.

COSTS. The expenses incident to a suit or action, paid in general by the defeated party. Costs in actions at common law were first given to plaintiffs by the Statute of Gloucester, passed in the sixth year of Edward I. And by subsequent statutes of Henry VIII. and James I. the defendant was declared entitled to costs in all cases in which the plaintiff would have been entitled thereto had he succeeded.

Costs in equity were in the discretion of the judge, but were in general given to the successful party.

Costs as between *party and party* are opposed to costs as between *solicitor and client*, in that the former are costs which in an action or suit are incurred of necessity : whereas costs as between solicitor and client, include many items of costs actually paid to the solicitor, though not strictly necessary for the suit. But see now R. S. C.

Costs in the cause are costs of an interlocutory application which are to abide the eventual result of the action, as opposed to *costs in any event* which are to be paid by the party failing on the interlocutory application, even though he be eventually successful on the trial of the action.

By R. S. C. 1883, Ord. LXV., the costs of and incident to all proceedings in the High Court are to be in the discretion of the court. See also Jud. Act, 1890 (53 & 54 Vict. c. 44), s. 5.

As to the taxation of solicitor's costs see 6 & 7 Vict. c. 73 ; 22 & 23 Vict. c. 127 ; and 33 & 34 Vict. c. 28. [TAXATION OF COSTS.]

COUCHANT. Lying down. [LEVANT AND COUCHANT.]

COUNSEL. A word frequently used to denote a barrister-at-law, especially in reference to the solicitors or clients who consult him. [BARRISTER.]

COUNT. 1. Count, as a title of honour, is from the Latin *comes*, a title used in the Roman empire to denote the *attendants* of the sovereign. After the Norman Conquest they were for some time called counts or *countees*, from the French; but they did not long retain that name themselves, though their shires are called counties to this day. They were also called earls, which name they have retained. 2 *Steph. Com.*
2. A section of a declaration or indictment.
3. A count of the House of Commons by the Speaker. *May's Parl. Pract.*

COUNT OUT. [COUNT, 3.]

COUNTÉE. [COUNT, 1.]

COUNTERCLAIM. By R. S. C. 1883, Ord. XIX. r. 3, a defendant in an action may set off or set up by way of counter-claim any right or claim whether such set-off or counterclaim sound in damages or not, and such set-off or counter-claim has the same effect as a statement of claim in a cross action so as to enable the court to pronounce a final judgment in the same action both on the original and on the cross claim. But if in the opinion of the court such set-off or counterclaim cannot be conveniently disposed of in the same action or ought not to be allowed, the court may refuse permission to the defendant to avail himself of it. See also SET-OFF and Jud. Act, 1873, s. 90.

COUNTER-DEED. A secret writing, either before a notary or under a private seal which destroys, invalidates, or alters a public one.

COUNTERFEIT. An imitation made without authority and with the object of defrauding. [COIN.]

COUNTERMAND. To revoke an act. As to countermanding notice of trial, see R. S. C. 1883, Ord. XXXVI. r. 19.

COUNTERPART. When the several parts of an indenture are interchangeably executed by the parties thereto, that part or copy which is executed by the grantor is called the *original*, and the rest are *counterparts*.

COUNTER-SECURITY. A security given to one who has entered into a bond or become surety for another.

COUNTER-SIGN. The signature of a secretary or other subordinate officer to vouch for the authenticity of a document signed by a superior.

COUNTING-HOUSE OF THE KING'S HOUSEHOLD is that which is commonly called the Board of Green Cloth, because the table stands covered with a green cloth. [BOARD OF GREEN CLOTH.]

COUNTRY. A word often used to signify a jury of the country. 3 *Steph. Com.*; 4 *Steph. Com.*

COUNTY. A division of the kingdom. made up of an indefinite number of hundreds. The word is plainly derived from *Comes*, the *Count* of the Franks; that is, the earl or alderman (as the Saxons called him) of a shire, to whom the government of it was entrusted. 1 *Steph. Com.*

COUNTY BOROUGHS. The 61 boroughs named in schedule 3 of the Local Government Act, 1888, which, either being counties themselves (see COUNTY CORPORATE) or containing a population of not less than 50,000 inhabitants, are constituted by s. 31 of the Act administrative counties of themselves.

COUNTY CORPORATE. A city or town with more or less territory annexed to it, to which, out of special grace and favour, the kings of England have granted the privilege to be counties of themselves, and not to be comprised in any other county; but to be governed by their own sheriffs and other magistrates, so that no officers of the county at large have any power to intermeddle therein. Such are London, York, Norwich, etc. Now, by stat. 38 Geo. 3, c. 52, and subsequent statutes, all causes of action arising, and offences committed, in a county corporate, may be tried in the next adjoining county at large. 1 *Steph. Com.*

COUNTY COUNCILS. The elective bodies established by the Local Government Act, 1888 (51 & 52 Vict. c. 41), to manage the administrative business of each county formerly managed by the justices of the peace in quarter sessions and other administrative business mentioned in the Act. 3 *Steph. Com.* They

COUNTY COUNCILS—_continued._

consist of the chairman, aldermen, and councillors. The chairman and aldermen are elected by the council: the aldermen are elected for six years and one half of their number goes out in every third year. The councillors are elected for separate electoral divisions under the County Electors Act, 1888. 3 _Steph. Com._

COUNTY COURT. 1. A court originally held every month or oftener by the sheriff, intended to try little causes not exceeding the value of forty shillings, in what part of the county he pleased to appoint for that purpose; also for the election of knights of the shire. The freeholders in the county were the real judges in this court; the sheriff being the officer appointed to carry its decisions into effect. It might be held also for the proclamation of outlawries, the election of coroners, and the like. 3 _Steph. Com._

But the local administration of justice in these courts is almost entirely obsolete; such jurisdiction in civil cases being now conferred by statute on the modern courts of the same name.

2. These latter so-called county courts were first established under the statute 9 & 10 Vict. c. 95, passed in 1846, by an Order in Council of the 9th of March, 1847. By the same order, as well as by the authority of the Lord Chancellor under a subsequent Act (21 & 22 Vict. c. 74), a certain number of county court _districts_ are appointed in each county. These districts are grouped in unequal numbers into a variety of circuits, over each of which is assigned a judge, chosen by the Lord Chancellor from amongst the serjeants, King's counsel, and barristers-at-law of seven years' standing and upwards; and for each district there is a registrar and other officers. The county courts are held, as a general rule, once in every calendar month, or at such other interval as is directed by the Lord Chancellor. The county courts have jurisdiction for the recovery of small debts and demands, and have also jurisdiction in equity and bankruptcy, defined by Acts of parliament passed for that purpose. To some county courts also, in the neighbourhood of the sea, a limited jurisdiction is given to Admiralty cases. 1 _Steph. Com._; 3 _Steph. Com._ The Act of 1846 was repealed and re-enacted with fourteen amending Acts by the County Courts Act, 1888 (51 & 52 Vict. c. 43).

COUNTY PALATINE. The counties Chester, Durham, and Lancaster, are called counties palatine. They are so called _a palatio_, because the owners thereof (the Earl of Chester, the Bishop of Durham, and the Duke of Lancaster) had formerly in those counties _jura regalia_ (royal rights) as fully as the king had in his palace. They might pardon treasons, murders, and felonies; all writs and indictments ran in their names, as in other counties in the king's; and all offences were said to be done against _their peace_, and not, as in other places, _contra pacem domini regis_ (against the peace of our lord the king). The Isle of Ely (says Blackstone) is not a county palatine, but only a royal franchise; the bishop having by grant of King Henry I. _jura regalia_ within the Isle of Ely, whereby he exercised a jurisdiction over all causes, as well criminal as civil.

These counties palatine have been now for the most part assimilated to the rest of England. And by the Supreme Court of Judicature Act, 1873 (36 & 37 Vict. c. 66), s. 16, the jurisdiction of the Court of Common Pleas at Lancaster and the Court of Pleas at Durham, was transferred to the High Court of Justice established by the Act. The jurisdiction of the Chancery Courts of Lancaster and Durham, however, was not affected by the Act. See 1 _Steph. Com._; 3 _Steph. Com._

COUNTY RATE. One levied on the occupiers of lands in a county for various local purposes. See 15 & 16 _Vict._ c. 81.

COUNTY SESSIONS. The Court of General Quarter Sessions of the Peace, held in every county once in every quarter of a year. By statute 11 Geo. 4 & 1 Will. 4, c. 70, s. 35, the quarter sessions are appointed to be held in the first week after the 11th day of October; the first week after the 28th day of December; the first week after the 31st day of March; and the first week after the 24th day of June; now, however, by 57 & 58 Vict. c. 6, the justices may fix or alter the time to any date within fourteen days before or after the week in which they would ordinarily be held. This court is held before two or more justices of the peace. For the county of Middlesex, however, it is enacted that there shall be holden two sessions or adjourned sessions of the peace in every calendar month. 4 _Steph. Com._ See _Shirley's Magisterial Law._

COURT (Lat. *Curia*) has various significations—

1. The house where the king remaineth with his retinue. *Cowel*.

2. The place where justice is judicially administered. 3 *Steph. Com.*

3. The judges who sit to administer justice : and, in jury trials, the judge or presiding magistrate, as opposed to the jury.

4. A meeting of a corporation, or the principal members thereof ; as when we speak of the Court of Aldermen, Court of Directors, etc.

See also the titles following.

COURT, BAIL. [BAIL COURT.]

COURT BARON. A court incident to every manor in the kingdom, to be holden by the steward within the said manor. [MANOR.] This Court Baron is of two natures. (1) The one is a customary court appertaining entirely to the *copyholders*, in which their estates are transferred by surrender and admittance, and other matters transacted relative to their tenures only. (2) The other is a court of common law, not of record, held before the *freehold* tenants who owe suit and service to the lord of the manor ; and of this court the steward of the manor is rather the registrar than the judge. The freeholders' court was anciently held every three weeks ; and its most important business was to determine, in the real action called the *writ of right*, all controversies relating to lands within the manor. It might also hold plea (*i.e.*, assume jurisdiction) of personal actions, where the debt or damages did not amount to 40*s*. This court, however, has long ago fallen into disuse, and its jurisdiction is practically abolished by s. 28 of the County Courts Act, 1867 (30 & 31 Vict. c. 142), by which no action or suit, which can be brought in any county court, shall henceforth be maintainable in any hundred or inferior court not being a court of record. 3 *Steph. Com.*

COURT, CONSISTORY. [CONSISTORY COURTS.]

COURT, COUNTY. [COUNTY COURT.]

COURT FOR CONSIDERATION OF CROWN CASES RESERVED. A court established by 11 & 12 Vict. c. 78, passed in 1848, for the purpose of deciding any question of law reserved for their consideration by any judge or presiding magistrate in any court of oyer and terminer, gaol delivery, or quarter sessions, before which a prisoner has been found guilty by verdict. Such question is stated in the form of a special case for the consideration of the judges. The jurisdiction given by this Act may now be exercised by the judges of the High Court or five of them at least. The judgment of such court is final and without appeal. *Jud. Act*, 1873, *s*. 47 ; 4 *Steph. Com.*

COURT FOR DIVORCE AND MATRIMONIAL CAUSES. A court established in 1857 by the Divorce Act of that year (20 & 21 Vict. c. 85), of which the judges were the Lord Chancellor and the judges of the Superior Courts at Westminster, together with the judge of the Probate Court ; which last judge was made *judge in ordinary* of the Divorce Court. To this court was transferred the matrimonial jurisdiction of the ecclesiastical courts, together with the power, hitherto exercised by private Acts of parliament, to grant divorces *a vinculo* in certain cases ; and, by the Legitimacy Declaration Act, 1858 (21 & 22 Vict. c. 93), persons might apply to this court for a declaration of their legitimacy, or of the validity of the marriages of their fathers and mothers, or of their grandfathers and grandmothers ; or for a declaration of their own right to be deemed natural-born subjects. 2 *Steph. Com.*

By the Supreme Court of Judicature Act, 1873, this court was merged in the Supreme Court of Judicature, and its business assigned to the Probate, Divorce and Admiralty Division. See 36 & 37 *Vict. c.* 66, *ss.* 3, 16, 34 ; 3 *Steph. Com.*

COURT, HUNDRED. A larger Court Baron, being held for all the inhabitants of a particular hundred, instead of a manor. 3 *Steph. Com.* 308. [COURT BARON ; HUNDRED.

COURT LANDS, *terræ curtiles*, otherwise called demesnes, *terræ dominicales*. Domains kept in the lord's hands to serve his family : called court-lands as being appropriated to the house or court of the lord, and not let out to tenants.

COURT LEET. A court of record held once in the year and not oftener within a particular hundred, lordship, or manor, before the steward of the leet : being the king's court granted by charter to the lords of those hundreds or manors. Its office was to view the *frankpledges*,

COURT LEET—*continued.*

that is, the freemen within the liberty; to present by jury crimes happening within the jurisdiction; and to punish trivial misdemeanors. It has now, however, for the most part fallen into desuetude (but see Sheriff's Act, 1887, s. 40); though in some manors a "court leet" is still periodically held for the transaction of the administrative business of the manor. 4 *Steph. Com.*

COURT-MARTIAL. A court with a jurisdiction to try and punish military offences under the provisions of the Army Act, 1881. Courts-martial are general, district and regimental. As to naval courts-martial, see 29 & 30 Vict. c. 109, ss. 58—69. 2 *Steph. Com.*

COURT OF ADMIRALTY. [ADMIRALTY.]

COURT OF ARCHDEACON. The most inferior court in the whole ecclesiastical polity, held before a judge appointed by the archdeacon himself, and called his *official.* Its jurisdiction comprises ecclesiastical causes in general arising within the archdeaconry. From the archdeacon's court an appeal generally lies to that of the bishop. 3 *Steph. Com.* [ARCHDEACON.]

COURT OF ARCHES. [ARCHES, COURT OF.]

COURT OF BANKRUPTCY. [BANKRUPTCY COURT.]

COURT OF CHANCERY. [CHANCERY.]

COURT OF CHIVALRY was a court which used to be held before the Lord High Constable and Marshal of England. It was not a court of record, but it had a jurisdiction relating to deeds of arms and war, and to the redressing of injuries of honour, and of encroachments in the matter of coat-armour, precedency, and other distinctions of families. From its sentences an appeal lay to the king in person. Now obsolete. 3 *Steph. Com.*

COURT OF CLERK OF THE MARKET. A court incident to every fair and market in the kingdom, to punish misdemeanors therein. 4 *Steph. Com.*

COURT OF COMMISSIONERS OF SEWERS. These courts are erected by virtue of a commission under the great seal pursuant to the Statute of Sewers (23 Hen. 8, c. 5), whose powers are confined to such county or particular place as their commission shall expressly name. Their jurisdiction is to overlook the repairs of the banks and walls of the sea coast and of navigable rivers, and to cleanse such rivers and the streams communicating therewith. They may also assess such rates or scots upon the owners of lands within their district as they shall judge necessary. 3 *Steph. Com.*

COURT OF COMMON PLEAS, or, as it was sometimes called, the Court of Common Bench, was one of the superior courts of common law. It took cognizance of all actions between subject and subject, without exception. It formerly had an exclusive jurisdiction over real actions, which excelled all others in importance. It was also entrusted with exclusive jurisdiction in appeals from the decisions of revising barristers, and in some other matters. 3 *Steph. Com.* By s. 16 of the Supreme Court of Judicature Act, 1873 (36 & 37 Vict. c. 66), the business of the Court of Common Pleas was transferred to the Common Pleas division of the High Court of Justice established under that Act, but by Order in Council of Dec. 16th, 1880, under s. 31 of the Act, that division was merged in the Queen's Bench Division (now King's Bench Division). 3 *Steph. Com.*

COURT OF CONSCIENCE. [CONSCIENCE, COURTS OF; COURT OF REQUEST.]

COURT OF CORONERS. A court of record held by a coroner. 4 *Steph. Com.* [CORONER.]

COURT OF ENQUIRY. See INQUIRY, COURT OF.

COURT OF EQUITY. [EQUITY.]

COURT OF ERROR. An expression formerly applied especially to the Court of Exchequer Chamber and the House of Lords, as taking cognizance of *error* brought. 3 *Steph. Com.* [ERROR.]

COURT OF EXCHEQUER, one of the superior courts of Westminster, was a very ancient court of record, intended principally to order the revenues of the Crown, and to recover the king's debts and duties. It was called the Exchequer, *scaccarium,* from the chequed cloth, resembling a chess-board, which covered the table there, and on which, when certain of the king's accounts were made up, the sums were marked and scored with counters. The Exchequer consisted of two divisions, the

COURT OF EXCHEQUER—*continued*.

receipt of the Exchequer, which managed the royal revenue, and the *court*, or judicial part of it. This court was, down to the year 1842, subdivided into a court of equity and a court of common law. But by 5 Vict. c. 5 all the equity jurisdiction of the Court of Exchequer was transferred to the Court of Chancery. The Court of Exchequer consisted, moreover, of a *revenue* side, and of a common law or *plea* side. On the *revenue* side it ascertained and enforced the proprietary rights of the Crown against the subjects of the realm. On the *plea* side it administered redress between subject and subject in all actions personal. 3 *Steph. Com.*

By the Supreme Court of Judicature Act, 1873, the business of the Court of Exchequer was transferred to the Exchequer Division of the High Court of Justice, and by Order in Council under s. 31 of that Act the Exchequer Division was in turn merged in the Queen's Bench Division (now King's Bench Division). 3 *Steph. Com.*

COURT OF EXCHEQUER CHAMBER. An intermediate court of appeal between the superior courts of common law and the House of Lords. When sitting as a court of appeal from any one of the three superior courts of common law, it was composed of judges of the other two courts. The powers of this court were, by s. 18 (4) of the Judicature Act, 1873, transferred to the Court of Appeal established by that Act. 3 *Steph. Com.*

COURT OF FACULTIES. [FACULTY.]

COURT OF FOREST. [FOREST COURTS.]

COURT OF GREAT SESSIONS IN WALES. A court formerly held twice every year in each county in Wales by judges appointed by the Crown, from which writs of error lay to the Court of King's Bench of Westminster. This court is abolished by 11 Geo. 4 & 1 Will. 4, c. 70, and the Welsh judicature entirely incorporated with that of England. 3 *Steph. Com.*

COURT OF HIGH COMMISSION. [HIGH COMMISSION COURT.]

COURT OF HUSTINGS. A court held within the City of London, before the Lord Mayor, Recorder, and Sheriffs. This court is the representative, within the City, of the ancient county court of the sheriff. It had exclusive juris-diction in all real and mixed actions for the recovery of land within the city, except ejectment. But now that all real and mixed actions, except ejectment, are abolished, the jurisdiction of this court has fallen into comparative desuetude. 3 *Steph. Com.; Pulling on the Customs of London.*

COURT OF KING'S BENCH. One of the superior courts of common law. It is so called because the sovereign used to sit there in person. This court may follow the sovereign's person wherever he goes; and we find that, after Edward I. had conquered Scotland, it actually sat at Roxburgh. This court keeps all inferior jurisdictions within the bounds of their authority, and may either remove their proceedings to be determined before itself, or prohibit their progress below. It superintends all civil corporations in the kingdom. It commands magistrates and others to do what their duty requires, in every case where there is no other specific remedy. It protects the liberty of the subject by speedy and summary inter-position. It takes cognizance both of criminal and civil causes; the former in what is called the *crown side* or *crown office;* the latter in the *plea side* of the court. 3 *Steph. Com.; 4 Steph. Com.*

By s. 34 of the Judicature Act, 1873, the jurisdiction of this court was assigned to the King's Bench Division of the High Court of Justice, and by Order in Council under s. 32 of the same Act, the Common Pleas and Exchequer Division were merged in the King's Bench Division in February, 1881.

The Lord Chief Justice of England is President of the Division (Judicature Act, 1873, s. 31).

COURT OF LORD HIGH STEWARD OF GREAT BRITAIN. A court instituted for the trial, during the recess of parliament, of peers or peeresses indicted for treason or felony, or for misprision of either. Into this court indictments against peers of parlia-ment are removed by *certiorari.* The office is created *pro hâc vice* only, whenever the occasion requires it. During a session of parliament the trial is not properly in the court of the Lord High Steward but before the High Court of Parliament; a Lord High Steward is, however, always appointed to regulate the proceedings. 4 *Steph. Com.*

COURT OF LORD STEWARD OF THE KING'S HOUSEHOLD. A court created by stat. 33 Hen. 8, c. 12, with jurisdiction to inquire of, hear, and determine all treasons, misprisions of treason, murders, manslaughters, and bloodshed. Now obsolete. *4 Steph. Com.*

COURT OF MARSHALSEA. A court which held plea (*i.e.*, had jurisdiction) of all trespasses committed within the verge (*i.e.*, within twelve miles) of the king's court, where one of the parties was of the royal household ; and of all debts and contracts, when both parties were of that establishment. Abolished by 12 & 13 Vict. c. 101, s. 13. *3 Steph. Com.*

COURT OF OYER AND TERMINER. [ASSIZE, COURTS OF ; OYER AND TERMINER.]

COURT OF PASSAGE. A court of record having jurisdiction over causes of action arising within the borough of Liverpool, similar in extent to the jurisdiction of county courts having admiralty jurisdiction.

COURT OF PECULIARS. A branch of the Court of Arches. The Court of Peculiars has jurisdiction over all those parishes, dispersed through the province of Canterbury, which are exempt from the ordinary's jurisdiction, and subject to the metropolitan only. *3 Steph. Com.*

COURT OF PIEDPOUDRE (*Curia pedis pulverizati*, or *Court of powdered foot*). A court of record incident to every fair and market, of which the steward of him who owned the toll of the market was the judge. Its jurisdiction extended to all commercial injuries done in that fair or market, and not in any preceding one. From this court a writ of error lay in the nature of an appeal to the courts at Westminster. Various explanations have been given of the name. The jurisdiction of this court is now practically obsolete. *3 Steph. Com.*

COURT OF POLICIES OF ASSURANCE. A court established under the stats. 43 Eliz. c. 12, and 13 & 14 Car. 2, c. 23, for the purpose of determining in a summary way all causes concerning policies of assurance in London, with an appeal by way of bill to the Court of Chancery. This court, having been for some time obsolete, was abolished by the repeal of the above statutes by 26 & 27 Vict. c. 125. *3 Steph. Com.*

COURT OF PROBATE. A court established in 1857 under the Probate Act of that year (20 & 21 Vict. c. 77). To this court was transferred, by that Act, the testamentary jurisdiction of the Ecclesiastical Courts. *2 Steph. Com.*

This is one of the courts merged in the Supreme Court of Judicature under s. 16 of stat. 36 & 37 Vict. c. 66, establishing the Supreme Court of Judicature. *3 Steph. Com.*

COURT OF QUARTER SESSIONS. [BOROUGH SESSIONS ; COUNTY SESSIONS.]

COURT OF RECORD. A court whose acts and judicial proceedings are enrolled in parchment for a perpetual memorial and testimony ; whose rolls are the *records* of the court. All courts of record are the king's courts, and no other court hath authority to fine and imprison ; so that the very erection of a new jurisdiction with the power of fine or imprisonment makes it instantly a court of record. Such common law courts as are *not* courts of record are of inferior dignity, and in a less proper sense the king's courts. And in these, the proceedings not being enrolled or recorded, as well their existence, as the truth of the matters therein contained, shall, if disputed, be tried and determined by a jury. A court not of record, says Blackstone, is the court of a private man, whom the law will not entrust with any discretionary power over the fortune or liberty of his fellow-subjects. *3 Steph. Com.*

COURT OF REQUEST, otherwise called a *Court of Conscience.* These courts are for the recovery of small debts, established by Acts of parliament in various parts of the kingdom, but now superseded by the county courts (*q.v.*). [CONSCIENCE, COURTS OF.]

COURT OF SESSION. The superior court, in Scotland, of law and equity, divorce and admiralty, having a universal civil jurisdiction.

COURT OF SHERIFF'S TOURN. [SHERIFF'S TOURN.]

COURT OF STANNARIES OF CORNWALL AND DEVON, established for the administration of justice among the tinners, was a court of record with a special jurisdiction, held before a judge called the vice-warden, with an appeal to the lord warden. All tinners

COURT OF STANNARIES—*continued.*
and labourers in and about the stannaries (*i.e.*, the mines and works in Devon and Cornwall where tin metal is dug and purified) might sue and be sued in this court in all matters arising within the stannaries, excepting pleas of land, life, and member. By the Stannaries Court Abolition Act, 1896, their jurisdiction was transferred to county courts. 3 *Steph. Com.*

COURT OF STAR-CHAMBER. [STAR-CHAMBER.]

COURT, PREROGATIVE. [PREROGATIVE COURT.]

COURT ROLLS. The rolls of a manor, whereon are entered all surrenders, wills, grants, admissions, and other acts relating to the manor. They are considered to belong to the lord of the manor, and are kept by the steward as his agent ; but they are in the nature of public books for the benefit of the tenants as well as the lord, so that it is a matter of course for the courts of law to grant an inspection of the court rolls in a question between two tenants. *Scriven on Copyholds.*

COURT, SUPREME, OF JUDICATURE. [SUPREME COURT OF JUDICATURE.]

COURTS OF THE UNIVERSITIES. [UNIVERSITY COURTS.]

COUSENAGE. [COSINAGE.]

COUSIN. This word, besides its ordinary sense, has a special meaning in writs and commissions and other formal instruments issued by the Crown, in which it signifies any peer of the degree of an earl. The appellation is as ancient as the reign of Henry IV., who, being related or allied to every earl then in the kingdom, acknowledged that connexion in all his letters and public acts ; from which the use has descended to his successors, though the reason has long ago failed. 2 *Steph. Com.*

COUTHUTLAUGH. A person that willingly and knowingly received an outlaw, and cherished and concealed him ; in which case he was in ancient time subject to the same punishment as the outlaw himself.

COVENANT. A clause of agreement contained in a deed whereby a party stipulates for the truth of certain facts, or binds himself to give something to another, or to do or not to do any act. 1 *Steph. Com.* [COVENANT RUNNING WITH THE LAND.]

COVENANT, ACTION OF. An action brought to recover damages for breach of a promise made by deed under seal. This is no longer a technical expression since the new rules of pleading under the Judicature Act, 1875. 3 *Steph. Com.*

COVENANT FOR TITLE. [TITLE, COVENANT FOR.]

COVENANT RUNNING WITH THE LAND is a covenant of which successive owners or lessees of the same land are, as such, entitled to the benefit, or liable to the obligation. Thus, a covenant by the lessee of a house to keep it in repair will in general "run with the land," and bind any person to whom the lessee may assign the lease. *Spencer's Case,* 1 *Smith's Leading Cases ;* 1 *Steph. Com.*

COVENANT TO STAND SEISED TO USES was where a person seised of land proposed to convey his estate to his wife, child, or kinsman. It was a voluntary assurance operating under the Statute of Uses, and had to be by deed and not by parol. In its terms it consisted of a covenant by the owner to stand *seised to the use* of the intended transferee. This conveyance was held to be ineffectual, unless the parties to it stood to one another in the relation of marriage, or of near consanguinity ; and it is now wholly obsolete. 1 *Steph. Com.*

COVERT BARON. An expression sometimes used of a wife, to indicate that she is under the protection or influence of her husband, who is her *baron* or lord.

COVERTURE. The condition of a wife during her marriage, involving certain disabilities on the one hand, and certain protections or privileges on the other. The disabilities of coverture in respect of property have been almost entirely removed by the Married Women's Property Act, 1882 (45 & 46 Vict. c. 75). 2 *Steph. Com.*

COVIN. A deceitful agreement between two or more to the prejudice of another.

COVINOUS. Fraudulent.

CRASSA NEGLIGENTIA. Gross neglect.

CRAVEN. A word of disgrace and obloquy, pronounced by the vanquished champion in trial by battel. [WAGER OF BATTEL.] We retain the word still for a coward. 4 *Steph. Com.* This form of trial is now abolished by 59 Geo. 3, c. 46.

CREDITOR. He that *trusts* another with any debt, be it in money or wares. But the word is generally (though less accurately) used in a larger sense, to signify anyone who has a legal claim against another.

CREDITORS' SUIT. A suit in Chancery instituted by a creditor of a deceased person on behalf of himself and all other creditors of the deceased, for the administration of the estate of the deceased for the benefit of his creditors.

CREMATION. The disposal of a dead body by burning instead of by burial. This is not illegal unless it be done so as to cause a nuisance, or with the intention of preventing a coroner's inquest.

CREPARE OCULUM. To put out an eye; the damages for which, under the laws of Henry I., were assessed at sixty shillings.

CRETIO, in the Roman law, was the time allowed (generally 100 days) to an appointed heir for deciding whether he would take the inheritance or not.

CRIER OF A COURT. An inferior officer of a court, who makes the proclamations required by law, and, in general, administers the oaths to the witnesses. An officer of this name existed in the Court of Chancery until the year 1852, when the office was abolished by 15 & 16 Vict. c. 87, s. 27. In the courts of common law the judge's clerk acts as crier. 15 *& 16 Vict. c.* 73, *s.* 8; *Judicature Act*, 1873, *s.* 77.

CRIME. A crime, as opposed to a civil injury, is the violation of a right, considered in reference to the evil tendency of such violation, as regards the community at large. Crimes consist either of felonies or misdemeanors. 4 *Steph. Com.*

CRIMINAL CONVERSATION, sometimes abbreviated into *crim. con.*, is adulterous conversation, or living with the wife of another man. An action for criminal conversation was formerly allowed by our law to the injured husband. This action is now abolished by s. 59 of the Divorce Act, 1857 (20 & 21 Vict. c. 85). But by s. 33 of the Act a husband may, in suing for a divorce, claim damages from the adulterer. 3 *Steph. Com.*

CRIMINAL INFORMATION. [INFORMATION.]

CRIMINAL LAW comprises: (1) The general criminal law administered throughout the kingdom. (2) The Crown law as administered by the King's Bench Division, which is principally *quasi* criminal, *e.g.*. indictments for nuisance, repair of roads, etc. See *Russell on Crimes.*

CRIMINAL LAW CONSOLIDATION ACTS. The stats. 24 & 25 Vict. cc. 94, 95, 96, 97, 98, 99, 100, passed in 1861, for the Consolidation of the Criminal Law of England and Ireland. See 4 *Steph. Com.*; and see 34 *& 35 Vict. c.* 32.

CRIMP. One who decoys and plunders sailors under cover of harbouring them.

CROFT. A little close adjoining to a house, either for pasture or arable land, as the owner pleases. *Cowel.*

CROSS ACTION. Where A. brings an action against B. in reference to any transaction, and B. brings an action against A. in reference to the same transaction, these are called "cross actions."

CROSS APPEAL. If both parties to a judgment are dissatisfied therewith, and each accordingly appeals, the appeal of each is called a cross appeal in relation to that of the other; it not being open to a respondent to an appeal, as such, to contend that the decision in the court below was not sufficiently favourable to him. But, by R. S. C. Ord. LVIII. rr. 6, 7, a respondent will be allowed so to contend, if he have within due time given notice of his intention so to do to any parties who may be affected by such contention. 3 *Steph. Com.*

CROSS BILL. A bill brought by a defendant in a Chancery suit against a plaintiff or a co-defendant, praying relief in reference to the same subject-matter.

CROSS DEMAND. A counter-claim.

CROSS-EXAMINATION. The examination of a witness by the opposing counsel. Leading questions are allowed, which is not the case in examination in chief. By R. S. C. 1883, Ord. XXXVI. r. 38, the judge may disallow vexatious and irrelevant questions. 3 *Steph. Com.*

Also, an examination of a *hostile* witness on behalf of the party producing him is sometimes called cross-examination.

CROSS REMAINDER is where each of two grantees has reciprocally a remainder in the share of the other. 1 *Steph. Com.*

Thus if an estate be granted, as to one half, to A. for life, with remainder to his children in tail, with remainder to B. in fee simple ; and, as to the other half, to B. for life, with remainder to his children in tail, with remainder to A. in fee simple ; these remainders are called cross remainders. They may be implied in a will, but must always be expressed in a deed, and should be expressly limited in a will. See *Theobald on Wills.* [REMAINDER.]

CROSSED CHEQUE. [CHEQUE.]

CROWN. A word often used for the king or queen as being the sovereign of these realms.

CROWN CASES RESERVED. [COURT FOR CONSIDERATION OF CROWN CASES RESERVED.]

CROWN COURT. The court in which the ordinary criminal trials take place at an assize, as opposed to the Nisi Prius Court, which is for the trial of civil actions.

CROWN DEBTS. Debts due to the Crown. These are, by various statutes, put upon a different footing from debts due to a subject, and they are recoverable by a summary process called an extent. By s. 30 (1) of the Bankruptcy Act, 1883, a bankrupt's discharge is not to relieve him from such debts unless the Commissioners of the Treasury certify in writing their consent to his being discharged therefrom. *Robson, Bkcy.*

CROWN LANDS (Lat. *Terræ dominicales regis,* the demesne lands of the Crown) include the share reserved to the Crown at the original distribution of landed property, and such as came to it afterwards by forfeitures or other means. In modern times the superintendence of the royal demesnes has been vested in the Commissioners of Woods, Forests, and Land Revenues, and it is now usual for the sovereign to surrender these lands at the commencement of his reign for its whole duration in consideration of the Civil List settled upon him. 2 *Steph. Com.*

CROWN LAW. The criminal law.

CROWN OFFICE. The *Crown side* of the Court of King's Bench, on which it took cognizance of criminal causes, from high treason down to the most trivial misdemeanor or breach of the peace. The Judicature Act, 1879, amalgamated the Crown Office with the Central Office of the Supreme Court. 4 *Steph. Com.*

CROWN PAPER. A paper containing the list of cases which await decision on the Crown side of the King's Bench Division.

CROWN SIDE. That jurisdiction of the King's Bench Division by which it takes cognizance of criminal causes, including many questions which are practically of a civil nature. 4 *Steph. Com.* It may be added, that any matter in the King's Bench Division, whether of a civil or criminal nature, and whether arising originally in that court, or removed thereto by *certiorari,* is, if sent down for trial at the assizes, tried in the *Nisi Prius* Court, or (as it is often somewhat inaccurately called) the *civil side,* and not in the Crown Court. 4 *Steph. Com.*

CROWN SOLICITOR. The Solicitor to the Treasury, called the Public Prosecutor (*q.v.*). In Ireland there are still officers called Crown Solicitors attached to each circuit, whose duty it is to get up the case for the Crown in all criminal prosecutions. In Scotland this duty is performed in every county by the Procurator-Fiscal, a subordinate of the Lord-Advocate.

CRUELTY. Such conduct on the part of husband or wife as entitles the other party to a judicial separation. For summary proceedings for aggravated assault or persistent cruelty, see 20 & 21 Vict. c. 85, s. 16, and 58 & 59 Vict. c. 39,

CRUELTY TO ANIMALS. This offence is committed where " any person shall cruelly beat, ill-treat, over-drive, abuse or torture any horse, mare, gelding, bull, ox, cow, heifer, steer, calf, mule, ass, sheep, lamb, hog, pig, sow, goat, dog, cat or any other domestic animal." 12 *&* 13 *Vict.* c. 92 ; 4 *Steph. Com.* See also 17 & 18 Vict. c. 60 ; 24 & 25 Vict. c. 97, ss. 40, 41 ; and 63 & 64 Vict. c. 33.

CRY DE PAIS. A " hue and cry " raised in the absence of the constable. [HUE AND CRY.]

CUCKING-STOOL. An engine of correction in which a common scold was placed, for the purpose of being plunged in water. 4 *Steph. Com.*

CUI ANTE DIVORTIUM. A writ for a woman divorced, whose husband *before the divorce* had disposed of her estate. Abolished in 1833 by 3 & 4 Will. 4, c. 27, s. 36.

CUI IN VITÂ. A writ similar to the preceding, for a widow whose husband *in his lifetime* had disposed of her estate. This writ is also abolished by 3 & 4 Will. 4, c. 27, s. 36.

CUJUS EST DARE, EJUS EST DISPONERE (whose it is to give, his it is to regulate the manner of the gift).

CUJUS EST SOLUM EJUS EST USQUE AD CŒLUM ET AD INFEROS (whose is the soil, his it is, even to heaven, and to the middle of the earth).

CULPA LATA DOLO ÆQUIPARATUR (gross negligence is held equivalent to intentional wrong).

CUM TESTAMENTO ANNEXO (with the will annexed). [ADMINISTRATOR.]

CUMULATIVE LEGACY. A legacy which is to take effect *in addition* to another disposition whether by the same or another instrument, in favour of the same party, as opposed to a *substitutional* legacy, which is to take effect as a *substitute* for some other disposition. See *Williams on Executors, 9th ed., Vol.* 2, *pp.* 1155 *et seq.*

CUMULATIVE SENTENCE. See ACCUMULATION.

CUR. ADV. VULT. An abbreviation often used in legal reports to indicate that the court wishes to deliberate (Lat. *curia adrisari vult*) before pronouncing judgment.

CURATOR. A person entrusted with the charge of an estate, or with the conduct of a minor past the age of pupillarity, or with the management of a lawsuit. For the appointment and duties of an *interim curator,* see the Felony Act, 1870 (33 & 34 Vict. c. 23), s. 21. [INTERIM CURATOR.]

CURE BY VERDICT is where some objection to a declaration or indictment, which might have been maintained before verdict given, is no longer maintainable after the jury have delivered their verdict. [AIDER BY VERDICT.]

CURFEW (Fr. *Couvre-feu,* cover-fire). The ringing of a bell, by which the Conqueror willed every man to take warning for the raking up, or covering up of his fire, and the putting out of his light.

CURIA. A court of justice. It is sometimes, however, taken for the persons who, as feudatory and other customary tenants, did suit and service at the lord's court, and who were also called *pares curtis* or *pares curiæ.* 1 *Steph. Com.*

CURIA ADVISARI VULT. [CUR. ADV. VULT.]

CURIA CLAUDENDA (the court to be closed). A writ that lay against him who, being bound to fence and close up his wall, should refuse or defer to do it. Abolished by 3 & 4 Will. 4, c. 27, s. 36.

CURIA DOMINI. The court of the lord of a manor.

CURIA REGIS. The king's court. A term applied to any of the superior courts, but principally to the *aula regia.* [AULA REGIA.]

CURIALITY. The Scotch name for curtesy. [CURTESY.]

CURSITOR (Lat. *Clericus de cursu,* clerk of the course). An officer or clerk belonging to the Chancery, who made out original writs. Abolished in 1835 by 5 & 6 Will. 4, c. 82.

CURSITOR BARON. An officer of the Exchequer, whose duty it was to examine sheriffs' accounts, to administer oaths to officers of excise, etc. *Manning's Exchequer Practice, p.* 322. Abolished in 1856 by 19 & 20 Vict. c. 86.

CURTESY OF ENGLAND is the life estate which a husband has in the lands of his deceased wife ; which by the common law takes effect where he has had issue by her born alive, and capable of inheriting the lands.

Thus, if a wife have lands in tail male, *i.e.,* descendible to her *male* issue only, the birth of a son will entitle the husband to curtesy, but the birth of a daughter will not. 1 *Steph. Com.*

CURTILAGE. A garden, yard or field, or other piece of ground lying near or belonging to a house or messuage.

CURTILES TERRÆ. [COURT LANDS.]

CUSTODE ADMITTENDO and **CUSTODE AMOVENDO.** Writs formerly used for the admitting and removing of guardians.

CUSTODES LIBERTATIS ANGLIÆ AUTHORITATE PARLIAMENTI (guardians of the liberty of England by the authority of parliament) was the style wherein writs and other judicial proceedings ran from the execution of King Charles I. to the usurpation of Cromwell.

CUSTODIAM, or **CUSTODIAM LEASE.** A lease from the Crown, under the seal of the Exchequer, whereby the custody of lands, seized into the king's lands, was demised or committed to some person as custodee or lessee thereof.

CUSTOM. Unwritten law established by long use. Custom is of two kinds :—
1. General custom, or the common law properly so called. [COMMON LAW.]
2. Particular custom, that is to say, the customs which affect only the inhabitants of particular districts. These it is usual to designate by the word *customs*, to distinguish them from the general customs just referred to.
These particular customs are probably the remains of local customs prevailing formerly over the whole of England, while it was broken into distinct dominions. Such is the custom of *garelkind* in Kent ; and the custom called *borough-English* which prevails in certain ancient boroughs ; also the customs of the city of London. All are contrary to the general law of the land, and are good by special usage. The requisites to make a particular custom good are : It must have been (1) used so long that the memory of man runs not to the contrary, (2) continuous, (3) peaceable, (4) reasonable, (5) certain, (6) compulsory, (7) consistent with other customs. 1 *Steph. Com.*

CUSTOM HOUSE. A house in several cities and seaports, where the king's customs are received, and all business relating thereunto transacted. [CUSTOMS ON MERCHANDISE.]

CUSTOM OF LONDON. The customs peculiar to the city of London. Formerly principally with reference (1) to the law of intestate succession ; (2) to the law of foreign attachment. The custom of London in respect to intestate succession is abolished by 19 & 20 Vict. c. 94. That with regard to foreign attachment has been extended to the whole of England and Wales. [GARNISHEE.] See also as to trial of particular customs in London. 1 *Steph. Com.;* also *Pulling's Customs of London.*

CUSTOM OF MERCHANTS (*Lex mercatoria*). The branch of law which comprises the rules relating to bills of exchange, partnership and other mercantile matters. Blackstone classes it under the head of *particular customs :* but Stephen disputes the propriety of this classification, as the custom is not local, nor is its obligation confined to a particular district. 1 *Steph. Com.*

CUSTOM OF THE COUNTRY means, in agriculture, the usage which, unless expressly excluded, governs the relations of agricultural landlords and tenants. It has reference to "away going crops," allowances for manure, drainage, etc.

CUSTOM OF YORK. A custom of intestacy in the province of York, similar to that of London [CUSTOM OF LONDON]. This custom also was abolished by 19 & 20 Vict. c. 94.

CUSTOMARY COURT BARON. A court in which the estates of copyholders are transferred by surrender and admittance, and other matters transacted relative to their tenures only. 3 *Steph. Com.* [COURT BARON.]

CUSTOMARY FREEHOLD. A kind of tenure of which the incidents are for the most part similar to those of common copyhold ; the principal difference being, that the building in a customary freehold is not said to be *at the will of the lord.* Called also *privileged copyholds.* 1 *Steph. Com.* [ANCIENT DEMESNE.]

CUSTOMARY TENANTS are such tenants as hold by the custom of the manor. Thus copyholders are said to hold " at the will of the lord, according to the custom of the manor " ; the will being no longer arbitrary and precarious, but restrained so as to be exerted according to the custom of the manor. 1 *Steph. Com.* [COPYHOLD.]

CUSTOMARY TENURE. A tenure depending on the custom of a manor. [CUSTOMARY TENANTS.]

CUSTOMS AND SERVICES. Duties which tenants owe to their lords by virtue of their tenure. A writ *de consuetudinibus et servitiis* formerly lay for neglect of these, but this writ is now abolished by 3 & 4 Will. 4, c. 27, s. 36.

CUSTOMS ON MERCHANDISE. The duties, toll, tribute or tariff payable upon merchandise exported and imported. 2 *Steph. Com.*

CUSTOS BREVIUM. The keeper of the writs; a principal clerk in the Court of Common Pleas, whose office was to receive and keep the writs returnable in that court, and to put them upon files. There was also a *custos brevium et rotulorum* (keeper of writs and rolls) in the Court of King's Bench. Both of these offices were abolished by 7 Will. 4 & 1 Vict. c. 30.

CUSTOS MORUM. An expression applied to the Court of King's Bench, as the *guardian of the morals* of the nation. 4 *Steph. Com.*

CUSTOS ROTULORUM is he that hath the custody of the rolls or records of the sessions of the peace. He is always a justice of the peace and of the quorum in the county where he hath his office. 2 *Steph. Com.* [JUSTICE OF THE PEACE; QUORUM.]

He is the first civil officer, as the lord lieutenant is the first military officer, of the county; but the two offices are usually held by the same person. *Archbold's Practice of Quarter Sessions.*

CUSTOS SPIRITUALIUM (guardian of the spiritualities) is he that exerciseth spiritual or ecclesiastical jurisdiction in any diocese during the vacancy of a see.

CUSTOS TEMPORALIUM (guardian of the temporalities). He to whose custody a vacant see or abbey was committed by the king as supreme lord. As steward of the goods and profits thereof, he had to give an account of the same to the escheator, and he into the exchequer.

CUSTUMA ANTIQUA SIVE MAGNA. Ancient duties on wool, sheep-skins, or woolfells, and leather. See the following title.

CUSTUMA PARVA SIVE NOVA. An impost of threepence in the pound, due from merchant-strangers only, for all commodities, as well imported as exported. This was usually called the alien's duty, and was granted in the 31st year of Edward I. 2 *Steph. Com.*

CUT-PURSE (Lat. *Saccularius*). One who privately steals from a man's person, as by picking his pocket or the like, privily without his knowledge. 4 *Steph. Com.*

CUTTER OF THE TALLIES. An officer in the Court of Exchequer, whose duty it was to provide wood for the tallies, and cut the sum paid upon them. [COURT OF EXCHEQUER; TALLEY.]

Provision was made by 23 Geo. 3, c. 82, s. 1, for the abolition of this office and other "useless, expensive, and unnecessary offices," upon the death, surrender, forfeiture, or removal of the then holders.

CY PRES. [CYPRES.]

CYPRES. When the intention of a donor or testator is incapable of being literally acted upon, or where its literal performance would be unreasonable, or in excess of what the law allows, the courts will often allow the intention to be carried into effect *cy près*, that is, *as nearly as may be* practicable, or reasonable, or consistent with law; as (1) when a testator attempts to settle his property on future generations beyond the bounds allowed by law; or (2) where a sum of money is found to be too large for a charitable purpose to which it has been devoted, or for some other reason cannot be applied thereto. 3 *Steph. Com.*; *Wms. R. P.*

D. P. (Lat. *Domus Procerum*). House of Lords.

DAMAGE FEASANT. Doing hurt or damage (Fr. *faisant*); that is, when one man's beasts are in another man's ground, without licence of the tenant of the ground, and there do seed, tread, and otherwise spoil the corn, grass, woods, and such like. In this case the owner of the soil may distrain them (*i.e.*, take possession of them) until satisfaction be made him for the injury he has sustained. 3 *Steph. Com.*

DAMAGES. The pecuniary satisfaction awarded by a judge or jury in a civil action for the wrong suffered by the plaintiff. 3 *Steph. Com.* [EXEMPLARY DAMAGES; NOMINAL DAMAGES.]

DAME. The proper legal title of the wife of a knight or baronet.

DAMNOSA HEREDITAS. A burdensome inheritance; that is to say, an inheritance of which the liabilities exceed the assets. In such case, in the Roman law, the heir, being liable to the full extent of the deceased's liabilities, was a loser by entering upon the inheritance.

DAMNUM ABSQUE INJURIA. A damage without injury, that is, effected without legal wrong. In such case, no action is maintainable. Thus, if I have a mill, and my neighbour builds another mill upon his own ground, whereby the profit of my mill is diminished, yet no action lies against him, for every one may lawfully erect a mill on his own ground. 3 *Steph. Com.*

DAMNUM FATALE. Fatal damage; that is, damage caused by a fortuitous event, or inevitable accident, and for which bailees are not liable.

DANEGELD, or **DANEGELT,** was a tribute levied by the Anglo-Saxons, of twelve pence upon every hide of land, for the purpose of clearing the seas of Danish pirates.

DANE-LAGE. Such customs of the Danes as were retained in this kingdom after the Danes had been expelled. 1 *Steph. Com.*; 4 *Steph. Com.*

DARBAR. [DURBAR.]

DARREIN. A corruption from the French *dernier*, last.

DARREIN CONTINUANCE. The plea *puis darrein continuance* alleges that "since the last continuance" new ground of defence has arisen. [CONTINUANCE.]

DARREIN PRESENTMENT. Last presentation. [ASSIZE OF DARREIN PRESENTMENT.]

DATIVE. A word derived from the Roman law, signifying "appointed by public authority." Thus, in Scotland, an executor-dative is an executor appointed by a court of justice, corresponding to an English *administrator*. [ADMINISTRATOR.]

DAUPHIN was formerly the title of the eldest sons of the kings of France.

DAY RULE. A certificate of permission given by the court to a prisoner to go beyond the "rules" of the King's Bench prison for the purpose of transacting his business. Abolished by 5 & 6 Vict. c. 22, s. 12.

DAY, YEAR AND WASTE. [YEAR, DAY AND WASTE.]

DAYS OF GRACE. 1. Three days of grace formerly allowed to a person summoned by writ, beyond the day named in the writ, in which to make his appearance.
2. Three days allowed for the payment of a bill of exchange or a promissory note after it has nominally become due. No such days of grace are allowed in the case of bills of exchange and promissory notes purporting to be payable on sight or on demand. 2 *Steph. Com.* See *Bills of Exchange Act,* 1882 (45 & 46 *Vict. c.* 61), *s.* 14.

DAYSMAN. In some northern parts of England, any arbitrator, umpire, or elected judge is commonly termed a Deies-man, or Daysman.

DE BENE ESSE may perhaps be translated "for what it is worth." To take or do a thing *de bene esse* is to allow or accept for the present, till it comes to be more fully examined, and then to stand or fall according to the merit of the thing in its own nature, so that *valeat quantum valere potest*. Thus, the taking evidence in a chancery suit "*de bene esse*" is the taking evidence out of the regular course, and is looked upon as a temporary and conditional examination, to be used only in case the witness cannot be afterwards examined in the suit in the regular way. See *R. S. C.* 1883, *Ord. XXXVII. r.* 5.

DE BONIS NON. [ADMINISTRATOR.]

DE DIE IN DIEM (from day to day); thus, we speak of a sitting *de die in diem* until a case is concluded.

DE DONIS. The statute of Westminster the Second, 13 Edw. 1, st. 1, c. 1, *De donis conditionalibus*, which provided that, in grants to a man and the heirs of his body or the heirs male of his body, so the will of the donor should be observed according to the form expressed in the deed of gift; and that the tenements so given should go, after the death of the grantee, to his issue (or issue male, as the case might be), if there were any; and, if there were none, should revert to the donor. This statute gave rise to the estate in fee tail, or *feudum talliatum*, generally called an estate tail or entail. 1 *Steph. Com.* [CONDITIONAL FEE.]

DE EXPENSIS CIVIUM ET BURGEN-SIUM. [DE EXPENSIS MILITUM.]

DE EXPENSIS MILITUM. A writ commanding the sheriff to levy so much a day for the expenses of a knight of the shire. A like writ to levy two shillings a day for every citizen and burgess was called *De Expensis Civium et Burgensium.*

DE FACTO. An expression indicating the actual state of circumstances, independently of any remote question of right or title; thus, a king *de facto* is a person acknowledged and acting as king, independently of the question whether some one else has a better title to the crown. See *Austin, Jur., Lecture VI.* By stat. 11 Hen. 7, subjects obeying a king *de facto* were excused thereby from any penalties of treason to a king *de jure.* [DE JURE.]

DE IDIOTA INQUIRENDO. A writ by the old common law, to inquire whether a man be an idiot or not. This writ has long been dormant. *2 Steph. Com.*

DE JURE. Sometimes used of a supposed right in contradistinction to actual fact; thus a government *de jure* is a so-called government which is not a government, but which, according to the speaker or writer, ought to be a government. *Austin, Jur., Lecture VI.* [DE FACTO.]

DE LA PLUS BELLE (of the fairest [land]). A form of dower, being a consequence of tenure by knight service. It was abolished in 1660 with the military tenures, by 12 Car. 2, c. 24. *1 Steph. Com.*

DE LUNATICO INQUIRENDO. An old writ to inquire whether a man be a lunatic or not. Now the Lord Chancellor, under the Lunacy Acts (16 & 17 Vict. c. 70, and 25 & 26 Vict. c. 86), which were repealed and re-enacted by the consolidating Lunacy Act, 1890 (53 & 54 Vict. c. 5), upon petition or information, grants a *commission* in the nature of this writ. *2 Steph. Com.*

DE MEDIETATE LINGUÆ. A jury composed half of foreigners; a privilege formerly allowed to aliens, but abolished in civil cases by 6 Geo. 4, c. 50, ss. 3, 47, and in criminal cases by 33 Vict. c. 14, s. 5. *3 Steph. Com.*

DE MINIMIS NON CURAT LEX (the law takes no account of very trifling matters).

DE NOVO. Anew. Thus, to begin *de novo* is to begin again from the beginning.

DE PRÆROGATIVA REGIS. The statute 17 Edw. 3, st. 1, c. 9, which directs that the king shall have ward of the lands of natural fools (*i.e.*, idiots), taking the profits without waste or destruction, and finding them necessaries. This Act was not repealed by the consolidating Lunacy Act, 1890. *2 Steph. Com.*

DE RATIONABILI PARTE BONORUM. A writ formerly given to the wife and children of a deceased person to recover *a reasonable part* of his personal estate. By the common law, as it stood in the reign of Henry II., a man's goods were to be divided into three equal parts, of which one went to his heirs or lineal descendants, another went to his wife, and a third was at his own disposal. But this restraint on the power of bequeathing has now, for a century and a half, been utterly abolished for the whole of England. *2 Steph. Com.* [DEAD'S PART.]

DE SON TORT. [EXECUTOR DE SON TORT.]

DE SON TORT DEMESNE (of his own wrong). Lat. *De injuriâ suâ propriâ.*

DE TALLAGIO NON CONCEDENDO. The stat. 25 Edw. 1, by which it was declared, that no tallage or aid should be taken or levied without the goodwill and assent of the archbishops, bishops, earls, barons, knights, burgesses, and other freemen of the land. *2 Steph. Com.*

DE VENTRE INSPICIENDO. [AD VENTREM INSPICIENDUM.]

DEACON. The lowest degree of holy orders in the Church of England. *2 Steph. Com.*

DEAD FREIGHT. When a merchant has shipped only a part of a cargo, the freight payable for the part not shipped is called *dead freight.*

DEAD MAN'S PART. The part of a deceased's estate which, according to the custom of London, formerly devolved on the administrator for his own use. This was abolished by 1 Jac. 2, c. 17; and the custom itself, as regards the distribution of intestates' effects, is abolished by 19 & 20 Vict. c. 94. *2 Steph. Com.*

DEAD RENT. A rent payable on a mining lease in addition to a royalty, so called because it is payable although the mine may not be worked.

DEAD'S PART. The part of a man's moveables which, by the law of Scotland, he may distribute by his testament. *Bell*. [DEAD MAN'S PART.]

DEAN. The chief of the clergy appointed for the celebration of divine service in the bishop's cathedral. 2 *Steph. Com*.

DEAN OF THE ARCHES. The judge of the Arches Court, so called because he anciently held his court in the Church of St. Mary-le-Bow (*Sancta Maria de arcubus*). 3 *Steph. Com*. [ARCHES, COURT OF.]

DEBENTURE. 1. A custom-house certificate to the effect that an importer of goods is entitled to "drawback." [DRAWBACK.]
2. A charge in writing (usually under seal), of certain property with the repayment at a time fixed of the money lent at a given interest. Being for a fixed sum and time it was found to be inconvenient to lenders, and has been superseded in many cases by *debenture stock*, which is frequently irredeemable and usually transferable in any amount. The issue of debenture stock in the case of companies incorporated by Act of parliament is regulated either by their special Acts or by the Companies Clauses Act, 1863 (26 & 27 Vict. c. 118). See also the Companies Act, 1900.

DEBET ET SOLET. Words formerly used in a "writ of right," implying that the demandant is suing for something that is now first of all denied him, because he himself, and his ancestors before him, usually enjoyed the thing sued for. The writ of right is abolished with other real actions, by stat. 3 & 4 Will. 4, c. 27, s. 36.

DEBT. A certain sum due from one person to another, either (1) by *record*, *e.g.*, judgment, (2) under *specialty*, or deed, or (3) under *simple* contract by writing or oral. With the exception of certain preferred debts, all debts are payable *pari passu* in bankruptcy. In the administration of the estate of a deceased person the order is, (1) Crown debts, (2) rates, taxes, etc., (3) judgments, (4) recognizances and statutes, (5) specialty and simple debts, (6) voluntary debts.

DEBT, ACTION OF, for certain sum under either simple contract or specialty. [ASSUMPSIT, COVENANT.]

DEBTEE EXECUTOR is where a person makes his creditor his executor.

DEBTOR EXECUTOR is where a creditor constitutes his debtor his executor.

DEBTOR'S SUMMONS. A summons granted under the Bankruptcy Act, 1869, against a debtor by a court having jurisdiction in bankruptcy, on the creditor proving that there is due to him from the debtor a liquidated sum of not less than 50*l.*, and that the creditor has failed to obtain payment of his debt after using reasonable efforts to do so. The Bankruptcy Act, 1883, has replaced this process by a "bankruptcy notice" which is applicable in the case of an unpaid *judgment* debt of *any* amount. *Robson, Bkcy*.

DECEIT. Fraud, craft, or collusion, employed for the purpose of gaining advantage over another. There was an old writ called a "writ of deceit." which was brought in the Court of Common Pleas to reverse a judgment obtained in a real action by fraud and collusion between the parties. This writ was abolished by 3 & 4 Will. 4, c. 27, s. 36. 3 *Steph. Com*. There is also an old action of deceit, to give damages in some particular cases of fraud. But the remedy in cases of fraud, whereby a man is injured, was in general by an action on the case for damages. *Pasley* v. *Freeman*, 2 *Smith's Leading Cases;* 3 *Steph. Com*.

DECEM TALES (ten such). [TALES.]

DECENNARY. The same as a tithing; so called because ten freeholders with their families composed one. 1 *Steph. Com*.

DECIMATION. The punishing of every tenth soldier by lot for mutiny, etc.

DECINERS (*Decennarii*). Such as were wont to have the oversight of ten households, and the maintenance of the king's peace.

DECLARANT. A person who makes a declaration.

DECLARATION. The first of the pleadings in an ordinary action, consisting of a written statement by the plaintiff of his ground of action. 3 *Steph. Com.* This declaration might be delivered at any time after an "appearance" has been entered on behalf of the defendant. A statement of claim now takes the place of the declaration. [STATEMENT OF CLAIM.]

DECLARATION BY DEBTOR OF INABILITY TO PAY HIS DEBTS. To make such a declaration is an act of bankruptcy. See *Bankruptcy Act,* 1883 (46 & 47 *Vict. c.* 52), *s.* 4 (8). *Robson, Bkcy.* [ACT OF BANKRUPTCY.]

DECLARATION IN LIEU OF OATH. See the *Statutory Declarations Act,* 1835, 5 & 6 *Will.* 4, *c.* 62. [AFFIRMATION.]

DECLARATION OF PARIS. This expression is generally used to denote a certain declaration respecting International Maritime Law, annexed to Protocol No. 23 of the Protocols drawn up at the Congress of Paris in April, 1856. The articles of this declaration were as follows :—

1. Privateering is and remains abolished.

2. The neutral flag covers enemy's goods except contraband of war.

3. Neutral goods, except contraband of war, are not liable to confiscation under a hostile flag.

4. Blockades, to be binding, must be effective. *Parliamentary Papers,* 1856, *Nos.* 2073, 2074; *Twiss's Law of Nations.*

DECLARATION OF TRUST. A declaration whereby a person admits that he holds property upon trust for another. A declaration of trust of land, whether freehold, copyhold, or leasehold, must, by the Statute of Frauds, be evidenced in writing, and signed by the party declaring the trust. But declarations of trust of money, or chattels personal, need not be so evidenced. *Sm. Man. Eq.*

DECLARATORY ACT. An Act of parliament which professes to *declare* existing law, and not to enact new law. Legislative declaration, however, like judicial, is frequently deceptive, and enacts new law under the guise of expounding the old. 1 *Steph. Com.*

DECLINATORY PLEA. A plea of sanctuary, or of benefit of clergy. Abolished, 6 & 7 Geo. 4, c. 28, s. 6. [BENEFIT OF CLERGY; SANCTUARY.]

DECREE. The sentence of the Court of Chancery delivered on the hearing of a cause ; corresponding to a judgment at law. Since the Judicature Acts the expression *judgment* is adopted in reference to the decisions of all the Divisions of the Supreme Court. The word is also used in Scotland to signify the final sentence of a court.

DECREE ARBITRAL. The Scotch term for the award of an arbitrator.

DECREE NISI. A decree made for a divorce, which is not to take effect till after the expiration of such time, not less than six months from the pronouncing thereof, as the court shall by any general or special order from time to time direct. During this period any person may show cause why the decree should not be made absolute. 2 *Steph. Com.*

DECRETAL ORDER. An order in a chancery suit made on motion or otherwise not at the regular hearing of a cause, and yet not of an interlocutory nature, but finally disposing of the cause, so far as a decree could then have disposed of it.

DECRETALS are books of the canon law, containing the decrees of sundry Popes. 1 *Steph. Com.* [CANON LAW.]

DEDI ET CONCESSI (I have given and granted). An expression formerly used in conveyances of land, and importing that the grantor *warranted* the goodness of his title to the land conveyed. But this is now so no longer. 8 & 9 *Vict. c.* 106, *s.* 4 ; *Wms. R. P.*

DEDICATION OF WAY. The giving up a private road to the use of the public.

DEED. A writing sealed and delivered. 1 *Steph. Com.; Wms. R. P.* [DELIVERY OF A DEED.]

A deed is either a *deed poll* or a *deed indented.* If a deed be made by more parties than one, there ought to be regularly as many copies of it as there are parties ; and the deed so made is called an indenture, because each part used formerly to be cut or *indented* in acute angles on the top or side, to tally or correspond one with the other. Such deeds were formerly called *syngrapha* by the canonists, and with us *chirographa.* Now, by 8 & 9 Vict. c. 106, s. 5, a deed, purporting to be an indenture, is to have the effect of an indenture, though not actually indented.

DEED—*continued*.

A deed made by one party only is not and never was indented, but *polled* or shaved quite even, and therefore called a *deed poll*, or a single deed. 1 *Steph. Com.*

DEED OF COMPOSITION. [COMPOSITION.]

DEED OF COVENANT. Covenants are often entered into by separate deed, *e.g.*, a deed of covenant for production of deeds (now generally replaced by an acknowledgment).

DEED OF SEPARATION. [SEPARATION DEED.]

DEED-POLL. [DEED.]

DEEMSTERS. A kind of judges in the Isle of Man, who, without process, writings, or any charge, decide all controversies there.

DEFAMATION. The general term for words, either spoken or written, which tend to injure a person's reputation. See SLANDER ; LIBEL.

DEFAULT is an offence in omitting that which we ought to do ; as in the expression " wilful neglect or default." It is often taken for non-appearance in court at a day assigned ; and judgment given against a party by reason of such non-appearance, or other neglect to take any of the steps required of him within due time, is called *judgment by default.* 3 *Steph. Com.*

DEFAULT SUMMONS. A procedure in the county courts, under s. 86 of the County Courts Act, 1888 (51 & 52 Vict. c. 43), for the summary recovery of a debt or liquidated demand.

DEFEASANCE. A collateral deed, made at the same time with a feoffment or other conveyance, containing certain conditions, upon the performance of which the estate then created may be defeated, or totally undone. 1 *Steph. Com.* So, a defeasance on a bond or recognizance, or judgment recovered, is a condition which, when performed, defeats or undoes it. It is inserted in a separate deed in the same manner as the defeasance of an estate above mentioned.

DEFECTUM, CHALLENGE PROPTER. [CHALLENGE.]

DEFECTUM SANGUINIS, ESCHEAT PROPTER. [ESCHEAT.]

DEFENCE. [STATEMENT OF DEFENCE.]

DEFENDANT. A person sued in an action or charged with a misdemeanor. A person who is charged with felony is called the *prisoner*.

DEFENDEMUS (we will defend). A word in a feoffment or donation binding the donor and his heirs to defend the donee, if any man go about to lay any servitude (*i.e.*, to claim any incumbrance) upon the thing given, other than is contained in the donation. [FEOFFMENT.]

DEFENDER, in Scotch law, is the same as defendant in the English law.

DEFENDER OF THE FAITH. A title given to the King or Queen of England. It was first given by Leo X. to King Henry VIII., for writing against Martin Luther on behalf of the Church of Rome.

DEFENSIVE ALLEGATION. The allegation by a defendant in an ecclesiastical suit of the facts and circumstances which he has to offer in his defence. 3 *Steph. Com.*

DEFENSUM. An inclosure of land or any fenced ground.

DEFERRED STOCK. The stock in a company is sometimes divided into " preferred " and " deferred." The " preferred " shareholders are entitled to a fixed preferential dividend. The residue of the net profits are thus divided between the holders of the deferred stock.

DEFINITIVE SENTENCE. The final judgment of a spiritual court, as distinguished from an interlocutory or provisional judgment.

DEFORCE. To deprive another of lands. [DEFORCEMENT.]

DEFORCEMENT, in English law, signifies, in its most extensive sense, the holding of lands or tenements to which another person hath a right. But, in its more limited sense, it is only such a detainer of the freehold from him that hath the right of property, but never had any possession under that right, as falls within none of the injuries called *abatement, intrusion,* and *disseisin.* [ABATEMENT ; DISSEISIN ; INTRUSION.] 3 *Steph. Com.*

DEFORCEOR. One who deforces. [DE-FORCEMENT.]

DEFORCIANT. The person against whom the fictitious action of fine was brought. Abolished by 3 & 4 Will. 4, c. 74.

DEGRADATION. 1. Of peers. Where a person who has been in the rank of peers has ceased to be such ; as when a peeress, who is such only by marriage, is married to a commoner ; or where a peer is deprived of his nobility by Act of parliament. 2 *Steph. Com.*
2. Of ecclesiastics. As thus applied, the word signifies an ecclesiastical censure, whereby a clergyman is deprived of his holy orders.

DEHORS (without). Foreign or extrinsic to the record or deed, or other matter in question.

DEI JUDICIUM (the judgment of God). The old Saxon trial by *ordeal* was so called, because it was regarded as an appeal to God for the justice of a cause.

DEL CREDERE COMMISSION is a commission for the sale of goods to an agent, who, for a higher reward than is usually given, becomes responsible to his principal for the solvency of the purchaser. In other words, the agent (who is then called a *del credere* agent) guarantees the due payment of the price of the goods sold. 2 *Steph. Com.*

DELEGATES. [COMMISSION OF DELEGATES.]

DELEGATUS NON POTEST DELEGARE (a delegate cannot delegate). A person on whom an office or duty is delegated cannot delegate the duty to another, unless he is specially authorised so to do.

DELICTO, ACTION EX. A phrase occasionally used to designate an action of *tort ;* that is, an action for a wrong which is such independently of contract, as for libel, assault, etc. [ACTIONS REAL AND PERSONAL, 2 ; TORT.]

DELICTUM, CHALLENGE PROPTER. [CHALLENGE.]

DELICTUM TENENTIS, ESCHEAT PROPTER. [ESCHEAT.]

DELIVERY OF A DEED. This is held to be performed by the person who executes the deed placing his finger on the seal, and saying, "I deliver this as my act and deed." A deed takes effect only from this tradition or delivery. A delivery may be either absolute, that is, to the other party or grantee himself ; or to a third person, to hold until some condition be performed by the grantee ; in which latter case it is called an *escrow.* 1 *Steph. Com.*

DEM., in such an expression as Doe dem. Smith, means *demise* in the sense of lease ; indicating that Doe as lessee of Smith is the nominal plaintiff. [EJECTMENT.]

DEMANDANT. The plaintiff in a "real action" was called the *demandant.* Real actions are now abolished by 3 & 4 Will. 4, c. 27, s. 36, and 23 & 24 Vict. c. 126, s. 26. [ACTIONS REAL AND PERSONAL.]

DEMESNE (Lat. *Dominicum*) is most frequently used to signify those lands which the lord of a manor keeps in his own hands, as opposed to those which are let out to tenants. The word, however, is very variously used. 1 *Steph. Com.*

DEMISE (Lat. *Demittere*). To lease. This word implies an absolute covenant on the part of the lessor for quiet enjoyment. The word was formerly applicable to the grant of a freehold estate, but it is not now so applied. 1 *Steph. Com.*

DEMISE OF THE CROWN. A phrase used to denote the death of the king or queen, because the kingdom is thereby transferred or *demised* to his successor.

DEMI-VILL. A town consisting of five freemen or frankpledges.

DEMONSTRATIVE LEGACY. A gift by will of a certain sum to be paid out of a specific fund. *Wms. P. P.*

DEMUR, TO. To deliver a demurrer. [DEMURRER.]

DEMURRAGE. The daily sum payable by a merchant, who, having hired a ship, detains it for a longer time than he is entitled to do by his contract. Sometimes the delay itself is called *demurrage.* 2 *Steph. Com. ; Smith's Mercantile Law.*

DEMURRER. A written formula, whereby a party objects to a bill or information, declaration, indictment, or other pleading of his adversary, on the ground that it is, on the face of it, insufficient in point of law. In civil matters this mode of pleading is abolished by R. S. C. 1883, Ord. XXV. r. 1, but subsequent rules of the same order allow points of law raised on the pleadings to be disposed of before trial by order of the court or a judge, and pleadings to be struck out if they disclose no reasonable cause of action.

In *criminal* cases a demurrer may be, but seldom is, still resorted to. 7 *Geo.* 4, c. 64, *ss.* 20, 21; 14 & 15 *Vict. c.* 100, *s.* 25; 3 *Steph. Com.*; 4 *Steph. Com.*

DEMURRER BOOK. A book containing at length a transcript of the proceedings in cases where questions of law arise as to the sufficiency of matters alleged in the pleadings. Demurrers are now abolished and demurrer books are not made up, but any party who enters an action for trial must deliver to the officer of the court two copies of the pleadings, one for the use of the judge at the trial. See *R. S. C.* 1883, *Ord. XXXVI. r.* 30; 3 *Steph. Com.*

DENELAGE. [DANELAGE.]

DENIZEN. An alien born who has obtained *ex donatione regis* (from the gift of the king) letters patent to make him an English subject. A denizen is in a kind of middle state, between an alien and natural-born subject, and partakes of them both.

The grant of letters of denization is not affected by the Naturalisation Act, 1870 (33 & 34 Vict. c. 14); see s. 14. 2 *Steph. Com.*

DEODAND. Any personal chattel which is the immediate occasion of the death of any reasonable creature: which was formerly forfeited to the king, to be applied to pious uses, and distributed in alms by his high almoner, though in earlier times it was destined to a more superstitious purpose. Deodands were abolished in 1846 by 9 & 10 Vict. c. 62. 2 *Steph. Com.*

DEPARTURE, in pleading, is the shifting of his ground by a party, or a variation from the title or defence which he has once insisted on. See *R. S. C.* 1883, *Ord. XIX. r.* 16; 3 *Steph. Com.*

DEPONENT. A person who gives evidence, whether orally or by affidavit.

DEPORTATION. Transportation, banishment.

DEPOSIT. 1. The act of entrusting money to a bank is called a *deposit* in a bank; and the amount of the money deposited is also called the *deposit.* 3 *Steph. Com.* [SAVINGS BANK.]
2. A species of bailment by which a person entrusts another with a chattel to keep safely without reward. In this sense, the Latin form of the word, *depositum*, is more frequently adopted. *Story on Bailments.* [BAILMENT.]
3. Money paid as earnest or security for the performance of a contract, *e.g.*, the money paid by the purchaser on signature of a contract for sale.

DEPOSIT OF TITLE DEEDS. This is when the title deeds of an estate are deposited (generally with a bank) as a security for the repayment of money advanced. This operates as an equitable mortgage. [EQUITABLE MORTGAGE; MORTGAGE.]

DEPOSITION. A word used to indicate written evidence, or oral evidence taken down in writing. This cannot be read at the trial except where the witness himself cannot be produced. See *R. S. C.* 1883, *Ord. XXXVII. rr.* 1, 5. As to depositions in criminal proceedings (in connection with which the term is most commonly used), see 11 & 12 Vict. c. 42, s. 17, and 30 & 31 Vict. c. 35, ss. 6, 7. The word is also used to signify the depriving a person of some dignity; and it seems to have been at one time taken to signify death.

DEPOSITUM. A species of bailment. [DEPOSIT, 2.]

DEPRIVATION. A depriving or taking away: as when a bishop, parson, vicar. etc. is deposed from his preferment. Deprivation is of two sorts; *deprivatio à beneficio*, whereby a man is deprived of his promotion or benefice; and *deprivatio ab officio* is that whereby a man is deprived of his orders, which is also called *depositio* or *degradatio*, and is commonly for some heinous crime meriting death, and performed by the bishop in a solemn manner. 2 *Steph. Com.* [DEGRADATION.]

DEPUTY. One who acts for another in some office. Judges of the Supreme Court cannot act by deputy, but county court judges may under s. 18 of the County Courts Act, 1888; also recorders

DEPUTY—*continued.*
under the Municipal Corporations Act, 1882 (45 & 46 Vict. c. 50, s. 166). See also 51 & 52 Vict. c. 23. By the Sheriffs Act, 1887, every sheriff must appoint a deputy having an office within a mile of the Inner Temple Hall for the receipt of writs, etc.

DEPUTY LIEUTENANT. The deputy of a lord lieutenant of a county, each of whom has several deputies.

DERELICT. A thing forsaken or thrown away by its owner, especially a vessel forsaken at sea.

DERELICTION is where the sea shrinks back below water-mark, so that land is gained from the sea. If this gain is gradual, it goes to the owner of the land adjoining : but if it is sudden, the land gained belongs to the Crown. 1 *Steph. Com.*

DERIVATIVE CONVEYANCE. A conveyance which presupposes some other conveyance precedent, and serves to enlarge, confirm, alter, restrain, restore, or transfer the interest granted by such original conveyance. 1 *Steph. Com.* [PRIMARY CONVEYANCE.]

DERIVATIVE SETTLEMENT. [SETTLEMENT.]

DESCENT. The title whereby a man on the death of his ancestor intestate acquires his estate by right of representation as his heir-at-law. Now governed by the Inheritance Act, 1833 (3 & 4 Will. 4, c. 106), and 22 & 23 Vict. c. 35. 1 *Steph. Com.*

DESCENT CAST was where one who had wrongfully possessed himself of another's lands by *abatement, disseisin,* or *intrusion,* died, and his estate descended to his heir. Prior to 3 & 4 Will. 4, c. 27, the effect of this *descent cast* (if the rightful owner were under no disability) was, that the heir of the wrongdoer was clothed with an *apparent right of possession,* not to be defeated by mere entry without action ; and the *estate* of the rightful owner was turned into a *right of action.* 3 *Steph. Com.* [ABATEMENT, 5 ; DISSEISIN ; INTRUSION.]

DESERTION. 1. The criminal offence of abandoning the naval or military service without licence. See *s.* 12 *et seq.* of the *Army Act,* 1881.

2. An abandonment of a wife which is a matrimonial offence. See 20 *&* 21 *Vict.* c. 85, *ss.* 16, 21, and the *Summary Jurisdiction (Married Women) Act,* 1895.

DESIGNS, if registered, are protected by statute.

DETAINER. The forcible detention of a man's person or property. 3 *Steph. Com.* [FORCIBLE DETAINER.]

DETERMINABLE FREEHOLDS. Freeholds which are terminable on a given contingency, specified in the deed creating them. 1 *Steph. Com.*

DETINUE. The form of action whereby a plaintiff seeks to recover a chattel personal unlawfully detained. It differs from *trover,* inasmuch as in *trover* the object is to obtain *damages* for a wrongful conversion of the property to the defendant's use ; but in *detinue* the object is to recover the *chattel itself,* or failing that, its value, and damages. And now by R. S. C. 1883, Ord. XLVIII. the court may, upon the application of the plaintiff, order execution to issue for the return of the chattel detained. And see also Sale of Goods Act, 1893, (56 & 57 Vict. c. 71), s. 52.

DEVASTAVIT. The waste or misapplication of the assets of a deceased person committed by an executor or administrator. 2 *Steph. Com.*

DEVIATION. A departure from a plan conceived and agreed upon.
1. The word is used principally in reference to policies of marine insurance, as to which it is held, that the slightest *deviation* from the voyage marked out in the policy, except under circumstances of absolute necessity, will render the insurance ineffectual. 2 *Steph. Com.* Delay in commencing and prosecuting the voyage, for purposes foreign to the adventure, is also called *deviation.*
2. By a railway in course of construction is only allowed within certain limits. See the *Railway Clauses Act,* 1845 (8 *Vict.* c. 20), *ss.* 11 *et seq.*

DEVISAVIT VEL NON. An issue or inquiry whether a man had in fact made a devise (*i.e.,* will of lands) or not, directed by the Court of Chancery upon a bill being brought by the party claiming as devisee to have the will established. Obsolete.

DEVISE (Lat. *Divisa*). A bequest by a man of his lands and goods by his last will and testament in writing. At present the term "devise" is principally used with reference to landed property, and "bequeath" and "bequest" with reference to personalty. The giver is called the *devisor* and the recipient the *devisee*.

DICKER OF LEATHER. A quantity consisting of ten hides. *Cowel.*

DICTORES. Arbitrators.

DICTUM. 1. Arbitrament.

2. A saying or opinion of a judge, during the hearing of a case, on a point of law, which, however, is not necessary for the decision of that case.

"DIE WITHOUT ISSUE." [DYING WITHOUT ISSUE.]

DIEM CLAUSIT EXTREMUM (he has closed the last day of his life).

1. An ancient writ that lay for the heir of him that held land of the king, either by knight-service or socage, and died. The writ was directed to the escheator of the county, to inquire of what estate the party died seised.

2. The name of a special writ of *extent*, issued in the event of the death of a Crown debtor, by which the sheriff is commanded to seize his chattels, debts, and land into the hands of the Crown. 3 *Steph. Com.* [EXTENT.]

DIES FASTI ET NEFASTI. *Dies fasti* were the days in heathen Rome in which it was lawful to conduct litigation. *Dies nefasti* were days in which it was not lawful. *Ovid, Fasti, I.* 47, 48. 3 *Steph. Com.*

DIES JURIDICUS. An ordinary day in court, as opposed to Sundays and other holidays, upon which the courts do not sit.

DIES NON (*scil.* **JURIDICUS**). A day on which legal proceedings cannot be carried on, as Sundays, etc. [DIES JURIDICUS.]

DIET. 1. A name sometimes given to a general assembly on the continent of Europe.

2. A day. [DIETS OF COMPEARANCE.]

DIETA RATIONABILIS. A reasonable day's journey.

DIETS OF COMPEARANCE, in Scotland, are the days within which parties in civil and criminal prosecutions are cited to appear. *Bell.*

DIEU ET MON DROIT ("God and my right"). The motto of the royal arms, introduced by Richard I., indicating that the king holds his dominions of none but God.

DIGEST. 1. The Digest of the Emperor Justinian (otherwise called the Pandects) was a collection of extracts from the most eminent Roman jurists. In A.D. 530 Justinian authorised Tribonian, with the aid of sixteen commissioners, to prepare such a collection, and allowed ten years for the work. It was, however, completed in three years, and published under the title of Digest or Pandects, on the 16th of December, 533, and declared to have the force of law from the 30th of that month. 1 *Steph. Com.*; *Sandars' Justinian, Introd. s.* 30.

2. A Digest of Cases is a compilation of the head-notes or main points of decided cases, arranged in alphabetical order, according to the branches or subjects of law which they respectively illustrate.

DIGNITIES. A species of incorporeal hereditament in which a man may have a property or estate. They were originally annexed to the possession of certain estates in land, and are still classed under the head of real property.

DILAPIDATION. 1. The name for ecclesiastical waste committed by the incumbent of a living; which is either voluntary, by pulling down; or permissive, by suffering the chancel, parsonage-house, and other buildings thereunto belonging, to decay. 3 *Steph. Com.* 346, 451.

2. Also used to signify a want of repair for which a tenant is liable who has agreed to give up the premises in good repair.

DILATORY PLEA is a plea by a defendant in an action, founded on some matter of fact not connected with the merits of the case, but such as may exist without impeaching the right of action itself. They are now, for the most part, obsolete. A dilatory plea is either—

1. A plea *to the jurisdiction*, showing that, by reason of some matter therein stated, the case is not within the jurisdiction of the court.

DILATORY PLEA—*continued*.

2. A plea *of suspension* showing some matter of temporary incapacity to proceed with the suit.

3. A plea *in abatement*, showing some matter for *abating* the action. Now abolished. [ABATEMENT, 6.]

The effect of a dilatory plea, if established, is, that it defeats the particular action, leaving the plaintiff at liberty to commence another in a better form.

A dilatory plea is opposed to a peremptory plea, otherwise called a *plea in bar*, which is founded on some matter tending to impeach the right of action. 3 *Steph. Com.*

DILIGENCE, besides its ordinary meaning, has a special meaning in the law of Scotland, in which it signifies the warrants issued by the courts for the attendance of witnesses, or the production of writings; also the process whereby persons or effects are attached or seized on execution, or in security for debt. *Bell.*

DIMISSORY LETTERS. Letters sent by one bishop to another, requesting him to ordain a candidate for holy orders, who has a title in the diocese of the former bishop, but is anxious to be ordained by the latter.

DIOCESAN COURTS. The consistory courts of the bishops for the trial of ecclesiastical causes arising within their respective dioceses. 3 *Steph. Com.* [CONSISTORY COURTS.]

DIOCESE, or **DIOCESS.** The circuit of a bishop's jurisdiction. See also 1 *Steph. Com.*

DIPLOMA. A royal charter or letters patent.

DIPLOMACY. The conduct of negotiations between nations, by means of correspondence or by ambassadors or the like.

DIRECT EVIDENCE is evidence directly bearing upon the point at issue, and which, if believed, is conclusive in favour of the party adducing it; and is opposed to *circumstantial* evidence, from which the truth as to the point at issue can be only inferentially deduced. [CIRCUMSTANTIAL EVIDENCE.]

DIRECTION TO A JURY is where a judge instructs a jury on any point of law, in order that they may apply it to the facts in evidence before them. See *Jud. Act*, 1873, *s.* 22. Misdirection is a ground for a new trial.

DIRECTIONS, SUMMONS FOR. One general summons which is issued in most actions at an early stage of the proceedings for directions as to pleadings, discovery, mode and place of trial, and the like. See *R .S. C., Ord. XXX.*

DIRECTORS. Persons appointed to manage the affairs of a corporation or company. If the company be incorporated by Act of parliament their powers are derived from their special Act and from ss. 90—100 of the Companies Clauses Act, 1845 ; if the company be incorporated under the Companies Act, 1862, from "articles of association," see s. 14 of that Act. They may receive a salary, but may make no personal profit from their company, being trustees. As to fraud, see 24 & 25 Vict. c. 96, ss. 81 *et seq.*, and the Directors' Liability Act, 1890 (53 & 54 Vict. c. 64). See also Companies Act, 1900.

DIRECTORY STATUTE. A statute is said to be merely directory when it directs anything to be done or omitted, without invalidating acts or omissions in contravention of it.

DISABILITY. At the present day the word is generally used to indicate an incapacity for the full enjoyment of ordinary legal rights ; thus married women, persons under age, insane persons, and felons convict are under disability. It may be either *absolute* or *partial*.

Sometimes the term is used in a more limited sense, as when it signifies an impediment to marriage ; or the restraints placed upon clergymen by reason of their spiritual avocations. 2 *Steph. Com.*

DISABLING STATUTE. A statute which disables or restrains any person or persons from doing that which formerly was lawful or permissible ; as the statute 1 Eliz. c. 19, disabling archbishops and bishops from making leases for more than twenty-one years or three lives, or without receiving the usual rent. 1 *Steph. Com.* ; 2 *Steph. Com.*

DISAFFORESTED. Exempted from the forest laws.

DISAGREEMENT. A word sometimes used to signify the *disclaimer* of an estate. [DISCLAIMER, 2.]

DISALT. *To disable* a person.

DISBAR. To deprive a barrister of his privileges and status as such.

DISBENCH. To deprive a bencher of his privileges. [BENCHERS.]

DISCHARGE. A word used in various senses :

1. Of the discharge of a bankrupt under s. 28 of the Bankruptcy Act, 1883, by which he is freed of all debts and liabilities provable under the bankruptcy, with certain specified exceptions. *2 Steph. Com.; Robson, Bkcy.*

2. Of the discharge of a surety, whereby he is released from his liability as surety. *2 Steph. Com.*

3. Of the release of a prisoner from confinement.

4. Of the payment of a debt, whereby the debtor is freed from further liability.

5. Of the release of lands, or money in the funds, from an incumbrance, by payment of the amount to the incumbrancer, or otherwise by consent of the incumbrancer.

6. Of an order of a court of justice dismissing a jury on the grounds that they have performed their duties, or are unable to agree in a case before them.

7. Of the reversal of an order of a court of justice; thus we say, such an order was "discharged on appeal," etc.

8. A rule *nisi* is discharged where the court decides it shall not be made absolute.

9. Of a jury, (*a*) by the act of God, on the death of one member, (*b*) on the giving of a verdict, or (*c*) on failure to agree to a verdict.

DISCLAIMER is a renunciation, denial, or refusal. It is used :—

1. Of an answer of a person made defendant to a bill in Chancery in respect of some interest he is supposed to claim, whereby he disclaims all interest in the matters in question. Now obsolete.

2. Of any act whereby a person refuses to accept an estate which is attempted to be conveyed to him; as, for instance, where land is conveyed to an intended trustee without his consent, and he refuses to accept it. This is called the disclaimer of an estate. *1 Steph. Com.*

3. Of the refusal by the trustee in a bankruptcy to accept a burdensome lease or other onerous property of the bankrupt. *Robson, Bkcy.; Bkcy. Act, 1883, s. 55.*

4. Of disclaimer of tenure; that was where a tenant, who held of any lord, neglected to render him the due services, and, upon an action brought to recover them, disclaimed to hold of the lord: which disclaimer of tenure in any court of record was a forfeiture of the lands to the lord. *1 Steph. Com.*

5. Of disclaimer of patent. See Patent Act, 1883, *s.* 19.

DISCLOSURE. Every solicitor whose name is on a writ must on demand in writing by a defendant declare whether the writ was issued with his privity. *R. S. C.* 1883, *Ord. VII., r.* 1.

As to disclosure of partners' names, etc., where writ issued in the name of the firm, see *Ibid., r.* 2.

DISCONTINUANCE OF ACTION is governed by *R. S. C.* 1883, *Ord. XXVI.* [WITHDRAWING THE RECORD.]

DISCONTINUANCE OF AN ESTATE, otherwise called discontinuance of possession, is defined in Bacon's Abridgment as "such an alienation of possession, whereby he who has a right to the inheritance cannot *enter*" (without bringing an action), "but is driven to his *action*;" as where a tenant in tail made a feoffment in fee simple, or for the life of the feoffee, or in tail; all which were beyond his power to make, for that by the common law extended no further than to make a lease for his own life. In such case the possession by the feoffee after the death of the feoffor was termed a "discontinuance;" the ancient legal estate being gone, or at least suspended, and for a while *discontinued*.

In such case the heir in tail, remainderman or reversioner was deprived of his *right of entry*, and driven to his *action* to recover the land. *3 Bl.; 3 Steph. Com.*

But from the 15th century to the year 1833, a tenant in tail could ordinarily bar *entirely* all future interests in the land by a *common recovery* [RECOVERY], and, since the year 1833, by a disentailing deed. [DISENTAILING DEED.] Discontinuances, therefore, prior to their express abolition, had long become obsolete and unmeaning; and they are now abolished by 3 & 4 Will. 4, c. 27. *1 Steph. Com.*

DISCOUNT. 1. An allowance made to bankers or others for advancing money upon bills before they become due.

2. An allowance frequently made at the settlement of accounts, by way of deduction from the amount payable.

DISCOVERT. A word applied to a woman who is a widow or unmarried, as not being under the disabilities of *coverture*. [COVERTURE.]

DISCOVERY. 1. Of *facts*, obtainable by either party to an action, in the form of answers on oath to questions known as interrogatories administered by the other after approval of the court, and on payment of deposit as security for the costs. The answers or any of them may be put in as evidence on the trial, and are obtained with the object of getting admissions or discovery of such material facts as relate to the case of the party interrogating.

2. Of *documents*, obtained as above. The party against whom an order for discovery of documents is made must file an affidavit setting out all the documents relating to the action which are or have been in his possession or power. See *R. S. C. Ord. XXXI.*, and *Bray on Discovery*.

The word is also used in reference to the disclosure by a bankrupt of his property for the benefit of his creditors. 2 *Steph. Com.; Robson, Bkcy.*

DISCREDIT. To show to be unworthy of credit. The term is employed chiefly in regard to witnesses in a court of justice. As a general rule, a party is not entitled to discredit his own witness.

DISENTAILING DEED. A deed executed by a tenant in tail under 3 & 4 Will. 4, c. 74, for the abolition of fines and recoveries; by which, if duly enrolled within six months of its execution, the tenant in tail is enabled, by s. 15 of the Act, to alienate the land for an estate in fee simple or any less estate, and thereby to destroy the entail. 1 *Steph. Com.*

DISFRANCHISE. To take away from one his privilege or franchise.

At the present day it is used to signify the depriving an individual of his right of voting, or a constituency of their right of returning a member to parliament. 2 *Steph. Com.; May's Parl. Pract.*

DISGAVEL. To abolish the custom of gavelkind as to any lands or tenements where it has previously existed. This can only be done by Act of parliament. [GAVELKIND.]

DISHERISON. The disinheriting of any person or persons.

DISHONOUR is where the drawee of a bill of exchange refuses to accept it, or, having accepted it, fails to pay it according to the tenor of his acceptance. See Bills of Exchange Act, 1882 (45 & 46 Vict. c. 61), s. 47; 2 *Steph. Com.; Byles on Bills.*

DISINHERISON. [DISHERISON.]

DISMES, DECIMÆ. Tithes; also the tenths of all spiritual livings formerly payable to the Pope, and afterwards to the Crown. 2 *Steph. Com.* [QUEEN ANNE'S BOUNTY.]

DISMISSAL OF ACTION. This may take place upon default in delivery of statement of claim, non-appearance at trial, etc. See *R. S. C.* 1883, *Ord. XXVII.; XXXVI., r.* 12.

DISMISSAL OF BILL IN EQUITY signified a refusal by the court to make a decree as prayed by a plaintiff's bill. This might be (1) *on the merits of the case*, or (2) *for want of prosecution*, that is to say, of due diligence on the part of the plaintiff or his advisers in taking the steps required by the practice of the court. The dismissal on the merits might be partial or entire, according to circumstances. *Dan. Ch. Pr.*

DISORDERLY HOUSES. The keeping of such is an indictable offence under 25 Geo. 2, c. 36, and is also punishable on summary conviction under s. 13 of the Criminal Law Amendment Act, 1885 (48 & 49 Vict. c. 69). Consult *Stone's Justices' Manual.*

DISPARAGEMENT. A word used to signify *inequality* or unsuitableness in marriage. 1 *Steph. Com.*

DISPAUPER. To prohibit a man who has once been admitted to sue *in formâ pauperis*, that is, as a pauper, from suing any longer as such. [FORMA PAUPERIS.]

DISPENSATION. 1. An exemption from some law.
2. An ecclesiastical licence.

DISSEISEE. A person disseised or put out of his freehold. [DISSEISIN.]

DISSEISIN is a wrongful putting out of him that is seised of the freehold. Now remedied by entry if it can be peaceably effected, and otherwise by action commonly called ejectment. 3 & 4 *Will.* 4, c. 27, s. 36; 1 *Steph. Com.;* 3 *Steph. Com.* [ENTRY, WRIT OF; OUSTER.]

DISSEISOR. A person who puts another out of his freehold. [DISSEISIN.]

DISSENTERS. Persons who do not conform to the Established Church. The word is usually confined to Protestant seceders from the Established Church, and their descendants. 2 *Steph. Com.*

DISSOLUTION. The act of breaking up.

1. Of *parliament* is where a final period is put to the existence of a parliament by the sovereign's will, expressed either in person or by representation, or by lapse of time. Parliaments were formerly dissolved by the death of the sovereign, but this doctrine is now abolished. 30 & 31 *Vict. c.* 102, *s.* 51 ; 2 *Steph. Com. ; May's Parl. Pract.*

2. Of *partnership*, by proper notice, by effluxion of time as agreed in the articles of partnership, by order of a court, by death, insolvency, etc., of a partner. Consult *Lindley on Partnership.*

3. Of *marriage*, by decree of divorce (*q.v.*).

4. Of *companies*, by winding up, etc. As to dissolution of railway companies, see 9 & 10 Vict. c. 28, and 13 & 14 Vict. c. 83.

DISSOLVING AN INJUNCTION is tantamount to discharging or reversing it. [INJUNCTION.]

DISTRAIN. To execute a distress. 3 *Steph. Com.* [DISTRESS.]

DISTRAINT. A distress. [DISTRESS.]

DISTRESS. The taking of a personal chattel out of the possession of a wrongdoer into the custody of the party injured, to procure satisfaction for the wrong committed. 3 *Steph. Com.* The word is most frequently (though not at all exclusively) used with reference to the taking by a landlord of goods for the non-payment of rent.

DISTRESS INFINITE. A distress that has no bounds with regard to its quantity, and may be repeated from time to time, until the stubbornness of the wrongdoer is overcome, *e.g.*, distress for fealty or suit of court, and for compelling jurors to attend. 3 *Steph. Com.*

DISTRIBUTION. A word used specially for the division of the personal estate of an intestate among the parties entitled thereto as next of kin. This is regulated by the Statute of Distribution, 22 & 23 Car. 2, c. 10, amended by 29 Car. 2, c. 3. See also the Intestates

Act, 1890 (53 & 54 Vict. c. 29). 2 *Steph. Com.*

DISTRICT REGISTRIES have been created by Order in Council under s. 60 of the Judicature Act, 1873, to facilitate proceedings in country districts. Power is reserved to a judge to remove proceedings from a district registry to the office of the High Court by s. 65. See generally *ss.* 60—66. Proceedings in district registries are regulated by R. S. C. 1883, Ord. XXXV.

DISTRINGAS (that you distrain). 1. A writ formerly issuing against the goods and chattels of a defendant who did not appear. 3 *Steph. Com.*

2. A writ after judgment for the plaintiff in the action of *detinue*, to compel the defendant, by repeated distresses of his chattels, to give up the goods detained. 3 *Steph. Com.; C. L. Proc. Act*, 1854, *s.* 78. [DETINUE.]

3. The name, in the Court of King's Bench, of an old writ commanding the sheriff to bring in the bodies of jurors who do not appear, or to distrain their lands and goods. This writ is now abolished.

4. The process in equity against a body corporate, refusing to obey the summons and direction of the court.

5. A writ issued under 5 Vict. c. 5, s. 5, by a party claiming to be interested in any stock in the Bank of England, restraining the bank from transferring the stock or paying any dividend on it, as the case may be. By R. S. C. 1883, Ord. XLVI., r. 2, no distringas under 5 Vict. c. 5, s. 5, can any longer be issued, but rr. 3—11 of the same order provide a procedure to be pursued in such a case.

6. *Distringas nuper vicecomitem* (that you distrain the late sheriff). A writ which may be issued when a sheriff, having levied execution by *fieri facias*, and being unable to sell the goods so levied, goes out of office. The writ is directed to his successor, commanding him to *distrain* the late sheriff, to compel him to sell the goods.

DISTURBANCE. A form of real injury done to some incorporeal hereditament, by hindering or disquieting the owners in their regular and lawful enjoyment of it. Blackstone enumerates five sorts of this injury :—(1) Disturbance of *franchises.* (2) Disturbance of *common.* (3) Disturbance of *ways.* (4) Disturbance of *tenure.* (5) Disturbance of *patronage.* 3 *Steph. Com.*

DISTURBER. A bishop is so styled who refuses or neglects to examine and admit a patron's clerk (*i.e.*, a clergyman presented by a patron to a living) without good reason assigned, or notice given. 2 *Steph. Com.*

DIVERSITE DES COURTES. A treatise, supposed to have been written early in the sixteenth century, giving a catalogue of the matters of conscience then cognizable by subpœna in Chancery. 3 *Steph. Com.*

DIVERSITY OF PERSON is where a prisoner pleads in bar of execution that he is not the same as the person convicted. 4 *Steph. Com.*

DIVESTING OF AN ESTATE is where an estate, vested in a man and his heirs, etc., ceases to be so. This may be—
1. By conveyance.
2. By forfeiture.
3. By the terms of the instrument under which the estate is held.
4. By the order of a court of justice; including those cases where property is divested by an order of adjudication in bankruptcy.

DIVIDEND. 1. *Dividenda.* A word used in the Statute of Rutland, 10 Edw. 1, to signify one part of an indenture.
2. The periodical income arising from stocks, shares, etc.
3. The proportion of a creditor's debt payable to him on the division of a bankrupt's or insolvent's estate.

DIVINE RIGHT, or **DIVINE RIGHT OF KINGS**, is the name generally given to the patriarchal theory of government, according to which the monarch and his legitimate heirs, being by *divine right* entitled to the sovereignty, cannot forfeit that right by any misconduct, however gross, or any period of dispossession, however long. It was by this right that the English sovereigns in the seventeenth century claimed to reign.

DIVINE SERVICE. A tenure by which the tenants were obliged to do some special divine services in certain; as to sing so many masses, to distribute such a sum in alms, and the like. 1 *Steph. Com.*
Tenure by *divine service* differed from tenure in *frankalmoign* in this: that in case of the tenure by *divine service*, the lord of whom the lands were holden might distrain for its non-performance, whereas in case of *frank-*

almoign the lord has no remedy by distraint for neglect of the service, but merely a right of complaint to the visitor to correct it.

DIVISA. 1. An award or decree.
2. A boundary.
3. A boundary court.
4. A devise (*q.v.*).

DIVISIONAL COURTS. Courts (which under the Judicature Act take the place of the sittings "in banc") constituted usually of two judges of the High Court, to transact certain business which cannot be disposed of by a single judge, *e.g.*, appeals from county courts, from judge in chambers, special cases from justices of the peace, Crown business, etc. All applications for new trials of King's Bench actions are, since the Judicature Act, 1890, to be made to the Court of Appeal, and so also are appeals from judge in chambers on questions of practice and procedure by the Judicature Act, 1894. There are no divisional courts of the Chancery Division. See *App. Jur. Act*, 1876, *s.* 17; *Judicature Act*, 1884, *s.* 4.

DIVISIONS OF THE HIGH COURT. The High Court of Justice created by the Judicature Act, 1873, was by s. 31 of that Act divided into five divisions, which were called the Chancery, the Queen's Bench, the Common Pleas, the Exchequer, and the Probate, Divorce, and Admiralty Divisions; but an Order in Council under s. 32 of the same Act, which came into operation on 26th February, 1881, united into one Queen's Bench (now King's Bench) Division, the judges attached to the Common Pleas and Exchequer Divisions; so that there are now *three* Divisions.

DIVORCE. A separation of man and wife. This is of three kinds:—
1. *A mensâ et thoro*, now generally called a *judicial separation*. Its effect is to place the parties in the position of single persons, except that neither party can lawfully marry again in the lifetime of the other.
2. Divorce *à vinculo* for some cause subsequent to the marriage, now called *dissolution*. This, by the law of England, make take place for adultery, combined, if the adultery be that of the husband, with some other circumstance of aggravation; as a wife cannot obtain a dissolution of the marriage for the simple adultery of the husband. The effect of this kind of divorce is to dissolve the marriage, and allow the

DIVORCE—*continued.*

parties to marry again; but it does not bastardise the issue. Now usually granted by Probate, Divorce, and Admiralty Division. For private Act of parliament see *May's Parl. Pract.*

3. Divorce *à vinculo* for some cause of impediment existing prior to the marriage; now called *nullity.* This is a declaration that the marriage is a nullity, as having been absolutely unlawful from the beginning. This kind of divorce not only enables the parties to contract marriage at their pleasure. but bastardises the issue, if any. 2 *Steph. Com.* Consult generally *Browne* or *Dixon on Divorce.*

DIVORCE ACT means either a private Act of parliament for dissolving a marriage, or the Public General Divorce Act of 1857, by which the Divorce Court was constituted. [DIVORCE.]

DIVORCE COURT, or **THE COURT FOR DIVORCE AND MATRIMONIAL CAUSES**, is the court erected by the Divorce Act, 1857. To this court (now a branch of the High Court of Justice) is transferred the matrimonial jurisdiction of the old ecclesiastical courts, together with power to grant divorces *à vinculo* in cases of adultery. [COURT FOR DIVORCE AND MATRIMONIAL CAUSES; DIVORCE.]

DOCK. The place in court where a prisoner is placed while on trial. He may, from the dock, instruct counsel without the intervention of a solicitor.

DOCK WARRANT. A document given to the owner of goods imported and warehoused in the docks, as a recognition of his title to the goods, on the bills of lading and other proofs of ownership being produced. Like a bill of lading, it passes by indorsement and delivery, and transfers the absolute right to the goods described in it.

DOCKET, or **DOCQUET**. A brief writing, on a small piece of paper or parchment, containing the effect of a larger writing. Also it is used to signify a register of judgments.

The name is also given to the copy of a decree in Chancery, made out and left with the Record and Writ Clerk, preparatory to enrolment. [ENROLMENT.]

DOCQUET OF DECREE. [DOCKET.]

DOCTORS' COMMONS. An institution near St. Paul's Churchyard, where the Ecclesiastical and Admiralty Courts used to be held until the year 1857. See 20 & 21 *Vict. c.* 77, *ss.* 116, 117; 3 *Steph. Com.*

DOCUMENT OF TITLE TO GOODS. See *Factors Act*, 1889, *s.* 1 (4); and *Larceny Act*, 1861, *s.* 1.

DOCUMENT OF TITLE TO LANDS. See *Larceny Act*, 1861, *s.* 1.

DOE, JOHN. Generally the name of the fictitious plaintiff in the old action of ejectment. 3 *Steph. Com.* [EJECTMENT.]

DOG-DRAW. An apprehension of an offender against venison in the forest, where any man hath stricken or wounded a wild beast, and is found with a hound or other *dog drawing* after him to recover the same. *Cowel.*

DOLE. A Saxon word signifying as much as *pars* or *portio* in Latin. It hath of old been attributed to a meadow, because divers persons had shares in it. We still retain the word to signify a share, as to deal a dole. *Cowel.*

DOLI CAPAX (capable of crime). An expression used to indicate that in any given case a child between the ages of seven and fourteen has, contrary to the ordinary presumption · in such cases, sufficient understanding to discern · between good and evil, so as to be criminally responsible for his actions. This is otherwise expressed by the maxim, *Malitia supplet ætatem* (malice supplies the want of age). 4 *Steph. Com.*

DOLI INCAPAX (incapable of crime).

DOM. PROC. An abbreviation for *Domus Procerum*, the House of Lords.

DOM-BOC. [DOME-BOOK.]

DOME, or **DOOM**. A judgment, sentence, or decree. We have several words that end in *dom*, as kingdom, earldom, etc., so that it may seem to signify the jurisdiction of a lord or a king.

DOME-BOOK (Lat. *Liber judicialis*). Probably a book of statutes proper to the English Saxons, wherein perhaps the laws of former Saxon kings were contained.

This book is said to have been compiled by Alfred, and to have been extant so late as the reign of Edward IV., but it is now lost. • 1 *Steph. Com.*

DOMESDAY-BOOK (Lat. *Liber judiciarius*). An ancient record made in the reign of William the Conqueror, containing a survey of the lands in England. It was begun by five justices, assigned for that purpose in each county in the year 1081, and was finished in 1086.

DOMESMEN. Judges or men appointed to doom, and determine suits or controversies.

DOMESTICS. Menial servants. So called from being employed *intra mœnia domus* (within the walls of a house).

DOMICELLUS. An old appellation given as an addition to the king's natural sons in France. John of Gaunt's natural sons are called *domicelli* in the charter of legitimation. *Domicellus* also signifies a private gentleman ; also a better sort of servant.

DOMICIL. The place in which a man has his fixed and permanent home, and to which, whenever he is absent, he has the intention of returning. It is of three sorts : (1) by birth ; (2) by choice ; (3) by operation of law. Upon domicil depend questions of personal status and the devolution of movable property. Domicil is also in general the test of national character for the purpose of war. *Story's Conflict of Laws; 2 Steph. Com.; Westlake's Private International Law ; Dicey on Domicile.*

DOMINA. A title given to honourable women, who anciently in their own right of inheritance held a barony.

DOMINANT TENEMENT. A tenement in favour of which a service or " servitude " is constituted. Thus an estate, the owner of which has, by virtue of his ownership, a right of way over another man's land is called the *dominant tenement* in respect thereof ; and the land over which the right of way exists is called the *servient tenement.* These terms are derived from the Roman civil law. Consult *Gale on Easements.*

DOMINICUM. A demesne. [DEMESNE.]

DOMINIUM. A term in the Roman law. used to signify *ownership of a thing*, as opposed (1) to a mere life interest or usufruct ; (2) to an equitable or " prætorian " right ; (3) to a merely possessory right ; (4) to a right *against a person*, such as a covenantee has against a covenantor.

DOMINUS. This word prefixed to a man's name usually denoted him a knight or a clergyman ; sometimes the lord of a manor.

DOMINUS LITIS. The controller of a suit or litigation.

DOMITÆ NATURÆ (of a tame disposition). An expression applied to animals of a nature tame and domestic, as horses, kine, sheep, poultry, and the like. In these a man may have as absolute a property as in any inanimate thing. *2 Steph. Com.*

DOMO REPARANDA (for repairing a house). An ancient writ that lay for a man against his neighbour, by the anticipated fall of whose house he feared damage to his own. The writ directed the neighbour to put his house in a proper state of repair.

DOMUS PROCERUM. The House of Lords.

DON, GRANT, ET RENDER. [FINE, 1.]

DONATIO MORTIS CAUSÂ (a gift by reason of death) is a gift of personal property made by one who apprehends that he is in peril of death, and evidenced by a manual delivery by him, or by another person in his presence and by his direction, to the donee or to some one else for the donee, of the means of obtaining possession of the same, or of the writings whereby the ownership thereof was created, and conditioned to take effect absolutely in the event of his not recovering from his existing disorder, and not revoking the gift before his death.

A *donatio mortis causâ* differs from a legacy mainly in its being wholly independent of the donor's last will and testament, and it therefore requires no assent on the part of his executor or administrator to give full effect to it. It is liable to the donor's debts in case of insufficiency of assets, and is subject to legacy and account duty. *Sm. Man. Eq.; 2 Steph. Com.*

DONATIVE, ADVOWSON. [ADVOWSON.]

DONEE. [DONOR.]

DONIS, DE. [DE DONIS.]

DONOR is he who makes a gift to another; and he to whom the gift is made is called the *donee*.

DOOM. [DOME.]

DORMANT PARTNER. One who takes no active part in the partnership affairs, nor is known to the world as a partner, but who receives the profits of the partnership. *Sm. Merc. Law;* see also *Lindley on Partnership.*

DOTE, or, more fully, **RECTO DE DOTE,** was a writ of right of dower, which lay for a widow who had received part of her dower, but was deprived of the residue, lying in the same town, by the wrong of the same tenant. For this writ, by s. 26 of the C. L. P. Act, 1860, a personal action is now substituted. [DOTE UNDE NIHIL HABET.]

DOTE ASSIGNANDA. A writ that lay for the widow of a tenant who held of the king *in capite* (*i.e.,* without the intervention of any mesne lord), for the assignment of her dower. In order to obtain this writ she had to make oath that she would not marry without the king's leave. [DOWER, 2.]

DOTE UNDE NIHIL HABET. or, more fully, **RECTO DE DOTE UNDE NIHIL HABET.** A writ which lay for a widow to whom no dower had been assigned. An ordinary action commenced by writ of summons is now substituted for this writ. 23 & 24 *Vict. c.* 126, *ss.* 26, 27 ; 3 *Steph. Com.* [DOWER, 2.]

DOTIS ADMENSURATIONE. An old writ for admeasurement of dower, against a widow who (it was alleged) held more lands than her proper share.

DOUBLE AVAIL OF MARRIAGE. [VALOR MARITAGII.]

DOUBLE COMPLAINT. [DUPLEX QUERELA.]

DOUBLE COSTS OR TREBLE COSTS, given in various cases by Act of parliament. All such provisions as were enacted for this purpose before the year 1842 are repealed by 5 & 6 Vict. c. 97. See also County Courts Act, 1888, s. 115.

DOUBLE ENTRY. A system of mercantile bookkeeping in which the entries are made so as to show the debit and credit of every transaction.

DOUBLE FINE. A fine *sur don, grant, et render* was so called, because it comprehended the fine *sur cognizance de droit come ceo,* etc., and the fine *sur concessit.* 2 *Bl.* ; 1 *Steph. Com.* [FINE, 1.]

DOUBLE INSURANCE is where a person, being fully insured by one policy, effects another with some other insurer or insurers, the risk and interest being the same in both. He may recover the amount of his actual loss from either insurer, but not both, as the contract is one of indemnity only. The insurer who pays is entitled to contribution from the other. 2 *Steph Com.*

DOUBLE PLEA is that wherein the defendant or tenant in any action pleads a plea in which two matters are comprehended, and each one by itself is a sufficient bar or answer to the action. Such double pleading, otherwise called duplicity in pleading, must be avoided; the rule being that every plea must be confined to one single point. The rule is much relaxed now, but such pleading is liable to be struck out if it tend to embarrass.

DOUBLE POSSIBILITY (*Potentia remota*). A possibility upon a possibility ; as where a remainder in land is limited to a son John or Richard of a man that hath no son of that name; the supposed "double" possibility being, (1) that the man would have a son ; (2) that the son would be called John or Richard, as the case might be. Such a remainder was formerly held illegal, but this doctrine is now quite exploded. 1 *Steph. Com.*

DOUBLE QUARREL. [DUPLEX QUERELA.]

DOUBLE RENT is payable by a tenant who continues in possession after the time for which he has given notice to quit, until the time of his quitting possession. 11 *Geo.* 2, c. 19, *s.* 18 ; *Woodfall's L. & T.*

DOUBLE VALUE. Double the yearly value of lands payable by a tenant who wilfully "holds over" (*i.e.,* continues in possession) after the expiration of his term, and after notice by the landlord requiring him to leave. 4 *Geo.* 2, c. 28 ; *Woodfall's L. & T.* For *double value of marriage,* see VALOR MARITAGII.

DOUBLE VOUCHER was where a common recovery was effected by first conveying an estate of freehold to an indifferent person, against whom the *præcipe* was brought, who then "vouched" the tenant in tail, and he the common vouchee. 1 *Steph. Com.* [RECOVERY ; VOUCHING TO WARRANTY.]

DOUBLE WASTE. When a tenant bound to repair, suffers a house to be wasted, and then unlawfully fells timber to repair it, he is said to commit double waste.

DOWAGER. A queen dowager is the widow of a king. 2 *Steph. Com.* So, a duchess dowager, countess dowager, etc., is the widow of a duke, earl, etc.

DOWER. 1. By the Roman law *dower* is that which a wife brings to her husband in marriage. It is sometimes spoken of as *dowry*.

2. By the law of England, *dower* is a portion which a widow hath of the lands of her husband. This extends by the common law to the third part of the freehold lands and tenements whereof the husband was solely seised for an estate of inheritance during the marriage ; and may be enjoyed for the life of the widow. But, in order to entitle a widow to dower out of the land, the husband's estate or interest therein must be such that their common issue might have inherited it. If, therefore, a man have lands to himself and the heirs of his body by his wife A., a second wife B. would not be entitled to dower out of such lands. Now, by the Dower Act of 1833, the dower of women married on or after the 1st of January, 1834, is placed entirely in the power of their husbands, as it is barred by the lands being disposed of by the husband during his life or by will, or by his giving the wife *any* lands out of which dower might have been claimed, or by declaration to bar dower either in the deed conveying the lands to the husband, or in any separate deed or by his will. Thus where the Act applies, dower can only be claimed where the husband died intestate and there was no declaration by deed barring dower. 1 *Steph. Com.*

As to copyholds, see FREEBENCH, to which the Dower Act does not apply.

DOWRESS. A widow entitled to dower; otherwise called a "tenant in dower."

DOWRY. That which the wife brings her husband in marriage. [DOWER, 1.] Not to be confounded with the *dower* of the English law. [DOWER, 2.]

DRAFT signifies a cheque or bill of exchange, or other negotiable instrument; also the rough copy of a legal document before it has been engrossed.

DRAWBACK. The repayment of duties or taxes previously charged on commodities, from which they are relieved on exportation.

DRAWEE. A person on whom a bill of exchange is *drawn*, as one who may be expected to "accept" it. [BILL OF EXCHANGE.]

DRAWER. A person who draws a bill of exchange.

DRAW-LATCHES were thieves and robbers.

DRIFT OF THE FOREST (Lat. *Agitatio animalium in forestâ*). An exact view or examination what cattle are in the forest, that it may be known whether it be over-charged or not, and whose the beasts be.

DRINKHAM, or **DRINKLEAN.** A contribution of tenants towards a *potatio* or ale, provided to entertain the lord or his steward.

DROFLAND, or **DRYFLAND,** or **DRIFT-LAND.** An ancient yearly payment made by some to their landlords, for driving their cattle through the manor to fairs and markets.

DROIT. A French word, answering to the Latin *jus*, and signifying either (1) a right ; or (2) law, as used in such phrases as "the law of nations," etc.

DROITS OF ADMIRALTY. A word applied to ships and property of the enemy taken by a subject in time of war without commission from the Crown. Any such prize would, by the effect of the prerogative, become an admiralty *droit*, or a right of the admiralty. The rights of the admiralty have been relinquished in favour of the captors. 2 *Steph. Com.*

DROITURAL ACTIONS include the "writ of right," and all actions in the nature of a writ of right, as opposed to *possessory* actions. [ACTIONS ANCESTRAL, POSSESSORY, AND DROITURAL; WRIT OF RIGHT.]

DRY EXCHANGE (Lat. *Cambium siccum* seemeth to be but a subtle term invented to disguise a foul usury, in which something is pretended to pass on both sides, whereas in truth nothing passes but on one side.

DUBITANTE (doubting). A word used in legal reports to signify that a judge cannot make up his mind as to the decision he should give.

DUCES TECUM (bring with thee). A subpœna commanding a person to appear at a certain day in court, and to *bring with him* some writings, evidences, or other things, which the court would view. 3 *Steph. Com.*

DUCES TECUM LICET LANGUIDUS. A writ formerly directed to a sheriff, upon a return (*i.e.*, upon his having made a statement endorsed on a previous writ) that he could not bring his prisoner without danger of death, commanding him to bring him nevertheless. Now quite obsolete.

DUCHY COURT OF LANCASTER. A special jurisdiction held before the chancellor of the duchy or his deputy concerning equitable interests in lands holden of the king in right of the Duchy of Lancaster. 3 *Steph. Com.* [CHANCELLOR, 2.]

DUEL is where two persons engage in a fight with intent each to murder the other. If either of them is killed the other and the seconds are guilty of murder. It is a misdemeanor to challenge another to fight or to provoke another to send a challenge. 4 *Steph. Com.* See also the next title.

DUEL, TRIAL BY. The same as trial by battel. 4 *Steph. Com.* [WAGER OF BATTEL.]

DUKE. 1. An ancient elective officer among the Germans, having an independent power over the military state. 2 *Steph. Com.*

2. The first title of nobility next to the royal family. No subject was honoured with this title till the time of Edward III., who, in the eleventh year of his reign, created his son, Edward the Black Prince, Duke of Cornwall. 2 *Steph. Com.*

DUM BENE SE GESSERIT (so long as he shall behave himself well). Words used to signify that the tenure of an office is to be held during good behaviour, and not at the pleasure of the Crown or the appointer.

DUM CASTA VIXERIT (so long as she shall live chaste). Deeds of separation between husband and wife often provide that the allowance to the wife is to be paid only so long as she lives a chaste life and may be inserted on a decree for dissolution or orders for maintenance. The clause to this effect is called the "*dum casta* clause."

DUM FUIT IN PRISONA. A writ similar to the preceding, for enabling a man to recover lands which he had conveyed away under duress of imprisonment. Abolished by 3 & 4 Will. 4, c. 27, s. 36.

DUM FUIT INFRA ÆTATEM (whilst he was within age). A writ that lay for him who, having, before he came of full age, made a conveyance of his lands, desired to recover them again from him to whom he conveyed them. Abolished by 3 & 4 Will. 4, c. 27, s. 36.

DUM FUIT NON COMPOS MENTIS. A writ that lay for a man who had aliened (*i.e.*, conveyed away) his lands while in an unsound state of mind. Abolished by 3 & 4 Will. 4, c. 27, s. 36.

DUM SOLA (while single). An expression used to indicate the period of a woman being unmarried or a widow, and therefore not labouring under the disabilities of "coverture." [COVERTURE.]

DUODECIMA MANU was when a man was defended by the oath of twelve persons, in the proceeding called *wager of law.* [WAGER OF LAW.]

DUPLEX QUERELA (double complaint or quarrel). A complaint in the nature of an appeal from the ordinary to his next immediate superior, as from a bishop to an archbishop. 3 *Steph. Com.* This complaint is available to a clergyman who, having been presented to a living, is refused institution by the ordinary.

DUPLICATE. 1. Second letters patent granted by the Lord Chancellor in a case wherein he had formerly done the same, when the first were void.

2. A copy or transcript of a deed or writing.

3. The ticket given by the pawnbroker to the pawner.

DUPLICITY IN PLEADING. [DOUBLE PLEA.]

DURANTE ABSENTIA. [ADMINISTRATOR.]

DURANTE LITE, or PENDENTE LITE. During the continuance of a suit. 2 Steph. Com. [ADMINISTRATOR.]

DURANTE MINORE ÆTATE. During minority. 2 Steph. Com. [ADMINISTRATOR.]

DURANTE VIDUITATE (during widowhood). Words used with reference to an estate granted to a widow until she marries again. 1 Steph. Com.; Wms. R. P.

DURBAR, in India, is a court, audience, or levee.

DURESS (Lat. Durities). A constraint. Of this there are two kinds.

1. Actual imprisonment, where a man actually loses his liberty.

2. Duress per minas (by threats), where the hardship is only threatened and impending. A contract made under duress is voidable at the option of the person upon whom it is practised, but the person who has employed the force cannot avail of it as a defence if the contract be insisted upon by the other party. 1 Steph. Com.

DURHAM. Formerly one of the counties palatine, in which the Bishop of Durham had jura regalia as fully as the king in his palace. [COUNTY PALATINE.] But the palatinate jurisdiction of the Bishop of Durham is taken away by 6 & 7 Will. 4, c. 19, and vested as a franchise or royalty in the Crown. And the jurisdiction of the Court of Pleas of Durham, the relic of the palatinate jurisdiction, is transferred by the Judicature Act, 1873, to the Supreme Court of Judicature. 1 Steph. Com. [SUPREME COURT OF JUDICATURE.]

"DYING WITHOUT ISSUE." These words, in a will executed since the 1st of Jan., 1838, are held, under s. 26 of the Wills Act, 1837 (7 Will. 4 & 1 Vict. c. 26), to refer only to the case of a person dying and leaving no issue behind him at the date of his death. Prior to that time the words were held to refer to the case of death and subsequent failure of issue at an indefinite time afterwards, however remote; by which interpretation many dispositions were held void for remoteness, and testators' intentions defeated in many ways. 1 Steph. Com.; Wms. R. P.

E CONVERSO. Conversely, contrariwise.

E.R. An abbreviation for Eduardus Rex (Edward, King.)

EALDERMAN, or EALDORMAN, among the Saxons, was as much as earl among the Danes. It is as much as an elder or statesman, called by the Romans senator. [ALDERMAN.]

EARL. An ancient title of nobility, equivalent to ealdorman among the Saxons. Earls were also called schiremen, because they had each the civil government of a several division or shire. The word is now a title of nobility ranking between a marquis and a viscount. 2 Steph. Com. [COUNT, 1; COUSIN.]

EARL MARSHAL. The officer who, jointly with the Lord High Constable, presided over the Court of Chivalry. Under him is the heralds' office or college of arms. The office is of great antiquity and has been for several ages hereditary in the family of the Howards. 3 Steph. Com. [COURT OF CHIVALRY.]

EARLDOM. The status of an earl; but originally the jurisdiction of an earl. [DOME.]

EARMARK. A mark for the purpose of identifying anything which is a subject of property.

EARNEST. The evidence of a contract of sale; money paid as part of a larger sum, or goods delivered as part of a larger quantity; or anything given as security to bind a bargain. Sale of Goods Act, 1893 (56 & 57 Vict. c. 71), s. 5. 2 Steph. Com.

EASEMENT. A right enjoyed by a man over his neighbour's property ; such as a right of way, or a right of passage for water ; called in the Roman law a *servitude.* Generally (and, according to some authorities, necessarily) it belongs to a man as being the owner of some specific house or land, which is then called the *dominant tenement.* 1 *Steph. Com.; Gale on Easements.* [DOMINANT TENEMENT ; SERVITUDE.]

EAST INDIA COMPANY. A body of persons originally incorporated for purposes purely commercial, who gradually acquired immense territorial dominions, by which they became effectively (though subject to the undoubted supremacy of the British Crown) the sovereigns of India. Their exclusive right of trading to India was abolished, in 1833, by 3 & 4 Will. 4, c. 85, and they were debarred from engaging, in the future, in commercial transactions. In 1858, by 21 & 22 Vict. c. 106, the political powers and rights of the East India Company were transferred to the Crown ; and by 36 & 37 Vict. c. 17, the company was dissolved as from the 1st of June, 1874. 1 *Steph. Com.*

EASTER DUES AND OFFERINGS are payments made by parishioners to their clergy at Easter as a composition for personal tithes or the tithes for personal labour. Recoverable under 7 & 8 Will. 3, c. 6. See 2 & 3 *Vict. c.* 62, *s.* 9 ; *R. v. Hall*, L. R. 1 Q. B. 632 ; *Cripps' Law of the Church and Clergy, Bk. II. ch. 3* ; *Phillimore's Eccl. Law.*

EASTERLING. [STERLING.]

EAT INDE SINE DIE. A form of words indicating that a defendant may be dismissed from an action, and "go without day," that is, without any future day appointed for his re-appearance.

EAVES-DROPPERS are such as listen under walls or windows, or the eaves of a house, to hearken after discourse, and thereupon to frame slanderous and mischievous tales. 4 *Steph. Com.*

ECCLESIA. A church or place set apart for the service of God. Sometimes it means a parsonage.

ECCLESIASTICAL COMMISSIONERS. A body of commissioners appointed to consider the state of the several dioceses, with reference to the amount of their revenues, and the more equal distribution of episcopal duties ; also the best means of providing for the cure of souls in parishes. The first commissioners for this purpose were Royal Commissioners, appointed in 1835 ; and the statute incorporating the Ecclesiastical Commissioners is 6 & 7 Will. 4, c. 77. It has been amended by various subsequent statutes. The Ecclesiastical Commissioners now comprise the bishops and the chief justices, and other persons of distinction. 2 *Steph. Com.*

ECCLESIASTICAL CORPORATION. A corporation of which the members are entirely spiritual persons, such as bishops, parsons, deans and chapters, archdeacons, etc. 3 *Steph. Com.* The visitor of an ecclesiastical corporation is the ordinary. 3 *Steph. Com.*

ECCLESIASTICAL COURTS are the Archdeacon's Court, the Consistory Courts, the Court of Peculiars, and the Court of Arches, the Prerogative Courts of the two archbishops in the Faculty Court. These are the ecclesiastical courts proper ; but there is also the Court of Final Appeal, which used to be the Court of Delegates, but is now the Judicial Committee of the Privy Council. 3 *Steph. Com.* [JUDICIAL COMMITTEE ; SUPREME COURT OF JUDICATURE.]

EFFECTS. Goods and chattels ; a man's property.

EFFRACTORES. Burglars that break open houses to steal.

EGYPTIANS. Wandering impostors and jugglers, using no craft nor feat of merchandise, pretending to tell men's and women's fortunes, and by craft and subtlety defrauding the people of their money. Such persons, remaining one month within this kingdom, were formerly liable to capital punishment. 22 *Hen.* 8, *c.* 10 ; 4 *Steph. Com.* They are now generally called gypsies.

EIGNE (Fr. *Aisné*, or *Aîné*). The eldest. [BASTARD EIGNE.]

EIRE (Lat. *Iter*). A journey. [EYRE.]

EJECIT INFRA TERMINUM (he ejected him before the end of his term). [QUARE EJECIT INFRA TERMINUM.]

EJECTIONE CUSTODIÆ. A writ which lay against him that cast out the guardian from any land during the minority of the heir.

EJECTIONE FIRMÆ. A writ which lay to eject a tenant from his holding. See next title. [ACTIONS MIXED; ACTIONS REAL AND PERSONAL; EJECTMENT.]

EJECTMENT. An action to try the title to land. The old action, which was very elaborate in procedure, was abolished by the Common Law Procedure Act, 1852, which, by ss. 168—170, directed that a writ, in a prescribed form, was to be addressed, on the part of the claimant, to the person or persons in possession, by name, and generally "to all persons entitled to defend the possession" of the premises therein described; commanding such of them as deny the claimant's title to appear in court and defend the possession of the property. Not only the person to whom the writ is directed, but any other person (on filing an affidavit that he or his tenant is in possession, and obtaining the leave of the court or a judge), is allowed to appear and defend. 3 *Steph. Com.*

According to the Judicature Rules, the plaintiff must indorse the writ of summons with a statement in accordance with the forms given in R. S. C., Appendix C., sect. vii. If the possession be vacant, service may, by Ord. IX. r. 9, be effected by posting the writ upon the door of the dwelling-house, or some conspicuous part of the property. The action is now called one for the recovery of land, and in certain cases by landlord against tenant may be by specially endorsed writ under Ord. III. r. 6.

EJUSDEM GENERIS (of the same kind or nature). Where in a statute, etc., particular classes are specified by name, followed by general words, the meaning of the general words is generally cut down by reference to the particular words, and the general words are taken to apply to those *ejusdem generis* with the particular classes.

ELDER BRETHREN. The masters of the Trinity House, by whom the affairs of the corporation are managed. [TRINITY HOUSE.]

ELECTION is when a man is left to his own free will to take or do one thing or another, which he pleases. But it is more frequently applied to the choosing between two rights by a person who derives one of them under an instrument in which an intention appears (or is implied by a court of law or equity) that he should not enjoy both. *E.g.*, where A. gives B. property, but by the same instrument gives to C. property which really belongs to B., B. would have to elect between retaining his own property and to that extent abandoning what A gave him, or taking what A gave him and allowing his (B.'s) property to go to C.

The word is also commonly applied to the choosing of officers or representatives; especially the choosing, by a constituency, of some person or persons to represent it in parliament.

ELECTION COMMITTEES. Committees of the House of Commons formerly appointed for the purpose of determining the validity of elections in cases where a petition had been presented to the House, impugning the validity of an election on the ground of corrupt practices, or for any other cause. This jurisdiction is now exercised by judges of the High Court. *May's Parl. Pract.; 2 Steph. Com.* [ELECTION JUDGES.]

ELECTION JUDGES. Judges of the High Court selected in pursuance of the Parliamentary Elections Act, 1868 (31 & 32 Vict. c. 125) s. 11, and the Jud. Act, 1873, s. 38, for the trial of election petitions.

ELECTION OF MEMBERS OF PARLIAMENT. See the *Reform Act*, 1832; the *Representation of the People Act*, 1867; the *Ballot Act*, 1872; the *Representation of the People Act*, 1884; the *Redistribution of Seats Act*, 1885; *Rogers on Elections*, etc.

ELECTION PETITION. A petition complaining of an undue return of a member to serve in parliament. Such petitions were, before the year 1868, presented to the House of Commons; they are now presented to the King's Bench Division of the High Court. *May's Parl. Pract.; 2 Steph. Com.* [ELECTION COMMITTEES.]

ELEEMOSYNÆ. The possessions belonging to churches.

ELEEMOSYNARY CORPORATION. A corporation constituted for the perpetual distribution of the free alms or bounty of the founder, to such persons as he has directed. Of this kind are hospitals and colleges. 3 *Steph. Com.*

ELEGIT. A species of execution, given by the Statute of Westminster the Second (13 Edw. 1, c. 18). Before that statute, a man could only have the *profits* of lands of a debtor in satisfaction of his judgment, but not the *possession* of the lands themselves. The statute granted this writ (called an elegit because it is in the *choice* of a judgment-creditor whether he will sue out this writ or a *fieri facias*), by which the judgment-debtor's goods and chattels are appraised and delivered to the creditor in satisfaction of his debt. If they should prove insufficient, then one half of the debtor's lands of freehold tenure was further to be delivered over to the judgment-creditor, to hold until the debt was levied, or the debtor's interest therein had expired. But by stat. 1 & 2 Vict. c. 110, s. 11, it was provided that, under an *elegit*, the sheriff should deliver execution of *all* the debtor's lands, including those of copyhold or customary tenure.

The creditor, while in the enjoyment of an estate under a writ of *elegit*, is called *tenant by elegit*; and his estate is called an estate held by *elegit*. 1 *Steph. Com.; 3 Steph. Com.*

ELEMENTARY EDUCATION ACTS. 1. The stat. 33 & 34 Vict. c. 75, passed in 1870, to provide for elementary education in England and Wales.

2. The stat. 36 & 37 Vict. c. 86, passed in 1873, for the purpose of making certain alterations in the Act of 1870, above mentioned.

ELISORS. Two officers appointed to name a jury, in case neither the sheriff nor the coroners are indifferent and unexceptionable persons for the performance of such a duty. 3 *Steph. Com.*

ELOIGN, or **ELOINE** (Fr. *Eloigner*). To remove or send away. 3 *Steph. Com.*

ELOIGNMENT. Removal; sending away.

ELONGATUS. Withdrawn; of a man withdrawn from the sheriff's jurisdiction.

EMANCIPATION. A word which, in the Roman law, originally signified selling out of one's possession by the form of *mancipation*. By a law of the Twelve Tables, a father was not allowed to sell his son more than three times; and if a son was manumitted after being three times sold by his father, he became free. Afterwards, a threefold sale became a matter of form for giving freedom to a son; and hence the modern use of the word *emancipation*.

EMBARGO ON SHIPS. A prohibition issued by the Crown upon ships, forbidding them to go out of any port. 2 *Steph. Com.*

The term "embargo" is borrowed from the Spanish law procedure, and signifies *arrest* of *sequestration*; and it is applied to the seizure or detention of persons or property which happen to be within the territory of the nation at the time of seizure. The seizure of ships and cargoes under the authority of municipal law is spoken of as a *civil* embargo. An *international* embargo, on the other hand, is an act not of civil procedure, but of hostile detention. It may be made for the same object as *reprisals* are made upon the high seas, namely, for the satisfaction of a debt or the redress of an injury; and it may also be made by way of prelude to war. *Twiss' Law of Nations, Part II. s. 12. Hall's International Law.*

EMBEZZLEMENT. The appropriation by a clerk or servant of the property of his master. It differs from *larceny* properly so called, inasmuch as embezzlement is committed in respect of property which is not, at the time, in the actual or legal possession of the owner. 4 *Steph. Com.* [LARCENY.]

EMBLEMENTS. The profits of a crop which has been sown, *i.e.*, any products created by *annual industry*, *e.g.*, corn as opposed to grass, *fructus industriales*, not *fructus naturales*. And see 14 & 15 Vict. c. 25, s. 1. The general rule as to emblements sown by an outgoing tenant, whose estate ends before harvest time, is, that the outgoing tenant or his representatives shall have the crop if the termination of the estate has arisen from the act of God or the will of the landlord, but not if the termination of the estate is due to effluxion of time, or any act of forfeiture committed by the tenant. 1 *Steph. Com.; Woodfall, L. & T.*

EMBRACEOR. A person guilty of embracery. [EMBRACERY.]

EMBRACERY. An offence consisting in the attempt to influence a jury corruptly. It is a misdemeanor punishable by fine and imprisonment by common law and by statute. 6 *Geo.* 4, *c.* 50, *s.* 61; 4 *Steph. Com.*

EMINENT DOMAIN (Lat. *Dominium eminens*) is the right which every state or sovereign power has to use the property of its citizens for the common welfare. This right is the true foundation of the right of taxation.

EMPANEL. [IMPANELLING A JURY.]

EMPARLANCE. [IMPARLANCE.]

EMPHYTEUSIS may be described as a perpetual lease. It was a right known in the Roman law, by which the perpetual use of land was given to a person for the payment of rent. *Bell; Maine's Ancient Law; 1 Steph. Com.*

EMPLEAD. [IMPLEAD.]

EMPTOR. A buyer. [CAVEAT EMPTOR.]

EN AUTER DROIT, or **EN AUTRE DROIT** (in another person's right); as, for instance, an executor holds property and brings actions in right of those entitled to his testator's estate.

ENABLING STATUTE. A statute enabling persons or corporations to do that which, before it was passed, they could not do. The phrase is used especially of the stat. 32 Hen. 8, c. 28, by which persons holding land in fee simple in right of their churches may make leases for three lives or twenty-one years, so as to bind their successors, provided they observe the several requisites and formalities prescribed by the statute. *2 Steph. Com.*

ENCROACHMENT. An unlawful gaining upon the possession of another.

ENDORSEE. [INDORSEMENT.]

ENDORSEMENT. [INDORSEMENT.]

ENDOWMENT signifies—
1. The giving or assigning dower to a woman. *1 Steph. Com.* [DOWER.]
2. The setting or severing of a sufficient portion for a vicar towards his perpetual maintenance. *2 Steph. Com.*
3. Also any permanent provision for the maintenance of schools is called an *endowment. 3 Steph. Com.*
4. And the word is now generally used of a permanent provision for any institution or person.

ENEMY GOODS, ENEMY SHIP. A maxim which would imply that goods of an enemy carried on board a neutral ship render the ship liable to confiscation as enemy's property. Such a doctrine was contended for by France in the 16th and 17th centuries, but never received general acceptance. *Twiss' Law of Nations, Part II., s. 83.*

ENEMY SHIP, ENEMY GOODS. A maxim which would imply that the fact of goods being in an enemy's ship renders them liable to confiscation as enemy's goods. The doctrine was sanctioned by various treaties between the years 1640 and 1780, but it has never been regarded as part of the general law of nations. It was repudiated at the Declaration of Paris of 1856, by which it is declared that neutral goods, other than contraband of war, are exempt from capture in enemy's ships. *Twiss' Law of Nations, Part II., ss. 83, 86.* [DECLARATION OF PARIS.]

ENFEOFF. To invest another with a freehold estate by the process of feoffment. [FEOFFMENT.]

ENFRANCHISE. To make free, to incorporate a man into a society or body politic.
Enfranchisement is a word which is now used principally in three different senses:—
1. Of conferring a right to vote at a parliamentary election.
2. Of giving to a borough or other constituency a right to return a member or members to parliament.
3. Of the conversion of copyhold into freehold, as to which see COPYHOLD. *1 Steph. Com.*

ENGLESCHERIE. The name given in the times of Canute and of William the Conqueror to the presentment of the fact that a person slain was an Englishman. This fact, if established, excused the neighbourhood from the fine they would have been liable to, had a Dane or a Norman been slain. *4 Steph. Com.*

ENGROSSING. 1. The getting into one's possession, or buying up, in gross or wholesale, large quantities of corn, or other dead victuals, with intent to sell them again. The total engrossing of any commodity, with intent to sell it at an unreasonable price, was an offence at common law. But this is abolished by 7 & 8 Vict. c. 24; it is also called *regrating*, or forestalling the market. *4 Steph. Com.*

2. The fair copying by a clerk of a deed or other legal instrument.

ENLARGE. To *enlarge* frequently means to put off or extend the time for doing anything. Thus, enlarging a rule signifies extending the time for doing that which by a rule of court is required to be done. See also the following title.

ENLARGING AN ESTATE (Fr. *Enlarger l'estate*) is where a man's *estate* (*i.e.*, interest) in land is increased ; as, for instance, where there is an estate in A. for life, with remainder to B. and his heirs, and B. releases his estate to A., A.'s estate is said to be *enlarged* into a fee simple. 1 *Steph. Com.*

ENQUEST. An inquisition by jurors. [INQUEST.]

ENQUIRY, WRIT OF. [WRIT OF INQUIRY.]

ENROLMENT is the registering, recording, on entering of any lawful act. Thus, for instance, bargains and sales of freeholds were, under the Statute of Enrolment (27 Hen. 8, c. 16), required to be enrolled ; so, by the Statute of Mortmain (9 Geo. 2, c. 36), are conveyances to corporations ; and so are disentailing deeds by the Act for the Abolition of Fines and Recoveries (3 & 4 Will. 4, c. 74). We also speak of the enrolment of decrees in Chancery, which might be done by a party who desired to appeal therefrom to the House of Lords, as there could be no further hearing in Chancery by way of appeal from an enrolled decree, except the enrolment were vacated by the Lord Chancellor, which would be done under special circumstances of fraud or irregularity, on the application of any party interested. The effect of the Judicature Act is practically to abolish enrolment of decrees.

ENROLMENTS, STATUTE OF. [ENROLMENT.]

ENTAIL, in legal treatises, is used to signify an estate tail, especially with reference to the restraint which such an estate imposes upon its owner, or, in other words, the points wherein such an estate differs from an estate in fee simple. [DISENTAILING DEED ; ESTATE, I.; FINE, 1 ; RECOVERY.] And this is often its popular sense ; but sometimes it is, in popular language, used differently, so as to signify a succession of life estates, as when it is said that " an entail ends with A. B.," meaning that A. B. is the first person

who is entitled to bar or cut off the entail, being in law the first tenant in tail.

ENTERING APPEARANCE. [APPEARANCE.]

ENTERING BILLS SHORT. This is when a banker, having received an undue bill from a customer, does not carry the amount to the credit of the latter, but notes down the receipt of the bill in the customer's account, with the amount and the time when due. Whether, however, any given bill is to be regarded as "a short bill " (that is, not to be treated as cash) must depend not so much upon whether it has been " entered short " as upon the surrounding circumstances, and the general mode of dealing between the parties.

ENTERING CAUSE FOR TRIAL. This is done by a plaintiff in an action, who has given notice of trial, depositing with the proper officer of the court the *nisi prius* record, with the panel of jurors annexed. 3 *Steph. Com.*; 38 & 39 *Vict. c. 77.* [NISI PRIUS RECORD.]

ENTERING JUDGMENT. The successful party to an action causes the judgment to be entered by the proper officer of the court. This is done upon his delivery to such officer the associates' certificate of the judge's directions at the trial, together with a copy of the pleadings. 3 *Steph. Com.*

ENTERING SHORT. [ENTERING BILLS SHORT.]

ENTERPLEADER. [INTERPLEADER.]

ENTIRE CONTRACT. A contract wherein everything to be done on one side is the consideration for everything to be done on the other. This is opposed to a severable or apportionable contract.

ENTIRE TENANCY signifies a sole possession in one man, in contradistinction to a several tenancy, which implies a tenancy jointly or in common with others.

ENTIRETIES, TENANCY BY. Where an estate was devised or conveyed to husband and wife during coverture, they were said to be *tenants by entireties, i.e.*, each was seised of the whole estate and neither of a part. They were seised *per tout*, and not *per my et per tout*. Now altered by the Married Women's Property Act, 1882.

ENTIRETY. Denotes the whole, as contradistinguished from a moiety, etc.

ENTRY signifies—

1. Putting down a mercantile transaction in a book of account.

2. The taking possession of lands or tenements. See the following titles.

ENTRY, FORCIBLE. [FORCIBLE ENTRY.]

ENTRY, RIGHT OF. A right to enter and take possession of lands or tenements without bringing an action to recover the same ; a remedy allowed in various cases by common or statute law, or the deed by which an estate (*i.e.*, a person's interest in land) is marked out and limited. See 3 *Steph. Com.*

ENTRY, WRIT OF. A writ by which a party claiming the right of possession to lands disproved the title of the tenant or possessor, by showing the unlawful means by which he entered or continued possession, by *intrusion*, or *disseisin*, or the like.

A writ of entry was called a writ of entry *sur disseisin sur intrusion*, *sur alienation*, etc., according to the circumstances of the case. 3 *Bl.;* 3 *Steph. Com.*

Writs of entry, having been long superseded in practice by the action of ejectment [EJECTMENT], were abolished in 1833 by 3 & 4 Will. 4, c. 27, s. 36.

ENUMERATORS. Persons appointed to take the census.

ENURE. To take effect, operate, result, or be available. When we say that a transaction enures to the benefit of A. B., we mean that A. B. gets the benefit of it.

ENVOY. A diplomatic agent despatched by one state to another.

EO NOMINE. In that name ; on that account.

EPISCOPALIA. Synodals and other customary payments from the clergy to their bishops or diocesan, which dues were formerly collected by the rural deans, and by them transmitted to the bishop.

Provision is now made by 23 & 24 Vict. c. 124, s. 2, for the payment of these emoluments to the Ecclesiastical Commissioners. [ECCLESIASTICAL COMMISSIONERS.]

EQUITABLE ASSETS. Assets of a deceased person, which cannot be made available to a creditor of the deceased but through the medium of a court of equity. [ASSETS.]

EQUITABLE DEFENCE. A defence to an action at common law on *equitable* grounds ; that is, on grounds which, prior to the passing of the Common Law Procedure Act, 1854 (17 & 18 Vict. c. 125), would have been cognizable only in a court of equity. 17 & 18 *Vict. c.* 125, *ss.* 83—85 ; see now Jud. Act, 1873, s. 24.

EQUITABLE ESTATE. An estate in land not fully recognised as such except in a court of *equity.* 1 *Steph. Com.; Wms. R. P.*

EQUITABLE MORTGAGE. A mortgage recognised in a court of equity only. An equitable mortgage may be effected either by a written instrument or by a deposit of title deeds with or without writing. 3 *Steph. Com.; Sm. Man. Eq.*

EQUITABLE WASTE. Waste hitherto cognizable only in a court of equity, as by a tenant for life pulling down a mansion-house, or felling timber standing for ornament, or doing other permanent injury to the inheritance. This kind of waste is forbidden, even to a tenant for life who holds *without impeachment of waste* ; and this doctrine is recognised in the Judicature Act, 36 & 37 Vict. c. 66, s. 25, sub-s. 3. 3 *Steph. Com.; Wms. R. P.*

EQUITY is described by *Cowel* as being of two sorts, and these of contrary effects ; for the one doth abridge and take from the letter of the law, the other doth enlarge and add thereto. And the instance of the first kind he gives is that of a person acquitted of a capital crime on the ground of insanity or infancy. The instance he gives of the latter is that of the application of a statute to *administrators*, which in its terms applies to *executors* only. [ADMINISTRATOR ; EQUITY OF A STATUTE ; EXECUTOR.]

But these usages of the term are comparatively rare at the present day, and equity in its technical sense has been defined as that portion of English jurisprudence which was formerly administered exclusively by the Court of Chancery and the Court of Exchequer, and subsequently by the Court of Chancery only ; concurrently in some

EQUITY—*continued.*

cases with local courts having a like jurisdiction, especially since 1865, when a so-called "equitable jurisdiction" was conferred upon the county courts.

The distinction (says Mr. Haynes) between equity in the technical sense and law, is truly matter of *history*, and not matter of *substance*. The short sum of the matter is this—that the Court of Chancery recognises certain rights and applies certain remedies, which the courts of law might have equally recognised and applied, but did not. *Haynes' Eq.*

Since the Judicature Act, 1873, every Division of the High Court and the judges thereof have all the jurisdiction of the other Divisions and of the judges thereof, in addition to their own original jurisdiction; and where there is any conflict between the rules of common law and equity, the latter are to prevail: but for reasons of practical convenience such matters as were formerly dealt with in the Court of Chancery are still assigned to the Chancery Division. [SUPREME COURT OF JUDICATURE.]

EQUITY OF A STATUTE. The sound interpretation of a statute, the words of which may be too general, too special, or otherwise inaccurate and defective. 3 *Steph. Com.*

EQUITY OF REDEMPTION. The right, cognizable in a court of equity, which a mortgagor has, on payment of the mortgage debt, with interest and costs, to *redeem* the mortgaged estate, even after the right of redemption is gone at law. 1 *Steph. Com.; Sm. Man. Eq.*

EQUITY TO A SETTLEMENT is the right which a wife has in equity to have a portion of her equitable property settled upon herself and her children. This right was originally granted to the wife when the husband sued in a court of equity for the purpose of reducing the property into his possession, on the principle that he who seeks equity must do equity. It has, however, now for at least a century been settled that this equity may be asserted actively by the wife. *Lady Elibank* v. *Montolieu* (1 *Wh. & T. L. C., Eq.*); *Smith's Man. Eq.* The amount to be settled on the wife and children is in the discretion of the court, and varies according to circumstances.

Now by the Married Women's Property Act, 1882, all a wife's property, both real and personal, vests in her as her separate estate.

ERRANT (Lat. *Itinerans*, journeying) is a word attributed to justices that go on circuit, and to bailiffs travelling from place to place to execute process.

ERROR signifieth especially an error in pleading, or in the process; and the writ which is brought for remedy of this oversight is called a writ of error, or, in Latin, *breve de errore corrigendo* (a writ for correcting an error). A writ of error is that properly which lieth to redress false judgment given in any court of record. *Cowel.* [FALSE JUDGMENT, WRIT OF.]

Proceedings in error are now abolished by the Judicature Act, 1875, Ord. LVIII. r. 1, except in criminal cases, the appeal system being substituted in civil cases. 3 *Steph. Com.*

Writ of error lies also in criminal cases for notorious mistakes in the judgment or other parts of the record. These writs of error to reverse judgments in case of misdemeanors are allowed, as a matter of course on sufficient probable cause shown to the Attorney-General, whose decision on the matter is final. Writs of error to reverse judgment in felonies are allowed only *ex gratiâ*, and not without express warrant under the sign manual, or at least by the consent of the Attorney-General. 4 *Steph. Com.*

ERRORS EXCEPTED. A phrase appended to an account stated, to excuse slight mistakes or oversights.

ESCAPE. A violent or privy evasion out of some lawful restraint. There are two kinds of escape: *voluntary*, which happens when a prisoner escapes with the consent of the keeper, sheriff, or other person who has him in charge; and *negligent*, when the escape is against the will of the sheriff or other such officer. Officers and others negligently permitting a felon to escape are punishable by fine, but voluntarily permitting an escape amounts to the same kind of offence as that of which the prisoner is guilty, and is punishable in the same degree. See 28 & 29. Vict. c. 126.

ESCAPE-WARRANT. A warrant addressed to all sheriffs, etc. throughout England, to re-take an escaped prisoner and to commit him to gaol when taken.

ESCHEAT. An obstruction of the course of descent, by which land naturally results back by a kind of reversion to the original grantor or lord of the fee.

Escheats are divided by Blackstone into escheats *propter defectum sanguinis*, and escheats *propter delictum tenentis;* the one sort, if a tenant dies without heirs ; and the other, if his blood be attainted. This latter form differs from a forfeiture of goods and chattels in that a forfeiture always went to the Crown, but an escheat to the immediate lord (who might or might not be the king).

Now, by s. 1 of the Felony Act, 1870 (33 & 34 Vict. c. 23), no confession, verdict. inquest, conviction or judgment of or for any treason, or felony, or *felo de se*, shall cause any forfeiture or escheat.

So that escheat *propter delictum tenentis* is now abolished. But escheat *propter defectum sanguinis* now applies to equitable interests as well as legal, viz., on death of the beneficiary intestate and without representatives. 47 & 48 *Vict. c.* 61, *s.* 4 ; 1 *Steph. Com.*

ESCHEATOR. An officer, formerly existing in every county, appointed by the Lord Treasurer to hold inquests with a view to enforcing right of escheat. Now superseded by procedure under the Escheat Procedure Act, 1887 (50 & 51 Vict. c. 53).

ESCROW (Lat. *Scriptum*). A scroll or writing sealed and delivered to a person not a party thereto, to be held by him till some condition or conditions be performed by the party intended to be benefited thereby ; and, on the fulfilment of those conditions, to be delivered to such party, and to take effect as a deed to all intents and purposes. 1 *Steph. Com.*

ESCUAGE (Lat. *Scutagium*) in law signifieth a kind of knight's-service, called *service of the shield*, whereby the tenant was bound to follow his lord into the Scotch or Welsh wars at his own charge. But the above form of *escuage*, which was *uncertain* in its burdens, was changed in process of time into an *escuage certain*, whereby a yearly rent was paid in lieu of all services; which latter was *escuage* merely in name. But knight's service, with other military tenures, was abolished by 12 Car. 2, c. 24. 1 *Steph. Com.; Wms. R. P.* [KNIGHT-SERVICE.]

ESLISORS. [ELISORS.]

ESNECY. A prerogative given to the eldest coparcener, to choose first after an inheritance is divided. [CO-PARCENARY.]

ESPLEES (Lat. *Expletia*) seem to be the full profits that the ground or land yieldeth ; as, the hay of the meadows, the feed of the pasture, the corn of the arable land ; the rents, service, and such like issues. *Cowel.*

ESQUIRE, or **ESQUIER** (Lat. *Armiger ;* Fr. *Escuier*, a word derived from the Latin *scutiger*, shield-bearer) was originally such a one as attended a knight in time of war, and carried his shield.

There are several sorts of esquires :—

1. The eldest sons of knights, and their eldest sons.

2. The younger sons of peers, and their eldest sons.

3. Esquires created by the king's letters patent, or other investiture, and their eldest sons.

4. Esquires by virtue of their offices ; as justices of the peace, and others who bear any office of trust under the Crown, and are named "esquires" by the Crown in their commission or appointment.

5. Barristers-at-law, and doctors in their several faculties.

6. Esquires of Knights of the Bath, each of whom constitutes three at his installation.

7. All foreign peers.

8. The chiefs of ancient families are so by prescription. 2 *Steph. Com.*

ESSOIN, ESSOIGN, ESSOINE, ESSOIGNE, or **ASSOIGN** (Lat. *Exoneratio*) signifieth in the common law the allegation of an *excuse* for him that is summoned or sought for to appear. Thus *casting an essoign* means alleging an excuse for failing to appear.

ESSOIN DAY OF TERM. The first day of term, on which the court sat to take *essoigns*, or excuses, for such as did not appear according to the summons of the writ. 11 Geo. 4 & 1 Will. 4, c. 70, s. 6, did away with the essoin day for all purposes as part of the term.

ESTATE. An interest in land.

Estates may be variously classified:—

I. According to the *quantity* of interest. The primary division of estates is into such as are *freehold* and such as are *not freehold*.

The principal freehold estates are :—

1. Estates in fee simple.

ESTATE—*continued*.

   2. Estates in fee tail, otherwise called estates tail.

   3. Estates for life.

An *estate in fee simple* is that which a man hath to hold to him and his heirs. It is the most extensive estate of inheritance that a man can possess ; it is the entire property in the land, and to it is attached the right of alienation to the full extent of the interest which is vested in the tenant himself, or for any smaller estate. For the limited form of this estate, called a " fee simple conditional," see CONDITIONAL FEE.

An *estate in fee tail* is that which a man hath to hold to him and the heirs of his body, or to him and particular heirs of his body. By the statute *De Donis conditionalibus* (13 Edw. 1, st. 1, c. 1, passed in 1285), an estate so limited devolved, at the death of the donee, on his issue ; and, on the failure of issue, reverted to the donor and his heirs. In the construction of this statute the judges held that the donee had an estate which they called a *fee tail*. This estate thus assumed the form of a perpetual entail until the reign of Edward IV., when, in a celebrated case called *Taltarum's case*, it was held by the judges that an estate tail might be *barred* by the collusive and fictitious proceeding called a *common recovery* [RECOVERY], and thus turned into an estate in fee simple. And, in the reign of Henry VIII., the process called a *fine* was made effectual to enable a tenant in tail to bar his issue, but not the remainderman or reversioner. [FINE, 1.] Fines and recoveries were abolished by 3 & 4 Will. 4, c. 74, and now an estate tail may in general be barred by a simple entailing deed to be inrolled in Chancery within six months, in cases where it could, previously to the Act, have been barred by fine or recovery.

But estates tail of which the reversion is in the Crown cannot be barred so far as regards the reversion ; and estates tail created by Act of parliament cannot in general be barred. So, a tenant in tail after possibility of issue extinct cannot bar his estate. [TENANT IN TAIL AFTER POSSIBILITY OF ISSUE EXTINCT.]

An *estate for life* is in general an estate to one for his own life. But an estate during widowhood is also reckoned among estates for life.

In addition to these three kinds of estate we may notice the following kinds, which are less than freehold,—

   4. An estate for years.

   5. An estate at will.

   6. An estate at sufferance.

An *estate for years* is often spoken of as "a term of years." The instrument by which it is created is called a *lease* or *demise*, and the estate itself is called a *leasehold interest*. It is generally made subject to covenants and conditions.

An *estate at will* is where lands and tenements are let by one man to another to have and to hold at the will of the lessor, and the tenant by force of this lease obtains possession.

An *estate at sufferance* is where one comes into possession under a lawful demise, and, after such demise is ended, wrongfully continues the possession.

Besides these several divisions of estates there is another species, called an *estate upon condition* ; which is an estate whose existence depends upon the happening or not happening of some event. Under these are included,—

   7. Estates held upon condition *implied*.

   8. Estates held upon condition *expressed*.

Under these last may be included,—

   9. Estates held in mortgage. [MORTGAGE.]

   10. Estates by statute merchant or statute staple. [STATUTE MERCHANT; STATUTE STAPLE.]

   11. Estates held by elegit. [ELEGIT.]

II. Estates may also be divided with regard to the *time* at which the quantity of interest is to be enjoyed. Thus, an estate may be,—

   1. An estate in possession.

   2. An estate in expectancy.

An estate in *possession* implies a right of present possession, involving a right of entry ; that is, the right of entering upon and taking possession of the land withheld, where that can be done without breach of the peace. [POSSESSION.]

An estate in *expectancy* is of two kinds—an estate in *reversion* and an estate in *remainder* ; the distinction between the two being as follows :—

   1. When a person grants an estate for life, or other estate of limited interest to another, such estate is called a *particular estate* ; and the residue remaining in the grantor is called his *reversion*.

   2. When a person grants an estate for life, or other *particular estate* to one man, and the residue to another, the interest of the latter

ESTATE—*continued.*

is called a *remainder*, though it is often popularly spoken of as a *reversion.*

III. Estates may further be divided, with respect to the number and connection of their owners, into,—

1. Estates in severalty. [SEVERALTY.]
2. Estates in joint-tenancy. [JOINT-TENANCY.]
3. Estates in coparcenary. [COPARCENARY.]
4. Estates in common. [COMMON, TENANCY IN.] 2 *Bl.*; 1 *Steph. Com.*; *Wms. R. P.*

ESTATE CLAUSE. An *express* clause in conveyances, added to the description of the parcels, passing all the estate, etc. of the grantor in the property conveyed. It is now *implied* by virtue of the Conveyancing Act, 1881, s. 63.

ESTATE DUTY. A duty levied upon the principal value of all property, real or personal, settled or not settled, which " passed " on the death of a person dying on or after August 2nd, 1894. The rate of duty is graduated according to the total value of the estate. See the *Finance Act*, 1894 (57 & 58 *Vict. c.* 30), and the *Finance Act*, 1900 (62 & 63 *Vict. c.* 7.) See also SETTLEMENT ESTATE DUTY.

ESTATES OF THE REALM are, according to *Blackstone* and *Hallam,*—

1. The lords spiritual.
2. The lords temporal, who sit together in one house of parliament.
3. The commons, who sit by themselves in the other.

Some writers, however, have argued, from the want of a separate assembly and separate negative of the prelates, that the lords spiritual and temporal are now in reality only one estate; which is unquestionably true in every effectual sense, though the ancient distinction between them still nominally continues.

ESTOP, TO. [ESTOPPEL.]

ESTOPPEL. An impediment or bar arising from a man's own conduct; whereby he is prohibited from averring or proving anything in contradiction to what he has either expressly avowed, or has by his conduct led others to believe to be the case.

It is of three kinds :—

1. By matter of record, which imports such absolute and incontrovertible verity that no person against whom it is producible shall be permitted to aver against it. 3 *Steph. Com.*

2. By deed. No person can be allowed to dispute his own solemn deed, which is conclusive against him and those claiming under him. 1 *Steph. Com.*; 2 *Steph. Com.*

3. In *pais*, *e.g.*, a tenant cannot dispute his landlord's title. 3 *Steph. Com.*

ESTOVERIIS HABENDIS, WRIT DE. [ESTOVERS.]

ESTOVERS (*Estoverium*) signifieth nourishment or maintenance (*Cowel*); or wood for fuel, which a tenant for life is entitled to out of the estate. 1 *Steph. Com.* [COMMON, IV.] Also, the alimony allowed by the Ecclesiastical Court to a wife was sometimes called her *estovers;* for which, if the husband refused payment, the wife had, at common law, a writ *de estoveriis habendis,* to recover them. 2 *Steph. Com.*

ESTRAYS are such valuable animals as are found wandering in any manor or lordship, and no man knoweth the owner of them, in which case the law gives them to the king as the general owner and lord paramount of the soil; and they now most commonly belong to the lord of the manor, by special grant from the Crown. 2 *Steph. Com.*

ESTREAT (Lat. *Extractum*). 1. A true copy, or duplicate, of an original writing. 2. The *estreat of a recognizance* means the *extracting*, or taking out from among the other records, of a recognizance or obligation which has become forfeited, and sending it to be enforced; or, in some cases, directing it to be levied by the sheriff, and returned by the clerk of the peace to the Lords of the Treasury. 2 *Steph. Com.*; *Oke's Mag. Syn.*

ESTREATED RECOGNIZANCE. [ESTREAT, 2.]

ESTREPE (Fr. *Estropier*, to maim). To commit waste. [ESTREPEMENT.]

ESTREPEMENT signifies waste or spoil made by a tenant for life upon any lands or woods, to the prejudice of the reversioner. For this there was a *writ of estrepement.* Abolished by 3 & 4 Will. 4, c. 27, s. 36. 3 *Steph. Com.* [ACTIONS REAL AND PERSONAL.]

ET HOC PARATUS EST VERIFICARE (and this he is prepared to verify). Words formerly used at the conclusion of a common law pleading containing new affirmative matter.

ETHELING, or **ATHELING**. A Saxon word signifying *noble*.

EVES-DROPPERS. [EAVES-DROPPERS.]

EVICTION. Dispossession ; also a recovery of land by form of law.

EVIDENCE. That which, in a court of justice, makes clear, or ascertains the truth of, the very fact or point in issue, either on the one side or on the other.

Any matter, lawfully deposed to on oath or affirmation, which contributes (however slightly) to the elucidation of any question at issue in a court of justice, is said to be *evidence*. [CIRCUMSTANTIAL EVIDENCE ; DIRECT EVIDENCE ; HEARSAY EVIDENCE.]

Evidence is either *written* or *parol* ; *written evidence* consists of records, deeds, affidavits, or other writings : *parol* or *oral evidence* consists of witnesses personally appearing in court, and in general sworn to the truth of what they depose. 3 *Steph. Com.*

EX ABUNDANTI CAUTELA. From excessive caution.

EX ÆQUO ET BONO. According to equity and good conscience.

EX CAPITE LECTI. [REDUCTION EX CAPITE LECTI.]

EX CATHEDRÂ. With the weight of one in authority ; originally applied to the decisions of the Popes from their *cathedra* or chair.

EX CONTRACTU. Actions *ex contractu* are actions arising out of breaches of contract, express or implied. 3 *Steph. Com.*

EX DEBITO JUSTITIÆ. As a matter of right ; in opposition to a matter for the favour or discretion of the court. Thus the improper rejection of evidence in an action is ground for a new trial as a matter of right, or *ex debito justitiæ*.

EX DELICTO, or **EX MALEFICIO**. Actions *ex delicto*, or *ex maleficio*, are actions founded on some wrong other than a breach of contract, express or implied.

EX DOLO MALO NON ORITUR ACTIO. No right of action arises out of a fraud.

EX GRATIA. As a matter of favour.

EX GRAVI QUERELA. A writ that lay for one to whom lands or tenements were devised by will, when the heir of the testator detained them from him. Abolished by 3 & 4 Will. 4, c. 27, s. 56.

EX MERO MOTU. Words used in the king's charters and letters patent, to signify that he grants them of his own mere motion, without petition or suggestion from any other. [EX PROPRIO MOTU.]

EX NUDO PACTO NON ORITUR ACTIO. No action arises from a bare pact, *i.e.*, one made without consideration. This applies to simple contracts, not to specialty, which are dependent upon sealing and delivery.

EX OFFICIO. By virtue of an office. Any prerogative or jurisdiction which a person in office has, by virtue of that office, he is said to exercise *ex officio*. See next title.

EX OFFICIO INFORMATION. 1. A criminal information filed by the Attorney-General *ex officio* on behalf of the Crown in the Court of King's Bench. This kind of information is filed for offences more immediately affecting the Government, and is to be distinguished from that class of informations in which the Crown is the nominal prosecutor at the suggestion of some private informer. 4 *Steph. Com.*

2. The expression is also applied, though not very frequently, to information filed by the Attorney-General in the Chancery Division to have a charity properly established. See 3 *Steph. Com.* [INFORMATION.]

EX PARTE. 1. Of the one part, one-sided. Thus, an *ex parte* statement is a statement of one side only. So, an injunction granted *ex parte* is an injunction granted after hearing one side only.

2. The phrase "*ex parte*" preceding a name in the heading of a reported case, indicates that the party whose name follows is the party on whose application the case is heard.

EX POST FACTO signifies something done so as to affect another thing that was committed before. Thus, a lease granted by tenant for life to endure beyond his life may be confirmed *ex post facto* by the reversioner or remainderman. An *ex post facto* law is one having a retrospective application.

EX PROPRIO MOTU. Of his own mere motion, spontaneously ; as when a judge, without application from any party, orders a witness to be prosecuted for perjury, or commits him for trial. [Ex MERO MOTU.]

EX PROVISIONE VIRI. Words used with reference to lands settled on a wife in tail by her husband, or on her and her husband by any of his ancestors. Obsolete. 3 *Steph. Com. ; Wms. R. P.* [DISENTAILING DEED ; RECOVERY.]

EX TURPI CAUSA NON ORITUR ACTIO (No right of action arises from a base cause), *e.g.,* on a contract founded on an immoral consideration.

EXACTION. A wrong done by an officer, or one pretending to have authority, in taking a reward or fee for that which the law allows not. [EXTORTION.]

EXAMINATION. 1. The interrogation of witnesses. The *examination-in-chief* of a witness is the interrogation of a witness, in the first instance, by the counsel of the party producing him. His examination by the opposing counsel is called his *cross-examination ;* and his further examination by his own side, on points arising out of the cross-examination, is called his *re-examination.*

2. The examination of a bankrupt is the interrogation of a bankrupt, by a court having jurisdiction in bankruptcy, as to the state of his property. 2 *Steph. Com. ; Robson, Bkcy.*

3. The examination of a prisoner is the inquiry into the charge made against him by a police magistrate or justice of the peace, preparatory to his being committed for trial, in case there should appear to be a *primâ facie* case against him. 4 *Steph. Com.*

EXAMINERS OF THE COURT. Barristers of not less than three years' standing appointed by the Lord Chancellor to examine witnesses out of court. *R. S. C., Ord. XXXVII.*

EXANNUAL ROLL. A roll into which the fines which could not be levied and the bad debts were formerly transcribed in the sheriffs' accounts in the exchequer.

EXCEPTION signifies—
1. An objection. Thus, for instance, an exception to a defendant's answer in Chancery was an objection taken to it for some cause allowed by the practice of the court, as insufficiency, or scandal and impertinence. 3 *Steph. Com. ; Hunt. Eq.*
2. A saving clause in a deed, preventing certain things passing which would otherwise pass thereby.
3. In the Roman law, and in the Scotch law, the word means a defence. *Bell.*
4. See 42 & 43 *Vict. c. 49, s. 39, sub-s. 2.*

EXCEPTIONS, BILL OF. [BILL OF EXCEPTIONS.]

EXCERPTA, or EXCERPTS. Extracts.

EXCHANGE. 1. The place appointed for the exchange of bullion, gold, silver, plate, etc., with the king's coin.
2. An exchange of land is a mutual grant of equal interest in lands or tenements, the one in consideration of the other ; and is used peculiarly in our common law for that compensation which the *warrantor* must make to the *warrantee,* value for value, if the land warranted be recovered from the warrantee. 1 *Steph. Com.*

EXCHANGE, BILL OF. [BILL OF EXCHANGE.]

EXCHEQUER. The department of state having the management of the royal revenue. It consisted formerly of two divisions, the first being the office of the receipt of the Exchequer, for collection of the royal revenue ; the second being a court for the administration of justice. 2 *Steph. Com.* [COURT OF EXCHEQUER.]

EXCHEQUER BILLS AND BONDS. Bills of credit issued by the Exchequer, under the authority, for the most part, of Acts of parliament passed for the purpose ; and containing an engagement, on the part of the Government, for the repayment of the principal sums advanced, with interest in the meantime. 2 *Steph. Com.*

EXCHEQUER CHAMBER. [COURT OF EXCHEQUER CHAMBER.]

EXCISE was a name formerly confined to the imposition upon beer, ale, cider, and other commodities, being charged sometimes upon the consumption of the commodity, but more frequently upon the retail sale of it. 2 *Steph. Com.*

Under recent Acts of parliament, however, many other imposts have been classed under excise. Such is the case with regard to the licence which must be taken out by every one who keeps a dog, uses a gun, or deals in game. 2 *Steph. Com.*

EXCLUSAGIUM. A payment due to the lord for the benefit of a sluice.

EXCOMMUNICATION, or **EXCOMMENGEMENT.** A spiritual censure for offences falling under ecclesiastical cognizance. It is described in the books as twofold : (1) The *lesser* excommunication, which is an ecclesiastical censure, excluding the party from the sacraments. (2) The *greater*, which excluded him from the company of all Christians, and rendered him incapable of any legal act. See 53 *Geo.* 3, *c.* 127 ; 3 *Steph. Com.* [CONTUMACE CAPIENDO ; EXCOMMUNICATO CAPIENDO.]

EXCOMMUNICATO CAPIENDO. When a person was excommunicated for contempt of an order of the ecclesiastical court, the bishop was allowed to certify the contempt to the sovereign in chancery, who thereupon issued a writ called a *significarit* or *de excommunicato capiendo*, directing the sheriff of the county to take the offender and imprison him in the county gaol until he was reconciled to the church. But by 53 Geo. 3, c. 127, it was provided that no person excommunicated should incur by the sentence any incapacity or penalty beyond six months' imprisonment, to be inflicted at the discretion of the court, and that such sentence should be signified to the sovereign in chancery, and enforced by a writ *de contumace capiendo*, which has the same force and effect as formerly belonged to a writ *de excommunicato capiendo*. See *Green* v. *Lord Penzance* (6 *App. Ca.* 657).

EXCOMMUNICATO DELIBERANDO. A writ to deliver and release one who, after being imprisoned on a writ *de excommunicato capiendo*, is reconciled to the church.

EXCOMMUNICATO RECAPIENDO (or **RECIPIENDO**). A writ for the retaking of excommunicated persons unlawfully released. [EXCOMMUNICATO CAPIENDO ; EXCOMMUNICATO DELIBERANDO.]

EXCUSABLE HOMICIDE is of two sorts : 1. Where one kills another *per infortunium*, i.e., by misadventure, in doing a lawful act ; or 2. *Se defendendo*, in defending one's self. 4 *Steph. Com.*

EXEAT. Leave to depart. [NE EXEAT REGNO.]

EXECUTE. 1. To carry into force an order made in a judicial proceeding. 2. To give legal effect to a deed or other writing by signature or otherwise.

EXECUTED and **EXECUTORY.** These words are used in law in a sense very nearly equivalent to *past* (or *present*) and *future* respectively. Thus,

1. A contract may be either *executed*, as if A. and B. agree to exchange horses, and they do it immediately ; here the possession and the right are transferred together ; or *executory*, as if they agree to exchange next week ; here the *right* only vests, and their reciprocal *property* in each other's horse is not in *possession* but in *action* ; for a contract executed, which differs nothing from a grant, conveys a *chose in possession* ; a contract executory conveys only a *chose in action.* 2 *Steph. Com.* [CHOSE.]

2. So, a *consideration* for a promise may be *executed* or *executory*, according as the consideration precedes the promise or not : and its character in this respect is determined by the relation which it bears in point of time to the promise, as being prior or subsequent. [CONSIDERATION.]

3. A *use* is also executed or executory. Thus, on a conveyance to A. to the use of B., the use in B. is said to be *executed* by the Statute of Uses. But a use in land, limited *in futuro*, on a condition independent of any preceding estate or interest in the land, is an *executory* use, because it is not *executed* by the Statute of Uses till the fulfilment of the condition on which it is to take effect. Such a use is also called a *springing* use. 1 *Steph. Com.* [EXECUTORY INTEREST ; SPRINGING USE ; USE.]

4. So, a *devise* (i.e., a disposition of land by will), by which a future estate is allowed to be limited contrary to the rules of the old common law, is called an *executory devise*. 1 *Steph. Com.* [EXECUTORY INTEREST.]

EXECUTED and **EXECUTORY**—*contd.*

5. Also, an estate in possession, whereby a present interest passes to the tenant, is sometimes called an *executed* estate, as opposed to the *executory* class of estates depending on some *subsequent* circumstances or contingency. *2 Bl.*

6. A trust may also be *executed* or *executory.* An *executed* trust is one where the trust estate is completely defined in the first instance, no future instrument of conveyance being contemplated. An *executory* trust is a trust where the party, whose benefit is designed, is to take through the medium of a future instrument of conveyance to be executed for the purpose. *1 Steph. Com.* The importance of the distinction lies in this, that an *executed* trust is construed strictly according to the technical meaning of the terms used ; an *executory* trust is construed according to the apparent meaning of the author of the trust, as gathered from the instrument by which it is created.

This is one of the most technical and difficult distinctions in English law. It might at first be supposed that an executed trust was a trust fully administered by the final distribution, on the part of the trustee, of the trust property among the parties entitled thereto ; and that an executory trust was a trust not yet fully administered. As Lord St. Leonards says in the case of the *Earl of Egerton* v. *Brownlow* (4 *House of Lords Cases*, 210) :—" All trusts are in a sense executory, because a trust cannot be executed except by conveyance, and therefore there is always something to be done. *But that is not the sense which a court of equity puts upon the term executory trust.*" And his lordship goes on to distinguish the two in this way :—An *executory* trust is where the author of the trust has left it to the court to make out from *general expressions* what his intention is. An executed trust is where " you have nothing to do but to take the limitations he has given you, and convert them into legal estates." Or, perhaps, we may express it in this way :—An *executory* trust is one of which the author indicates, either by the vagueness and generality of the words he has used, or by his intention expressed in the instrument creating the trust, that some further conveyance should be executed for expressing the trusts in proper legal form. Whereas, an *executed* trust is a trust itself expressed in proper legal form. An exe-

cutory trust thus bears to an executed trust the same relation which the heads of a settlement bear to the settlement itself. This use of the term "executed " may, perhaps, be illustrated by such expressions as "the execution of a will," "execution of a deed."

EXECUTION. 1. The putting in force the sentence of the law in a judicial proceeding. *3 Steph. Com.* It is styled *final process*, and is regulated by R. S. C. 1883, Ord. XLII. See also 23 & 24 Vict. c. 38, 27 & 28 Vict. c. 112. *4 Steph. Com.* [For the various writs of execution, see under their several titles.]

2. The signing of a deed or will, or other written instrument, in such manner as to make it (so far as regards form) legally valid.

EXECUTIONE FACIENDA IN WITHER-NAMIUM (for doing execution in withernam). [WITHERNAM.]

EXECUTIONE JUDICII. An ancient writ directed to the judge of an inferior court of record, or to the sheriff or bailiff of an inferior court not of record, to do execution upon a judgment therein, or to return some reasonable cause wherefore he delays execution.

EXECUTIVE. That branch of government which is entrusted with enforcing the laws. The supreme executive power in this kingdom is vested in the king or queen for the time being. *1 Steph. Com.; 2 Steph. Com.*

EXECUTOR. One to whom another, by his last will and testament, commits the execution of the directions and dispositions thereof. His duties are :—

1. To bury the deceased in a manner suitable to the estate which he leaves behind him.

2. To prove the will of the deceased.

3. To make an inventory of the goods and chattels of the deceased, and to collect the goods so inventoried ; and, for this purpose, if necessary, to take proceedings against debtors to his testator's estate.

4. To pay, *first*, the debts of his testator, and *then* the legacies bequeathed by his will ; and to distribute the residue, in default of any residuary disposition, among the next of kin of the testator.

An executor is the legal personal representative of his testator, and the testator's rights and liabilities devolve

EXECUTOR—*continued.*

for the most part upon him. A person appointed executor is not on that account bound to accept the office. 2 *Steph. Com.; Wms. P. P.; Williams on Executors.* See also REAL RE-PRESENTATIVE.

EXECUTOR DE SON TORT. One who, without any just authority, intermeddles with the goods of a deceased person, as if he had been duly appointed executor. An *executor de son tort* is liable to the trouble of an executorship without its profits and advantages. He cannot bring an action himself in right of the deceased, but actions may be brought against him. 2 *Steph. Com.*

EXECUTORY INTEREST. In one sense, any future estate in land is an executory estate or interest. [EXECUTED and EXECUTORY.] But the term "executory interest" is especially applied to such an interest in real estate as is "limited" to commence at a future time, upon some contingency not depending on the determination of a prior estate. As, if land be limited by deed to A. and his heirs to the use of B. and his heirs until C. shall return from Rome, and then to the use of D. and his heirs; D.'s interest is called an *executory interest. Wms. R. P.* [EXECUTED and EXECUTORY, 3, 4, 5.]

EXECUTRIX. Feminine of executor. By the Married Women's Property Act, 1882, s. 18, a married woman may be executrix.

EXEMPLARY DAMAGES. Damages on an unsparing scale, given in respect of tortious acts, committed through malice or other circumstances of aggravation.

EXEMPLI GRATIA (abbrv. *ex. gr.* or *e. g.*) For the sake of example.

EXEMPLIFICATION. 1. A copy.

2. A certified transcript under the seal of a court.

EXEQUATUR. A rescript or order given by the foreign department of a state to which a consul is accredited, authorising the functionaries of the home department to recognise the official character of the consul. [CONSUL.] It may be revoked at any time at the discretion of the government wherein he is established. *Twiss' Law of Nations.*

EXHIBIT. A document or other thing shown to a witness while giving evidence and sworn to by him.

Usually applied to a document referred to in an affidavit and shown to the deponent when being sworn. The exhibit is marked by the commissioner or other person before whom it is sworn.

EXHIBITION, in the law of Scotland, signifies the production of deeds; and an *action of exhibition* is an action for compelling production of the same.

EXIGENT, or **EXIGI FACIAS.** A writ issued to the sheriff that lay where the defendant in a personal action could not be found, charging him to appear on pain of outlawry. It lay also in an indictment of felony, where the party indicted could not be found. 4 *Steph. Com.*

EXIGENTER. An officer in the Courts of King's Bench and Common Pleas, whose duty it was to make out *exigents.* Abolished by 7 Will. 4 & 1 Vict. c. 30. [EXIGENT.]

EXIGI FACIAS. [EXIGENT.]

EXITUS. 1. Issue, child or children, offspring.

2. The rents or profits of land.

3. The conclusion of the pleadings.

EXOINE. [ESSOIGN.]

EXONERATION generally signifies relieving part of the estate of a deceased person, charged with a debt, by the payment of the debt out of another part thereof. This may be by law, or by the special direction of the deceased in his will. For instance, prior to the Act called Locke King's Act (17 & 18 Vict. c. 113), passed in 1854, the heir of a deceased mortgagor, or person claiming the mortgaged estate under the will of the deceased, was entitled to be repaid, or *exonerated,* out of the personal estate of the deceased.

EXONERETUR (let him be discharged). An entry formerly made on the bail-piece upon render of a defendant to prison in discharge of his bail. [BAIL-PIECE.]

EXPATRIATION. The forsaking one's own country and renouncing allegiance, with the intention of becoming a permanent resident and citizen in another country. See *Naturalization Act,* 1870 (33 *Vict.* c. 11, *ss.* 4, 6).

EXPECTANCY, ESTATES IN, are interests in land which are limited or appointed to take effect in possession at some future time. [ESTATE.]

EXPECTANT HEIR. One who has a prospect of coming into property on the death of another person.

Such persons have always been peculiarly under the protection of courts of equity, who have relieved them from unconscionable bargains.

EXPECTATION OF LIFE. In matters of life insurance, and the granting of annuities, this expression is used to signify the length of time that any specified person may expect, according to the tables of averages, to live.

EXPENDITORS. Disbursers of taxes raised for the repairs of sewers.

EXPENSÆ LITIS. The costs of a suit or action, allowed generally to the successful party. [COSTS.]

EXPENSIS MILITUM LEVANDIS. An old writ directed to the sheriff for levying the allowance for the knights of parliament.

EXPENSIS MILITUM NON LEVANDIS AB HOMINIBUS DE ANTIQUO DOMINICO NEC A NATIVIS. An old writ to prohibit the sheriff from levying any allowance for knights of the shire upon such as held lands in ancient demesne. [ANCIENT DEMESNE.]

EXPERT. A skilled witness called to give evidence on the art or mystery with which he is especially conversant.

EXPIRING LAWS CONTINUANCE ACT. An Act passed at the end of each session of parliament for the purpose of continuing—usually for one full year more—temporary Acts which would otherwise expire.

EXPLEES (*Expletiæ*). Rents or profits of land, otherwise called *esplees*.

EXPLOSIVE SUBSTANCES. Injuries by, see 24 & 25 Vict. c. 97, ss. 9, 10, 54, 55 ; c. 100, ss. 28-30, 64, 65. Manufacture and sale, see Explosives Act, 1875. Causing dangerous explosions, see Explosive Substances Act, 1883.

EXPOSING, in a public thoroughfare, a person infected with a contagious disease, is punishable as a common nuisance. See also 38 & 39 Vict. c. 55, s. 126.

2. Exposing child under the age of two years. See 24 & 25 Vict. c. 100, s. 27.

3. Exposing the person. See INDECENT EXPOSURE.

EXPRESS. That which is not left to implication : as express promise or covenant.

EXPRESS COLOUR. [COLOUR.]

EXPRESS CONTRACT OR CONVENTION. A contract or convention expressed in words, or by signs which custom or usage has made equivalent to words. *Austin, Jur. Lect. VI.*

EXPRESS TRUST. A trust which is clearly expressed by the authors thereof, or may fairly be collected from a written document. *Sm. Man. Eq.*

EXPRESSIO UNIUS EST EXCLUSIO ALTERIUS (the mention of one is the exclusion of another). See *Broom's Max.*

EXPRESSUM FACIT CESSARE TACITUM (what is expressed makes what is implied to cease). *E.g.,* an express covenant in a lease destroys that which would otherwise be implied by the use of the word "demise."

EXPROPRIATION. The surrender of a claim to exclusive property.

EXTEND. To value the lands or tenements of a judgment debtor, or one whose recognizance is forfeited, so that by the yearly rent the creditor may in time be paid his debt. *Cowel.* [EXTENT.]

EXTENDI FACIAS is a writ ordinarily called a writ of extent. [EXTENT.]

EXTENT. A writ or commission to the sheriff for the *valuing* of lands and tenements and goods and chattels of a judgment-debtor.

Extents are of several kinds, as follows:

1. A process of execution under the laws relating to statute staple and statutes merchant, by which the lands and goods of a person whose recognizance had been forfeited, or whose debt had been acknowledged on statute staple or statute merchant, might be appraised and delivered to the creditor. 1 *Steph. Com.; 3 Steph. Com.*

2. An *extent in chief,* a writ issuing out of the Court of Exchequer, for the recovery of debts of record due to the Crown ; by which the sheriff was

EXTENT—*continued.*

directed to cause the lands, goods and chattels of the debtor to be appraised at their full value, and to be seized into the hands of the sovereign.

3. An *extent in aid*, issued at the suit or instance of a *Crown debtor* against a person indebted to the Crown debtor himself.

4. A special writ of extent directing the sheriff to seize the lands and goods of a *deceased* Crown debtor. This writ is called *diem clausit extremum.* 3 *Steph. Com.*

EXTINGUISHMENT signifies an effect of consolidation. Thus, if a man purchase lands out of which he has a rent, then the property and the rent are consolidated, and the rent is said to be extinguished. So, if a lessee or tenant for life purchases the reversion, his estate for years or life is *extinguished*, being merged in the reversion. So, an extinguishment of copyhold is effected when the freehold and copyhold interest are united in the same person ; as in the tenant by enfranchisement, or in the lord by escheat, forfeiture, descent, or surrender to his use. Similarly, an extinguishment of right of way is effected by the purchase, on the part of the owner of the right of way, of the land wherein the way lies. 1 *Steph. Com.*

Also, a parol contract is said to be *extinguished* by a contract *under seal* between the same parties to the same effect. 2 *Steph. Com.*

EXTORTION. An unlawful or violent wringing of money or money's worth from any man. The word is used especially as follows :—

1. In reference to demanding money or other property by threats and menaces of various kinds. This offence is severely punishable. 24 & 25 *Vict. c.* 96, *ss.* 45, 46 ; 4 *Steph. Com.*; *Cox & Saunders' Cr. Law,* 50.

2. In reference to the unlawful taking by an officer, under colour of his office, of money not due to him, or more than is due. See the *Sheriffs Act,* 1887 (50 & 51 *Vict. c.* 55); 4 *Steph. Com.*

EXTRA COSTS. [INCREASE, AFFIDAVIT OF.]

EXTRADITION. The surrender of a person by one state to another. The word is generally applied to the surrender of a person charged with an offence to the state having jurisdiction to try the same. The Acts by which this subject is at present regulated are the Extradition Act, 1870 (33 & 34 Vict. c. 52), and the Extradition Act, 1873 (36 & 37 Vict. c. 60). The former Act empowers his Majesty to enter into arrangements with foreign states for the mutual surrender of fugitive criminals in the cases therein specified. The Act of 1873 is supplementary, and enlarges the scope of the former Act. 4 *Steph. Com.*

EXTRAJUDICIAL. Any act done or word spoken by a judge, outside the authority and jurisdiction which for the time being he is exercising, is called *extrajudicial.* [OBITER DICTUM.]

EXTRAORDINARY RESOLUTION. [RESOLUTION.]

EXTRAPAROCHIAL PLACES. Places not united to, or forming part of, any parish. 1 *Steph. Com.*

EXTRA-TERRITORIALITY. Immunity from a country's laws, such as that enjoyed by an ambassador. Consult *Wheaton Inter. Law.*

EXTRAVAGANTES. Twenty constitutions or decrees of Pope John XXII. were called *Extravagantes Joannis.* To these have been added some decrees of later popes, in five books, called *Extravagantes Communes.* 1 *Steph. Com.*

EYE-WITNESS. One who gives evidence as to facts seen by himself.

EYRE. The justices in eyre, or justices *in itinere,* were regularly established by the parliament of Northampton, A.D. 1176, with a delegated power from the king's court or *aula regia,* being looked upon as members thereof ; and they afterwards made their circuit round the kingdom once in seven years for trying causes. They were afterwards directed by *Magna Charta,* c. 12, to be sent into every county once a year to take or receive the verdict of jurors or "recognitors" in certain actions, then called *recognitions* or *assizes,* the most difficult of which they were directed to adjourn into the Court of Common Pleas, to be there determined. [ASSIZE, WRIT OF.] The itinerant justices were sometimes mere justices of assize, or of dower, or of gaol delivery, and the like: but they sometimes had a more general commission, being constituted *justitiarii ad omnia placita.* These were superseded by the justices of assize and *nisi prius,* established in 1280 by the Statute of Westminster the Second. 3 *Steph. Com.* [ASSIZE. COURTS OF.]

F.O.B. (free on board). A term often inserted in contracts for sale of goods to be shipped. It signifies that the cost of shipping, *i.e.*, putting on board at port or place of shipment, is to be paid by the vendor.

FABRIC LANDS. Lands given to the rebuilding, repair, or maintenance of the fabrics of cathedrals or other churches.

FAC SIMILE PROBATE. This is where the probate copy of a will is a *fac simile* of the original will. It is allowed in cases where the construction of the will may be affected by the appearance of the original paper. *Wms. Exors.*

FACIO UT DES. I do that you may give ; as when I agree to perform anything for a price. This is one of the considerations for contracts mentioned in the Roman law. 2 *Steph. Com.* [DO UT DES ; DO UT FACIAS.]

FACIO UT FACIAS. I do that you may do ; as when I agree with a man to do his work for him, if he will do mine for me. 2 *Bl.* ; 2 *Steph. Com.* See preceding title.

FACTOR. An agent remunerated by a commission, who is entrusted with the possession of goods to sell in his own name, as apparent owner. The Factors Acts were amended and consolidated by the Factors Act, 1889 (52 & 53 Vict. c. 45) ; extended to Scotland by 53 & 54 Vict. c. 40. See also ss. 75 & 78 of the Larceny Act; 1861 (24 & 25 Vict. c. 96); 2 *Steph. Com.*

FACTORAGE, also called " commission," is an allowance given to factors by a merchant who employs them.

FACTORY. 1. A place where a considerable number of *factors* reside, in order to negotiate for their masters or employers.

2. A building in which goods are manufactured.

The Factory and Workshop Act, 1878 (41 Vict. c. 16), consolidated and amended the various Acts whereby the management of factories and the labour of persons employed in them have been regulated from time to time.

This Act was amended by the Factory and Workshop Acts of 1883, 1891, and 1895. A further consolidation has been effected by the Act of 1901.

FACTUM. An act or deed.

FACULTIES, COURT OF. [FACULTY.]

FACULTY. A privilege or special dispensation, granted to a man by favour and indulgence to do that which by the common law he could not do, *e.g.*, to marry without banns, or erect a monument in a church, etc. And for the granting of these there is an especial court under the Archbishop of Canterbury called the Court of the Faculties, and a chief officer thereof, called the Master of the Faculties (Lat. *Magister ad Facultates*), whose power to grant as aforesaid was given by 25 Hen. 8, c. 21. See *Phillimore's Eccl. Law.*

In Scotch law, "faculty" means a power which any person is at liberty to exercise. *Bell.*

FACULTY OF ADVOCATES. The college of advocates in Scotland, *i.e.*, the barristers entitled to practise in the Supreme Court.

FAGGOT VOTE is where a man has a formal right to vote for members of parliament without possessing the substance which the vote should represent, the vote being acquired for the mere purpose of influencing the result of an election. See now the Representation of the People Act, 1884 (48 Vict. c. 3, s. 4).

FAILING OF RECORD is where a defendant, having pleaded any matter of record, fails to prove it, or brings in such a one as is no bar to the action.

FAINT ACTION. or **FEIGNED ACTION.** An action in which the words of the writ are true, yet for certain causes the party bringing it hath no title to recover thereby. Whereas in a *false action* the words of the writ are false.

FAINT PLEADER, or **FAINT PLEADING.** A false, covinous, or collusory manner of pleading, to the deceit of a third party. 3 *Edw.* 1, c. 19.

FAIR. A solemn or greater sort of market granted to any town by privilege, for the more speedy and commodious provision of such things as the subject needeth. *Cowel.* See 36 & 37 *Vict. c.* 37 ; 31 & 32 *Vict.* c. 106 (*Metropolitan Fairs*) ; 38 & 39 *Vict. c.* 55, *s.* 157 (*Powers of Local Authorities*) ; 34 *Vict. c.* 12 (*Abolition of Fairs by Home Secretary*).

FAIT. A deed.

FALCATURA. One day's mowing of grass : a customary service to a lord from his inferior tenants.

FALDAGE, or **FOLDAGE.** A privilege which anciently several lords reserved to themselves, of setting up folds for sheep within their manors, the better to manure them.

FALDFEY, or **FALDAGE FEE.** A fee or rent paid by some customary tenants for liberty to fold their sheep upon their own land.

FALDSTOOL, or **FOLDSTOOL.** A place at the south side of the altar, where the sovereign kneels at his coronation.

FALK LAND, or **FOLKE LAND.** [FOLK LAND.]

FALSA DEMONSTRATIO NON NOCET (a false demonstration does not injure). [FALSE DEMONSTRATION.]

FALSE ACTION. [FAINT ACTION.]

FALSE DEMONSTRATION. An erroneous description of a person or thing in a written instrument. The import of the maxim that "a false demonstration does not injure," is this,—that where there is an adequate naming or definition, with a convenient certainty, of any person or thing in a written instrument, a subsequent erroneous addition will not vitiate it. *Broom's Legal Maxims ; Jarman on Wills.*

FALSE IMPRISONMENT is a trespass committed against a man by imprisoning him without lawful cause. Every confinement of the person is an imprisonment, whether it be in a common prison, or in the stocks, or even by forcibly detaining one in the public streets. False imprisonment is usually made the subject of a civil action, but is also indictable at the suit of the Crown. *3 Steph. Com. ; 4 Steph. Com. ; Addison on Torts.*

FALSE JUDGMENT, WRIT OF. A writ which lay to amend errors in the proceedings of an inferior court, *not being a court of record.* 3 Steph. Com.

FALSE PERSONATION. The offence of personating another for the purpose of fraud. This is a misdemeanor at common law, and is made highly penal in many cases under various statutes. 4 *Steph. Com.*

The stat. 37 & 38 Vict. c. 36, makes it felony, punishable with penal servitude for life, to personate any person, or the heir, executor, etc. of any person, with intent to claim succession to real or personal property, or falsely to claim relationship to any family. Personation of a voter is made felony by the Ballot Act, 1872, and personation of a master for the purpose of giving a false character to a servant is a misdemeanor by 32 Geo. 3, c. 56.

FALSE PLEA. [SHAM PLEA.]

FALSE PRETENCE. Any false statement whereby a person knowing it to be false, obtains from another, for himself or for his own benefit, any chattel, money, or valuable security, with intent to cheat or defraud any person, is a misdemeanor at common law, and punishable by fine and imprisonment. 24 & 25 *Vict. c.* 96, *s.* 88 : 4 *Steph. Com.* See also the Summary Jurisdiction Act, 1899 (62 & 63 Vict. c. 22).

For the distinction between false pretence and larceny by a trick, see LARCENY.

FALSE RETURN by a sheriff, etc., to a writ, renders him liable to an action for damages.

FALSE SIGNAL, or **LIGHTS,** exhibited with intent to bring ships into danger is a felony. See 24 & 25 Vict. c. 97. s. 47.

FALSE VERDICT formerly rendered a jury liable to be prosecuted by writ of attaint at the instance of the injured party. Abolished, 6 Geo. 4, c. 50, s. 60.

FALSIFY signifies, 1. To prove a thing to be false. 4 *Steph. Com.*

2. To tamper with any document, whether of record or not, by interlineation, obliteration, or otherwise. 24 & 25 *Vict. c.* 98, *s.* 28 ; 4 *Steph. Com.*

3. To represent facts falsely, as for instance to state a pedigree falsely. 22 & 23 *Vict. c.* 35, *s.* 24 ; 4 *Steph. Com.*

FALSO RETORNO BREVIUM. A writ which lay against the sheriff for a false return to a writ. [RETURN.]

FAMILIA signifies all the servants belonging to a particular master; but in another sense it is taken for a portion of land sufficient to maintain one family. Sometimes it is taken for a *hide* of land, which is also called a *manse*; sometimes for *carucata*, or *plough-land*, containing as much as one plough and oxen can till in one year.

FARDEL OF LAND (*Fardella terræ*) is, according to some authors, the fourth part of a yard-land; yet Noy, in his "Compleat Lawyer," page 57, will have two fardels make a *nook*, and four *nooks* make a yard-land.

FARDINGDEAL, or **FARUNDEL OF LAND**. The fourth part of an acre.

FARE. Money paid for a passage by land or water. Railway fares must be published at stations, by 31 & 32 Vict. c. 119, s. 6.

Travelling without prepayment, and with intent to defraud, is punishable by the Regulation of Railways Act, 1889.

FARINAGIUM. Toll of meal or flour.

FARLEU. Money paid by a tenant in lieu of a heriot.

FARM, FERM, or **FEORME** (Fr. *Ferme*) is said by Blackstone to be an old Saxon word signifying *provisions;* and he says that it came to be used of rent or render, because anciently the greater part of rents were reserved in provisions, till the use of money became more frequent. So that a farmer, *firmarius*, was one who held his lands upon payment of a rent or *feorme;* though at present, by a gradual departure from the original sense, the word "farm" is brought to signify the very estate so held upon farm or rent. "To farm let" are usual, though not necessary, words of operation in a lease. 1 *Steph. Com.* [FERME.]

FARO. An unlawful game of chance. 12 *Geo.* 2, c. 28.

FARUNDEL OF LAND. [FARDINGDEAL.]

FARYNDON INN. The old name for Serjeants' Inn. 3 *Steph. Com.* [INNS OF CHANCERY.]

FAST-DAY. A day of abstinence appointed by the Church. They may also be appointed on special days by royal proclamation. On such days no legal business is transacted. See *R. S. C. Ord. LXIII.* r. 6.

See also ss. 14 to 92 of Bills of Exchange Act, 1882.

FAUTORS. Favourers, supporters, or abettors.

FAVOUR, CHALLENGE TO. [CHALLENGE.]

FEAL. Faithful. [FEALTY.]

FEALTY. Faith, fidelity. An oath, taken at the admittance of every tenant, to be true to the lord of whom he holds his land. In the usual oath of fealty there was frequently an exception of the faith due to a superior lord; but when the acknowledgment was made to the superior himself, who was vassal to no man, it was no longer called the oath of fealty, but the oath of allegiance.

The term *fealty* is applied not only to the oath, but to the actual tie which binds the vassal to his lord. 1 *Steph. Com.*; 2 *Steph. Com.*

The oath of fealty is in practice never exacted. *Wms. R. P.*

FEDERAL GOVERNMENT. A government formed by the aggregation of several states, previously independent, in such a manner that the sovereignty over each of the states resides thenceforth in the aggregate of the whole, while each of the states, though losing its individual sovereignty, retains nevertheless important political powers within its own territory, and shares the sovereignty of the entire federation with the other states, and (in general) with a new legislative or executive body having a limited jurisdiction over the entire area of the federation, and called "the general government." If the individual states retain severally their sovereign character, the federation is called a *permanent confederacy of supreme governments.* At what point this sovereign character is to be held to be lost cannot be discussed here. See *Austin on Jurisprudence, Lecture VI.; De Tocqueville's Democracy in America; Freeman's History of Federal Government.*

A "Federal Council of Australasia Act" (48 & 49 Vict. c. 60) was passed in 1885. It is now superseded by the Commonwealth of Australia Constitution Act, 1900 (63 & 64 Vict. c. 12).

FEE. 1. The true meaning of this word is the same with that of *feud* or *fief*. In the northern languages it signified a conditional stipend or reward. These feuds, fiefs, or fees, were large districts or parcels of land allotted by the conquering general to the superior officers of the army, and by them dealt out again in smaller parcels to the inferior officers and deserving soldiers. The condition annexed to them was that the possessor should do service faithfully, both at home and in the wars, to him by whom they were given. A fee or feud is therefore defined as being the right which the vassal or tenant hath in land, to use the same and take the profits thereof to him and his heirs, rendering to the lord his due services.

2. Hence the word *fee* is used to signify an estate of inheritance, being the highest and most extensive interest which a man can have in a feud ; and when the term is used simply, without any adjunct, or has the adjunct of *simple* annexed to it, it is used in contradistinction to a fee conditional at the common law, or a fee tail under the *Statute de Donis*, importing an absolute inheritance descendible to heirs general, and liable to alienation at the pleasure of the owner, whether by will or deed, to the full extent of his interest, or for a smaller estate. 1 *Steph. Com. ; Wms. R. P.* [CONDITIONAL FEE ; DE DONIS ; ESTATE.]

FEE CONDITIONAL. [CONDITIONAL FEE.]

FEE FARM is when a tenant holds of his lord in fee simple, paying to him the value of half or other proportion of the land by the year.

FEE FARM RENT is where an estate in fee is granted subject to a rent in fee of at least one-fourth of the value of the land at the time of its reservation. 1 *Steph. Com.*

FEE SIMPLE. An estate limited to a man and his heirs ; the most absolute interest which a subject can possess in land. [ESTATE ; FEE, 2.]

FEE SIMPLE CONDITIONAL. [CONDITIONAL FEE.]

FEE TAIL. An estate limited to a man and the heirs of his body, generally called an *estate tail.* 1 *Steph. Com.* [ESTATE.]

FEED. To lend additional support to. Thus an accruing interest is said to feed an estoppel in cases where a person is thereby enabled to give effect to a grant previously made, which grant had, prior to such accruer, no effect except by way of estoppel.

FEIGNED ACTION. [FAINT ACTION ; FEIGNED ISSUE.]

FEIGNED ISSUE. An issue formerly directed in the same form as if an action had been commenced at common law upon a *bet* or *wager* involving the fact in dispute; the issue joined thereon was referred to a jury. Now obsolete. 3 *Steph. Com.*

FELE, or **FEAL HOMAGERS.** Faithful subjects, from the Saxon *fai*, faith.

FELLOW-SERVANT. [SERVANT.]

FELO DE SE. He that commits felony by murdering himself. The goods of a *felo de se* were forfeited to the Crown, until the passing of the Felony Act, 1870 (33 & 34 Vict. c. 23). 2 *Steph. Com. ;* 4 *Steph. Com.*

FELON. A person who commits felony. [FELONY.]

FELON CONVICT. [CONVICT.]

FELONICE CEPIT ET ASPORTAVIT (he feloniously took and carried away). Words in an indictment for larceny. [LARCENY.]

FELONY, in the general acceptation of our English law, comprises every species of crime which at common law occasioned a forfeiture of lands and goods. Treason, therefore, was a species of felony. At the time when Blackstone wrote, an Act of parliament making an offence felony without benefit of clergy, meant that the offender, if convicted, was to suffer death, and incur a forfeiture of his lands and goods. But, as capital punishment never entered into the true idea of felony, so it has now long ceased to have any necessary connection with it in practice. And by s. 1 of the Felony Act, 1870, forfeiture for treason and felony is abolished ; so that the essence of the distinction between felony and misdemeanor is lost, though such other differences between the two classes of offences, whether in procedure or otherwise, as existed before that Act, exist still. The Act also sanctioned the appointment of

FELONY—*continued.*
interim curators and *administrators* of the property of felons, and provided for other matters in connection therewith. 4 *Steph. Com.*

FEME (Fr. *Femme*). A woman.

FEME COVERT (Lat. *Fœmina viro co-operta*). A married woman; opposed to *feme sole*, which means a single woman. 2 *Steph. Com.*

FEME SOLE. A single woman, including those who have been married, but whose marriage has been dissolved by death or divorce, and (for most purposes) those women who are judicially separated from their husbands. 2 *Steph. Com.*

FENCE-MONTH, or **DEFENCE-MONTH.** A forest word, signifying a *close time* during the space of thirty-one days in the year, that is to say, fifteen days before Midsummer, and fifteen days after, in which time it was forbidden for any man to hunt in the forest, or to go into it to disturb the beasts. The reason was, because the female deer did then fawn.

FENGELD. A tax or imposition for the repelling of enemies.

FEOD, FEUD, FIEF, or **FEE.** [FEE, 1.]

FEODAL, or **FEUDAL.** Of or belonging to a feud or fee. [FEE.] "Feodal actions" is the name given in the Mirror to real actions. [ACTIONS REAL AND PERSONAL; FEUDAL SYSTEM.]

FEODAL SYSTEM. [FEUDAL SYSTEM.]

FEODALITY. Fealty.

FEODARY. [FEUDARY.]

FEODATORY. [FEUDATORY.]

FEODUM. Same as feod or feud. [FEE; FEUDUM.]

FEODUM ANTIQUUM, NOVUM, etc. [FEUDUM ANTIQUUM, NOVUM, etc.]

FEOFFEE. A person to whom a feoffment is made. [FEOFFMENT.]

FEOFFEE TO USES. A person to whom a feoffment of lands is made to the use of some other person. Prior to the Statute of Uses (27 Hen. 8, c. 10), passed in 1536, the feoffee to uses had the *legal estate* in the lands so conveyed by feoffment; the claim of the person to whose *use* they were conveyed being enforceable by the Court of Chancery. But since, by that statute, uses are turned into legal estates, the feoffee to uses has no longer even a legal estate in the land; he has only what is called a *scintilla juris.* 1 *Steph. Com.*; *Wms. R. P.* [FEOFFMENT; LEGAL ESTATE; SCINTILLA JURIS; USES.]

FEOFFMENT (Lat. *Feoffamentum*) is properly *donatio feudi*, the gift of the fee; and it may (says Blackstone) be defined as the gift of any corporeal hereditament to another. [CORPOREAL PROPERTY.]
 But in practice we never use the word in this extensive sense; for by a *feoffment* is always meant the feudal mode of transferring estates called *feoffment with livery of seisin.* This "livery of seisin" is the pure feudal investiture. It is either "in deed" or "in law."
 Feoffments, having long been disused, were practically abolished by 8 & 9 Vict. c. 106, ss. 2, 3. For, by s. 2 of that Act, all corporeal hereditaments are, as regards the conveyance of the immediate freehold, to be deemed to lie *in grant* as well as *in livery.* That is to say, they may be conveyed by deed of grant without anything else. And, by s. 3, a feoffment other than a feoffment made under a custom by an infant (*i.e.*, made under some special local custom by a minor) is void at law, unless evidenced by deed. Thus a deed is necessary in any case, so that a feoffment is quite useless. 1 *Steph. Com.*; *Wms. R. P.*

FEOFFOR. A person who makes a *feoffment.* [FEOFFMENT.]

FEORME. The same as farm. [FARM.] 1 *Steph. Com.*

FERÆ NATURÆ. Of a wild disposition; an expression applied to animals which are generally found at liberty, though it may happen that they are sometimes tamed and confined by the art and industry of man. They are not whilst living the subjects of absolute property, so that they cannot be the subject of larceny. 24 & 25 *Vict.* c. 96, ss. 11—24. But see GAME. 2 *Steph. Com.*; 4 *Steph. Com.*

FERDELLA TERRÆ. Ten acres. It is thus apparently synonymous with *ferlingata terræ.*

FERLING (*Ferlingus*). The fourth part of a penny. Also used as synonymous with *ferlingata terræ*.

FERLINGATA TERRÆ. The fourth part of a yard-land. Ten *acres* (it is said) make one *ferling*; four *ferlings* one *virgate* (or *yard-land*); four *virgates* one *hide*; and five *hides* a knight's fee. [KNIGHT'S FEE.]

FERMARY (from the Saxon *Feorme*, provisions) signifies an hospital.

FERME (Fr.). A farm. [FARM.]

FERMIER. A farmer: of public revenue in France.

FERMISONA. The winter season for killing deer.

FERRY. A liberty or franchise by prescription, or by the king's grant or Act of parliament, to have a boat for passage upon a great stream for carriage of horses and men for reasonable toll. This right, where it exists, involves a right of action on the part of the owner of the ferry against those who set up a new one so near as to diminish his custom. On the other hand, the existence of the right implies also a duty, on the part of the grantee, to keep up a boat over the stream, if not otherwise fordable, for the convenience of the public: and neglect of this duty will render him liable to a criminal prosecution. 1 *Steph. Com.*

FEU, or **FEW**. The prevailing tenure of land in Scotland, where the vassal, in place of military service, makes a return in grain or in money. It is in the nature of a perpetual lease.

FEUD. The same as fee. [FEE.]
Also it signifies implacable hatred, not to be satisfied but with the death of the enemy; and especially a combination of the kindred of a murdered man to avenge his death upon the slayer and all his race.

FEUD BOTE. A recompense for engaging in a feud or faction fight, and the contingent damages, it having been the custom in ancient times for all the kindred to engage in the kinsman's quarrel. [FEUD.]

FEUDAL SYSTEM. The system of military tenures, perfected in this country by the Conqueror. The main incidents of the feudal system continued until the abolition of military tenures, by 12 Car. 2, c. 24. 1 *Steph. Com.*

FEUDARY, or **FEODARY**, was an officer in the Court of Wards, appointed by the master of that court by virtue of 32 Hen. 8, c. 46, to be present with the escheator in every county at the "finding of offices" [OFFICE FOUND], and to give in evidence for the king as well for the value as the tenure; also to survey the lands of the ward after office found, and to return the true value into the court. This office was abolished by 12 Car. 2, c. 24 (the Act for the abolition of military tenures).

FEUDATORY, or **FEODATORY**. He that holdeth lands by feudal service. [FEE; FEUDAL SYSTEM.]

FEUDUM (or **FEODUM**) **ANTIQUUM**. An ancient feud; that is, a feud which has descended to a man from his ancestors. 1 *Steph. Com.*

FEUDUM (or **FEODUM**) **LAICUM**. A lay fee, as opposed to such a tenure as frankalmoign, in which the service is of a spiritual nature.

FEUDUM MILITIS, or **FEUDUM MILITARE**. A knight's fee. [KNIGHT'S FEE.]

FEUDUM NOVUM. A feud newly acquired by a man, and not descended upon him from his ancestors. 2 *Steph. Com.* See next title.

FEUDUM NOVUM UT ANTIQUUM. A *feudum novum*, or newly-acquired fee, granted to a man to hold *ut feudum antiquum*; that is, with all the qualities annexed to a feud derived from one's ancestors, so as to admit the succession of *collateral relations* of the purchaser, even *in infinitum*, because they might have derived their blood from the first *imaginary* purchaser. 1 *Steph. Com.*

FI. FA. [FIERI FACIAS.]

FIAT. A short order or warrant of a judge for making out and allowing certain processes; or an indorsement by the Lord Chancellor or Attorney-General, on behalf of the Crown, upon a petition for any purpose for which the consent of the Crown is necessary. (*E.g.*, under sect. 3 of the Newspaper Libel and Registration Act, 1881.)

FIAT JUSTITIA RUAT CŒLUM (let justice be done though the heavens should fall).

FICTION OF LAW (Lat. *Fictio juris*) is defined as a supposition of law that a thing is true, without inquiring whether it be so or not, that it may have the effect of truth so far as is consistent with justice. There are many instances of fictions used in English law, *e.g.*, *Ejectment, Fine, Trover*, etc. (*q.v.*).

The phrase "implied by law" is frequently used to cover a legal fiction. For instance, when it is said that a contract or request is "implied by law," it is frequently meant that no such contract or request has ever been made, but that, for certain legal purposes, it must be held to have been made. But the phrase is applied equally to the most rational and obvious inferences of fact. [IMPLIED.]

FIDEJUSSORES. Sponsors, sureties; a word derived from the Roman law. 4 *Steph. Com.*

FIDUCIARY ESTATE. The estate or interest of a trustee in lands or money, as opposed to the beneficial interest or enjoyment thereof.

FIEF. [FEE, 1.]

FIEF D'HAUBERT. The Norman phrase for tenure by knight-service. 1 *Steph. Com.* [KNIGHT-SERVICE.]

FIERDING COURTS were local courts under the ancient Gothic constitutions. They were so called, because *four* were instituted within every superior district or hundred.

FIERI FACIAS, or **FI. FA.** A writ of execution for him that hath recovered in an action of debt or damages, addressed to the sheriff, to command him to levy the debt or damages from the goods of the party against whom judgment is recovered. It is opposed to a *levari facias*, which affects the *profits* of a man's lands as well as his goods; to an *elegit*, which affects lands and goods; and to a *capias ad satisfaciendum*, which is directed against the person. *R. S. C. Ord. XLIII. r.* 1; 3 *Steph. Com.* See EXECUTION. *See* next title.

FIERI FACIAS DE BONIS ECCLESIASTICIS. A writ of execution issued when a judgment debtor is a clerk in holy orders, and the sheriff returns (*i.e.*, endorses on the writ), that the debtor has no lay fee within his county. *R. S. C. Ord. XLIII. r.* 3.

FIERI FECI. A return to the writ of *fieri facias*, denoting that the sheriff or other officer to whom it is directed has levied the sum named in the writ, either wholly or as to that part to which the return is applicable. [RETURN.]

FILACER. An officer in the superior courts at Westminster, so called because he *filed* those writs whereon he made process. Abolished by 7 Will. 4 & 1 Vict. c. 30.

FILING BILL IN EQUITY signified placing a copy of the bill on the files of the court. This was done by one of the clerks of records and writs. [CLERK OF RECORDS AND WRITS.] The filing of the bill was the commencement of the formal proceedings in a Chancery suit : now superseded under the Judicature Act, 1875, by the "general indorsements" in Appendix (A.), Part III., or such similarly concise forms as the nature of any given case may require. *R. S. C. Ord. III. r.* 3.

FILIUS MULIERATUS. The same as *mulier puisné*. 1 *Steph. Com.* [MULIER PUISNÉ.]

FILIUS NULLIUS. FILIUS POPULI. (Son of no man. Son of the people.) Expressions used of a bastard. 2 *Steph. Com.*

FILUM AQUÆ MEDIUM. The thread or middle part of a stream which divides the jurisdictions or properties. Riparian owners possess the bed of a river *usque ad medium filum*.

FINAL JUDGMENT is a judgment awarded at the *end* of an action, so opposed to an *interlocutory judgment*. 3 *Steph. Com.* [INTERLOCUTORY JUDGMENT.]

FINAL PROCESS. The expression used to denote execution on final judgment. 3 *Steph. Com.* [FINAL JUDGMENT; PROCESS.]

FINDER OF GOODS has a special property in them, good against everyone but the true owner.

FINDING OF A JURY. The verdict of a petty jury. But the expression may also be applied to the presentment of a grand jury; thus we say that a true bill was *found* against such a party. 4 *Steph. Com.*

FINE. 1. Fine of lands and tenements.

This is sometimes called a *feoffment of record;* though it might with more accuracy be called an *acknowledgment of a feoffment on record.* [FEOFF-MENT.] It was an amicable composition or agreement of a suit, either actual or fictitious, by leave of the king or his justices, whereby lands in question became, or were acknowledged to be, the right of one of the parties. In its original it was founded on an actual suit commenced at law for recovery of possession of lands. It was called a *fine,* because it put an *end,* not only to the suit thus commenced, but also to all other suits and controversies concerning the same matter. *Cowel;* 2 *Bl.;* 1 *Steph. Com; Hallam's Const. Hist. ch.* 1.

2. Fine on alienation.

This was a sum of money paid in ancient times to the lord by a tenant whenever he had occasion to make over his land to another; and so, even to the present day, fines are payable by the custom of most manors, to the lord, upon every descent or alienation of a copyhold tenement. 2 *Bl.;* 1 *Steph. Com.*

3. Fine for endowment.

This was a fine anciently payable to the lord by the widow of a tenant, without which she could not be endowed of her husband's lands. It was abolished under Henry I., and afterwards by *Magna Charta.* 2 *Bl.*

4. A sum of money payable by a lessee on a renewal of the lease.

5. A pecuniary mulct inflicted by way of penalty for an offence. 4 *Steph. Com.*

FINE FORCE signifies an unavoidable constraint. To do a thing *de fine force* is to do it under constraint. *Cowel.*

FINES FOR ALIENATION. [FINE, 2.]

FINES IN COPYHOLD. [FINE, 2.]

FIRE INSURANCE POLICY. [INSURANCE.]

FIRE ORDEAL. An ancient form of ordeal confined to persons of high rank. [ORDEAL.]

FIREBOTE, otherwise called house-bote, signifies a sufficient allowance of wood to burn in a house. 1 *Steph. Com.*

FIRM. The name or style under which a house of trade is carried on; also the collective name of the partners. See the *Partnership Act,* 1890, s. 3. As to suing partners in the name of the firm, see Ord. XLVIIIA, R.S.C. 1891.

FIRMA. Victuals or provisions; a farm; also rent. [FARM.]

FIRMA NOCTIS. A customary tribute formerly paid towards the entertainment of the king for one night.

FIRST CLASS MISDEMEANANT. By s. 67 of the Prisons Act, 1865 (28 & 29 Vict. c. 126), it is provided that, in every prison to which that Act applies (*i.e.*, the county, city and borough prisons of England and Wales), prisoners convicted of misdemeanor, and not sentenced to hard labour, shall be divided into two divisions, one of which shall be called the *first division;* and whenever any person convicted of misdemeanor is sentenced to imprisonment, without hard labour, it shall be lawful for the court or judge, before whom such person has been tried, to order, if such court or judge think fit, that such person shall be treated as a *misdemeanant of the first division;* and a misdemeanant of the first division is not to be deemed a "criminal prisoner" within the meaning of the Act.

A misdemeanant of the first division, referred to in the above section, is usually called a "first class misdemeanant," and, as above stated, he is not treated as a "criminal prisoner," that is, by s. 4, a prisoner charged with, or convicted of, any crime He now falls under Division I. of the Prisons Act, 1898 (61 & 62 Vict. c. 41).

FIRST FRUITS. The first year's whole profits of every spiritual living in one year, given in ancient times to the Pope throughout all Christendom. These payments were restrained by various Acts of parliament, but they were made notwithstanding, until in the year 1535 they were annexed to the Crown by 26 Hen. 8, c. 3. In the year 1703 they were restored to the Church by Queen Anne, under the name of Queen Anne's Bounty. 2 & 3 *Ann. c.* 11; 1 *Steph. Com.,* 2 *Steph. Com.* 670. [QUEEN ANNE'S BOUNTY.]

IRST IMPRESSION. A case of *first impression* (Lat. *primæ impressionis*) is a case for which there is no precedent applicable in all respects.

FIRST INSTANCE, COURT OF. That before which an action is first tried. Thus distinguished from a court of appeal.

FISC, or FISCUS. The treasury of a state.

FISCAL. Belonging to the exchequer or revenue.

FISH ROYAL. Whale and sturgeon, which, when thrown ashore, or caught near the coast, are the property of the sovereign. 2 *Steph. Com.*

FISHERY is a word often used to denote a right of fishing. The right is of three kinds : (1) A free fishery. (2) A several fishery. (3) A common of piscary. A *free fishery* is an exclusive right of fishing in a public river. A *free fishery* differs from a *several* fishery, because he that has a *several* fishery, must be owner of the soil, which in a free fishery is not requisite. It differs also from a *common of piscary* in that a *free fishery* is an exclusive right, and a *common of piscary* is not so. 1 *Steph. Com.*

FITZHERBERT. Sir Anthony Fitzherbert, of Norbury, in Derbyshire, was born in the latter part of the fifteenth century. He was the author of a work called "The Grand Abridgment," containing an abstract of the Year-Books till his time, the first edition of which was published in 1514 ; also of a publication called *Natura Brevium* (generally referred to as "F. N. B."), which is a comment upon the writs existing in his time, and issuing out of the king's courts. He was called to the degree of serjeant in 1510 ; in 1516 he was made one of the king's serjeants, and received the honour of knighthood ; and about Easter, 1522, he was made a judge of the Court of Common Pleas. His signature is the last but one of the seventeen subscribers to the articles of impeachment against Cardinal Wolsey, and he was one of the commissioners appointed on the trials both of Sir Thomas More and Bishop Fisher.

Sir Anthony Fitzherbert died, as appears by his epitaph in the church at Norbury, on May 27th, 1538. 1 *Steph. Com.*

FIVE MILE ACT is a name given to the stat. 35 Eliz. c. 2, passed in 1593, whereby popish recusants convicted for not going to church were compelled to repair to their usual place of abode and not to remove above five miles from thence under certain penalties. Repealed by 7 & 8 Vict. c. 102.

FIXTURES. Things of an accessory character, annexed to houses or lands ; including not only such things as grates in a house, or steam engines in a colliery, but also windows and palings. To be a fixture, a thing must not constitute part of the principal subject, as in the case of the walls or floors of a house ; but, on the other hand, it must be in actual union or connection with it, and not merely brought into contact with it, as in the case of a picture suspended on hooks against a wall. As a general rule the property, by being annexed to the land, immediately belongs to the freeholder, but there are three exceptions to the rule. (*a.*) In favour of trade fixtures. (*b.*) For agricultural purposes. See *Agricultural Holdings Act*, 1883, *s.* 34. (*c.*) For ornament and convenience. See *Woodfall Land and Tent.*, *14th ed., ch. XVI., s.* 8 ; 2 *Steph. Com. ; Amos and Ferard on Fixtures.*

FLAGRANTE DELICTO. An expression applied to the apprehension of a man red-handed in the act of committing a crime.

FLEET. 1. A place where the tide flows— a creek, hence Northfleet, etc.

2. A famous prison in London, so called from a river or ditch that was formerly there, and on the site whereof it stood. By 5 & 6 Vict. c. 22 it was abolished, and it was pulled down in 1845.

FLEET-BOOKS contain the entries of marriages solemnised in the Fleet Prison from 1686 to 1754. They are not admissible in evidence to prove a marriage. They are now deposited in the Registrar-General's office. 3 & 4 *Vict. c.* 92 *ss.* 6, 20.

FLETA. A feigned name of a learned lawyer, who lived in the time of Edward I. He wrote a book of the common law of England, as it existed in his time. The work is entitled " Fleta, seu Commentarius Juris Anglicani." He is supposed to have been confined in the Fleet Prison, hence the name. 1 *Steph. Com. ; 4 Steph. Com.*

FLOATING CAPITAL. Capital retained for the purpose of meeting current expenditure.

FLOOR OF THE COURT. That part between the judge and the first row of counsel. Parties who appear in person stand there.

FLOTSAM, or **FLOATSAM,** signifies any goods that by shipwreck be lost, and lie *floating* or swimming upon the top of the water. These, with other wreck, belong to the Crown, if no owner appears to claim them within a year and a day. See the *Merchant Shipping Act,* 1894; 2 *Steph. Com.;* 3 *Steph. Com.* [WRECK.]

FŒNUS NAUTICUM. The extraordinary rate of interest, proportioned to the risk, demanded by a person lending money on a ship, or on *bottomry* as it is termed. The agreement for such a rate of interest is also called *fœnus nauticum.* 2 *Steph. Com.* [BOTTOMRY.]

FOLCLAND. [FOLKLAND.]

FOLCMOTE. [FOLKMOTE.]

FOLDAGE. [FALDAGE.]

FOLIO signifies generally seventy-two words of a legal document. But for some purposes ninety words are reckoned to the folio.

FOLKLAND, in the times of the Saxons, was land held in villenage, being distributed among the common *folk,* or people, at the pleasure of the lord of the manor, and resumed at his discretion. Not being held by any assurance in writing, it was opposed to *book* land, or *charter* land, which was held by deed. 1 *Steph. Com.*

FOLKMOTE. A word which, in its meaning, included two kinds of courts; the old county court, and the sheriff's tourn. Some think that it was a common council of all the inhabitants of a city, town, or borough, convened by sound of bell to the mote-hall or house.

FOOT OF A FINE. The conclusion of a fine. [FINE, 1.]

FORBARRE, or **FORBAR,** is for ever to deprive. 9 *Rich.* 2, *c.* 2, and 6 *Hen.* 6, *c.* 4.

FORCE generally means unlawful violence.

FORCE AND ARMS (Lat. *Vi et armis*). Words sometimes inserted in indictments, and in declarations for trespass,

but now no longer necessary. 3 *Steph. Com.*

FORCIBLE DETAINER. A forcible holding possession of any lands or tenements, whereby the lawful entry of justices, or others having a right to enter, is barred or hindered. 4 *Steph. Com.*

FORCIBLE ENTRY. The violent entering and taking possession of lands or tenements with menaces, force, and arms, which is both a civil and a criminal injury. 3 *Steph. Com.;* 4 *Steph. Com.*

FORECHEAPUM. Pre-emption; forestalling the market; from the Saxon *fore,* before; and *ceapan,* to buy.

FORECLOSURE. The forfeiture by a mortgagor of his equity of redemption, by reason of his default in payment of the principal or interest of the mortgage debt within a reasonable time. Foreclosure may be enforced in equity by a proceeding called a *foreclosure action.* 1 *Steph. Com.;* *Sm. Man. Eq.;* *Wms. R. P.*

FOREGIFT. A payment in advance; a word generally applied to money paid down, in consideration of a lease, by the intended lessee. See 5 & 6 *Vict. c.* 108, *s.* 30.

FOREHAND RENT. Rent payable in advance.

FOREIGN ATTACHMENT. A process by which a debt due to a judgment debtor from a person not a party to the action or suit is made available for satisfying the claim of the judgment creditor. Such a process has been immemorially used in London, Bristol, and other cities. 3 *Steph. Com.* [CUSTOM OF LONDON.]

FOREIGN BILL OF EXCHANGE is a bill *not* drawn in any part of the United Kingdom of Great Britain, the Isle of Man and the Channel Islands, or not made payable in, or drawn upon, any person resident therein. See *Bills of Exchange Act,* 1882, *s.* 4; 2 *Steph. Com.*

FOREIGN ENLISTMENT ACTS are statutes for preventing British subjects serving foreign states in war. The Foreign Enlistment Act of 1870 (33 & 34 Vict. c. 90) provides that if any British subject shall, without the licence of His Majesty, accept any commission in the military or naval service of any foreign state at war with any friendly state (*i.e.,* a state at peace with His

FOREIGN ENLISTMENT ACTS—*contd.* Majesty) he shall be punishable by fine or imprisonment to the extent of two years, or both. And any person who, without licence from the Crown, shall build or equip any ship for the service of a foreign state at war with a friendly state, is punishable in like manner. 4 *Steph. Com.*

FOREIGN JURISDICTION ACT, 1890, regulates the exercise by the Crown of the powers and jurisdictions acquired by it in countries out of the dominions of the British Crown. 1 *Steph. Com.*

FOREIGN LAW is a question of fact which must be proved by the evidence of expert witnesses. See 24 *Vict. c.* 11, and *Chitty's Statutes, vol. II., p.* 827, *and note.*

FOREIGN PLEA. A plea objecting to the judge on the ground that the matter in hand is not within his jurisdiction.

FOREJUDGER (Lat. *Forisjudicatio*). A judgment whereby a man is deprived of a thing in question. To be forejudged the court is when an officer or attorney of any court is expelled from the same for some offence.

FOREMAN. The presiding member of a jury.

FORENSIC MEDICINE. The science of medical jurisprudence, comprising those matters which may be considered as common ground to both medical and legal practitioners; as, for instance, inquiries relating to suspected murder or doubtful sanity. 1 *Steph. Com.*

FORESHORE. That part of the shore which is covered by an ordinary tide. It *primâ facie* belongs to the Crown.

FOREST. As a legal right, it is defined as the right of keeping, for the purpose of hunting, the wild beasts and fowls of forest, chase, park, and warren, in a territory or precinct of woody ground or pasture set apart for the purpose. 1 *Steph. Com.*

FOREST COURTS. The courts instituted for the government of the king's forests in different parts of the kingdom. They are now obsolete.

FOREST LAW. The old law relating to the forest; under colour of which the most horrid tyrannies and oppressions were exercised, in the confiscation of lands for the purposes of the royal forests. 1 *Steph. Com.*

FORESTALLING. [ENGROSSING, 1.]

FORFEITURE is defined by Blackstone as a punishment annexed by law to some illegal act or negligence, in the owner of lands, tenements, or hereditaments, whereby he loses all his interest therein, and they go to the party injured, as a recompense for the wrong which either he alone, or the public together with himself, hath sustained. *E.g.,* alienation in mortmain, disclaimer by tenant of lord's title, breach of copyhold customs, breach of covenants in a lease. (See, however, relief given in case of lease, Conveyancing Acts, 1881, s. 14, and 1892, s. 2 (2).) 1 *Steph. Com.*

Many of the grounds of forfeiture which formerly existed are now obsolete. And, especially, forfeitures to the Crown for treason and felony are abolished by s. 1 of the Felony Act, 1870 (33 & 34 Vict. c. 23).

FORFEITURE OF MARRIAGE (Lat. *Forisfactura maritagii*). A writ which lay against him who, holding by knight's service, and being under age and unmarried, refused her whom the lord offered him without disparagement, and married another. *T. L.; Cowel.* [DISPARAGEMENT; VALOR MARITAGII.]

FORGABULUM, or **FORGAVEL.** A quit rent, or a small reserved rent in money.

FORGERY. The fraudulent making or alteration of a writing to the prejudice of any man's right; or of a stamp, to the prejudice of the revenue. 4 *Steph. Com.* It is a common mistake to suppose that if a deed is really executed by the parties by whom it purports to be executed, it cannot be a forgery. So far from this being the case, any material alteration of a written instrument, however slight, made with intent to defraud, is a forgery. 24 & 25 *Vict. c.* 98. See also the Forged Transfers Acts, 1891 and 1892.

FORINSECUM MANERIUM. That part of a manor which lies without a town, and is not included within the liberties thereof.

FORISFAMILIARI. A word applied to a son who accepts part of his father's lands in discharge of any further claim upon him.

FORISFAMILIATION. The separation of a child from the father's family.

FORMÂ PAUPERIS (in the character of a pauper). A litigant applying to sue *in formâ pauperis* must swear that he is not worth £25, except his wearing apparel and the subject-matter of the cause in question. It is discretionary with the court to grant the indulgence of suing *in formâ pauperis*, but when granted it exempts the litigant from all court, counsel's and solicitor's fees. See *R. S. C.* 1883, *Ord. XVI. rr.* 22—31. 3 *Steph. Com.*

FORMEDON (Lat. *Brere de forma donationis*) was a writ in the nature of a "writ of right," granted to persons claiming by virtue of any entail under the Statute of Westminster the Second (13 Edw. 1, c. 1). [WRIT OF RIGHT.] It was of three kinds.
  1. A *formedon* in the *descender.*
  2. A *formedon* in the *remainder.*
  3. A *formedon* in the *reverter.* 3 *Steph. Com.*
  Abolished by 3 & 4 Will. 4, c. 27, s. 36.

FORSPEAKER. An attorney or advocate in a cause.

FORSTALLING. [ENGROSSING, 1.]

FORTHWITH. When a defendant is ordered to plead *forthwith* he must plead within twenty-four hours. In a statute the word means within a reasonable time.

FORTUNA is sometimes used for *treasure trove.* [TREASURE TROVE.]

FORTUNE-TELLERS. Persons professing to tell fortunes are punishable as rogues and vagabonds. See 5 *Geo.* 4, c. 83.

FORUM. A word frequently used to signify the place where jurisdiction is exercised in a given case. Thus, if a person be sued in England, on a contract made in France, England in the given case, is the *forum*, and the law of England is, accordingly, the *lex fori.*

FORUM ORIGINIS. The court of the country of a man's domicile by birth.

FORWARDING MERCHANT. One who receives and forwards goods, taking upon himself the expenses of transportation, for which he receives a compensation from the owners, having no concern in the vessels or wagons by which they are transported, and no interest in the freight, and not being deemed a common carrier, but a mere warehouseman and agent. *Story on Bailments.*

FOSTER-LAND. Land given for finding food or victuals for any person or persons, as for monks in a monastery.

FOSTER-LEAN (Sax.) A nuptial gift; the jointure or stipend for the maintenance of a wife; the remuneration fixed for the rearing of a foster-child.

FOUR CORNERS of an instrument; that which is contained on the face of a deed (without any aid from the knowledge of the circumstances under which it was made) is said to be within its four corners, because every deed is supposed to be written on one entire skin.

FOUR SEAS. The seas surrounding England; divided into the western, including the Scotch and Irish; the northern, or North Sea; the eastern, or German Ocean; and the British Channel. [BEYOND SEAS.]

FOXHUNTING upon the land of another is a trespass. *Paul* v. *Summerhayes* (4 Q. B. D. 9).

FOX'S ACT. The stat. 32 Geo. 3, c. 60, and extended to Ireland by 33 Geo. 3, c. 43, by which it was enacted that, in every trial of indictment for libel, the jury might give a general verdict of guilty or not guilty upon the whole issue; and that they should not be required by the court or judge to find a defendant guilty merely on proof of publication, by such defendant, of the paper charged to be a libel, and of the sense ascribed to it in the indictment. 3 *Steph. Com.*

FRACTION OF A DAY, the law does not recognise, except in cases of necessity and for the purposes of justice. When therefore a thing is to be done on a certain day, all that day is allowed for doing it.

FRANCHISE. A royal privilege, or branch of the king's prerogative, vested in the hands of a subject. It arises either from royal grant or from prescription which presupposes a grant. It is an incorporeal hereditament and is synonymous with liberty. There are many kinds, *e.g.*, bodies corporate, the

FRANCHISE—*continued.*

right to hold fairs, markets, ferries, fisheries. 1 *Steph. Com.* At the present day, the word is most frequently used to denote the right of voting for a member to serve in parliament, which is called the parliamentary franchise ; or the right of voting for an alderman or town councillor, which is called the municipal franchise.

FRANK. To *frank* a letter means to send it post-free, so that the person who receives it shall have nothing to pay. This is now done in the ordinary way by prepaying the postage. Formerly members of parliament, peers, etc., had the privilege of franking their letters by autograph. This right was abolished on the establishment of the penny postage by 3 & 4 Vict. c. 96. 2 *Steph. Com.* For other senses of the word, see the following titles.

FRANKALMOIGN. Tenure in *frankalmoign*, or free alms, was a spiritual tenure, whereby religious corporations held lands of the donors to them and their successors for ever. They were free of all other but religious services, and the *trinoda necessitas.* This tenure is expressly excepted in the 12 Car. II. c. 24, s. 7, and therefore still subsists. It differs from *tenure by divine service*, in which the tenants were obliged to do some special divine service in certain, for neglect of which the lord might distrain, without any complaint to the visitor. 1 *Steph. Com.*

FRANK-BANK. The same as *freebench*. [FREEBENCH.]

FRANK-FEE. A tenure in which no service is required. This is sometimes called an *improper feud*, because free from all services, but not from homage.

FRANK-FOLD. [FALDAGE.]

FRANK-MARRIAGE, or **FREE MARRIAGE**. A tenure in tail special, which arises when a man seised of land in fee simple gives it to another man and his wife, who is the daughter or sister or otherwise of kin to the donor, *in free marriage (in liberum maritagium)*, by virtue of which words they have an estate in special tail, and hold the land of the donor quit of all manner of services, except fealty, till the fourth degree of consanguinity be past between the issues of the donor and donee. This tenure has now grown out of use, but is still capable of subsisting. 1 *Steph. Com.*

FRANK-PLEDGE. A pledge or surety to the sovereign for the good behaviour of free men. 1 *Steph. Com.* [COURT LEET.]

FRANK-TENEMENT (Lat. *Liberum tenementum*). The same as *freehold ;* used in old time in opposition to *villenage.* 1 *Steph. Com.* [FREEHOLD.]

FRATER CONSANGUINEUS, in a narrow sense, indicates a brother by the father's side, as opposed to *frater uterinus*, a brother by the mother's.

FRATER NUTRICIUS. An expression used in ancient deeds for a bastard brother.

FRATER UTERINUS. A brother by the mother's side. 1 *Steph. Com.*

FRAUD. The modes of fraud are infinite, and it has been said that the courts have never laid down what shall constitute fraud, or any general rule, beyond which they will not go in giving equitable relief on the ground of fraud. Fraud is, however, usually divided into two large classes, actual fraud and constructive fraud.

An actual fraud may be defined to be something said, done or omitted by a person with the design of perpetrating what he must have known to be a positive fraud.

Constructive frauds are acts, statements or omissions which operate as virtual frauds on individuals, or which, if generally permitted, would be prejudicial to the public welfare, and yet may have been unconnected with any selfish or evil design ; as, for instance, bonds and agreements entered into as a reward for using influence over another, to induce him to make a will for the benefit of the obligor. For such contracts encourage a spirit of artifice and scheming and tend to deceive and injure others. *Sm. Man. Eq.*

FRAUD ON A POWER is such an exercise of a power of appointment as defeats the intention of the person creating it.

FRAUDS, STATUTE OF. The statute 29 Car. 2, c. 3, passed for the prevention of frauds and perjuries. This is attempted to be done by enactments providing that various transactions therein specified shall be in writing, or evidenced by some memorandum in writing, signed by the party who is sought to be made liable thereon ; else they shall, for most or all purposes, be deemed invalid. The statute also required *three* witnesses to a will of real property, a provision altered by the Statute of Wills, passed in the year 1837. This statute is one of the most important statutes ever passed by the legislature, especially with reference to mercantile contracts. Section 4 is specially important. Section 17 (relating to sale of goods for 10*l*. or upwards) has been superseded by the Sale of Goods Act, 1893. 1 *Steph. Com.; Chitty on Contracts; Smith on Contracts; Wms. R. P.*

FRAUDULENT CONVEYANCES. See 13 Eliz. c. 5, and 27 Eliz. c. 4.

FRAUDULENT PREFERENCE. [PREFERENCE, FRAUDULENT.]

FREE BOROUGH MEN. [FRIBORGH.]

FREE CHAPEL. Places of worship of royal foundation exempted from the jurisdiction of the ordinary, or founded by private persons to whom the Crown has thought fit to grant the same privilege. 2 *Steph. Com.*

FREE FISHERY. [FISHERY.]

FREE SERVICES were such as were not unbecoming the character of a soldier or a *freeman* to perform ; as to serve under his lord in the wars, to pay a sum of money, and the like. [FREEHOLD.]

FREE SHIPS, FREE GOODS. A maxim implying that, in time of war, neutral vessels are to impart a neutral character to the goods of belligerents carried therein, so as to exempt them from capture. This doctrine, except so far as relates to contraband of war, is recognised in the document generally known as the Declaration of Paris, 1856. [DECLARATION OF PARIS.]

FREE WARREN. A franchise or royalty derived from the Crown, empowering the grantees to take and kill beasts and fowls of warren ; also for the preservation and custody thereof. 1 *Steph. Com.* [WARREN.]

FREEBENCH (*Francus bancus*). The right which a widow has in her husband's copyhold lands, corresponding to dower in the case of freeholds. The extent of the right to freebench, and the conditions under which it is to be enjoyed, vary according to the custom of the manor. 1 *Steph. Com.; Wms. R. P.* [DOWER.]

FREEDOM OF A BOROUGH. [FREEMAN.]

FREEHOLD, or **FRANK - TENEMENT** (Lat. *Liberum tenementum*), is that land or tenement which a man holdeth in fee, fee tail, or at the least for term of life. It is said that freehold is of two sorts, freehold *in deed* and freehold *in law*. Freehold *in deed* is the real possession of land or tenements in fee, fee tail, or for life ; and freehold *in law* is the right that a man hath to such tenements before entry. It hath likewise been extended to those offices which a man holdeth either in fee or for term of life. A less estate than an estate for life was not deemed worthy of the acceptance of a free man. But an estate which may come to an end by the voluntary act of the tenant in his lifetime may nevertheless be a freehold. Thus an estate during widowhood is regarded as a freehold.

The term freehold is used (1) in opposition to leasehold, *i.e.*, to indicate *estate* ; (2) in opposition to copyhold, *i.e.*, to indicate *tenure*.

A leasehold interest, being an estate for a term of years, is but a chattel interest, and in law is less than an estate of freehold, however long the term may be.

A copyhold interest was originally an estate *at the will of the lord of the manor*, as it is still in name though not in fact ; and an estate at will is the smallest estate known to the law. And in their origin copyholds were deemed worthy the acceptance only of villeins and slaves. Freehold is even yet spoken of in contradistinction to copyhold, though the word *freehold* in a will, if obviously used in contradistinction to *leasehold*, may sometimes be held to include *copyhold*. 1 *Steph. Com.; Wms. R. P.*

We often hear a freehold spoken of as if it were such an estate as a man is *free* to do what he likes with. This is

FREEHOLD—*continued.*

probably owing to the comparative absence in freeholds, of those restrictions and liabilities which, in the case of copyholds, are imposed by custom, and, in the case of leaseholds, by covenants in the lease. But the notion of rights of property in land, without corresponding duties, is abhorrent to the general spirit of our old common law. The distinguishing marks of a freehold were—(1) that it should last for life (unless sooner put an end to by the voluntary act, neglect, or default of the tenant); (2) that the duties or services should be *free*, that is, worthy the acceptance of a free man. To fulfil this latter condition, it was necessary that the services by which the land was held, and by the non-performance of which it would be forfeited, should be *honourable* (*i.e.*, not servile) in respect of their quality, and *certain* in respect both of their quality and quantity. [COPYHOLD; CUSTOMARY FREEHOLD; PRIVILEGED VILLENAGE; TENURE.]

FREEHOLD, CUSTOMARY. [CUSTOMARY FREEHOLD.]

FREEMAN. An allodial proprietor, one born or made free to enjoy certain municipal immunities and privileges.

Previous to the Municipal Corporations Act, 1835, these privileges could be sold or given away. See also the Municipal Corporations Act, 1882, which however is qualified in certain respects by the Honorary Freedom of Boroughs Act, 1885. 3 *Steph. Com.*

FREEMAN OF LONDON. The freedom of the city of London can be obtained in three different methods: (1) By *patrimony*, that is, as the son of a freeman born after the father has acquired his freedom: (2) By *servitude*, that is, by serving an apprenticeship of seven years to a freeman; and, (3) By *redemption*, that is, by purchase.

The last method includes the case where the freedom of the city is obtained by honorary gift, as a mark of distinction for public services. 2 *Steph. Com.*

FREIGHT. The sum payable for the hire of a vessel, or for the carriage of goods therein. It may also, in a policy of marine insurance, include the benefit which a shipowner expects to derive from carrying his goods in his own vessel. As to shipowner's lien for freight, see Merchant Shipping Act, 1894, ss. 494, 495. 2 *Steph. Com.*; 3 *Steph. Com.*; *Sm. Merc. Law.*

FREIGHTER. The hirer of a vessel. 2 *Steph. Com.*

FRESH DISSEISIN. That disseisin which was so recent that a man might formerly seek to defeat it of himself, without resorting to the king or the law; as where it was not above fifteen days' old.

FRESH FINE. A fine of lands, levied within a year past, is so called in the Statute of Westminster the Second (13 Edw. 1, st. 2, c. 45). [FINE, 1.]

FRESH PURSUIT, or **FRESH SUIT** (Lat. *Recens persecutio*). Instant and immediate following with intent to recapture a thing lost, as a bird or beast escaped, or goods stolen, etc. In this latter case the party pursuing then had back his stolen goods which otherwise were forfeited to the Crown. 2 *Steph. Com.*

FRIARS. The name of an order of religious persons, of which there were four principal branches: (1) Minors, Grey Friars, or Franciscans. (2) Augustines. (3) Dominicans, or Black Friars. (4) White Friars, or Carmelites.

FRIBORGH, FRIBURGH, or **FRITHBURGH.** The same as *frank-pledge;* the one being in the time of the Saxons, and the other since the Conquest. [FRANK-PLEDGE.]

FRIENDLESS MAN was the old Saxon word for what we call an outlaw.

FRIENDLY SOCIETY. An association for the purpose of affording relief to the members in sickness, and assistance to their widows and children at their deaths. Friendly societies are governed by numerous Acts of parliament. See 38 & 39 *Vict. c.* 60; 39 & 40 *Vict. c.* 32; 42 *Vict. c.* 9; 50 & 51 *Vict. c.* 56; 59 & 60 *Vict. c.* 25 (a consolidating Act).

FRIENDLY SUIT. A suit brought not in a hostile manner, the object being to settle some point of law, or do some act which cannot safely be done except with the sanction of a court of justice.

FRITHBORGH. [FRIBORGH.]

FRITHMAN. A member of a company or fraternity.

FROM. Generally excludes the day from which the time is to be reckoned.

FRUCTUS INDUSTRIALES. [EMBLEMENTS.]

FUAGE, FOCAGE, or FUMAGE. [CHIMNEY-MONEY.]

FUER. To fly ; which may be by bodily flight, or by non-appearance when summoned to appear in a court of justice, which is flight in the interpretation of the law.

FUGITIVE OFFENDERS ACT (44 & 45 Vict. c. 69) provides for the apprehension and sending back of persons accused of any offence, punishable with twelve months or more hard labour, to that part of the Crown's dominions where the offence is alleged to have been committed.

FULL AGE. The age of twenty-one years. 2 *Steph. Com.* [AGE.]

FULL COURT. A court composed of all the judges, members thereof, *e.g.*, the full court in divorce and matrimonial causes consisted of the judge ordinary and at least two other members of the court. Its jurisdiction was transferred to the Court of Appeal by the Judicature Act, 1881 (44 & 45 Vict. c. 68), s. 9. 3 *Steph. Com.*

FUMAGE. [CHIMNEY-MONEY.]

FUNCTUS OFFICIO. A person who has discharged his duty, or whose office or authority has come to an end, is said to be *functus officio*.

FUND, CONSOLIDATED. [CONSOLIDATED FUND.]

FUNERAL EXPENSES. It is the first duty of an executor or administrator to bury the testator in a manner suitable to the estate he has left, and the expenses will form a first charge on the estate ; if, however, he is extravagant he commits a *devastavit*, for which he is answerable to the creditors or legatees.

FUNGIBLES. Movable goods which may be estimated by weight, number or measure, as grain or coin. They are opposed to jewels, paintings, etc. *Bell ; Toml.*

FURANDI ANIMUS. The intention of stealing ; that is, the intention, in one who takes goods, of unlawfully depriving the right owner of his property

therein. 4 *Steph. Com. ; Russell on Crimes.* [LARCENY.]

FURTHER ADVANCE or CHARGE. A second or subsequent loan of money to a mortgagor by a mortgagee, either on the same, or on an additional security.

FURTHER ASSURANCE. A covenant for further assurance, in a deed of conveyance, means a covenant to make to the purchaser any additional " assurance " which may be necessary to complete his title. It is *implied* in conveyances made on and after the 1st of January, 1882, by virtue of the Conveyancing Act, 1881. [ASSURANCE, 1.]

FURTHER CONSIDERATION. It frequently happens that a judgment in Chancery directs accounts and inquiries to be taken before the master, and reserves the further consideration. The hearing on the master's certificate is called a hearing on *further consideration.*

FURTHER DIRECTIONS. When accounts in Chancery were taken before masters ordinary, a hearing after a master had made his report in pursuance of the directions of the decree was called a hearing on *further directions.* This stage of a suit is now called a hearing on *further consideration.* [FURTHER CONSIDERATION.]

FURTUM. Theft, robbery.

FUTURE ESTATE. An estate to take effect in possession at a future time. The expression is most frequently applied to contingent remainders and executory interests ; but it would seem to be also applicable to vested remainders and reversions. See 1 *Steph. Com.* [CONTINGENT REMAINDER ; EXECUTORY INTEREST ; VESTED REMAINDER.]

GABALET. [GAVELET.]

GABEL, or GABLE. [GAVEL.]

GAGE (*Vadium*). A pawn or pledge.

GAGE, ESTATES IN. Estates held in pledge ; such pledge being of two kinds : *vivum vadium*, living pledge, or *vifgage* (a phrase now obsolete) ; and *mortuum vadium*, dead pledge, or *mortgage*. 1 *Steph. Com.* [MORTGAGE ; VIVUM VADIUM.]

GAGER DELIVERANCE. To wage deliverance; that is, to give security for the re-delivery of cattle or other goods illegally distrained and removed out of the jurisdiction. The ordinary remedy in such cases was by *withernam*, which was a reciprocal distress of the goods of the wrong-doer; but if the latter was sued and appeared, he was allowed to *gage deliverance* instead.

GALE. The payment of a rent or annuity. [GAVEL.]

GALE DAY. The day on which rent is payable.

GAME. A name used to denote animals and birds that are objects of the chase, *feræ naturæ*.

This word is defined under the Game Acts as including hares, pheasants, partridges, grouse, heath or moor game, black game and bustards; though some of the provisions of these Acts are directed to deer, woodcocks, snipes, quails, landrails, and rabbits. 2 *Steph. Com.*

At common law game belongs to a tenant and not to a landlord, but the right to game is frequently reserved to the landlord in the lease.

A game licence must be taken out by anyone killing or taking game. 2 *Steph. Com.* As to the right of occupier to kill hares and rabbits, see Ground Game Act, 1880. 2 *Steph. Com.*

GAMING, or **GAMBLING**. The playing of any game of chance for money or money's worth. The following games are prohibited under various statutes :— Faro, basset, ace of hearts, hazard, passage, roly poly, and roulette; all games with dice, except backgammon. By various acts of the present reign, provision is made for the punishment of those who keep or frequent common gaming-houses. See 8 & 9 *Vict. c.* 109; 16 & 17 *Vict. c.* 119; 17 & 18 *Vict. c.* 38; 35 & 36 *Vict. c.* 94; 36 & 37 *Vict. c.* 38; 37 & 38 *Vict. c.* 49; 37 *Vict. c.* 15; 55 & 56 *Vict. c.* 9.

GANGS (AGRICULTURAL) ACT (30 & 31 Vict. c. 130) regulates the employment of children, young persons and women by gangmasters upon agricultural work.

GAOL DELIVERY, COMMISSION OF. A commission empowering the judges and others to whom it is directed to try every prisoner who shall be in the gaol when they arrive at the circuit town. 3 *Steph. Com.*; 4 *Steph. Com.* [ASSIZE, COURTS OF.]

GARNISHEE. A person who is *garnished* or warned. The word is especially applied in law to a debtor who is *warned* by the order of a court to pay his debt, not to his immediate creditor, but to a person who has obtained a final judgment against such creditor. The order is called a *garnishee order.* See *R. S. C. Ord. XLV.*; 3 *Steph. Com.* [ARRESTMENT; ATTACHMENT, FOREIGN; CUSTOM OF LONDON.]

GARNISHMENT. Warning, notice, or instruction; as, a warning or notice given to a person to furnish the court with information material to a case before it; or to interplead with the plaintiff. [INTERPLEADER.] But the term is now generally used in connection with the attachment of debts in the hands of a third party. See preceding title.

GARTER. The honourable ensign of a great and noble society of knights, called knights of the Order of St. George, or of the Garter. This order was first instituted by Edward III. upon good success in a skirmish, wherein the king's garter, it is said, was used as a token. The Order of the Garter is the first dignity after the nobility. 2 *Steph. Com.*

GARTH. A little backside or close in the north of England; an enclosure about a house or church; also a dam or weir in a river, for the catching of fish, vulgarly called a fishgarth.

GAVEL signifies tribute, toll, custom, annual rent or revenue, of which there were of old several sorts.

GAVELET. An ancient and special kind of *cessavit* used in London and in Kent, where the custom of gavelkind prevails, whereby a tenant, withholding the rent and services due to his lord, forfeited his land, if no sufficient distress could be found on the premises. The word in its original signification imported *rent.*

The remedy of *gavelet*, as well as that by *cessavit*, has fallen wholly into disuse. [CESSAVIT.]

GAVELGELD. Payment of tribute or toll.

GAVELKIND. A tenure which obtains by custom in the county of Kent, almost the whole of which is subject to it. It is also to be found in some other parts of the kingdom, and is supposed to have been the general custom of the realm in Saxon times. It is said to be a species of socage tenure, modified by the custom of the country. The principal characteristics of this tenure are these :

1. The tenant is of age sufficient to alien his estate by feoffment at the age of fifteen. [FEOFFMENT.]

2. The estate never escheated in case of an attainder for felony ; the maxim being "the father to the bough, the son to the plough." [ATTAINDER ; ESCHEAT ; FELONY.]

3. The tenant always enjoyed the power of disposing by will of the lands and tenements so held.

4. The lands descend on an intestacy, not to the eldest son, but to all the sons together.

5. The widow is endowed of half the lands of which her husband died seised, and the husband is tenant by curtesy of the half, although he have no issue by his wife ; but the estate of the husband and wife ceases by a second marriage. [CURTESY ; DOWER.]

1 *Steph. Com.*

GAZETTE. The official publication of the Government, also called the *London Gazette.* It is evidence of acts of state, and of everything done by the King in his political capacity. Orders of adjudication in bankruptcy are required to be published therein ; and the production of a copy of the *Gazette*, containing a copy of the order of adjudication, is conclusive evidence of the fact, and of the date thereof. 2 *Steph. Com. ; Robson, Bkcy.*

GELD, among the Saxons, signified money or tribute ; also the compensation for a crime ; also a fine or amerciament.

GEMOTE. A Saxon word, signifying an assembly or court.

GENERAL AGENT. An agent empowered to act *generally* in the affairs of his principal, or at least to act for him *generally* in some particular capacity ; as opposed to one authorised to act for him in a particular manner. 2 *Steph. Com.*

GENERAL AVERAGE. [AVERAGE, 3.]

GENERAL DEMURRER. A demurrer not setting forth any special cause of demurrer. 3 *Steph. Com.* A general demurrer admits all the facts as alleged to be true, and refers the case to the judgment of the court upon the substantial merits. [DEMURRER ; SPECIAL DEMURRER.]

GENERAL ISSUE, PLEA OF. A plea which traverses, thwarts, and denies *generally* the whole of the declaration, information, or indictment, without offering any special matter whereby to evade it. Such was the plea of *not guilty* in an action of tort or an indictment for a criminal offence ; a plea of *never indebted* in an action of debt, etc. Such pleas are called the general issue, because, by importing an absolute and general denial of what is alleged in the declaration, they amount at once to an issue ; by which we mean a fact affirmed on one side and denied on the other. 3 *Steph. Com. ; 4 Steph. Com.* Since the Judicature Acts, the plea of the general issue is not admissible in ordinary civil actions, except in cases where it is expressly sanctioned by statute. See *R. S. C.* 1883, *Ord. XIX., rr.* 4, 12, 17 ; *Ord. XXI., r.* 19. In criminal proceedings the general issue is "not guilty" which is pleaded *vivâ voce* by the prisoner at the bar. [NOT GUILTY.]

GENERAL LIEN. The right of a bailee to detain a chattel from its owner until payment be made, not only in respect of that particular article, but of any balance that may be due, on a general account between the bailor and bailee, in the same line of business. 2 *Steph. Com. ; Wms. P. P.* [BAILMENT.]

GENERAL SHIP. A merchant ship which is open *generally* to the conveyance of goods belonging to different owners ; as opposed to a ship *chartered* or *freighted*, that is, a ship which is hired entirely by a single individual. 2 *Steph. Com. ; Wms. P. P.* [CHARTERPARTY.]

GENERAL TAIL. [TAIL GENERAL.]

GENERAL VERDICT. A verdict which, in a civil suit, is absolutely for the plaintiff or for the defendant, or, in a criminal case, is a verdict of guilty or not guilty ; opposed in either case to a special verdict, in which the naked facts are stated, and the inference of law left to be determined by the court. 3 *Steph. Com.*

GENERAL WARRANT. A warrant to apprehend all persons suspected, without naming or describing any person in special. Such a warrant is illegal and void for uncertainty. 4 *Steph. Com.*

GENERAL WORDS. These used generally to be added in conveyances, to convey the easements and rights subsisting in the grantor.

They are now implied by s. 6 of the Conveyancing Act, 1881.

GENTLEMAN. Under this name be comprised all above the rank of yeomen. 2 *Steph. Com.* [YEOMAN.]

GENTLEMAN USHER OF THE BLACK ROD. [BLACK ROD.]

GIFT. A conveyance which passeth either land or goods. As to things immovable, when strictly taken, it is said to be applicable only to lands and tenements given in tail. This limitation of the word is, however, quite obsolete. Blackstone distinguishes a *gift* from a *grant* in that a gift is always gratuitous without binding considerations and therefore void in certain cases, whereas a grant is made upon some consideration or equivalent. 2 *Steph. Com.* [DONATIO MORTIS CAUSÂ ; GRANT.]

GILD. A voluntary association or fraternity. 3 *Steph. Com.* [GUILD.] Also used as synonymous with *geld*, in such compounds as *weregild*. [GELD.]

GILDA MERCATORIA. A mercantile meeting or assembly, by the grant of which from the Crown to any set of men they become an incorporated society. 3 *Steph. Com.*

GIST OF ACTION. The cause for which an action lieth, without which it is not maintainable.

GLANVILLE. The author of a book, written about 1181, entitled *Tractatus de legibus et consuetudinibus regni Angliæ*, probably the first work of the kind.

GLEBE signifies the land of which a rector or vicar is seised in right of the church. By 5 & 6 Vict. c. 54 it is provided that the Tithe Commissioners shall have power to ascertain and define the boundaries of the glebe lands of any benefice. As to sale of glebe see the Glebe Lands Act, 1888. 2 *Steph. Com.*

GLEBÆ ADSCRIPTITII. Villein-socmen who could not be removed from the soil so long as they performed the services due from them.

GOD'S ACRE. A churchyard.

GOD'S PENNY. Earnest money given to a servant when hired.

GOOD ABEARING (Lat. *Bonus gestus*). See next title.

GOOD BEHAVIOUR. Blackstone speaks of this as synonymous with *good abearing*, and as implying a restraint from acts that be *contra bonos mores*, as well as *contra pacem*, as the haunting of bawdy-houses ; also words tending to scandalise the government, and abuse of the officers of justice, especially in the execution of their office. 4 *Steph. Com.* 253. [KEEPING THE PEACE.]

GOOD CONSIDERATION. A consideration founded on relationship, or natural love and affection. This is not a *valuable* consideration, and will not "sustain a promise" ; that is, that whereas in certain cases a "consideration" is necessary to give legal validity to a promise, so that an action may be brought for breach of the same, a merely "good" consideration will not be sufficient for this purpose. 2 *Steph. Com.* [CONSIDERATION ; CONTRACT.]

GOOD JURY. A jury selected from the special jury list by the order of a judge, for the purpose of assessing the damages on a writ of inquiry. 3 *Steph. Com.* [WRIT OF INQUIRY.]

GOODS AND CHATTELS, in the fullest sense, include any kind of property which, regard being had either to the subject-matter, or to the quantity of interest therein, is not freehold. 1 *Steph. Com.; Wms. P. P. Introd.; Wms. R. P. Introd.* But in practice the expression is most frequently limited to things movable, especially things movable in possession. 2 *Steph. Com.*

GOODWILL. The *goodwill* of a trade or business comprises every advantage which has been acquired by carrying on the business, whether connected with the premises in which the business has been carried on, or with the name of the firm by whom it has been conducted. *Wms. P. P.*

GOVERNMENT. This word is most frequently used to denote the principal executive officer or officers of a state or territory. Thus, when we in England speak of "the government," we generally understand the ministers of the Crown for the time being. But sometimes the word is used differently, so as to indicate the supreme legislative power in a state, or the legislature in a dependent, or semi-independent territory. The word is also used to indicate the art or science of governing. See *Aust. Jur.*, *Lect. VI.*

GRACE, ACT OF. [ACT OF GRACE.]

GRACE, DAYS OF. [DAYS OF GRACE.]

GRAFFER. A scrivener, attorney, or notary.

GRAFFIUM. A writing book or register of deeds and evidences.

GRAMMATICA FALSA NON VITIAT CHARTAM (bad grammar does not vitiate a deed).

GRAND ASSISE. A peculiar species of trial by jury, introduced by King Henry II. with consent of parliament, as an alternative open to the tenant or defendant in the action called a *writ of right*, which he might demand in lieu of trial by battel, which up to that time had been the only means of deciding upon writs of right. Abolished by 3 & 4 Will. 4, c. 42, s. 13. 3 *Steph. Com.*; 4 *Steph. Com.* [WAGER OF BATTEL; WRIT OF RIGHT.]

GRAND CAPE. [CAPE.]

GRAND COUSTUMIER OF NORMANDY. An ancient book containing the ducal customs of Normandy, by which the Channel Islands are for the most part governed. 1 *Steph. Com.*

GRAND DISTRESS. A more extensive kind of distress than ordinary, extending to all the goods and chattels of the party distrained within the county; it lay in those cases when the tenant or defendant was attached, and appeared not, but made default; and also when the other party made default after appearance.

It was thus more extensive than the writs of *grand* and *petit cape*. Obsolete. [CAPE.]

GRAND JURY. A body of from twelve to twenty-three men which the sheriff of every county is bound to return to every session of the peace, and every commission of *oyer* and *terminer*, and of general gaol-delivery.

The grand jury are instructed in the articles of their inquiry by a charge from the judge who presides upon the bench. They then withdraw, to sit and receive indictments, to hear evidence on behalf of the prosecution, and to inquire, upon their oaths, whether there be sufficient cause to call upon the party accused to answer it on trial before a petty jury. 4 *Steph. Com.* [BILL, 3.]

GRAND LARCENY. The name formerly given to the offence of stealing goods above the value of twelve pence. Abolished by 7 & 8 Geo. 4, c. 29, s. 2. 4 *Steph. Com.* [LARCENY.]

GRAND SERJEANTY. A tenure whereby the tenant was bound, instead of serving the king *generally* in the wars, to do some *special* honorary service to the king in person, as to carry his banner, his sword, or the like; or to be his butler, champion, or other officer at his coronation. It was in most other respects like knight-service. 1 *Steph. Com.*

GRANT (Lat. *concessio*). 1. A grant may be defined generally as the transfer of property by an instrument in writing without the delivery of the possession of any subject-matter thereof. This may happen (1) where there is no subject-matter capable of delivery, as in the case of an advowson, patent right, or title of honour; (2) where the subject-matter is not capable of *immediate* delivery, as in the case of a reversion or remainder; (3) where, by reason of the subject-matter of the property being in the custody of another, or for any other cause, it is impracticable or undesirable to transfer the immediate possession. The person making the grant is called the *grantor*; the person to whom it is made, the *grantee*. Where the grantor transfers his whole interest in any subject-matter, the grant is generally called an *assignment*.

A grant has always been the regular method of transferring incorporeal hereditaments, as an advowson, etc., and estates in expectancy, because no "livery," that is, physical delivery, could be made of such estates. For this reason they were said to *lie in grant*; while corporeal hereditaments in possession were said to *lie in livery*.

GRANT—*continued.*

The word "grant" formerly implied a warranty of title, unless followed by a covenant imposing on the grantor a less liability. Now by 8 & 9 Vict. c. 106, s. 4, the word grant is not to imply any covenant, except so far as it may do so by force of any Act of parliament. By the same statute it is provided that all corporeal tenements and hereditaments shall, as regards the conveyance of the immediate freehold thereof, be deemed to lie *in grant* as well as *in livery*. So that the method of conveyance by deed of grant is no longer confined to incorporeal hereditaments and future estates. 1 *Steph. Com.*

According to Blackstone, a *grant* is distinguished from a *gift* as being made upon some consideration or equivalent, whereas a gift is gratuitous. 2 *Steph. Com.* [GIFT.]

2. The word *grant* is also frequently used in reference to public money devoted by parliament for special purposes. *May's Parl. Pract.*

GRANT TO USES. This is the usual mode of transferring realty. It is a grant with uses superadded.

GRATUITOUS. Made without consideration or equivalent.

GRAVAMEN. 1. When we speak of the *gravamen* of a charge or accusation, we mean that part of it which weighs most heavily against the accused.

2. But the word is applied specially to grievances alleged by the clergy, and made by them a subject of complaint to the archbishop and bishops in Convocation. See *Phillimore's Eccl. Law.*

GRAY'S INN. One of the Inns of Court. [INNS OF COURT.]

GREAT SEAL. A seal by virtue of which a great part of the royal authority is exercised. The office of the Lord Chancellor, or Lord Keeper, is created by the delivery of the Great Seal into his custody. 1 *Steph. Com.* By art. 24 of the union between England and Scotland it was provided that there should be one Great Seal for Great Britain, for sealing writs to summon parliaments, for sealing treaties with foreign states, and all public acts of state which concern the United Kingdom.

GREAT TITHES are generally held to include tithes of corn [TITHES], hay and wood, otherwise called *predial* tithes. In *appropriated* livings, they are for the most part reserved to the appropriators. No clear line of demarcation has been drawn between *great* and *small* tithes. 2 *Steph. Com.* [APPROPRIATION; TITHES; VICAR.]

GREEN CLOTH. The counting house of the royal household; so called from the green cloth on the table. [BOARD OF GREEN CLOTH.]

GREEN WAX signified originally the wax in which the seal of the Court of Exchequer was affixed to the estreats (*i.e.*, the extracted and authorised copies) of fines and amerciaments which the sheriff was directed to levy. Hence the expression "green wax" is applied to the estreats themselves.

GRETNA GREEN MARRIAGES. An expression formerly applied to marriages contracted in Scotland by parties who had gone there for the purpose of being married without the delay and formalities required by the law of England. They were usually celebrated at Gretna Green in Dumfriesshire, as being the nearest and most convenient place for the purpose; they have been practically abolished by 19 & 20 Vict. c. 96, which requires that one at least of the parties contracting it should have, at the date thereof, his or her usual place of residence in Scotland, or should have lived there for twenty-one days preceding such marriage.

GROSS. A word indicating independent ownership of incorporeal property. A right *in gross* is one which does *not* belong to the party invested with it *as being the owner or occupier of specifically-determined land* (*i.e.*, which is not *appendant* or *appurtenant* to another thing), but is annexed to, or inheres in, his person; being quite unconnected with anything corporeal, and existing as a separate subject of transfer; thus we speak of a common *in gross*, an advowson *in gross*, etc. 1 *Steph. Com.*

GROSS ADVENTURE. A loan on bottomry, that is, on mortgage of a ship. [BOTTOMRY.]

GROUND GAME ACT, 1880. [GAME.]

GROUND RENT. A rent payable on a building lease.

GROUNDAGE. A tribute paid for the ground on which a ship stands in port. *Cowel ; Pulling on the Customs of London.*

GUARANTEE, in the strict sense, is where one man contracts as surety on behalf of another an obligation to which the latter is also liable as the proper and primary party. See the *Statute of Frauds* (29 *Car.* 2, *c.* 3) and *Mercantile Law Amendment Act*, 1856 (19 & 20 *Vict. c.* 97). 2 *Steph. Com.* ; 3 *Steph. Com.*

GUARDIAN. One who hath the charge or custody of any person or thing ; but commonly he who hath the custody and education of such persons as are not of sufficient discretion to manage their own affairs. 2 *Steph. Com.*

I. GUARDIAN OF A CHILD OR CHILDREN. Of this there are several species :—

1. *A Guardian by Nature.* A father is so called in respect of the guardianship which belongs to him over the person of his *heir apparent*, or of his *heiress presumptive.* 2 *Steph. Com.*

2. *Guardian for Nurture.* A father is so called in respect of the guardianship of all his children ; and, after the father's decease, the mother. This guardianship is said to last only to the age of fourteen years. But though after that age the father or mother may not be properly designated as guardian for nurture, yet the parent is understood to stand substantially in the capacity of guardian to his children so long as they are minors, by having the care and control of their persons during that period. 2 *Steph. Com.*

3. *Guardian in Socage* is one who has the care of the *estate* as well as the *person* of a minor. This species occurs where the legal estate in lands or other hereditaments held in socage descends upon a minor ; in which case the guardianship devolves upon his next of blood, to whom the inheritance cannot descend. This guardianship lasts till the age of fourteen years. 1 *Steph. Com.* ; 2 *Steph. Com.*

4. *Guardian in Chivalry.* If the heir of an estate held by chivalry (or knight service) was under twenty-one, or, being a female, was under fourteen, the lord of whom the land was held was entitled to the wardship of the heir, and was called *guardian in chivalry.* 1 *Steph. Com.* This kind of guardianship entitled the lord to receive the profits of the heir's land without accounting for them. It ceased to exist in 1660,

when the military tenures were abolished by 12 Car. 2, c. 24.

5. *Guardian by Statute* is a guardian appointed by virtue of 12 Car. 2, c. 24, or by virtue of the Guardianship of Infants Act, 1886. The former statute provides that a father may, by deed or will, dispose of the custody, after his death, of such of his children as should be infants (*i.e.*, under age) and unmarried at his death, or should be born posthumously, to any person he pleases, in such manner as to be effectual against all persons claiming as guardians in socage or otherwise. By s. 2 of the Act of 1886, on the death of the father, the mother, if surviving, becomes guardian, either alone, when no guardian is appointed by the father, or jointly with any guardian appointed by the father, or by the High Court or county court. 2 *Steph. Com.*

6. *Guardian by Election* is one appointed by an infant having lands in socage, when the guardianship in socage has terminated by the infant attaining the age of fourteen. This guardianship is now almost wholly disused. 2 *Steph. Com.*

7. *Guardian by Appointment of the High Court of Justice.* This happens where a father has died without exercising his power of appointing guardians ; also where the father's misconduct is such as to make it improper that his children should continue under his control. But the court will not in general appoint a guardian to an infant not possessed of property. See also the Acts 49 & 50 Vict. c. 27 ; 54 & 55 Vict. c. 3 ; and 57 & 58 Vict. c. 41. 2 *Steph. Com.*

8. *Guardian ad Litem.* A guardian appointed by a court of justice to represent an infant in an action or suit. 2 *Steph. Com.* ; 3 *Steph. Com.*

9. *Guardian by Custom.* A guardian who is such by local custom. In copyholds this belongs of common right to the next of blood, to whom the copyhold cannot descend ; and in London to the mayor and aldermen. It is said, however, to have fallen into disuse. 2 *Steph. Com.*

II. GUARDIAN DE L'ESTEMARY. The guardian or warden of the stannaries, or mines in the county of Cornwall. [COURT OF STANNARIES OF CORNWALL AND DEVON.]

III. GUARDIAN OF THE CINQUE PORTS. The warden of the cinque ports. [CINQUE PORTS ; WARDEN OF THE CINQUE PORTS.]

GUARDIAN—*continued.*

IV. GUARDIAN OF THE PEACE. A person entrusted with the keeping of the peace as conservator thereof. [CONSERVATOR OF THE PEACE.]

V. GUARDIANS OF THE POOR. Persons having the management of parish workhouses and unions. The guardians are elected by the owners of property and ratepayers in the parish ; and in the case of two or more parishes being consolidated into one union for the relief of the poor, are elected by the owners and ratepayers of the component parishes. See the *Local Government Act,* 1894 ; 3 *Steph. Com.*

VI. GUARDIAN OF THE SPIRITUALITIES (Lat. *Custos spiritualium*).. The person to whom the spiritual jurisdiction of a diocese is committed during the vacancy of a see.

VII. GUARDIAN OF THE TEMPORALITIES (Lat. *Custos temporalium*). The person to whose custody a vacant see or abbey was committed by the king.

GUILD. A voluntary association or fraternity, usually for some commercial purpose. 3 *Steph. Com.*

GUILD HALL means the place of meeting of a guild. 3 *Steph. Com.* [GUILD.]

GUILD MERCHANT. A mercantile meeting of a guild. 1 *Bl.*; 3 *Steph. Com.* [GUILD.]

GUILDHALL SITTINGS. The sittings held in the Guildhall of the city of London for city of London causes.

GULE OF AUGUST. The first of August, being the day of *St. Peter ad Vincula.*

GUN LICENCE. A duty of 10*s.* is imposed for every such licence by 33 & 34 Vict. c. 57.

GUNPOWDER. As to making, sale, carriage, etc., see 38 Vict. c. 17.

HABEAS CORPORA JURATORUM. The name given to a compulsive process issuing out of the Court of Common Pleas for the bringing in of a jury, or of so many of them as refuse to come upon a *venire facias,* upon the trial of a cause brought to issue. Abolished by s. 104 of the C. L. Proc. Act, 1852.

The corresponding process in the Court of King's Bench was called a *distringas.* [DISTRINGAS.]

HABEAS CORPUS. This is the most celebrated writ in the English law, being the great remedy which that law has provided for the violation of personal liberty.

The most important species of *habeas corpus* is that of *habeas corpus ad subjiciendum,* which is the remedy used for deliverance from illegal confinement. This is directed to any person who detains another in custody, and commands him to produce the body, with the day and cause of his caption and detention, *ad faciendum, subjiciendum, et recipiendum,*—to do, submit to, and receive whatsoever the judge or court awarding such writ shall direct. This writ existed at common law, though it has been improved by statute. By stat. 25 & 26 Vict. c. 20, passed in 1862, no writ of *habeas corpus* shall issue out of England, by authority of any judge or court therein, into any colony or foreign dominion of the Crown, where her Majesty has a lawfully-established court with power to grant and issue such writ, and with power to ensure its due execution throughout such colony or dominion. It has been held that this statute does not extend to the Isle of Man. 1 *Steph. Com.* ; 3 *Steph. Com.*

There are also other kinds of *habeas corpus* mentioned in the books.

1. *Ad respondendum ;* which was to bring up a prisoner confined by the process of an inferior court to charge him with a fresh action in the court above. 3 *Steph. Com.*

2. *Ad satisfaciendum,* with a similar object when *judgment* in an inferior court has been obtained against the prisoner. 3 *Steph. Com.*

3. *Ad faciendum et recipiendum* (otherwise called a *habeas corpus cum causâ*). This writ was applied for when, in an action in an inferior court, the defendant had been arrested ; and it had for its object to remove the proceedings and bring up the body of the defendant to the court above, " to do and receive what the king's court shall deliver in that behalf." 3 *Steph. Com.*

4. *Ad prosequendum, testificandum, deliberandum,* etc., which was issued for bringing up a prisoner to bear testimony in any court, or to be tried in the proper jurisdiction. 3 *Steph. Com.*

But the present law of arrest for debt has lessened the importance of all these species except the last ; and, with regard to the last, the occasions for its use have diminished now that, by various recent enactments, its objects can be attained by order of a judge or of a secretary of state. 3 *Steph. Com.*

HABEAS CORPUS ACTS. The statutes regulating the granting of the writ of *habeas corpus* [HABEAS CORPUS], of which the most celebrated is the Habeas Corpus Act of 1679, 31 Car. 2, c. 2. This Act has been amended and supplemented by 56 Geo. 3, c. 100. 3 *Steph. Com.*

HABENDUM. That clause of a deed which determines the estate or interest granted by the deed. 1 *Steph. Com.*

HABERE FACIAS POSSESSIONEM. A writ of execution to recover possession of a chattel interest in real estate. Now, by R. S. C. 1883, Ord. XLVII., a judgment that a party recover possession of land may be enforced by writ of possession. [CHATTEL INTEREST IN LAND.] See also 3 *Steph. Com.*

HABERE FACIAS SEISINAM. A writ of execution that lay to recover possession of the freehold in an action real or mixed. [ACTIONS MIXED; ACTIONS REAL AND PERSONAL.]

HABERE FACIAS VISUM. A writ that lay in divers cases where *view* (*i.e.*, a personal inspection) was to be taken of lands and tenements in question in an action.

HABITUAL CRIMINALS ACT. [PREVENTION OF CRIMES ACT.]

HÆREDA was the name, under the Gothic constitutions, of the hundred court. 3 *Steph. Com.* [HUNDRED COURT.]

HÆREDE ABDUCTO. A writ that lay for a lord who, having the legal wardship of his tenant under age, could not obtain access to him by reason of the ward having been conveyed away by some other person.

HÆREDE DELIBERANDO ALII QUI HABET CUSTODIAM TERRÆ. An ancient writ, directed to the sheriff, requiring him to command one who had taken away an heir under age to deliver him up to the lawful guardian of his person and estate.

HÆREDIPETA. The next heir to lands.

HÆREDITAS JACENS. A vacant inheritance; that is, an estate upon which no heir has entered, so that no title has been completed to it. This may happen in systems founded on the Roman law, as, for instance, in the law of Scotland; but by the law of England an *heir* (in the English sense of that word) cannot disclaim the inheritance.

HÆRES FACTUS. An heir appointed by will.

HÆRES NATUS. An heir who is such by his birth or descent. This is the only form of heirship recognised in the English law. *Wms. R. P.* [HEIR.]

HÆRETICO COMBURENDO. A writ that lay for burning him who, having once been convicted of heresy by his bishop, afterwards fell again into the same or some other heresy, and was thereupon delivered over to the secular power. It was not till 29 Car. 2, c. 9, that is, the year 1677, that the writ was totally abolished. 2 *Steph. Com.*; 4 *Steph. Com.*

HALF-BLOOD. The relationship between two persons who have but one *nearest* common ancestor, and not a pair of *nearest* common ancestors.

In the succession to personal property, the law makes no difference between relationship by the half-blood and that by the whole blood; but in the succession to land the rule is that the kinsman of the half-blood succeeds next after the kinsman in the same degree of the whole blood when the common ancestor is a male, and next after the common ancestor when the common ancestor is a female. *Stat.* 3 & 4 *Will.* 4, c. 106, s. 9. Until the year 1833, when this statute was passed, kinsmen of the half-blood were entirely excluded from the succession to lands by descent. 1 *Steph. Com.*; 2 *Steph. Com.*

HALF-TIMER. A child who is employed for less than the full time in a factory or workshop, in order that he may attend some "recognised efficient school." See *Elementary Education Act*, 1876, s. 11; *Factory and Workshop Act*, 1901, s. 68.

HALLAMSHIRE. A part of Yorkshire in which the town of Sheffield stands.

HALLMOTE, or **HALIMOTE**. The meeting of tenants of one hall or manor. A Saxon court answering to our court-baron.

HALYMOTE. A holy or ecclesiastical court. Also the same as hallmote. [HALLMOTE.]

HAM. A house; also a village or little town.

HAMESECKEN, or **HAMSOKEN.** The ancient word for burglary or house-breaking. *4 Steph. Com.*

HAMLET. The diminutive of *ham*. [HAM.]

HANAPER OFFICE. An office in the Court of Chancery on its *common law side* (*i.e.*, within what was formerly called the "ordinary jurisdiction" of the court : see CHANCERY). Of the writs issuing out of this "common law side," those having exclusive reference to the affairs of the *subject* were formerly kept in a *hamper* (*in hanaperio*) ; while those relating to matters in which the Crown was mediately or immediately concerned were kept in a little sack or bag (*in parvâ bagâ*). Hence the *hanaper office* signifies the office on the common law side of the Court of Chancery devoted to business relating to the affairs of the subject. *5 & 6 Vict. c. 103 ; 3 Steph. Com.*

HAND-BOROW. A surety, or manual pledge, one of the frankpledges inferior to the headborough. [FRANKPLEDGE ; HEADBOROUGH.]

HAND-HABEND. A thief caught in the very act, having the stolen goods in his hand.

HAND-SALE. A sale made by shaking of hands. (Lat. *venditio per mutuam manuum complexionem*). In process of time the word was used to signify the price or earnest given immediately after the shaking of hands, or instead thereof. *2 Steph. Com.*

HARD LABOUR. A punishment most usually inflicted in company with im-prisonment, first introduced in 1706, by *5 Ann. c. 6.* There are a few cases even now in which it is not lawful to add hard labour to the punishment of imprisonment. The subject is governed now by the Prison Act, 1898, and the rules of the Home Secretary thereunder. *4 Steph. Com.*

HARE. A beast of warren. Is "game" within the Game Acts and Game Certificate Acts, but by 11 & 12 Vict. c. 29, the occupier and owner may kill hares without a certificate. There is no close time for hares, but (except foreign hares) they may not be sold or exposed for sale between March and July, both inclusive. See *55 & 56 Vict. c. 8.* See also the Ground Game Act, 1880, as to right of occupier to kill hares and rabbits. *1 Steph. Com. ; 2 Steph. Com. ; 4 Steph. Com.* [GAME.]

HARIOT. The same as heriot. [HERIOT.]

HAWKERS. Persons who carry their goods from place to place for sale. See, however, *52 & 53 Vict. c. 33.*

HAYBOTE, or **HEDGEBOTE.** Necessary stuff to make and repair hedges, or to make rakes and forks, and such like instruments ; or a permission, expressed or implied, to take the same. *1 Steph. Com.*

HEADBOROUGH, or **HEADBOROW,** signi-fied him that was chief of the frank-pledge, tithing, or decennary, appointed to preside over the rest, being supposed the discreetest man in the borough, town, or tithing. *1 Steph. Com.* [DE-CENNARY ; FRANKPLEDGE ; TITHING.] The office of headborough was united with that of petty constable, on the institution of the latter office, about the reign of Edward III. *2 Steph. Com.* [CONSTABLE, 1.]

HEALFANG, or **HALSFANG** (Lat. *Col-listrigium*). The pillory. Sometimes it is taken for a pecuniary mulct, as a commutation for standing in the pillory.

HEALGEMOTE. [HALYMOTE.]

HEARING. The trial of an action.

HEARSAY EVIDENCE. A statement by a witness of what has been said or declared out of court by a person not party to the suit. Hearsay evidence is in general excluded by our law, but may, in certain cases, be admitted. Consult *Taylor on Evid. : 3 Steph. Com. : 4 Steph. Com.*

HEARTH MONEY. [CHIMNEY MONEY.]

HEDGEBOTE. [HAYBOTE.]

HEIR, in the common law, is he that succeeds by right of blood to any man's lands and tenements in fee ; that is, he upon whom, by right of blood, the law casts the real estate of a deceased person intestate. *1 Steph. Com. ; Wms. R. P.* See also the following titles.

HEIR APPARENT and **HEIR PRE-SUMPTIVE.** It is a rule in law, that no one is the heir of a living person (*nemo est hæres viventis*). The heir is called into existence by the death of his ancestor, for no man, in his lifetime can have an heir.

HEIR APPARENT—*continued.*

The *heir apparent* is the person who, if he survive the ancestor, must certainly be his heir, as the eldest son in the lifetime of his father.

The *heir presumptive* is the person who would be the heir in case of the ancestor's immediate decease. Thus, an only daughter, there being no sons, is the heiress presumptive of her father ; for if he were now to die, she would at once be his heir ; but he may have a son who would supplant her. *Wms. R. P.;* 1 *Steph. Com.*

HEIR AT LAW. The person who succeeds as heir by right of blood, according to the disposition of the law. [HEIR.]

HEIR BY CUSTOM. One upon whom a local custom casts the inheritance of a deceased ancestor.

HEIR IN TAIL. The person selected by law to succeed to the estate tail of an ancestor dying intestate.

HEIRESS. A female heir. Sometimes the word is used in a more extended sense, as in the expression *stealing an heiress ;* an offence which is now punishable by penal servitude for fourteen years. See 24 *&* 25 *Vict. c.* 100, *s.* 53 ; 4 *Steph. Com.* 68.

HEIRESS-STEALING. [HEIRESS.]

HEIRLOOM signifies, strictly, a *limb* or member of the inheritance. By *heirlooms,* we generally mean implements or ornaments of a household, or other personal chattels, which accrue to the heir with the house itself by custom ; or else such chattels as are directed by will or settlement to follow the limitations thereby made of some family mansion or estate. But the last mentioned, though the most usual, is not the strict and proper sense of the term. See also the Settled Land Act, 1882, s. 37. 2 *Steph. Com. ; Wms. P. P.*

HEIRS. A term used in conveyances of estates in which it is intended that the fee-simple should pass : thus, a conveyance to "A. and his heirs," gives A. an estate in fee-simple. And see now Conveyancing Act, 1881, s. 51. The word as thus used is called a word of *limitation* and not of *purchase,* because the heirs of A. take nothing *directly* under the grant but the word is used

to *limit* or *mark out* the estate taken by A.

Similarly, "heirs of the body" is a phrase importing a grant of an estate tail. And see now Conveyancing Act, 1881, s. 51.

"Heirs male of the body " imports a grant of an estate in tail male. [TAIL MALE.]

" Heirs male " is an expression which, in an ordinary deed, will (it is said) confer an estate in fee simple ; but in a will, or in a grant of arms by the Crown, the same phrase will confer an estate in tail male. *Wms. R. P.*

HERALD. [KINGS-AT-ARMS.]

HERALDS' COLLEGE. An ancient royal corporation instituted by Richard III. in 1483. The heralds' books are good evidence of pedigrees. The heralds' office is still empowered to make grants of arms and to permit change of names. 3 *Steph. Com.* [KINGS-AT-ARMS.]

HERBAGE. The fruit of the earth, produced by nature for the bite and food of cattle. But it is also used for a liberty that a man hath to feed his cattle in another man's ground.

HERBAGIUM ANTERIUS. The first crop of grass or hay, in opposition to *aftermath,* or second cutting. [AFTERMATH.]

HEREDITAMENTS are such things, whether corporeal or incorporeal, as a man may have to himself and his heirs by way of inheritance. 1 *Steph. Com.* The word includes everything which may descend to the heir. [HEIR ; HEIRLOOM ; CORPOREAL PROPERTY ; INCORPOREAL HEREDITAMENTS ; REAL AND PERSONAL PROPERTY.]

HERESY. An offence which consists not in a total denial of Christianity, but of some of its essential doctrines, publicly and obstinately avowed. [HÆRETICO COMBURENDO.] Heresy is now subject only to ecclesiastical correction, by virtue of stat. 29 Car. 2, c. 9. 4 *Steph. Com.*

HERETIC. [HÆRETICO COMBURENDO ; HERESY.]

HERETICO COMBURENDO. [HÆRETICO COMBURENDO.]

HERIOT. The best beast or other chattel of a tenant, seized on his death by the lord. The heriot of a military tenant was his arms and habiliments of war, which belonged to the lord for the purpose of equipping his successor. Heriots from freeholders are rare; but heriots from copyholders remain to this day, in many manors, a badge of the ancient servility of the tenure. But the right of the lord, in this as in other respects, is controlled by the custom of the manor. In some cases the heriot consists merely of a money-payment. *Wms. R. P.* The above kind of heriot is called *heriot custom*; but there is another kind, called *heriot service*, which is due upon a special reservation in a grant or lease of lands; but this kind of heriot scarcely ever exists except where it forms part of the service by which a particular tenement has been held from time immemorial. As to valuation of heriots on a compulsory enfranchisement, see s. 6 of Copyhold Act, 1894. 1 *Steph. Com.*, 3 *Steph. Com.*

HEYBOTE. [HAYBOTE.]

HIDAGE. An extraordinary tax paid for every hide of land.

HIDE OF LAND. A certain quantity of land, such as might be ploughed with one plough in a year. According to some it was sixty acres; others say eighty, and others a hundred. The quantity probably was always determined by local usage.

HIGH BAILIFFS. Officers appointed under s. 33 of the County Court Act, 1888, to serve summons, execute warrants, etc. 3 *Steph. Com.*

HIGH COMMISSION COURT. A court of ecclesiastical jurisdiction, erected and united to the regal power by 1 Eliz. c. 1. It was intended to vindicate the peace of the Church, by reforming, ordering, and correcting the ecclesiastical state and persons, and all manner of errors, heresies, schisms, abuses, offences, contempts, and enormities. Under the shelter of these very general words, the High Commission Court exercised extraordinary and despotic powers of fine and imprisonment. Nor did it confine its jurisdiction altogether to cases of spiritual cognizance. For these reasons the court was abolished in 1641 by 16 Car. 1, c. 11. James II. afterwards attempted to revive it. 3 *Steph. Com.*

HIGH CONSTABLES. [CONSTABLE.]

HIGH COURT OF CHANCERY. [CHANCERY.]

HIGH COURT OF JUSTICE. [SUPREME COURT OF JUDICATURE.]

HIGH SEAS. That part of the sea which is more than three miles distant from the coast. The territorial jurisdiction of a country does not extend beyond the three-mile limit. Offences committed on board a British ship on the high seas are punishable by English law the same as if committed on British soil, such a ship being in law part of the territory of the United Kingdom. *Arch. Crim. Pleading; 4 Steph. Com.*

HIGH STEWARD. An expression used—
1. Of the Lord High Steward, who holds a court appointed, *pro hâc vice*, during the recess of parliament, for the trial of a peer indicted for treason or felony, or for misprision of either. 4 *Steph. Com.* [COURT OF LORD HIGH STEWARD.]
2. Of the Lord High Steward of the Royal Household. 4 *Steph. Com.* [COURT OF LORD STEWARD OF THE KING'S HOUSEHOLD.]
3. Of the Lord High Steward of the University of Oxford or Cambridge, an officer of the University appointed to preside at the trial of any scholar or privileged person of the University, on any indictment for treason or felony, of which the Vice-Chancellor of the University may have claimed and been allowed cognizance. Before the office of the High Steward is called into action he must have been approved by the Lord High Chancellor of England. 4 *Steph. Com.* [UNIVERSITY COURTS.]

HIGH TREASON. [TREASON.]

HIGHWAY. A public road which all the subjects of the realm have a right to use. Highways exist by prescription, by local Act of parliament, or by dedication to the public on the part of individuals. The parish is, as a rule, bound to keep in repair any highway within its boundaries. 3 *Steph. Com.* [DEDICATION OF WAY; PRESCRIPTION.]

HIGHWAY RATE. A tax for the maintenance and repair of highways, chargeable upon the same property that is liable to the poor-rate. 3 *Steph. Com.*

HINDE PALMER'S ACT (32 & 33 Vict. c. 46). Abolished the priority of specialty over simple contract debts in the administration of the estate of a person dying after January 1st, 1870.

HIRING (Rom. law, *locatio, conductio*) is a contract which differs from borrowing only in this, that hiring is always for a price, stipend, or additional recompense ; whereas borrowing is merely gratuitous. It is a bailment for reward whereby the possession of goods, with a transient property therein, is transferred for a particular time or use, on condition to restore the goods so hired as soon as the time is expired or use performed. It is of four kinds. The hiring (1) of a thing for use (*locatio rei*) ; (2) of work and labour (*locatio operis faciendi*) ; (3) of services to be performed on the thing delivered (*locatio custodiæ*) ; (4) of the carriage of goods (*locatio operis mercium vehendarum*). 2 *Steph. Com.* [BAILMENT.]

HIRE-PURCHASE SYSTEM. Under this system the person who hires the goods, becomes, upon payment of the last instalment of the amount fixed, the owner of them. The instrument effecting this arrangement does not usually require registration as a Bill of Sale. See *Helby* v. *Matthews*, [1895] A. C. 471.

HOLDER. A payee or indorsee in possession of a bill of exchange or a promissory note.

HOLDER IN DUE COURSE. One who has taken a bill of exchange, cheque or note, complete and regular on the face of it, and who became the holder of it before it was overdue and without notice of previous dishonour and who took it in good faith and for value without notice of any defect in the title of the person who negotiated it. See *s.* 29, *Bills of Exchange Act*, 1882.

HOLDING, in the Agricultural Holdings Act, means a farm.

HOLDING OVER is where a man, having come into possession of land under a lawful title, continues possession after the title has expired ; as if a man takes a lease for a year, and after the year is expired continues to hold the premises without any fresh lease from the owner of the estate. 1 *Steph. Com.* ; 3 *Steph. Com.* [DOUBLE RENT ; DOUBLE VALUE.]

HOLOGRAPH is a deed or writing written entirely by the "grantor's" own hand. On account of the difficulty with which the forgery of such a document can be accomplished it is held by the Scotch law valid without witnesses. So, a holograph will is a will written in the testator's own hand.

HOLY ORDERS in the English Church are the orders of bishops (including archbishops), priests and deacons. 2 *Steph. Com.*

HOMAGE. A ceremony performed by a vassal or tenant upon investiture, in which, openly and humbly kneeling, being ungirt, uncovered, and holding up his hands both together between those of his lord, who sat before him, he professed that " he did become his *man*, from that day forth, of life and limb and earthly honour ; " and then he received a kiss from his lord. The ceremony was denominated *homagium* or *manhood* by the feudists, from the stated form of words, *derenio rester homo*. 1 *Steph. Com.* ; *Wms. R. P.*

Homage Auncestrel was where a man and his ancestors had immemorially bolden land of another and his ancestors by the service of homage.

The word *homage* is also used to signify the tenants of a manor present at the lord's court, and a jury consisting of such tenants is called a *homage jury.*

HOMAGE JURY. [HOMAGE.]

HOMAGER. One that does, or is bound to do, homage to another.

HOMAGIO RESPECTUANDO was a writ directed to the escheator, commanding him to deliver seisin of lands to the heir of full age, notwithstanding his *homage* not done, which ought to be performed before the heir have livery (*i.e.*, have his lands delivered over to him).

HOMAGIUM REDDERE. To renounce homage ; which took place when the vassal made a solemn declaration of disowning and defying his lord, for which there was a set form and method prescribed by the feudal laws.

HOME OFFICE. The department of state through which most of the internal affairs of the kingdom are administered. It deals specially with the regulation of the police, the supervision of prisons, etc.

HOMICIDE. The killing of a human being. It was usually divided into three kinds—*justifiable, excusable,* and *felonious.*

1. *Justifiable homicide* is of divers kinds :—

  1. The putting a man to death pursuant to a legal sentence.

  2. The killing, by an officer of justice, of a person who assaults or resists him, and cannot otherwise be taken.

  3. The killing of persons for the dispersion of riots or rebellious assemblies, or the prevention of atrocious crimes, such as murder and rape.

2. *Excusable homicide* is of two sorts : either—

  1. *Per infortunium*, by misadventure.

  2. *Se defendendo*, in self-defence.

This kind of self-defence is to be distinguished from that included under the head of justifiable homicide, to hinder the perpetration of a capital crime, by the fact that, in the case now supposed, the person killing has himself to blame (though ever so slightly) for the circumstances which have led to the killing. There is now no practical difference between justifiable and excusable homicide.

3. *Felonious homicide.* This is either killing one's self—suicide—or another, which is again divided into two kinds, *manslaughter* and *murder*, which will be found discussed under their respective titles. 4 *Steph. Com.*

HONORARIUM. A gratuity given for professional services. 3 *Steph. Com.*

HONORARY FEUDS. Titles of nobility, which were not of a divisible nature, but could be inherited only by the eldest son ; whereas, originally, the *military* feuds descended to all the sons alike. 1 *Steph. Com.* [FEUDAL SYSTEM.]

HONORARY SERVICES were such as were incident to grand-serjeanty. They were commonly annexed to some *honour.* [HONOUR.]

HONORIS RESPECTUM, CHALLENGE PROPTER. [CHALLENGE.]

HONOUR, besides its general signification, is a word used more especially—

  1. For the nobler sort of seigniories, whereupon other inferior lordships and manors do depend. It seems that originally none were "honours" but such as belonged to the king, though afterwards given in fee to noblemen. 1 *Steph. Com.*

  2. The word is also used in reference to the acceptance *for honour* of a bill of exchange. [ACCEPTANCE SUPRA PROTEST.]

  3. It is also used generally in regard to bills of exchange. To honour a bill, is to pay it.

HONOUR COURTS are courts held within *honours.* [HONOUR, 1.]

HORNGELD, or **HORNEGELD.** A tax within a forest to be paid for horned beasts.

HOSTILE WITNESS. If a witness under examination in chief shows himself "hostile" to the party who called him he may by leave of the judge be cross-examined by the party who called him, as though he had been called by the opposite party. 17 & 18 *Vict. c.* 128, *s.* 22. As to discrediting a witness in criminal cases, see 28 & 29 Vict. c. 18, s. 3.

HOTCHPOT literally signifies a pudding mixed with divers ingredients ; but, by a metaphor, it signifieth a commixture or putting together of lands of several tenures, for the equal division of them. The word is frequently applied in reference to settlements which give a power to a parent of appointing a fund among his or her children, wherein it is provided that no child, taking a share of the fund under any appointment, shall be entitled to any share in the un appointed part without bringing his or her share into "hotchpot," and accounting for the same accordingly. The effect of such a clause would be to prevent a child who takes under an appointment from claiming his full share in the unappointed part, in addition to his appointed share. 1 *Steph. Com.* ; 2 *Steph. Com.* ; *Wms. P. P.*

HOUSE OF COMMONS. The lower house of parliament, consisting of the representatives of the nation at large, exclusive of the peerage. 2 *Steph. Com.* ; *May's Parl. Pract. Bk. I. ch.* 1.

HOUSE OF CORRECTION. A species of prison, originally designed for the penal confinement, after conviction, of paupers refusing to work, and other persons falling under the legal description of vagrants. See 5 & 6 *Will.* 4, *c.* 38, *ss.* 3, 4 ; 14 & 15 *Vict. c.* 55, *ss.* 20, 21 ; and *s.* 56 of the *Prisons Act*, 1865 (28 & 29 *Vict. c.* 126). 3 *Steph. Com.*

HOUSE OF KEYS. [KEYS.]

HOUSE OF LORDS. The upper house of the legislature, consisting of the lords spiritual and the lords temporal. The lords spiritual consist of the archbishops of Canterbury and York ; of the bishops of London, Durham, and Winchester ; and of twenty-one other bishops. The lords temporal sit, for the most part, in their own right ; but a certain number of them are elected, under the Acts of Union with Scotland and Ireland, to represent in the House of Lords the body of the Scottish and Irish nobility respectively. The Scottish representative peers are sixteen in number, and are elected for one parliament only. The Irish representative peers are twenty-eight, and are elected for life. The aggregate number of the lords temporal is indefinite, and may be increased at will by the Crown. The House of Lords is also the court of final appeal in all civil causes except from the Colonial courts, appeals from which are heard by the Judicial Committee of the Privy Council as a court of final appeal. 2 *Steph. Com.; May's Parl. Pract.*

HOUSEBOTE signifies estovers, or an allowance of necessary timber out of the lord's wood, for the repair and support of a house or tenement. This belongs, of common right, to a lessee for years or for life. 1 *Steph. Com.*

HOUSEBREAKING is the offence of breaking and entering a house with the intention of committing a felony therein ; or, after committing a felony therein, breaking out of the same. It differs from burglary in that (1) burglary is committed by night, and only in respect of a dwelling-house ; (2) it may be by day and in respect of other buildings. 4 *Steph. Com.* [BURGLARY.]

HOUSE-DUTY. A tax on inhabited houses imposed by 14 & 15 Vict. c. 36, in lieu of window-duty, which is abolished.

HUE AND CRY (Lat. *Hutesium et clamor*) is the old common law process of pursuing, with horn and with voice, all felons, and such as have dangerously wounded another. If a man wantonly and maliciously raises a hue and cry without cause he is liable to fine and imprisonment, and also to an action at the suit of the party injured. See the *Sheriff's Act*, 1887 (50 *&* 51 *Vict. c.* 55) ; 4 *Steph. Com.*

HUNDRED is part of a county or shire, probably so called because at first it contained ten tithings, composed each of ten families ; or else because the king found therein a hundred able men for his wars. The hundred was originally governed by a high constable or bailiff ; and formerly there was regularly held in it the hundred court for the trial of causes, though now fallen into disuse. 1 *Steph. Com.* [CONSTABLE, 1 ; HUNDRED COURT.]

HUNDRED COURT. A larger Court Baron, being held for all the inhabitants of a particular hundred instead of a manor. The free suitors are here also the judges, and the steward the registrar, as in the case of the Court Baron. Causes might be removed from it, and its decisions reviewed by a writ of false judgment. [FALSE JUDGMENT, WRIT OF.] It had been long obsolete when its jurisdiction was practically abolished by s. 28 of the County Courts Act, 1867, by which it was enacted that no action which can be brought in a county court shall thenceforth be maintainable in any hundred or other inferior court not being a court of record. 3 *Steph. Com.; 4 Steph. Com.*

HUNDREDERS, or **HUNDREDORS**, were men empanelled, or fit to be empanelled, as jurors upon a controversy, dwelling in the hundred where the land in question lay, or the cause of action arose, or accusation was tried. It was formerly necessary that there should be a competent number of hundreders on every panel. 3 *Steph. Com. ; 4 Steph. Com.* Until 1886 hundredors were liable for damage done by rioters, but see the Riot Damages Act, 1886 (49 & 50 Vict. c. 38).

HUSBAND AND WIFE. At common law they were for the most part treated as one person. The property of a wife became, with few exceptions, that of the husband. At common law a husband could not make a conveyance directly to his wife. This could be effected, however, through the medium of a use or trust, or by will. The *property* distinction between a married woman and an unmarried woman has been almost entirely removed by statute. See the *Married Women's Property Acts*, 1870 *and* 1882. As to the contracts of a married woman, see 56 & 57 Vict. c. 63, s. 1. Upon the whole subject consult *Lush on Husband and Wife*.

HUSH-MONEY. A bribe to hinder the giving of information.

HUSTINGS. A *house* of *things* or causes, from *hus*, house, and *thing*, cause. A platform from which parliamentary candidates addressed the electors prior to the Ballot Act, 1872. [COURT OF HUSTINGS.]

HUTESIUM ET CLAMOR. Hue and cry. [HUE AND CRY.]

HYPOTHECA, HYPOTHEC, or **HYPOTHEK.** A security for a debt which remains in the possession of the debtor; differing thus from a *pledge*, which is handed over to the creditor :—
1. Thus, a mortgage of land, where the mortgagee does not take possession, is in the nature of a *hypotheca*. 2 *Bl.* 159.
2. So, to mortgage a ship for necessaries is called *hypothecation*. 2 *Bl.*; 2 *Steph. Com.*

I. O. U. (I owe you) is a written acknowledgment of a debt. It operates merely as evidence of a debt due by virtue of some antecedent contract. It does not require to be stamped. *Byles on Bills.*

IBIDEM, IBID., ID. (in the same place or case).

ID CERTUM, ET C. See CERTUM, ETC.

IDEM SONANS (sounding alike). The courts will not set aside proceedings on account of misspelling of names, provided the variance is so slight as not to mislead, or the name as spelt be *idem sonans, e.g.,* Lawrance for Lawrence.

IDENTITY OF PERSON. A phrase applied especially to those cases in which the issue before the jury is, whether a man be the same person with one previously convicted or attainted.

IDIOT. A natural fool, or one who, from his birth, is *non compos mentis ;* to be distinguished from a *lunatic*, who is one that hath had understanding, but by disease, grief, or other cause, has lost use of his reason. See the *Idiots Act,* 1886 (49 & 50 *Vict. c.* 25); 2 *Steph. Com.* [LUNATIC.]

IDLE AND DISORDERLY PERSON. [VAGRANT.]

IGNIS JUDICIUM. The ordeal of fire. [ORDEAL.]

IGNORAMUS. A word formerly written by the grand jury on the back of a bill preferred to them, when they considered the evidence too defective or too weak to support an indictment. Now, in such cases, they indorse in English "no bill," "no true bill," or "not found," and the bill is thus said to be " thrown out." 4 *Steph. Com.* [BILL, 3 ; INDICTMENT.]

IGNORANTI FACTI EXCUSAT, IGNORANTIA JURIS NON EXCUSAT (ignorance of a fact excuses, ignorance of the law excuses not).

IGNORE means properly to be ignorant of. The word is used especially with reference to the throwing out of a bill of indictment by a grand jury. [IGNORAMUS.]

ILLEGITIMACY. [BASTARD.]

ILLUSORY APPOINTMENT was where a person, having power to appoint any real or personal property among a limited class of persons, appointed to any one of them a merely nominal share (as one shilling) of the property subject to the power of appointment. This in equity made the exercise of the power bad. This was altered by 11 Geo. 4 & 1 Will. 4, c. 46, and now, by 37 & 38 Vict. c. 37, it is provided that under a power to appoint among certain persons, appointments may be made wholly excluding one or more of the objects of the power. [POWER.]

IMBARGO. A stop or stay put upon ships by public authority. [EMBARGO ON SHIPS.]

IMBASING OF MONEY is mixing the species with an alloy below the standard of sterling, which the king by his prerogative may do.

IMBEZZLE. [EMBEZZLEMENT.]

IMBRACERY. [EMBRACERY.]

IMMEMORIAL USAGE. A practice which has existed from before the time of legal memory. 1 *Steph. Com.*

IMMORAL CONTRACTS. Those founded upon immoral considerations (*contra bonos mores*) are void. *Ex turpe causa non oritur actio* (*q.v.*).

IMPANELLING A JURY signifies the writing and entering into a parchment schedule, by the sheriff, of the names of a jury. [PANEL, 1.]

IMPARL. To confer with. 1 *Steph. Com.*; *Wms. R. P.* [IMPARLANCE.]

IMPARLANCE (Lat. *Licentia loquendi*) was a licence formerly given to a defendant for a respite until some further day to put in his answer, to see if he could end the matter amicably without further suit, by talking with the plaintiff.

IMPEACHMENT. A prosecution of an offender before the House of Lords by the Commons of Great Britain in parliament. The articles of impeachment are a kind of indictment found by the House of Commons, and afterwards tried by the House of Lords.

It has always been settled law that a peer could be impeached for any crime.

As regards commoners, however, Blackstone lays it down that a commoner cannot be impeached before the lords for any capital offence, but only for high misdemeanors. 4 *Steph. Com.* The contrary doctrine, however, was laid down when Chief Justice Scroggs, a commoner, was impeached of high treason. And when, on the 26th of June, 1689, Sir Adam Blair and four other commoners were impeached of high treason, the lords resolved that the impeachment should proceed. And this is the clear opinion of Sir Erskine May, *Parl. Prac. ch.* 23.

This form of prosecution has rarely been called into action in modern times. the last memorable cases are those of Warren Hastings in 1788, and Lord Melville in 1805.

IMPEACHMENT OF WASTE. A restraint from committing waste upon lands and tenements. The phrase is intended to denote the ordinary legal liability incurred by a tenant for life or other limited interest, in committing waste on the property. [WASTE; WITHOUT IMPEACHMENT OF WASTE.]

IMPERFECT OBLIGATIONS. Moral duties not enforceable at law, such as charity, gratitude, or the like.

IMPERFECT TRUST. An executory trust (*q.v.*).

IMPERTINENCE. Irrelevancy in pleading or evidence, by the allegation of matters not pertinent to the question at issue. Any unnecessary or scandalous pleading may be struck out by order of the court or a judge, and the costs occasioned by such pleading imposed on the party making it. *R. S. C.* 1883, *Ord. XIX. rr.* 23 to 27.

IMPLEAD. To sue, arrest, or prosecute by course of law.

IMPLICATION. A legal inference of something not directly declared.

IMPLIED. This term could only be properly used to signify "established by indirect or circumstantial evidence," or, which comes to the same thing, "presumed under certain circumstances to exist, in the absence of evidence to the contrary," especially with reference to inward intentions or motives as inferred from overt acts.

Thus, Mr. Josiah Smith, in his "Manual of Equity," Tit. II. ch. 5, defines an *implied trust* as "a trust which is founded in an unexpressed but presumable intention"; and afterwards, in ch. 6, after remarking that implied trusts and constructive trusts are frequently confounded together, observes that a *constructive* trust is one raised by construction of a court of equity without reference to the presumable intention of any party: and that in this it differs both from an *express* and from an *implied* trust.

But the general use of this word "implied" by our legal text-writers is far more indiscriminate. The phrase "implied contract" is often applied indiscriminately to all those events which in law are treated as contracts, whether they arise from a presumed mutual consent or not, provided only they be not express contracts.

Thus the phrase is used to signify *sometimes* a genuine consensual contract not expressed in words, or in signs which usage has rendered equivalent to words; *sometimes* an event to which, though not a genuine consensual contract, the law annexes most or all of the incidents of a genuine contract as against any person or persons.

The implied but genuine contract is frequently spoken of as a *tacit* contract. It may be defined, in opposition to an express contract, as "a contract not expressed in words, or in signs which usage has rendered equivalent to words." As, if I order a coat from a tailor, without saying anything as to the price or quality. He, in undertaking the order, tacitly promises me that the coat shall

IMPLIED—*continued.*

be reasonably fit for wear. I tacitly promise him to pay a reasonable price for it. In implied contracts of this class there is no agreement as to precise terms and conditions, but there *is* an agreement, though of a vague and general character.

The implied contract which is such by fiction of law is frequently called a *quasi*-contract. Thus a person saves my goods on board a ship which is being wrecked, and claims from me "salvage-money" for doing so. This claim is said to arise "*quasi ex contractu*" (*as if* from a contract). It is totally independent of any consent on the part of the owner to pay for the saving of his goods. In implied contracts of this class there is no agreement at all; the supposed agreement being a pure fiction of law, adopted for the purposes of what is called "substantial justice." See *Austin's Fragments.*

The expression "implied request" is used in a manner analogous to "implied contract." A request is said to be "implied by law" sometimes when it has been in fact made, though not in express words: sometimes when it has never been made at all, but, by a fiction of law, is supposed or imagined to have been made.

IMPLIED COLOUR. [COLOUR.]

IMPLIED CONTRACT. [IMPLIED.]

IMPLIED MALICE. [MALICE.]

IMPLIED REQUEST, IMPLIED TRUST. [IMPLIED.]

IMPOSSIBILITY. If a man contract to do a thing which is absolutely impossible such contract will not bind him; but where the contract is to do a thing which is possible in itself but becomes impossible, he will be liable for the breach.

IMPOTENCE. Physical inability of a man or woman to perform the act of sexual intercourse. A marriage is void if at the time of the celebration either party is incurably impotent, and may be declared void by a decree in a suit of nullity of marriage.

IMPOTENTIAM, PROPTER, PROPERTY. A qualified property which may exist in animals *feræ naturæ.* [ANIMALS.]

IMPOUND. To place in a pound goods or cattle distrained. 3 *Steph. Com.* [POUND.]

Also, to retain in the custody of the law: which is ordered when a forged or otherwise suspicious document is produced at a trial, so that the document may be produced in case criminal proceedings should be subsequently taken.

IMPRESSMENT. The arresting and retaining mariners for the king's service. 3 *Steph. Com.*

IMPRISONMENT. [FALSE IMPRISONMENT.]

IMPROPER FEUD. A feud held otherwise than by military service. 1 *Steph. Com.*

IMPROPRIATION. [ADVOWSON; APPROPRIATION.]

IMPROVEMENT OF LAND ACTS are various Acts of parliament passed in recent years to enable tenants for life to expend money in improving their estates, and tò charge the expenses upon the inheritance. The chief Acts are the Improvement of Land Act, 1864 (27 & 28 Vict. c. 114), and the Settled Land Act, 1882 (45 & 46 Vict. c. 38).

IN ACTION. [CHOSE.]

IN ÆQUALI JURE MELIOR EST CONDITIO POSSIDENTIS (where the rights are equal the condition of the possessor is best).

IN ALIENO SOLO (in another's ground).

IN ARBITRIO JUDICIS (in the discretion of the judge).

IN ARTICULO MORTIS (in a dying state).

IN AUTER (or **AUTRE**) **DROIT** (in another's right). As where an executor sues for a debt in right of his testator.

IN BANCO. [BANC.]

IN CAMERA. [CAMERA.]

IN CAPITE. Tenants who held their land *immediately* of the king were said to hold it *in capite*, or *in chief.*

In theory, all the land in the country

IN CAPITE—*continued*.

is held originally of the Crown. The immediate tenants of the Crown under the feudal system frequently granted out portions of their lands to inferior persons, and those inferior persons became tenants to them, as they were of the king ; and it was in contradistinction to such inferior tenants that those who held immediately of the king were called tenants *in capite*. 1 *Steph Com.* [FEUDAL SYSTEM ; SUBINFEUDATION.]

IN CASU CONSIMILI. [CASU CONSIMILI.]

IN CASU PROVISO. [CASU PROVISO.]

IN CHIEF. A phrase used variously. [CHIEF, TENANTS IN : EXAMINATION, 1 ; IN CAPITE.]

IN COMMENDAM. [COMMENDAM.]

IN CUSTODIA LEGIS (in the custody of the law). An expression used with regard to goods which, on account of having been already seized by the sheriff under an execution, are exempt from distress for rent.

IN ESSE. In being, as opposed to a thing *in posse*, which may be, but is not. Thus a child, before he is born, is said to be *in posse* ; but after he is born, and for many purposes after he is conceived, he is said to be *in esse*, or in actual being.

IN EXTENSO. In full ; a copy of a document made *verbatim*.

IN EXTREMIS. On the point of death.

IN FORMA PAUPERIS (in the character of a pauper). A person may be admitted to sue or defend as a pauper on proof that he is not worth 25*l.*, his clothes and the subject-matter of the cause excepted ; and the court may assign him if necessary counsel and solicitor and exempt him from all court fees. See *R. S. C.* 1883, *Ord. XVI. rr.* 22—31.

IN GROSS is that which belongs to the person of a lord or other owner, and not to any manor, lands, etc. The phrase, applied to an incorporeal interest in land, signifies that the incorporeal interest in question is not appendant or appurtenant to any corporeal thing, but is enjoyed by its owner as an independent subject of property. [APPENDANT ; APPURTENANCES ; GROSS.]

IN INVITUM (against a person's will).

IN LIMINE (on the threshold). An objection *in limine* is a preliminary objection.

IN LOCO PARENTIS (in the place of a parent).

IN PAIS (done without legal proceedings). [ESTOPPEL.]

IN PARI DELICTO MELIOR EST CONDITIO POSSIDENTIS (where both parties are equally in the wrong, the position of the possessor is the more favourable).

IN PERSONAM. A proceeding *in personam* is one in which relief is sought against, or punishment sought to be inflicted upon, a specific person.

IN RE (in the matter of). These words used at the beginning of a lawyer's letter indicate the subject of the letter. And, in headings to legal reports, they are applied especially (though by no means exclusively) to estates or companies which are being wound up, or to the owners of such estates.

IN REM. A proceeding *in rem* is one in which relief is not sought against, or punishment sought to be inflicted upon, any person. Actions *in rem* are generally instituted to try claims to some property or title or status ; as, for instance, where it is sought to condemn a ship in the Court of Admiralty, or to recover land in an action of ejectment, etc.

IN TERROREM (for the purpose of intimidation). A condition which the law will not enforce is so called.

IN TRANSITU (in passage from one place to another). Generally it is used of goods in their passage from the vendor to the purchaser. [STOPPAGE IN TRANSITU.]

IN VENTRE SA MERE (in his mother's womb).

INADEQUACY OF CONSIDERATION does not affect the validity of a contract. [CONSIDERATION.]

INALIENABLE. Not transferable.

INCEST. Carnal intercourse between persons within the Levitical degrees of kindred ; at one time a capital offence, but afterwards left to the action of the spiritual courts.

INCIDENT. A thing appertaining to or following upon another as principal, and passing by a general grant thereof.

Thus, rent may be made incident to a reversion ; and, when so incident, it passes by a general grant of the reversion. Formerly the rent so incident was destroyed when the reversion was destroyed by surrender or merger ; but this doctrine, so far as regards cases of surrender or merger, is abolished by 8 & 9 Vict. c. 106, s. 9. 1 *Steph. Com. ; Wms. R. P.*

INCLOSURE. 1. The extinction of commonable rights in fields and waste lands. 1 *Steph. Com.*
2. Land inclosed.

INCLOSURE COMMISSION ACT, 1845. The stat. 8 & 9 Vict. c. 118, by which a Board of Commissioners, called the Inclosure Commissioners for England and Wales, was established, and empowered, on the application of persons interested to the amount of one-third of the value of land subject to be inclosed, and provided the consent of persons interested to the amount of two-thirds of the land, and of the lord of the manor (in case the land be waste of a manor), be ultimately obtained, to inquire into the case, and to report to parliament as to the expediency of making the inclosure. Their powers are now vested in the Board of Agriculture. 1 *Steph. Com.*

INCLOSURE COMMISSIONERS. Now the Inclosure Department of the Board of Agriculture. 52 & 53 *Vict. c.* 30. [INCLOSURE COMMISSION ACT.]

INCOME TAX. A tax of so much in the pound on income. It is levied under five heads in respect of : (A) ownership of land, etc. ; (B) occupation of land, etc. ; (C) dividends ; (D) professional or trade earnings or profits ; (E) official and other salaries.

INCORPORATE. 1. To declare that one document shall be taken as part of the document in which the declaration is made as much as if it were set out at length therein.

2. To establish as a corporation by grant from the Crown or Act of parliament.

INCORPOREAL CHATTELS are personal rights and interests which are not of a tangible nature,—such as personal annuities, stocks and shares, patents and copyrights. 2 *Steph. Com. ; Wms. P. P. Part III.*

INCORPOREAL HEREDITAMENT is any possession or subject of property which is capable of being transmitted to heirs, and is not the object of the bodily senses. It is in general a right annexed to, or issuing out of, or exercisable within, a corporeal hereditament ; as a right of common of pasture, or a right of way over land. 1 *Steph. Com. ; Wms. R. P.*

INCORPOREAL PROPERTY. [CORPOREAL PROPERTY ; INCORPOREAL CHATTELS ; INCORPOREAL HEREDITAMENT.]

INCREASE. [AFFIDAVIT OF INCREASE.]

INCUMBENT. A clergyman in possession of an ecclesiastical benefice. 2 *Steph. Com.*

INCUMBER. To charge with an incumbrance. [INCUMBRANCE.]

INCUMBRANCE. A charge or mortgage upon real or personal estate.

INCUMBRANCER. A person entitled to enforce a charge or mortgage upon real or personal estate.

INDEBITATUS ASSUMPSIT. An action alleging that the defendant, being indebted to the plaintiff, undertook or promised to pay, but failed, whereupon the plaintiff claimed damages for the non-performance by the defendant of his undertaking. Obsolete since the Judicature Acts. [ASSUMPSIT.]

INDECENT ASSAULT. See 24 & 25 *Vict. c.* 100, *ss.* 52, 62. 4 *Steph. Com.*

INDECENT EXPOSURE is an indictable offence at common law. See also 5 Geo. 4, c. 83, s. 5. 4 *Steph. Com.*

INDECENT PRINTS OR BOOKS. The sale or obtaining, or procuring with intent to sell, is a misdemeanor. See 20 & 21 *Vict. c.* 83. 4 *Steph. Com.*

INDEFEASIBLE. That cannot be made void.

INDEFINITE PAYMENT is where a debtor owes several debts to the same creditor, and makes a payment without specifying to which of the debts the payment is to be applied.

INDEMNITY. Compensation for wrong done, or trouble, expense, or loss incurred. An undertaking, usually by deed, to indemnify another. As to the indemnity of trustees, see 22 & 23 Vict. c. 35, s. 31.

INDEMNITY ACT. An Act of parliament formerly passed every year to relieve from forfeiture persons who had accepted office without taking certain oaths then required by law. Rendered unnecessary by 31 & 32 Vict. c. 72, s. 16. 2 *Steph. Com.* Also any Act for pardon or oblivion of past offences against the law.

INDENTURE. A deed made by more parties than one; so called because there ought regularly to be as many copies of it as there are parties; and formerly each was cut or indented like the teeth of a saw, or in a waving line, to tally or correspond with the other. Now, by 8 & 9 Vict. c. 106, s. 5, a deed purporting to be an indenture is to have the effect of an indenture, though not actually indented. 1 *Steph. Com.; Wms. R. P.* [DEED.]

INDICAVIT. A writ or prohibition that lies for a patron of a church, when the clergyman presented by him to a benefice is made defendant in an action of tithes commenced in the ecclesiastical court by another clergyman, where the tithes in question extend to the fourth part of the benefice; for in this case the suit belongs to the "king's court" (*i.e.,* the common law court) by the stat. Westm. 2, c. 5.

The person sued may also avail himself of this writ.

INDICTMENT. A written accusation that one or more persons have committed a certain felony or misdemeanor, such accusation being preferred to, and (being found true) presented to the court upon oath by, a grand jury. *Arch. Crim. Plead.; 4 Steph. Com.* [BILL, 3.]

INDIRECT EVIDENCE. The same as circumstantial evidence. [CIRCUMSTANTIAL EVIDENCE; EVIDENCE.]

INDORSEE. [INDORSEMENT.]

INDORSEMENT. A writing on the back of a document. Thus we speak of an indorsement on a deed, on a bill of exchange, on a writ, etc.

An *indorsement in blank* is where a person, to whom a bill or note is payable, writes his name on the back simply. The effect of such an indorsement is that the right to sue upon the bill will be transferred to any person to whom the bill is delivered.

A *special* indorsement, or indorsement in full, is an indorsement directing payment of the bill to a specified person or his order; such person is thereupon called the *indorsee*. In this case the bill or note, in order to become transferable, must be again indorsed by the indorsee. For the requisites of a valid indorsement, see Bills of Exchange Act, 1882, c. 32. 3 *Steph. Com.*

For a special indorsement on a writ of summons in an action, see SPECIAL INDORSEMENT.

INDORSEMENT OF ADDRESS. By R. S. C. 1883, Ord. IV. r. 1, it is provided that the solicitor of a plaintiff suing by a solicitor shall indorse upon every writ of summons the address of the plaintiff, and also his own name or firm and place of business, and also an *address for service* if his place of business be more than three miles from the Royal Courts of Justice.

INDORSEMENT OF CLAIM. By R. S. C. 1883, Ord. II. r. 1, every writ of summons in the High Court must be indorsed with a statement of the nature of the claim made; and by Ord. III. r. 1, such indorsement must be made on the writ before it is issued. See also SPECIAL INDORSEMENT.

INDORSEMENT OF SERVICE. By R. S. C. 1883, Ord. IX. r. 15, the date of service must be indorsed upon every writ within three days of such service.

INDORSER. A person who indorses any document. [INDORSEMENT.]

INDOWMENT. [ENDOWMENT.]

INDUCEMENT. 1. The motive or incitement to any act.

2. Inducement, in pleading, is matter brought forward by way of explanatory introduction to the main allegations of the pleading.

INDUCTION. A ceremony performed, after a clergyman has been instituted to a benefice, by a mandate from the bishop to the archdeacon. It is done by giving the clergyman corporal possession of the church. This is the investiture of the temporal part of the benefice, as *institution* is of the spiritual. 2 *Steph. Com.*

INDUSTRIAL AND PROVIDENT SOCIETIES. See 56 & 57 *Vict. c.* 39.

INDUSTRIAL SCHOOLS. See 29 & 30 *Vict. c.* 118; 35 & 36 *Vict. c.* 21; 54 & 55 *Vict. c.* 23.

INDUSTRIAM, PER. *Per industriam* is a phrase applied to the reclaiming animals *feræ naturæ*, and making them tame by art, industry, and education; or else by confining them that they cannot escape and use their natural liberty. 2 *Steph. Com.* [ANIMALS.]

INFAMY does not now incapacitate from giving evidence. 7 & 8 *Vict. c.* 85, *s.* 1.

INFANT, in law, is a person under the age of twenty-one years; an age at which persons are considered competent for all that the law requires them to do, and which is therefore designated as *full age.* This age is gained on the day preceding the twenty-first anniversary of a person's birth. 2 *Steph. Com.* [AGE; MINOR; see also the following titles.]

INFANTICIDE. The killing of a child immediately after it is born. The felonious destruction of the *fœtus in utero* is called fœticide, or criminal abortion.

INFANTS' RELIEF ACT, 1874. The stat. 37 & 38 Vict. c. 62, for making contracts by infants (*i.e.*, persons under age), for goods supplied (other than necessaries), accounts stated, or money lent, absolutely void and incapable of ratification by the party on his attaining his full age.

INFANTS' SETTLEMENT ACT. The stat. 18 & 19 Vict. c. 43, for enabling persons under age to make settlements on their marriage, with the concurrence of the Court of Chancery. Any such person, if a male, must be at least twenty years of age; and, if a female, of seventeen years.

INFECTIOUS DISEASES See the *Public Health Act,* 1875 (38 & 39 *Vict. c.* 55), *ss.* 120—139; the *Infectious Diseases Notification Acts,* 1889 (52 & 53 *Vict. c.* 72), and 1899 (62 & 63 *Vict. c.* 8); the *Infectious Diseases Prevention Act,* 1890 (53 & 54 *Vict. c.* 34). As to London, see the Public Health (London) Act 1891.

INFERIOR COURTS. The courts which are subject to and controllable by the superior courts by writ of prohibition. They are:

1. The Courts Baron.
2. The Hundred Courts.
3. The Sheriffs' County Courts, which are the old County Courts.
4. The modern County Courts, established in 1846, by stat. 9 & 10 Vict. c. 95.
5. The Courts which in many cities and boroughs are held by prescription, charter, or Act of parliament.
6. The Courts of the Commissioners of Sewers.
7. The Stannary Courts (now merged in the County Courts).
8. The University Courts.
9. The Mayor's Court, London.

INFEUDATION OF TITHES. The granting of tithes to laymen. 2 *Steph. Com.*

INFORMATION. A proceeding on behalf of the Crown against a subject otherwise than by indictment.

Informations are of various kinds :—

1. An information in Chancery, which differed from a bill only by the fact that it was instituted in the name of the Attorney-General on behalf of the Crown, or of those who partake of its prerogative, or whose rights are under its particular protection; whereas a bill was filed on behalf of a subject merely. It often happened, however, that the proceeding by way of information was prosecuted in the name of the Attorney-General by some private person interested in the maintenance of the public right which it was intended to enforce. Such private person was then called the *relator,* and was responsible for the conduct of the suit and for the costs. 3 *Steph. Com.* This species of information is superseded by action in the High Court of Justice. *R. S. C.* 1883, *Ord. I. r.* 1.

2. An information in the Exchequer on behalf of the Crown, to recover money due to the Crown, or to recover

INFORMATION—*continued.*
damages for an intrusion upon Crown property. 3 *Steph. Com.* [INTRUSION, 2.]

3. An information in the King's Bench Division in the nature of a *quo warranto,* for the purpose of trying the right to a franchise. 3 *Steph. Com.*

4. An information on a penal statute, which gives the informer a share in the penalty. 3 *Steph. Com.*

5. A criminal information in the King's Bench Division. This may be by the Attorney-General *ex officio,* or by a private prosecutor in the name of the Crown. But in the latter case the information cannot be filed but by the express direction of the Court itself. 4 *Steph. Com.*

6. A charge laid before a justice or justices of the peace, with a view to a summary conviction. See *Summary Jurisdiction Act,* 1848 (11 & 12 *Vict. c.* 43), *ss.* 1, 10, 11 ; 4 *Steph. Com.*

Of these six classes, the first two are civil in their nature, and differ from ordinary suits and actions by the fact of their being instituted on behalf of the Crown. The third class is in its origin a criminal proceeding, but even in Blackstone's time it had assumed the character of a civil proceeding for the purpose of trying a right. The fourth class is partly a civil, partly a criminal proceeding. In its form it partakes more of the civil character : but its object is a penal one, and not the redress of any private wrong. The last two classes of informations are purely criminal in their nature.

INFORMATION IN REM. An information *in rem* is a proceeding in the King's Bench Division, claiming property on behalf of the Crown. 3 *Steph. Com.* [INFORMATION, 2.]

INFORMER. Any one who informs or prosecutes in any of the courts of law those that offend against any law or penal statute. Especially of one who informs for the purpose of sharing in the money to be paid by way of penalty on conviction. [COMMON INFORMER ; INFORMATION, 4.]

INFORTUNIUM. Misadventure or mischance. [HOMICIDE.]

INFRINGEMENT. A violation of another's right ; a word used principally with reference to the violation of another's patent or copyright.

INGRESS, EGRESS, and **REGRESS.** Free entry into, going forth of, and returning from a place.

INGRESSU. A writ of entry, whereby a man sought entry into lands or tenements. [ENTRY, WRIT OF.] The various writs of entry were abolished by 3 & 4 Will. 4, c. 27, s. 36.

INGROSSING. [ENGROSSING.]

INHERITANCE. A perpetuity in lands or tenements to a man and his heirs. The word is mostly confined to the title to lands and tenements by *descent.* 1 *Steph. Com.; Wms. R. P.* ; 3 & 4 *Will.* 4, *c.* 106 ; 22 & 23 *Vict. c.* 35, *ss.* 19, 20. [DESCENT ; ESTATE, 1.]

INHERITANCE ACT, 1833. The stat. 3 & 4 Will. 4, c. 106, by which the present law of inheritance is regulated. 1 *Steph. Com.; Wms. R. P.*

INHIBITION signifies a writ to *inhibit* or forbid a judge from farther proceeding in a cause depending before him ; an ancient synonym for *prohibition.* In ecclesiastical law it signifies a command from a bishop or ecclesiastical judge that a clergyman shall cease from taking any duty.

INITIATE TENANT BY CURTESY. A husband becomes *initiate tenant by curtesy* in his wife's estate of inheritance upon the birth of issue capable of inheriting the same. The husband's estate by curtesy is not said to be *consummate* till the death of the wife. 1 *Steph. Com.* [CURTESY.]

INJUNCTION. A writ issuing, prior to the Judicature Acts, only out of Chancery, in the nature of a prohibition, by which the party enjoined or prohibited is commanded not to do, or to cease from doing, some act not amounting to a crime. Injunctions may now be granted by all Divisions of the High Court and by the Court of Appeal. They are either (1) *interlocutory, i.e., provisional* or temporary until the hearing of the cause, or (2) *perpetual.* By the Judicature Act of 1873, s. 24, sub-sect. 5, no cause or proceeding at any time pending in the High Court of Justice, or before the Court of Appeal, shall be restrained by prohibition or injunction. And, by s. 25, sub-sect. 8, an injunction may be granted by an interlocutory order of the court in all cases in which it shall appear just or convenient. See *R. S. C.* 1883, *Ord. L. r.* 6. See *Kerr on Injunctions ; Joyce on Injunctions.*

INJURIA. An actionable wrong,

INJURY. A violation of another's right; or a violation of legal duty to the prejudice of another.

INLAGARY, or **INLAGATION.** A restitution of one outlawed to the king's protection, and to the benefit or estate of a subject.

INLAND BILL OF EXCHANGE. "A bill which on the face of it purports to be (*a*) both drawn and payable within the British Islands; or (*b*) drawn within the British Islands upon some person resident therein." Any other is a foreign bill, but unless the contrary appear on the face of the bill the holder may treat it as an inland bill. *Bills of Exchange Act*, 1882, *s.* 4; 2 *Steph. Com.*

INLAND REVENUE. "The revenue of the United Kingdom collected or imposed as stamp duties, taxes, and duties of excise and placed under the care and management of the Inland Revenue Commissioners." *Inland Revenue Regulation Act*, 1890 (53 & 54 *Vict. c.* 21).

INN. An inn is defined to be a house, the owner of which holds out that he will receive all travellers and sojourners who are willing to pay a price adequate to the sort of accommodation provided, and who come in a condition in which they are fit to be received. He is bound to accommodate and entertain all properly conducted persons provided there is room in the house. He has a lien upon the goods of his guests for board and lodging, etc. See 41 *Vict. c.* 38. His liability for the loss of their goods, etc., is regulated by 26 & 27 *Vict. c.* 41. [LICENSING ACTS.]

INNER TEMPLE. One of the Inns of Court. [INNS OF COURT.]

INNINGS. Lands recovered from the sea in Romney Marsh by draining. When they are rendered profitable, they are termed *gainage* lands.

INNKEEPERS. [INN.]

INNOCENT CONVEYANCE. A conveyance which could not operate by wrong. Thus, a lease and release, and a bargain and sale, and a covenant to stand seised, were called *innocent conveyances*, because they could not, like a feoffment, have a tortious operation. But see 8 & 9 *Vict. c.* 106, s. 4. 1 *Steph. Com.*; *Wms. R. P.* [TORTIOUS OPERATION.]

INNOTESCIMUS. Letters patent so called, being always of a charter or feoffment, or other instrument not of record; so called from the words of the conclusion, *innotescimus per præsentes.*

INNOVATION. [NOVATION.]

INNS OF CHANCERY were Clifford's Inn, Clement's Inn, New Inn, Staple Inn, Barnard's Inn, Furnival's Inn, the Strand Inn, Lyon's Inn, and Thavies' Inn. There was also Serjeants' Inn, which consisted of serjeants only. The Inns of Chancery and the Inns of Court were originally two sorts of collegiate houses in the same juridical university, the Inns of Chancery being those in which the younger students of the law were usually placed. The Inns of Chancery have now sunk into insignificance, and an admission to them is no longer of any avail to a student in his progress to the bar. 1 *Steph. Com.* [INNS OF COURT.]

INNS OF COURT are Lincoln's Inn, the Inner Temple, the Middle Temple, and Gray's Inn. They enjoy the exclusive privilege of conferring the rank or degree of barrister-at-law, the possession of which constitutes an indispensable qualification for practising as an advocate or counsel in the superior courts. The Inns of Court are governed by officers called "benchers," to whom application is made by students desirous to be called to the bar. The benchers have also authority to deprive a bencher or a barrister of his *status*, which proceedings are called respectively "disbenching" and "disbarring." An appeal from decisions of the benchers lies to the judges in their capacity of visitors. Full information as to the regulations, examinations, fees, etc., imposed previous to call to the bar can be obtained by application to the Treasurer of any of the Inns. 1 *Steph. Com.*

INNUENDO (from *innuo*, to beck or nod with the head) is a word the office of which is only to declare and ascertain the person or thing which was named or left doubtful before; as to say, he (*innuendo*, the plaintiff) is a thief, where there was mention before of another person. The word *innuendo* is most frequently applied to signify, in a proceeding for libel, the averment of a particular meaning in a passage *primâ facie* innocent, which, if proved, would establish its libellous character. 3 *Steph. Com.*

INOFFICIOUS TESTAMENT. A will made contrary to the natural duty of the testator and without proper regard to the claims of kindred. *Williams on Executors ; 2 Steph. Com.*

INQUEST. An inquisition or inquiry.

1. The inquest of office is an inquiry made by the king's officer, his sheriff, coroner, or escheator, either *virtute officii*, or by writ to them sent for that purpose, or by commissioners specially appointed, concerning any matter that entitles the king to the possession of lands or tenements, goods or chattels. This is done by a jury of no determinate number, being either twelve, or less, or more. 3 *Steph. Com.*

2. A coroner's inquest is an inquiry into the manner of the death of any one who has been slain, or has died suddenly, or in prison. It is held before a jury, who must consist of twelve at least. See *Coroners Act*, 1887 ; 2 *Steph. Com.*

3. Inquisition as to lunacy. See *Lunacy Act*, 1890, *ss.* 90—107.

4. Inquisition under the Lands Clauses Acts as to the amount of purchase money or compensation due to a claimant under those Acts. See *Lands Clauses Act*, 1845.

INQUIRY, COURT OF. 1. A court occasionally directed by the Crown to inquire into the conduct of officers, with a view to further proceedings by court-martial or otherwise.

2. Also, a court for hearing the complaints of private soldiers. [COURT OF ENQUIRY.]

INQUIRY, WRIT OF. [WRIT OF INQUIRY.]

INQUISITION. [INQUEST.]

INQUISITORS are sheriffs, coroners, or the like, who have power to inquire in certain cases.

INROLMENT. [ENROLMENT.]

INSANITY. [LUNATIC.]

INSOLVENCY. Inability to pay debts.

Prior to the year 1861, there was a distinction between bankruptcy and insolvency ; an insolvent debtor was a person, *not a trader*, who was unable to meet his liabilities, whereas only *traders* could be made bankrupt. And the term " insolvency " was frequently applied to the means of getting rid of pecuniary engagements, afforded by Acts of parliament passed for the relief of insolvent debtors.

All the Acts relating to insolvent debtors were repealed by the Bankruptcy Act, 1861 (24 & 25 Vict. c. 134), which also abolished the Insolvent Debtors Court. This Act has in turn been repealed by the Bankruptcy Act, 1869 (32 & 33 Vict. c. 71), and the latter by that of 1883 (46 & 47 Vict. c. 52). *Robson, Bkcy.* [ACT OF BANKRUPTCY ; BANKRUPT.]

INSOLVENT DEBTOR. [INSOLVENCY.]

INSPECTION. A mode of trial formerly in use for the greater expedition of a cause, in which the point at issue was one capable of being easily settled by the use of the bodily senses. 3 *Steph. Com.*

INSPECTION, COMMITTEE OF. [COMMITTEE OF INSPECTION.]

INSPECTION OF DOCUMENTS. The right of a party in an action or suit to inspect and take copies of documents material to his case, which may be in the possession of the opposite party. Either party is, as a rule, entitled (after notice) to inspect documents referred to in the pleadings or affidavits of the other. With regard to other documents the party desiring to inspect takes out a summons requiring his opponent to state what documents he has in his possession, and to make an affidavit in a prescribed form for that purpose. See *R. S. C.* 1883, *Ord. XXXI. rr.* 15—18.

INSPECTION OF PROPERTY. Any party to a cause may by order of the Court or a judge inspect any property or thing which is the subject of the cause. See *R. S. C.* 1883, *Ord. L. rr.* 3—5.

INSPECTORSHIP DEED. A deed by which inspectors are appointed to watch a debtor's affairs on behalf of the creditors, the creditors undertaking not to sue the debtor, and the debtor agreeing to pay the creditors a composition of so much in the pound. [COMPOSITION.]

INSTALMENT. 1. The ceremony by which possession is given of an ecclesiastical dignity. 1 *Steph. Com.*

2. A sum of money less than the whole sum due, paid by a debtor in partial liquidation of the debt.

INSTANCE COURT OF ADMIRALTY is the court in which the judge of the Admiralty sits by virtue of a commission from the Great Seal which enumerates the objects of his jurisdiction, but which has no jurisdiction in matter of prize. The *Prize Court* is a court presided over by the same judge, but by a different commission, which issues in every war under the Great Seal to the Lord High Admiral. [ADMIRALTY, THE HIGH COURT OF.]

INSTANTER. Immediately, without delay.

INSTITUTES. 1. Justinian's Institutes. [CORPUS JURIS CIVILIS ; JUSTINIAN.]

2. Sir Edward Coke's Institutes. This work was published by Sir Edward Coke in the year 1628. They have little of the institutional method to warrant such a title. The first volume is an extensive comment upon a treatise of tenures, compiled by Judge Littleton in the reign of Edward IV. The second volume is a comment upon many old Acts of parliament, without any systematic order ; the third, a more methodical treatise of the pleas of the Crown ; and the fourth an account of the several species of courts. 1 *Steph. Com.* [COKE, SIR EDWARD.]

INSTITUTION. The ceremony by which a clergyman presented to a living is invested with the spiritual part of his benefice. Before institution, the clergyman must renew the declaration of assent to the Book of Common Prayer, as required by stat. 28 & 29 Vict. c. 122 ; he must also subscribe the declaration against simony, and must take the oath of allegiance to the King before the archbishop or bishop, or their commissary, and he must also take the oath of canonical obedience to the bishop. See also 61 & 62 Vict. c. 48. 2 *Steph. Com. ;* 3 *Steph. Com.*

INSTRUCT. To convey information as a client to a solicitor, or as a solicitor to counsel ; to authorise one to appear as advocate.

INSTRUMENT. A deed, will, or other formal legal document in writing.

INSUFFICIENCY, prior to the Judicature Acts, was where a defendant's answer in Chancery did not fairly answer the interrogatories of the plaintiff. Where this was the case, the plaintiff might *except* to it for insufficiency.

By R.S.C. 1883, Ord. XXXI., interrogatories are to be answered by affidavit ; and if the party interrogated answers insufficiently, the party interrogating may apply to the court or a judge, by motion or summons, for an order requiring him to answer further.

INSURANCE, or **ASSURANCE**, is a contract by which one party, in consideration of a premium, engages to pay money on a given event, *e.g.* death, or indemnify another against a contingent loss. The party who pays the premium is called the *insured* or *assured ;* the party giving the security is termed the *underwriter* or *insurer*, and the instrument is called a policy of insurance.

Insurances are mainly of three kinds :

1. Marine insurances, which are insurances of ship, goods, and freight, against the perils of the sea, and other dangers therein mentioned.

2. Fire insurances, which are insurances of a house or other property against loss by fire, not exceeding a sum mentioned in the policy.

3. Life insurances, which are engagements to pay to the representatives of the assured, within a limited period from the date of his death, a specified sum of money, or to pay any such sum to the assured or his representatives, within a limited period of the death of some other person, specified in the policy of assurance, or to pay to the assured on his attaining a certain age or to his representatives if he die earlier (endowment policy). Though a life policy is not a contract of indemnity (as fire and marine policies are), a person can only insure a life in which he has an interest, viz. his own, his debtors', trustees', or a wife her husband's. See *Married Women's Property Act*, 1882, *s.* 11.

INTENDMENT. The understanding, intention, and true meaning of any document. Thus, intendment of law is the intention and true meaning of law. [INTENTION, 1.]

INTENTION. 1. In reference to the construction of wills and other documents.

The *intention* of a document is the sense and meaning of it as gathered from the words used therein. Parol evidence is not ordinarily admissible to explain it; the main exceptions to the rule being in the case of a latent ambiguity [AMBIGUITY], and in the case of a word or expression having acquired by local

INTENTION—*continued.*

custom a sense different from the ordinary sense. See *Broom's Legal Maxims, ch.* 8, 10.

2. In reference to civil and criminal responsibility.

Where a person contemplates any result as not unlikely to follow from a deliberate act of his own, he may be said to *intend* that result, whether he desire it or not. Thus, if a man should, for a wager, discharge a gun among a multitude of people, and any should be killed, he would be deemed guilty of *intending* the death of such person ; for every man is presumed to *intend* the natural consequence of his own actions.

Intention is often confounded with *motive*, as when we speak of a man's " good intentions."

INTER ALIA. Amongst other things.

INTERCOMMONING is where the commons of two manors lie together, and the inhabitants of both have, time out of mind, depastured their cattle promiscuously in each.

INTERDICTION. An ecclesiastical censure prohibiting the administration of divine service.

INTERESSE TERMINI. The right of entry on lands demised which the demise gives to the lessee, before he has entered upon the lands. 1 *Steph. Com. ; Wms. R. P.*

INTEREST. 1. A right or title to, or estate in, any real or personal property.

2. The income of a fund invested ; or the annual profit or recompense on a loan of money.

3. Such a personal advantage derivable from his judgment as disqualifies a judge by virtue of the rule " *Nemo debet judex esse in causâ suâ propriâ,*" as where a judge is a shareholder in a company which is plaintiff or defendant in an action.

4. Interest does not now exclude a witness from giving evidence. 6 *& 7 Vict. c.* 85 : 14 *& 15 Vict. c.* 99 ; 1 *Steph. Com. ;* 3 *Steph. Com.*

INTEREST REIPUBLICÆ UT SIT FINIS LITIUM (it is to the interest of a state that there should be an end of litigation).

INTEREST SUIT. An action in the Probate Division to determine which party is entitled to a grant of letters of administration of the estate of a deceased person.

INTERIM CURATOR. A person appointed by justices of the peace to take care of the property of a felon convict until the appointment by the Crown of an administrator or administrators for the same purpose. 33 *& 34 Vict. c.* 23, *ss.* 21—26 ; 4 *Steph. Com.*

INTERIM ORDER. An order to take effect provisionally, or until further directions. The expression is used especially with reference to orders given pending an appeal.

INTERLINEATION. Writing between the lines in a deed, will, or other document. A deed may be avoided by interlineation, unless a memorandum be made thereof at the time of the execution or attestation. An interlineation in a deed is presumed, in the absence of proof to the contrary, to have been made at or before the time of execution. In a will, the presumption is the other way. 1 *Steph. Com.* As to interlineation in affidavits, see R. S. C. 1883, Ord. XXXVIII. r. 12.

INTERLOCUTORY. Intermediate, with especial reference to a suit or action.

INTERLOCUTORY DECREE or **ORDER** is a decree or order which does not conclude a cause, *e.g.*, an order for inspection of documents. 3 *Steph. Com.*

INTERLOCUTORY INJUNCTION is an injunction granted for the purpose of keeping matters *in statu quo* until a decision is given on the merits of the case. 3 *Steph. Com.* [INJUNCTION.]

INTERLOCUTORY JUDGMENT is a judgment in an action at law, given upon some defence, proceeding, or default, which is only intermediate, and does not finally determine or complete the action. The phrase is most frequently applied to those *judgments* whereby the *right* of the plaintiff to recover in the action is established, but the *quantum* of damages sustained by him is not ascertained. This happens when the defendant suffers judgment to go against him by *confession* or for *default of plea*, in any action brought for recovery of damages. 3 *Steph. Com. ;* R. S. C. 1883, *Ord. XIII. rr.* 5, 6.

INTERNATIONAL COPYRIGHT. See COPYRIGHT, and 2 *Steph. Com.*

INTERNATIONAL LAW (Lat. *Jus inter gentes*). The positive morality which obtains between nations or sovereigns. International law is divided into two branches :—

1. Public international law, which comprises the rights and duties of sovereign states towards each other.

2. Private international law, which comprises the rights and duties of the *citizens* of different states towards each other, and is mainly conversant with questions as to the particular law governing doubtful cases. This is otherwise called the " conflict of laws." [CONFLICT OF LAWS.]

Consult, on Public International Law, Wheaton's International Law ; Phillimore's International Law ; Twiss' Law of Nations, and Woolsey on International Law ; and on Private International Law, Story's Conflict of Laws, Westlake's Private International Law, and Dicey, Conflict of Laws.

INTERPLEADER. A motion by way of interpleader is a motion for relief from adverse claims. It often happens that a man finds himself exposed to the adverse claims of two opposite parties, each requiring him to pay a certain sum of money or to deliver certain goods, and that he is unable to comply safely with the requisition of either, because a reasonable doubt exists as to which of them is the rightful claimant. Formerly it was necessary to institute a suit in Chancery in order to obtain relief in such a case ; but by 1 & 2 Will. 4, c. 58, a defendant, sued by either party in the case above mentioned, may apply to the court or a judge to order the other party so claiming the money or goods to appear and state the particulars of his claim, and either to maintain or relinquish the same, and, if he maintains it, to make himself the defendant in the action.

The process of interpleader was enlarged and made more beneficial by the Common Law Procedure Act, 1860, and in 1883 these two Acts were put expressly into the form of rules by R. S. C. 1883, Ord. LVII., and the Acts themselves repealed. 3 *Steph. Com.*

INTERPRETATION CLAUSE. A clause frequently inserted in Acts of parliament, declaring the sense in which certain words used therein are to be understood.

INTERREGNUM. In kingdoms where the monarch is elected, the time during which the throne is vacant is called an interregnum. Where sovereignty is hereditary, no interregnum can occur.

INTERROGATORIES. 1. Questions in writing administered by a plaintiff to a defendant, or by a defendant to a plaintiff, on points material to the suit or action. *R. S. C.* 1883, *Ord. XXXI.*, *rr.* 1, 26 ; 3 *Steph. Com.* [DISCOVERY.]

2. Questions administered to a person suspected of, or charged with, contempt of court, now probably obsolete. 4 *Steph. Com.*

INTERVENER, A person who intervenes in a suit, either on his own behalf or on behalf of the public. This is allowed in certain cases, especially in suits for divorce and nullity of marriage, by 23 & 24 Vict. c. 144, and 36 Vict. c. 31. In these suits it is usual for the King's Proctor to intervene where collusion is suspected. [KING'S PROCTOR.]

INTESTATE. Without making a will. See *Williams on Executors ;* 47 & 48 *Vict. c.* 71 ; 53 & 54 *Vict. c.* 29 ; 2 *Steph. Com.*

INTIMIDATION. The using of violence, threats, etc., to compel a person to do or abstain from doing that which he has a legal right to do or abstain from doing is a misdemeanor. 4 *Steph. Com.* ; 38 & 39 *Vict. c.* 86, *s.* 7.

INTRA VIRES (within its powers). The converse of *ultra vires* (*q.v.*).

INTRUSION. 1. A species of injury to freehold, which happens when a tenancy for life, or other " particular estate of freehold," has come to an end, and a stranger enters, before the person entitled in remainder or reversion. 3 *Steph. Com.* There was formerly a writ of *entry sur intrusion*, which is abolished by 3 & 4 Will. 4, c. 27, s. 36.

2. Trespass committed on the lands of the Crown ; as, by entering thereon without title ; holding over after a lease is at an end, etc. For this the remedy is by an *information of intrusion* in the King's Bench Division. 3 *Steph. Com.*

INUENDO. [INNUENDO.]

INURE. To take effect. [ENURE.]

INVENTION, TITLE BY. See PATENT ; COPYRIGHT.

INVENTORY. 1. A description or repertory made by an executor or administrator of all the goods and chattels of the deceased, which he is bound to deliver to the Court of Probate, if and when thereunto lawfully required. 2 *Steph. Com.*

2. Any account of goods sold, or exhibited for the purpose of sale. *Toml.*

INVESTITURE. The giving possession or seisin. 1 *Steph. Com.* [HOMAGE.]
    The word is also often applied to a ceremonial introduction to some office or dignity. [INDUCTION; INSTITUTION; LAY INVESTITURE OF BISHOPS.]

INVESTMENT. As to the securities in which trustees are authorised by law to invest trust moneys, see the Trustee Act, 1893 (56 & 57 Vict. c. 53). 3 *Steph. Com.*

INVITO DOMINO (without the assent of the lord or owner).

INVOICE. A list of goods that have been sold by one person to another, stating the particulars and prices. The invoice is sent by the seller to the buyer, either along with the goods or separately by post.

IPSE DIXIT. He himself said; words used to denote an assertion resting on the authority of an individual.

IPSO FACTO. By the very act. These words are often applied to forfeitures, indicating that when any forfeiture is incurred, it shall not be necessary to declare such forfeiture in a court of law, but that the penalty shall be incurred by the doing of the act prohibited. And so, when it is enacted that any proceeding shall be *ipso facto* void, it means that such a proceeding is to have not even *primâ facie* validity, but may be treated as void for all purposes *ab initio.* [VOID AND VOIDABLE.]

IRREGULARITY. A departure from rule, or neglect of legal formalities. In practice the term is most frequently (though not exclusively) applied to such departure, neglect, or informality as does not affect the validity of the act done. Thus an *irregular distress* is not now vitiated, so as to make the distrainer a trespasser *ab initio*, and so to render all his proceedings illegal from the first; but where distress is made for rent justly due, any subsequent irregularity will do no more than give an action for damages to the party grieved, and not even that, if tender of amends is made before action brought. This is by 11 Geo. 2, c. 19, s. 19. Formerly, any irregularity made the party distraining a trespasser *ab initio.* 3 *Steph. Com.* [AB INITIO; DISTRESS; SIX CARPENTERS' CASE.]

IRREPLEVIABLE, or IRREPLEVISABLE. That which cannot be replevied or set at large upon sureties. [REPLEVIN.]

IRREVOCABLE. That cannot be revoked; powers of appointment are sometimes executed so as to be irrevocable. A will is never irrevocable.

ISSUABLE PLEA. A plea which raises a defence on the merits of the case, so that the plaintiff may take issue thereon, and go to trial. [ISSUE, 5.]

ISSUE hath divers significations in law :—
    1. The children begotten between a man and his wife.
    2. Descendants generally. 7 *Will.* 4 & 1 *Vict. c. 26, s. 33; Wms. R. P.*
    3. The profits growing from amerciaments and fines.
    4. The profits of lands and tenements.
    5. The point of matter issuing out of the allegations and pleas of the plaintiff and defendant in a cause, whereupon the parties join, and put their cause upon trial. 3 *Steph. Com.* See *R. S. C.* 1883, *Ord. XIX. r.* 18, *Ord. XXIII. r.* 5, and *Ord. XXVII. r.* 13. [SETTLING ISSUES.]
    6. Also the putting out of bank-notes and other paper money for public circulation. 3 *Steph. Com.*

ITINERANT. Travelling or taking a journey; ·and those were anciently called justices *itinerant*, or justices *in eyre* (*in itinere*), who were sent into divers counties with commission to hear causes. 3 *Steph. Com.* [EYRE.]

JACENS. In abeyance. [HÆREDITAS JACENS.]

JACTITATION. Boasting of something which is challenged by another. Specially with reference to the suit of *jactitation of marriage*, where one of two parties has falsely boasted or given out that he or she was married to the other, whereby a common reputation

JACTITATION—*continued.*

of their matrimony might ensue, and the other sues for an order enjoining perpetual silence on that head. Now almost obsolete. 3 *Steph. Com.*; 20 *&* 21 *Vict. c.* 85, *s.* 6.

JACTUS, or **JACTURA MERCIUM.** [JETTISON.]

JAVELIN-MEN. Yeomen retained by the sheriff to escort the judge of assize.

JEOFAIL (from the old French *j'ay faillé*, I have failed), in a legal sense, denotes an oversight in pleading. Various statutes, called statutes of amendment and jeofails, allow a pleader to amend any slip which he may have made in the form of his pleadings. Formerly, the most trifling objection in point of form might be alleged in arrest of judgment. [AMENDMENT.]

JETSAM. [WRECK ; JETTISON.]

JETTISON, or **JACTUS**, or **JACTURA MERCIUM.** The act of throwing goods overboard for the purpose of lightening a ship in danger of wreck. Such goods are styled jetsam. 2 *Steph. Com.*; *Sm. Merc. Law.*

JOBBER. [STOCKBROKER.]

JOHN DOE. The name generally given to the fictitious plaintiff in an action of ejectment, before the passing of the C. L. P. Act, 1852. [EJECTMENT.]

JOINDER IN PLEADING. [ISSUE, 5.]

JOINDER OF CAUSES OF ACTION. Joining in one action several causes of action. By R. S. C. 1883, Ord. XVIII., the plaintiff may unite in the same action several causes of action subject to powers of the court or a judge to order separate trials.

JOINDER OF PARTIES. All persons may be joined as plaintiffs in whom the right to any relief claimed is alleged to exist, whether jointly, severally or in the alternative. Two or more defendants may be joined in case the plaintiff is in doubt as to the person from whom he is entitled to redress. *R. S. C.* 1883, *Ord. XVI.*

JOINT AND SEVERAL. When two or more persons declare themselves jointly and severally bound, this means that they render themselves liable to a joint action against all, as well as to a separate action against each, in case the conditions of the bond or agreement be not complied with. And the party to whom they are so jointly and severally bound is called a joint and several creditor.

JOINT STOCK BANK. The ordinary name given to banking companies other than the Bank of England. 3 *Steph. Com.*

JOINT STOCK COMPANY. [COMPANY.]

JOINT TENANCY is where an estate is acquired by two or more persons in the same land, by the same title, not being a title by descent, and at the same period ; and (if created by a written instrument) without any words importing that the parties are to take in distinct shares. The principal feature of this tenancy is that on the death of one of the parties his share accrues to the others by survivorship. Joint tenants are said to be seised *per my et per tout*. In joint tenancy there are four unities, viz., of possession, interest, title and time. 1 *Steph. Com.* ; *Wms. R. P.*

A joint tenancy is distinguished from a tenancy in common, as to which see COMMON, TENANCY IN. See also CO-PARCENARY.

The phrase is also applied to the holding of personal property under the like conditions. 2 *Steph. Com.*

JOINTRESS. A woman entitled to jointure. [JOINTURE, 2.]

JOINTURE. 1. A name sometimes given to an estate in joint tenancy. 1 *Steph. Com.*

2. But, in common speech, the term *jointure* is usually confined to that estate, which, by virtue of ss. 6—9 of 27 Hen. 8, c. 10 (commonly called the Statute of Uses), is settled upon a husband and wife before marriage, as a full satisfaction and bar of the woman's dower. It should be, strictly speaking, a joint estate, limited to both husband and wife ; but, in common acceptance it extends also to a sole estate, limited to the wife only ; and is defined by Sir Edward Coke as "a competent livelihood of freehold for the wife of lands and tenements, to take effect, in profit or possession, presently after the death of the husband, for the life of the wife at least." 1 *Steph. Com.*

JOURNALS OF THE HOUSES OF PAR-LIAMENT. The daily records of the proceedings of the Houses. They are evidence in courts of law of the proceedings in parliament, but are not conclusive of facts alleged by either House, unless they be within their immediate jurisdiction. *May's Parl. Pract.*

JUDGE. One invested with authority to decide questions in dispute between parties, and to award the proper punishment to offenders.

The judges of the Supreme Court (except the Lord Chancellor) hold their offices during good behaviour, subject to a power of removal by the Crown upon the address of both houses of parliament. They may not sit in the House of Commons. See *Jud. Act*, 1875, *s.* 5.

As to county court judges, see the County Courts Act, 1888, ss. 5, 8, 24.

No action lies against a judge for anything said or done in his judicial capacity, but if he act without jurisdiction, he may be made answerable for the consequences. *Scott* v. *Stansfield*, L. R. 3 Ex. 220. [INTEREST, 3.]

JUDGE ORDINARY. The judge of the Court of Probate, sitting as judge of the Court of Divorce under sect. 9 of the Divorce Act, 1857 (20 & 21 Vict. c. 85), was so called, as being the *ordinary* judge of the Divorce Court. [COURT FOR DIVORCE AND MATRIMONIAL CAUSES ; DIVORCE COURT.]

JUDGE-ADVOCATE-GENERAL. An officer appointed to advise the Crown in reference to courts martial and other matters of military law. 2 *Steph. Com.*

JUDGE'S ORDER. An order made on summons by a judge at chambers. [CHAMBERS ; SUMMONS.]

JUDGMENT. The sentence or order of the court in a civil or criminal proceeding. [FINAL JUDGMENT ; INTERLOCUTORY JUDGMENT.]

JUDGMENT CREDITOR. A creditor who claims to be such by virtue of a judgment ; that is, a party entitled to enforce execution under a judgment.

JUDGMENT DEBT. A debt due under a judgment.

JUDGMENT DEBTOR. A person against whom a judgment ordering him to pay a sum of money stands unsatisfied, and who is liable therefore to have his property taken in execution under the judgment.

JUDGMENT SUMMONS. A summons issued under the Debtors Act, 1869, and the rules framed in pursuance thereof, on the application of a plaintiff who has obtained a judgment or order in a county court for the payment of any sum or sums of money, but has not succeeded in obtaining payment from the defendant of the sum or sums so ordered to be paid. The judgment summons cites the defendant to appear personally in court, and be examined on oath touching the means he has, or has had since the date of the judgment, to pay the sum in question, and also to show cause why he should not be committed to prison for his default. *Robson, Bkcy.*

JUDICATURE ACTS. [SUPREME COURT OF JUDICATURE.]

JUDICIAL COMMITTEE. This expression is used to denote the Judicial Committee of the Privy Council. The Judicial Committee, as constituted by 3 & 4 Will. 4, c. 41, and 14 & 15 Vict. c. 83, s. 15, consisted of the Lord President of the Council, the Lord Chancellor, the Lords Justices of Appeal, and such other members of the Privy Council as should hold, or have held, certain judicial or other offices enumerated in the Acts, or should be specially appointed by the Crown to serve on the committee. But see 34 & 35 Vict. c. 91, and the Appellate Jurisdiction Act, 1876, s. 14. 2 *Steph. Com.*; 3 *Steph. Com.*

To the Judicial Committee were referred all appeals to the Crown from Admiralty and Ecclesiastical Courts and from courts in His Majesty's colonies and dependencies ; also petitions for the prolongation of patents. See 3 *Steph. Com.*

A portion of the jurisdiction of this court, viz., in appeals from the Court of Admiralty or orders in lunacy, was taken away by s. 18 of the Judicature Act, 1873. But see 54 & 55 Vict. c. 53, s. 4.

JUDICIAL NOTICE. Of many things the court takes judicial notice, and of them no proof is required. See *Best on Evidence*.

JUDICIAL SEPARATION. A separation of man and wife by the Divorce Court, which has the effect, so long as it lasts, of making the wife a single woman for all legal purposes, except that she cannot marry again ; and similarly the husband, though separated from his wife, is not by a judicial separation empowered to marry again. It thus corresponds somewhat to a divorce *à mensâ et thoro* under the old law, but is more complete in its effects. 20 *& 21 Vict. c.* 85, *ss.* 16, 25, 26. By 58 & 59 Vict. c. 39, it may be granted to a wife on conviction of the husband of aggravated assault. 2 *Steph. Com.* [DIVORCE, 1.]

JUDICIAL WRIT. [WRIT.]

JUDICIUM DEI. The judgment of God ; a term applied by our ancestors to the trial by ordeal. 4 *Steph. Com.* [ORDEAL.]

JUNIOR BARRISTER. A barrister under the rank of King's counsel. Also, the junior of two counsel employed on the same side in any judicial proceeding.

JURA REGALIA. Royal rights, or rights in the nature of royal rights ; especially civil and criminal jurisdiction. 1 *Steph. Com.* ; 3 *Steph. Com.* [COUNTY PALATINE.]

JURAT. 1. A short statement at the foot of an affidavit, *when, where,* and *before whom* it was sworn. See *R. S. C.* 1883, *Ord. XXXVIII. rr.* 9, 12, 13, 14, and the *Oaths Act,* 1888, *s.* 4.

2. An officer in the island of Jersey. 1 *Steph. Com.*

3. Officers in the nature of aldermen in some corporations in Kent and Sussex.

JURATA was formerly the conclusion of every *nisi prius* record, which stated in effect that the proceedings were respited till some day therein named, unless the judge who was to try the cause should before that day come (as he always did) to the place appointed for the trial. Now abolished.

JURE DIVINO. By divine right. [DIVINE RIGHT.]

JURE UXORIS. In right of his wife.

JURIS ET DE JURE (of law and from law). A presumption which may not be rebutted is so called.

JURIS UTRUM, sometimes called the parson's writ of right, was a writ that lay for an incumbent whose predecessor had alienated the lands belonging to his benefice, to recover the same.

JURISDICTION. An authority or power which a man hath to do justice in causes of complaint brought before him : it may be limited either locally, *e.g.*, that of a county court, or as to amount or as to the character of the questions to be determined.

JURISPRUDENCE. 1. The science of law. 2. Sometimes used of a body of law.

JUROR. A member of a jury.

JURORS' BOOK. A book annually made out in each county, out of lists returned from each parish by the churchwardens and overseers, of persons therein qualified to serve as jurors. From this book the sheriff takes the names of the jurors to be summoned. 3 *Steph. Com.* [JURY.]

JURY signifies a body of men sworn to inquire of a matter of fact, and to declare the truth upon such evidence as shall be delivered them. Juries are of two kinds : grand juries, to inquire whether there is a *primâ facie* ground for a criminal accusation [BILL, 3 ; GRAND JURY ; INDICTMENT] ; and petty juries, for determining disputed matters of fact in civil and criminal cases. [PETTY JURY.] 3 *Steph. Com. ;* 4 *Steph. Com.*

The principal Acts of parliament at present in operation, relating to juries in England and Wales, are :

1. The County Juries Act, 1825 (6 Geo. 4, c. 50).
2. The Juries Act, 1862 (25 & 26 Vict. c. 107).
3. The Juries Act, 1870 (33 & 34 Vict. c. 77).

Under these Acts the property qualification of a juryman is as follows :— For a common juror, 10*l.* a year freehold or 20*l.* a year leasehold or assessment to the poor rate or house duty for a house of 30*l.* a year in Middlesex and 20*l.* a year in other counties. A special juror either must have the property qualification above-mentioned, and, in addition, be legally entitled to be called an esquire, or he must be a person of higher degree, or be a banker or merchant, or occupy a house of a certain rateable value. Further, a juror m

JURY—*continued.*

be between the ages of 21 and 60 years. Various classes of persons are exempted from serving on juries ; the persons exempted including judges ; members of parliament ; clergymen, and other ministers of religion ; practising barristers and solicitors ; officers of courts of law and equity ; and many others.

A coroner's jury and a grand jury may consist of any number above 11. In criminal trials and in civil trials in the High Court of Justice, the number is 12 ; in county courts, 5.

The churchwardens and overseers of each parish are bound annually to make out a list of every man within the parish who is qualified and liable to serve on juries, and to cause a copy of such list to be affixed on the doors of every church and chapel in the parish on the first three Sundays in September. The churchwardens and overseers must produce their lists at a special petty sessions of the justices, held within the last seven days of September for the purpose of revising the same. Any person desirous of having his name removed from the list on the ground of any legal disqualification or exemption must insist on his claim at the special sessions of the justices held for the purpose of revising the lists, as no person whose name is once down in the jury-book for the year is to be excused from attendance for any cause other than illness, not claimed by him at the time of the revision of the list by the justices. See also CHALLENGE.

JURY BOOK. [JURORS' BOOK ; JURY.]

JURY BOX. The place in which jurors sit for the trial of matters submitted to them.

JURY OF MATRONS. A jury of twelve matrons appointed to inquire whether a woman, who pleads pregnancy in bar of execution, is quick with child. 4 *Steph. Com.*

JURY PROCESS, now abolished, consisted of two writs for the summoning of juries. A jury is now summoned by precept. 33 *&* 34 *Vict. c.* 77.

JUS. Law or right. In the Roman law, the whole of civil procedure was expressed by the two words *jus* and *judicium*, of which the former comprehended all that took place before the

prætor or other magistrate (*in jure*), and the latter all that took place before the judex (*in judicio*) : the judex being a juryman appointed to try disputed facts. In many cases a single judex was considered sufficient : in others, several were appointed, and they seem to have been called *recuperatores*, as opposed to the single judex. *Smith's Dict. Ant.* For other meanings of *jus*, see the following titles.

JUS ACCRESCENDI. The right of survivorship between joint tenants. 1 *Steph. Com.* [JOINT TENANCY.]

JUS ACCRESCENDI INTER MERCATORES LOCUM NON HABET, PRO BENEFICIO COMMERCII (the right of survivorship does not exist among merchants, for the benefit of commerce).

JUS ACCRESCENDI PRÆFATUR ONERIBUS ET ULTIMA VOLUNTATI (the right of survivorship prevails as against debts and against the last will). [JOINT TENANCY.]

JUS AD REM. An inchoate and imperfect right ; such, for instance, as a clergyman presented to a living acquires, before induction, by presentation and institution. 1 *Steph. Com.*

Jus ad rem is merely an abridged expression for *jus ad rem acquirendam ;* and it properly denotes a right to the *acquisition* of a thing.

JUS CIVILE. The civil law. It is defined by Justinian as the law which each state has established for itself : but the term is now almost exclusively appropriated to the Roman civil law. [CORPUS JURIS CIVILIS.]

JUS DISPONENDI. The right of disposing of property.

JUS GENTIUM. The law of nations, which is thus described in the opening passages of Justinian's Institutes :— " Quod vero naturalis ratio inter omnes homines constituit, id apud omnes populos peræque custoditur, vocaturque jus gentium, quasi quo jure omnes gentes utuntur " (that law which natural reason has established among men is maintained equally by all nations, and is called the law of nations, as being the law which all nations adopt).

JUS HABENDI ET RETINENDI. The right to have and retain the profits, tithes, and offerings of a rectory or parsonage.

JUS HONORARIUM. The body of Roman law made up of the edicts of the supreme magistrates, particularly of the prætors.

JUS IN PERSONAM. A right availing against a determinate person or persons, as opposed to a right *in rem*, which avails against all the world.

JUS IN RE. Full and complete right, accompanied by corporal possession. 1 *Steph. Com.*

JUS IN REM. A right availing against all the world. Thus the phrase denotes the *compass* and not the *subject* of the right.

JUS MARITI. The right acquired by a husband in the movable estate of his wife, by virtue of the marriage prior to the Married Women's Property Act, 1882.

JUS PATRONATUS. 1. The right of patronage or presentation to a benefice. 2. A commission from the bishop awarded when two rival presentations are made to him upon the same avoidance of a living. This commission is directed to the bishop's chancellor, and others of competent learning, who are to summon a jury of six clergymen and six laymen to inquire who is the rightful patron. 3 *Steph. Com.*

JUS POSTLIMINII. [POSTLIMINIUM.]

JUS TERTII. The right of a third party. If A., who *primâ facie* is liable to restore property to B., alleges that C. has a paramount title, A. is said to set up the *jus tertii.* This may not be done by an agent as against his principal.

JUSTICE OF THE PEACE. A subordinate magistrate appointed to keep the peace within a given jurisdiction, and to inquire of felonies and misdemeanors; with a statutory jurisdiction to decide summarily in many cases, and in some cases to adjudicate upon claims of a civil nature.

Justices of the peace for counties are selected on the recommendation of the Lord Lieutenant, and appointed by special commission under the Great Seal by the Lord Chancellor. 2 *Steph. Com.*

Justices of the peace for boroughs are also in general selected by the Lord Chancellor. 3 *Steph. Com.* [CONSERVATOR OF THE PEACE; CUSTOS ROTULORUM; QUORUM.]

JUSTICES. Officers deputed by the Crown to administer justice, and do right by way of judgment. The judges of the Supreme Court are called justices since the Judicature Act, but the word is usually applied to justices of the peace. [JUSTICE OF THE PEACE.]

JUSTICES IN EYRE. Justices who formerly made a circuit every seven years round the kingdom to try causes. Superseded by the more modern justices of assize. 3 *Steph. Com.* [EYRE; ITINERANT.]

JUSTICES OF ASSIZE were originally judges appointed to try the real actions called *assizes.* The present justices of assize are judges of the superior courts sent with other commissioners to try causes in the respective counties. 1 *Steph. Com.*; 3 *Steph. Com.* [ASSIZE, COURTS OF; ASSIZE, WRIT OF.]

JUSTICES OF GAOL DELIVERY. [ASSIZE, COURTS OF; GAOL DELIVERY, COMMISSION OF.]

JUSTICES OF NISI PRIUS are now practically the same as the justices of assize. [ASSIZE, COURTS OF; NISI PRIUS.]

JUSTICES OF OYER AND TERMINER. Justices of assize are so called in respect of their commission to *hear and determine* all treasons, felonies, and misdemeanors. 3 *Steph. Com.*; 4 *Steph. Com.* [ASSIZE, COURTS OF; OYER AND TERMINER.]

JUSTICIARY (or JUSTICIAR), CHIEF. The old name of judge, before the *Aula Regia* was divided. 3 *Steph. Com.*

JUSTICIES. A special writ empowering the sheriff, for the sake of despatch, to do the same justice in his county court as might otherwise be had at Westminster. The jurisdiction of the sheriff's county court is now almost wholly superseded. 3 *Steph. Com.* [COUNTY COURT.]

JUSTIFIABLE HOMICIDE. [HOMICIDE.]

JUSTIFICATION is showing a sufficient reason in court by a defendant why he did what he is called upon to answer, particularly in an action of libel, *e.g.*, by showing the libel to be true and to have been published for the public benefit; or in an action of assault showing the violence to have been necessary. 3 *Steph. Com.*

JUSTIFICATORS. [COMPURGATORS.]

JUSTIFYING BAIL. Showing the sufficiency of persons tendering themselves as bail.

JUVENILE OFFENDERS. Children under 12 and young persons under 14 may be summarily tried for certain indictable offences instead of being committed for trial by jury. See *ss.* 10 *and* 11 *of the Summary Jurisdiction Act,* 1879 (42 *&* 43 *Vict. c.* 49); 4 *Steph. Com.* [INDUSTRIAL SCHOOLS.]

K.B. King's Bench.

KANTREF. An old Welsh word signifying one hundred towns. *Cowel.*

KEELAGE. A custom to pay money for ships resting in a port or harbour.

KEEPER OF THE GREAT SEAL is, since 5 Eliz. c. 18, the Lord Chancellor. 3 *Steph. Com.*

KEEPER OF THE PRIVY SEAL, now called the Lord Privy Seal; the officer through whose hands all charters, pardons, etc., pass, before they come to the Great Seal. 1 *Steph. Com.* The office is always held by a Cabinet Minister. 2 *Steph. Com.*

KEEPING HOUSE, as an act of bankruptcy, is when a man absents himself from his place of business and retires to his private residence, so as to evade the importunity of creditors. The usual evidence of "keeping house" is denial to a creditor who has called for money. *Robson, Bkcy.* [ACT OF BANKRUPTCY.]

KEEPING TERM, by a student of law, consists in eating a sufficient number of dinners in hall to make the term count for the purpose of being called to the bar. [CALL TO THE BAR.]

KEEPING THE PEACE. Avoiding a breach of the peace; or persuading or compelling others to refrain from breaking the peace,

Security for keeping the peace consists in being bound with one or more securities in a recognizance or obligation to the Crown, whereby the party acknowledges himself to be indebted to the Crown, in a given sum, with condition to be void if he shall keep the peace either generally, towards the sovereign and all his liege people, or particularly to the person who craves the security. 4 *Steph. Com.* [GOOD BEHAVIOUR.]

KENTLEDGE, or **KENTLAGE.** The permanent ballast of a ship, consisting usually of pigs of iron cast in a particular form, or other weighty material, which, on account of its superior cleanliness and the small space occupied by it, is frequently preferred to ordinary ballast. *Abbott on Shipping.*

KEYS, in the Isle of Man, are the twenty-four chief commoners, who form the local legislature. 1 *Steph. Com.*

KIDNAPPING. The forcible taking away of a man, woman, or child from their own country, and sending them into another. As to children, see 24 & 25 Vict. c. 100, s. 56. 4 *Steph. Com.* [STEALING CHILDREN.] See also 35 & 36 Vict. c. 19.

KIN. Legal relationship.

KIN-BOTE. Compensation for the murder of a kinsman.

KING. The King or Queen is the person in whom the supreme executive power of this kingdom is vested. In domestic affairs the sovereign is a constituent part of the supreme legislative power, and may negative all new laws, and is bound by no statute unless specially named therein. The sovereign is also considered as the general of the kingdom, and as such may raise armies, fleets, etc. He is also the fountain of justice and general conservator of the peace, and may erect courts, prosecute offenders, pardon crimes, etc. The sovereign is also head of the Church, and as such nominates bishops, etc., and receives appeals in ecclesiastical causes. 2 *Steph. Com.* [CIVIL LIST.] As the statutes of the realm and the older law cases and other records are in general referred to as being of such a year of such a reign, we append a list of the kings and queens of England, with the dates of their accessions and

KING—*continued.*

deaths, from the Conqueror to the present time.

King.	Accession.	Reigned until
William I. (the Conqueror)	1066 ...	1087
William II. (William Rufus, son of William I.)	1087 ...	1100
Henry I. (youngest son of William I.)	1100 ...	1135
Stephen	1135 ...	1154
Henry II.	1154 ...	1189
Richard I. (otherwise called Richard Cœur de Lion)	1189 ...	1199
John	1199 ...	1216
Henry III.	1216 ...	1272
Edward I.	1272 ...	1307
Edward II.	1307 ...	1327
Edward III.	1327 ...	1377
Richard II.	1377 ...	1399
Henry IV.	1399 ...	1413
Henry V.	1413 ...	1422
Henry VI.	1422 ...	1461
Edward IV.	1461 ...	1483
Edward V.	1483 ...	1483
Richard III.	1483 ...	1485
Henry VII.	1485 ...	1509
Henry VIII.	1509 ...	1547
Edward VI.	1547 ...	1553
Mary (married in 1554 to Philip of Spain; hence the subsequent statutes of her reign are referred to as those of Philip and Mary)	1553 ...	1558
Elizabeth	1558 ...	1603
James I.	1603 ...	1625
Charles I.	1625 ...	1649
Commonwealth declared	1649	
Oliver Cromwell, Protector	1653 ...	1658
Richard Cromwell ...	1658 ...	1659
Charles II.	1660 ...	1685

The statutes of the reign of Charles II. are dated as if from the year 1649, when his father was beheaded, on the fiction that, as heir to the Crown, he began to reign immediately on his father's death. Hence, the statute for the abolition of military tenures, passed in 1660, is called 12 Car. 2, c. 24; the Statute of Frauds, passed in 1677, 29 Car. 2, c. 3; etc.

James II.	1685 ...	1688
William III. and Mary	1689 .. 1702 / 1689 ... 1694	
Anne	1702 ...	1714
George I.	1714 ...	1727
George II.	1727 ...	1760
George III.	1760 ...	1820
George IV.	1820 ...	1830
William IV.	1830 ..	1837
Victoria	1837 ...	1901
Edward VII.	1901	

KING CAN DO NO WRONG. This maxim means that the king is not responsible legally for aught that he may please to do, or for any forbearance or omission. It does not, therefore, mean that every thing done by the government is just and lawful; but that whatever is exceptional in the conduct of public affairs is not to be imputed to the king. 2 *Steph. Com.*

KING'S ADVOCATE. [ADVOCATE, KING'S.]

KING'S BENCH. [COURT OF KING'S BENCH.]

KING'S BOOKS. Books containing the valuation of ecclesiastical benefices and preferments. pursuant to 26 Hen. 8, c. 3, and 1 Eliz. c. 4. 2 *Steph. Com.*

KING'S CORONER AND ATTORNEY. An officer of the Court of King's Bench, usually called "The Master of the Crown Office," whose duty it is to file informations at the suit of a private subject by direction of the court. He is now the "Master of the Crown Office." 4 *Steph. Com.* [CROWN OFFICE; INFORMATION, 5.]

KING'S COUNSEL is a name given to barristers appointed by letters patent to be his Majesty's counsel learned in the law. Their selection and removal rests in practice with the Lord Chancellor. A King's counsel may not, except by licence from the Crown, take a brief against the Crown in any civil or criminal case; but such licence will generally be given, unless the Crown requires his services in that case. A King's counsel, in taking that rank, renounces the preparation of written pleadings, and other chamber practice. 3 *Steph. Com.*

KING'S EVIDENCE. Evidence for the Crown. When we say that an accused person turns king's evidence, we mean that he confesses his guilt, and proffers himself as a witness against his accomplices. His admission, however, in that capacity requires the sanction of the court; and, unless his statements be corroborated in some material part by unimpeachable evidence, the jury are usually advised by the judge to acquit the prisoner notwithstanding. If his evidence is unsatisfactory he may still be convicted on his original confession or other evidence. 4 *Steph. Com.* [APPROVER.]

KING'S PROCTOR is the proctor or solicitor representing the Crown in the Courts of Probate and Divorce. In petitions for dissolution of marriage, or for declarations of nullity of marriage, the King's Proctor may, under the direction of the Attorney-General, and by leave of the court, intervene in the suit for the purpose of proving collusion between the parties. 23 & 24 *Vict. c.* 144, *s.* 7; 36 & 37 *Vict. c.* 31; 3 *Steph. Com.*

KING'S REMEMBRANCER. [REMEM-BRANCERS.]

KING'S SILVER. A name given to the money formerly payable to the king in the Court of Common Pleas, for the licence there granted to any man to pass a fine. [FINE, 1.]

KING'S WIDOW. A widow of the king's tenant in chief, who could not marry without the king's leave. [IN CAPITE.]

KINGS-AT-ARMS. The principal heralds. There are three existing in England: Garter, Clarencieux, and Norroy. *Lyon* King-at-Arms is the chief in Scotland, and *Ulster* in Ireland. 3 *Steph. Com.*

KLEPTOMANIA. A species of insanity in the form of an irresistible mania for thieving.

KNIGHT. A commoner of rank, originally one that bore arms, who, for his martial powers, was raised above the ordinary rank of gentleman. The following are different degrees of knights:—
1. Knight of the Order of St. George, or of the Garter: first instituted, in the opinion of Selden, by Edward III. in the 18th year of his reign. [GARTER.]
2. A Knight Banneret: who ranks after privy councillors and judges; and, unless created by the king in person in the field, under royal banners, in time of open war, he ranks after baronets. [BANERET.]
3. A Knight of the Order of the Bath: an order instituted by King Henry IV. They are so called from the ceremony, formerly observed, of bathing the night before their creation.
4. Knight Bachelor: the most ancient, though the lowest order of knighthood among us. We have an instance of King Alfred conferring this order on his son Athelstan.

5. Knight of the Order of St. Michael and St. George: an order instituted the 27th of April, 1818, for the United States of the Ionian Islands, and for the ancient sovereignty of Malta and its dependencies. This order is often conferred on persons who have distinguished themselves in the colonies and dependencies of the British Empire.
6. Knight of the Thistle: an order instituted by King Achias, of Scotland, and re-established by Queen Anne, on the 31st of December, 1703. 2 *Steph. Com.*

KNIGHT OF THE BATH. [KNIGHT, 3.]

KNIGHT OF THE CHAMBER. A knight bachelor, so made in time of peace. [KNIGHT, 4.]

KNIGHT OF THE SHIRE. A gentleman of worth chosen by the freeholders of a county to represent it in parliament. 1 *Steph. Com.*; 2 *Steph. Com.*

KNIGHTHOOD. The dignity of a knight.

KNIGHT-SERVICE (Lat. *Servitium militare*). The most universal and most honourable species of tenure under the feudal system. It was entirely military. To make a tenure by knight-service, a determinate quantity of land was necessary, which was called a knight's fee. [KNIGHT'S FEE.] And he who held this proportion of land by knight-service was bound to attend his lord to the wars for forty days in every year, if called upon. There were other burdens attached to this tenure, under the name of aids, reliefs, primer seisins, etc.
Knight-service was abolished, with other military tenures, by 12 Car. 2, c. 24. 1 *Steph. Com.* [AID; PRIMER SEISIN; RELIEF.]

KNIGHT'S FEE (Lat. *Feudum militare*). A quantity of land sufficient to maintain a knight with convenient revenue. In the reign of Henry III. it was 15*l.* per annum. In the reign of Edward I. it was estimated at twelve plough-lands, and its value in that and the following reign was stated at 20*l.* per annum. But there are many different opinions as to its extent and value at various times. 1 *Steph. Com.*
Also, the rent that a knight paid to his lord of whom he held. [KNIGHT-SERVICE.]

L. S. [LOCUS SIGILLI.]

LA REYNE LE VEULT. [LE ROY LE VEULT.]

LABOURERS' DWELLINGS. All the Acts relating to this subject are consolidated by the Housing of the Working Classes Act, 1890 (53 & 54 Vict. c. 70).

LABOURERS, STATUTE OF. The stat. 23 Edw. 3 enacted that every able-bodied person (whether free or bond) within the age of threescore years, not exercising any craft, nor having of his own whereby he might live, nor any land of his own, should, if required to serve in a station that suited his condition, be bound to serve for the wages usual in the twentieth year of the king, on pain of being committed to gaol.

This statute, having been partially repealed by 5 Eliz. c. 4, was finally repealed in 1863 by 26 & 27 Vict. c. 125.

LAC or **LAKH.** A hundred thousand; thus a lac of rupees is 100,000 rupees, or about 10,000*l.* of our money.

LACHES. Slackness or negligence. In general it signifies neglect in a person to assert his rights, or long and unreasonable acquiescence in the assertion of adverse rights. This neglect or acquiescence will often have the effect of barring a man of the remedy which he might have had if he had resorted to it in proper time. Thus, by certain statutes called Statutes of Limitations, the time is specified within which various classes of actions respectively therein mentioned may be brought. And, independently of these statutes, a Court of Equity will often refuse relief to a plaintiff who has been guilty of unreasonable delay in seeking it. [LIMITATIONS, STATUTE OF.]

LADY-DAY. 1. When speaking of Lady-Day, we ordinarily mean the 25th of March, being the Feast of the Annunciation of the Blessed Virgin Mary, and one of the quarter-days for the payment of rent. [QUARTER-DAYS.]

2. Sometimes, however, a different meaning is given to the phrase by local custom. And, particularly, in parts of Ireland they speak of the 15th of August as Lady-Day, that day being, in the Roman Catholic Church, the festival of the Assumption of the Virgin. Under the old style Lady-Day was 6th April.

LÆSÆ MAJESTATIS CRIMEN. The name in Roman Law for high treason; called also *majestas.*

LÆSIONE FIDEI. Suits *pro læsione fidei* were suits for non-payment of debts or breaches of civil contracts, which, in the reign of Stephen, were brought in the Ecclesiastical Courts. This attempt to turn the Ecclesiastical Courts into Courts of Equity, on the ground that such acts were offences against conscience, was checked by the Constitutions of Clarendon, A.D. 1164, which provided that such matters should be within the jurisdiction of the King's Court. 3 *Steph. Com.* [CLARENDON, CONSTITUTIONS OF.]

LAGAN or **LAGON.** [LIGAN.]

LAGON. [LIGAN.]

LAMBETH DEGREES. Degrees conferred by the Archbishop of Canterbury. 2 *Steph. Com.*

LAMMAS DAY. The first of August. On that day the tenants that held land of York Cathedral were bound by their tenure to bring a living lamb into the church at high mass. [GULE OF AUGUST.]

LAMMAS LANDS. Lands over which there is a right of pasturage, from about Lammas or reaping time until sowing time by persons other than the owner of the land.

LANCASTER COUNTY PALATINE was erected into a county palatine in the fiftieth year of Edward III., and granted by him to his son John for life, that he should have *jura regalia*, and a kinglike power therein. 1 *Steph. Com.* [COUNTY PALATINE; DUCHY COURT OF LANCASTER; JURA REGALIA.]

LAND signifies generally not only arable ground, meadow, pasture, woods, moors, waters, etc., but also messuages and houses; comprehending everything of a permanent and substantial nature. Thus an action to recover possession of a pool must be brought for so much land covered with water, etc. 1 *Steph. Com.*

LAND CHARGE. Principal moneys, or a rent or an annuity charged upon land otherwise than by deed, by virtue of various Acts of Parliament. As to registration and searches, see s. 4 of the Land Charges Registration and Searches Act, 1888 (51 & 52 Vict. c. 51):

LAND COMMISSIONERS, formerly called the Copyhold Inclosure and Tithe Commissioners. See the *Settled Land Act*, 1882, *s.* 48.

LAND TAX. A tax upon land, the original of which may be traced, Blackstone says, to our military tenures. The personal attendance required of tenants of knights' fees growing troublesome, the tenants found means of compounding for it, first, by sending others in their stead, and in process of time by making a pecuniary satisfaction to the Crown in lieu of it. This pecuniary satisfaction at last came to be levied by assessments, under the name of *escuage* or *scutage*. [ESCUAGE.] It was promised by King John in *Magna Charta*, and provided by several statutes under Edward I. and Edward III., that no taxes should be levied but by consent of the Commons and great men in parliament.

Of the same nature with scutages upon knights' fees were assessments of *hidage* upon all other land, and of *talliage* in cities and boroughs. But they all fell into disuse upon the introduction of *subsidies*, about the time of Richard II. and Henry IV. These were a tax, not immediately imposed upon property, but upon persons in respect of their reputed estates. These taxes did not extend to spiritual preferments, such preferments being usually taxed by the clergy themselves in convocation. The last subsidies were given in 15 Car. II. (A.D. 1664); but periodical assessments upon the counties of the kingdom continued to be levied and granted as the national emergencies required. In the year 1692 there was a new assessment or valuation of estates throughout the kingdom, according to which the land tax was imposed by 4 Will. 3, c. 1, and has ever since continued a permanent charge on land; for, by stat. 38 Geo. 3, c. 60, this tax, which had long been annual, was converted into a perpetual one, and fixed at four shillings in the pound; but made subject, on the other hand, to redemption by the landowner. As between landlord and tenant, the tax is a charge upon the former, in the absence of any special engagement. Yet if the tenant has, to any extent, a beneficial interest, and does not hold at a rack-rent, he becomes liable, *pro tanto*, and can only charge the residue on his landlord. 1 *Bl.*; 2 *Steph. Com.* As to redemption of land tax, see 59 & 60 Vict. c. 28, s. 32.

LAND TRANSFER ACTS (25 & 26 Vict. c. 53, 38 & 39 Vict. c. 87, and 60 & 61 Vict. c. 65), for the establishment of a land registry for the registration of titles to land; with various provisions in reference to the transmission of land, and unregistered dealings with registered land, etc. Under the last-mentioned Act registration is, to some extent, compulsory. *Brickdale and Sheldon's Land Transfer Act.*

LANDED ESTATES COURT. A court in Ireland created in 1858 by 21 & 22 Vict. c. 72, in succession to the Encumbered Estates Court, for the purpose of deciding questions relating to the title to land.

LANDLORD. He of whom lands and tenements are holden; who has a right to distrain for rent in arrear, etc., the *tenant* being the person holding the lands. See *Woodfall, Landlord and Tenant.*

LANDS CLAUSES CONSOLIDATION ACTS, 1845. 1. The stat. 8 & 9 Vict. c. 18, for England and Ireland; amended by 23 & 24 Vict. c. 106, and by 32 & 33 Vict. c. 18.

2. Stat. 8 & 9 Vict. c. 19, for Scotland. amended by 23 & 24 Vict. c. 106.

The object of these general Acts is to provide legislative clauses in a convenient form for incorporation by reference in future special Acts of Parliament for taking land, with or without the consent of their respective owners, for the promotion of railways and other public undertakings. 1 *Steph. Com.*; 3 *Steph. Com.*

LANDWAITER. An officer of the Custom-house.

LAPSE. 1. A species of forfeiture, whereby the right of presentation to a benefice accrues to the ordinary, by neglect of the patron to present; to the metropolitan, by neglect of the ordinary; and to the Crown, by neglect of the metropolitan. 2 *Steph. Com.*; 3 *Steph. Com.* It is in the nature of a spiritual escheat.

2. The failure of a testamentary disposition in favour of any person, by reason of the death of the intended beneficiary in the lifetime of the testator.

In two cases, however, of the intended beneficiary dying in the testator's lifetime, there is now no lapse. The first case is that of a devise of real

LAPSE—*continued.*

estate to any person for an *estate tail*, where any issue who would inherit under such entail are living at the testator's death. The second case is that of a devise or bequest to a *child* or *other issue* of the testator, leaving issue, any of whom are living at the testator's death. See the *Wills Act* (1 *Vict. c.* 26), *ss.* 32 *and* 33 ; 1 *Steph. Com.*; 2 *Steph. Com.*

LAPSED DEVISE. [LAPSE, 2.]

LAPSED LEGACY. [LAPSE, 2.]

LARBOARD. The left side of a ship or boat when you stand with your face towards the bow. The term *port* is now ordered by the Lords Commissioners of the Admiralty to be used in the Royal Navy instead of *larboard*. Larboard is opposed to *starboard*, which is the right hand side looking forward.

LARCENY. The unlawful taking and carrying away of things personal, with intent to deprive the right owner of the same. The taking must be *animo furandi* (*i.e.*, with the intention of stealing), in order to constitute larceny. [FURANDI ANIMUS.] There must also be an "asportation," that is, a "carrying away"; but for this purpose the smallest removal is sufficient.

Larceny may be *simple*, that is, not combined with any circumstances of aggravation ; or, if so combined, it is called *compound* larceny. Under the latter are included :—

1. Larceny in a *dwelling-house* of goods above the value of 5*l.*

2. Larceny in *ships*, *wharves*, etc.

3. Larceny *from the person;* which is either by *privately stealing*, or by open and violent assault, usually called *robbery*. And a robbery may be committed, either directly from the person, or merely in the presence of the injured party by putting him in fear.

4. Larceny *by clerks and servants*, etc.

5. Larcenies, etc., *in relation to the Post Office*, by servants employed therein, which are punishable under the express provision of the Post Office Acts.

Distinction between Larceny and False Pretences.—Where a man, being desirous to possess himself fraudulently of another's goods, obtains possession of the goods by some trick or artifice, the owner not intending to part with the entire right of property, but with the temporary possession only ; this is held to constitute larceny. In *larceny* the owner of the thing stolen has no intention to part with his *property* therein to the person taking it, although he may intend to part with the *possession;* whereas in *false pretences* the owner does intend to part with his property in the money or chattel, but it is obtained from him by fraud.

Distinction between Larceny and Embezzlement.—Larceny by a servant is where a servant appropriates his master's property after it has come into the possession of the latter. Embezzlement is where a servant, having received property in the name of or on account of his master, appropriates the same before it reaches his master. As to misappropriation of property by persons entrusted with it for safe custody, or application for any particular purpose, see Larceny Act, 1901 ; 1 Edw. 7, c. 10.

See 24 & 25 *Vict. c.* 96 ; 4 *Steph. Com.*; *Archbold's Crim. Plead.*; *Russell on Crimes.* [EMBEZZLEMENT ; ROBBERY.]

LAST COURT. A court held by the twenty-four jurats in the marshes of Kent, and summoned by the bailiffs. [JURAT, 3.]

LAST HEIR (Lat. *Ultimus hæres*). He to whom land comes by escheat, for want of lawful heirs ; that is, in some cases, the lord of whom they are held ; in others, the king.

LAST RESORT. A court from which there is no appeal is called a court of last resort.

LASTAGE. 1. A custom exacted in some fairs and markets, to carry things bought where one will.
2. The ballast of a ship.
3. Stowage room for goods in a vessel.
4. A custom paid for wares sold by the last.

LATA CULPA DOLO ÆQUIPARATUR (Gross negligence is tantamount to fraud).

LATENT AMBIGUITY. [AMBIGUITY ; INTENTION, 1.]

LATHE, LATH, or **LETH.** A great part of a county containing three or four hundreds, as in Kent and Sussex. 1 *Steph. Com.* [HUNDRED.]

LATH REEVE. An officer who, under the Saxons, had authority over the *lath* or *lathe.* 1 *Steph. Com.* [LATHE.]

LATITAT. A writ sued out on a supposed bill of Middlesex, when the defendant did not reside in Middlesex, alleging that the defendant *latitat et discurrit* in the county in which he really resided. 3 *Steph. Com.* [AC ETIAM ; BILL OF MIDDLESEX.]

LAUDIBUS LEGUM ANGLIÆ. The treatise *De Laudibus Legum Angliæ* was a panegyric on the laws of England written by Sir John Fortescue in the reign of Henry VI. 1 *Steph. Com.*

LAW is defined by Blackstone as a rule of action prescribed or dictated by some superior, which an inferior is bound to obey.

Austin describes a law as being a *command* to *a course of conduct ;* a *command* being the expression of a wish or desire conceived by a rational being that another rational being shall do or forbear, coupled with the expression of an intention in the former to inflict some evil upon the latter, in case he comply not with the wish. But besides laws properly so called, Austin alludes to laws improper, imposed by public opinion ; also laws metaphorical or figurative, such as the laws regulating the movements of inanimate bodies, or the growth or decay of vegetables ; or that uniformity in the sequence of things or events which often goes by the name of *law.* Law is also sometimes used as opposed to equity ; now, however, by the Judicature Act, 1873, ss. 24, 89 and 91, full effect is given to all equitable rights in all branches of the Supreme Court and in inferior courts.

LAW AGENT. Any person entitled to practise as an agent (solicitor) for another in a court of law in Scotland. 36 *&* 37 *Vict. c.* 63.

LAW DAY signifies a day for holding a leet or sheriff's tourn. [COURT LEET ; HUNDRED ; SHERIFF'S TOURN.]

LAW LIST. An annual publication of a quasi-official character containing a list of barristers, solicitors, and other legal practitioners. It is *primâ facie* evidence that the persons therein named as solicitors or certified conveyancers are such. 23 *&* 24 *Vict. c.* 127, *s.* 22.

LAW LORDS are peers who hold or have held high judicial office, *i.e.,* a puisne judgeship of the High Court or higher office.

LAW MERCHANT (*Lex mercatoria*). The general body of European usage in matters relative to commerce, comprising rules relative to bills of exchange, partnership, and other mercantile matters, incorporated into the law of England. 1 *Steph. Com.*

LAW OF MARQUE. A law of reprisal, by which persons who have received wrong, and cannot get ordinary justice within the precincts of the wrong-doers, take their ships and goods. [LETTERS OF MARQUE AND REPRISAL.]

LAW OF NATIONS (Lat. *Jus gentium*). [INTERNATIONAL LAW ; JUS GENTIUM.]

LAW OF THE STAPLE. The same with law merchant. [LAW MERCHANT.]

LAW REPORTS are the authorised monthly reports of decided cases commencing from 1866 inclusive. They are published under the direction of a body called the Incorporated Council of Law Reporting. 1 *Steph. Com.*

LAW SOCIETY. A society of solicitors, whose function it is to carry out the Acts of parliament and orders of court with reference to the examinations of articled clerks ; to keep an alphabetical roll of solicitors ; to issue certificates to persons duly admitted and enrolled; also to exercise a general control over the conduct of solicitors in practice, and to bring cases of misconduct before the judges. See 6 *&* 7 *Vict. c.* 73, *s.* 21; and 51 *&* 52 *Vict. c.* 65 ; 3 *Steph. Com.*

LAW SPIRITUAL. The ecclesiastical law, according to which the ordinary, and other ecclesiastical judges, do proceed in causes within their cognizance. *Cowel.*

LAWS OF OLERON. [OLERON, LAWS OF.]

LAWSUIT. This is not a legal expression, but it is generally used to denote a case before the courts of law or equity in which there is a controversy between two parties.

LAY. A word opposed to *professional.* It is generally, but not necessarily, used in opposition to *clerical.*

LAY CORPORATIONS. Corporations not composed wholly of spiritual persons, nor subject to the jurisdiction of the ecclesiastical courts. Lay corporations are either *civil* or *eleemosynary.* Eleemosynary corporations are such as are constituted for the perpetual distribution of the free alms or bounty of the founder of them, to such purpose as he has directed. All other lay corporations are civil corporations. 3 *Steph. Com.* [CORPORATION.]

LAY DAYS. The days ordinarily allowed to the charterer of a vessel for loading and unloading the cargo. Also called *running* days. 2 *Steph. Com.* [DEMURRAGE.]

LAY FEE. Lands held in fee of a lay lord, involving services of a temporal character, as opposed to *frankalmoign*, which is a tenure of a spiritual character. 1 *Steph. Com.* [FEE; FRANKALMOIGN.]

LAY IMPROPRIATORS. [APPROPRIATION.]

LAY INVESTITURE OF BISHOPS. The formal act whereby the Crown invested a bishop with the temporalities of his office. 2 *Steph. Com.*

LE ROY LE VEULT, or LA REINE LE VEULT. "The king (or queen) wills it so to be." The form of words by which the sovereign assents to a public bill which has passed through both Houses of Parliament. The form of assent to a private bill is in the words "soit fait comme il est desiré," and to a money bill or grant of supply to the Crown in the words "Le Roy (or La Reine) remercie ses bons sujets accepte leur bénévolence et ainsi le veult." 2 *Steph. Com.*

LE ROY S'AVISERA, or LA REINE S'AVISERA. "The king (or queen) will consider." The form for refusing the royal assent to a bill passed by both Houses of Parliament. This power of refusal was last exercised in the year 1707, when Queen Anne refused her assent to a Scotch militia bill. 2 *Steph. Com.; May's Parl. Prac.*

LEADER. The leading counsel in a case, as opposed to a *junior*.

LEADING A USE. This was an expression used of a deed whereby a person covenanted to levy a fine, or suffer a recovery of lands, to certain uses upon which it was intended to settle the lands. The deed was then said to *lead* to the uses of the fine; and the fine, when levied, would, by virtue of the Statute of Uses, enure (*i.e.*, take effect) to the uses so specified. Or, if a fine or recovery were had without any previous settlement, and a deed were afterwards made between the parties, *declaring* the uses to which the same would be applied; this would be equally good as if the fine had been expressly levied, or the

recovery suffered, in consequence of a deed directing its operation to those particular uses. So that the difference between a deed *leading* the use, and a deed *declaring* the use, was that the former was made previous to the fine or recovery, and the latter subsequently thereto. 1 *Steph. Com.* [ENURE; FINE, 1; RECOVERY; USE; USES, STATUTE OF.]

LEADING CASES are the cases which have had the most influence in settling the law.

LEADING QUESTIONS. Questions which suggest the answer which is expected: as "Did you not see this?" or "Did you not hear that?" Such questions are not allowed except in cross-examination; but see HOSTILE WITNESS.

LEASE. A demise or letting of lands or tenements, rights of common, rent, or any hereditament, by one person, called the *lessor*, to another, called the *lessee*, for a term of years or life, or at will, usually for a rent reserved. The interest created by the lease must be *less* than the lessor hath in the premises, else it is not a *lease*, but an *assignment*. By the joint effect of the Statute of Frauds and of 8 & 9 Vict. c. 106, s. 3, all leases except those not exceeding three years and with a rent of not less than two-thirds of the improved annual value must be by deed. 1 *Steph. Com.* [INTERESSE TERMINI.]

LEASE AND RELEASE. 1. At common law consisted of first a lease to a proposed alienee, which demise, if perfected by entry, conferred on him a complete estate of leasehold, and then, being tenant of the "particular estate" on which the reversion was expectant, he became capable of receiving a *release* of the reversion, which was accordingly executed to him and his heirs. 1 *Steph. Com.* [PARTICULAR ESTATE.]
2. The conveyance of the same name under the Statute of Uses is much better known. It consisted of:—First, a bargain and sale; secondly, a common law conveyance of release. The bargain and sale would not have been sufficient under the Statute of Enrolments (27 Hen. 8, c. 16) to transfer the *freehold* unless the same were by deed indented, and enrolled within six months after its date. [BARGAIN AND SALE.] The practitioners of that day, being anxious to

LEASE AND RELEASE—*continued.*

effect secret conveyances, made the conveying party execute a bargain and sale for some *leasehold* interest, generally for a year, which passed the legal estate for a year to the bargainee (the Statute of Enrolments not extending to leaseholds), and the estate so transferred was complete without entry. The transferee, therefore, was capable of receiving a release of the freehold and reversion ; which release was accordingly granted to him on the next day. This form of conveying a freehold estate soon became so generally established as to supersede every other. By 4 & 5 Vict. c. 21, the release was made effectual without the previous lease ; and by 8 & 9 Vict. c. 106, s. 2, it was provided that corporeal hereditaments should, as regards the conveyance of the immediate freehold thereof, be deemed to *lie in grant* as well as *in livery*, and so become transferable by deed of grant, which is now the ordinary method of transferring such estates. 1 *Steph. Com.* ; *Wms. R. P.* [ENROLMENT ; GRANT, 1 ; LIE IN GRANT ; LIE IN LIVERY ; USES, STATUTE OF.]

LEASEHOLD. Any interest in land less than freehold might be so called ; but in practice the word is generally applied to an estate for a fixed term of years.

LEAVE AND LICENCE. A defence to an action for trespass, setting up the consent of the plaintiff to the trespass complained of.

LEAVE TO DEFEND. By R. S. C. 1883, Ord. III. r. 6, where a plaintiff seeks to recover a debt or liquidated demand in money or possession where a tenancy has expired or been determined by notice to quit, the writ of summons may be specially indorsed with the particulars of the amount sought to be recovered, and if the defendant fail to appear judgment may be signed for the amount claimed ; and by Ord. XIV., where the defendant does so appear, the plaintiff may, on affidavit swearing that in his belief there is no defence to the action, call on the defendant to show cause why the plaintiff should not be at liberty to sign final judgment for the amount indorsed on the writ with interest and costs ; and unless the defendant satisfy the court or judge that he has a good defence on the merits, or disclose sufficient facts to

entitle him to be permitted to defend the action, the court or judge may make an order empowering the plaintiff to sign final judgment accordingly.

LEDGRAVE. The chief man of a *lath*, the same as *lath-reeve*. [LATHE.]

LEEMAN'S ACTS. 1. 30 Vict. c. 29, by which contracts for the sale of bank shares are void unless the numbers of the shares sold are set out in the contract. See *Neilson* v. *James*, 9 *Q. B. D.* 546.

2. 35 & 36 Vict. c. 91, which authorises the application of funds of municipal corporations and other governing bodies, under certain conditions, towards promoting or opposing parliamentary and other proceedings for the benefit of the inhabitants.

LEET. A court of local jurisdiction. [COURT LEET.]

LEGACY. A bequest or gift of goods and chattels by testament. 2 *Steph. Com.*

A legacy may be either specific, demonstrative, or general.

1. A *specific legacy* is a bequest of a specific part of the testator's personal estate.

2. A *demonstrative legacy* is a gift by will of a certain sum directed to be paid out of a specific fund.

3. A *general legacy* is one payable out of the general assets of the testator. *Wms. P. P.* [ADEMPTION OF A LEGACY.]

LEGACY DUTY. A duty payable by an executor out of the legacies bequeathed by his testator, under certain statutes called the Legacy Duty Acts. The proportion of legacy duty varies from 1 to 10 per cent. according to the relationship which the legatee bears to the testator. 2 *Steph. Com.*

Legacy duty must not be confounded with probate or estate duty. [PROBATE DUTY ; ESTATE DUTY.]

LEGAL ASSETS. Assets of a deceased person available in a court of law to satisfy the claims of creditors. [ASSETS.]

LEGAL ESTATE. An estate in land, fully recognised as such in a court of common law, has been hitherto called the "legal estate." 1 *Steph. Com.* [EQUITABLE ESTATE.]

LEGAL MEMORY. The time of "legal memory" runs back to the commencement of the reign of Richard I. 1 *Steph. Com.*

LEGAL TENDER is a tender in payment of a debt which will be held valid and sufficient. Gold coin is always a legal tender, so far as a debt admits of being paid in gold; silver coin is a legal tender in payment of a sum not exceeding forty shillings; and bronze coin is a legal tender in payment of a sum not exceeding one shilling. See the *Coinage Act*, 1870 (33 & 34 *Vict. c.* 10), *s.* 4; and 3 & 4 *Will.* 4, c. 98, *s.* 6; 2 *Steph. Com.*

LEGANTINE CONSTITUTIONS, or **LEGATINE CONSTITUTIONS** were ecclesiastical laws, enacted in national synods, held under the cardinals Otho and Othobon, legates from Pope Gregory IX. and Pope Clement IV., about the years 1220 and 1268. 1 *Steph. Com.*

LEGATE. An ambassador or Pope's nuncio. *Toml.*

LEGATEE. One to whom anything is bequeathed by will.

LEGES POSTERIORES PRIORES CONTRARIAS ABROGANT (Later laws abrogate prior contrary ones).

LEGITIMACY DECLARATION. A party may apply to the Divorce Division of the High Court for a declaration of his legitimacy, or his right to be deemed a natural-born subject. 21 & 22 *Vict. c.* 93; 2 *Steph. Com.*

LEGITIMATION *per subsequens matrimonium.* A legitimation of children by the subsequent marriage of their parents. This may be done according to the civil and canon law, and the systems founded thereon, including the law of Scotland. 2 *Steph. Com.*

LEONINA SOCIETAS. A partnership in which one partner has all the loss, and another all the gain. It is so called, because the lucky partner has the "lion's share" of the profits.

LESSEE. A person to whom a lease is made. [LEASE.]

LESSOR. A person by whom a lease is made. [LEASE.]

LESSOR OF THE PLAINTIFF. The claimant in an action of ejectment was so called, as being the lessor of the fictitious plaintiff Doe, Goodright, or Goodtitle, etc. 3 *Steph. Com.* [EJECTMENT.]

LETTER MISSIVE. 1. A letter from the king or queen to a dean and chapter, containing the name of the person whom he would have them elect as bishop. 2 *Steph. Com.* [CONGE D'ELIRE.]
2. A letter sent by the Lord Chancellor to a peer, who was made a defendant to a bill in Chancery, to request his appearance.

LETTER OF ATTORNEY. [POWER OF ATTORNEY.]

LETTER OF CREDIT. A letter written by one man (usually a merchant or banker) to another, requesting him to advance money, or entrust goods to the bearer, or to a particular person by name, and for which the writer's credit is pledged. It may be either *general*, addressed to all merchants or other persons, or *special*, addressed to a particular person by name. It is not negotiable.

LETTER OF LICENCE was an instrument or writing made by creditors to a man that had failed in his trade, allowing him longer time for the payment of his debts, and protecting him from arrests in going about his affairs. Imprisonment for debt was abolished by 32 & 33 Vict. c. 62.

LETTERS OF ADMINISTRATION. [ADMINISTRATION; ADMINISTRATOR.]

LETTERS OF MARQUE AND REPRISAL. These words, *marque* and *reprisal*, are used as synonymous; *reprisal* signifying a *taking in return*, and *marque* the passing over the *marches* or frontiers in order to do so. Letters of marque and reprisal are granted by the law of nations whenever the subjects of one State are oppressed and injured by those of another, and justice is denied by that State to which the oppressor belongs.

The term is now applied to commissions granted in time of war to merchants and others to fit out *privateers* or armed ships, authorising them to take the ships of the enemy, and directing that the prizes captured by them shall be divided between the owners, the captains and the crew. 2 *Steph. Com.* [DECLARATION OF PARIS.]

LETTERS OF REQUEST. 1. Letters formerly granted by the Lord Privy Seal preparatory to granting letters of marque. [LETTERS OF MARQUE AND REPRISAL.]

2. Letters whereby a bishop, within whose jurisdiction an ecclesiastical cause has arisen, and who is desirous to waive such jurisdiction, requests the Dean of Arches to take cognizance of the matter. The acceptance of such letters on the part of the Dean of Arches is not optional. 2 *Steph. Com.* ; 3 *Steph. Com.*

LETTERS OF SAFE CONDUCT. [SAFE CONDUCT.]

LETTERS PATENT (Lat. *Literæ patentes*) are writings sealed with the Great Seal of England, whereby a man is authorised to do or to enjoy anything that otherwise of himself he could not. They are so termed by reason of their form, because they are open (*patentes*) with the seal affixed, ready to be shown for confirmation of the authority given by them. 1 *Steph. Com.* ; 2 *Steph. Com.* [PATENT.]

LEVANT AND COUCHANT (Lat. *Levantes et cubantes*). A law term for cattle that have been so long in the ground of another, that they have lain down, and are risen up to feed, until which time they cannot be distrained by the owner of the lands, if the lands were not sufficiently fenced so as to keep out cattle. 1 *Steph. Com.* ; 3 *Steph. Com.*

LEVARI FACIAS. A writ of execution directed to the sheriff, for the levying a sum of money upon the lands and tenements of the judgment debtor. Abolished by the Bankruptcy Act, 1883, s. 146. 3 *Steph. Com.* [FIERI FACIAS ; SEQUESTRARI FACIAS.]

LEVITICAL DEGREES. Degrees of kindred within which persons are prohibited to marry, set forth in the eighteenth chapter of Leviticus. See also 32 Hen. 8, c. 38.

LEX BREHONIA. The Brehon or Irish law, overthrown by King John in the twelfth year of his reign.

LEX DOMICILII. The law of the place of a man's domicile. [DOMICILE.]

LEX FORI. The law of the *forum*, that is, the law of the place in which any given case is tried. [FORUM ; LEX LOCI CONTRACTUS.]

LEX LOCI CONTRACTÛS. The law of the place in which a contract was made. Thus, if an action were brought in England upon a contract made in France, the law of England would, as regards such action, be the *lex fori*, and the law of France the *lex loci contractûs*.

LEX LOCI REI SITÆ, or LEX SITÛS. The law of the place in which a thing in question happens to be. Thus it is said that the descent of immovable property is regulated according to the *lex loci rei sitæ* ; that is, according to the law of the place where it is situated.

LEX MERCATORIA signifies the law or custom of merchants. [CUSTOM ; LAW MERCHANT.]

LEX NON SCRIPTA. The unwritten or common law which includes general and particular customs. 1 *Steph. Com.* [CUSTOM.]

LEX SCRIPTA. The written (or statute) law.

LEX TALIONIS. The law of retaliation. See 4 *Steph. Com.*

LEZE - MAJESTY (*Læsæ Majestatis Crimen*). An offence against sovereign power ; treason, rebellion.

LIBEL (Lat. *Libellus*). A little book. Hence it signifies—

1. The original declaration of an action in the civil law.

2. Articles drawn out in a formal allegation in the Ecclesiastical Court, setting forth the complainant's ground of complaint. 3 *Steph. Com.*

3. The charge on which, in Scotland, a civil or criminal prosecution takes place.

4. An obscene, blasphemous, or seditious publication, whether by printing, writing, signs, or pictures. 4 *Steph. Com.*

5. A defamatory publication upon a person by writings, pictures, or the like. All contumacious matter that tends to degrade a man in the opinion of his neighbours, or to make him ridiculous, will, if published, amount to libel. Thus libel differs from slander, in that slander consists in oral defamation only, whereas a libel must consist of matter published ; also the scope of the offence of libel is more extensive than that of slander. Libel may be punished criminally, whereas a person guilty o-

LIBEL—*continued.*
slander can only be proceeded against civilly. As to libels in newspapers, see 44 & 45 Vict. c. 60 and 51 & 52 Vict. c. 64; and 3 *Steph. Com.*; 4 *Steph. Com.* [DEFAMATION; FOX'S ACT; SLANDER.]

LIBERAM LEGEM AMITTERE. To lose the *status* of a free citizen, and to become infamous. 4 *Steph. Com.*

LIBERTIES, or **FRANCHISES**, are royal privileges subsisting in the hands of subjects, as a liberty to hold pleas in a court of one's own; also districts in regard to which such privileges have been granted by the Crown to individuals, conferring on them or their bailiffs the exclusive jurisdiction of executing legal process therein. Such districts are, in consequence, exempt from the sheriff's jurisdiction; but the practical importance of this exemption is diminished by the fact that it is now usual to insert a *non omittas* clause in the writs directed to the sheriff ("that you omit not by reason of any liberty within your bailiwick," etc.), specially authorising him to enter into such privileged places. And by 13 & 14 Vict. c. 105, a liberty may, on petition to the Crown by the Court of Quarter Sessions, be made to merge for the future in the general county jurisdiction. See also the Sheriffs Act, 1887, s. 34, and the Local Government Act, 1888, s. 48, sub-s. 1. 2 *Steph. Com.*

LIBERTY TO HOLD PLEAS. [See preceding title.]

LIBERUM TENEMENTUM. A freehold. [FREEHOLD.]

LICENCE. A power or authority to do some act which, without such authority, could not lawfully be done.

LICENCE TO MARRY. [MARRIAGE LICENCE.]

LICENSING ACTS. This expression is applied by Hallam (*Const. Hist. ch.* 13) to Acts of parliament for the restraint of printing, except by licence. It may also be applied to any Act of parliament passed for the purpose of requiring a licence for doing any act whatever.
But when we speak of the Licensing Acts, we generally mean the Acts regulating the sale of intoxicating liquors. These Acts are of two kinds. The first

class of these enactments has in view the subject of revenue, and requires excise licences to be taken out for the sale of certain liquors. The second class has in view the proper regulation of the places where such sale is carried on, and the prevention of the abuses to which they are naturally liable. By these Acts, a magistrate's licence is required, in addition to the excise licence. The statutes of the latter and more important class, now wholly or partially in operation, are the following:—
1. Stat. 9 Geo. 4, c. 61, being the Intoxicating Liquors Licensing Act, 1828.
2. Stat. 32 & 33 Vict. c. 27, being the Wine and Beerhouse Act, 1869.
3. Stat. 33 & 34 Vict. c. 29, being the Wine and Beerhouse Act Amendment Act, 1870.
4. Stat. 35 & 36 Vict. c. 94, being the Licensing Act, 1872.
5. Stat. 37 & 38 Vict. c. 49, being the Licensing Act, 1874, for England.
6. Stat. 37 & 38 Vict. c. 69, being the Licensing Act, 1874, for Ireland; 45 & 46 Vict. c. 34, being the Beer Dealers' Licences Amendment Act, 1882; 2 Ed. 7, c. 28.
See 3 *Steph. Com.*

LICENTIA CONCORDANDI. [FINE, 1.]

LICENTIA LOQUENDI. A licence to imparl. [IMPARLANCE.]

LIE. An action is said *to lie*, if it is legally maintainable.

LIE IN FRANCHISE. Waifs, wrecks, estrays, and the like, which the persons entitled thereto may seize without the aid of a court, are said to *lie in franchise.* 3 *Steph. Com.*

LIE IN GRANT. To *lie in grant*, when said of property, means to be capable of passing by deed of grant, as opposed to the passing of property by physical delivery. [FEOFFMENT; GRANT, 1; LEASE AND RELEASE, 2; LIE IN LIVERY.]

LIE IN LIVERY. To *lie in livery* is to be capable of passing by physical delivery. [CORPOREAL PROPERTY; FEOFFMENT; LIE IN GRANT.]

LIEGE, bound by some feudal tenure. 2 *Steph. Com.* [ALLEGIANCE.]

LIEN. 1. As applied to personalty, a lien is understood to be the right of a bailee to retain the possession of a chattel entrusted to him until his claim upon it be satisfied. 2 *Steph. Com.* [BAILMENT ; GENERAL LIEN ; PARTICULAR LIEN.]

2. As applied to realty, a *vendor's lien* for unpaid purchase-money is his right to enforce his claim upon the land sold ; a right which is recognised in a court of equity, subject to the doctrines of that court for the protection of *bonâ fide* purchasers for valuable consideration without notice.

LIEUTENANCY, COMMISSION OF. A commission for mustering the inhabitants of a district for the defence of the country. These commissions of lieutenancy were introduced by the Tudors, and superseded the old commissions of array. 2 *Steph. Com.*

LIFE ANNUITY. An annual payment during the continuance of any life or lives. [ANNUITY.]

LIFE ASSURANCE. A transaction whereby in consideration of a single or periodical payment of premium a sum of money is secured to be paid upon the death of the person whose life is assured. 33 & 34 *Vict. c.* 61, amended by 34 & 35 *Vict. c.* 58, and 35 & 36 *Vict. c.* 41 ; 2 *Steph. Com.* [INSURANCE.]

LIFE ESTATE. [ESTATE.]

LIFE PEERAGE. Letters patent conferring the dignity of baron for life only, do not enable the grantee to sit and vote in the House of Lords, not even with the usual writ of summons to the house. But see LORDS OF APPEAL IN ORDINARY.

LIGAN. Goods sunk in the sea, but tied to a buoy, in order to be found again. 2 *Steph. Com.* [JETTISON.]

LIGEANCE, LIGEANCY. The same as *allegiance.* [ALLEGIANCE.]

LIGHTS. The right which a man has to have the access of the sun's rays to his windows, free from any obstruction on the part of his neighbours. It is a species of easement. [EASEMENT.] This is sometimes spoken of as "the right to light and air ;" sometimes as " ancient lights," because the possessor must have enjoyed them for a certain time before the right is indefeasible.

This period is now twenty years. 2 & 3 *Will.* 4, *c.* 71, *s.* 3 ; 1 *Steph. Com.*

LIMITATION OF ACTIONS. [LIMITATIONS, STATUTE OF.]

LIMITATION OF ESTATES. The " limitation " of an estate is the marking out, in a deed or other instrument in writing, of the estate or interest which a person is intended to hold in any property comprised therein. Thus when it is said, with reference to a conveyance to A. and his heirs, that the word *heirs* in a deed is a word of *limitation* and not of *purchase*, it means that the word *heirs* marks out the nature of the estate taken by A., which is an estate in fee simple : and that the *heirs* of A. take nothing *directly* (*i.e.*, take nothing "by purchase") under such a "limitation." 1 *Steph. Com.* [RULE IN SHELLEY'S CASE.]

LIMITATIONS, STATUTE OF. A statute of limitations is one which limits a time for bringing actions after a ground for action has arisen. Various statutes have been passed with this object ; but the two principal statutes of limitation are 21 Jac. 1, *c.* 16, and the Real Property Limitation Act, 1874 (37 & 38 Vict. *c.* 57). The former of these Acts limits the right to bring personal actions in general to *six years* after the cause of action accrued. Actions for assault and false imprisonment are limited to *four years ;* and actions for slander to *two years.* But to these limitations there are exceptions in favour of persons labouring under disabilities. By 37 & 38 Vict. *c.* 57, actions to recover land must generally be brought within *twelve years* from the time that the right of action accrued ; arrears of rent cannot be recovered for a longer period back than *six years.* 3 *Steph. Com.*

LIMITED ADMINISTRATION means an administration of certain specific effects of a deceased person, the rest being committed to others. 2 *Steph. Com.* [ADMINISTRATION.]

LIMITED COMPANY. A company in which the liability of each shareholder is limited by the number of shares he has taken, so that he cannot be called on to contribute beyond the amount of his shares. By the Companies Act, 1879 (42 & 43 Vict. c. 76), the unlimited liability of banks in respect of their notes is continued. 3 *Steph. Com. ; Lindley on Partnership.* As to the liability of shipowners see s. 503 of the Merchant Shipping Act, 1894, and as to railways see s. 7 of the Railway and Canal Traffic Act, 1854.

LIMITED EXECUTOR. An executor of a deceased person for certain limited purposes, or for a certain limited time. [EXECUTOR.]

LIMITED LIABILITY. [LIMITED COMPANY.]

LIMITED OWNER. A tenant for life, in tail or by curtesy, or other person not having a fee simple in his absolute disposition. See *Settled Land Act*, 1882, *s.* 58. [SETTLED LAND.]

LINCOLN'S INN. One of the Inns of Court. [INNS OF COURT.]

LINEAL CONSANGUINITY. The relationship between ascendants and descendants; as between father and son, grandfather and grandson, etc.

LINEAL DESCENT. Direct genealogical descent.

LIQUIDATED DAMAGES. The ascertained amount, expressed in pounds, shillings, and pence, which an injured party has sustained, or is taken to have sustained. The term is used in contradistinction to a penalty. 2 *Steph. Com.*

LIQUIDATION. This method by which, under the Bankruptcy Act, 1869, an insolvent debtor could escape being made a bankrupt, was abolished by the Bankruptcy Act, 1883.

LIQUIDATOR. An officer appointed to conduct the winding-up of a company; to bring and defend actions and suits in its name, and to do all necessary acts on behalf of the company. 3 *Steph. Com.* He may be appointed either by resolution of the shareholders in a voluntary winding-up, or by the court in a compulsory winding-up. [OFFICIAL LIQUIDATOR.]

LIS MOTA. A lawsuit put in motion.

LIS PENDENS. A pending suit; an expression used especially of pending suits relating to land, as affecting the title to the land in question.

LITE PENDENTE. While a suit is pending. [LIS PENDENS.]

LITIGIOUS. A church is said to be *litigious*, when two rival presentations are offered to the bishop upon the same avoidance of the living. 3 *Steph. Com.* [AVOIDANCE; JUS PATRONATUS.]

LITIS CONTESTATIO. 1. In Ecclesiastical Courts, the issue of an action.
2. In Roman law, the submission to the decision of a judge.

LITTLETON. A judge in the reign of Edward 1V., who wrote a treatise of tenures upon which Chief Justice Coke has written an extensive comment.

LIVERPOOL COURT OF PASSAGE. [PASSAGE COURT.]

LIVERY (Lat. *Liberatura*). 1. A delivery of possession to tenants who held of the king *in capite*, or by knight-service. [IN CAPITE; KNIGHT-SERVICE.]
2. A writ which lay for the heir to obtain the possession or seisin of land at the king's hands. [FEOFFMENT; LIVERY OF SEISIN.]
3. The members of a company of the city of London chosen out of the freemen. [LIVERYMAN.]

LIVERY OF SEISIN. A delivery of feudal possession, part of the ceremony called a *feoffment*. [FEOFFMENT.]

LIVERYMAN. A member of a company in the city of London, chosen out of the freemen, to assist the master and wardens in the government of the company.

LLOYD'S. An association in the city of London, the members of which underwrite each other's policies. 2 *Steph. Com.* [UNDERWRITER.]

LLOYD'S BONDS are instruments under the seal of a company admitting the indebtedness of the company in a specified amount to the obligee, with a covenant to pay him such amount with interest on a future day. 2 *Steph. Com.* The validity of these instruments depends on the considerations for which they are given; they are *primâ facie* binding on the company as admissions of indebtedness; but when issued by railway companies for money borrowed after their statutory powers for borrowing are exhausted, they are altogether illegal and void. 7 & 8 *Vict. c.* 85, *s.* 17.

LOAD-LINE. This word indicates the depth to which a ship is loaded so as to sink in salt water, and beyond which it may not be loaded. See the *Merchant Shipping Act*, 1894.

LOAN SOCIETIES. Those established for advancing money on loan to the industrial classes. See 3 *& 4 Vict. c.* 110 ; 26 *& 27 Vict. c.* 56.

LOCAL ACTION. An action founded on such a cause as refers necessarily to some particular locality, as in the case of trespasses to land, and in which the venue must as a rule have been laid in the county where the cause of action arose. 3 *Steph. Com.* [VENUE.]

LOCAL ALLEGIANCE. Such as is due from an alien or stranger born so long as he continues within the sovereign's dominions and protection.

LOCAL AND PERSONAL ACTS. This expression is applied to the second category of Acts of parliament as classified for publication, comprising generally Acts which have been passed as private bills, except that they receive the royal assent in the form of public Acts. These Acts when passed are to be judicially noticed as public Acts. See the *Interpretation Act*, 1889, *s.* 9.

LOCAL COURTS are courts whose jurisdiction is confined to certain districts, as the county courts, police courts, etc.

LOCAL GOVERNMENT. [COUNTY COUNCILS.]

LOCAL GOVERNMENT BOARD. A department of the Government, established by 34 & 35 Vict. c. 70. To this department were transferred all the powers and duties of the Poor Law Board, which then ceased to exist, as well as certain powers that had been exercised by the Home Secretary, or in the Privy Council, under certain Acts of parliament specified in the schedule to the above Act. 3 *Steph. Com.*

LOCATIO. The contract of letting and hiring, also called *locatio-conductio ; locatio* expressing the letting out to hire, and *conductio* the hiring. This contract is a species of bailment. [BAILMENT.]

LOCATIO OPERIS FACIENDI. The letting to hire of work to be done ; a species of bailment, which consists in one man delivering to another any article of property for the latter to expend work and labour upon it ; or, in other words, *let his work to hire ;* as when one gives a tailor a coat to be repaired. [BAILMENT.]

LOCATIO OPERIS MERCIUM VEHENDARUM. The hire of a person's labour for the purpose of carrying goods or merchandise from one place to another.

LOCATIO REI. The letting of anything to hire for temporary use. This also is a species of bailment. [BAILMENT.]

LOCKE KING'S ACTS (now called Real Estate Charges Acts). The stat. 17 & 18 Vict. c. 113, amended by 30 & 31 Vict. c. 69 and 40 & 41 Vict. c. 34, for making a mortgage debt of a deceased person a burden in the first instance upon the land subject to the mortgage, in the absence of any declaration having been made by the deceased to the contrary.

LOCUM TENENS. A deputy or substitute.

LOCUS IN QUO. The place in which anything is alleged to be done.

LOCUS PŒNITENTIÆ. A place or chance of repentance ; a phrase generally applied to a power of drawing back from a bargain before anything has been done to confirm it in law.

LOCUS REGIT ACTUM. The place governs the act, *i.e.*, the act is governed by the law of the place where it is done.

LOCUS SIGILLI. The place of the seal; the initials (L.S.) are also used in a copy of a document, to indicate the place where the seal was in the original document.

LOCUS STANDI (a place of standing) signifies a right of appearance in a court of justice, or before parliament, on any given question. In other words, it signifies a right *to be heard*, as opposed to a right *to succeed on the merits.*

LODGER. A tenant having exclusive possession of a part of a house, the general dominion over which remains in the landlord or his agent. A lodger's goods are protected against distraint by the superior landlord by 34 & 35 Vict. c. 79. 3 *Steph. Com.*

LODGER - FRANCHISE. Occupiers of lodgings of the yearly value of 10l. (unfurnished) are entitled to the parliamentary franchise by 30 & 31 Vict. c. 102, s. 4, and 48 Vict. c. 3, s. 2, but this franchise must be claimed anew every year. 2 *Steph. Com.*

LODGING HOUSES. See the *Public Health Act*, 1875, *ss.* 76 *et seq.*

LOG, or **LOG-BOOK**, is a journal kept by the chief mate or first officer of a ship, in which the situation of the ship from time to time, the winds, weather, courses, and distances, the misconduct or desertion of any of the crew, and every thing of importance, are carefully noted down.

An *official log-book* is a book required by law to be kept in every ship (except those employed exclusively in the coasting trade of the United Kingdom) in a form sanctioned by the Board of Trade, either in connection with, or distinct from, the ordinary log-books. 3 *Steph. Com.*

LONG VACATION. By the "Long Vacation Order" of December, 1883, the Long Vacation begins on the 13th August, and ends on the 23rd October. 3 *Steph. Com.*

LORD ADVOCATE. [ADVOCATE, LÓRD.]

LORD CAMPBELL'S ACTS. 1. Stat. 6 & 7 Vict. c. 96, for amending the law respecting defamatory words and libel, by allowing a defendant in pleading to an *indictment* or *information* for defamatory libel to allege the truth of the matters charged and that their publication was for the public benefit. 3 *Steph. Com.*

2. Stat. 9 & 10 Vict. c. 93 (amended by 27 & 28 Vict. c. 95, and now called Fatal Accidents Act), for enabling the executors or administrators of persons killed by negligence to bring actions for the benefit of the wife, husband, parent, or children of the deceased, against the parties guilty of the negligence. 3 *Steph. Com.*

3. Stat. 20 & 21 Vict. c. 83, authorising magistrates to issue warrants for the seizure of obscene books, papers, writings, or representations kept in some place for the purpose of being sold, distributed, lent on hire, or otherwise published for gain. 4 *Steph. Com.*

LORD CHAMBERLAIN. [CHAMBERLAIN.]

LORD CHANCELLOR. [CHANCELLOR.]

LORD CHIEF JUSTICE OF ENGLAND. The presiding judge of the King's Bench Division, and, in the absence of the Lord Chancellor, President of the High Court. He is also an *ex-officio* judge of the Court of Appeal. *Jud. Act*, 1873, *s.* 5; *Jud. Act*, 1875, *s.* 4. [CHIEF JUSTICE.]

LORD HIGH ADMIRAL. [ADMIRAL.]

LORD HIGH STEWARD. [HIGH STEWARD.]

LORD JUSTICE. [LORDS JUSTICES.]

LORD KEEPER. [KEEPER OF THE GREAT SEAL.]

LORD LIEUTENANT. 1. The Viceroy of the Crown in Ireland.

2. The principal officer of a county, originally appointed for the purpose of mustering the inhabitants for the defence of the country. It is at his recommendation that magistrates are appointed. 2 *Steph. Com.*

LORD MAYOR'S COURT. A local court within the city of London, presided over by the Recorder, or, in his absence, by the Common Serjeant. By the stat. 20 & 21 Vict. c. clvii., the practice and procedure of this court were amended, and its powers enlarged. 3 *Steph. Com.*

LORD OF A MANOR. [COPYHOLD; MANOR.]

LORD PARAMOUNT. [PARAMOUNT.]

LORD PRIVY SEAL. One of the members of the Cabinet, through whose hands all charters, etc., pass before they come to the Great Seal. 2 *Steph. Com.*

LORD TENTERDEN'S ACT. The stat. 9 Geo. 4, c. 14, for the amendment and extension of the Statute of Frauds, and for other purposes. 2 *Steph. Com.* [FRAUDS, STATUTE OF.]

LORD TREASURER, otherwise called the Lord High Treasurer of England, was a high officer of State, who had the charge and government of the king's wealth contained in the Exchequer. The office of Lord Treasurer has now for a long time been entrusted to commissioners, who are called the Lords Commissioners of the Treasury. The chief of the commissioners is called the

LORD TREASURER—*continued.*

First Lord, and the Chancellor of the Exchequer is the second, and there are three others, who usually act as "Whips" for the political party in power.

LORD WARDEN OF THE CINQUE PORTS. The principal officer of the cinque ports having the custody thereof, and having, until lately, a civil jurisdiction therein. 3 *Steph. Com.* [CINQUE PORTS.]

LORDS COMMISSIONERS. When a high public office in the State, formerly executed by an individual, is put into commission, the persons charged with the commission are called Lords Commissioners, or sometimes Lords or Commissioners simply. Thus we have, in lieu of the Lord Treasurer and Lord High Admiral of former times, the Lords Commissioners of the Treasury, and the Lords Commissioners of the Admiralty: and whenever the Great Seal is put into commission, the persons charged with it are called Commissioners or Lords Commissioners of the Great Seal.

LORDS COMMISSIONERS OF THE ADMIRALTY. [ADMIRAL; LORDS COMMISSIONERS.]

LORDS COMMISSIONERS OF THE TREASURY. [LORD TREASURER; LORDS COMMISSIONERS.]

LORDS, HOUSE OF. [HOUSE OF LORDS.]

LORDS JUSTICES OF APPEAL. Two judges appointed, under 14 & 15 Vict. c. 83, to assist the Lord Chancellor in hearing appeals from the Master of the Rolls and the Vice-Chancellors. They also heard appeals from the Chief Judge in Bankruptcy, and had original jurisdiction in lunacy. The Lords Justices sometimes sat separately from the Lord Chancellor, and sometimes with him. In the latter case the court was called the Full Court of Appeal.

By s. 4 of the Judicature Act, 1875, the then existing Lords Justices of Appeal were made judges of the Court of Appeal under that Act.

LORDS OF APPEAL. Peers who hold, or have held, " high judicial office," three of whom at least must be present to constitute a sitting of the House of Lords for judicial business. See the *Appellate Jurisdiction Act*, 1876, *s.* 5 ; 3 *Steph. Com.*

LORDS OF APPEAL IN ORDINARY. Two persons having held high judicial office or practised at the Bar for not less than fifteen years, to aid the House of Lords and the Judicial Committee of the Privy Council in hearing appeals. They rank as barons for life, but sit and vote in the House of Lords during the time of their office only. *Appellate Jurisdiction Act*, 1876, *s.* 6 ; 3 *Steph. Com.*

LORDS SPIRITUAL. The bishops who have seats in the House of Lords : being the Archbishops of Canterbury and York, the Bishops of London, Durham, and Winchester, and twenty-one other bishops. 2 *Steph. Com.*

LORDS TEMPORAL. The peers of the realm who have seats in the House of Lords, other than the bishops. 2 *Steph. Com.*

LOST BILL OF EXCHANGE, CHEQUE, etc. See the *Bills of Exchange Act*, 1882, *ss.* 69, 70.

LOST OR NOT LOST. These words are often inserted in a policy of marine insurance. They enable the insurer to recover although, unknown to both parties, the vessel was lost at the time of effecting the insurance.

LUCRI CAUSA. For the sake of gain.

LUNATIC. A person who has become insane as distinguished from an idiot who is born so. 2 *Steph. Com.*

The existing law as to lunatics is contained in the consolidating Lunacy Act, 1890, as amended by the Lunacy Act, 1891. The main provisions are :—

1. The requirement of an order of a judicial authority, *e.g.*, county court judge, stipendiary magistrate or justice of the peace, for the detention of any lunatic not so found by inquisition.

2. The periodical examination of all such detained lunatics with a view to their discharge if recovered.

3. The partial application of the laws of lunacy to persons incapable through mental infirmity of managing their affairs.

4. The gradual substitution of public for private asylums.

See 2 *Steph. Com.; 3 Steph. Com.*

LUNATIC ASYLUM. See the *Lunacy Acts,* 1890, *Parts VIII. and IX.;* 3 *Steph. Com.*

LUNATICO INQUIRENDO. An ancient writ to inquire whether a person be a lunatic. At the present day a commission may be granted by the Lord Chancellor under the Lunacy Act, 1890, in the nature of this writ. 2 *Steph. Com.*

LYING BY. Neglecting to assert rights, or allowing persons to deal with land or other property as if one had no interest in it ; as when a mortgagee allows his mortgagor to retain the title deeds and raise money upon a fresh mortgage of the land, without notice to the new mortgagee of the prior mortgage. [LACHES.]

LYING IN FRANCHISE. [LIE IN FRANCHISE.]

LYING IN GRANT. [GRANT ; INCORPOREAL HEREDITAMENT ; LIE IN GRANT.]

LYING IN LIVERY. [LIE IN LIVERY.]

LYNCH LAW. The execution of summary justice by a mob without reference to the process of ordinary municipal law.

LYON KING AT ARMS. An officer who takes his title from the armorial bearing of the Scotch king, the lion rampant. [KINGS-AT-ARMS.]

LYON'S INN. [INNS OF CHANCERY.]

LYTTLETON. [LITTLETON.]

MAGISTRATE. A person entrusted with the commission of the peace for any county, city, borough or other jurisdiction. [CONSERVATOR OF THE PEACE ; JUSTICE OF THE PEACE ; STIPENDIARY MAGISTRATE.]

MAGNA CARTA was a charter granted by King John in the year 1215, at Runningmead, and confirmed in Parliament in the 9th year of Henry III., A.D. 1225, and again by the *Confirmatio Chartarum,* in the 25th year of Edward I., A.D. 1297. [CONFIRMATIO CHARTARUM.]
This Great Charter is based substan-

tially on the Saxon Common Law and contains thirty-eight chapters on various subjects, especially with reference to landed estates and their tenures. Many of its provisions are now repealed.

MAIDEN ASSIZE. One at which there are no prisoners to be tried.

MAIHEM or **MAYHEM.** The violently depriving another of the use of a member proper for his defence in fight. 3 *Steph. Com. ;* 4 *Steph. Com.*

MAIMING. [MAIHEM.]

MAINOUR or **MEINOUR.** Anything that a thief taketh or stealeth. To be taken with the *mainour* is to be taken with the thing stolen about him, *in manu* (in his hand). 4 *Steph. Com.*

MAINPERNABLE signifies that which may be held to bail. 3 *Edw.* 1, *c.* 15. [MAINPERNORS.]

MAINPERNORS (Lat. *Manucaptores*). Those persons to whom a person is delivered out of custody or prison, and they become security for his appearance. [MAINPRISE.] Mainpernors, unlike bail, cannot surrender him up before the stipulated day of appearance, but are sureties for his appearance at the day, though they are bound to produce him to answer all charges whatsoever. 3 *Steph. Com.*

MAINPRISE (Lat. *Manucaptio*). A writ directed to the sheriff, commanding him to take sureties for a prisoner's appearance, usually called *mainpernors,* and to set him at large. As opposed to bailing him or giving him into their custody. Obsolete. [MAINPERNORS.]

MAINTAINORS. Persons guilty of *maintaining* a lawsuit. [MAINTENANCE, 1.]

MAINTENANCE. 1. An officious intermeddling in a suit that in no way belongs to one, by maintaining or assisting either party, with money or otherwise, to prosecute or defend it. 4 *Steph. Com.*
2. Providing children, or other persons in a position of dependence, with food, clothing, and other necessaries. 2 *Steph. Com.* [See next title.]

MAINTENANCE AND EDUCATION CLAUSES, in a deed or will wherein property is conveyed or bequeathed upon trust, are clauses empowering the trustee or trustees to expend the income of the trust property in the maintenance and education of the children who are to participate in the property when they come of age. This power is given to all trustees of settled property by 44 & 45 Vict. c. 41.

MAJORI REGALIA. The king's dignity, power. and royal prerogative ; as opposed to his *rerenue*, which is comprised in the *minora regalia.* 2 *Steph. Com.*

MAJORITY. Full age, twenty-one. A minor comes of age in the eye of the law on the day preceding the twenty-first anniversary of his birth.

MAKER, of a promissory note, is he who signs it. By so doing he engages to pay it according to its tenor. See *Bills of Exchange Act*, 1882, *s.* 88.

MAL. A prefix meaning bad, wrong, fraudulent.

MALA FIDES. Bad faith.

MALA GRAMMATICA NON VITIAT CHARTAM. Bad grammar does not vitiate a deed.

MALA IN SE. Acts which are wrong in themselves, such as murder, whether prohibited by human laws or not, as distinguished from *mala prohibita*, which are indifferent in themselves, but are wrongs by reason of being expressly prohibited by human laws, *e.g.*, playing at unlawful games. 1 *Steph. Com.* ; 2 *Steph. Com.*

MALA PRAXIS is improper or unskilful management of a case by a surgeon, physician, or apothecary, whereby a patent is injured ; whether it be by neglect, or for curiosity and experiment. 3 *Steph. Com.*

MALA PROHIBITA. [MALA IN SE.]

MALESWORN. Forsworn. *Cowel.*

MALFEASANCE. The commission of some act which is in itself unlawful, as opposed to *nonfeasance*, which is the omission of an act which a man is bound by law to do ; and to *misfeasance*, which is the improper performance of some lawful act. 3 *Steph. Com.*

MALICE. 1. The wicked and mischievous purpose. which is of the essence of the crime of murder. Also called "malice aforethought," " malice and forethought," " malice prepense." It exists where any one contemplates the death of any person or persons as a probable consequence of an act done by himself without lawful justification or excuse, or of some unlawful omission, and is implied where he does any act the natural or probable consequence of which is to cause the death of a person. [MURDER.]

2. As regards malicious injuries to persons or property, especially the latter, a "malicious act" has been defined by Mr. Justice Bayley, as a wrongful act, intentionally done without just cause or excuse. *Bromage* v. *Prosser,* 4 B. & C. 247, 255. Under the Malicious Injuries Act (24 & 25 Vict. c. 97) it must be understood in a more restricted sense than the malice which is of the essence of murder. An act lawful in itself is not converted by malice into an actionable wrong. *Allen* v. *Flood,* [1898] A. C. 1.

MALICE AFORETHOUGHT. [MALICE, 1.]

MALICE PREPENSE. [MALICE, 1.]

MALICIOUS INJURIES TO THE PERSON. See 24 & 25 *Vict. c.* 100.

MALICIOUS INJURIES TO PROPERTY. See 24 & 25 *Vict. c.* 97 ; 4 *Steph. Com.*

MALICIOUS PROSECUTION. A prosecution undertaken against a person without reasonable or probable cause. In an action for malicious prosecution, the burden lies upon the plaintiff to show that no probable cause existed. 3 *Steph. Com.*

MALUM IN SE. [MALA IN SE.]

MALINS' ACTS. The Infants' Settlement Act, 1855 (18 & 19 Vict. c. 43), and the Married Women's Reversionary Interest Act, 1857 (20 & 21 Vict. c. 57).

MALVERSATION. Misbehaviour in an office, commission, or employment.

MANDAMUS. 1. The prerogative writ of mandamus. This is, in its form, a command issuing in the king's name, and directed to any person, corporation, or inferior court of judicature, requiring them to do some particular thing which

MANDAMUS—*continued.*

appertains to their office and duty. In its application, it may be considered as confined to cases where relief is required in respect of the infringement of some *public* right or duty, and where no effectual relief can be obtained in the ordinary course of an action. For the rules of procedure, see *Crown Office Rules,* 1886, 60—80. 3 *Steph. Com.*

2. A mandamus incidental to an action. Even prior to the C. L. P. Act, 1854, there was a *mandamus* for the purpose of examining witnesses in India and the other dependencies of the Crown. By that Act, a plaintiff might in any action, except replevin and ejectment, indorse upon the writ of summons a notice that he intended to claim a writ of mandamus commanding the defendant to perform some duty in which the plaintiff is interested. Now, by R. S. C. 1883, Ord. LIII. r. 3, mandamus in an action is by judgment or order, which shall have the same effect as a writ of mandamus formerly had. 3 *Steph. Com.* Under the Judicature Acts the court may, by an interlocutory order, grant a mandamus in any case in which it shall appear just and convenient that such order should be made. 3 *Steph. Com.*

MANDATE. 1. A command of the king or his justices, to have anything done for despatch of justice.

2. A contract by which one man employs another gratuitously in the management of his affairs. 2 *Steph. Com.* [BAILMENT.]

MANDATORY or **MANDATARY.** 1. He to whom a charge or commandment is given.

2. He that obtains a benefice by *mandamus.*

MANDATUM. [MANDATE, 2.]

MANDAVI BALLIVO. A return to a writ whereby a sheriff states that he has committed its execution to the bailiff.

MANIFEST. A document signed by the master of a ship giving a description of the ship, of the goods laden in her, etc.

MANOR was originally a district of ground held by a lord or great personage, who kept to himself such parts of it as were necessary for his own use,

which were called *terræ dominicales,* or *demesne lands,* and distributed the rest to freehold tenants. Of the demesne lands, again, part was retained in the actual occupation of the lord, and other portions were held in villenage ; and there was also a portion which, being uncultivated, was called the lord's waste, and served for public roads and for common of pasture to the lord and his tenants. Manors were also called baronies, as they still are lordships, and each baron or lord was empowered to hold a domestic court called the *court baron,* for redressing misdemeanors and nuisances within the manor, and for settling disputes of property among the tenants. In most manors at the present day we find that species of tenants called *copyholders,* whose lands, though substantially their own property, are nominally part of the lord's demesnes. But a manor, in its proper and perfect state, also comprises land occupied by *freehold tenants* holding of the manor in perpetuity. The essence of a manor seems to consist in the jurisdiction exercised by the lord in his court ; and it has been said that if the number of suitors should so fail as not to leave sufficient to make a jury or homage, that is, two tenants at least to attend in the court, the manor itself is lost. 1 *Steph. Com.* But by 4 & 5 Vict. c. 35, s. 86, this attendance is now unnecessary.

The civil and criminal jurisdiction of these local courts is now practically obsolete (3 *Steph. Com.*) ; though they are held for the admittances of tenants and surrenders, etc. *Wms. R. P.* [COMMON ; COPYHOLD ; COURT BARON ; DEMESNE ; FREEHOLD ; VILLENAGE.]

MANSION or **MANSION-HOUSE.** The lord's chief dwelling-house within his fee, otherwise called the *capital messuage* or manor-place.

Under the Settled Land Act, 1882, the principal mansion-house (unless it be usually occupied as a farm house, or its park, etc., do not exceed twenty-five acres in extent) may not be sold, exchanged, or leased by a tenant for life without the consent of the trustees of the settlement or the order of the Chancery Division. 1 *Steph. Com. ; Wms. R. P.*

MANSLAUGHTER is defined as the unlawful killing of another without malice express or implied ; which may be either voluntarily, upon a sudden

MANSLAUGHTER—*continued.*

heat, or involuntarily, but in the commission of some unlawful or negligent act. 4 *Steph. Com.*

The absence of such malice as would constitute the act murder may be inferred under the following circumstances :—

1. Where there is not time for one to consider consequences ; as when one, having a deadly weapon in his hand, throws it in the heat of passion at another who has provoked him.

2. Where there is time to consider the probable consequences of an unlawful act wilfully done, and yet the death of any person is by no means a natural or probable consequence of such unlawful act ; as if two parties fight without deadly weapons ; or as if a stationmaster, contrary to orders, starts a train before the proper time, having no reason to expect any obstacle, and yet a collision happens whereby some person is killed ; or other case of negligence, provided that the negligence in question be not such as to indicate a wanton and palpable disregard of human life, in which case it will amount to murder. [MURDER.] This definition would imply that the difference between murder and manslaughter is often one of degree, which is in fact the case. 4 *Steph. Com.*

MAN-TRAPS, to catch trespassers, are unlawful except in a dwelling-house for defence between sunset and sunrise. 24 & 25 *Vict. c.* 100, *s.* 31.

MANUMISSION. The freeing of a villein or slave out of his bondage. 1 *Steph. Com.*

MARCHERS. [MARQUIS.]

MARCHES. Boundaries or frontiers.

The boundaries and limits between England and Wales, or between England and Scotland ; or generally the borders of the dominions of the Crown. 2 *Steph. Com.*

MARCHETA, or **MARCHET.** A word interpreted by some as a *cheta* or fine for marriage ; by some as the composition or acknowledgment by the sokeman or villein for the lord's permission to give his daughter in marriage to one not subject to the lord's jurisdiction, or the fine for giving her away without such permission. 1 *Steph. Com.*

MARINE INSURANCE. [INSURANCE.]

MARITAL. Pertaining to a husband.

MARITIME COURTS. Courts having jurisdiction in maritime causes, formerly the Court of Admiralty, and the Judicial Committee of Privy Council on appeal therefrom. By the Judicature Act, 1875, this jurisdiction is vested in the Probate, Divorce, and Admiralty Division of the High Court with an appeal to the Court of Appeal. 3 *Steph. Com.* The maritime courts in our colonies and dependencies are called Vice-Admiralty Courts. 3 *Steph. Com.* ; 4 *Steph. Com.*

MARITIME LAW. The law relating to harbours, ships, and seamen.

MARK. [TRADE MARK.]

MARKET. An emporium of commerce or place of buying and selling ; or the liberty to set up such a place, which any person or body corporate may have by Act of parliament, grant, or prescription. 1 *Steph. Com.* ; 2 *Steph. Com.* ; 3 *Steph. Com.*

MARKET OVERT. Open market ; an expression applied to the open sale of goods as opposed to a clandestine or irregular sale. Market overt, in the country, is held only on the special days provided for particular towns ; but in the city of London every day, except Sunday, is market day. Also in the country the market-place is the only market overt ; but in London every shop in which goods are exposed publicly for sale is market overt for the sale by the occupier of such things as he professes to trade in. See *Hargreave* v. *Spink* [1892], 1 Q. B. 25. See also s. 22 of the Sale of Goods Act, 1893.

The effect of a sale in market overt is that it will in general give the purchaser a secure title to the goods which he has bought, though the vendor has had no property therein. To this rule, however, there are some exceptions ; as, if the goods be Crown property ; or if the goods be stolen, and the owner have prosecuted the thief to conviction. 2 *Steph. Com.*

MARKET TOWNS are towns entitled to hold markets. 1 *Steph. Com.*

MARKSMAN. A deponent who cannot write, and therefore, instead of signing his name, makes his mark, generally a cross. In practice it is desirable that the mark should be attested by a witness.

MARLBRIDGE, STATUTE OF. A statute made at Marlbridge, Marleberge, or Marlborough, in the 52nd year of Hen. III., A.D. 1267, directed chiefly against excessive distress. 3 *Steph. Com.*

MARQUE. [LETTERS OF MARQUE AND REPRISAL.]

MARQUIS or **MARQUESS** is a title of honour next before an earl, and next after a duke. It first came up in the time of Richard II., when it was applied to those lords who had the charge and custody of *marches* or limits, and who before that time were called *marchers* or *lords marchers*. 2 *Steph. Com.*

MARRIAGE (*Maritagium*), besides its ordinary meaning, signifies the right, formerly enjoyed by the lord of whom lands were held in knight-service, of disposing of his infant wards in matrimony, at their peril of forfeiting to him, in case of their refusing a suitable match, a sum of money equal to the value of the marriage ; that is, what the suitor was willing to pay down to the lord as the price of marrying his ward ; and double the market value was to be forfeited if the ward presumed to marry without the lord's consent. 1 *Steph. Com.* ; *Wms. R. P.* [VALOR MARITAGII.]

In socage tenure, however, marriage, or the *valor maritagii*, was of no advantage to the guardian. For, if the guardian married his ward under the age of fourteen, he was bound to account to the ward for the value of the marriage, even though he took nothing for it, unless he married him to advantage. 1 *Steph. Com.* As to the marriage ceremony, see MARRIAGE LICENCE.

MARRIAGE ARTICLES. Heads of an agreement for a marriage settlement.

MARRIAGE BROKAGE CONTRACTS are agreements whereby a party engages to give another a remuneration if he will negotiate a marriage for him. Such agreements are void, as tending to introduce marriages not based on mutual affection, and therefore contrary to public policy.

MARRIAGE LICENCE is of the following kinds :—

1. A common licence, granted by the ordinary or his surrogate.
2. A special licence from the Archbishop of Canterbury.
3. A licence from the registrar of the district.

A licence obtained in either of the forms (1) or (2) will enable the parties to marry without banns, according to the forms of the Church of England ; and a licence obtained in form (3) will enable the parties to marry in any other lawful manner. In this case the presence of the registrar was formerly necessary. His presence is now dispensed with in many cases. See the *Marriage Act*, 1898 (61 & 62 *Vict. c.* 58). 2 *Steph. Com.*

MARRIAGE SETTLEMENT. A settlement of property between an intended husband and wife, made in consideration of their marriage.

MARRIED WOMEN'S PROPERTY. [HUSBAND AND WIFE.]

MARSHAL. 1. An officer (paid by the Treasury) who attends on each judge of assize, and whose duty it is to swear in the grand jury, and, on the civil side, to receive records and enter causes.

2. The marshal of the King's Bench, who had the custody of the King's Bench Prison. An officer called the Keeper of the King's Prison was substituted by 5 & 6 Vict. c. 22.

3. An official of the Admiralty Court, having duties very similar to a sheriff at common law.

MARSHALLING OF ASSETS. An adjustment of the assets of a deceased person so as to pay as many claims upon his estate as possible. Thus if A. has a claim on funds X. and Y., and B. only upon X. ; and A. goes against X. and thus disappoints B. of his fund, B. under this doctrine may go against Y. fund to the extent that A. has drawn upon X. fund.

MARSHALSEA COURT. [COURT OF MARSHALSEA.]

MARTIAL COURTS. [COURT-MARTIAL.]

MARTIAL LAW. The law imposed by the military power. 2 *Steph. Com.*

MARTINMAS. The 11th of November.

MASTER AND SERVANT. [SERVANT.]

MASTER IN CHANCERY. Masters were abolished by 15 & 16 Vict. c. 80, s. 59, and their duties relegated to Chief Clerks. Since 1897 the officials previously called Chief Clerks have been called "Masters." 3 *Steph. Com.*

MASTER IN LUNACY. The Masters in Lunacy are judicial officers appointed by the Lord Chancellor for the purpose of conducting inquiries into the state of mind of persons alleged to be lunatics, and making orders as to the administration of their estates. The inquiries usually take place before a jury. See the *Lunacy Acts*, 1890 *and* 1891. 2 *Steph. Com.*

MASTER OF A SHIP. A chief officer of a merchant ship, having a certificate from the Board of Trade, which is either a certificate of competency obtained in an examination, or a certificate of service obtained by his having attained a certain rank in the service of his Majesty. 3 *Steph. Com.*

MASTER OF THE CROWN OFFICE. The coroner and attorney of the sovereign, whose duty it is to file criminal informations in the Court of King's Bench under the direction of the court, upon the complaint or relation of a private person. He is now an officer of the Supreme Court. 4 *Steph. Com.*

MASTER OF THE FACULTIES is an officer under the Archbishop of Canterbury, appointed to grant licences, dispensations, etc. [FACULTY.]

MASTER OF THE MINT is an officer whose duty it is to receive in the silver and bullion from the goldsmiths to be coined, and to pay them for it, and to superintend everything belonging to the Mint. By 33 & 34 Vict. c. 10, the Chancellor of the Exchequer for the time being is made Master of the Mint. 2 *Steph. Com.*

MASTER OF THE ROLLS is one of the judges of the Court of Chancery, and keeper of the rolls of all patents and grants that pass the Great Seal, and of all records of the Court of Chancery. He was formerly but one of the Masters in Chancery, and his earliest judicial attendances seem to have been merely as assessor to the Chancellor, with the other Masters. His character as an independent judge was fully established in the reign of George II. 3 *Steph Com.* By the Judicature Act, 1881, s. 2, he sits in the Court of Appeal only. 3 *Steph. Com ; 2 Steph. Com.* [ROLLS COURT.]

MASTERS OF THE COURTS OF COMMON LAW were the most important officers of the respective courts, appointed to record the proceedings of the court to which they belonged, to superintend the issue of writs, and the formal proceedings in an action; to receive and account for the fees charged on legal proceedings, and moneys paid into court. There were five to each court. They were appointed under stat. 7 Will. 4 & 1 Vict. c. 30. These officers became, under the Judicature Acts, officers of the Supreme Court and may, with certain exceptions, transact all such business as may be done by a judge at chambers. See *R. S. C.* 1883, *Ord. LIV. rr.* 12 *et seq.* 3 *Steph. Com.*

MATRICIDE. The murder of a mother.

MATRIMONIAL CAUSES are causes respecting the rights of marriage, which were formerly a branch of the ecclesiastical jurisdiction, but were placed by the Divorce Act, 1857, under the cognizance of the Court for Divorce and Matrimonial Causes, now a branch of the High Court of Justice. They are either for—

    (1) Restitution of conjugal rights.
    (2) Judicial separation.
    (3) Dissolution of marriage.

2 *Steph. Com.*; 3 *Steph. Com.* [COURT FOR DIVORCE AND MATRIMONIAL CAUSES; DIVORCE.]

MATRIMONIUM signifies—

    1. Marriage.
    2. Inheritance descending to a man from his mother or her relatives. *Toml.*

MATRONS, JURY OF. [JURY OF MATRONS.]

MATTER. 1. *Matter in Deed* is a truth to be proved by some deed or "specialty," *i.e.*, writing under seal.

2. *Matter in Pais*, strictly speaking a thing done in the country, is matter to be proved by witnesses, and tried by a jury of the country. This is otherwise called *nude matter*. The expression, however, is also used so as to include *matter in deed*. [ESTOPPEL.]

3. *Matter of Record* is matter which may be proved by some record, as having been done in some court of record.

    1 *Steph. Com.*

MATURITY. A bill or note is said to be at *maturity* when the time arrives at which it is payable. 2 *Steph. Com.*

MAYHEM. [MAIHEM.]

MAYOR. The chief magistrate of a municipal borough elected annually by the councillors. His chief duties are to act as returning officer at parliamentary and municipal elections, as chairman of the council, and as a justice of the peace for the borough. 45 & 46 *Vict.* c. 50, s. 15. 3 *Steph. Com.*

MAYOR'S COURT. [LORD MAYOR'S COURT.]

MEASURE OF DAMAGE. The rule by which the *amount* of damage in any given case is to be determined.

MEDIETAS LINGUÆ. [DE MEDIETATE LINGUÆ.]

MELIUS INQUIRENDO, or **MELIUS INQUIRENDUM,** was a writ that lay for a *second* inquiry of what lands and tenements a man died seised of, where partial dealing was suspected upon the writ of *diem clausit extremum*, or where the facts were insufficiently specified in the inquisition upon such writ. See also the Coroners Act, 1887 (50 & 51 Vict. c. 71), s. 6. [DIEM CLAUSIT EXTREMUM; EXTENT, 4.]

MEMORANDUM OF ASSOCIATION. A document to be subscribed by seven or more persons associated for a lawful purpose, by subscribing which, and otherwise complying with the requisitions of the Companies Acts in respect of registration, they may form themselves into an incorporated company, with or without limited liability. See 25 & 26 *Vict.* c. 89, s. 8. It must give name, particulars of capital, objects, etc., and cannot be varied even by the whole body of shareholders except under the special provisions of the Companies (Memorandum of Association) Act, 1890 (53 & 54 Vict. c. 62). See also *Astbury Rly., etc., Co.* v. *Riche,* L. R. 7 H. L. 653. 3 *Steph. Com.*

MEMORIAL. A document containing particulars of a deed, etc., for purposes of registration.

MEMORY, TIME OF LEGAL. [LEGAL MEMORY.]

MENIALS (from Lat. *Mænia*, the walls of a house) are household servants, that is, such as live within the walls of their master's house. *T. L.; Cowel;* 1 *Bl.;* 2 *Steph. Com.*

MENSA ET THORO ("from bed and board"). [DIVORCE; JUDICIAL SEPARATION.]

MENSURA, in a legal sense, is taken for a bushel, as *mensura bladi,* a bushel of corn. *Cowel.*

MERCHANDISE MARKS ACT. The stat. 25 & 26 Vict. c. 88, for punishing the forgery of trade marks, and for some other purposes in connection therewith, was repealed and re-enacted with amendments by the Act of 1887 (50 & 51 Vict. c. 28), which was further amended by the Merchandise Marks Act, 1891. 2 *Steph. Com.;* 4 *Steph. Com.* [TRADE MARKS.]

MERCHANT SHIPPING ACTS. The Merchant Shipping Act, 1894 (57 & 58 Vict. c. 60), supersedes and consolidates the provisions of the Merchant Shipping Acts, 1854 to 1892.

By s. 713 of this Act, the Board of Trade is charged with the general superintendence of matters relating to Merchant Shipping. See 3 *Steph. Com.*

MERCHETA. [MARCHETA.]

MERE RIGHT signifies a right of property without possession. 3 *Steph. Com.*

MERGER. The sinking or drowning of a less estate in a greater, by reason that they both coincide and meet in one and the same person. Thus, if there be a tenant for years, and the reversion in fee simple descends to or is purchased by him, the term of years is *merged* in the inheritance, and shall never exist any more. 1 *Steph. Com.; Wms. R. P.*

The Judicature Act, 1873, s. 25 (4), provides that there shall no longer be any merger by operation of law only of any estate the beneficial interest in which would not be deemed to be merged or extinguished in equity. 3 *Steph. Com.*

MERITORIOUS CONSIDERATION. [CONSIDERATION.]

MERITS. The substantial question at issue in an action or other proceeding.

MERTON, STATUTE OF. Stat. 20 Hen. 3, so called, because passed at Merton, in Surrey. 1 *Steph. Com.*

By this statute, passed in 1235, it is provided *inter alia* that one born before the marriage of his parents should not be legitimate ; that any freeman might make suit by attorney at his lord's court, or any county or hundred court. Lords of the Manor also were authorised to enclose or "approve" commons provided the freeholders were left sufficient pasture. 1 *Steph. Com.*

MESNE. Middle, intermediate.

A *mesne lord* is a lord who has tenants holding under him, and yet himself holds of a superior lord. *T. L.; 1 Steph. Com.*

Mesne process was a phrase applied to the writs issued in an action subsequently to the first or original writ, but prior to the writ of execution, that is, all such process as intervened between the beginning and end of a suit. 3 *Bl.;* 3 *Steph. Com.*

Mesne profits are profits of land taken by a tenant in wrongful possession, from the time that the wrongful possession commenced to the time of the trial of an action of ejectment brought against him. *R. S. C.* 1883, *Ord. XVIII. r.* 2 *;* 3 *Steph. Com.*

MESNE, WRIT OF. An obsolete writ in the nature of a writ of right, brought by a tenant paravail (or undertenant) against the mesne lord (of whom the tenant paravail immediately held the land), when the mesne lord had allowed the tenant paravail to be distrained for rent or services due from the mesne lord to the superior lord. 3 *Steph. Com.*

MESSUAGE. A house, comprising the outbuildings, the orchard, and curtilage or court yard, and, according to the better opinion, the garden also. *Wms. R. P.*

METRIC SYSTEM. A decimal subdivision of weights and measures. See *s.* 21 of the *Weights and Measures Act,* 1878, and 60 & 61 *Vict. c.* 46. 2 *Steph. Com.*

METROPOLITAN BOARD OF WORKS. A board established in 1855, by stat. 18 & 19 Vict. c. 120, called the Metropolis Local Management Act, passed for the general local management of the metropolis. The powers, etc., of the Board were transferred to the London County Council by the Local Government Act, 1888, s. 40, sub-s. 8. 3 *Steph. Com.*

MICHAELMAS DAY. [QUARTER DAYS.]

MICHAELMAS HEAD COURT. A meeting of the heritors in Scotland, when the roll of freeholders is revised. *Bell.*

MICHAELMAS SITTINGS. [SITTINGS.]

MICHAELMAS TERM. [SITTINGS.]

MICHEL GEMOTE. The Great Council of the English nation in the Saxon times ; more frequently called *wittenagemote.* 1 *Bl.;* 2 *Steph. Com.* [WITTENA-GEMOTE.]

MIDDLE MAN. A person intermediate between two others ; a word often used of a person who leases land (especially in Ireland) which he lets out again to tenants. The phrase is thus used as analogous to the "mesne lord" of feudal times. [MESNE.]

MIDDLESEX, BILL OF. [BILL OF MIDDLESEX.]

MIDDLESEX REGISTRY. A registry established in 1709 by 7 Anne, c. 20, for the registration of deeds and wills affecting lands in the county of Middlesex. By 54 & 55 Vict. c. 64, the Middlesex Registry is transferred to the Land Registry. Yorkshire is the only other county in England having similar registries. 1 *Steph. Com.*

MIDSUMMER DAY. [QUARTER DAYS.]

MILEAGE. Travelling expenses allowed according to scale.

MILITARY COURTS. 1. The Court of Chivalry, which was a court of honour, and is now practically obsolete. 3 *Steph. Com.* [COURT OF CHIVALRY.]
2. Courts martial, having jurisdiction to try and to punish offences committed against the Articles of War, and the Mutiny Acts. 2 *Steph. Com.* [COURT MARTIAL ; MUTINY ACT.]
3. The courts which, under the name of courts martial, execute martial law upon offenders in time of war.

MILITARY FEUDS. [FEE ; FEUDAL SYSTEM ; KNIGHT-SERVICE.]

MILITARY TENURES. The tenures by :—
1. Knight-service ; 2. Grand serjeanty ; 3. Cornage. [See under their respective titles.] These were all abolished by 12 Car. 2, c. 24, except the honorary services of grand serjeanty. 1 *Steph. Com.; Wms. R. P.* [FEE ; FEUDAL SYSTEM.]

MILITARY TESTAMENT. A will made by a soldier in active service, without those forms which in ordinary cases are required by statute. 1 *Vict. c.* 26, *s.* 11; 2 *Steph. Com.*

MILITIA. A force for the defence of the country; raised, in default of voluntary enlistment, by compulsory levy in the way of ballot. Compulsory service is, however, practically at an end; and by the Militia Acts the militia has been re-established as a volunteer force, and is annually called out for training. The present system is chiefly founded on the General Militia Act (42 Geo. 3, c. 90), and the Militia Act, 1882 (45 & 46 Vict. c. 49). 2 *Steph Com.*

MILK. See *Public Health Act,* 1875, *ss.* 116—119, and *Sale of Food and Drugs Acts,* 1875 *and* 1879.

MINERAL COURTS. [BARMOTE COURTS.]

MINIMENTS, otherwise called *muniments,* are the evidences or writings whereby a man is enabled to defend the title of his own estate. [MUNIMENTS OF TITLE.]

MINISTRI REGIS (servants of the king). Persons having ministerial offices under the Crown; also the judges of the realm. *Cowel.*

MINOR. A person under the age of twenty-one years. In probate for the purpose of a grant of administration *durante minore ætate,* it means a person above seven and under twenty-one as opposed to an infant, a person under seven. [INFANT.]

MINOR CANONS are officers of a cathedral appointed to conduct the cathedral services. Their appointment is vested in the chapter. 2 *Steph. Com.*

MINORA REGALIA. The king's revenue, as opposed to his dignity and regal power. 2 *Steph. Com.*

MINT. 1. The place where money is coined, near the Tower. The constitution of the Mint was remodelled in the year 1815, and again in 1870 (33 & 34 Vict. c. 10), when the Chancellor of the Exchequer was made the Master of the Mint; the custody of the standard weights committed to the Board of Trade; and the general superintendence of the Mint entrusted to the Treasury. 2 *Steph. Com.*

2. Formerly a pretended place of privilege in Southwark. *Toml.*

MINUTES. 1. The record kept of a meeting.

2. *Of an order or judgment.* An outline of the order or judgment, drawn by one party and agreed to by the other party. Afterwards embodied in a formal order or judgment of the court.

MIRROR OF JUSTICE, generally spoken of as the Mirror, or Mirrour, is a work generally ascribed to the reign of Edward II. It is stated to have been written by one Andrew Horne. 1 *Steph. Com.*

MISADVENTURE. An unfortunate mischance arising out of a lawful act. It is a word generally used with reference to accidental homicide. 4 *Steph. Com.*

MISCARRIAGE. 1. A failure of justice.

2. Abortion (*q.v.*).

MISDEMEANOR. An offence not amounting to felony. The word is generally confined to indictable offences. 4 *Steph. Com.*

The punishment of a misdemeanor at common law was by fine and imprisonment at the discretion of the court; and this is therefore the law at the present day in cases to which no statutory enactment applies. But the misdemeanors most frequently committed are punishable with hard labour under various statutes, and in many cases with penal servitude, for terms specified in the Acts relating to them. The distinction between misdemeanor and felony is now in great measure unmeaning; but it is not yet entirely obsolete. Consult *Archbold's Crim. Plead.* and *Russell on Crimes.* [FELONY; LARCENY.]

MISDIRECTION. The wrong direction of a judge to a jury on a matter of law. 3 *Steph. Com.*

A new trial on the ground of misdirection is not a matter of right in all cases. See *R. S. C.* 1883, *Ord. XXXIX. r.* 6; *Judicature Act,* 1875, *s.* 22; 3 *Steph. Com.* [NEW TRIAL.]

MISE. 1. A gift or customary present formerly made by the people of Wales to a new king or prince on his entrance into that principality.

2. A tax or tallage.

3. Costs and expenses.

4. A writ of right so called.

5. The issue in a writ of right.

6. Cast, or put upon.

7. For *mease,* a messuage or tenement. 3 *Steph. Com.*

MISERICORDIA. An arbitrary amercia-ment or mulct set upon any person for an offence.

MISERICORDIA COMMUNIS. A fine levied on a whole county or hundred.

MISFEASANCE. [MALFEASANCE.]

MISJOINDER OF PARTIES. The wrong-ful joining of parties in a cause. Under the Judicature Act, 1875, no action is to be defeated by the misjoinder of parties. See *R. S. C.* 1883, *Ord. XVI. r.* 1; 3 *Steph. Com.*

MISNOMER. Calling a person by a wrong name in a declaration or other pleading. Any mistake of this kind may now be amended in civil proceed-ings under R. S. C. 1883, Ord. XXVIII. and in criminal pleading by 7 Geo. 4, c. 64, s. 19. 4 *Steph. Com.*

MISPLEADING is the omission, in plead-ing, of anything essential to the action or defence. The word was especially applied to such an error in pleading as could not be *cured by verdict.* [AIDER BY VERDICT; AMENDMENT.]

MISPRISION (from the French *Mépris*). Contempt, neglect, or oversight. Thus, 1. Misprision of treason or felony is a neglect or light account shown of treason or felony by not revealing it; or by letting any person committed for felony go before he be indicted. 2. Also, in every treason and felony misprision is held to be included. 3. The word has also been applied to coining foreign coin, the reason given being that the offence was at one time visited with the same punishment as misprision. 4. It has also been applied to the neglect of clerks in writing and keeping records. 4 *Steph. Com.*

MISREPRESENTATION, *i.e., suggestio falsi,* whether by acts, words, or by positive assertions. It is immaterial whether the person making the mis-representation knew the matter to be false or asserted it without knowing if it were false or true.

The courts will grant relief against a contract induced by misrepresentation if it be shown that such misrepresenta-tion was material, and that the party claiming relief was misled by it. 3 *Steph. Com.* [DECEIT; FRAUD.]

MISTAKE. In criminal law, where a man intending to do a lawful act does, by reason of ignorance of fact, some-thing which is unlawful, he is excused, one of the ingredients necessary to form a criminal act (*mens rea*) being absent. 4 *Steph. Com.*

Mistake, as it has been understood in equity, is defined to be an act which would not have been done, or an omis-sion which would not have occurred, but from ignorance, forgetfulness, inad-vertence, mental incompetence, surprise, misplaced confidence, or imposition. Mistake is either of law or fact. As to the former, the maxim *Ignorantia legis neminem excusat* applies. As to the latter, the rule is that an act done under a mistake or ignorance of a material fact, and an efficient cause of its being done, is relieved against in equity, provided compensation can be made for the injury occasioned by it, and provided also the exercise of reason-able diligence could not have ascertained the fact.

Clearly proved and obvious mistakes in written instruments, etc., will also be relieved against by the court. The rectification, setting aside, etc., of written instruments, is part of the business assigned to the Chancery Division of the High Court by the Judicature Act, 1873.

MISTRIAL. A false or erroneous trial.

MISUSER. Such use of an office or grant as is contrary to the express or implied condition upon which it may have been made, and which works a forfeiture of it. 1 *Steph. Com.;* 3 *Steph. Com.*

MITIGATION. Abatement of anything penal, or of damages. 3 *Steph. Com.*

An address in mitigation is a speech made by the defendant or his counsel to the judge after verdict or plea of guilty, and which may be followed by a speech in *aggravation* from the opposing counsel.

MITTER LE DROIT. MITTER L'ESTATE.
1. *Mitter le Droit.* A form of release by *passing a right.* 1 *Steph. Com.*
2. *Mitter l'Estate.* A release by way of *passing an estate.* 1 *Steph. Com.* [COPARCENARY; RELEASE.]

MITTIMUS. 1. A writ by which records are directed to be transferred from one court to another.

2. A warrant under the hand and seal of a justice, committing a prisoner to gaol to take his trial.

MIXED ACTIONS. [ACTIONS MIXED.]

MIXED JURY. A jury *de medietate linguæ*, now abolished. [DE MEDIETATE LINGUÆ.]

MIXED LARCENY, also called *compound larceny*, signifies larceny combined with circumstances of aggravation. 4 *Steph. Com.* [LARCENY.]

MIXED POLICY is a policy of marine insurance in which not only the time is specified for which the risk is limited, but the voyage also is described by its local termini, *e.g.*, "at and from London to Cadiz for six months," as opposed to policies of insurance for a particular voyage without any limits as to time, and also to purely time policies, in which there is no designation of local termini at all. *Arnould, Mar. Ins.*

MIXED PROPERTY. 1. Property which, though falling under the definition of things real, is attended with some of the legal qualities of things personal, *e.g.*, emblements.

2. Property which, though falling under the definition of things personal, is attended with some of the legal qualities of things real, *e.g.*, heirlooms. 2 *Steph. Com.*

MIXED QUESTIONS OF LAW AND FACT. Cases in which a jury finds the facts, and the court decides, by the aid of established rules of law, what is the legal result of those facts.

MIXED TITHES are tithes consisting of natural products, but nurtured and preserved in part by the care of man; as tithes of cheese, milk, etc. 2 *Steph. Com.*

MOBILIA SEQUUNTUR PERSONAM. Movables follow the person.

MODO ET FORMA. Words signifying that the defendant, in his pleading, denied having done the thing for which he was sued *in manner and form* as in the declaration alleged. This evasive kind of pleading is abolished under the Judicature Act, 1875. See *R. S. C.* 1883, *Ord. XIX. r.* 19.

MODUS DECIMANDI, generally called simply a *modus*, is a partial exemption from tithes; which is where by immemorial usage the general law of tithing is altered, and a new method of taking tithes is introduced. This may be by a pecuniary composition as satisfaction for tithes in kind; or by a compensation in work and labour; or in other ways. 2 *Steph. Com.* [TITHES.]

MOLLITER MANUS IMPOSUIT (he laid hands on him gently). A plea by a defendant, who is sued in an action for an assault and battery, to the effect that he used no more violence upon the plaintiff than was necessary and justifiable under the circumstances. 3 *Steph. Com.*

MOLMUTIAN LAWS. The laws of Dunvallo Molmutius, sixteenth king of the Britons, who began his reign about 400 B.C. These laws were famous in the land till the time of William the Conqueror.

MONEY BILL. A bill for granting aids and supplies to the Crown. 2 *Steph. Com.*

MONEY COUNTS, otherwise called the *indebitatus* or "common counts," are the counts hitherto used in a plaintiff's declaration expressing the most usual grounds of action; as (1) for money lent; (2) for money paid by the plaintiff for the defendant at his request; (3) for money received by the defendant for the use of the plaintiff; and (4) for money found to be due from the defendant to the plaintiff, upon an account stated between them. 3 *Steph. Com.*

MONEY LAND. A phrase sometimes used to signify money held upon trust to be laid out in the purchase of land.

MONEY, PAYMENT OF, INTO COURT. [PAYMENT OF MONEY INTO COURT.]

MONEY-LENDER. By the Act of 1900 (63 & 64 Vict. c. 51), a money-lender, for the purposes of the Act, is defined as "every person whose business is that of money-lending, or who advertises or announces himself or holds himself out in any way as carrying on that business." The term, however, does not apply to pawnbrokers, loan societies, banking or insurance companies, and some others. Money-lenders to whom the Act applies are placed under an obligation to be registered, and they are liable to have their contracts judicially varied.

MONITION. A warning; generally a warning to a defendant in an ecclesiastical court not to repeat an offence of which he has been convicted. 2 *Steph. Com.*

MONOPOLY. A licence or privilege allowed by the sovereign for the buying and selling, making, working, or using of anything, to be enjoyed exclusively by the grantee. Monopolies were, by 21 Jac. 1, c. 3 (Statute of Monopolies), declared to be illegal and void, subject to certain exceptions therein specified, including patents in favour of the authors of new inventions. 2 *Steph. Com.; Wms. P. P.* [PATENT.]

MONSTER is one which hath not the shape of mankind, but in any part evidently resembles the brute creation; it cannot inherit land. 1 *Steph. Com.*

MONSTRANS DE DROIT. Manifestation or plea of right; which is a claim made against the Crown when the Crown is in possession of a title the facts of which are already set forth upon record. This proceeding was extended by statutes of Edward III. and Edward VI. to almost all cases where a subject claims against the right of the Crown founded on an inquisition of office. 3 *Steph. Com.* [INQUEST, 1; PETITION OF RIGHT.]

The judgment in a *monstrans de droit* or other proceeding against the Crown is called *amoreas manus*, or *ouster-le-main*.

MONTH is a space of time containing by the week twenty-eight days, and by the calendar twenty-eight, thirty, or thirty-one days. At common law the meaning of the term "month" is twenty-eight days, otherwise called a *lunar month*. [LUNAR MONTH.] But, in ecclesiastical and mercantile matters, a month is interpreted to mean a calendar month; also, by 13 Vict. c. 21 (repealed and re-enacted by the Interpretation Act, 1889), in an Act of parliament it is henceforth to mean a calendar month; as also in the Rules of Court. See *R. S. C.* 1883, *Ord. LXIV. r.* 1; 1 *Steph. Com.*

MOOT. 1. A court, plea, or convention.

2. An exercise, or arguing of cases, which was formerly practised by students in the Inns of Court, the better to enable them to defend their clients. The places where moot-cases were argued was anciently called a *moot-hall*; and those who argued the cases were called *moot-men.*

Hence a *moot point* signifies a point open to argument and discussion.

MORATUR, or DEMORATUR IN LEGE, signifies "he delays in law," or demurs. [DEMURRER.]

MORE OR LESS. These words, appended to measurements in a conveyance of land, import a vagueness, within certain small limits, in the measurements of the land referred to: if there be a considerable deficiency the purchaser will be entitled to an abatement on the price.

MORGANATIC MARRIAGE. The marriage which a prince or nobleman contracts with a woman of humble birth, on the express condition that the ordinary civil effects shall not result therefrom, and that the wife and children shall be contented with certain specified advantages. The restrictions relate only to the rank of the parties and succession to property, and do not affect the nature or validity of the matrimonial engagement.

MORT D'ANCESTOR. A real action or assize available to a demandant who complained of an "abatement" to or entry upon his freehold, effected by a stranger on the death of the demandant's father or mother, brother or sister, uncle or aunt, nephew or niece. Abolished in 1833 by stat. 3 & 4 Will. 4, c. 27, s. 36. 3 *Steph. Com.* [ABATEMENT, 5; ASSIZE, WRIT OF.]

MORTGAGE (Lat. *Mortuum radium, i.e.,* dead pledge) is a conveyance, assignment, or demise of real or personal estate as security for the repayment of money borrowed. 1 *Steph. Com.; Wms. R. P.*

If the conveyance, assignment, or demise be of land or any estate therein, the transaction is called a mortgage, notwithstanding that the creditor enters into possession; but the transfer of the possession of a moveable chattel to secure the repayment of a debt is called not a *mortgage*, but a *pledge*. [GAGE; PLEDGE; VIVUM VADIUM.] Mortgages are either (*a*) legal, including statutory, or (*b*) equitable.

The term "mortgage" is applied indifferently: (1) to the mortgage transaction; (2) to the mortgage deed; and (3) to the rights conferred thereby on the mortgagee.

MORTGAGEE. The creditor to whom a mortgage is made. [MORTGAGE.]

MORTGAGOR. The debtor who makes a mortgage. [MORTGAGE.]

MORTIS CAUSA DONATIO. [DONATIO MORTIS CAUSA.]

MORTMAIN (Lat. *Mortuâ manu*). An alienation of lands in mortmain is an alienation of lands or tenements to any corporation, sole or aggregate, ecclesiastical or temporal. The name is thought to have been derived from the fact that the religious houses, to whom principally in former days alienations in mortmain were made, were composed of persons dead in law. [MORTMAIN ACTS.]

MORTMAIN ACTS. The statutes whereby the rights of corporations to take lands by grant or devise are abridged. The Act which is usually known as the "Mortmain" Act is the stat. 9 Geo. 2, c. 36, passed in 1735. At the time of the passing of that Act, no devise of lands to a corporation was good, except for charitable uses. By that statute no lands or hereditaments or money to be laid out therein might be given or conveyed, charged or incumbered, for any charitable use whatever, unless by deed executed in the presence of two witnesses, twelve calendar months before the death of the donor, and enrolled in Chancery within six calendar months of its execution, and unless such gift was made to take effect immediately, and was without power of revocation. Gifts to the Universities of Oxford and Cambridge, and their colleges, or in trust for the scholars on the foundations of Eton, Winchester and Westminster, were excepted from the operation of the Act ; so were *bonâ fide* purchases for valuable consideration paid down. Various other exceptions have been introduced by subsequent statutes. The above Act was repealed and re-enacted, with amendments, by 51 & 52 Vict. c. 42, which, in turn, has been amended by 54 & 55 Vict. c. 73. 1 *Bl.*; 2 *Bl.*; 1 *Steph. Com.*; 3 *Steph. Com.*; *Wms. R. P.*

MORTUARY. 1. A mortuary was originally a gift left by a man at his death to his parish church, for the recompense of his personal tithes and offerings not duly paid in his lifetime. Also a kind of ecclesiastical heriot. 2 *Steph. Com.*

2. A place for the temporary reception of the dead.

MORTUUM VADIUM. Dead pledge or mortgage. 1 *Steph. Com.* [MORTGAGE.]

MOTE. A court ; a plea ; an assembly. [MOOT, 1.]

MOTION. An application made to a court or judge *vivâ voce* in open court. Its object is to obtain an order or rule, directing some act to be done in favour of the applicant. 3 *Steph. Com.*

A motion must in general be preceded by notice to any party intended to be affected thereby. See *R. S. C.* 1883, *Ord. LII. rr.* 1—9.

MOTION FOR JUDGMENT. A proceeding whereby a party to an action moves for the judgment of the court in his favour ; which he may adopt under various circumstances enumerated in Ord. XL. of the R. S. C. 1883.

MOVEABLES. Goods, furniture, etc., which may be moved from place to place. 1 *Steph. Com.*; 2 *Steph. Com.*; *Wms. P. P.*

MULCT. A fine or penalty.

MULIER PUISNE. The lawful issue preferred before an elder brother born out of matrimony. 1 *Steph. Com.* [BASTARD EIGNE.]

MULMUTIN LAWS. [MOLMUTIAN LAWS.]

MULTA or **MULTURA EPISCOPI.** A fine given formerly to the king, that the bishop might have power to make his own last will and testament, and to have the probate of other men's, and the granting administrations.

MULTIFARIOUSNESS, in a bill in equity, was the improperly joining distinct subjects in the same bill of complaint. See now JOINDER OF CAUSES OF ACTION.

MULTIPLICITY OF SUITS or **ACTIONS** is where several different suits or actions are brought upon the same issue. This was obviated sometimes by a proceeding in equity called a Bill of Peace ; sometimes by a rule of a Court of Common Law for the consolidation of different actions. See *Judicature Act*, 1873, *s.* 24 (7). [BILL OF PEACE ; CONSOLIDATION ORDER.]

MULTURE. A toll paid to a miller for grinding corn; the grist or grinding; the corn ground.

MUNICIPAL CORPORATION. A town corporation consisting of a mayor, aldermen, and councillors, who together form the council of the borough. Under the Municipal Corporations Act, 1835 (5 & 6 Will. 4, c. 76), in the boroughs to which that Act applies, which are the great majority of the boroughs in England and Wales, the town councillors are elected by the burgesses, and the mayor and aldermen by the council. The council is directed to meet once a quarter (and oftener if due notice be given) for the transaction of the general business of the borough. 3 *Steph. Com.*

The Act of 1835 has been amended by various statutes from time to time, which were finally consolidated by the Municipal Corporations Act, 1882 (45 & 46 Vict. c. 50). See also 46 & 47 Vict. c. 18.

MUNICIPAL LAW means strictly the law of a municipality. The expression is, however, generally used to denote the positive law of a particular state as opposed to the law of nations or international law.

MUNIMENTS OF TITLE. The deeds and other evidences which fortify or protect a man's title to his estates.

MURDER. We may define murder as "the causing the death of any one by some act done without lawful justification or excuse, or by some unlawful omission, of which act or omission a probable consequence is to cause the death of some person or persons." But to this definition some authorities would add, "or in the commission of a felony." 4 *Steph. Com.* [CONSTRUCTIVE MURDER; MALICE; HOMICIDE; MANSLAUGHTER.]

MURDRUM. The secret killing of another; or the fine or amerciament imposed by the Danish and Norman conquerors upon the town or hundred wherein the same was committed. 4 *Steph. Com.* [ENGLESCHERIE.]

MUTATIS MUTANDIS. With the necessary changes in points of detail.

MUTE. Speechless, who refuses to speak; a word applied formerly to a prisoner who, being arraigned of treason or felony,

1. Made no answer at all; or
2. Answered foreign to the purpose; or
3. Having pleaded not guilty, refused to put himself upon his country. (This last formality is now unnecessary.)

Standing mute was, in high treason, in petty larceny, and in misdemeanors, held to be equivalent to conviction. But in other felonies, and in petty treason, it exposed the prisoner to the *peine forte et dure.* [PEINE FORTE ET DURE.] Now the court may order the proper officer to enter a plea of "not guilty" on behalf of the prisoner so standing mute. 7 & 8 *Geo.* 4, c. 28, s. 2; 4 *Steph. Com.*

MUTINY ACT. An Act passed annually by parliament "for punishing mutiny and desertion, and for the better payment of the army, and their quarters."

By the Bill of Rights (1 Will. & Mary, s. 2, c. 2) the keeping of a standing army in time of peace without consent of parliament is against law. The definite establishment of a standing army by an Act of parliament of unlimited duration, would be in effect a revocation of the above provision, as in that case no further "consent of parliament" would be required for its continuance. Such consent is accordingly given by Acts of parliament appointed to continue in force for one year only, called the Mutiny Acts. 2 *Steph. Com.*

MUTUAL DEBTS. Debts due on both sides, as between two persons. See SET-OFF.

MUTUAL PROMISES. Concurrent considerations which support one another, unless one or the other be void. In that case, as there is no consideration one side, no contract can arise.

MUTUAL TESTAMENTS. Wills made by two persons who leave their effects reciprocally to the survivor.

MUTUALITY. Reciprocity of obligation, two persons being mutually bound.

MUTUUM. The contract of a loan to be repaid in kind; as, so much barley, wine, etc.

N. L. [NON LIQUET.]

N. P. [NISI PRIUS.]

NAAM. The taking another man's moveable goods, either by lawful distress or otherwise.

NAM or **NAAM**. [NAAM.]

NAMATION. Taking or impounding.

NAMES. Either christian or surname. A man may change his surname, but not his christian name. By *a name and arms clause* in a settlement or will is meant one by which a gift is made conditionally on the donee assuming the name and arms of the donor.

NAMIUM. A pledge or distress. [NAAM.]

NAMIUM VETITUM. [WITHERNAM.]

NARRATIO. A declaration or count. [COUNT, 2 ; DECLARATION.]

NATIONAL DEBT. The debt due by the nation to individual creditors, whether our own people or foreigners. This national debt is in part *funded* and in part *unfunded ;* the former being that which is secured to the national creditor upon the public funds ; the latter, that which is not so provided for. The unfunded debt is comparatively but of small amount, and is generally secured by Exchequer bills and bonds. See the *National Debt Act*, 1870 ; 2 *Steph. Com.* [CONSOLIDATED FUND ; EXCHEQUER BILLS AND BONDS ; PUBLIC FUNDS.]

NATIONS, LAW OF. [JUS GENTIUM ; LAW OF NATIONS.]

NATIVI. Bondmen ; strictly, persons born servants, as opposed to bondmen by contract, *nativi conventionarii*. 1 *Steph. Com.*

NATIVI DE STIPITE. Bondmen by birth or descent.

NATIVO HABENDO. A writ for the apprehension of a villein or bondman who had run away from his lord.

NATURA BREVIUM. [FITZHERBERT.]

NATURAL AFFECTION. Often used in deeds for the motive, or consideration for a gift arising from relationship. In many cases this consideration is not sufficient to "sustain a promise," *i.e.*, to give an action to the promisee against the promisor for its non-fulfilment. 2 *Steph. Com.*

NATURAL ALLEGIANCE. The perpetual allegiance due from natural-born subjects, as distinguished from *local* allegiance, which is temporary only. 2 *Steph. Com.*

NATURAL CHILD. The child of one's body, whether legitimate or illegitimate. The word, however, in popular language, is usually applied only to an illegitimate child.

NATURAL LIFE. That which terminates by natural death, as opposed to civil death. [CIVIL DEATH.]

NATURAL PERSONS. Persons in the ordinary sense of the word, as opposed to *artificial* persons or corporations.

NATURAL-BORN SUBJECTS include by the common law :—
1. All persons born within the United Kingdom, or in the colonies and dependencies, except such as are born of alien enemies in time of war.
2. The children of the sovereign, wherever born.
3. The children of our ambassadors born abroad.
But the class of natural-born subjects has been considerably extended by statutory enactments, 25 Edw. 3, stat. 2 ; 7 Ann. c. 5 ; 4 Geo. 2, c. 21 ; and 13 Geo. 3, c. 21. 2 *Steph. Com.* [ALIEN.]

NATURALIZATION. The giving to a foreigner the *status* of a natural-born subject. This may be done either by Act of parliament, or by a certificate of the Secretary of State under the Naturalization Act, 1870 (33 Vict. c. 14), on his taking the oath of allegiance provided for by 33 & 34 Vict. c. 102. 2 *Steph. Com.* [ALIEN ; ALLEGIANCE ; NATURAL-BORN SUBJECTS.]

NAVAL DISCIPLINE ACTS. The method of ordering seamen in the royal fleet. and keeping up a regular discipline there, was first directed by certain express rules, articles and orders, enacted by the authority of parliament soon after the Restoration. The Act at present in force is the Naval Discipline Act, 1866 (29 & 30 Vict. c. 109), as amended by 47 & 48 Vict. c. 39. 2 *Steph. Com.*

NAVIGATION LAWS. Acts of Parliament (now repealed) regulating the trading intercourse of foreign countries with the United Kingdom and the British possessions in general. 3 *Steph. Com.*

NAVY BILLS. Those drawn by officers of the Royal Navy for their pay, etc.

NE ADMITTAS (do not admit him). A prohibitory writ which lay for the plaintiff in a *quare impedit* to restrain the bishop from admitting the clerk of a rival patron until the contention be determined. 3 *Steph. Com.* Now practically obsolete. [QUARE IMPEDIT.]

NE EXEAT REGNO (that he leave not the kingdom). A prerogative writ whereby a person is prohibited from leaving the realm, even though his usual residence is in foreign parts. The writ is directed to the sheriff of the county in which the defendant is resident, commanding him to take bail from the defendant not to quit England without leave of the court. It is granted on motion, supported by affidavit showing that a sum of money is due from the defendant to the plaintiff, or will be due on taking accounts between them, and that the defendant intends to abscond.

The writ was formerly applied to great political purposes, but it is now applied in civil matters only, and is almost superseded by orders under the Debtors Act, 1869 (32 & 33 Vict. c. 62), s. 6. 1 *Steph. Com.*; 2 *Steph. Com.*

NE UNQUES ACCOUPLE was a defence by a tenant (or defendant) in an action of dower, to the effect that the demandant and her alleged husband were never joined in lawful matrimony, and that therefore she could not claim dower as his widow. 3 *Steph. Com.*

NE UNQUES EXECUTOR, or ADMINISTRATOR. A phrase indicating the defence by which a person, sued as executor or administrator, denies that he ever was executor or administrator.

NE UNQUES SEISIE. A defence to an action of dower, whereby it was alleged that the deceased husband of the demandant had never been seised of such an estate as would give the demandant a legal claim to dower. 3 *Steph. Com.* [DOWER, 2.]

NEAT CATTLE. Oxen and heifers.

NECESSARIES, in the case of an infant, include meat, drink, apparel, physic, and likewise good teaching and instruction, whereby he may profit himself afterwards ; and, in general, things suitable to his circumstances, degree, and station in life. For the supply of all such things an infant may bind himself by contract. 2 *Steph. Com.* [INFANTS' RELIEF ACT.]

Similarly, necessaries for a married woman are things suitable for her station in life, and for the supply of these her husband will in general be responsible. 2 *Steph. Com.*

NECESSITY is a constraint upon the will, whereby a man is urged to do that which his judgment disapproves, and is thereby excused from responsibility which might be otherwise incurred. It includes—

1. The obligation of civil subjection.

2. In certain cases, the coercion of a wife by her husband.

3. In certain cases also *duress per minas*, which impels a man to act in a given way from fear of death or personal injury. [DURESS.]

4. Where a man is constrained to choose the lesser of two evils. 4 *Steph. Com.*

NEGLIGENCE. A culpable omission of a positive duty. It differs from *heedlessness*, in that heedlessness is the doing of an act in violation of a *negative* duty, without adverting to its possible consequences. In both cases there is inadvertence, and there is breach of duty.

Negligence is often said to be of three kinds—

1. Gross negligence, which is the want of that care which every man of common sense takes of his own property.

2. Ordinary negligence, which is the omission of that care which men of prudence take of their concerns ; and,

3. Slight negligence, which is the omission of that diligence which very circumspect and careful persons employ.

The question of negligence is usually one of fact for the jury. 2 *Steph. Com.* [CONTRIBUTORY NEGLIGENCE.]

NEGLIGENT ESCAPE is where a prisoner escapes without his keeper's knowledge or consent. It is thus opposed to a *voluntary* escape, which is an escape by consent or connivance of the officer. 4 *Steph. Com.*

NEGOTIABLE INSTRUMENTS are instruments purporting to represent so much money, in which the property passes by mere delivery, such as bills of exchange, promissory notes, etc. See Bills of Exchange Act, 1882. Such instruments constitute an exception to the general rule that a man cannot give a better title than he has himself. 2 *Steph. Com.*

NEGOTIORUM GESTOR is a person who does an act to his own inconvenience for the advantage of another, but without the authority of the latter, or any promise to indemnify him for his trouble. The *negotiorum gestor* was entitled, by the Roman law, to recover compensation for his trouble; and this is so by the law of England in cases of salvage, and in some other cases.

NEMINE CONTRADICENTE (abbrev., *nem. con.*). No one contradicting; that is, unanimously; a phrase used with especial reference to votes and resolutions of the House of Commons; *nemine dissentiente* being the corresponding expression as to unanimous votes of the House of Lords.

NEMO DAT QUOD NON HABET (no one can give that which he has not, *i.e.*, no one can give a better title than he has). But see NEGOTIABLE INSTRUMENT.

NEMO DEBET ESSE JUDEX IN PROPRIA CAUSA (no one should be judge in his own cause).

NEMO EST HÆRES VIVENTIS (no one is the heir of a living man).

NEPOS. A grandson.

NEPTIS. A granddaughter.

NEUTRALITY LAWS are the Acts otherwise called the Foreign Enlistment Acts. [FOREIGN ENLISTMENT ACTS.]

NEVER INDEBTED. A plea in actions of contract which denies the matters of fact from which the liability of the defendant arises; thus, in actions for goods bargained and sold, the plea operates as a denial of the bargain and sale. 3 *Steph. Com.*

Denials must now be specific, general denials being no longer admitted in pleading. See *R. S. C.* 1883, *Ord. XIX. r.* 17.

NEW ASSIGNMENT. A reply by the plaintiff to a defendant's plea, by which the plaintiff alleged that he brought his action not for the cause supposed by the defendant, but for some other cause to which the plea pleaded was irrelevant. 3 *Steph. Com.*

Ord. XXIII. r. 6, R. S. C. 1883, provides that no new assignment shall hereafter be necessary or used. But everything which was formerly alleged by way of new assignment is to be introduced by amendment.

NEW INN. One of the Inns of Chancery. 1 *Steph. Com.* [INNS OF CHANCERY.]

NEW STYLE. [OLD STYLE.]

NEW TRIAL has been held to be grantable in civil cases on motion, on any of the following among other grounds:—

1. That the judge misdirected the jury on a point of law.

2. That he admitted or rejected evidence improperly.

3. That he improperly discharged the jury.

4. That he refused to amend the record when an amendment ought to have been made.

5. That the defendant did not receive due notice of trial.

6. That the successful party misbehaved.

7. That the jury, or any of them, have misbehaved, as by drawing lots for the verdict.

8. That the damages are excessive.

9. That the damages are too slight.

10. That the verdict has been obtained by a surprise.

11. That the witnesses for the prevailing side are manifestly shown to have committed perjury.

12. That the verdict was against the weight of evidence.

13. That new and material facts have come to light since the trial.

The court must, however, be satisfied in all cases that the merits have not been fairly and fully discussed, and that justice has not been done. See *R. S. C.* 1883, *Ord. XXXIX.* 3. *Steph. Com.*

A new trial is not quite the same thing as a *venire de novo*, which is a much more ancient proceeding. [VENIRE DE NOVO.]

A new trial is seldom obtainable in criminal cases, being confined to informations for misdemeanor tried in the King's Bench Division. [MISDIRECTION.]

NEXT FRIEND. An adult under whose protection an infant or a married woman institutes an action or other legal proceeding, and who is responsible for the conduct and the costs of the same. The Married Women's Property Act, 1882, s. 1, sub-s. 2, by allowing a married woman to sue in all respects as if she were a *feme sole*, has rendered the "next friend" in her case unnecessary. See *R. S. C.* 1883, *Ord. XVI. r.* 16.

Lunatics and persons of unsound mind sue by their committee or next friend, and defend by their committee or guardian *ad litem*. *Ibid. r.* 17.

NEXT OF KIN. 1. An expression generally used for the persons who, by reason of kindred, are, on the death of a person intestate, entitled to his personal estate and effects under the Statute of Distributions. 2 *Steph. Com.* ; *Wms. P. P.*

2. Those who are, lineally or collaterally, related in the nearest degree to a given person.

NEXT PRESENTATION. The right to present to a living on the next vacancy. The purchase of the next presentation to a vacant benefice is illegal and void ; so is the purchase by a clergyman, either in his own name or in another's, of the next presentation simply, with the view of presenting himself to the living, though the benefice be not vacant at the time of purchase. And see further restrictions under the Benefices Act, 1898 (61 & 62 Vict. c. 48). 2 *Steph. Com.* [SIMONY.]

NIENT COMPRISE. An exception formerly sometimes taken to a petition as unjust, because the thing desired is not contained in the act or deed whereon the petition is granted.

NIENT CULPABLE. Not guilty. 4 *Bl.* ; 4 *Steph. Com.*

NIENT DEDIRE. To suffer judgment by not denying or opposing it, that is, by default.

NIENT LE FAIT. Not his deed.

NIGHT. Night was anciently accounted to be the time from sunset to sunrise.

Now, by the Larceny Act (24 & 25 Vict. c. 96), s. 1, the night, in the offence of burglary, is deemed to commence at 9 o'clock in the evening, and to end at 6 o'clock in the morning on the following day. 4 *Steph. Com.*

By 9 Geo. 4, c. 69, s. 15, night, for the purposes of night poaching, is to be considered to commence at the expiration of one hour after sunset, and to conclude at the beginning of the last hour before sunrise. 4 *Steph. Com.*

NIHIL (nothing). A return made by the sheriff in some cases. [NULLA BONA.]

NIHIL DEBET, or **NIL DEBET** (he owes nothing). The plea of the general issue in an action of debt. Abolished. [NEVER INDEBTED.]

NIHIL DICIT, or **NIL DICIT,** means a failure on the part of a defendant to put in his defence. 3 *Steph. Com.* [DEFAULT.]

NIHIL HABUIT, or **NIL HABUIT, IN TENEMENTIS.** A plea which could sometimes be pleaded by a lessee, when an action of debt was brought against him by a party claiming as landlord for rent due. The import of it was that the plaintiff had no title in the land demised, and that the defendant was not "estopped" by deed or otherwise from disputing the plaintiff's title. [ESTOPPEL.]

NISI PRIUS. A writ judicial, whereby the sheriff of a county was commanded to bring the men impanelled as jurors in any civil action to the court at Westminster on a certain day, unless before that day (*nisi prius*) the justices of assize came into the county, in which case, by the statute of Nisi Prius, 13 Edw. 1, c. 30, it became his duty to return the jury, not to the court at Westminster, but before the justices of assize. The *nisi prius* business was thus at first a mere adjunct to the *assizes*, or real actions. Now these real actions are abolished altogether, though the name *assizes* is retained ; and the judges in civil cases at the assizes are said to sit at *nisi prius*. And a trial at *nisi prius* is generally understood to mean a trial, before a judge and jury, of a civil action, which has been brought in one of the superior courts. It is thus to be distinguished from (1) a trial at bar, (2) a criminal trial, (3) a trial in an inferior court. 3 *Steph. Com.;* 4 *Steph. Com.* [CROWN SIDE.]

NISI PRIUS COURT. The court in which civil actions are tried at the assizes. [ASSIZE, COURTS OF.]

NISI PRIUS RECORD. The parchment roll on which the issue in a civil action, consisting of a record of the pleadings which have taken place, was formerly transcribed for the purpose of being delivered to the proper officer of the court, for the use of the judge who is to try the case. 3 *Steph. Com.*

By R. S. C. 1883, Ord. XXXVI. r. 30, the party entering the action for trial is to deliver to the officer two copies of the pleadings and particulars (if any) for the use of the judge, and if no pleadings two copies of the writ must be lodged.

NOBILITY. The rank or dignity of peerage, comprising—1. Dukes. 2. Marquesses. 3. Earls. 4. Viscounts. 5. Barons. 2 *Steph. Com.*

NOLENS VOLENS. Whether willing or unwilling.

NOLLE PROSEQUI (to be unwilling to prosecute) was a formal averment by the plaintiff in an action, that he will not further prosecute his suit as to one or more of the defendants, or as to part of the claim or cause of action. Its effect is to withdraw the cause of action, in respect of which it is entered, from the record. 3 *Steph. Com.*

A *nolle prosequi* may only be entered in a criminal prosecution by leave of the attorney-general.

NOMINAL DAMAGES. A trifling sum recovered by verdict, in cases where, although the action is maintainable, it is nevertheless the opinion of the jury that the plaintiff has not suffered substantial damage. [INJURIA SINE DAMNO.] 3 *Steph. Com.*

NOMINAL PARTNER. [OSTENSIBLE PARTNER.]

NOMINATIM. By name.

NOMINATION, of candidates at an election. See the *Ballot Act*, 1872, and *Municipal Corporations Act*, 1882, *s.* 55.

NOMINATION TO A LIVING. A power that a man hath by virtue of a manor, or otherwise, to appoint a clerk to a patron of a benefice, to be by him presented to the ordinary.

NON ASSUMPSIT (he did not promise). The plea of the general issue in an action of assumpsit, to the effect that the defendant did not promise as alleged in the plaintiff's declaration. 3 *Steph. Com.* [ASSUMPSIT; GENERAL ISSUE, PLEA OF.]

NON CEPIT. The plea of the general issue in the action of *replevin;* that the defendant did not take the goods as alleged by the plaintiff. 3 *Steph. Com.* [GENERAL ISSUE, PLEA OF; REPLEVIN.]

NON CLAIM. The omission or neglect of him that ought to challenge his right within a time limited, by which neglect he is barred of his right. See 3 *&* 4 *Will.* 4, *c.* 27, *s.* 11 ; 1 *Steph. Com.*

NON COMPOS MENTIS. A phrase applied to a man to indicate that he is of unsound mind, so as to be incapable of managing himself or his affairs. 2 *Steph. Com.*

NON CONSTAT (it is not evident). This phrase is often used as importing that an alleged inference is not deducible from given premises. [NON SEQUITUR.]

NON CUL. Short for *non culpabilis*, not guilty. [NOT GUILTY.]

NON DAMNIFICATUS (not damnified). A plea to an action on a bond of indemnity, whereby the defendant alleges that the plaintiff has suffered no such damage as to warrant him in bringing the action.

NON DECIMANDO. A claim to be entirely exempt from tithes, and to pay no compensation in lieu of them. [DE NON DECIMANDO.]

NON DEMISIT (he did not demise). The name of a plea on an action of debt for rent under a lease, denying the fact of the lease.

NON DETINET (he does not detain). The plea of the general issue in an action of detinue, which operates as a denial of the detention of the goods, but not of the plaintiff's property therein. [DETINUE; GENERAL ISSUE, PLEA OF.]

NON DIRECTION. Omission on the part of a judge to enforce a necessary point of law upon a jury. See *Jud. Act*, 1875, *s.* 22.

NON EST FACTUM (it is not his deed). The plea of the general issue in an action on a deed, denying the *fact* of the deed having been executed. [GENERAL ISSUE, PLEA OF.]

NON EST INVENTUS (he has not been found). A return by the sheriff to a writ of *capias*, when he cannot find the defendant within his bailiwick. [BAILIWICK; CAPIAS AD SATISFACIENDUM.]

NON INTROMITTANT CLAUSE. A clause in the charter of a borough by which it is exempted from the jurisdiction of the county justices. 3 *Steph. Com.*

NON ISSUABLE PLEA. A plea which does not raise an issue on the merits of the case. [ISSUABLE PLEA.]

NON LIQUET (it is not clear). A verdict given by a jury when a matter was to be deferred to another day of trial.

NON OBSTANTE (notwithstanding). A clause by which the Crown occasionally attempted to give effect to grants and letters-patent, notwithstanding any statute to the contrary. The doctrine of *non obstante*, which set the prerogative above the laws, was demolished by the Bill of Rights at the Revolution. 1 *Steph. Com.*, 4 *Steph. Com.*

NON OBSTANTE VEREDICTO (notwithstanding the verdict). A motion for judgment *non obstante veredicto* is a motion made on the part of a plaintiff for judgment in his favour after verdict found for the defendant, *e.g.*, where the jury has found for the defendant contrary to law. Disused. 3 *Steph. Com.*

NON OMITTAS PROPTER ALIQUAM LIBERTATEM. A clause now generally inserted in writs directed to a sheriff, by which he is commanded "not to omit, by reason of any liberty within his bailiwick," to execute the process which the writ enjoins, but to execute the same within liberties and privileged places as well as in the county at large. 2 *Steph. Com.* [BAILIWICK ; LIBERTY.]

NON PROS. or NON PROSEQUITUR. The delay or neglect by a plaintiff in proceeding with his action. So a judgment for the defendant by reason of such neglect in the plaintiff is called judgment of *non pros.* Now, by *R. S. C.* 1883, *Ord. XXVII.*, the defendant may apply for a dismissal of the action for want of prosecution.

NON RESIDENCE. The neglect by a clergyman to reside on his benefice. The cases in which non residence is to be permitted to the clergy are now regulated by statute. See 2 *Steph. Com.*

NON SANE MEMORY means generally unsoundness of mind.

NON SEQUITUR (it does not follow). An expression used in argument to indicate that the premises do not warrant the inference drawn from them.

NON SUM INFORMATUS. I have no instructions. [INFORMATUS NON SUM.]

NON TENURE. An exception to the plaintiff's count in a real action, to the effect that the defendant did not hold the land mentioned in the count. *Cowell.* [ACTIONS REAL AND PERSONAL.]

NON VIDENTUR QUI ERRANT CONSENTIRE (they are not considered to consent who act under a mistake).

NONAGE. The absence of full age, which is for most purposes twenty-one years.

NONAGIUM, or **NONAGE**. The ninth part of movable goods formerly payable to the clergy on the death of persons in their parish.

NONCONFORMISTS. Dissenters from the Church of England ; a word used more especially of the Protestant bodies who have seceded from the Church. 2 *Steph. Com.*

NONFEASANCE. [MALFEASANCE.]

NON-JOINDER. A plea in abatement by which it is alleged that the plaintiff has omitted to *join* in the action all the persons who ought to be parties to it. Under the R. S. C. 1883, Ord. XVI., r. 11, no action is to be defeated by the misjoinder or non-joinder of parties ; and by Ord. XXI., r. 20, pleas in abatement are abolished in civil actions. 3 *Steph. Com.*

NON-JURORS. Persons who after the abdication of James II. refused to take the oaths to William III. and his successors in the government.

NON-SUIT. A renouncing of a suit by the plaintiff ; most commonly upon the discovery of some error or defect, when the matter is so far proceeded with, as that the jury is ready at the bar to deliver their verdict. So, if the plaintiff does not appear at all he is said to be non-suit or non-suited. A non-suit may, however, be entered by the court where the plaintiff fails to make out a legal cause of action. 3 *Steph. Com.*

Since the Judicature Act, 1875, a non-suit has the same effect as a judgment upon the merits for the defendant and a plaintiff cannot now elect to be non-suited and bring his action over again.

NOT FOUND. [IGNORAMUS.]

NOT GUILTY. The plea of the general issue in actions of trespass (or trespass on the case), and in criminal trials. But there is this difference between the two cases. In criminal cases special matter, as, for instance, matter by way of justification, may in general be given in evidence on a plea of not guilty; whereas in civil actions special matter must in general be specially pleaded. 3 *Steph. Com.*; 4 *Steph. Com.*

Under the present rules of pleading, it is not sufficient for a defendant in his defence to deny generally the facts alleged by the plaintiff's statement of claim, but he must deal specifically with each allegation of fact of which he does not admit the truth. *R. S. C.* 1883, *Ord. XIX. r.* 17. But by rule 12 of the same Order, nothing in these rules contained is to affect the right of any defendant to plead "not guilty by statute.". [GENERAL ISSUE, PLEA OF.]

NOT GUILTY BY STATUTE. A plea of the general issue by a defendant in a civil action, when he intends to give special matter in evidence by virtue of some Act or Acts of parliament; in which case he must add the reference to such Act or Acts, and state whether such Acts are public or otherwise. *R. S. C.* 1883, *Ord. XXI., r.* 19. But if a defendant so plead, he will not be allowed to plead any other defence without the leave of the court or a judge. *Ibid., Ord. XIX., r.* 12.

NOT PROVEN. A verdict of a jury in a Scotch criminal trial, to the effect that the guilt of the accused is not made out, though his innocence is not clear. The legal effect of such a verdict is the same as that of a verdict of Not Guilty.

NOTARY, or **NOTARY PUBLIC** (Lat. *Registrarius, Actuarius, Notarius*), is one that attests deeds or writings to make them authentic in another country. He is generally a solicitor. 3 *Steph. Com.*

It is the office of a notary, among other things, at the request of the holder of a bill of exchange of which acceptance or payment is refused, to *note* and *protest* the same. *Byles on Bills*; 2 *Steph. Com.* [NOTING A BILL.]

NOTE OF A FINE. An abstract which used to be made by the chirographer of the proceedings in a fine, before it was engrossed. Abolished by 3 & 4 Will. 4, c. 74. 1 *Steph. Com.* [FINE, 1.]

NOTE OF HAND is the same as a promissory note. 2 *Steph. Com.* [PROMISSORY NOTE.]

NOTICE is a word which sometimes means knowledge, either actual, or imputed by construction of law; sometimes a formal notification of some fact, or some intention of the party giving the notice; sometimes the expression of a demand or requisition. See the following titles.

NOTICE OF ACTION is a notice to a person of an action intended to be brought against him, which is required by statute to be given in certain cases. Thus a justice of the peace was entitled to one calendar month's notice of an action to be brought against him for an oversight in the discharge of his office. See now 56 & 67 Vict. c. 61; 2 *Steph. Com.*

NOTICE OF DISHONOUR is a notice that a bill of exchange has been dishonoured. This notice the holder of a dishonoured bill is bound to give promptly to those to whom, as drawers or indorsers, he wishes to have recourse for payment of the bill. The rules as to notice of dishonour are contained in the 49th section of the Bills of Exchange Act, 1882. 2 *Steph. Com.*; *Byles on Bills.* [BILL OF EXCHANGE; DISHONOUR.]

NOTICE OF MOTION. [MOTION.]

NOTICE OF TITLE is where an intending mortgagee or purchaser has knowledge, by himself or his agent, of some right or title in the property adverse to that of his mortgagor or vendor. Thus we speak of a *bonâ fide* purchaser for valuable consideration *without notice*; meaning that the purchaser of the property has paid the price to those who, he believed, had the right to sell.

"Notice" does not of necessity imply actual knowledge. For whatever is sufficient to put a man of ordinary prudence on an inquiry is constructive notice of everything to which that inquiry might have led. Thus, negligence in investigating a title will not exempt a purchaser from responsibility for knowledge of facts stated in the deeds which are necessary to establish the title.

In reference to real property, the doctrine of notice is mainly important as between a prior owner or incumbrancer of an *equitable* interest in the land, and a subsequent purchaser of the

NOTICE OF TITLE—*continued.*

legal estate. The subsequent purchaser will be preferred, if, when he advanced his money, he had no notice of the equitable incumbrance; but not otherwise.

As between incumbrancers on a fund in the hands of trustees, it is notice to the trustees which regulates the respective priorities of the incumbrancers; so that a prior incumbrancer neglecting to give notice of his claim will be postponed to a subsequent incumbrancer who gives notice. *Sm. Man. Eq.* [Constructive Notice.]

NOTICE OF TRIAL. The notice given by a plaintiff to a defendant that he intends to bring on the cause for trial. It may be given with the reply (if any), or at any time after the issues of fact are ready for trial, and must be a ten days' notice at least, unless the defendant be under terms to take "short notice," in which case a four days' notice is sufficient. 3 *Steph. Com.; R. S. C.* 1883, *Ord. XXXVI. rr.* 11, 14.

NOTICE TO ADMIT is where one party in an action calls on another to admit a document, saving all just exceptions, or to admit certain facts. If the party so called on should neglect or refuse to give the admission, he will bear the cost of proving the same, unless the judge certify that such refusal was reasonable. 3 *Steph. Com.; R. S. C.* 1883, *Ord. XXXII. rr.* 2 and 4.

NOTICE TO PRODUCE. A notice by one party in an action to the other to produce, at the trial, certain documents in his possession or power relating to any matter in question in the action. If, after receiving this notice, the party do not produce them, then secondary evidence of their contents may be given. 3 *Steph. Com.*

NOTICE TO QUIT. A notice often required to be given by landlord to tenant, or by tenant to landlord, before the tenancy can be terminated. In cases of a tenancy from year to year, the notice required is generally a six months' notice. The length of notice may vary according to special agreement between the parties or by local custom, or under the Agricultural Holdings Act, 1883; s. 33 of which requires a year's notice in cases where the Act applies. 1 *Steph. Com.; Woodfall, L. & T.*

NOTICE TO THIRD PARTY. [Third Party.]

NOTICE TO TREAT. A notice given under the Lands Clauses Consolidation Act, 1845, by public bodies having compulsory powers of purchasing land, to the persons interested in the land which they propose to purchase for the purposes of their undertaking. *Ibid., ss.* 18 *et. seq.*

NOTING A BILL. When a bill of exchange is not duly paid on presentation the holder applies to a notary-public, who again presents the bill; if not paid, he makes a memorandum of the non-payment, which is called *noting the bill.* Such memorandum by the officer consists of his initials, the month, day and year, and his charges for minuting; and is considered as the preparatory step to a protest. *Byles on Bills.* [Protesting a Bill.]

NOVA STATUTA (new statutes). An appellation sometimes given to the statutes which have been passed since the beginning of the reign of Edw. III. 1 *Steph. Com.*

NOVATIO NON PRÆSUMITUR (novation is not presumed).

NOVATION. The substitution of a new obligation for an old one, or of a new debtor for an old one, with the consent of the creditor. See 35 & 36 *Vict. c.* 41, *s.* 7

NOVEL DISSEISIN originally signified a disseisin committed since the last eyre or circuit of justices. [Assize of Novel Disseisin; Disseisin; Eyre.]

NOVELS (Lat. *Novellæ Constitutiones*) were Constitutions of the Emperor Justinian, published after the completion of the Code. [Constitution; Corpus Juris Civilis.]

NUDE CONTRACT, or **NUDUM PACTUM**. A bare promise of a thing without any "consideration" or equivalent. 2 *Steph. Com.* [Consideration.]

NUISANCE. Whatsoever unlawfully annoys or doth damage to another. Nuisances are of two kinds: (1) public or common nuisances, which affect the public and are an annoyance to all, or at least to an indefinite number, of the King's subjects, *e.g.*, the obstructing of a highway; the remedy is usually by indictment; (2) private nuisances, which cause special damage to particular persons, or a limited and definite number of persons, and do not amount to trespasses, *e.g.*, where one man so

NUISANCE—*continued.*
uses his own property as to injure another : the remedy in this case is usually by action for an injunction and damages. 3 *Steph. Com. ;* 4 *Steph. Com.*

NUL DISSEISIN. A plea of the general issue in the action of *novel disseisin,* now abolished. [ASSIZE OF NOVEL DISSEISIN ; GENERAL ISSUE, PLEA OF.]

NUL TIEL AGARD or **RECORD** (no such award or record). A plea by a defendant in an action traversing an award or record, *i.e.,* denying the existence of the award or record. 3 *Steph. Com.*

NUL TORT was, like *nul disseisin,* a plea of the general issue in the action of *novel disseisin,* now abolished. [ASSIZE OF NOVEL DISSEISIN.]

NULLA BONA (no goods). A return made by the sheriff to the writ of *fieri facias,* when there are no goods within the county out of which to levy the distress. [RETURN.]

NULLITY OF MARRIAGE. A matrimonial suit instituted for the purpose of obtaining a decree declaring a supposed marriage null and void, *e.g.,* on the ground that one of the parties is impotent. 2 *Steph. Com.*

NULLIUS FILIUS (the son of no man). An expression sometimes applied to a bastard. 1 *Steph. Com. ;* 2 *Steph. Com.*

NULLUM TEMPUS OCCURRIT REGI (no time can prejudice the king). The Statutes of Limitations do not, as a rule, run against the sovereign. This rule has been modified by the Nullum Tempus Act (9 Geo. 3, c. 16), and by 24 & 25 Vict. c. 62.

NUNC PRO TUNC. Now instead of then ; meaning that a judgment is entered, or document enrolled, so as to have the same legal force and effect as if it had been entered or enrolled on some earlier day. See 3 *Steph. Com.*

NUNCUPATIVE WILL. A will declared by a testator before a sufficient number of witnesses, and afterwards reduced into writing. *Wms. Exors.* Nuncupative wills are not now allowed, except in the case of soldiers and sailors on actual service. 2 *Steph. Com.*

NUNQUAM INDEBITATUS. [NEVER INDEBTED.]

NURTURE, GUARDIAN FOR. [GUARDIAN, 1., 2.]

O. NI (*Oneratur, nisi habet sufficientem exonerationem*—Let him be charged, unless he have sufficient excuse). A mark formerly set against a sheriff when he had entered into his accounts in the Exchequer, to indicate that he thenceforth became the king's debtor for such accounts.

O YES. [OYEZ.]

OATH EX OFFICIO was the oath by which a clergyman charged with a criminal offence was formerly allowed to swear himself to be innocent ; also the oath by which the compurgators swore that they believed in his innocence. 3 *Steph. Com.* [COMPURGATORS.]

OATH OF ALLEGIANCE. An oath to bear true allegiance to the sovereign, required from most officers of the Crown. 2 *Steph. Com.* [ALLEGIANCE ; NATURALIZATION.]

OATHS. The Oaths Act, 1888 (51 & 52 Vict.), allows an affirmation instead of an oath to be made in all places and for all purposes where an oath is or shall be required by law. 2 *Steph. Com.*

OBITER DICTUM. A dictum of a judge on a point not directly relevant to the case before him.

OBJECTS OF A POWER. Where property is settled subject to a power given to any person or persons to appoint the same among a limited class, the members of the class are called the *objects of the power.* Thus, if a parent has a power to appoint a fund among his children, the children are called the objects of the power. [POWER.]

OBJURGATRIX. A common scold. [CUCKING-STOOL.]

OBLATIONS. Offerings to the Church, part of the revenues of the clergy. 2 *Steph. Com.*

OBLIGATION. 1. Legal or moral duty as opposed to physical compulsion. *Aust. Jur., Lect. XXIII.*

2. A bond containing a penalty, with a condition annexed, for the payment of money, performance of covenants, or the like.

OBLIGOR. The person bound by an obligation to another person, called the *obligee,* who is entitled to the benefit of the bond or obligation. 2 *Steph. Com.*

OBSCENE BOOKS, ETC. [INDECENT PRINTS.]

OBVENTIONS. Offerings or tithes. 2 *Steph. Com.*

OCCUPANCY. The taking possession of those things which before belonged to nobody. 1 *Steph. Com.; 2 Steph. Com.*

OCCUPANT. One who takes property by occupancy. [OCCUPANCY.] Especially one who entered upon land on the death of tenant *pur auter vie*, living *cestui que vie.* That is, A. having an estate during the life of B., and dying in B.'s lifetime, C. entered ; C. was called an *occupant.* If C. had no right prior to his entry, he was called a *general occupant*, and his occupancy was called *common occupancy*, but if he entered as A.'s heir under a grant to A. and his heirs, he was called a *special occupant.* Common occupancy cannot now exist. See Wills Act (7 Will. 4 & 1 Vict. c. 26), ss. 3, 6. 1 *Steph. Com.* [ADMINISTRATOR ; AUTRE VIE ; CESTUI QUE VIE ; CHATTELS ; EXECUTOR.]

OCCUPATION. 1. The putting a man out of his freehold in time of war, corresponding to disseisin in time of peace.
2. The use, tenure, or possession of land.
3. An usurpation upon the king, as when one uses liberties which one has not. [LIBERTY.]

OCCUPIER. The person residing or having the right to reside in or upon any house, land or place. He is rateable to the poor rate, and as the "inhabitant occupier" is entitled to the parliamentary franchise. See the *Representation of the People Acts*, 1867 & 1884. 2 *Steph. Com.; 3 Steph. Com.*

OFF-GOING CROP. [AWAY-GOING CROP.]

OFFICE. A species of incorporeal hereditament, consisting in the right to exercise a publc or private employment. But, in its more limited sense, it is a right which entitles a man to act in the affairs of others without their appointment or permission. 2 *Steph. Com.*

OFFICE COPY is a copy, made under the sanction of a public office, of any deed, record, or other instrument in writing deposited therein.

OFFICE FOUND is when, by an *inquest of office*, facts are found entitling the Crown to any real or personal property by forfeiture or otherwise. 3 *Steph. Com.* [INQUEST.]

OFFICE, INQUEST OF. [INQUEST.]

OFFICE OF A JUDGE. A criminal suit in an ecclesiastical court, not being directed to the reparation of a private injury, is regarded as a proceeding emanating from the *office of the judge*, and may be instituted by the mere motion of the judge. But in practice these suits are instituted by private individuals, with the permission of the judge or his surrogate ; and the private prosecutor in any such case is, accordingly, said to *promote the office of the judge.*

OFFICIAL, or OFFICIAL PRINCIPAL, in the ancient civil law signified him who was the minister of, or attendant upon, a magistrate. In the canon law, it is especially taken for him to whom any bishop doth generally commit the charge of his spiritual jurisdiction, and in this sense the chancellor of the diocese is called the official principal. The word official also includes the deputy of an archdeacon. *Phillimore's Eccl. Law; 3 Steph. Com.*

OFFICIAL ASSIGNEES. Officers of the bankruptcy courts appointed by the Lord Chancellor under the Bankruptcy Acts for the purpose of acting, as occasion might require, with other assignees in the winding up of bankrupts' estates.
By the Bankruptcy Act, 1869 (32 & 33 Vict. c. 71), these officers are abolished ; but the "Official Receivers" established by the Act of 1883 resemble them. 2 *Steph. Com.; Robson, Bkcy.*

OFFICIAL LIQUIDATOR. The Official Receiver or one of the same nominated by the Board of Trade in case of an order for the compulsory winding up of a company, is to bring and defend suits and actions in the name of the company, and generally to do all things necessary for winding up the affairs of the company, until he or any other person shall on the application of the creditors or contributories be appointed by the court as liquidator. If *he* be appointed he is then called Official Receiver and Liquidator. 3 *Steph. Com.* [LIQUIDATOR.]

OFFICIAL RECEIVERS. Officials appointed by the Board of Trade, who act as interim receivers and managers of bankrupts' estates. See *s.* 66 of the *Bankruptcy Act*, 1883.

OFFICIAL LOG BOOK. [LOG.]

OFFICIAL PRINCIPAL. [OFFICIAL.]

OFFICIAL REFEREES are officers attached to the Supreme Court of Judicature, to whom the trial of any question arising in any civil proceeding before the High Court of Justice may be referred by the court. The law as to references has been amended and consolidated by the Arbitration Act, 1889 (52 & 53 Vict. c. 49). 3 *Steph. Com.*

OLD BAILEY SESSIONS. Superseded by Central Criminal Court.

OLD STYLE. The mode of reckoning time which prevailed in this country until the year 1752. This method differed from the *New Style* at present in use in the following particulars :—
1. The year commenced on the 25th of March, instead of, as now, on the 1st of January.
2. The reckoning of days was based on the assumption that every fourth year was a leap-year, no exception being admitted ; instead of, as now, but 97 leap-years in 400 years.
3. The rules for determining the feast of Easter were far less elaborate than at present.
So far as regards the second point above mentioned, the Old Style is still observed in Russia.
The New Style was introduced into the British dominions by stat. 24 Geo. 2, c. 23, passed in 1751, and came into operation in the following year. It had prevailed in the Roman Catholic countries of the Continent since the year 1582.

OLD TENURES. A treatise on tenures in the reign of Edw. III. It is called " Old Tenures," to distinguish it from Littleton's book on the subject of tenures. [LITTLETON.]

OLERON, LAWS OF. A code of maritime laws compiled in the twelfth century by King Rich. I. at the isle of the bay of Aquitaine, on the coast of France, then part of the possessions of the Crown of England. 2 *Steph. Com.*; 3 *Steph. Com.*

OMNE MAJUS CONTINET IN SE MINUS (the greater contains the less).

OMNE QUOD SOLO INÆDIFICATUR SOLO CEDIT (everything built upon the soil belongs to the soil).

OMNIA PRÆSUMUNTUR CONTRA SPOLIATOREM (all things are presumed against a wrong-doer).

OMNIA PRÆSUMUNTUR SOLEMNITER (or **RITE**) **ESSE ACTA** (all things are presumed to have been done rightly).

OMNIS RATIHABITIO RATIO-TRAHITUR ET MANDATO PRIORI ÆQUIPARATUR (every ratification has a retrospective effect, and is equivalent to a previous request).

OMNIUM. A term used on the Stock Exchange, to express the aggregate value of the different stocks in which a loan is usually funded.

ONUS PROBANDI. The burden of proof. [BURDEN OF PROOF.]

OPEN POLICY. An *open policy* is one in which the value of the subject insured is not fixed or agreed upon in the policy, but is left to be estimated in case of loss. An *open policy* is opposed to a *valued policy*, in which the value of the subject insured is fixed for the purpose of the insurance, and expressed on the face of the policy. *Arnould, Mar. Ins.* [INSURANCE.]

OPENING A COMMISSION is the commencement of the judicial proceedings at an assize, by the reading of the commissions by virtue of which the judges sit to try cases.

OPENING BIDDINGS is where an estate having been put up and sold by auction, it is again put up to competition. This practice long prevailed in sales under the authority of the Court of Chancery, if, after the sale, an intending purchaser offered a large increase over the price at which the estate had been actually knocked down ; so that a *bonâ fide* purchaser was never sure of his bargain. This practice is abolished by 30 & 31 Vict. c. 48, s. 7 ; and the opening of biddings is now allowed only in cases of fraud or misconduct in the sale. *Wms. R. P.*

OPENING PLEADINGS is the statement, in a concise form, of the pleadings in a case by the junior counsel for the plaintiff, for the instruction of the jury. 3 *Steph. Com.*

OPERATIVE PART OF A DEED is that part whereby the object of the deed is effected, as opposed to the recitals, etc. [RECITALS.]

OPTION. 1. The archbishop has a customary prerogative, when a bishop is consecrated by him, to name a clerk or chaplain of his own to be provided for by such bishop ; in lieu of which the bishop used to make over by deed to the archbishop, his executors and assigns, the next presentation of such dignity or benefice in the diocese within the bishop's disposal, as the archbishop himself should choose ; which, therefore, was called his *option*. Disused. 2 *Steph. Com.*

2. The word is also used on the Stock Exchange to express a right to take or sell stock on a future day. [TIME BARGAIN.]

3. An option of purchase in a lease is the right given to the lessee to purchase, during the term, the reversion.

OPTIONAL WRIT. Original writs were either *optional* or *peremptory*. An optional writ, otherwise called a *præcipe*, was a writ commanding a defendant to do a thing required, or else to show the reason wherefore he had not done it ; thus giving the defendant his choice, either to redress the injury, or to stand the suit. [ORIGINAL WRIT.]

ORAL PLEADINGS. Pleadings put in *virâ voce* in court, which was formerly done in civil cases until the reign of Edw. III.

ORATOR. A word formerly used in bills in Chancery to denote the plaintiff ; *oratrix* being the word used to denote a female plaintiff.

ORDEAL, or **ORDEL.** The most ancient species of trial, called also *judicium Dei* (the judgment of God), and based generally on the notion that God would interpose miraculously to vindicate an earthly right. This was of four sorts : (1) fire ordeal, (2) hot water ordeal (3) cold water ordeal, (4) ordeal by combat or battle. 4 *Steph. Com.*

ORDER. Any command of a superior to an inferior may be so called. But the word is frequently applied to those acts of courts of justice which do not dispose of the merits of any case before them, *e.g.*, in interlocutory proceedings.

Besides these orders, which are applicable merely in particular instances, there are what are called General Orders, which are framed by courts of justice, sometimes by virtue of their inherent jurisdiction, but now more frequently under the express authority of some statute ; such are the Consolidated "Rules of the Supreme Court 1883," which are divided into Orders and subdivided into rules.

ORDER AND DISPOSITION is a phrase denoting the apparent possession, on the part of a bankrupt, of goods not his own, with the consent of the true owner. In such case the title of the trustee in the bankruptcy, as representing the creditors, will in general prevail over that of the person claiming the goods as owner. See *Bankruptcy Act*, 1883, *s.* 44 ; and *Bills of Sale Act*, 1882, *s.* 15. 2 *Steph. Com.* ; *Robson, Bkcy.*

ORDER OF DISCHARGE. An order obtainable by a bankrupt after passing his public examination, made by a court of bankruptcy, which has the effect of releasing the bankrupt from his debts, except such as are due to the Crown, and such as have been incurred by fraud. *Bankruptcy Act*, 1883, *s.* 28 ; 2 *Steph. Com.; Robson, Bkcy.*

ORDER OF REVIVOR. [ABATEMENT, 4 ; REVIVOR.]

ORDER, PAYABLE TO. A bill or note payable to order is a bill or note payable to a given person, or as he shall direct by any indorsement he may make thereon. Until he has so indorsed it, no one else can maintain an action upon it ; and in this respect it differs from a bill or note *payable to bearer*. 2 *Steph. Com.*

ORDINANCE OF PARLIAMENT. In ancient times there seems to have been a distinction between the *statutes* and *ordinances* of parliament. A *statute* was drawn up with the advice and deliberation of the judges and other learned men, and was entered on a roll called the *statute roll* ; whereas *ordinances* appear to have been answers of the king to the great men and commons in parliament, entered upon the parliament roll. Ordinances were, in theory, merely declaratory of the existing law.

ORDINARY. 1. In the civil law, an *ordinary* signifies any judge that hath authority to take cognizance of causes in his own right, and not by deputation.

2. In the common law, it is taken for him that hath exempt and immediate jurisdiction in causes ecclesiastical, who is generally the bishop of the diocese. 2 *Steph. Com.*

ORDINATION. The admission by the bishop of any person to the order of priest or deacon. 2 *Steph. Com.*

ORDNANCE OFFICE, or **BOARD OF ORDNANCE,** was a public department consisting of six officers, under the control of the Master General. It was the duty of the Master General and the Board to direct all matters relating to the Corps of Artillery and Engineers, and to superintend the construction and repair of fortifications, barracks, and military buildings in the United Kingdom and in the Colonies, and of the Colonial Government Buildings ; also the supply of arms, ammunition, and military stores for the army and navy.

By stat. 18 & 19 Vict. c. 117, these powers and duties were transferred to the Secretary of State for War.

ORDNANCE SURVEY, THE, of Great Britain and the Isle of Man was first authorised in 1841, and has since been continued from time to time.

ORIGINAL AND DERIVATIVE ESTATES. An original estate is contrasted with a derivative estate ; the latter is a particular interest carved out of a larger estate.

ORIGINAL BILL IN EQUITY was a bill filed otherwise than by way of supplement or revivor. [BILL, 2; FILING BILL IN EQUITY ; REVIVOR ; SUPPLEMENT.]

ORIGINAL WRIT was formerly the beginning or foundation of every action. When a person had received an injury for which he desired satisfaction at law, the first step in the process of obtaining redress was to sue out, or purchase, by paying the stated fees, an *original*, or *original writ*, from the Court of Chancery. This original writ was a mandatory letter from the king on parchment, sealed with his Great Seal, and directed to the sheriff of the county wherein the injury was supposed to have been committed, requiring him to command the wrongdoer or party accused either to do justice to the complainant, or else to appear in court, and answer the accusation against him. Whatever the sheriff did in pursuance of the writ, he was bound to *return* or certify to the Court of Common Pleas, together with the writ itself, which was the foundation of the jurisdiction of that court, being the king's warrant for the judges to proceed to the determination of the causes. Various devices were in course of time resorted to by the connivance of the judges, in order to avoid the expense of an original writ, until, in 1831, an Act of parliament (stat. 2 & 3 Will. 4, c. 39) was passed, called the Uniformity of Process Act, by which a comparatively simple and uniform system was introduced into actions at common law. 3 *Steph. Com.* [JUDICIAL WRIT ; WRIT.]

ORIGINATING SUMMONS. A summons whereby proceedings are commenced in the Chancery Division, and in some cases even in King's Bench Division, without the issue of a writ. Such summonses are used in a variety of matters, *e.g.*, to determine particular questions arising in the administration of a trust, where a general administration is not required. See *R. S. C. 1883, Ord. LV.*

OSTENSIBLE or **NOMINAL PARTNER** is a man who allows his credit to be pledged as a partner ; as in the case where a man's name appears in a firm, or where he interferes in the management of the business, so as to produce in strangers a reasonable belief that he is a partner. The person so acting is answerable as a partner to all who deal with the firm without having notice at the time that he is a stranger to it in point of interest. 2 *Steph. Com.*

OSTIUM ECCLESIÆ. The door of the church. [AD OSTIUM ECCLESIÆ.]

OUSTER. The dispossession of a lawful tenant, whether of freehold or chattels real, giving remedy at law, in order to gain possession, with damages for the injury sustained. 3 *Steph. Com.*

OUSTER LE MAIN (out of the hand). 1. A delivery of lands out of the king's hands by judgment given in favour of the petitioner in a *monstrans de droit.* 3 *Steph. Com.* [MONSTRANS DE DROIT.]

2. A delivery of the ward's lands out of the hands of the guardian on the former arriving at the proper age, which was twenty-one in males, and sixteen in females. Abolished by 12 Car. 2, c. 24. 1 *Steph. Com.*

OUT OF COURT. This is a colloquial phrase often applied to a litigant party, which may be otherwise expressed by saying that " he has not a leg to stand on." Thus, when the principal witness, who was expected to prove a party's case, breaks down, it is often said, " that puts him *out of court*."

OUTER BAR. A phrase applied to the junior barristers who plead " ouster " or outside the bar, as opposed to King's Counsel, who are admitted to plead within the bar.

OUTLAWRY. Putting a man out of the protection of the law, so that he became incapable of bringing an action for redress of injuries, and forfeited all his goods and chattels to the king. Now abolished except against an absconding defendant in a proceeding for treason or felony. Pleas in abatement being abolished in ordinary civil actions under the Judicature Rules, it would seem that an outlaw is no longer disabled to sue. *R. S. C.* 1883, *Ord. XXI. r.* 20 ; 3 *Steph. Com. ;* 4 *Steph. Com.*

OUTSTANDING TERM. A term of years (that is, an interest for a definite period of time [TERM, 2]) in land, of which the legal estate was vested in some person other than the owner of the inheritance, in trust for such owner ; such a term was said to *attend* or *protect* the inheritance, because it took priority of any charges which might have been made upon the inheritance, of which the owner had no notice when he took his conveyance and paid his purchase-money. [NOTICE OF TITLE.] But in such case if the owner took an assignment of the term for himself, it would become merged and lost in the inheritance [MERGER] ; and he would lose the benefit of its protection. The Satisfied Terms Act, 1845 (8 & 9 Vict. c. 112), provided that such terms should for the future cease and determine, on becoming attendant upon the inheritance. 1 *Steph. Com. ; Wms. R. P.*

OVER. In conveyancing, a gift or limitation *over* signifies one which is to come into existence on the determination of a particular estate.

OVER INSURANCE is where the whole amount insured in different policies is greater than the whole value of the interest at risk. *Arnould, Mar. Ins.*

OVERDUE BILL OR NOTE. A bill or note is said to be *overdue* so long as it remains unpaid after the time for payment is past.

OVERSEERS. Officers appointed in each parish, under stat. 43 Eliz. c. 2, to provide for the poor of the parish. By that statute it was enacted that the churchwardens of the parish should be overseers. In rural parishes the jurisdiction of the churchwardens as overseers has been put an end to by the Local Government Act, 1894, the overseers now being appointed by the parish council or parish meeting.

The duty of making and levying the poor rate belongs to the overseers (it being signed by two magistrates) ; and the concurrence of the inhabitants is not necessary. The overseers are charged with the duty of preparing the lists of parliamentary and municipal voters.

OVERT (Fr. *Ouvert*). Open : thus, an overt act is an open act, as opposed to an intention conceived in the mind, which can be judged of only by overt acts. 4 *Steph. Com.* [MARKET OVERT ; POUND.]

OYER. 1. To hear. 2. Assizes.

OYER AND TERMINER. To hear and determine ; a commission issued to judges and others for hearing and determining cases upon indictments found at the assizes, being the largest of the commissions by which our judges of assize sit in their several circuits. 3 *Steph. Com. ;* 4 *Steph. Com.* [ASSIZE, COURTS OF.]

OYER OF DEEDS AND RECORDS. The hearing them read in court. Formerly, a party suing upon or pleading any deed was bound to make *profert* of the same, that is, to bring it into court (Lat. *profert in curiam*), and the opposite party was entitled to crave *oyer* of the same ; that is, to have it read by the officer of the court. Abolished by the C. L. P. Act, 1852.

OYEZ (hear ye). Now generally pronounced O yes. It is used by criers in courts and elsewhere when they make proclamation of anything.

PACKAGE. A duty formerly charged in the port of London on goods imported and exported by aliens.

PACT. A promise or contract.

PAINS AND PENALTIES, ACTS OF, for attainting particular persons of treason or felony, or for inflicting pains and penalties beyond or contrary to the common law. It is an incident of such bills that persons to be affected by them have, by custom, the right to be heard at the bar of the House in opposition to the bill.

PAIRING OFF. A kind of system of negative proxies, by which a member whose opinions would lead him to vote on one side of a question agrees with a member on the opposite side that they both shall be absent at the same time, so that a vote is neutralised on each side. This practice has been resorted to for many years in the House of Commons. Sometimes members of opposite parties pair with each other, not only upon particular questions, but even for weeks or months at a time. *May's Parl. Pract.*

PAIS, or **PAYS.** The country. A trial *per pais* is a trial by the country, that is, by a jury; and matter *in pais* is matter triable by the country; that is, an ordinary matter of fact. 3 *Steph. Com.* [MATTER, 2.] A conveyance of land *in pais* meant originally a conveyance on the spot to be transferred. 1 *Steph. Com.*

PALATINE. [COUNTY PALATINE.]

PANDECTS. A name given to the Digest of Roman Law, compiled by order of the Emperor Justinian. [CORPUS JURIS CIVILIS.]

PANEL. A schedule or roll of parchment containing the names of jurors which the sheriff hath returned to pass upon any trial. 3 *Steph. Com.;* 4 *Steph. Com.*

PANNAGE, or **PAWNAGE.** 1. The food which swine feed on in the woods, as mast of beech, acorns, etc.
2. Money taken by the *agisters* for the same. [AGIST.]

PANNEL. [PANEL.]

PAPER BLOCKADE. When a blockade is proclaimed in time of war, and the naval force on watch is not sufficient to repel attempts to enter or get out, the blockade is called a **paper blockade** as opposed to a *good* or *effective* blockade.

PAPER BOOKS. Copies of the demurrer-book taken for the perusal of the judges. [DEMURRER BOOK.]

PAPER OFFICE. 1. An ancient office within the palace of Whitehall, wherein state papers are kept.
2. An ancient office belonging to the Court of King's Bench, where the records of the court were kept.

PARAGE. Equality of name, blood, or dignity; also of lands to be partitioned. Hence comes the word *disparagement*, which signifies inequality. [DISPARAGEMENT.]

PARAMOUNT. 1. The supreme lord of a fee. Thus, the king is lord paramount of all the lands in the kingdom. 1 *Steph. Com.*
2. The word is also frequently used in a *relative* sense, to denote a superior lord as opposed to a mesne lord holding under him.

PARAPHERNALIA (Gr. παρὰ φερνήν). *Things besides dower;* the goods which a wife, besides her dower or jointure, is, after her husband's death, allowed to have, as furniture for her chamber, and wearing apparel. 2 *Steph. Com.*

PARAVAIL. The lowest tenant; being he who was supposed to make *avail* or profit of the land. It is thus the reverse of *paramount*. 1 *Steph. Com.* [PARAMOUNT.]

PARCEL (Lat. *Particula*). A small piece of land.
A description of *parcels*, in a deed, is a description of lands with reference to their boundaries and local extent.
A *bill of parcels* is an account of the items composing a parcel or package of goods, transmitted with them to a purchaser.

PARCENERS. The same as *coparceners;* those who hold an estate in coparcenary. [COPARCENARY.]

PARDON is either (1) by the sovereign in virtue of the prerogative, or (2) by Act of parliament.
(1) Must be pleaded specially and at a proper time; it cannot however be pleaded in bar of an impeachment by the Commons.
(2) Need not be pleaded, but the court is bound to take notice of it. 4 *Steph. Com.*

PARENS PATRIÆ (parent of his country). A title sometimes applied to the king or queen. *2 Steph. Com.*

PARENTELA. Kindred. *De parentelâ se tollere* was to renounce one's kindred. This was done in open court before a judge, and in the presence of twelve men, who made oath that they believed it was done lawfully, and for a just cause. This renunciation incapacitated the person from inheriting from any of his kindred.

PARES. Peers, equals. Thus, the various tenants of the same manor were called *pares curtis* or *pares curiæ*, as being *equals* in attendance upon the lord's court. *1 Steph. Com.* [PEERS.]

PARI PASSU. On an equal footing, or proportionately. A phrase used especially of the creditors of an insolvent estate, who (with certain exceptions) are entitled to payment of their debts in shares proportioned to their respective claims. [PRIVILEGED DEBTS.]

PARISH. A circuit of ground committed to the charge of one parson or vicar, or other minister having the cure of souls therein. *1 Steph. Com.* See also the definition in sect. 5 of the Interpretation Act, 1889.

PARISH APPRENTICES. The children of parents unable to maintain them may by law be *apprenticed*, by the guardians or overseers of their parish, to such persons as may be willing to receive them as apprentices. Such children are called *parish apprentices*. The reception of a parish apprentice was formerly compulsory, but, by 7 & 8 Vict. c. 101, s. 13, this is no longer so. *2 Steph. Com.*

PARISH CLERK. An officer of a church, generally appointed by the incumbent. By custom, however, he may be chosen by the inhabitants. Formerly, the parish clerk was very frequently in holy orders, and was appointed to officiate at the altar ; but now his duty consists chiefly in making responses in church to the minister. By the common law he has a freehold in his office. *2 Steph. Com.* The office seems now to be falling into desuetude.

PARISH COUNCILS. Established by the Local Government Act, 1894 (56 & 57 Vict. c. 73), for rural parishes with populations of 300 and upwards. Their principal duties are to appoint overseers of the poor and to manage parish property.

PARISH MEETING. Established for every rural parish by the Local Government Act, 1894. Its principal duty is to elect the parish council (if any), and if none, it takes the place of the parish council.

PARISH OFFICERS. Churchwardens, overseers, and constables.

PARK, in a legal sense, is a piece of ground enclosed, and stored with beasts of chase, which a man may have by prescription, or the king's grant. *1 Steph. Com.*

PARLIAMENT. A solemn conference of all the estates of the kingdom, summoned together by the authority of the Crown, to treat of the weighty affairs of the realm. The constituent parts of the parliament are the sovereign and the three estates of the realm, namely, the lords spiritual and lords temporal, who sit, together with the sovereign, in one house, and the commons, who sit by themselves, in another. *2 Steph. Com.; May's Parl. Pract.* [ESTATES OF THE REALM ; HOUSE OF COMMONS ; HOUSE OF LORDS ; LORDS SPIRITUAL ; LORDS TEMPORAL.]

PARLIAMENTARY AGENTS are agents (generally solicitors) who, in parliament, promote or oppose the passing of private bills, and conduct other proceedings for pecuniary reward. No member or officer of the house may act as an agent. *May's Parl. Pract.*

PARLIAMENTARY COMMITTEE. A committee appointed by either house for making enquiries, *e.g.*, in the case of private bills.

PAROL. Anything done by word of mouth.

PAROL AGREEMENT. An agreement by word of mouth. Sometimes, however, the phrase is used to include writings not under seal ; since at common law, prior to the Statute of Frauds, there was no difference between an agreement by word of mouth and one in writing without seal. *2 Steph. Com.* [FRAUDS, STATUTE OF.]

PAROL ARREST. An arrest, ordered by a justice of the peace, of one who is guilty of a breach of the peace in his presence.

PAROL EVIDENCE, otherwise called *oral evidence*, is evidence given *vivâ voce* by witnesses, as opposed to that given by affidavit. As a general rule parol evidence cannot be given to contradict, alter, or vary a written instrument. Consult *Taylor on Evidence*.

PARRICIDE. He that kills his father ; or the crime of murdering a father. 4 *Steph. Com*.

PARS RATIONABILIS. A reasonable part. [DE RATIONABILI PARTE.]

PARSON (*Persona ecclesiæ*). The rector or incumbent of a parochial church, who hath full possession of all the rights thereof. He is called parson, *persona*, because by his person the church, which is an invisible body, is represented ; and he is himself a body corporate, in order to protect and defend the rights of the church, which he personates, by a perpetual succession. There are four requisites to his appointment : holy orders, presentation, institution, and induction. 2 *Steph. Com*.

PARSONAGE. A certain portion of lands, tithes, and offerings, established by law, for the maintenance of the minister who hath the cure of souls. The word is generally used for the *house* set apart for the residence of the minister. 2 *Steph. Com*.

PART OWNERS. Persons who have a share in anything, especially those who have an interest in a ship.

PARTIAL LOSS, in marine insurance, otherwise called an *average* loss, is one in which the damage done to the thing insured is not so complete as to amount to a *total loss*, either actual or constructive. In every such case the underwriter is liable to pay such proportion of the sum which would be payable on total loss, as the damage sustained by the subject of insurance bears to the whole value at the time of insurance. 2 *Steph. Com.* ; *Arnould, Mar. Ins*. [TOTAL LOSS.]

PARTICEPS CRIMINIS. An accomplice or partaker in wrongdoing.

PARTICULAR AVERAGE. [AVERAGE, 4.]

PARTICULAR ESTATE is an estate in land which precedes an estate in remainder or reversion, so called because it is a *particula*, or small part, of the inheritance. 1 *Steph. Com.* ; *Wms. R. P.* [CONTINGENT REMAINDER ; ESTATE, 2 ; REMAINDER ; REVERSION ; VESTED REMAINDER.]

PARTICULAR LIEN, as opposed to a *general lien*, is a lien upon a particular article for the price due or the labour bestowed upon that article. 2 *Steph. Com.* [GENERAL LIEN ; LIEN.]

PARTICULAR TENANT. The tenant of a particular estate. 1 *Steph. Com.* [PARTICULAR ESTATE.]

PARTICULARS OF CLAIM OR DEFENCE. By Ord. XIX. r. 4 of R. S. C., a plaintiff or defendant is required to give a statement in summary form of all material facts on which he relies for his claim or defence, and certain forms are given in the Appendices to the Rules, and in cases in which particulars may be necessary beyond those given in the forms, they are to be stated in the pleading (*r.* 6), and in default the other party may apply for further or better particulars (*r.* 7). On the summons for directions under Ord. XXX. r. 1, the master now usually orders statement of claim and defence with all necessary particulars, and if these are not given the cost of obtaining them by a further application will usually fall upon the party failing to give them.

PARTICULARS OF SALE are the particulars of the property which is to be sold, and the terms and conditions on which the sale is to take place.

PARTIES. 1. Persons who voluntarily take part in anything, in person or by attorney, as the parties to a deed.

2. Persons required to take part in any proceeding, and bound thereby, whether they do so or not ; as the defendants in a suit or action. The rules as to parties in actions will be found in R. S. C. 1883, Ord. XVI.

PARTITION. A dividing of land held in joint tenancy, in coparcenary, or in common, between the parties entitled thereto ; so that the estate in joint tenancy, coparcenary or common is destroyed, and each party has henceforth an undivided share. This may be done by agreement, by deed of partition, or compulsorily by an action in the Chancery Division. There was a *writ* of partition, but that was abolished by 3 & 4 Will. 4, c. 27, s. 36. 1 *Steph. Com*.

Under the Judicature Act, 1873, the partition of real estates is assigned to the Chancery Division of the High Court of Justice. 36 & 37 *Vict. c.* 66, *s.* 33, *sub-s.* 3. See also the Settled Land Act, 1882.

PARTNERSHIP is where two or more persons agree to carry on any business or adventure together, upon the terms of mutual participation in its profits and losses. It is generally constituted by a deed, the provisions of which are usually denominated *articles of partnership*. The law on the subject was codified by the Partnership Act, 1890. 2 *Steph. Com.* ; *Lindley on Partnership.*

PARTY AND PARTY, COSTS AS BE-TWEEN. [COSTS.]

PARTY-WALL. A wall adjoining lands or houses belonging to two different owners. The common user of such a wall by the adjoining owners is *primâ facie* evidence that it belongs to them in equal moieties as tenants in common. *Gale on Easements* ; *Fawcett, L. & T.*

PASSAGE COURT. An ancient court of record in Liverpool, originally called the Mayor's Court of Pays Sage, but now usually called the Court of the Passage of the Borough of Liverpool. It has jurisdiction in causes of action arising within the borough and also in Admiralty matters. 3 *Steph. Com.*

PASSIVE TRUST. A trust in which the trustee has no active duty to perform. 1 *Steph. Com.* [BARE TRUSTEE.]

PASSPORT means strictly a licence to *pass* a *port* or haven ; that is, a licence for the safe passage of any man from one place to another. 2 *Steph. Com.*

PASTURE. Any place where cattle may feed ; also feeding for cattle. [COMMON, I.]

PATENT. Letters patent from the Crown. 1 *Steph. Com.* [LETTERS PATENT.] These are granted for various purposes ; among other things, for conferring a peerage. But the term *patent*, or *patent right*, is usually restricted to mean a privilege granted by letters patent from the Crown to the first inventor of any new contrivance in manufacture, that he alone shall be entitled, during a limited period, to benefit by his own invention. This is one of the exceptions reserved in the Statute of Monopolies, 21 Jac. 1, c. 3, passed in 1623, by which the granting of monopolies is in general forbidden. From this general prohibition are excepted all letters patent for the term of fourteen years or under, by which the privilege of sole working or making any new manufactures within this realm, which others at the time of granting the letters patent shall not use, shall be granted to the true and first inventor thereof ; "so as they be not contrary to law, nor mischievous to the State, nor to the hurt of trade, nor generally inconvenient." The grant of a patent right is not *ex debito justitiæ*, but is an act of royal favour ; though in a fit case it is never refused.

The mode in which a patent is to be obtained is prescribed by the Patent Acts, 1883 and 1888.

PATENT OF PRECEDENCE. Letters patent granted to such barristers as the Crown thinks fit to honour with that mark of distinction, whereby they are entitled to such rank and pre-audience as are assigned in their respective patents, which is sometimes next after the Attorney-General, but more usually next after his Majesty's counsel then being. These rank promiscuously with the king's (or queen's) counsel, but are not the sworn servants of the Crown. 3 *Steph. Com.*

PATENT RIGHT. [PATENT.]

PATENTEE. A person to whom a patent is granted. 2 *Steph. Com.*

PATRICIDE. [PARRICIDE.]

PATRIMONY. An hereditary estate. The legal endowment of a church or religious house was called ecclesiastical patrimony.

PATRON. In the canon and common law, signifies him that hath the gift of a benefice. 2 *Steph. Com.*

PAUPER. 1. A person who, on account of his poverty, becomes chargeable to the parish. 3 *Steph. Com.*
2. A person who, on account of his poverty, is admitted to sue or defend *in formâ pauperis*. [FORMA PAUPERIS.]

PAWN. The transfer of a chattel as security for a debt. [PLEDGE.]

PAYEE. A person to whom, or to whose order, a bill of exchange or promissory note is expressed to be payable. 2 *Steph. Com.*

PAYMASTER-GENERAL. A public officer whose duties consist in the payment of all the voted services for the army and navy, and all charges connected with the naval and military expenditure. The Paymaster-General likewise makes payments for the civil services in England, and for some in Scotland. By the Court of Chancery (Funds) Act, 1872 (35 & 36 Vict. c. 44), the office of Accountant-General is abolished, and its duties transferred to that of the Paymaster-General. See *Jud. Act*, 1875, *s.* 24.

PAYMENT OF MONEY INTO COURT. 1. *At Common Law.* This is when a defendant in an action at law pays money into court (with or without a denial of liability), together with the costs already incurred, in order to save the expense of further proceedings. 3 *Steph. Com.* If the plaintiff does not accept the amount paid in, and the jury find that it is sufficient, the defendant will be entitled to the judgment and his costs of suit.

A defendant may, in an action brought to recover a debt or damages, pay into court a sum of money in satisfaction or amends. He may do so even after delivering his defence, by leave of the court or a judge. A defendant may not, however, pay money into court in actions for libel and slander with a defence denying liability. *R. S. C.*, 1883, *Ord. XXII.*

2. *In Equity.* It frequently happens that, when there is a clear admission by a party to a suit that he holds money on trust, an order is made for payment of the sum into court. This is done through the medium of the Paymaster-General, and the department which has to deal with these payments is called the Chancery Pay Office. The payment is made in the first instance to the Bank of England, and by the Bank placed to the credit of the Chancery Pay Office Account. See sect. 30 of the Judicature Act, 1875. [PAYMASTER-GENERAL.]

PAYMENT OF MONEY OUT OF COURT. When money is to be paid out of court the order directing the payment is taken to the Chancery Pay Office, and in due course a cheque for the amount will be given by the Paymaster-General. [PAYMENT OF MONEY INTO COURT, 2.]

PEACE, BILL OF. [BILL OF PEACE.]

PEACE OF THE KING. That peace and security, both for life and goods, which the king promiseth to all his subjects, or others taken under his protection.

PECULIAR. A particular parish or church exempt from the jurisdiction of the ordinary. All ecclesiastical causes arising within them are cognizable in the Court of Peculiars. 3 *Steph. Com.* [COURT OF PECULIARS.]

PEERAGE. The dignity of the lords or peers of the realm. A *peerage case* is a case in which a question of the right to that dignity is involved. [PEERS, 2.]

PEERESS. A woman who has the dignity of peerage, either in her own right or by right of marriage. In the latter case she loses the dignity by a second marriage with a commoner. 2 *Steph. Com.*

PEERS (Lat. *Pares*). Equals. 1. Those who are impanelled in an inquest upon any man, for the convicting or clearing him of any offence for which he is called in question. "The co-vassals by whose verdict a vassal is condemned of felony."

2. Those that be of the nobility of the realm and lords of parliament. [ESTATES OF THE REALM; LORDS TEMPORAL; NOBILITY.]

PEINE FORT ET DURE. This was the punishment for standing mute of malice on an indictment of felony. Before it was pronounced the prisoner had a threefold admonition (*trina admonitio*), and also a respite of a few hours; and the sentence was distinctly read to him that he might know his danger. The sentence was that he be remanded to the prison and loaded with weights, etc., till he died or answered. It was abolished in 1772. 4 *Steph. Com.* [MUTE.]

PENAL ACTIONS. [ACTIONS CIVIL AND PENAL.]

PENAL LAWS. Laws imposing penalties or punishments for the doing of prohibited acts. 3 *Steph. Com.*

The question whether a given provision in an Act of parliament is a penal one or not, is sometimes important. For instance, it is a rule that penal statutes must be construed *strictly* (that is, narrowly).

PENAL SERVITUDE. A punishment introduced in 1853 by 16 & 17 Vict. c. 99, in lieu of transportation beyond seas. It ranges in duration from a minimum period of three years to the life of the convict. See 54 & 55 Vict. c. 69; 4 *Steph. Com.*

PENAL STATUTES. [PENAL LAWS.]

PENALTY. 1. Punishment; especially used of a pecuniary fine.

2. Money recoverable by virtue of a penal statute.

3. A sum named in a bond as the amount to be forfeited by the obligor in case he comply not with the conditions of the bond. Notwithstanding that a sum may be so named, still, in an action on the bond, a jury is directed to inquire what damages the plaintiff has sustained by breach of the condition; and the plaintiff cannot take out execution for a larger amount than the jury shall so assess. See 8 & 9 *Will.* 3. c. 11; 57 & 58 *Vict.* c. 16.

4. A sum agreed to be paid on breach of an agreement, or some stipulation in it. See LIQUIDATED DAMAGES.

PENDENTE LITE. While a suit is pending. Thus letters of administration may be granted *pendente lite*, where a suit is commenced touching the validity of a will. 2 *Steph. Com.* [ADMINISTRATOR.]

PENSION. The payment of a sum of money; especially a periodical payment for past services.

PEPPERCORN RENT. A rent of a peppercorn, that is, a nominal rent. 1 *Steph. Com.*

PER AUTER VIE. For another's life. [OCCUPANT; PUR AUTRE VIE.]

PER CAPITA. [CAPITA, DISTRIBUTION PER.]

PER CURIAM (by the court). An expression implying that such a decision was arrived at by the court, consisting of one or more judges, as the case may be.

Similarly, the word *per*, preceding the name of a judge, signifies that a dictum which follows is quoted on the authority of the judge.

PER, IN THE. To come in the *per* is to claim by or through the person last entitled to an estate; to come in the *post* is to claim by a paramount and prior title, as the lord by escheat. [ENTRY, WRIT OF; POST, WRIT OF ENTRY.]

PER INCURIAM. Through want of care.

PER INFORTUNIUM. By mischance.

PER MY ET PER TOUT (by the half and by all). An expression applied to occupation in joint-tenancy, indicating, according to some, that the joint-tenants have each of them the entire possession as well of every parcel as of the whole. *Wms. R. P.* But Mr. Serjeant Stephen considers the meaning to be, that the joint-tenants are all jointly seised of the whole, with the right to transfer in equal shares. 1 *Steph. Com.*

PER PAIS (Lat. *Per patriam*). By the country. A trial *per pais* is a trial by jury of the country. 3 *Steph. Com.*

PER PROCURATIONEM. By means of procuration or agency. The phrase is often used, either in full or abbreviated into "p. p.," where one man signs a receipt or other written document as agent for another. But the phrase is especially applied to the acceptance, etc. of a bill of exchange by one man as agent for another.

The words "per procuration," attached to a signature on a bill of exchange, are held to be an express intimation of a special and limited authority; and a person who takes a bill so drawn, accepted, or indorsed, is bound to inquire into the extent of the authority. See *Bills of Exchange Act,* 1882, *ss.* 25, 26.

PER QUÆ SERVITIA (by which services). A writ judicial issuing from the note of a fine, which lay for the cognizee of a manor, seigniory, etc. to compel the tenant of the land to attorn unto him. Abolished. [ATTORN, 1.]

PER QUOD (by reason of which). A phrase indicating special damage sustained by the plaintiff by reason of the defendant's conduct. In most cases of slander, for instance, it is necessary for the plaintiff to aver special damage to have happened by reason of the alleged slander, which is called laying his action with a *per quod.* 3 *Steph. Com.*

PER QUOD CONSORTIUM or SERVITIUM AMISIT. An allegation by a husband or master that he has lost the benefit of his wife's society or of his servant's assistance; being the special damage shown by a husband or master who brings a separate action against a person for grossly maltreating the wife or servant, whereby he is deprived of her or his company or assistance. 3 *Steph. Com.*

PER SE. Of itself, taken alone.

PER STIRPES. [STIRPES, DISTRIBUTION PER.]

PER TOTAM CURIAM. By the whole court. [PER CURIAM.]

PERAMBULATION. A walking of boundaries.

PEREMPTORY signifies a final and determinate act, without hope of renewing or altering. See also the following titles.

PEREMPTORY CHALLENGE is where a party challenges a juror without showing cause. 4 *Steph. Com.* [CHALLENGE.]

PEREMPTORY MANDAMUS. A *mandamus* to do a thing at once, directed to a person to whom a previous writ of *mandamus* has issued to do the thing in question, and who has made some excuse, either insufficient in law, or false in fact, for not doing it. 3 *Steph. Com.*

PEREMPTORY PLEAS, more usually termed *pleas in bar*, are pleas by a defendant tending to impeach the plaintiff's right of action, as opposed to what are called *dilatory pleas.* 3 *Steph. Com.* [DILATORY PLEA.]

PEREMPTORY UNDERTAKING. An undertaking by a plaintiff to bring on a cause for trial at the next sittings or assizes.

PEREMPTORY WRIT. An original writ not optional. [OPTIONAL WRIT; ORIGINAL WRIT.]

PERFECT TRUST. An executed trust.

PERFECTING BAIL is a phrase used to signify the completion of the proceedings whereby persons tendering themselves as sureties for the appearance of a party in court on a day assigned are admitted in that capacity, when they have established their pecuniary sufficiency. [BAIL.]

PERFORMANCE. The doing wholly or in part of a thing agreed to be done. [SATISFACTION, 2; SPECIFIC PERFORMANCE.]

PERILS OF THE SEA. Policies of marine insurance include all fortuitous occurrences which are incident to navigation: the law has extended the phrase considerably. See *Hamilton, Fraser & Co. v. Pandorf & Co.*, 12 App. Ca. 518. 2 *Steph. Com.*

PERJURY is the swearing, wilfully, absolutely, and falsely, in a judicial proceeding, in a matter material to the issue or cause in question. By many statutes, however, false oaths in certain cases, not of a judicial kind, are to be deemed to amount to perjury, and to be visited with the same penalties. The penalties of perjury also attach to wilful falsehood in an affirmation by a Quaker, Moravian. or Separatist, or any other witness, where such affirmation is in lieu of an oath, and would, if believed, have the same legal consequences. 4 *Steph. Com.; Oke's Mag. Syn.*

PERMISSIVE WASTE. [WASTE.]

PERMIT. A licence or warrant for persons to pass with and sell goods, on having paid the duties of customs or excise for the same.

PERNANCY. A taking or receiving tithes in kind. A pernancy of profits is a taking of profits. [PERNOR OF PROFITS.]

PERNOR OF PROFITS. He who receives the profits of land. Thus, a *cestui que use* was said to be a *pernor of profits.*

PERPETUAL CURATE. A permanent minister in holy orders of an "appropriated" church in which no vicar had been endowed, was, until the year 1868, called a *perpetual curate.* But by the stat. 31 & 32 Vict. c. 117, it is provided that every incumbent of a church (not being a rector), who is entitled to perform marriages, etc., and to claim the fees for his own use, shall for the purpose of style and designation, be deemed and styled a *vicar*, and his benefice a vicarage. 2 *Steph. Com.* [APPROPRIATION, 1; VICAR.]

PERPETUAL INJUNCTION. An injunction which is not merely temporary or provisional, and which cannot be dissolved except by appeal, or some proceeding in the nature of an appeal. An interim injunction granted on motion is sometimes made *perpetual* by the decree. [INJUNCTION.]

PERPETUATING TESTIMONY. Proceedings in equity to enable a person to take evidence, otherwise in danger of being lost, for the purpose of quieting his title, where the facts likely to come into dispute cannot be immediately investigated by legal process; for instance, where the person filing it has merely a future interest. See also 21 & 22 Vict. c. 93, and in criminal cases 30 & 31 Vict. c. 35, s. 6. 3 *Steph. Com.*

PERPETUITY. 1. The settlement of an estate in tail so that it cannot be undone or made void. This is contrary to the policy of the law, and is not allowed, except in certain cases, e.g., mortmain.

2. And, generally, the attempt, by deed, will, or other instrument, to control the devolution of an estate beyond the period allowed by law, is spoken of as an attempt to create a *perpetuity*, and the disposition so attempted to be made is *void for remoteness*, though in some cases the courts will, by the operation of the *cyprès* doctrine, give effect to the disposition to the extent permitted by law. 1 *Steph. Com.*; 2 *Steph. Com.*; *Tudor L. C. R. P.*; *Wms. R. P.* [CYPRES.]

PERSON is used variously as follows :—
1. A human being capable of rights, also called a *natural* person.
2. A corporation or legal person, otherwise called an *artificial* person. See the *Interpretation Act*, 1889, *s.* 19.

PERSONA IMPERSONATA. [PARSON IMPARSONEE.]

PERSONAL ACTION signifies :—
1. An action which can be brought only by the person himself who is injured, and not by his representatives. [ACTIONS PERSONAL.]
2. An action which is not an action for the recovery of land. [ACTIONS REAL AND PERSONAL.]

PERSONAL CHATTELS are things movable, as opposed to interests in land. [CHATTELS.]

PERSONAL PROPERTY. [REAL AND PERSONAL PROPERTY.]

PERSONAL REPRESENTATIVE. This phrase is used to denote an executor or administrator, who has the charge of the personal property of the deceased. [REPRESENTATION, 2.]

PERSONAL RIGHTS. Right of personal security, *i.e.*, those of life, limb, body, health, reputation and liberty.

PERSONAL TITHES. Tithes paid out of the fruits of personal labour, as of manual occupations, trades, fisheries, and the like. 2 *Steph. Com.* [TITHES.]

PERSONALTY. Personal property. Personalty is either *pure* or *mixed*. Pure personalty is personalty unconnected with land; mixed personalty is a personal interest in land, or connected therewith. [CHATTELS REAL.] The distinction is important with reference to the Statutes of Mortmain, as pure personalty is not within the operation of those statutes. [MORTMAIN.]

PERSONATION. Pretending to be some other particular person. Personation to obtain property is felony by 37 & 38 Vict. c. 36. 4 *Steph. Com.*
Personation of a voter is felony under the Ballot Act, 1872.

PERVERSE VERDICT. A verdict given by a jury who refuse to follow the direction of the judge on a point of law.

PETER-PENCE, or **PETER'S PENCE,** was a tribute formerly paid to the Pope through the papal legates : also called Romescot and Hearth-Penny.

PETIT CAPE. [CAPE.]

PETIT JURY. [JURY ; PETTY JURY.]

PETIT LARCENY. [PETTY LARCENY.]

PETIT SERJEANTY. Holding lands of the king by the service of rendering to him annually some small implement of war, as a bow, a sword, a lance, an arrow, or the like. The services of this tenure being free and certain, it is in all respects like free socage. 1 *Steph. Com.*; *Wms. R. P.*

PETIT TREASON. A lower kind of treason, which might be committed :
1. By a servant killing his master.
2. By a wife killing her husband.
3. By an ecclesiastical person killing his superior, to whom he owes faith and obedience.
The crime of petit treason is now abolished by 9 Geo. 4, c. 31, s. 2, and 24 & 25 Vict. c. 100, s. 8 ; and any killing which formerly amounted to petit treason now amounts to murder only. 4 *Steph. Com.*

PETITIO PRINCIPII. A begging of the question.

PETITION has a general signification for all kinds of supplications made by an inferior to a superior, especially one having jurisdiction and authority. Thus we speak of petitions to the king; petitions to parliament, etc.

PETITION—*continued.*

The subject has a right to petition the sovereign, or parliament, subject to certain restrictions. See TUMULTUOUS PETITIONING.

A petition in Chancery is an application, addressed to a judge, stating the matters on which it is founded, put in the same manner as a bill, and concluding with a prayer for the specific order sought; or for such other order as the judge shall think right. See *R. S. C.* 1883, *Ord. LII. rr.* 16 *et seq.*

The word "petition" is variously used in English legal proceedings. Thus we speak of a *petition* for a receiving order in bankruptcy, a *petition* for a divorce. Petitions against the election of members of parliament used formerly to be addressed to the House of Commons, but now under the Parliamentary Elections Act, 1868, and amending Acts, they are tried by two judges of the King's Bench Division. 2 *Steph. Com.*

PETITION DE DROIT. [PETITION OF RIGHT, 1.]

PETITION OF RIGHT. 1. A petition for obtaining possession or restitution of property, either real or personal, from the Crown, which suggests such a title as controverts the title of the Crown, grounded on facts disclosed in the petition itself, in which case the petitioner must be careful to state truly the whole title of the Crown, otherwise the petition shall abate. As if a disseisor of lands dies without heir, and the Crown enters, the disseisee has remedy by petition of right.

The modern practice in a petition of right is regulated by stat. 23 & 24 Vict. c. 34, which provides that the petition shall be left with the Home Secretary for his Majesty's consideration; who, if he shall think fit, may grant his fiat that right be done; whereupon (the fiat having been served on the solicitor to the Treasury) an answer, plea, or other defence, shall be made on behalf of the Crown, and the subsequent pleadings be assimilated so far as practicable to the course of an ordinary action. 3 *Steph. Com.*

2. The stat. 3 Car. 1, being a parliamentary declaration of the liberties of the people, including personal liberty and immunity from arbitrary taxation, assented to by King Charles I. in the beginning of his reign. 1 *Steph. Com.*; 2 *Steph. Com.*; 3 *Steph. Com.*

PETITIONING CREDITOR. A creditor who petitions that his debtor may be adjudicated bankrupt. The creditor's debt must be a liquidated one of not less than 50*l.*, and grounded on an act of bankruptcy within three months before the petition. See *Bankruptcy Act,* 1883, *s.* 6. 2 *Steph. Com.*; *Robson, Bkcy.*

PETTY BAG OFFICE. The office belonging to the common law side of the Court of Chancery, out of which writs issued in matters wherein the Crown was mediately or immediately concerned; so called because the writs were kept originally in a little sack or bag, *in parva baga.* 3 *Steph. Com.* The Petty Bag Office was also formerly used for suits for and against officers of the Court of Chancery. The common law jurisdiction of the Court of Chancery is now transferred to the High Court of Justice (Judicature Act, 1873, s. 16), and the office of Clerk of the Petty Bag abolished. 3 *Steph. Com.* [CHANCERY; HANAPER OFFICE.]

PETTY JURY. Twelve good and lawful men of a county impanelled by the sheriff for the trial of issues of fact in criminal cases; so called in opposition to the grand jury. 4 *Steph. Com.* [GRAND JURY; JURY.]

PETTY LARCENY. Theft under the value of twelve pence, formerly distinguished from *grand* larceny, which was theft to a higher amount. This distinction is now abolished. [GRAND LARCENY.]

PETTY SERJEANTY. [PETIT SERJEANTY.]

PETTY SESSIONS. The meeting of two or more justices for trying offences in a summary way under various Acts of parliament empowering them to do so; for committing offenders for trial; for making orders in bastardy, hearing poor-rate appeals, and other similar purposes. See also Interpretation Act, 1889, s. 13, sub-s. 12. 2 *Steph. Com.*; 3 *Steph. Com.*

PETTY TREASON. [PETIT TREASON.]

PEW. An enclosed seat in a church. The right to sit in a particular pew in a church arises either from prescription, the pew being appurtenant to a messuage, or from a faculty or grant from the ordinary, who has the disposition of all pews which are not claimed by prescription. 2 *Steph. Com.*

PHARMACY ACTS. The stats. 15 & 16 Vict. c. 56; 31 & 32 Vict. c. 121, amended by 32 & 33 Vict. c. 117; regulating the examination of chemists, the sale of poisons, etc. 3 *Steph. Com.; Oke's Mag. Syn.*

PICCAGE, PICAGE, or **PICKAGE.** Money paid in fairs, for breaking the ground to set up booths or stalls. 1 *Steph. Com.* 610.

PICKETING. The posting of persons outside a manufactory or place of business to molest or intimidate workmen.

PIE POUDRE COURT. [COURT OF PIED-POUDRE.]

PILOT. He who hath the government of a ship, under the master. See next title.

PILOTAGE AUTHORITIES are various bodies of persons in different parts of the kingdom, having powers and jurisdictions with regard to the appointment and regulation of pilots for the districts in which they respectively act. [TRINITY HOUSE.]

The Board of Trade constitutes the pilotage authority in districts where none already exists.

The employment of a properly qualified and licensed pilot is in general compulsory upon the masters of ships within the limits of the pilotage jurisdictions. Where such pilotage is compulsory the owner and master of the ship are not answerable for any damage caused by the fault or neglect of the compulsory pilot. *Abbott on Shipping.* See also the Merchant Shipping Act, 1894. 3 *Steph. Com.*

PIN-MONEY. A sum payable by a husband to a wife for her separate use, in virtue of a particular arrangement, to be applied by the wife in attiring her person in a manner suitable to the rank of her husband, and in defraying other personal expenses. 2 *Steph. Com.*

PIRACY. 1. The crime of piracy consists in committing those acts of robbery and depredation upon the high seas, which, if committed upon land, would amount to felony there.

By statute law, the following offences are also to be deemed piratical :—

Hostilities by a natural-born subject against any of His Majesty's subjects, under colour of a commission from a foreign power.

The betrayal of his trust by a commander or other seafaring person.

Endeavouring to make a revolt on board ship.

Trading with known pirates, or fitting out a vessel for a piratical purpose, etc. 4 *Steph. Com.*

2. The infringement of a copyright. 2 *Steph. Com.*

PISCARY. A liberty of fishing in another man's waters. 1 *Steph. Com.* [COMMON, II. ; FISHERY.]

PIXING THE COIN signifies the ascertaining whether coin is of the proper standard. For this purpose, resort is had on stated occasions to an ancient mode of inquisition called the *trial of the pyx*, before a jury of members of the Goldsmiths' Company. 33 & 34 Vict. c. 10 ; 2 *Steph. Com.*

PLACITA. Pleas or pleadings. Formerly it signified the public assemblies at which the king presided.

PLAINT. The written statement of an action in the county court, which is entered by the plaintiff in a book kept by the registrar for the purpose. See the *County Court Act*, 1888, *s.* 73 ; 3 *Steph. Com.*

PLAINTIFF. By the Judicature Act, 1873, " plaintiff " includes every person asking any relief (otherwise than by way of counter-claim as a defendant) against any other person by any form of proceeding, whether the same be taken by action, suit, petition, motion, summons, or otherwise.

PLEA. 1. The defendant's answer to the declaration of the plaintiff in an action at common law. The general division of pleas was into dilatory pleas and peremptory pleas, or, which is nearly the same thing, pleas in abatement and pleas in bar. Pleas in abatement in civil actions are now abolished. 3 *Steph. Com.*

2. A short statement, in answer to a bill in equity, of facts which, if inserted in the bill would render it demurrable. It differed from an answer, in that an answer was a complete statement of the defendant's case, and contained answers to any interrogatories the plaintiff might have administered.

The pleas formerly used in civil proceedings in the Superior Courts are superseded by the "statement of defence" (*q.v.*). Pleas in civil causes were called common pleas and in criminal prosecutions pleas of the Crown. For the pleas in criminal law see 4 *Steph. Com.*

PLEADER. One who pleads. [SPECIAL PLEADER.]

PLEADING is a word used : 1. Of drawing the written pleadings in a suit or action. 2. Of advocating a client's cause *vivâ voce* in court.

PLEADING OVER is where a party pleads without taking advantage, by demurrer or otherwise, of a defect in his adversary's pleading. Also where a defendant, having demurred or specially pleaded, has judgment given against him on such demurrer or special plea, and proceeds to plead the general issue, he is said to plead over. 4 *Steph. Com.* [DEMURRER; GENERAL ISSUE, PLEA OF; SPECIAL PLEA.]

PLEADINGS are the mutual formal altercations in writing or print between the parties in a suit or action, with a view to the development of the point in controversy between them, and include the proceedings from the statement of claim to issue joined. The general rules of pleading at present in use are contained in the R. S. C. 1883, Ord. XIX. The delivery of pleadings is now dealt with on the summons for directions and subject to any order thereon is governed by R. S. C. XIX.—XXIII.

PLEAS OF THE CROWN. [PLEA.]

PLEDGE. 1. The transfer of a chattel by a debtor to his creditor to secure the repayment of the debt.
2. The chattel so transferred.
3. A surety. [FRANK-PLEDGE.]

PLENA PROBATIO. [SUPPLETORY OATH.]

PLENARTY. Fulness ; a word indicating that an ecclesiastical benefice is occupied and not vacant. 3 *Steph. Com.*

PLENE ADMINISTRAVIT. A plea by an executor or administrator to an action brought against him as representing the deceased, on the ground that he has already fully administered the estate of the deceased, and that the assets come to his hands have been exhausted in the payment of debts. 2 *Steph. Com.* See next title.

PLENE ADMINISTRAVIT PRÆTER. A plea by an executor or administrator that he has fully administered the testator's estate, with the exception of certain assets acknowledged to be still in his hands. If the plea is good the plaintiff should enter judgment in respect of the assets acknowledged to be in the executor's hands and in respect of assets *in futuro* for the residue of his claim.

PLENIPOTENTIARY. A person who is fully empowered to do anything.

PLEVIN. A warrant or assurance.

PLIGHT. An old English word, signifying the estate held by any one in land ; also the habit and quality thereof.

PLOUGH BOTE. Wood to be employed in repairing instruments of husbandry. 2 *Bl.* ; 1 *Steph. Com.*

PLOUGH LAND is the same with a hide of land or carucate.

PLUNDERAGE. Embezzling goods on board ship.

PLURALITY. The having two, three, or more benefices. The holder thereof is called a *pluralist.* Pluralities are now abolished, except in certain cases. See 1 & 2 *Vict. c.* 106, *s.* 2 ; 48 & 49 *Vict. c.* 54 ; and 50 & 51 *Vict. c.* 68. 2 *Steph. Com.*

PLURIES. A *pluries* writ is a writ that issues in the third place, after two former writs have been disregarded.

POACHING. The unlawful destruction of game, especially by night ; also trespassing by night on land in pursuit of game. See 9 *Geo.* 4, *c.* 69, extended by 7 & 8 *Vict. c.* 19. See also the Poaching Prevention Act (25 & 26 Vict. c. 114). 4 *Steph. Com.*

POCKET SHERIFFS. Sheriffs appointed by the sole authority of the Crown, not having been previously nominated in the Exchequer. The practice of occasionally naming pocket sheriffs continued until the reign of George III. 2 *Steph. Com.* [PRICKING FOR SHERIFFS ; SHERIFF.]

POLICE. The due regulation and domestic order of the kingdom. Especially that part of it which is connected with the prevention and detection of crime. [CONSTABLE.]

POLICE SUPERVISION. It is provided by the Prevention of Crimes Act, 1871 (34 & 35 Vict. c. 112), that where a person is convicted on indictment of a crime, and a previous conviction of a crime is proved against him, the court may, in addition to any other punishment, direct that he be subject to the *supervision of the police* for a period not exceeding seven years, commencing immediately after the expiration of the sentence passed on him for the last of such crimes; and that any person, so subject to supervision as aforesaid, who shall remain in any place for forty-eight hours without notifying the place of his residence to the chief officer of police for the district, or who shall fail to comply with the requisitions of the Act, in periodically reporting himself to such chief officer, shall, unless he can show that he did his best to act in conformity to the law, be liable to be imprisoned, with or without hard labour, for any period not exceeding one year. *4 Steph. Com.*

POLICIES OF ASSURANCE, COURT OF. [COURT OF POLICIES OF ASSURANCE.]

POLICY OF ASSURANCE or **INSURANCE.** [INSURANCE.]

POLL. The process of giving and counting votes at an election. See *2 Steph. Com.* [POLLING; POLLS.]

POLL, DEED. [DEED.]

POLL MONEY, POLL SILVER, or **POLL TAX.** A tax by which every person in the kingdom was assessed by the head or poll, according to his degree. It has been imposed at various periods in our history.

POLLING. Counting heads; especially used of counting voters at an election.

POLLS. Heads or individuals; also the place where polling takes place for the purpose of an election. For *challenges to the polls*, see CHALLENGE, 2.

POLYGAMY. The having more wives than one. *4 Steph. Com.*

PONDUS REGIS. The king's weight; signifying the original standard of weights and measures in the time of Richard I. *2 Steph. Com.*

PONE. 1. A writ whereby a cause depending in an inferior court might be removed into the Court of Common Pleas. Obsolete. *3 Steph. Com.*
2. *Pone per radium et plegios* was a writ whereby the sheriff was commanded to take security of a man for his appearance at a day assigned. It generally issued when a defendant failed to appear. Obsolete.

PONTAGE. A toll or tax for the maintenance or repair of bridges.

POOR LAW BOARD. A Government Board appointed in 1847 to take the place of the Poor Law Commissioners, under whose control the general management of the poor, and the funds for their relief throughout the country, had been for some years previously administered. The Poor Law Board is now superseded by the Local Government Board, which was established in 1871 by stat. 34 & 35 Vict. c. 70. *3 Steph. Com.* [LOCAL GOVERNMENT BOARD.]

POOR LAWS. The laws relating to the relief of the poor. The most important of such laws passed in recent times is the Poor Law Amendment Act, 1834 (4 & 5 Will. 4, c. 76). It has been amended by several subsequent Acts. *3 Steph. Com.* [OVERSEERS; and see preceding title.]

POOR RATE. The rate levied by churchwardens and overseers for the relief of the poor. [OVERSEERS; RELIEF, 2.]

POPULAR ACTION. [QUI TAM ACTIONS.]

PORT. A place where persons and merchandise are allowed to pass into and out of the realm. The duty of appointing ports and sub-ports, and declaring the limits thereof, is confided, by the Customs Consolidation Act, 1853 (16 & 17 Vict. c. 107), to the Commissioners of His Majesty's Treasury. *2 Steph. Com.*

PORTION. A part of a person's estate which is given or left to a child or person to whom another stands in *loco parentis*. The word is especially applied to payments made to younger children out of the funds comprised in their parents' marriage-settlement, and in pursuance of the trusts thereof. [ADVANCEMENT; SATISFACTION.]

POSITIVE LAW is properly synonymous with law properly so called. For every law is *put* or set by its author. But in practice the expression is confined to laws set by a sovereign to a person or persons in a state of subjection to their author; that is, to laws enacted by sovereign States, or by their authority, disobedience to which is *malum prohibitum*. [MALA IN SE.]

POSSE. A word signifying a possibility. A thing *in posse* means a thing which may be; as opposed to a thing *in esse*, or in being.

POSSE COMITATUS. The power of the county; that is, the people of the county which the sheriff may command to attend him for keeping of the peace and pursuing felons; also for defending the county against the king's enemies. To this summons all persons, except peers, women, clergymen, persons decrepit, and infants under the age of fifteen, are, by stat. 2 Hen. 5, c. 8, bound to attend, under pain of fine and imprisonment. See also 50 & 51 Vict. c. 55, s. 8. *2 Steph. Com.; 4 Steph. Com.*

POSSESSIO FRATRIS FACIT SOROREM ESSE HEREDEM (the possession of the brother makes the sister heir). A maxim indicating that if a man, having a son and daughter by a first wife, and a son (with or without other children) by a second wife, died intestate, and his eldest son died after him without entering on the land; then the younger son would inherit as heir to their common father, who was the last person actually seised. But if the eldest brother, before his death, entered and took possession, and died seised of the land and intestate, that possession enabled the sister to succeed in exclusion of the brother; because the descent was traced from the person last seised. This maxim would not now apply; for, by sect. 2 of the Inheritance Act of 1833 (3 & 4 Will. 4, c. 106), the descent is to be traced from the *purchaser*; that is, the last person who acquired the land *otherwise than by descent*. So that, in the case above put, there could be no descent traced from the eldest son, as he himself succeeded to the land by descent; and the younger brother would inherit, as from the father, on the death of the elder brother intestate. *1 Steph. Com.; Wms. R. P.*

POSSESSION. 1. When a man actually enters into lands and tenements. This is called actual possession.
2. When lands and tenements descend to a man, and he hath not yet entered into them. This is called possession in law. Thus we speak of estates in possession as opposed to estates in remainder or reversion. Into the former a man has a right to enter at once; of the latter the enjoyment is delayed. *1 Steph. Com.*
3. The exercise of the right of ownership, whether rightfully or wrongfully. [See the following titles.] This is defined by Sir H. S. Maine as "physical detention, coupled with the intention to use the thing detained as one's own." *Maine's Ancient Law.*

POSSESSION, WRIT OF. A writ giving a person possession of land. A phrase used especially with reference to the fictitious plaintiff in the old action of ejectment. *R. S. C.* 1883, *Ord. XLVII.; 3 Steph. Com.* [EJECTMENT.]

POSSESSORY ACTION was an action brought for the purpose of regaining possession of land whereof the demandant or his ancestors had been unjustly deprived by the tenant or possessor of the freehold, or those under whom he claimed. [ACTIONS ANCESTRAL, POSSESSORY, AND DROITURAL; ASSIZE, WRIT OF; ENTRY, WRIT OF.]
These actions belonged to the class of real actions, and, having been for some time obsolete, were abolished in the year 1833 by 3 & 4 Will. 4, c. 27. *3 Steph. Com.*

POSSIBILITY. A chance or expectation. Possibilities are of two kinds:—
1. A bare possibility, such as that of the eldest son succeeding, on his father's decease intestate, to the inheritance of his lands.
2. A possibility *coupled with an interest*, or in other words, a possibility recognised in law as an estate or interest; as the chance of B. succeeding to an estate, held by A. for his life, in the event of C. not being alive at A.'s death. In this sense it includes a contingent remainder. *1 Steph. Com.* [CONTINGENCY WITH DOUBLE ASPECT; DOUBLE POSSIBILITY.]

POST. After. Occurring in a book it refers to a later page or line.

POST DISSEISIN. A writ for him who, having recovered lands by *novel disseisin*, was again disseised by the former disseisor.

POST ENTRY. When goods are weighed or measured, and the merchant has got an account thereof at the Custom House, and finds his entry already made too small, he must make a *post* or additional *entry* for the surplusage, in the same manner as the first was done. Post entries are usually confined to cargoes of grain. *M'Culloch's Com. Dict.*

POST FINE. A duty formerly paid to the king by the cognisee in a fine, when the same was fully passed. 1 *Steph. Com.* [FINE, 1.]

POST LITEM MOTAM. After a suit has been in contemplation ; or, "after an issue has become, or appeared likely to become, a subject of judicial controversy."

POST MORTEM (after death), *e.g.*, a *post mortem* examination of a corpse, to ascertain the cause of death.

POST OBIT BOND. A bond executed by a person on the receipt of money from another, whereby the borrower binds himself to pay to the lender a sum exceeding the sum so received, and the ordinary interest thereof, upon the death of a person upon whose decease he (the borrower) expects to become entitled to some property.

POSTDATING AN INSTRUMENT. The dating of an instrument as of a date after that on which it is executed. A bill, note or cheque may be postdated. See *Bills of Exch. Act*, 1882, *s.* 13.

POSTEA. According to the practice formerly observed in actions at common law, the *postea* was the record of that which was done subsequently to the joining of issue ; it stated the appearance of the parties, judge and jury, at the place of trial, and the verdict of the latter on the issues joined, and was indorsed on the *nisi prius* record by the associate. The associate's certificate now forms the substitute for the postea. 3 *Steph. Com.* [NISI PRIUS RECORD.]

POSTLIMINIUM. A fiction in the Roman law by which a person who, having been taken captive by the enemy, returned from captivity, was deemed never to have lost his liberty or his *status* as a citizen. A similar fiction is applied in some cases in international law, *e.g.*, by prize courts in the case of goods captured in war by an enemy, and afterwards rescued. 2 *Steph. Com.*; 3 *Steph. Com.*

POSTMASTER GENERAL. The minister of State who is at the head of the department of the Post Office. He may now sit in the House of Commons. 29 & 30 *Vict. c.* 55. [POST OFFICE.]

POSTNUPTIAL. After marriage ; thus a post-nuptial settlement is a settlement made after marriage, and, not being made on the consideration of marriage, it is in general considered as *voluntary*, that is, as having been made on no valuable consideration. 2 *Steph. Com.* [CONSIDERATION.]

POSTPONEMENT OF TRIAL may be applied for on sufficient grounds which must appear by affidavit. See as to civil trials, R. S. C. 1883, Ord. XXXVI.: and as to criminal, 14 & 15 *Vict. c.* 100. *s.* 27. 4 *Steph. Com.*

POSTREMOGENITURE. The right of the youngest born. [BOROUGH ENGLISH.]

POTENTIA PROPINQUA is a common possibility, which may reasonably be expected to happen. 1 *Steph. Com.*

POTENTIA REMOTA is a remote possibility, which cannot reasonably be expected to happen. 1 *Steph. Com.*

POTWALLERS, or **POTWALLOPERS.** Such as cooked their own diet in a fireplace of their own, and were on that account entitled, by the custom of some boroughs, to vote in the parliamentary election for the borough. The rights of such persons as were entitled, on this account, at the time of the passing of the Reform Act, 1832, to exercise the franchise, are preserved during their lives. 2 *Steph. Com.*

POUND (Lat. *Parcus*) is an enclosure for keeping cattle or other goods distrained. By stat. 11 Geo. 2, c. 19, any person distraining for rent may turn any part of the premises, upon which a distress is taken, into a pound, *pro hâc vice*, for securing of such distress. A pound is either pound *overt*, that is, open overhead ; or pound *covert*, that is, close. 3 *Steph. Com.* [DISTRESS.]

POUNDAGE. 1. A subsidy to the value of twelve pence in the pound on all manner of merchandise, formerly granted to the king. 2 *Steph. Com.*

2. A sheriff's allowance on the amount levied by him in execution. See the *Sheriffs Act,* 1887, *s.* 20, *sub-s.* 1; *R. S. C.* 1883, *Ord. XLII. r.* 15.

POUNDBREACH. The destruction of a pound, or any part, lock, or bolt thereof, or the taking of cattle or other goods from the place where they are impounded. As to the penalties for the same, see 2 W. & M. c. 5 and 6 & 7 Vict. c. 30. 3 *Steph. Com.*

POURPARTY. The part or share of an estate held by coparceners, which is by partition allotted to them.

POURPRESTURE (from Fr. *Pourpris,* an enclosure) is the wrongful enclosing of another man's property, or of the property of the public. According to Skene, there are three sorts of this offence, one against the king, a second against the lord of the fee, a third against a neighbour by a neighbour.

POURSUIVANT. The king's messenger; those attending upon him in his wars were called *Poursuivants-at-Arms.*

There are four poursuivants in the Heralds Office, called respectively, *Rouge Croix, Blue Mantle, Rouge Dragon,* and *Portcullis.*

POWER is an authority to dispose of any real or personal property independently of or even in defeasance of any existing estate or interest therein. The person entitled to exercise the power (who is called the *donee of the power*) may have no interest in the property in question, in which case the power is called a power *collateral* or *in gross*; or he may himself have an interest in the property, and the power is then called a power *coupled with an interest,* or a power *appendant* or *appurtenant, e.g.,* in case of a parent having a life interest in property, with power to appoint the property (either by deed or will) to his children after his death. The exercise of the power is called an *appointment*; and the persons taking the property under such an appointment are called *appointees,* and not grantees or assigns. See 1 *Steph. Com.*

Powers may be *general,* giving right to appoint as the donee may think fit, or *special* only in favour of some or all of certain persons or classes of persons. Also they may be powers of *revocation, e.g.,* in voluntary settlements, or of *revo-*cation and new appointment, *e.g.,* in marriage settlements to enable shares of children to be rearranged. [ILLUSORY APPOINTMENT.]

POWER OF ATTORNEY. An authority given by one to another to act for him in his absence, *e.g.,* to convey land, receive debts, sue, etc. See *Conveyancing Acts,* 1881 *and* 1882. The party so authorised to act is called the *attorney* of the party giving the authority.

POYNINGS' LAW was an Act of parliament (otherwise called the Statute of Drogheda) made in Ireland by Henry VII., in the year 1495, whereby it was enacted that all the statutes in England then in force should be in force in Ireland. It was called Poynings' Law because Sir Edward Poynings was at that time Lord Lieutenant of Ireland. Other Poynings' laws are mentioned. See 1 *Steph. Com.*

PRACTICE is the procedure in a court of justice, through the various stages of any matter, civil or criminal, depending before it.

The practice in the Supreme Court of Judicature is now mainly regulated by the Judicature Acts, 1873 and 1875, and the Rules of the Supreme Court, 1883, which may be found in "The Annual Practice." As to the practice of the county courts, see the County Courts Act, 1888, and the County Court Rules of 1889 and amending rules.

PRACTICE COURT. A name sometimes given to the Bail Court. [BAIL COURT.]

PRACTICE MASTER. One of the ordinary King's Bench Masters, sitting by rotation for the purpose of answering queries as to points of practice. *R. S. C., Ord. LXI. r.* 2.

PRÆCIPE. 1. An original writ commanding a person to do a thing, or show the reason wherefore he hath not done it. Abolished.

2. A note of instructions delivered by a plaintiff or his solicitor to the officer of the court who stamps the writ of summons, specifying the county in which the defendant is supposed to reside, the nature of the writ, the names of the plaintiff and defendant, and the name of the solicitor issuing the writ, and the date. The *præcipe* is filed by the officer.

No writ of *execution* can be issued without the party issuing it, or his solicitor, filing a præcipe for the purpose. See *R. S. C.* 1883, *Ord. XLII. r.* 12.

PRÆCIPE IN CAPITE. A writ of right, brought by one of the king's immediate tenants *in capite*, was called a *præcipe in capite*. [IN CAPITE; WRIT OF RIGHT.]

PRÆCIPE QUOD REDDAT (command that he restore). A writ by which a person was directed to restore the possession of land ; a phrase used especially of the writ by which a *common recovery* was commenced. Abolished. [RECOVERY.]

PRÆCIPE QUOD TENEAT CONVENTIONEM. The writ which commenced the action of covenant in fines.

PRÆCIPE, TENANT TO THE, signified a tenant in a real action, against whom a *præcipe* or writ was sued. But the phrase was especially used of the person against whom, in the proceeding called a *common recovery*, the fictitious action was to be brought. [RECOVERY.]

PRÆDIAL TITHES. Tithes paid out of the produce of land. 2 *Steph. Com.* [TITHES.]

PRÆFINE. The same as *primer fine.* [FINE, 1 ; PRIMER FINE.]

PRÆMUNIRE (by stat. 16 Rich. 2, c. 5, called the Statute of *Præmunire*) is the offence of procuring, at Rome or elsewhere, any translations, processes, excommunications, bulls, instruments or other things, against the king, his crown and realm, to which, by stat. 2 Hen. 4, c. 3, is added the offence of accepting any provision of the Pope, to be exempt from obedience to the proper ordinary. The offence was so called from the words *præmunire facias* (cause him to be forewarned, *præmunire* being a barbarous word for *præmoneri*), by which the writ for the citation of the party charged with any such offence was commenced. 1 *Steph. Com.* ; 4 *Steph. Com.*

PRÆPOSITUS. 1. A person in authority ; hence the word *provost.* A *præpositus regius* was an officer of a hundred.

2. The person from whom descent is traced under the old canons.

PRÆSCRIPTION. [PRESCRIPTION.]

PRAY IN AID is a phrase often used to signify "claiming the benefit of an argument." Especially in suits or actions in which there are several

parties, the above phrase is sometimes used by a counsel who claims the benefit, on behalf of his own client, of an argument already used on behalf of some other party in the suit or action.

PREAMBLE OF A STATUTE. The recital at the beginning of an Act of parliament, to explain the minds of the makers of the Act, and the mischiefs they intend to remedy by the same. 1 *Steph. Com.*

In the case of private bills, if the Committee of either House, before whom the bill comes, find the preamble "not proven," the bill is lost.

PRE-AUDIENCE. The priority of right of being heard in a court of justice, as the Attorney and Solicitor General before King's Counsel, and King's Counsel before junior barristers, etc.

PREBEND. A fixed portion of the rents and profits of a cathedral church set apart for the maintenance of the prebendaries. 2 *Steph. Com.*

PRECEDENCE, PATENT OF. [PATENT OF PRECEDENCE.]

PRECEDENCE, TABLE OF. The table of rules regulating the respective priorities of the various orders and dignities within the realm. 2 *Steph. Com.*

PRECEDENT CONDITION. [CONDITIONS PRECEDENT AND SUBSEQUENT.]

PRECEDENTS are examples which may be followed. The word is used principally, though by no means exclusively, to indicate one of the two following things :—

1. A decision in a court of justice, cited in support of any proposition for which it is desired to contend. A prior decision of the House of Lords is binding not only upon all inferior courts, but also upon the House of Lords itself, and nothing but an Act of parliament can alter it.

2. Drafts of deeds, wills, mortgages, pleadings, etc., which may serve as patterns for future draftsmen and conveyancers.

PRECEPT. 1. A commandment in writing sent out by a justice of the peace or other like officer for the bringing of a person or record before him.

2. An instigation to murder or other crime. In this sense the word is quite obsolete.

3. The direction issued by a sheriff to the proper returning officers of cities and boroughs within his jurisdiction for the

PRECEPT—*continued.*
election of members to serve in parliament.

4. The direction by the judges or commissioners of assize to the sheriff for the summoning a sufficient number of jurors. 3 *Steph. Com.*

5. The direction issued by the clerk of the peace to the overseers of parishes for making out the jury lists. 3 *Steph. Com.*

6. The direction issued by guardians of the poor and other local authorities to overseers of parishes for money to be raised by rates.

PRECINCT. Boundary. Hence it signifies—
1. A certain limited district round some important edifice, as a cathedral.
2. The local district for which a high or petty constable is appointed. [CONSTABLE.]
3. A place formerly privileged from arrests.

PRE-CONTRACT. A contract made before another contract ; especially with reference to a contract of marriage, which, according to the ancient law, rendered void a subsequent marriage solemnized in violation of it. 2 *Steph. Com.*

PREDIAL TITHES. [PRÆDIAL TITHES.]

PRE-EMPTION. 1. A right of purchasing before another ; a privilege formerly allowed to the king's purveyor. 2 *Steph. Com.*

2. A right given to the owner from whom lands have been acquired by compulsory powers in case such lands should become *superfluous* for the undertaking for which they were acquired. See *Lands Clauses Consolidation Act*, 1845, *ss.* 127—129.

3. In international law it signifies the right of a belligerent to compulsorily purchase merchandise of a neutral at its mercantile value to prevent its falling into the hands of the enemy. See *Hall's Int. Law.*

PREFER often means to bring a matter before a court of justice ; as when we say that A. preferred a charge of assault against B.

PREFERENCE (FRAUDULENT). A term used in connection with payments, transfers, conveyances, etc., made by a person unable to pay his debts by way of preference to some of his creditors over others. All such payments, etc., are fraudulent and void as against the trustee in bankruptcy if the debtor become bankrupt within three months. See *Bankruptcy Act*, 1883, *s.* 49. As to fraudulent settlements, see *ibid.*, s. 29. 2 *Steph. Com.*

PREFERENCE SHARES in a joint-stock company are shares entitling their holders to a preferential dividend ; so that a holder of preference shares is entitled to have the whole of his dividend (or so much thereof as represents the extent to which his shares are, by the constitution of the company, to be deemed preference shares) paid before any dividend is paid to the ordinary shareholders.

PREFERENTIAL PAYMENTS, in bankruptcy, winding up of companies, or administration of estates of persons dying insolvent :—One year's rates and taxes, four months' salaries of clerks up to fifty pounds, and two months' wages of labourers up to twenty-five pounds. are payable in priority to all other debts. See the *Preferential Payments in Bankruptcy Act*, 1888 (51 & 52 Vict. c. 62), and 60 & 61 Vict. c. 19. 3 *Steph. Com.* [PREFERENCE, FRAUDULENT.]

PREGNANCY, PLEA OF. [JURY OF MATRONS.]

PREJUDICE. Prejudging a matter. Thus, for instance, a court may decide that A. is entitled for his life to the income of a fund "without prejudice" to any question between B. and C., who claim adversely to each other the income of the fund after his death. And generally, the expression "without prejudice" implies that the consideration of the question to which it refers is postponed to a future time. And the phrase is often used in a lawyer's letter for the purpose of guarding himself as to anything therein contained being construed as an admission of liability.

PRELIMINARY ACT. In actions for damage by collision between vessels a sealed document giving all particulars of the collision must be filed by the solicitor for each side before any pleadings are delivered : such document is called a preliminary act. See *R. S. C.* 1883, *Ord. XIX. r.* 28. 3 *Steph. Com.*

PREMISES (Lat. *Præmissa*). 1. The commencement of a deed, setting forth the number and names of the parties, with their additions or titles, and the recital, if any, of such deeds and matters of fact as are necessary to explain the reasons upon which the deed is founded; the consideration upon which it is made; and, if the deed be a disposition of property, the particulars of the property intended to be thereby transferred; also the operative words, with the exceptions and reservations (if any). 1 *Steph. Com.; Woodfall, L. & T.*

2. Hence it has come to signify the lands granted; and hence any specified houses or lands.

3. Propositions antecedently supposed or proved.

PREMIUM. 1. A reward.

2. The periodical payment for the insurance of life or property.

3. A lump sum or fine paid for the granting of a lease.

4. A sum paid in excess of the nominal value of shares or stock..

PRÆMUNIRE. [PRÆMUNIRE.]

PRENDER. The power or right of taking a thing before it is offered. Thus heriot-custom is said to lie in *prender* and not in *render*, because the lord may seize the identical thing itself; but he cannot distrain for it. 3 *Steph. Com.* [DISTRESS; HERIOT.]

PREPENSE. Aforethought. Thus, malice prepense is equivalent to malice aforethought. [MALICE.]

PREROGATIVE. The special power, preeminence or privilege which the king hath, over and above other persons, in right of his crown. 2 *Steph. Com.*

PREROGATIVE COURTS. The courts of the provinces of Canterbury and York respectively, presided over by judges appointed by the respective archbishops. The jurisdiction of these courts has become practically obsolete since, by the Probate Act of 1857 (20 & 21 Vict. c. 77) the testamentary jurisdiction of the ecclesiastical courts was transferred to the Court of Probate. 2 *Steph. Com.; 3 Steph. Com.*

PREROGATIVE WRITS are writs which in their origin arise from the extraordinary powers of the Crown. They differ from other writs mainly in the two following points:—

1st. They do not issue as of mere course, nor without some probable cause being shown why the extraordinary powers of the Crown should be called in to the party's assistance.

2nd. They are generally directed, not to a sheriff or other public officer, but to the parties themselves whose acts are the subject of complaint.

They are the writs of *procedendo, mandamus, prohibition, quo warranto, habeas corpus,* and *certiorari.* See these titles. 3 *Steph. Com.*

PRESCRIBE TO. To assert or claim anything by title of prescription. [PRESCRIPTION.]

PRESCRIPTION. 1. *Præscriptio,* in the Roman law, was an exception *written in front* of the plaintiff's pleading. Afterwards it became applied exclusively to the *præscriptio longi temporis,* etc., or the prescription founded on length of possession. *Sandars' Justinian.* Hence its modern meaning. It was allowed by way of equitable plea where a defendant, sued in reference to the possession of property, had complied with the main conditions of *usucapion,* without having acquired ownership by usucapion. [USUCAPION.]

2. Prescription at common law, as defined by Blackstone, is where a man can show no other title to what he claims than that he, and those under whom he claims, have immemorially used and enjoyed it. The difference between prescription and custom is, that custom is a *local* usage, and not annexed to any *person,* whereas prescription is a *personal* usage. Prescription may, perhaps, in this sense be defined as the presumption of a grant arising from long usage.

This still applies to the acquisition of rights not included in the Prescription Act (2 & 3 Will. 4, c. 71), *e.g.,* right of support for buildings. For rules, see 1 *Steph. Com.*

The Act provides that a thirty years' enjoyment of rights of *common,* and other profits or benefits to be taken or enjoyed upon any land, shall no longer be defeated by proof that the enjoyment commenced at a period subsequent to legal memory [LEGAL MEMORY]; and that a prescriptive claim of sixty years' enjoyment shall be absolute and indefeasible except by proof that such

PRESCRIPTION—*continued.*

enjoyment took place under some deed, or written consent or agreement. In the case of *ways* and *watercourses*, the periods are twenty and forty years respectively. In the case of *lights*, the period is twenty years absolute.

The above is styled *positive* or *acquisitive prescription*, namely, that by which a title is acquired (as the *usucapio* of the Roman law), and in the English law properly applies to incorporeal hereditaments only. *Negative* prescription is that by which a right of challenge is lost (as the prescription under the Statutes of Limitation), and this is applicable to corporeal rights ; thus if an owner of land in the wrongful possession of another does not sue within twelve years from the time when such wrongful possession was obtained, he will usually lose his right to the property. Real Property Limitation Act, 1874.

PRESENTATION. The act of a patron in offering his clerk to the bishop, to be instituted in a benefice of his gift. 2 *Steph. Com.* ; 3 *Steph. Com.* [AD-VOWSON.]

PRESENTATIVE ADVOWSON. [ADVOW-SON.]

PRESENTEE. A clerk presented by the patron of a living to the bishop. [AD-VOWSON ; PRESENTATION.]

PRESENTMENT. 1. Presentation to a benefice. [PRESENTATION.]

2. The formal information to the lord, by the tenants of a manor, of anything done out of court. 1 *Steph. Com.*

3. An information made by a jury in a court before a judge who hath authority to punish an offence. Especially is it used of notice taken by a grand jury of anything from their own knowledge or observation. 4 *Steph. Com.*

4. The presenting a bill of exchange to the drawee for acceptance, or to the acceptor for payment. See *Bills of Exchange Act*, 1882, *ss.* 39, 40, 42, 45, 46. 2 *Steph. Com.* [ACCEPTANCE OF A BILL ; BILL OF EXCHANGE.]

PRESENTS. A word in a deed signifying the deed itself, which is expressed by the phrase " these presents." It is especially used in a deed-poll, which cannot be described as " This Indenture."

PRESIDENT OF THE COUNCIL. A high officer of the State, whose office is to attend on the sovereign, and to propose business at the council table. He is a member of the Judicial Committee and of the Cabinet. 2 *Steph. Com.* [JUDI-CIAL COMMITTEE.]

PRESUMPTION. That which comes near, in greater or less degree, to the proof of a fact. It is called violent, probable, or light, according to the degree of its cogency. Presumptions are also divided into—(1) *præsumptiones juris et de jure*, otherwise called irrebuttable presumptions (often, but not necessarily, fictitious), which the law will not suffer to be rebutted by any counter-evidence ; as, that an infant under seven years is not responsible for his actions ; (2) *præsumptiones juris tantum*, which hold good in the absence of counter-evidence. but against which counter-evidence may be admitted ; and (3) *præsumptiones hominis*, which are not necessarily conclusive, though no proof to the contrary be adduced. 3 *Steph. Com.*

PRESUMPTION OF DEATH. The presumption that a man is dead where there is no direct evidence of the fact. This presumption takes place when a man has not been heard of for seven years ; but the presumption is simply that the man is dead, and not that he died at the end of the seven years, or any other specified time. So that if B., a legatee under A.'s will, have been last heard of six years before A.'s death, B.'s representatives will not, after A. has been dead a year, be entitled to presume that B. survived A., so as to claim the legacy for themselves. See 3 *Steph. Com.*

PRESUMPTION OF SURVIVORSHIP is the presumption that A. survived B., or B. survived A., when there is no evidence which died first, *e.g.*, when both perish in the same shipwreck. The law of England recognises no such presumption, and survivorship must be proved. [COMMORIENTES.]

PRESUMPTIVE EVIDENCE. A term especially used of evidence which, if believed, would not be necessarily conclusive as to the fact in issue, but from which, according to the ordinary course of human affairs, the existence of that fact might be presumed. In this sense it is synonymous with circumstantial evidence. 3 *Steph. Com.*

PRESUMPTIVE HEIR. [HEIR APPA-RENT.]

PRESUMPTIVE TITLE. One which arises out of the mere occupation of property without any apparent right or pretence of right.

PRETENDED, or **PRETENSED, RIGHT** or **TITLE** (Lat. *Jus prætensum*) is the right or title to land set up by one who is out of possession against the person in possession. The stat. 32 Hen. 8, c. 9, forbids the sale of a pretended right or title to land, unless the vendor hath received the profits for one whole year before the grant, or have been in actual possession of the land, or of the reversion or remainder, on pain that both purchaser and vendor shall each forfeit the value of such land to the king and the prosecutor. See, however, 8 *&* 9 *Vict. c.* 109, and *s.* 11 of the *Land Transfer Act*, 1897. 4 *Steph. Com.*

PREVARICATION originally signified the conduct of an advocate who betrayed the cause of his client, and by collusion assisted his opponent ; hence it signifies collusion between an informer and a defendant in a feigned prosecution ; also any secret abuse committed in a public office or private commission. At the present day when we say that a witness *prevaricates*, we mean that he gives quibbling and evasive answers to questions put to him.

PREVENTIVE JUSTICE is that portion of law which has reference to the direct prevention of offences. It generally consists in obliging those persons, whom there is probable ground to suspect of future misbehaviour, to give full assurance to the public that such offence as is apprehended shall not happen, by finding pledges or securities to keep the peace, or for their good behaviour. 4 *Steph. Com. ; Oke's Mag. Syn.* [GOOD BEHAVIOUR ; KEEPING THE PEACE.]

PRICKING FOR SHERIFFS. The custom with regard to the appointment of sheriffs is, that all the judges, together with the other great officers, meet in the Court of Exchequer (*scil.*, King's Bench Division of the High Court of Justice) on the morrow of St. Martin (that is, on the 12th of November), and then and there the judges propose three persons for each county, to be reported (if approved of) to the king or queen, who afterwards appoints one of them for sheriff. This appointment is made by marking each name with the prick of a pin, and is therefore called "pricking for sheriffs." This mode of appointment is continued by the Sheriffs Act, 1887, which consolidates the. law relating to sheriffs. 3 *Steph. Com.* The sheriffs of London and Middlesex are now appointed by the king. See the *Local Government Act*, 1888 (51 *&* 52 *Vict. c.* 41), *ss.* 40, 46.

PRIMÂ FACIE CASE. A litigating party is said to have a *primâ facie* case when the evidence in his favour is sufficiently strong for his opponent to be called on to answer it. A *primâ facie* case, then, is one which is established by sufficient evidence, and can be overthrown only by rebutting evidence adduced on the other side. In some cases, the only question to be considered is whether there is a *primâ facie* case or no. Thus a grand jury are bound to find a true bill of indictment if the evidence before them creates a *primâ facie* case against the accused ; and for this purpose, therefore, it is not necessary for them to hear the evidence for the defence.

PRIMÂ FACIE EVIDENCE. A phrase sometimes used to denote evidence which establishes a *primâ facie* case in favour of the party adducing it. [PRIMÂ FACIE CASE.]

PRIMÆ IMPRESSIONIS (of first impression). A case of first impression is one as to which there is no precedent directly in point.

PRIMAGE. A payment due to mariners and ailors, for the loading of a ship at the setting forth from any haven.

PRIMARY CONVEYANCES, as opposed to derivative conveyances, are conveyances which do *not* take effect by way of enlarging, confirming, altering, or otherwise affecting other conveyances ; they are feoffments, grants, gifts, leases, exchanges, partitions. 1 *Steph. Com.*

PRIMARY EVIDENCE. The best evidence, *i.e.*, evidence which is not secondary, second-hand, or hearsay evidence. 3 *Steph. Com.* [SECONDARY EVIDENCE ; SECOND-HAND EVIDENCE.]

PRIMATE. A title given to the archbishops of Canterbury and York, and of Dublin and Armagh.

PRIMER FINE. [FINE, 1.]

PRIMER SEISIN. A burden incident to the king's tenants *in capite*, by which the king was entitled, when any of such tenants died, to receive of the heir, if he were of full age, one whole year's profits of the lands, if they were in immediate possession; and half a year's profits if they were in reversion expectant upon an estate for life. 1 *Steph. Com.* [IN CAPITE.]

PRIMITIÆ. The first year's profits of a benefice, formerly payable to the Crown. 1 *Steph. Com.*; 2 *Steph. Com.* [FIRST FRUITS.]

PRIMOGENITURE. The title of the eldest son in right of his birth, whereby in the United Kingdom he succeeds to all the real estate of an intestate parent.

Primogeniture is almost unknown except in the United Kingdom; it arose owing to the exigencies of military service under the feudal system. 1 *Steph. Com.*

PRINCE OF WALES. The eldest son of the reigning sovereign. Edward II., being born at Carnarvon, was the first English Prince of Wales. The heir apparent to the Crown is made Prince of Wales and Earl of Chester by special creation and investiture. He is also Duke of Cornwall by inheritance. 1 *Steph. Com.*; 2 *Steph. Com.*

PRINCIPAL. 1. An heirloom (*q.v.*).

2. The amount of money which has been borrowed, as opposed to the interest payable thereon. [INTEREST, 2.]

3. The head of a college or other institution.

4. The person directly concerned in the commission of a crime, as opposed to an accessory. 4 *Steph. Com.* [ACCESSORY.]

5. A person who employs an agent. 2 *Steph. Com.* [AGENT.]

6. A person for whom another becomes surety. 2 *Steph. Com.*

PRINCIPAL CHALLENGE. A challenge to a juror for such a cause assigned as carries with it *primâ facie* marks of suspicion. 3 *Steph. Com.* [CHALLENGE; FAVOUR, CHALLENGE TO.]

PRINTING. As to the requirement of printing of pleadings, affidavits, special cases, etc., see R. S. C. 1883 Ord. XIX. r. 9 (pleadings); Ord. XXXI. r. 9, Ord. XXXVIII. r. 30 (affidavits); Ord. XXXIV. r. 3 (special case).

PRIORITY. 1. An antiquity of tenure, in comparison with one not so ancient.

2. Any legal precedence or preference; as when we say that certain debts are paid in *priority* to others: or that certain incumbrancers of an estate are allowed *priority* over others, that is, are to be allowed to satisfy their claims out of the estate before the others can be admitted to any share therein, etc. The priority of specialty over simple contract debts was taken away by 32 & 33 Vict. c. 46 in the administration of the estates of persons dying on or after 1st January, 1870. 2 *Steph. Com.* See also PREFERENTIAL PAYMENTS.

PRISAGE. 1. An ancient hereditary duty belonging to the Crown, being the right of taking two tuns of wine from every ship importing into England twenty tuns or more. But, by charter of Edward I., this was exchanged into a duty of two shillings for every tun imported by merchant strangers, and was then called *butlerage* because paid to the king's butler. Abolished, 51 Geo. 3, c. 15. 2 *Steph. Com.*

2. The share which belongs to the Crown of such merchandises as are taken at sea by way of lawful prize.

PRIVATE ACT OF PARLIAMENT. A local and personal Act affecting particular persons and private concerns. By stat. 13 & 14 Vict. c. 21, every statute made after the commencement of the then next session of parliament is to be taken to be a public one, and judicially noticeable as such, unless the contrary be therein expressly declared; this statute is repealed by the Interpretation Act, 1889, but the provision is re-enacted by s. 9 of that Act. 1 *Steph. Com.* [BILL, 4; LOCAL AND PERSONAL ACTS; PRIVATE BILLS.]

PRIVATE BILLS are bills brought into parliament on the petition of parties interested, and on payment of fees. Such bills are brought in generally in the interest of individuals, parishes, cities, counties, or other localities, and are distinguished from measures of public policy in which the whole community are interested. 2 *Steph. Com.* [BILL, 4; LOCAL AND PERSONAL ACTS; PRIVATE ACT OF PARLIAMENT.]

PRIVATE CHAPELS are chapels owned by noblemen and other privileged persons, and used by themselves and their families. They are thus opposed to *public chapels*, otherwise called *chapels of ease*, which are built for the accommodation of particular districts within a parish, in *ease* of the original parish church. 34 & 35 *Vict. c.* 66 ; 2 *Steph. Com.*

PRIVATEERS are defined as armed ships fitted out by private persons, commissioned in time of war by the Lords of the Admiralty, or other lawful authority acting for the Crown in that behalf, to cruise against the enemy. These commissions, when granted, have been usually denominated " letters of marque." 2 *Steph. Com.* [DECLARATION OF PARIS ; LETTERS OF MARQUE AND REPRISAL.]

PRIVATION. [DEPRIVATION.]

PRIVIES. [PRIVITY OF CONTRACT ; PRIVITY OF ESTATE.]

PRIVILEGE. That which is granted or allowed to any person, or any class of persons, either against or beyond the course of the common law ; as, for instance, the non-liability of a member of the legislature to any court other than the parliament itself, for words spoken in his place in parliament. 2 *Steph. Com.* See also the following titles.

PRIVILEGE, WRIT OF. A writ formerly in use whereby a member of parliament, when arrested in a civil suit, might claim his deliverance out of custody by virtue of his parliamentary privilege. 1 *Bl.* 165, 166.

PRIVILEGED COMMUNICATION. 1. A communication which, though *primâ facie* libellous or slanderous, yet, by reason of the circumstances under which it is made, is protected from being made the ground of proceedings for libel or slander ; as in the case of confidential communications without malice, etc. 3 *Steph. Com.*
2. A communication which is protected from disclosure in evidence in any civil or criminal proceeding ; as in the case of confidential communications between a party and his legal adviser in reference to the matter before the court. 3 *Steph. Com.*

PRIVILEGED COPYHOLDS. [CUSTOMARY FREEHOLD.]

PRIVILEGED DEBTS. [PREFERENTIAL PAYMENTS.]

PRIVILEGED VILLENAGE, otherwise called villein-socage, is a tenure described by Bracton, in which the services were *base* as in villenage, but were *certain*, as in free and common socage. It seems principally to have prevailed among the tenants of the king's demesnes : and is supposed by some to be the same as the tenure in *antient demesne*. 1 *Steph. Com.* [ANCIENT DEMESNE ; FREEHOLD ; SOCAGE.]

PRIVILEGIUM. 1. A law, *ex post facto*, conferring rights or inflicting a punishment in respect of an act already done.
2. *Property propter*, a qualified property in animals *feræ naturæ, i.e.*, a privilege of hunting and taking them in exclusion of others. 2 *Steph. Com.*

PRIVILEGIUM CLERICALE. [BENEFIT OF CLERGY.]

PRIVITY OF CONTRACT is the relation subsisting between the parties to the same contract. Thus if A., B. and C. mutually contract, there is privity of contract between them ; but if A. contract with B., and B. make an independent contract with C. on the same subject matter, there is no privity of contract between A. and C.

PRIVITY OF ESTATE between two persons is where their estates are so related to each other that they make but one estate in law, being *derived at the same time* out of the *same original seisin*. Thus if A., the owner of an estate, convey it to B. for a term of years, with remainder to C. for his life, there is privity of estate between B. and C. But if A. conveys to B. for his life, and B. makes a lease for years to C., there is no privity between A. and C. 1 *Steph. Com.*

PRIVITY OF TENURE is the relation subsisting between a lord and his immediate tenant.

PRIVY. A partaker ; he that hath an interest in any action or thing. See the several titles immediately preceding this title.

PRIVY COUNCIL is the principal council belonging to the sovereign. Privy councillors are made such by the sovereign's nomination, without either patent or grant ; and, on such nomination, they become privy councillors, with the title of Right Honorable during the life of the sovereign who has chosen them, but subject to removal at his discretion. 2 *Steph. Com.* [COMMITTEE OF COUNCIL ON EDUCATION ; JUDICIAL COMMITTEE.]

PRIVY PURSE is that portion of the public money voted to the sovereign and his consort, which they may deal with as freely as any private individual may with his property. A sum of 110,000*l.* a year is assigned by parliament for this purpose. 1 *Edw.* 7, *c.* 4. 1 *Steph. Com.* ; 2 *Steph. Com.*

PRIVY SEAL and **PRIVY SIGNET.** The seal used for such grants from the Crown, or other things, as pass the Great Seal ; first they pass the privy signet, then the privy seal, and, lastly, the Great Seal of England. The Privy Seal is also used in matters of small moment which never pass the Great Seal. The Privy Signet is one of the sovereign's seals used for private letters and for grants which pass his hand by bill signed ; it is always in the custody of the king's secretaries. 1 *Steph. Com.* [LORD PRIVY SEAL.]

PRIZE COMMISSION. A commission issued in every war under the Creat Seal, requiring the Court of Admiralty to adjudicate upon all and all manner of captures, seizures, prizes and reprisals, and determine the same according to the law of nations. 3 *Steph. Com.* [ADMIRALTY, THE HIGH COURT OF ; INSTANCE COURT OF ADMIRALTY.]

PRIZE COURT. The Admiralty Court sitting under a Prize Commission to adjudicate on captures by land and sea. 2 *Steph. Com.* ; 3 *Steph. Com.* See preceding title.

PRIZE OF WAR. Things captured in time of war. As opposed to *booty of war*, it signifies prize taken *at sea*. It belongs to the Crown, but is given to the forces capturing it. See 2 *Will.* 4, *c.* 53. 3 *Steph. Com.*

PRIZE-FIGHTING in a public place is an affray, and an indictable misdemeanor on the part both of combatants and backers. *Mere presence* at a prize-fight, however, would seem not to be sufficient to render a person guilty of assault. 4 *Steph. Com.*

PRO FORMA. For form's sake.

PRO HAC VICE. For this occasion. An appointment *pro hâc vice* is an appointment for a particular occasion, as opposed to a permanent appointment. 3 *Steph. Com.*

PRO INDIVISO. For an undivided part ; a phrase used in reference to lands, the occupation of which is in joint tenancy, in coparcenary, or in common. [COMMON, TENANCY IN ; COPARCENARY ; JOINT TENANCY.]

PRO INTERESSE SUO. For his own interest. These words are used, especially of a party being admitted to intervene *for his own interest* in a suit instituted between other parties.

PRO LÆSIONE FIDEI. [LÆSIONE FIDEI.]

PRO RATA. Proportionately.

PRO RE NATA. For the matter which has arisen ; a phrase used especially to denote an unprecedented course, adopted to serve the exigencies of a given occasion.

PRO SALUTE ANIMÆ. For the salvation of his soul ; a phrase used to denote that the judgments and monitions in the Ecclesiastical Courts are intended for the reformation of the offender, being given in respect of matters unconnected with private injuries. 3 *Steph. Com.*

PRO TANTO. For so much, or so far as it will go ; as if a tenant for life make a lease for 100 years, the lease is good *pro tanto*, that is, for such an estate or interest as the tenant for life may lawfully convey.

PROBATE. The exhibiting and proving wills by the executors, which formerly took place before the ecclesiastical judge, upon which the original is deposited in the registry of the court, and a copy in parchment, called the *probate copy*, is made out under the seal of the court, and delivered to the executor, together with a certificate of its having been proved. It may be either *in common form* or *in solemn form per testes*, where the will is disputed or irregular. 2 *Steph. Com.* [SOLEMN FORM.]

PROBATE COURT. The court established in 1857 by the stat. 20 & 21 Vict. c. 77, amended by 21 & 22 Vict. c. 95. To this court was transferred by sect. 23 of the principal Act, the testamentary jurisdiction which up to that time had been exercised by the ecclesiastical courts. The Probate Court was merged in the Supreme Court of Judicature by the Judicature Act, 1873; and its jurisdiction is now exercised by the Probate, Divorce and Admiralty Division of that court. 2 *Steph. Com.*; 3 *Steph. Com.*

PROBATE DUTY. The duty payable on proving a will: it is now merged in the estate duty. See the *Finance Act, 1894 (57 & 58 Vict. c. 30)*; *Coote's Probate Practice*; 2 *Steph. Com.* [ESTATE DUTY.]

PROCEDENDO. 1. The writ of *procedendo ad judicium* is a writ which issues when the judge of any subordinate court doth delay the parties in refusing to give judgment. The writ commands him, in the name of the Crown, to proceed to judgment, but without specifying any particular judgment. 3 *Steph. Com.*

2. A writ whereby a cause which has been removed on insufficient grounds from an inferior to a superior court by *certiorari* or otherwise is removed back again to the inferior court. 3 *Steph. Com.* [CERTIORARI.]

3. A writ to revive a commission of the peace which has been superseded by writ of *supersedeas.* 2 *Steph. Com.* [COMMISSION OF THE PEACE; CONSERVATOR OF THE PEACE; JUSTICE OF THE PEACE.]

PROCEDURE. The steps taken in an action or other legal proceeding. [PRACTICE.]

PROCESS. 1. The writ commanding the defendant's appearance in an action. This is sometimes called *original* process. Since the Judicature Acts the process for the commencement of all actions is the same in all Divisions of the High Court. It is either a writ of summons or an originating summons. 3 *Steph. Com.* [SUMMONS, 4.]

2. The various writs formerly issued in the course of an action. Those issued subsequently to the first or original writ, and prior to the writs of execution, were called the *mesne process,* and the writs of execution were called the *final process.* 3 *Steph. Com.* [EXECUTION, 1.]

3. The steps taken upon an indictment or other criminal proceeding. 4 *Steph. Com.*

PROCESSUM CONTINUANDO. A writ for the continuance of a process after the death of the chief justice, or other justices, in the writ of *oyer and terminer.* [ASSIZE, COURTS OF; OYER AND TERMINER.]

PROCHEIN AMY. [NEXT FRIEND.]

PROCLAMATION. A notice publicly given of any thing, whereof the king thinks fit to advertise his subjects. 2 *Steph. Com.*

PROCLAMATION OF FINES. The proclamation of a fine was a notice openly and solemnly given at all the assizes held in the county where the lands lay, within one year after engrossing the fine; all claims not put in within the time allowed subsequent to the proclamation were barred. 1 *Steph. Com.* [FINE, 1.]

PROCTOR. 1. One chosen to represent a cathedral or collegiate church, or the clergy of a diocese, in the Lower House of Convocation.

2. One who prosecutes or defends a suit for another; especially certain officers who formerly were exclusively entitled to conduct suits in the ecclesiastical and admiralty courts. 3 *Steph. Com.* [KING'S PROCTOR.] All such officers are now, by sect. 87 of the Judicature Act, 1873, entitled to be called solicitors of the Supreme Court.

3. An executive officer of the University. 4 *Steph. Com.*

PROCURATION. [PER PROCURATIONEM.] For procurations payable by the clergy, see PROCURATIONS.

PROCURATION FEE. The fee which a scrivener or broker was allowed to take for making a bond. Also the fee charged for obtaining a loan on mortgage.

PROCURATION OF WOMEN. The providing of women for the purpose of illicit intercourse is an offence under the Criminal Law Amendment Act, 1885. 4 *Steph. Com.*

PROCURATIONS are certain sums of money which parish priests pay yearly to the bishop or archdeacon for his visitation. They were anciently paid in necessary victuals for the visitor and his attendants, but afterwards turned into money.

PRODITORIE. Traitorously.

PROFERT IN CURIA. [OYER OF DEEDS AND RECORDS.]

PROFITS À PRENDRE are rights exercised by one man in the soil of another, accompanied with participation in the profits of the soil thereof, as rights of pasture, or of digging sand. *Profits à prendre* differ from easements in that the former are rights of profit, and the latter are mere rights of convenience without profit. *Gale on Easements.* [COMMON ; EASEMENT.]

PROHIBITION. A writ to forbid an inferior court from proceeding in a cause there depending, upon suggestion that the cognizance thereof belongs not to that court.

Now, by 1 Will. 4, c. 21, an application for a writ of prohibition is made by motion, supported by affidavits. See *Crown Office Rules*, 1886, *rr.* 81, 82 ; *R. S. C.* 1883, *Ord. LXVIII., Ord. LIV. r.* 12.

Prohibition differs from injunction. in that prohibition is directed to a court as well as to the opposite party, whereas an injunction is directed to the party alone.

By the Judicature Act, 1873, s. 24, sub-s. 5, no cause or proceeding at any time pending in the High Court of Justice, or before the Court of Appeal, shall be restrained by prohibition or injunction. 3 *Steph. Com.*

PROLICIDE. The destruction of human offspring. See INFANTICIDE.

PROLIXITY. Unnecessary, superfluous, or impertinent statement. It renders an affidavit liable to be taken off the file, and in pleadings the offending party may be made to pay the costs. See *R. S. C.* 1883 ; *Orders XIX. rr.* 2, 5, 27 ; *XXXVIII. r.* 3 ; *LXV. r.* 20. 3 *Steph. Com.*

PROLOCUTOR. The officer who, in each House of Convocation, is chosen to preside over the deliberations of that House.

PROMISE. A voluntary engagement by one man to another for the performance or non-performance of some particular thing. A promise is in the nature of a verbal covenant ; and in strictness it differs from a contract, in that a contract involves the idea of mutuality, which a promise does not. 2 *Steph. Com.* [CONTRACT ; COVENANT.]

PROMISSORY NOTE, otherwise called a *note of hand,* is defined by s. 83 of the Bills of Exchange Act, 1882, as an unconditional promise in writing, made by one person to another, signed by the maker, engaging to pay on demand or at a fixed or determinable future time, a sum certain in money, to or to the order of a specified person or to bearer. The person who makes the note is called the maker, and the person to whom it is payable is called the payee. It differs from a bill of exchange, in that the maker stands in the place of drawer and acceptor. 2 *Steph. Com.* [BILL OF EXCHANGE ; INLAND BILL OF EXCHANGE.]

PROMOTERS. 1. Those who, in popular and penal actions, prosecute offenders in their own name and the king's ; common informers. The term is now only applied to the prosecutor of an ecclesiastical suit. [ACTIONS, CIVIL AND PENAL ; QUI TAM ACTIONS.]

2. Persons or corporations at whose instance private bills are introduced into, and passed through, parliament. *May's Parl. Pract.* [BILL, 4.]

3. Especially those who press forward bills for the taking of land for railways and other public purposes ; who are then called *promoters of the undertaking.*

4. Persons who assist in establishing joint stock companies.

PROMOTING THE OFFICE OF JUDGE. [OFFICE OF A JUDGE.]

PROMOTION MONEY. Money paid to the promoters of a joint stock company for their services in launching the concern. [PROMOTERS, 4.]

PROMULGATION OF A LAW. The publication of a law already made. 1 *Steph. Com.*

PROOF, in Scotch law, corresponds to *evidence* in English law ; and *to lead proof* is to produce evidence. See also the following titles.

PROOF OF DEBT means generally the establishment by a creditor of a debt due to him from an insolvent estate, whether of a bankrupt, a deceased person, or a partnership or company in liquidation. 2 *Steph. Com.; Robson, Bkcy.* [PROVE, 2.]

PROOF OF WILL. [PROBATE.]

PROPER FEUDS. The genuine or original feuds in the hands of military persons, and held by military services. 1 *Steph. Com.*

PROPERTY. The highest right a man can have in any thing ; which right, according to *Cowel,* no man can have in any lands and tenements, save only the king in right of his Crown ; or, according to *Blackstone,* the sole and despotic dominion which one man claims and exercises over the external things of the world, in total exclusion of the right of any other individual in the universe.

The five following applications of the term are enumerated by Austin in his 47th Lecture.

1. A right indefinite in point of user —unrestricted in point of disposition— and unlimited in point of duration. In this sense, it is nearly synonymous with the meaning of the term as given above, and is distinguished from a life interest or an interest for years on the one hand, and from a servitude or easement on the other.

2. The subject of such a right : as when we say, that horse or that field is my property.

3. A right indefinite in point of user, but limited in duration ; as, for instance, a life interest.

4. Right as opposed to possession.

5. A right availing against the world at large, as opposed to rights arising out of contract or quasi-contract.

PROPERTY IN ACTION, as opposed to property in immediate possession, is the right to recover any thing (if it should be refused) by suit or action at law. 2 *Steph. Com.* [CHOSE.]

PROPERTY TAX. [INCOME TAX.]

PROPOSITUS. An expression sometimes used of a person from whom, dying intestate, descent is to be traced, so as to ascertain who is to inherit his land. 1 *Steph. Com.*

PROPOUNDER. The person who, as executor under a will, or claiming administration with a will annexed, proposes it as genuine in the Court of Probate, or other court having jurisdiction for the purpose. [ADMINISTRATOR ; EXECUTOR ; PROBATE.]

PROPRIETARY CHAPELS. Chapels of ease, which are the property of private persons, who have purchased or erected them with a view to profit or otherwise. 34 & 35 *Vict. c.* 66 ; 2 *Steph. Com.* [PRIVATE CHAPELS; PUBLIC CHAPELS.]

PROPRIETATE PROBANDA. A writ which lay for a person upon whom a distress was made, where the distrainor claimed that the goods distrained were his own property. [DISTRESS.]

PROPRIO VIGORE (by its own force).

PROPTER AFFECTUM. PROPTER DEFECTUM. PROPTER DELICTUM. PROPTER HONORIS RESPECTUM. [CHALLENGE.]

PROROGATION OF PARLIAMENT. A putting off by the Crown of the sittings of parliament, the effect of which is to put an end to the session. It differs from an *adjournment,* in that an adjournment is effected by each house separately (though it may be at the instigation of the Crown) ; and after it all things continue as they were at the time of the adjournment made ; whereas, after a *prorogation,* bills introduced and not passed are as if they had never been begun at all. 2 *Steph. Com. ; May's Parl. Pract.*

PROSECUTION. 1. The proceeding with, or following up, any matter in hand.

2. The proceeding with any suit or action at law. By a caprice of language, a person instituting *civil* proceedings is said to prosecute *his action or suit ;* but a person instituting *criminal* proceedings is said to prosecute *the party accused.*

3. The party by whom criminal proceedings are instituted ; thus we say, such a course was adopted by the prosecution, etc.

PROSECUTOR means properly any person who prosecutes any proceeding in a court of justice, whether civil or criminal ; but the caprice of language has confined the term so as to denote in general a party who institutes criminal proceedings by way of indictment or information on behalf of the Crown, who is nominally the prosecutor in all criminal cases. [PUBLIC PROSECUTOR.]

PROSPECTUS is defined by the Companies Act, 1900, as "any prospectus, notice, circular, advertisement, or other invitation, offering to the public for subscription or purchase any shares or debentures of a company."

PROTECTION. 1. The benefit or safety which is secured to every subject by the laws.

PROTECTION—*continued.*

2. A special exemption or immunity given to a person by the king, by virtue of his prerogative, against suits in law or other vexations, in respect of the party being engaged in the king's service. It is now rarely granted.

3. The giving advantages in respect of duties to home over foreign commodities.

PROTECTION ORDER is an order for the protection of a wife's property, granted by the Divorce Court or by a magistrate, under the Divorce Act of 1857, to a wife whose husband has deserted her without reasonable cause. By virtue of the protection order she becomes entitled, during the continuance of such order, to enjoy her own property and to bring actions as if unmarried. The occasions for such an order are now very much fewer since the passing of the Married Women's Property Acts. 2 *Steph. Com.*

PROTECTOR OF SETTLEMENT. The person or persons whose consent, under the Fines and Recoveries Abolition Act, 1833 (3 & 4 Will. 4, c. 74), is necessary to enable a tenant in tail in remainder to bar the subsequent estates in remainder or reversion. The protector takes the place of the old tenant to the *præcipe* and is generally the prior tenant for life, but the author of the settlement may, in lieu of such prior tenant, appoint any number of persons, not exceeding three, to be together protector of the settlement. A protector is under no restraint in giving or withholding his consent. 1 *Steph. Com.* ; *Wms. R. P.*

PROTECTORATE. 1. The period in English history during which Cromwell was protector.

2. A relation sometimes adopted by a strong country towards a weak one, in the nature of a feudal sovereignty, whereby the former protects the latter from hostile invasion, and interferes more or less in its domestic concerns. *Hall's International Law.*

PROTEST. 1. A caution, by which a person declares that he does either not at all, or only conditionally, yield his consent to any act to which he might otherwise be deemed to have yielded an unconditional assent.

2. The dissent of a peer to a vote of the House of Peers, entered on the journals of the house, with his reasons for such

dissent. 2 *Steph. Com.* ; *May's Parl. Pract.*

3. A formal declaration by the holder of a bill of exchange, or by a notary public at his request, that the bill of exchange has been refused acceptance or payment, and that the holder intends to recover all the expenses to which he may be put in consequence thereof. In the case of a foreign bill, such a protest is essential to the right of the holder to recover from the drawer or indorsers. 2 *Steph. Com.* [BILL OF EXCHANGE.]

4. A document drawn up by a master of a ship and attested by a justice of the peace, consul, or notary public, stating the circumstances under which injury has happened to the ship or cargo.

PROTESTANDO. [PROTESTATION.]

PROTHONOTARY. [PROTONOTARY.]

PROTOCOL (Fr. *Protocole* ; Gr. πρωτόκολλον). 1. A Byzantine term applied to the first sheet pasted on a MS. roll, stating by whom it was written, etc. Gr. πολλάω, to glue, paste.

2. The first or original copy of anything.

3. The entry of any written instrument in the book of a notary or public officer, which, in case of the loss of the instrument, may be admitted as evidence of its contents.

4. A document serving as the preliminary to, or opening of, any diplomatic transaction.

PROTONOTARY. A chief scribe in a court of law. There were formerly three of such officers in the Court of Common Pleas, and one in the Court of King's Bench. He of the King's Bench recorded all civil actions in that court. Those of the Common Pleas entered all declarations, etc., and made out judicial writs. These officers were abolished in 1837, by stat. 7 Will. 4 & 1 Vict. c. 30. 1 *Steph. Com.*

PROVE. 1. To establish by evidence ; but specially,

2. To establish a debt due from an insolvent estate, and to receive a dividend thereon. See also PROVING A WILL.

PROVINCE. 1. The circuit of an archbishop's jurisdiction. *Cowel ;* 1 *Steph. Com.* ; 2 *Steph. Com.*

2. A colony or dependency.

PROVING A WILL. Procuring probate of a will. [PROBATE.]

PROVISION was a word applied to the providing a bishop or any other person (called the *provisor*) with an ecclesiastical living by the Pope, before the incumbent was dead. The word was subsequently applied to any right of patronage usurped by the Pope. The purchasing "provisions" at Rome or elsewhere exposed the offender to the penalties of *præmunire*. 4 *Steph. Com.* [PRÆMUNIRE.]

PROVISIONAL ASSIGNEE was an assignee formerly appointed provisionally by the Court of Bankruptcy until regular assignees should be appointed by the creditors.

PROVISIONAL ORDERS. Orders by a Government department authorising public undertakings under the authority of Acts of parliament, *e.g.*, under the Public Health Act, 1875, s. 279, for the "union of districts." Such orders are termed "provisional" because they do not come into force until confirmed by a further Act of parliament.

PROVISO. A condition inserted into a deed, upon the observance whereof the validity of the deed depends.

PROVISO, TRIAL BY, is where a defendant, being apprehensive of delay on the part of the plaintiff, himself undertakes to bring on the cause for trial, giving proper notice thereof to the plaintiff. It is called the trial by proviso by reason of the clause formerly inserted in the sheriff's *venire facias*, namely, "provided (*proviso*) that if two writs come to your hands" (one from the plaintiff and another from the defendant), "you shall execute only one of them." 3 *Steph. Com.*
By R. S. C. 1883, Ord. XXXVI. r. 12, a defendant may give notice of trial if the plaintiff fails to do so. But the phrase "trial by proviso" is not mentioned in the Rules, and is now become obsolete.

PROVISOR. [PROVISION.]

PROVOST MARSHAL. 1. An officer in the king's navy having charge of prisoners at sea.

2. An officer appointed in time of martial law to arrest and punish offenders. Execution parties are placed under his orders. *Simmons on Courts Martial.*

PROXIES. 1. Payments made to a bishop by a religious house, or by parish priests, for the charges of his visitation. [PROCURATIONS.]

2. By a *proxy* we generally understand a person deputed to vote in the place or stead of the party so deputing him. As in the House of Lords (*May's Parl. Pract.*); at meetings of creditors of a bankrupt (*Robson's Bkcy.*); at meetings of the shareholders of a company; and on various other occasions.

PUBERTY. The age of fourteen in men and twelve in women, at which they are deemed physically capable of contracting marriage.

PUBLIC ACT OF PARLIAMENT. An Act to be judicially noticed, which is now the case with all Acts of parliament, except the very few in which a declaration is inserted to the contrary. 1 *Steph. Com.*; 13 & 14 *Vict. c.* 21. [ACT OF PARLIAMENT; BILL, 4; LOCAL AND PERSONAL ACTS.]

PUBLIC AUTHORITIES PROTECTION ACT, 1893. This Act provides that actions brought against public officers for any alleged default in the execution of their duties must be commenced within six months of the act complained of. Notice of action is no longer necessary, but time must be given to the defendant to tender amends. 3 *Steph. Com.*

PUBLIC CHAPELS are chapels of ease designed for the benefit of particular districts within a parish. They are opposite to *private chapels*, which are erected for the use of persons of rank, to whom the privilege has been conceded by the proper authorities; also to *proprietary chapels*, which are the property of private persons, and are erected with a view to profit or otherwise. 2 *Steph. Com.*

PUBLIC HEALTH ACTS. The law relating to the public health was consolidated and amended by the Public Health Act, 1875 (38 & 39 Vict. c. 55), which Act is in turn amended by the Public Health Act, 1890 (53 & 54 Vict. c. 45). Under these Acts the whole of England is divided into districts called "urban" and "rural" sanitary districts, each having a "sanitary authority" governing the district according to the provisions contained in the Acts. 3 *Steph. Com.* [URBAN SANITARY AUTHORITY.]

PUBLIC MEETING. Any number of persons may meet for any lawful purpose in any place with the consent of the owner of the place, but there is no "right of public meeting" known to English law, and persons have only a right to pass and repass in the public streets, etc. *Dicey's Law of the Constitution.*

Political meetings within a mile of Westminster Hall during the session of Parliament are prohibited by 57 Geo. 3, c. 19.

Newspaper reports of public meetings are "privileged" by the Law of Libel Amendment Act, 1888 (*q.v.*).

PUBLIC PROSECUTOR. The Director of Public Prosecutions, appointed under the Prosecution of Offences Act, 1879, whose duty it is to undertake the prosecution in all cases where the magnitude of the offence makes it desirable, *e.g.*, in cases of murder, etc. By the Prosecution of Offences Act, 1884, the solicitor to the Treasury is constituted the Director of Public Prosecutions.

PUBLIC WORSHIP REGULATION ACT, 1874 (37 & 38 Vict. c. 85). An Act for the better administration of the laws respecting the regulation of public worship.

PUBLICATION. 1. The declaration by a testator that a given writing is intended to operate as his last will and testament. This was formerly necessary to give legal effect to a will. But, by sect. 13 of the Wills Act, 1837 (7 Will. 4 & 1 Vict. c. 26), no publication is necessary beyond the execution attested by two witnesses as required by sect. 9 of that Act. 1 *Steph. Com.*

2. The communication of a libellous statement to any person or persons other than the party of whom it is spoken. 4 *Steph. Com.*

PUBLICI JURIS (of public right).

PUBLISH. [PUBLICATION.]

PUERITIA. The age from seven to fourteen years. 4 *Steph. Com.*

PUFFER. A person employed to bid at a sale by auction on behalf of the owner of the land or goods sold. The employment of a puffer is illegal, unless a right to bid is reserved to the owner by the conditions or particulars of sale. See *stat.* 30 & 31 *Vict. c.* 48, as to land, and the *Sale of Goods Act,* 1893, *s.* 58, as to goods.

PUIS DARREIN CONTINUANCE (since the last continuance). A plea *puis darrein continuance* is a plea alleging some matter of defence which has arisen since the last "*continuance*" or *adjournment* of the court. 3 *Steph. Com.* [CONTINUANCE.]

Now, under R. S. C. 1883, Ord. XXIV., a ground of defence arising after action brought, but before the defendant has delivered his statement of defence, and before the time limited for his doing so has expired, may be pleaded by the defendant in his statement of defence. And any ground of defence arising after the defendant has delivered his statement of defence, or after the time limited for his doing so has expired, may be pleaded within eight days after such ground of defence has arisen.

PUISNE. Younger; thus, *mulier puisné* is the younger legitimate brother. [MULIER PUISNE.] So, the judges of the High Court, other than those having a distinctive title, are called the *puisne* judges. 3 *Steph. Com.*

PUR AUTER VIE, or PUR AUTRE VIE. For another's life; thus a tenant *pur autre vie* is a tenant whose estate is to last during another person's life.

PURCHASE, besides its ordinary meaning, has a more extensive technical meaning in reference to the law of real property. The meaning is twofold :—

1. The word signifies any lawful mode of coming to an estate by the act of the *party* as opposed to the act of *law*; that is to say, in any manner except by descent, escheat, curtesy, and dower. 1 *Steph. Com.*

2. Any mode, other than descent, of becoming seised of real estate. 1 *Steph. Com.* [PURCHASER.]

PURCHASER. 1. One who acquires real or personal estate by the payment of money.

2. One who acquires real estate by his own act and not by act of law.

3. One who acquires real estate otherwise than by descent. Thus, in sect. 1 of the Inheritance Act (3 & 4 Will. 4, c. 106), the "purchaser" is defined as the person who last acquired the land otherwise than by descent. 1 *Steph. Com.*

PURE VILLENAGE. Villenage in which the service was base in its nature and uncertain. 1 *Steph. Com.* [COPYHOLD; FREEHOLD; PRIVILEGED VILLENAGE.]

PURGATION was a word applied to the methods by which, in former times, a man cleared himself of a crime of which he was accused. This was either *canonical*, by the oaths of twelve neighbours that they believed in his innocence ; or *vulgar*, by fire or water ordeal, or by combat. 4 *Steph. Com.* [BENEFIT OF CLERGY ; COMPURGATORS.

PURGING. Atoning for an offence. Thus *purging a contempt of court* is atoning for a contempt. The party then ceases to be "in contempt," that is to say, liable to the disabilities of one who refuses to obey the orders of the court.

PURLIEU. A word variously derived from *pur lieu* (exempt place), or *pourallée* (perambulation), and signifying all that ground which, having been made forest by Henry I., Richard I., or John, was by Henry III. *disafforested*, so as to remit to the former owners their rights. 1 *Steph. Com.*

PURPARTY. [POURPARTY.]

PURPRESTURE. [POURPRESTURE.]

PURSUER. The Scotch name for a plaintiff or prosecutor.

PURVEYANCE AND PRE-EMPTION, PREROGATIVE OF. [PRE-EMPTION.]

PURVIEW. 1. That part of an Act of parliament which begins with the words, *Be it enacted.*

2. The scope of an Act of parliament.

PUT. An option which a party has of delivering stock at a certain time, in pursuance of a contract, the other party to the contract being bound to take the stock at the price and time therein specified.

PUTATIVE FATHER. The man who is supposed to be the father of a bastard child ; and, especially, one who is adjudged to be so by an order of justices, under the Bastardy Acts. See 2 *Steph. Com.*

PYX. [PIXING THE COIN.]

Q. V. (*Quod vide*, Latin for " which see "). This abbreviation directs a reader to consult some passage referred to.

QUÆ SERVITIA. [PERQUÆ SERVITIA.]

QUALIFICATION. That which makes a person eligible to do certain acts or to hold office. See 29 & 30 *Vict. c.* 22.

QUALIFIED. Limited ; thus a qualified fee is equivalent to a base fee, being one which hath a qualification subjoined thereto, and which must be determined (*i.e.*, put an end to) whenever the qualification annexed to it is at an end. 1 *Steph. Com.*

QUALIFIED INDORSEMENT, on a bill of exchange or promissory note, is an endorsement which restrains, limits, or enlarges the liability of the indorser. in a manner different from that which the law generally imports as his true liability, deducible from the nature of the instrument. [BILL OF EXCHANGE: INDORSEMENT ; PROMISSORY NOTE.] A particular species of this indorsement is one whereby the indorser repudiates liability, which may be made by annexing in French the words *sans recours.* or in English "without recourse to me," or other equivalent expression. *Byles on Bills ; Bills of Exchange Act,* 1882, *ss.* 16 (1) and 35.

QUALIFIED PROPERTY. A limited right of ownership ; as, for instance—

1. Such right as a man has in animals *feræ naturæ*, which he has reclaimed. 2 *Steph. Com.* [FERÆ NATURÆ ; INDUSTRIAM, PER.]

2. Such right as a bailee has in the chattel transferred to him by the bailment. 2 *Steph. Com.* [BAILMENT.]

QUAMDIU BENE SE GESSERIT (as long as he shall behave himself well). These words imply that an office or privilege is to be held during good behaviour (as opposed to *durante bene placito,* during the pleasure of the grantor), and therefore is not to be lost otherwise than by the misconduct of the occupant ; except of course by his death or voluntary resignation.

This is otherwise expressed by the phrase *ad vitam aut culpam.* 2 *Steph. Com.*

QUANDO ACCIDERINT (when they shall fall in). A judgment by which the creditor of a deceased person, who, having brought an action against the executor or administrator, has been met with a plea of *plene administravit,* is entitled to any assets which may in future fall into the hands of the defendant as legal representative of the deceased. 2 *Steph. Com.* [PLENE ADMINISTRAVIT.]

QUANTUM MERUIT (how much he has deserved). An action on a *quantum meruit* is an action of *assumpsit* grounded on a promise, express or implied, to pay the plaintiff for work and labour so much as his trouble is really worth. It no longer exists as a special form of action, but the phrase is still in use.

QUANTUM VALEBAT (as much as it was worth). A phrase applied to an action on an implied promise to pay for goods sold as much as they were worth, where no price had been previously fixed.

QUARANTINE. Forty days. 1. The space of forty days after the death of a husband seised of land, during which his widow was entitled to remain in her husband's capital mansion-house, and during which time her dower was to be assigned. 1 *Steph. Com.* [ASSIGNMENT OF DOWER; DOWER, 2.] 2. Forty days' probation for ships coming from infected countries, or such other time as may be directed by Order in Council. 3 *Steph. Com.*

QUARE CLAUSUM FREGIT (wherefore he broke the close). A phrase applied to an action for trespass in breaking and entering the plaintiff's close, which includes every unwarrantable entry on another's soil. 3 *Steph. Com.*

QUARE EJECIT INFRA TERMINUM (wherefore he ejected him within the term). A writ which lay for a lessee who had been ejected from his farm before the expiration of his term. It differed from the writ of *ejectment* in being brought, not against the original wrongdoer, but against a feoffee or other person in possession claiming under the wrongdoer, for keeping out the lessee during the continuance of the term. Long obsolete. [EJECTMENT.]

QUARE IMPEDIT (wherefore he hinders). A writ which lay for him whose right of advowson was disturbed. [ADVOWSON.]

The writ of *quare impedit*, which survived the general abolition of real actions in 1833, was finally extinguished by sects. 26 and 27 of the C. L. Proc. Act, 1860, by which it was provided that in the cases where such a writ would lie, an action should be commenced by writ of summons as in an ordinary action, there being indorsed upon such writ a notice that the plaintiff intends to claim in *quare impedit*. 3 *Steph. Com.* The practice in this respect is not altered under the Judicature Acts.

QUARE INCUMBRAVIT (wherefore he has incumbered). On the suing out of a *quare impedit*, if the plaintiff suspected that the bishop would admit some other clerk, he might have a prohibitory writ, called a *ne admittas;* and if the bishop, after receiving the same, nevertheless admitted any person other than the presentee of the plaintiff, then the plaintiff, having obtained judgment in the *quare impedit*, was entitled to a special action against the bishop, called a *quare incumbravit*, to recover the presentation, and also satisfaction in damages for the injury done.

Abolished by stat. 3 & 4 Will. 4, c. 27, s. 36. 3 *Steph. Com.* [NE ADMITTAS: QUARE IMPEDIT.]

QUARE NON ADMISIT (wherefore he has not admitted him). A writ by which a patron might recover damages against a bishop for not admitting the plaintiff's clerk, in obedience to a writ *ad admittendum clericum*, ordering him to admit such clerk. [ADMITTENDO CLERICO.]

QUARREL. A word anciently used for an action.

QUARTER DAYS are, in England, the four following days :—
1. The 25th of March, being the Feast of the Annunciation of the Blessed Virgin Mary, commonly called Lady Day. [LADY DAY.]
2. The 24th of June, being the Feast of St. John the Baptist, otherwise called Midsummer Day.
3. The 29th of September, being the Feast of St. Michael and All Angels, commonly called Michaelmas Day.
4. The 25th of December, being the Feast of the Nativity of Christ, commonly called Christmas Day.

QUARTER SESSIONS are the General Sessions of the peace held quarterly before the justices of the peace in counties, and before the recorder in boroughs. [BOROUGH SESSIONS; COUNTY SESSIONS; JUSTICE OF THE PEACE; RECORDER.]

In stat. 5 & 6 Vict. c. 38, s. 1, various offences are mentioned as not being within the jurisdiction of the quarter sessions. Among other offences so enumerated we may mention treason, murder, perjury, forgery, bigamy, abduction, and bribery. See *Oke's Mag. Syn.* 4 *Steph. Com.*

QUASH (Lat. *Cassum facere*) signifies to make void or annul. As when we say that an order of justices, or a conviction in an inferior court, is *quashed* by the judgment of a superior court.

QUASI-CONTRACT is an act or event from which, though not a consensual contract, an obligation arises *as if* from a contract (*quasi ex contractu*). Thus, for instance, an executor or administrator is bound to satisfy the liabilities of the deceased to the extent of his assets received, *as if* he had contracted to do so. [IMPLIED.]

QUASI-ENTAIL is an estate *pur autre vie* granted to a man and the heirs of his body. 1 *Steph. Com.*; *Wms. R. P.* [PUR AUTER VIE.]

QUASI-PERSONALTY. Things which are movables in point of law, though fixed to things real, either actually, as emblements, etc., or fictitiously, as chattels-real, leases for years, etc.

QUASI-REALTY. Things which are fixed in contemplation of law to realty, but are movable in themselves, *e.g.*, heirlooms, title deeds, etc.

QUASI-TRUSTEE. A person who reaps a benefit from a breach of trust, and so becomes answerable as a trustee. *Lewin on Trusts.*

QUE ESTATE was an expression formerly used in pleading to avoid prolixity in setting out titles to land; as if B., claiming a lawful title to land, pleads a conveyance of the land to A., which estate (*quem statum*) B. hath, without setting out at length how the estate came from A. to B. Hence the expression came to signify an estate acquired otherwise than by descent. Such an estate enabled a man, at common law, to acquire by prescription such rights as were appendant or appurtenant to lands enjoyed by himself and those whose estate he had. 1 *Steph. Com.* [PRESCRIPTION.]

QUEEN. 1. A queen regent, regnant, or sovereign, is one who holds the crown in her own right.

2. A queen consort is the wife of a reigning king.

3. A queen dowager is the widow of a deceased king. 2 *Steph. Com.*

QUEEN ANNE'S BOUNTY. A perpetual fund for the augmentation of poor livings, created by a charter of Queen Anne, out of the tenths and first fruits formerly payable by the beneficed clergy

to the Pope, and, after the Reformation, to the English sovereigns. 2 *Steph. Com.* [FIRST FRUITS.]

QUEEN CONSORT. [QUEEN, 2.]

QUEEN DOWAGER. [QUEEN, 3.]

QUEEN GOLD (Lat. *Aurum Reginæ*). [AURUM REGINÆ.]

QUERELA. An action preferred in a court of justice. [DUPLEX QUERELA; AUDITA QUERELA.]

QUEST. Inquest or inquiry. [INQUEST.]

QUI APPROBAT NON REPROBAT (he who accepts cannot reject).

QUI FACIT PER ALIUM FACIT PER SE (he who does a thing through another does it himself).

QUI HÆRET IN LITERÂ, HÆRET IN CORTICE (he who sticks to the letter of an instrument goes but skin deep into its meaning).

QUI MANDAT IPSE FACISSE VIDETUR (he who gives the order is considered to be the doer).

QUI PRIOR EST TEMPORE POTIOR EST JURE (he who is first in time is better in law).

QUI SENTIT COMMODUM, SENTIRE DEBET ET ONUS (he who receives the advantage ought also to suffer the burthen).

QUI TACET, CONSENTIRE VIDETUR (he who is silent, is understood to consent).

QUI TAM ACTIONS are actions brought by a person, under a penal statute, to recover a penalty, partly for the king or the poor, or some other public use, and partly for himself; so called because it is brought by a person who, as well for our lord the king as for himself, sues in this behalf: "*Qui tam pro domino rege, etc., quam pro se ipso in hâc parte sequitur.*" 3 *Steph. Com.*

QUIA EMPTORES. The stat. 18 Edw. 1, c. 1, which was passed in 1290, to put a stop to the practice of subinfeudation. That statute provided that it should be lawful for every freeman to sell at his own pleasure his lands and tenements, or part thereof, so nevertheless that the feoffee (or purchaser) should hold the same lands or tenements of the same chief lord of the fee, and by the same services and customs, as his feoffee held them before. 1 *Steph. Com.*; *Wms. R. P.*

QUIA TIMET (because he fears). A *quia timet* bill was a bill filed in Chancery for guarding against a future injury of which a plaintiff was apprehensive ; as by a person entitled to property in remainder, for the purpose of securing it against any accident which might befall it previously to the time when it should fall into possession ; or by a person who feared that some instrument really void but apparently valid might hereafter be used against him, and which he wished to be cancelled. The jurisdiction to entertain questions of this kind, so far as it consists in the rectification, setting aside, or cancellation of deeds and other written instruments, is, by s. 34 of the Judicature Act, 1873, (36 & 37 Vict. c. 66), assigned to the Chancery Division of the High Court. So far as it consists in the granting of a mandamus or injunction, it may, by s. 25, sub-s. 8, be exercised in any division.

QUICQUID PLANTATUR SOLO, SOLO CEDIT (whatever is affixed to the soil, belongs to the soil). See FIXTURES.

QUICQUID SOLVITUR, SOLVITUR SECUNDUM MODUM SOLVENTIS (whatever is paid, is paid according to the direction of the payer).

QUID PRO QUO. A compensation, or the giving of one thing of value for another thing of like value. 2 *Steph. Com.* [CONSIDERATION.]

QUIET ENJOYMENT is a phrase applied especially to the undisturbed enjoyment, by a purchaser of landed property, of the estate or interest so purchased. A general covenant, by a vendor or lessor, for quiet enjoyment by the purchaser or lessee, extends only to secure the covenantee against the acts of persons claiming under a *lawful* title, for the law will never adjudge that a lessor (or vendor) covenants against the wrongful acts of strangers, unless his covenant is express to that purpose. The construction, however, is different where an individual is named, for there the covenantor is presumed to know the person against whose acts he is content to covenant, and may therefore be reasonably expected to stipulate against any disturbance from him, whether by lawful title or otherwise. See also s. 7 of Conveyancing Act, 1881. *Woodfall, L. & T. ;* 1 *Steph. Com.*

QUIETUS. 1. Acquitted or discharged : a word used especially of the sheriffs and other accountants to the Exchequer, when they had given in their accounts.

2. An acquittance or discharge.

QUIETUS REDDITUS. Quit rent. [QUIT RENT.]

QUINTO EXACTUS. The fifth and last call of a defendant sued for outlawry, when, if he appeared not, he was declared outlawed. 4 *Steph. Com.* [EXIGENT ; OUTLAWRY.]

QUIT CLAIM. A release or acquitting of a man of any action or claim which might be had against him.

QUIT RENT. Fixed rent paid by the freeholders and copyholders (specially the latter) of a manor in discharge or acquittance of other services. 1 *Steph. Com.* [RENT.]

QUO ANIMO (with what intention). A phrase often used in criminal trials, where there is no question of certain overt acts having been committed by the accused, and the only question is with what intention (*quo animo*) they were done. [FURANDI ANIMUS.]

QUO JURE (by what right). A writ that lay for him in whose lands another claimed common of pasture time out of mind, calling on the latter to show by what title he claimed.

QUO LIGATUR, EO DISSOLVITUR (by the same mode by which a thing is bound by that it is released).

QUO MINUS. 1. A writ that lay for him who had a grant of housebote or haybote in another man's woods, to prevent the grantor making such waste that the grantee could not enjoy his grant. [HAYBOTE ; HOUSEBOTE.]

2. The allegation formerly made in civil actions in the Exchequer, that the plaintiff was the king's lessee or debtor. and that the defendant had done him the injury complained of, *quo minus sufficiens existeret, etc.,* "by reason whereof he was the less able to pay the king his rent or debt." By this fiction the Court of Exchequer usurped the jurisdiction of the ordinary courts of justice. 3 *Steph. Com.* [COURT OF EXCHEQUER.]

QUO WARRANTO. 1. A writ that lay against him that usurped any franchise or liberty against the king ; also against

QUO WARRANTO—*continued.*

him that intruded himself as heir into any land. This writ is now obsolete, its place being taken by 2, *infra.*

2. An information in the nature of a writ of *quo warranto* was originally a criminal information for the wrongful use of a franchise, but is now the usual method of trying the existence of the civil right, and is regarded practically as a civil proceeding. Under the Municipal Corporations Act, 1882, s. 87, an election petition is substituted for proceedings by *quo warranto* in all cases where an election is sought to be questioned on the ground of bribery, etc., disqualification or undue return.

Quo warranto still lies in cases of disqualification arising *after election* under s. 225 of the Act of 1882 (*q.v.*)

See also Crown Office Rules, 1882, rr. 51—9. 3 *Steph. Com.* [INFORMATION, 3, 5.]

QUOAD HOC (in respect of this matter). A term used in law reports to signify, *as to this matter* the law is so. *Toml.*

QUOD AB INITIO NON VALET, IN TRACTU TEMPORIS NON CONVALESCET (that which is invalid from the commencement, gains no strength by lapse of time).

QUOD FIERI DEBET FACILE PRÆSUMITUR (that which ought to be done is easily presumed).

QUOD FIERI NON DEBET FACTUM VALET (that which ought not to be done is valid when done).

QUOD NULLIUS EST, EST DOMINI REGIS (that which is the property of nobody, belongs to our lord the king).

QUOD RECUPERET (that he recover). The old form of final judgment for a plaintiff in a personal action.

QUOD SEMEL PLACUIT IN ELECTIONE AMPLIUS DISPLICERE NON POTEST (when election is once made, it cannot be revoked).

QUORUM. 1. A word used in commissions of the peace, by which it is intended to indicate that some particular justices, or some or one of them, are always to be included in the business to be done, so that no business can be done without their presence ; the words being " *quorum aliquem vestrum,*

A. B. C. D., etc., *unum esse volumus.*" The particular justices so named are called justices of the *quorum.* Formerly it was the custom to appoint only a select number of such justices : but even in Blackstone's time it had become the custom to advance all of them to that dignity, except perhaps only some one inconsiderable person, for the sake of propriety. 2 *Steph. Com.*

2. The *minimum* number of persons necessarily present in order that business may be proceeded with, at any meeting for the despatch of business, in the Houses of Parliament, or elsewhere, *e.g.,* the quorum of three justices under s. 37 of the Licensing Act, 1872. *May's Parl. Pract. ; Robson, Bkcy.*

QUOUSQUE. A word implying a temporary state of things. Thus the lord of a manor, after making due proclamation at three consecutive courts of the manor for a person to come in as heir or devisee of a deceased tenant, is entitled to seize the lands *quousque,* that is, until some person claims admittance. 1 *Steph. Com. ; Wms. R. P.* So, a prohibition *quousque* is a prohibition which is to take effect until some act be performed, or event happen, or time be elapsed, according as is specified in the prohibition.

R. S. C. Rules of the Supreme Court made by a committee of the judges under the authority of the Judicature Act, 1881. The rules were consolidated and amended in 1883, and may be found in the " Annual Practice."

RABBIT. A beast of warren, also termed a " coney." As to the right of a tenant to shoot rabbits on his farm, see the Ground Game Act, 1880.

RABIES ORDER, 1886. An order of the Privy Council whereby dogs were brought within the scope of the Contagious Diseases (Animals) Acts, and various provisions were made for preventing the spread of rabies. By the Board of Agriculture Act, 1889, the powers of the Privy Council in regard to dogs were transferred to the Board of Agriculture.

RACECOURSE. By the stat. 42 & 43 Vict. c. 18, no racecourse within ten miles of Charing Cross is allowed without an annual licence from the justices of the peace.

RACK. Torture for the purpose of extorting confession from an accused person. It is also called *question*. 4 *Steph. Com.*

RACK-RENT. Rent of the full annual value of the tenement on which it is charged, or as near to it as possible. 1 *Steph. Com.*

RAILWAY AND CANAL COMMISSION. A body established by 51 & 52 Vict. c. 25, to supersede the Railway Commissioners and exercise their jurisdiction with enlarged powers. It consists of two appointed and three *ex-officio* commissioners, one each for England, Scotland and Ireland, each being a judge of a superior court of their own country, in which alone they are required to serve. The *ex-officio* commissioner presides, and his opinion on a point of law prevails. As to appeals, see ss. 17 and 55 of the Act of 1888.

RAILWAY COMMISSIONERS. [RAILWAY AND CANAL COMMISSION.]

RAILWAYS CLAUSES CONSOLIDATION ACT (8 Vict. c. 20), and **RAILWAYS CLAUSES ACT, 1863** (26 & 27 Vict. c. 92.) These Acts contain general provisions as to the construction and management of railways, and were passed to avoid the necessity of repeating such provisions in the special Acts, by which each railway company is incorporated. 3 *Steph. Com.*

RANK MODUS. Every *modus* of tithes is presumably based on a composition on fairly equitable terms, by which the *modus* is substituted for the payment of tithe. [MODUS DECIMANDI ; TITHES.] If, then, a *modus* be so large that it, beyond dispute, exceeds the value of the tithes in the time of Richard I. (the date of legal memory), the *modus* is called a *rank modus*, and will not be accepted as a legal *modus*. For, as it would be destroyed by any direct evidence proving its non-existence at any time since that era, so also it is destroyed by carrying in itself this internal evidence of a much later origin. 2 *Steph. Com.*

RANSOM. 1. The sum paid for the redeeming of one taken prisoner. *T. L. ; Cowel ;* 2 *Bl.* 402.
2. A fine in the king's court, or the redemption of corporal punishment due by law for any offence. *T. L. ; Cowel ;* 4 *Bl.*

RANSOM-BILL. A security given by the master of a captured vessel to the captor for the ransom of the vessel, or any goods therein.

RAPE. 1. Part of a county, being in a manner the same with a hundred. The county of Sussex is divided into six rapes : those of Chichester, Arundel, Bramber, Lewes, Pevensey, and Hastings ; each of which, besides their hundreds, hath a castle, river, and forest belonging to it. They seem to have been military governments in the time of the Conqueror. 1 *Steph. Com.*
2. Trespass committed in the forest by violence. This is called *rape of the forest.*
3. The ravishment of a woman without her consent. Under stat. 24 & 25 Vict. c. 100, s. 48, this offence is punishable with penal servitude for life ; and see 48 & 49 Vict. c. 69, s. 4. 4 *Steph. Com. ; Oke's Mag. Syn.*

RAPINE. Robbery, *i.e.*, the unlawful taking of property from the owner by violence, or putting him in fear. *Cowel ;* 4 *Bl. ;* 4 *Steph. Com.*

RASURE. An erasure or obliteration in a deed or other instrument.

RATE. The generic name for local taxes. The principal of these are the *county rate*, the *borough rate*, and the *poor rate*.
1. The *county rate* is levied by the county council, who are authorised and empowered by law to assess and tax every parish, township and other place, whether parochial or extra-parochial, within the respective limits of the county, according to the annual value of the property, messuages, lands, tenements, and hereditaments rateable to the relief of the poor therein.
The finance committee having found the proportion due from each parish sends a precept to each poor law union for the amounts due from the parishes in it. The board of guardians then add the amount required in each case to their precepts for poor relief, etc., and pay the county council its due. *Atkinson's Local Government Law ;* 1 *Steph. Com.*
2. A *borough rate* is levied by the town council : and the town council may direct the churchwardens and overseers of each parish or place, within which the rate may be levied, to pay the same out of the poor rate, or to collect a pound rate for the purpose from the occupiers and possessors of rateable property

RATE—*continued.*

within such parish or place. *Archbold's Justice of the Peace; Oke's Mag. Syn.*

3. The *poor rate* is levied by the churchwardens and overseers within each parish. [OVERSEERS.]

RATE-TITHE. Tithe paid *pro ratâ*, according to the custom of the place, for sheep or other cattle kept in a parish for less time than a year.

RATIFICATION. Confirmation, *e.g.*, of a contract. [INFANTS' RELIEF ACT, 1874.]

RATIO DECIDENDI. The ground of a decision; a phrase often used in opposition to *obiter dictum*. [OBITER DICTUM.]

RATIONABILE ESTOVERIUM. Reasonable estovers or alimony. [ESTOVERS.]

RATIONABILI PARTE. [DE RATIONABILI PARTE.]

RATIONE TENURÆ (by reason of tenure or occupation). An individual or particular borough may be liable to repair a bridge *ratione tenuræ* though such liability is in general upon the county at large. 3 *Steph. Com.*

RAVISHMENT. [ABDUCTION.]

RE. In the matter of. [IN RE.]

READER. 1. The chaplain of the Temple. 2. A lecturer.

READING IN is a phrase used to denote the reading of the Thirty-nine Articles of Religion, and repeating the Declaration of Assent prescribed by stat. 28 & 29 Vict. c. 122, which is required of every incumbent on the first Lord's Day on which he officiates in the church of his benefice, or such other Lord's Day as the ordinary shall appoint and allow. 2 *Steph. Com.*

REAL, besides its ordinary meaning, has, in law, two special meanings :—

First, as being applicable to a thing in contradistinction to a person :

Secondly, as applicable to land, and especially freehold interests therein, as opposed to other rights and interests. See the following titles.

REAL AND PERSONAL PROPERTY. By *real property*, or *real estate*, we understand such interests in land as, on the death of their owner intestate, descend to his heir-at-law; or, if the land be copyhold or customary freehold, to the heir or heirs pointed out by the custom. By *personal property*, or *personal estate*, we understand such property as, on the owner's death, devolves on his executor or administrator, to be distributed (in so far as the owner has not made any disposition thereof by will) among his next of kin according to the Statutes of Distributions.

The origin of the names *real property* and *personal property* is explained as follows by Mr. Joshua Williams in the introduction to his treatise on the Law of Real Property :—Land of which the owner was deprived could always be restored, but goods could not. As to the one, the *real* land could be recovered; but, as to the other, proceedings must be had against the *person* who had taken them away. The remedies for the recovery of land were accordingly in old times called *real* actions, and those for the loss of goods were called *personal* actions.

Real property is not, however, precisely synonymous with property in land, nor is personal property synonymous with movable property. Thus, a title of honour, though annexed to the person of its owner, is real property, because in ancient times such titles were annexed to the ownership of various lands. On the other hand, shares in canals and railways are in general made personal property by the different Acts of parliament under the authority of which they have originated. And a lease for years is personal property, because, in ancient times, an ejected lessee could not recover his lease by real action : but he could bring a personal action for damages against his landlord, who was bound to warrant him possession. [ACTIONS REAL AND PERSONAL; CHATTELS; EJECTMENT.]

REAL REPRESENTATIVE. 1. The representative (whether heir or devisee) of a deceased person in respect of his real property. 2 *Steph. Com.* 2. By the Land Transfer Act, 1897, the executor or administrator of any person dying after the commencement of that Act is constituted the real representative. Real estate except copyhold vests in him as trustee for the person beneficially entitled.

REALTY. Real estate; that is, freehold interests in land ; or, in a larger sense (so as to include chattels real), things substantial and immovable, and the rights and profits annexed to or issuing out of these. 1 *Steph. Com.*

REASONABLE AND PROBABLE CAUSE is a phrase often used in connection with the usual ground of defence to an action for false imprisonment, that the defendant had reasonable and probable cause for arresting the plaintiff. Also in an action for malicious prosecution plaintiff must prove that there was no reasonable and probable cause for the prosecution. The question of reasonable and probable cause is, in England, a question for the judge, but in Scotland for the jury. 3 *Steph. Com.*

RE-ASSURANCE POLICY is a contract whereby an insurer seeks to relieve himself from a risk which he may have incautiously undertaken, by throwing it upon some other underwriter. Re-assurance was, except in certain specified cases, forbidden by stat. 19 Geo. 2, c. 37, s. 4, but this Act was repealed by 30 & 31 Vict. c. 23. 2 *Steph. Com.*

RE-ATTACHMENT. A second attachment of him that was formerly attached and dismissed the court without day, as by the not coming of the justices, or some such casualty. [EAT INDE SINE DIE.]

REBATE. Discount ; a deduction from a payment in consideration of its being made before due.

REBELLIOUS ASSEMBLY. A gathering together of twelve persons or more, going about of their own authority to change any laws or statutes of the realm ; or to destroy any park or ground enclosed, or the banks of any fish-pond, pool, or conduit, or to destroy any deer, or burn stacks of corn, or to abate rents, or prices of victuals, etc.

REBUTTER. The pleading by the defendant in answer to the plaintiff's surre-joinder. 3 *Steph. Com.*; *Steph. on Pleading.* [REJOINDER.]

REBUTTING EVIDENCE is evidence adduced to *rebut* a presumption of fact or law, that is, to avoid its effect. But the word is also used in a larger sense to include any evidence adduced to destroy the effect of prior evidence, not only in explaining it away while admitting its truth, but also by direct denial, or by an attack upon the character of the witness who has given it. 3 *Steph. Com.*

RECAPTION signifies :—1. A second distress of one formerly distrained for the same cause. 2. A writ that lay for the party thus distrained twice over for the same thing. 3. A reprisal taken by one man against another, who hath deprived him of his property, or wrongfully detained his wife, child, or servant. 3 *Steph. Com.*

RECEIPT. 1. That branch of the Exchequer in which the royal revenue is managed. 3 *Steph. Com.* [COURT OF EXCHEQUER.]

2. A written acknowledgment of the payment of money. As to stamping receipt see the Stamp Act, 1891. A receipt for the purchase money of land may be embodied in the purchase-deed. See the *Conveyancing Act*, 1881, ss. 54, 55. 1 *Steph. Com.*

RECEIVER. 1. One who receives stolen goods, knowing them to be stolen. 4 *Steph. Com.*

2. An officer appointed by the Court of Chancery to receive the rents and profits of a trust or mortgaged estate, and to account for the same to the court. Under the Jud. Act, 1873, s. 25 (8), a receiver may be appointed by an interlocutory order of the court in all cases in which it shall appear to be just or convenient. 3 *Steph. Com.* As to the power of a mortgagee to appoint a receiver see s. 19 of the Conveyancing Act, 1881. 1 *Steph. Com.* Under the Bankruptcy Act, 1883, a *receiver* of a debtor's estate may be appointed by the court after the presentation of a bankruptcy petition. 2 *Steph. Com.* See also the following titles.

RECEIVERS AND TRIERS OF PETI-TIONS. Officers appointed to examine petitions presented to the parliament. The appointment of these officers at the opening of every parliament has been continued by the House of Lords without interruption ; but their functions have now long since given way to the immediate authority of parliament at large. *May's Parl. Pract.*

RECEIVERS OF WRECK. Officers appointed by the Board of Trade in different districts to summon as many men as may be necessary, to demand help from any ship near at hand, or to press into their service any waggons, carts, or horses, for the purpose of preserving or assisting any stranded or distressed vessel, or her cargo, or for the saving of human life. See the *Merchant Shipping Act*, 1894, *ss.* 511—514. 2 *Steph. Com.* [WRECK.]

RECITAL. That part of a deed which recites the deeds, arguments, and other matters of fact, which may be necessary to explain the reasons upon which it is founded. 1 *Steph. Com.*; *Wms. R. P.*

Recitals are not essential to the validity of a deed, and are often dispensed with.

RECLAIMED ANIMALS. Wild animals made tame by art, industry and education. 2 *Steph. Com.* [FERÆ NATURÆ.]

RECOGNITORS. A word formerly used of a jury empannelled upon an assize or real action. [ASSIZE, WRIT OF.]

RECOGNIZANCE. An obligation of record, which a man enters into before some court of record, or magistrate duly authorised, binding himself under a penalty to do some particular act ; as to appear at the assizes, to keep the peace, to pay a debt, or the like. 4 *Steph. Com.*

RECOGNIZEE. He to whom another is bound in a recognizance.

RECOGNIZOR. A person bound in a recognizance.

RE-CONVERSION. The restoration, in contemplation of equity, to its actual original quality of property which has been constructively converted.

RE-CONVEYANCE. A deed by which, on the payment off of a mortgage, the legal estate in the mortgaged property is re-vested in the mortgagor.

RECORD. 1. An authentic testimony in writing, contained in rolls of parchment, and preserved in a court of record. 3 *Steph. Com.* [COURT OF RECORD.]
2. Of *nisi prius*—" the record." [NISI PRIUS RECORD.]

RECORD AND WRIT CLERKS were officers of the Court of Chancery, whose duty it was to file bills brought to them for that purpose. Business was distributed among them according to the initial letter of the surname of the first plaintiff in a suit. These officers are now transferred to the High Court of Justice under sect. 77 of the Judicature Act. 1873, and were made " masters " thereof by s. 8 of the Judicature Act, 1879.

RECORD, CONVEYANCES BY, are conveyances evidenced by the authority of a court of record. [COURT OF RECORD.] The principal conveyances by matter of record, are conveyances by private Act of parliament and royal grants. The now abolished assurances by fine and recovery were also by matter of record. 1 *Steph. Com.*

RECORD, COURT OF. [COURT OF RECORD.]

RECORD, DEBT OF. A sum of money which appears to be due by the evidence of a court of record, such as a judgment, etc. 2 *Steph. Com.*

RECORD, TRIAL BY, was where some matter of record was alleged by one party, which the opposite party denied : then the party pleading the record had a day given him to bring in the record, which if he failed to do, judgment was given for his antagonist. 3 *Steph. Com.*

RECORDARI FACIAS LOQUELAM (that you cause the plaint to be recorded) was an old writ in the nature of a *certiorari* directed to the sheriff to make a record of the proceedings of a cause depending in an inferior court, and to remove the same to the King's Bench or Common Pleas.

RECORDER. The principal legal officer of a city or borough. The Recorder of London is appointed by the Lord Mayor and aldermen ; but see s. 42, sub-s. 14 of the Local Government Act, 1888. He is judge of the Lord Mayor's Court, and one of the commissioners of the Central Criminal Court. In other cities and boroughs the Recorder (where there is one) is appointed by the Crown, under s. 163 of the Municipal Corporations Act, 1882. He is the judge of the Court of Quarter Sessions, and of the Borough Court of Record. and must be a barrister of not less than five years' standing. 3 *Steph Com.*; 4 *Steph. Com.*

RECOVERY is either a true or a feigned recovery.

1. A true recovery is an actual or real recovery of a thing, or the value thereof, by judgment.

2. A feigned recovery, otherwise called a *common recovery*, was a proceeding formerly resorted to by tenants in tail for the purpose of barring their entails, and all remainders and reversions consequent thereon, and making a conveyance in fee simple of the lands held in tail. [ESTATE.] The common recovery was a supposed real action carried on through every stage of the proceeding, and was as follows :—

Let us suppose Daniel Edwards, tenant in tail in possession of land, to be desirous of suffering a common recovery for the purpose of conveying the land to Francis Golding in fee simple. Golding then sued out a writ against him called a *præcipe quod reddat* (command that he restore), alleging that Edwards had no legal title to the land. The tenant Golding then appeared, and called on one Jacob Morland, who was supposed to have warranted the title to the tenant; and thereupon the tenant prayed that Jacob Morland might be called in to defend the title which he had so warranted. This was called *vouching to warranty*, and Morland was called the *vouchee*. Morland appeared and defended the title, whereupon Golding desired leave of the court to *imparl* or confer with the vouchee in private, which was allowed him; but the vouchee disappeared, and made default, whereupon judgment was given for the demandant Golding, and the tenant Edwards had judgment to recover from Jacob Morland lands of equal value in recompense for the land warranted by him, and lost by his default; which was called the recompense or recovery in value. But this recompense was only nominal, as Jacob Morland was a person having no land of his own, being usually the crier of the court. The land was then, by judgment of law, vested in the recoveror, Golding, in fee simple.

In later times it was usual to have a recovery with *double voucher*, by first conveying an estate of freehold to any indifferent person against whom the *præcipe* was brought (which was called making a tenant to the *præcipe*); and then the tenant in *præcipe* vouched the tenant in tail, who vouched over the common vouchee.

This cumbrous fiction was abolished in 1833 by 3 & 4 Will. 4, c. 74, by which a tenant in tail is now, in all cases, empowered to convey lands in fee simple by deed, enrolled within six months in the Court of Chancery, now the central office. 1 *Steph. Com.*; *Wms. R. P.*

RECTO. Writ of right. [WRIT OF RIGHT.]

RECTO DE DOTE. [DOTE.]

RECTO DE DOTE UNDE NIHIL HABET. [DOTE UNDE NIHIL HABET.]

RECTO DE RATIONABILI PARTE. [DE RATIONABILI PARTE.]

RECTOR. 1. He that hath full possession of the rights of a parochial church. As opposed to a *vicar*, a rector is an incumbent of an unappropriated church. A rector (or parson) has for the most part the whole right to all the ecclesiastical dues in his parish, both great and small tithes, and the chancel is vested in him : whereas, in theory of law, a vicar has an appropriator over him, entitled to the best part of the profits, to whom the vicar is, as it were, a perpetual curate, with a standing salary. 2 *Steph. Com.* Where the appropriator is a layman, he is called lay impropriator, or lay rector. [APPROPRIATION, 1; IMPROPRIATION ; VICAR.]

2. In some of the colleges in Oxford, the head is called by the title of rector.

RECTOR SINECURE. [SINECURE.]

RECTORIAL TITHES are those tithes which, in a benefice unappropriated, are paid to the rector, and, in a benefice appropriated, to the appropriator. Great as opposed to small tithes, generally in respect of hay, corn and wood. 2 *Steph. Com.* [APPROPRIATION, 1; VICAR.]

RECTORY. 1. A parish church, with its rights, glebes, tithes, and other profits.

2. The rector's mansion or parsonage-house.

RECTUS IN CURIA. Right in court; said of a man who, having been outlawed, had obtained a reversal of the outlawry, so as to be again able to participate in the benefit of the law. [OUTLAWRY.]

RECUSANTS. Those who separate from the church established by law, and wilfully absent themselves from the parish church; they were liable to penalties under the statutes of James I. and Elizabeth.

RECUSATIO JUDICIS, by the civil and canon law, was an objection to a judge on suspicion of partiality, or for other good cause.

REDDENDO SINGULA SINGULIS. A phrase indicating that different words in one part of a deed or other instrument are to be applied respectively to their appropriate objects in another part.

REDDENDUM. That clause in a lease whereby rent is reserved to the lessor. 1 *Steph. Com.* It usually specifies the periods at which the rent is to be paid or rendered. No special form of words is essential. *Fawcett, L. & T.*

RE-DEMISE signifies a re-granting of lands demised or leased.

The old way of granting a rent-charge was by *demise* and *re-demise.* That is, A. demised land to B., and B. re-demised it to A., reserving the sum agreed upon by way of rent.

REDEMPTION. 1. A ransom.

2. Especially, the buying back a mortgaged estate by payment of the sum due on the mortgage. [EQUITY OF REDEMPTION.]

3. Redemption of land tax; which is the payment by the landowner of such a lump sum as shall exempt his land from the land tax. 2 *Steph. Com.* [LAND TAX.]

REDISSEISIN. A disseisin made by him that once before was found and adjudged to have disseised the same man of his lands and tenements. [DISSEISIN.]

REDITUS ALBI. Quit rents paid in silver. [ALBA FIRMA; QUIT RENT.]

REDITUS ASSISUS. Rents of assize. [ASSIZE, RENTS OF; RENT, 4.]

REDITUS CAPITALES. Chief rents. [CHIEF RENTS; RENT, 4.]

REDITUS NIGRI. Quit rents paid in grain or base money. [ALBA FIRMA; BLACK MAIL; QUIT RENT.]

REDITUS QUIETI. Quit rents. [QUIT RENT.]

REDITUS SICCUS. [RENT, 3.]

REDUCTIO AD ABSURDUM. A method of proving the fallacy of an argument by showing that it leads to an absurd result.

REDUCTION INTO POSSESSION. The turning of a *chose in action* into a *chose in possession;* as when a man takes money out of a bank at which he has a balance, or procures the payment of a debt due. But the phrase is used especially with reference to a husband taking lawful possession of his wife's *choses in action,* as he thereupon makes them his own property to all intents and purposes, so that if he dies they go to his representatives; whereas the wife's *choses in action,* not reduced into possession, come back to her on her husband's death. But see the Married Women's Property Act, 1882, s. 2, as to persons married since January 1st, 1883. [CHOSE.]

REDUNDANCY. Matter introduced into the pleadings of an action which is foreign to the scope of the action.

RE-ENTRY. The resuming or retaking of possession lately had.

A *proviso for re-entry* is a clause in a deed of grant or demise providing that the grantor or lessor may re-enter on breach of condition by the grantee or lessee. A proviso for re-entry will be construed according to the letter, unless a decisive reason is shown for departing from it. 1 *Steph. Com.; Fawcett, L. & T.* [FORFEITURE.]

REEVE. A termination signifying an executive officer. 1 *Steph. Com.* Thus we have *shire-reeve* signifying sheriff: *church-reeve* for churchwarden, etc.

RE-EXAMINATION is the examination of a witness by the counsel of the party on whose behalf he has given evidence. in reference to matters arising out of his cross-examination. 3 *Steph. Com.* [EXAMINATION, 1.]

RE-EXCHANGE is the expense incurred by a bill being dishonoured in a foreign country where it is made payable and returned to that country in which it was drawn or indorsed. For this expense the drawer is liable. 2 *Steph. Com.* [BILL OF EXCHANGE.]

RE-EXTENT. A second extent (or valuation) made upon lands and tenements upon complaint that the former extent was but partially performed. [EXTENT.]

REFEREE. A person to whose judgment a matter is referred, whether by consent of parties or by compulsory reference under the Arbitration Act, 1889. 3 *Steph. Com.* [OFFICIAL REFEREE.]

REFERENCE. Referring a matter to an arbitrator, or to a master or other officer of a court of justice, for his decision thereon. 3 *Steph. Com.* [ARBITRATION ; OFFICIAL REFEREE.]

REFERENDUM. 1. A note addressed by an ambassador to his own Government with regard to a matter upon which he is not instructed.

2. A mode of appealing from an elected body to the whole electorate. See *Borough Funds Act*, 1872.

REFERRING A CAUSE. A phrase generally used of references to arbitration. [REFEREE.]

REFORM ACT, 1832. The stat. 2 Will. 4, c. 45, passed to amend the representation of the people in England and Wales. Amended by the Representation of the People Acts, 1867, 1884. 2 *Steph. Com.*

REFORMATORY SCHOOLS, to which juvenile offenders under sixteen may be sent for not less than two nor more than five years. 3 *Steph. Com.*

REFRESHER. A further or additional fee paid to counsel where a case is adjourned from one term or sittings to another, or where the hearing lasts over the first day and for more than five hours. It may be allowed on taxation. See *R. S. C.* 1883, *Ord. LXV. r.* 48.

REGAL FISHES. [FISH ROYAL.]

REGALIA. The royal rights of a king, comprising, according to the civilians—
1. Power of judicature.
2. Power of life and death.
3. Power of war and peace.
4. Masterless goods.
5. Assessments.
6. Minting of money.

[MAJORA REGALIA ; MINORA REGALIA.]

Also the crown, sceptre with the cross, and other jewels and ornaments used at a coronation, are called the *regalia*.

REGARDANT. A villein *regardant* was a villein *annexed to a manor*, having charge to do all base services within the same, and to see the same freed from all things that might annoy his lord. A villein *regardant* was thus opposed to a villein *in gross*, who was transferable by deed from one owner to another. 1 *Steph. Com.*

REGENT. A person appointed to conduct the affairs of State in lieu of the reigning sovereign, in the absence, disability, or minority of the latter. 2 *Steph. Com.*

REGICIDE. A slayer of a king ; or the murder of a king.

REGIO ASSENSU. A writ whereby the king gives his royal assent to the election of a bishop or abbot.

REGISTER. 1. The name of a book, wherein are mentioned most of the forms of the writs used at common law. 3 *Steph. Com.* [ORIGINAL WRIT.]

2. The register of a parish church, wherein baptisms. marriages, and burials are registered. Instituted by Cromwell, vicar-general of Henry VIII., in the year 1538. [REGISTRAR, 1.]

3. A record of deeds and other documents relating to land, such as exists in Middlesex and Yorkshire, and in Scotland and Ireland. 1 *Steph. Com.* [MIDDLESEX REGISTRY ; YORKSHIRE REGISTRY.]

4. A record of titles to land. [LAND TRANSFER ACTS.]

5. The General Register and Record Office for Seamen, containing, *inter alia*, the number and date of the register of each foreign-going ship and her registered tonnage ; the length and general nature of her voyage or employment ; the names, ages and places of birth of the master, the crew, and the apprentices ; their qualities on board their last ships or other employment ; and the dates and places of their joining the ship. *Merchant Shipping Act*, 1894, *s.* 251. 3 *Steph. Com.*

6. And, generally, a register signifies an authentic catalogue of names or events, *e.g.*, the register of joint-stock companies under the Companies Act, 1862, etc.

REGISTER OF ORIGINAL WRITS. [ORIGINAL WRIT ; REGISTER, 1.]

REGISTER OF PATENTS. A book of patents kept at the Specification Office for public use. See 46 & 47 *Vict. c.* 57. 2 *Steph. Com.* [PATENT.]

REGISTRAR. An officer appointed to register the decrees of a court of justice, or in any manner to keep a register of names and events. Of these we may mention—

1. The Registrar-General of births, deaths and marriages in England, to whom, subject to such regulations as shall be made by a principal secretary of state, the general management of the system of registering births, deaths, and marriages is entrusted. 3 *Steph. Com.*

2. The superintendent registrars of each parish or district union. This office is filled as of right by the clerk to the guardians of the union, in case of his due qualification and acceptance, and is held during the pleasure of the Registrar-General. 3 *Steph. Com.*

3. The registrars of the several registration districts, into which every poor-law union or parish is divided. 3 *Steph. Com.*

4. The Registrar of Solicitors, whose duty it is to keep an alphabetical list or roll of solicitors, and to issue certificates to persons who have been duly admitted and enrolled under 51 & 52 *Vict. c.* 65, *s.* 5. These duties are now performed by the Law Society. 3 *Steph. Com.* [ATTORNEY-AT-LAW : SOLICITOR.]

5. The Registrar of Joint-Stock Companies (an officer appointed by the Board of Trade) whose business it is to certify when a company is incorporated, &c. 3 *Steph. Com.*

6. The Registrars in Bankruptcy of the High Court, who are required to exercise such judicial powers as may be delegated to them from time to time by the judge of the court; and to perform various duties in connection with bankruptcy. 2 *Steph. Com.; Robson, Bkcy.*

7. Chancery Registrars are officers of the Chancery Division whose duty it is to enter causes for trial, to attend in court and take minutes of decisions given, and afterwards draw the same up in proper form, and settle them in the presence of the different parties or their solicitors.

8. Registrars of the Probate, Divorce, and Admiralty Division take interlocutory applications, enter judgments and decrees, and tax costs.

9. District Registrars. [DISTRICT REGISTRARS.]

10. The Registrar of a County Court, who is an officer appointed by the judge, subject to the approval of the Lord Chancellor. 3 *Steph. Com.* If the county court be one having jurisdiction in bankruptcy, he will be a registrar in bankruptcy.

11. The Deputy-Registrar of a County Court, who is an officer appointed by the registrar, subject to the approval of the judge. 3 *Steph. Com.*

12. The Registrar of Friendly Societies; an officer whose duty it is to examine the rules of friendly societies, and, if he find them conformable to law, to certify them as being so. 38 & 39 *Vict. c.* 60. 3 *Steph. Com.*

13. The Registrar of the Privy Council, whose duty it is to summon the members of the Judicial Committee when their attendance is required, and to transact other business relating to the Privy Council.

14. The Registrar-General of Shipping and Seamen. 3 *Steph. Com.* [REGISTER, 4.]

REGISTRATION OF TITLE. [LAND TRANSFER ACTS.]

REGISTRY. A place where anything is laid up. *Cowel.*

Or it may be defined as a place where a register is kept.

REGIUS PROFESSOR. This title, when applied to a professor, or reader of lectures in the universities, indicates that his office was founded by the king. King Henry VIII. was the founder of five professorships in each university, namely, the professorships of Divinity, Greek, Hebrew, Law, and Physic.

REGULÆ GENERALES (general rules). Published by the Courts from time to time for the regulation of their practice.

RE-HEARING was formerly a hearing again of a matter which had been decided by a judge in Chancery, either (1) by the same judge or his successor, or (2) by the Lord Chancellor or the Lords Justices. In the latter case, the hearing was spoken of as a hearing on appeal; but in strictness it was a re-hearing, being a hearing in the same Court of Chancery. 3 *Steph. Com.*

Now, by R. S. C. 1883, Ord. LVIII. r. 1, all appeals to the Court of Appeal are by way of *re-hearing*, and are brought by notice of motion in a summary way, and no petition, case, or

RE-HEARING—*continued.*
other formal proceeding other than such notice of motion is necessary, and a judge of the High Court has now no power to re-hear an order made by himself or any other judge after the order has been drawn up. The term re-hearing as opposed to new trial indicates that the original hearing was before a judge alone, and not with a jury. [APPEAL.]

RE-INSURANCE. Re-assurance. [RE-ASSURANCE POLICY.]

RE-ISSUABLE NOTES. Notes payable to bearer on demand for any sum between 5*l.* and 100*l.*, which may be re-issued after payment without being re-stamped; an annual licence is necessary for this purpose. 55 *Geo.* 3, *c.* 184. *Byles on Bills.*

REJOINDER. The defendant's answer to the plaintiff's replication, and therefore the fourth stage in pleading in an action at law in cases where the pleadings reach to this stage. 3 *Steph. Com.*
By R. S. C. 1883, Ord. XXIII. r. 3, no pleading subsequent to reply, other than a joinder of issue, can be pleaded without leave of the court or a judge.

RELATION. 1. Relation is where, in consideration of law, two times or other things are considered as if they were one, and by this the thing subsequent is said to take its effect *by relation* at the time preceding; as when it is said that an adjudication in bankruptcy has relation back to the act of bankruptcy upon which the adjudication is made. 2 *Steph. Com.; Robson, Bkcy.* [ACT OF BANKRUPTCY; ADJUDICATION.]

2. The act of a *relator* at whose instance an information is filed. [RELATOR.]

RELATOR. A relator is a private person at whose instance the Attorney-General allows an information to be filed—
1. In Chancery. 3 *Steph. Com.* By the Judicature Act, 1875, Ord. I. r. 1, the proceeding for this purpose is by action in the High Court of Justice.
2. In informations in the King's Bench in the nature of a *quo warranto.* 3 *Steph. Com.*
3. In strictly criminal cases, such person is generally called the *prosecutor* or the *private prosecutor;* but he might be called a *relator.* [INFORMATION.]

RELEASE (Lat. *Relaxatio*). 1. A discharge or conveyance by one who has a right or interest in lands, but not the possession, whereby he extinguishes his right for the benefit of the person in possession. The former is called the *releasor,* the latter the *releasee.* 1 *Steph. Com.* [PARTICULAR TENANT; PRIVITY OF ESTATE; LEASE AND RELEASE.]

2. An instrument whereby a party beneficially entitled to any estate held upon trust discharges his trustee from any further claim or liability in respect of the same.

RELEGATION. A temporary banishment, not involving civil death.

RELICT. A widow.

RELICTA VERIFICATIONE (his verification abandoned) is an old phrase denoting that a defendant having pleaded withdraws his plea, and confesses the plaintiff's right of action, and thereupon judgment is given for the plaintiff. [VERIFICATION.]

RELIEF. 1. A payment made by an heir who succeeded to a feud which his ancestors had possessed. It was in horses, arms, money, or the like; and was called a *relief,* because it raised up and re-established the inheritance. Reliefs, which originated while feuds were only life estates, were continued after feuds became hereditary. A relief may still be payable in respect of freeholds. 1 *Steph. Com.*

2. Assistance given by poor law authorities to paupers in distress. It is either *indoor relief,* the condition of which is, that the party relieved shall reside in the workhouse; or *outdoor relief,* to which no such condition is attached, and which consists generally in the supply of articles of general necessity, and sometimes in medical attendance. 3 *Steph. Com.* [OVERSEERS.]

3. The specific assistance prayed for by a party who institutes an action in Chancery. 3 *Steph. Com.* [STATE-MENT OF CLAIM; SUMMONS, 4.]

RELIEVING OFFICER. An overseer or other officer charged with the duty of administering immediate relief to paupers who apply for it. [OVER-SEERS.]

REM. [IN REM; INFORMATION IN REM; JUS IN REM.]

REMAINDER is where any estate or interest in land is granted out of a larger one, and an ulterior estate expectant on that which is so granted is at the same time conveyed away by the original owner. The first estate is called the *particular estate*, and the ulterior one the *remainder*, or the *estate in remainder*. Thus, if land be conveyed to A. for life, and after his death to B., A.'s interest is called a *particular* estate, and B.'s a *remainder*. 1 *Steph. Com.* The word, though properly applied to estates in land, is also applicable to personalty. 2 *Steph. Com.* [CONTINGENT REMAINDER; REVERSION; VESTED REMAINDER.]

REMAINDER MAN. A person entitled to an estate in remainder. [REMAINDER.]

REMAND is the recommittal of an accused person to prison, or his readmission to bail, on the adjournment of the hearing of a criminal charge in a police court. The remand, in the case of a person charged with an indictable offence, must not exceed eight days. A remand may be granted for securing the attendance of witnesses, for making inquiries into the previous career of the accused, or other reasonable cause. 11 & 12 *Vict. c.* 42, *s.* 21; *Oke's Mag. Syn.* As to the remand in cases of summary jurisdiction, see 11 & 12 Vict. c. 43, s. 16; *Oke's Mag. Syn.*

REMANENT PRO DEFECTU EMPTORUM (they remain unsold for want of buyers). This is a sheriff's return to a writ of *fi. fa.*, when he finds himself unable to sell the goods distrained. [FIERI FACIAS.]

REMANET. A cause put off from one sittings or assizes to another.

REMEDIAL STATUTES are such as supply some defect in the existing law, and redress some abuse or inconvenience with which it is found to be attended, without introducing any provision of a penal character; as, for instance, the Dower Act of 1833. 1 *Steph. Com.*

REMEDY. The means given by law for the recovery of a right, or of compensation for the infringement thereof.

REMEMBRANCERS. 1. Officers of the Exchequer, of which there were formerly three: the King's Remembrancer, the Lord Treasurer's Remembrancer, and the Remembrancer of First Fruits. Their duty was to put the Lord Treasurer and the justices of that court in remembrance of such things as were to be called on and dealt with for the king's benefit.

The duty of the King's Remembrancer is to enter in his office all recognizances taken for debts due to the Crown, etc.; to take bonds for such debts, and to make out process for breach of them; also to issue process against the collectors of customs and other public payments for their accounts. He is now an officer of the Supreme Court. *Jud. Act*, 1873, *s.* 77.

2. The Remembrancer of the City of London is an ancient officer of the Corporation, whose original duties were mainly ceremonial, it being his office to see to the due observance of all presentations, public processions, and other matters affecting the privileges of the Corporation. In this character he was their agent in Parliament, and at the Council and Treasury Boards; and at this day he performs the duty of parliamentary solicitor to the Corporation. He attends the Houses of Parliament, and examines bills likely to affect the privileges of the City, and reports upon the same to the Corporation. He also attends the Courts of Aldermen and Common Council, and committees, when required.

REMISSION. Pardon of an offence.

REMITTER is where he, who hath the true property or *jus proprietatis* in lands, but is wrongfully out of possession thereof, hath afterwards the freehold cast upon him by some subsequent, and of course defective, title; in this case he is *remitted* or sent back, by operation of law, to his ancient and more certain title. 3 *Steph. Com.*

As if a man dies intestate leaving two sons, A. the elder and B. the younger. B. wrongfully enters into possession and dies childless, leaving A. his heir-at-law. Then A. will be in as of his former estate, and so will take the land free of any incumbrances created or debts incurred by B.

REMITTER OF ACTIONS TO COUNTY COURTS. See 51 & 52 Vict. c. 43, s. 65.

REMITTIT DAMNA, otherwise called a *remittitur damna*, is an entry on the record of an action whereby a plaintiff remits the whole or a portion of the damages awarded to him by the verdict of the jury. It has been held that where a jury give greater damages than have been claimed by the plaintiff in his declaration, the error may be cured before judgment by entering a *remittitur* for the surplus.

REMOTENESS is—1. Where an attempt is made by any instrument in writing to tie up, or to dictate the devolution of, property, or to keep the same in suspense without a beneficial owner, beyond the period allowed by law. [PERPETUITY.] 2. *Remoteness of damage.* This expression is used to denote a want of sufficiently direct connection between a wrong complained of and the injury alleged to have been sustained thereby. 3 *Steph. Com.*

RENDER. 1. To give up again ; to restore.

2. A word used in connection with rents and heriots. Goods subject to rent or *heriot-service* are said to *lie in render*, when the lord may not only seize the identical goods, but may also distrain for them. 3 *Steph. Com.* [HERIOT ; PRENDER.]

RENEWAL OF LEASE. A re-grant of an expiring lease for a further term. Leases may be surrendered in order to be renewed without a surrender of under-leases by virtue of 4 Geo. 2, c. 28, s. 6. 1 *Steph. Com.*

RENEWAL OF WRITS. No writ of summons remains in force for more than twelve months, but may be renewed before the expiration of the twelve months for a further period of six months, and so on from time to time. See *R. S. C.* 1883, Ord. VIII.

RENOUNCING PROBATE is where a person appointed executor of a will refuses to accept the office. 2 *Steph. Com.*

RENT (Lat. *Reditus*). A compensation, or return ; that is, a profit issuing periodically out of lands or tenements. It does not necessarily consist in the payment of money. Rents are of various kinds :—1. *Rent-service*, which hath some corporeal service incident to it ; for non-performance of which the lord may distrain, if he hath in himself

the reversion after the lease or particular estate of the lessee or grantee is expired. This is the ordinary rent. 2. *Rent-charge*, which is where the owner hath no future interest in the land, but is enabled to distrain by virtue of a clause in the grant or lease reserving the rent. 3. *Rent-seck* (*reditus siccus*), or barren rent, is where there is merely a rent reserved by deed, but without any clause of distress, nor any right of distress at the common law. 4. *Rents of assize*, which are certain established rents payable by freeholders and ancient copyholders of a manor. Those of the freeholders are called *chief rents* (*reditus capitales*) ; and both sorts are called *quit rents* (*quieti reditus*), because thereby the tenant goes quit and free of other services. When these rents were reserved in silver or white money, they were anciently called *white* rents, or *blanch farms* (*reditus albi*) ; in contradistinction to rents reserved in work, grain, or baser money, which were called *reditus nigri* or black-mail. 5. *Rack-rent* is a rent of the full value of a tenement, or near it. 6. *A fee farm rent* is a rent issuing out of an estate in fee, of at least one-fourth of the value of the lands at the time of its reservation. 7. *Forehand rent* is one payable in advance. The difference which formerly existed between the various kinds of rent is now of little practical importance ; for it is provided by 4 Geo. 2, c. 28, that all persons may have the like remedy by distress for rents-seck, rents of assize, and chief-rents, as in case of rents reserved upon lease. See also the Conveyancing Act, 1881, ss. 44, 45. 1 *Steph. Com.* ; *Wms. R. P.* ; *Fawcett, L. & T.* [APPORTIONMENT.]

RENTS OF ASSIZE. [RENT, 4.]

REPEAL (Fr. *Rappel*). A calling back. The revocation of one statute, or a part of it, by another. See the *Interpretation Act*, 1889, ss. 11, 38.

REPLEADER was an order of the court that the parties *replead* ; granted when the parties in the course of pleading raised an issue immaterial or insufficient to determine the true question in the case.

Repleaders are now out of use, as the courts have almost unlimited power of allowing amendments for the purpose of determining the real question in controversy between the parties. 3 *Steph. Com.* [AMENDMENT.]

REPLEGIARE. To replevy; that is, to redeem a thing detained or taken by another, by putting in legal sureties.

REPLEGIARI FACIAS. A writ of replevin which issued out of Chancery, commanding the sheriff to deliver the distress (*i.e.*, the thing taken by way of distress) to the owner, and afterwards to do justice in respect of the matter in dispute in his own county court. Now superseded by ordinary action of replevin. 3 *Steph. Com.* [REPLEGIARE; REPLEVIN.]

REPLEVIABLE, or **REPLEVISABLE.** Capable of being replevied. [REPLEGIARE; REPLEVIN.]

REPLEVIN is defined as a re-delivery to the owner of his cattle or goods distrained upon any cause upon security that he will prosecute the action against him that distrained, denominated an action of replevin. The "replevisor" is the party who takes back his goods. The action, if intended to be commenced in a county court, must, according to the condition of the bond, be commenced within a month; if in a superior court, then within a week. It should be brought in the latter where there is good ground for believing that the title to some corporeal or incorporeal hereditament, or to some toll, fair, market or franchise is in question, or that the rent or damage exceeds 20*l.* The action is now tried in the same way as other actions. 3 *Steph. Com.*

REPLEVISH. To let one to mainprise on surety. [MAINPRISE.]

REPLICATION signified generally a pleading of the plaintiff whereby he replied (otherwise than by a legal or formal objection) to a defendant's plea or answer. See now REPLY. In the action of replevin [REPLEVIN], the replication was the *defendant's* second pleading; the plaintiff's second pleading being called his *plea.* In divorce the replication is the reply to the respondent's *answer.* 3 *Steph. Com.*

REPLY. 1. The *reply* of a plaintiff is that statement in his pleading whereby he *replies* to the defence. Now only when ordered. See *R. S. C.* 1883, *Ord. XXIII. r.* 112.

2. The speech of counsel for the plaintiff in a civil case, or for the prosecution in a criminal case, in answer in either case to the points raised by the defence, is generally called the *reply.*

REPORTS. 1. Histories of legal cases, with the arguments used by counsel and the reasons given for the decision of the court.

2. The reports of Chief Justice Coke are especially styled The Reports, and are in general cited without the author's name, as "Rep." 1 *Steph. Com.* [LAW REPORTS.]

The following is a catalogue of the Reports which have appeared up to the present time, together with the periods over which they extend and the abbreviations by which they are usually referred to. In the first column we give the names of the Reports in alphabetical order; in the second the abbreviation or abbreviations by which they are or may be referred to; in the third the period over which the Reports extend, or, in some cases, the date of publication; and, in the fourth, the courts or jurisdictions whose decisions are embraced in the several series of Reports respectively.

Reports.	Abbreviations.	Date.	Court.
Acton (Prize Causes) ...	Acton	1809—1811	Privy Council.
Addams	Add.	1822—1826	Ecclesiastical.
Adolphus & Ellis... ...	Ad. & Ell. *or* A. & E.	1834—1842	King's (*or* Queen's) Bench.
Adolphus & Ellis, New Series	Ad. & Ell., N. S. *or* Q. B. (for Queen's Bench).	1841—1852	Queen's Bench.
Alcock's Registry Cases ...	Alc.	1837 ...	Common Law, Ireland.
Alcock & Napier ...	Alc. & N. ...	1831—1833	Common Law, Ireland.
Aleyn	Aleyn	1646—1649	King's Bench.
Ambler	Amb. *or* Ambl..	1737—1783	Chancery.
Anderson, Sir E. ...	And.	16th century	Common Pleas.
Andrews, George	Andr.	1737—1738	King's Bench.

REPORTS—*continued.*

Reports.	Abbreviations.	Date.	Court.
Annaly	Ann.	... ...	King's Bench.
Anstruther ·	Anst.	1792—1796	Exchequer.
Arkley	Arkl.	1846—1848	Court of Justiciary, Scotland.
Armstrong, MacArtney & Ogle	Arm. Mac. & O.	1840—1842	Civil and Criminal Courts, Ireland.
Arnold	Arn.	1838—1839	Common Pleas.
Arnold & Hodges... ...	Arn. & H. ...	1839—1841	Queen's Bench.
Aspinall's Maritime Cases	Asp. M. C. ...	1870 to the present time	Admiralty.
Atkyns	Atk.	1736—1754	Chancery.
Bail Court Reports, by Lowndes & Maxwell, and by Saunders & Cole (*infra*).			
Ball & Beatty	Ball & B. *or* B. & B.	1807—1814	Chancery, Ireland.
Bankruptcy and Insolvency Reports	... ...	1853—1855	Bankruptcy, etc.
Barnardiston (Ch.) ...	Barnard. (Ch.)	1740—1741	Chancery.
Barnardiston (K. B.) ...	Barnard. (K.B.)	1726—1734	King's Bench.
Barnes' Notes of Cases ...	Barnes	1733—1756	Common Pleas.
Barnewall & Adolphus ...	Barn. & Ad. *or* B. & Ad.	1830—1834	King's Bench.
Barnewall & Alderson ...	Barn. & Ald. *or* B. & A.	1817—1822	King's Bench.
Barnewall & Cresswell ...	Barn. & Cress. *or* B. & C.	1822—1830	King's Bench.
Barron & Arnold	Bar. & Arn. ...	1843—1846	Election Committees.
Barron & Austin	Bar. & Aust. ...	1842 ...	Election Committees.
Batty	Batty	1825—1826	King's Bench, Ireland.
Beatty	Beat.	1827—1830*	Chancery, Ireland.
Beavan	Beav.	1838—1866	Rolls.
Bell (Crown Cases) ...	Bell	1858—1860	Crown Cases Reserved.
Bell (Scotch Appeals) ...	Bell	1841—1850	House of Lords.
Bell (Scotch Decisions) ...	Bell	1790—1792 1794—1795	Court of Session.
Bellew's Reports (published 1585)	Bellew	1377—1400	Common Law.
Belt's Supplement to Vesey, sen.	Belt	1746—1756	Chancery.
Benloe	Benl.	1535—1627	Common Law.
Benloe & Dalison ...	Ben. & D. ...	1440—1574	Common Pleas.
Best & Smith	B. & S. ...	1861—1870	Queen's Bench.
Bingham	Bing.	1822—1834	Common Pleas.
Bingham's New Cases ...	Bing. N. C. ...	1834—1840	Common Pleas.
Blackham, Dundas and Osborne	B., D. & O. ...	1846—1848	Exchequer, Ireland.
Blackstone, Henry ...	H. Bl.	1788—1796	Common Pleas.
Blackstone, Sir W. ...	W. Bl.	1746—1779	Common Law.
Bligh	Bligh	1819—1821	House of Lords.
Bligh's New Series ...	Bligh, N. S. ...	1827—1837	House of Lords.
Bluett's Notes of Cases ...	Blu.	1720—1847	Isle of Man Courts.
Bosanquet & Puller ...	Bos. & Pull. *or* B. & P.	1796—1804	Common Pleas.
Bosanquet & Puller's New Reports	B. & P. N. R. ...	1804—1807	Common Pleas.

·* Including also some earlier cases.

REPORTS—*continued.*

Reports.	Abbreviations.	Date.	Court.
Bridgman, Sir John ...	J. Bridg. ...	1615—1620	Common Law.
Bridgman, Sir Orlando ...	O. Bridg. ...	1660—1667	Common Pleas.
Broderip & Bingham ...	Bro. & B. *or* B. & B.	1818—1822	Common Pleas.
Brooke's New Cases ...	Brooke, N. C. *or* B. N. C.	1514—1557	Common Law.
Broun	Broun	1842—1845	Court of Justiciary, Scotland.
Brown's Reports of Cases in Chancery	Bro. C. C. ...	1778—1794	Chancery.
Brown's Reports of Cases in Parliament	Bro. P. C. ...	1702—1800	House of Lords.
Browne & Macnamara Railway Cases	Bro. & MN. ...	1881—1900	Railway and Canal Cases.
Browning & Lushington...	B. & L.	1863—1865	Admiralty and Privy Council.
Brownlow & Goldesborough	B. & G.... ...	1608—1625	Common Pleas.
Bruce's Reports	Bruce	1714—1715	Court of Session.
Buck's Cases in Bankruptcy	Buck	1816—1820	Bankruptcy, etc.
Bulstrode	Bulstr.	1609—1626	King's Bench.
Bunbury	Bunb.	1713—1741	Exchequer.
Burrow's Reports ...	Burr.	1756—1772	King's Bench.
Burrow's Settlement Cases	Burr. S. C. ...	1732—1776	King's Bench.
Cababe & Ellis	Cab. & El. ...	1882—1885	Queen's Bench.
Caldecott's Settlement Cases	Cald. S. C. ...	1776—1785	King's Bench.
Calthrop's Cases on the Customs of London	Calthrop ...	Published 1670	King's Bench.
Campbell	Camp.	1809—1816	Nisi Prius.
Carpmael's Patent Cases...	Carp. P. C. ...	1602—1844	All the Courts.
Carrington & Kirwan ...	Car. & K. *or* C. & K.	1843—1853	Nisi Prius and Criminal Courts.
Carrington & Marshman .	Car. & M. *or* C. & M.	1841—1842	Nisi Prius and Criminal Courts.
Carrington & Payne ...	Car. & P. *or* C. & P.	1823—1840	Nisi Prius and Criminal Courts.
Carrow, Hamerton & Allen's New Sess. Cases	C. H. & A. *or* New Sess. Cas.	1844—1847	All the Courts.
Carter	Cart.	1664—1675	Common Pleas.
Carthew	Carth.	1688—1700	King's Bench.
Cary	Cary	1471—1603	Chancery.
Cases in Chancery ...	Ch. Ca. ...	1660—1679	Chancery.
Cases in Equity Abridged	Cas. Eq. Ab. ...	Published 1756	Chancery.
Cases in the time of Finch	Cas. temp. Finch	1673—1680	
Cases in the time of Lord Hardwicke	Cas. temp. Hardwicke	1733—1737	Chancery.
Cases in the time of Lord Talbot	Cas. temp. Talbot	1733—1737	Chancery.
Cases of Practice, King's Bench	Cas. Pra. K. B.	1558—1774	King's Bench.
Chitty	Chit.	1819—1820*	King's Bench.
Choice Cases in Chancery	Cho. Ca. Ch. ...	1558—1605	Chancery.

* Including also some earlier cases.

REPORTS—*continued*.

Reports.	Abbreviations.	Date.	Court.
Clark & Finnelly...	Cl. & Fin. ...	1831—1846	House of Lords.
Clayton	Clay. ...	1631—1651	York Assizes.
Cockburn & Rowe ...	C. & R. ...	1833 ...	Election Committees.
Coke, Sir Edward ...	Co. Rep. *or* Rep.	1579—1615	Common Law.
Colles	Colles ...	1697—1713	House of Lords.
Collyer	Coll. ...	1844—1846	Chancery.
Coltman's Registration Cases	Colt. ...	1879—1885	Registration Cases.
Comberbach	Comb. ...	1685—1698	King's Bench.
Commercial Cases ...	Com. Cas. ...	1895 to the present time	The Commercial Court.
Common Bench Reports	C. B. ...	1845—1856	Common Pleas.
Common Bench Reports, New Series	C. B., N. S. ...	1856—1865	Common Pleas.
Common Law Reports ...	C. L. R. ...	1853—1855	Common Law Courts.
Comyns	Com. ...	1695—1740	Common Law Courts.
Connor & Lawson ...	Conn. & Law. *or* C. & L.	1841—1843	Chancery, Ireland.
Cooke	Cook. ...	1706—1740	Common Pleas.
Cooke & Alcock ...	C. & A. ...	1833—1834	King's Bench, Ireland.
Cooper, George ...	G. Coop. ...	1814—1815	Chancery.
Cooper's Cases in Chancery	Coop. ...	1833—1834	Chancery (Lord Brougham).
„ „ „	„	1837—1838	Chancery.
„ „ „	„	1846—1848	Chancery (Lord Cottenham).
Corbett & Daniell ...	Corb. & D. ...	1819 ...	Election Committees.
County Courts Cases ...	C. C. Cas. ...	1847—1852	Common Law Courts.
Couper	Coup. ...	1868 to present time	Court of Justiciary, Scotland.
Court of Session Cases ...	Court Sess. Ca.	1821 to present time	Court of Session, Scotland.
Cowell's Indian Appeals (Law Rep. vol. ii.)	L. R., 2 Ind. App.	Publication commenced March, 1875	Privy Council.
Cowper	Cowp. ...	1774—1778	King's Bench.
Cox & Atkinson's Registration Appeals	Cox & Atk. ...	1843—1845	Common Pleas.
Cox (Chancery)	Cox ...	1783—1797	Chancery.
Cox (Criminal Law) ...	Cox's C. L. ...	1843—1857	Criminal Courts.
Craig & Phillips ...	Cr. & Ph. ...	1840—1841	Chancery.
Craigie, Stewart & Paton's Scotch Appeals	Cr. St. & P. ...	1727—1757 (publ. 1849)	House of Lords.
Crawford & Dix ...	Cr. & D. ...	1837—1846	Irish Courts.
Cresswell's Insolvent Cases	... ...	1827—1829	Insolvency.
Cripps' Church Cases ...	... ...	1847—1850	All the Courts.
Croke, time of Charles I. .	Cro. Car. ...	1625—1641	Common Law.
Croke, time of Elizabeth .	Cro. Eliz. ...	1581—1603	Common Law.
Croke, time of James I. ...	Cro. Jac. ...	1603—1625	Common Law.
Crompton & Jervis ...	Cr. & J. *or* C. & J.	1830—1832	Exchequer.
Crompton & Meeson ...	Cr. & M. ...	1832—1834	Exchequer.
Crompton, Meeson & Roscoe	Cr. M. & R. ...	1834—1836	Exchequer.
Cunningham	Cunn. ...	1734—1735	King's Bench.
Curties	Curt. ...	1834—1844	Ecclesiastical.
Dalrymple, Sir Hew ...	Dalr. ...	1698—1718	Court of Session, Scotland.
Daniell	Dan. ...	1817—1823	Exchequer, Equity.

REPORTS—*continued.*

Reports.	Abbreviations.	Date.	Court.
Danson & Lloyd	D. & L. ...	1828—1829	Common Law.
Davies' Patent Cases ...	D. P. C. ...	Publd. 1866	Common Law Courts.
Davis, Sir John	Davis	1604—1611	Common Law, Ireland.
Davison & Merivale ...	D. & M. ...	1843—1844	Queen's Bench.
Deacon	Deac.	1835—1840	Bankruptcy, etc.
Deacon & Chitty ...	Deac. & Chit. ...	1832—1835	Bankruptcy.
Deane's Reports, completed by Swabey	Deane *or* Dea. & Sw.	1855—1857	Ecclesiastical.
Dearsley	Dears.	1852—1856	Criminal Courts.
Dearsley & Bell	Dearsl. & B. *or* D. & B.	1856—1858	Criminal Courts.
Deas & Anderson... ...	Deas & And. ...	1829—1833	Court of Session, Scotland.
De Gex	De G.	1844—1848	Bankruptcy.
De Gex & Jones	De G. & Jo. *or* D. & J.	1857—1862	Chancery (Appeals).
De Gex & Smale	De G. & Sm. ...	1846—1852	Chancery.
De Gex, Fisher & Jones ...	De G., F. & Jo. *or* D. F. & J.	1859—1862	Chancery (Appeals).
De Gex, Jones & Smith ...	De G., J. & Sm. *or* D. J. & S.	1862—1865	Chancery (Appeals).
De Gex, Macnaghten & Gordon	De G., Mac. & G. *or* D. M. & G.	1851—1857	Chancery (Appeals).
Delane	Delane	1832—1836	Revising Barristers.
Denison	Den. C. C. ...	1844—1852	Criminal Courts.
Dickens	Dick.	1559—1792	Chancery.
Dodson	Dods.	1811—1822	Admiralty.
Douglas' Election Cases...	Doug.	1775—1776	Election Committees.
Douglas' King's Bench ...	Doug.	1778—1785	King's Bench.
Dow	Dow	1812—1818	House of Lords.
Dow & Clarke	Dow & Cl. ...	1827—1832	House of Lords.
Dowling's Practice Reports	Dowl. *or* D. P. C.	1830—1841	Common Law.
Dowling's Practice Reports, New Series	Dowl., N. S. ...	1841—1843	Common Law.
Dowling & Lowndes ...	Dowl. & L. *or* D. & L.	1843—1849	Common Law.
Dowling & Ryland, King's Bench	Dowl. & Ry. *or* D. & R.	1822—1827	King's Bench.
Dowling & Ryland, Nisi Prius	D. & R., N. P. .	1822 ...	Nisi Prius Cases.
Dowling & Ryland, Magistrates' Cases	D. & R. M. C. ...	1822—1827	King's Bench.
Drewry	Drew.	1852—1859	V.-C. Kindersley.
Drewry & Smale... ...	Dr. & Sm. ...	1859—1865	V.-C. Kindersley.
Drinkwater	Drink.	1840—1841	Common Pleas.
Drury	Dru.	1843—1844	Chancery, Ireland.
Drury & Walsh	Dru. & Wal. ...	1837—1840	Chancery, Ireland.
Drury & Warren	Dru. & War. ...	1841—1843	Chancery, Ireland.
Dunlop, Bell & Murray ...	... ...	1834—1840	Court of Session.
Durie	Durie	1621—1642	Court of Session.
Durnford & East's Term Reports	Durn. & E. *or* T. R.	1785—1800	King's Bench.
Dyer	Dy.	1512—1582	Common Law.
Eagle & Young's Collection of Tithe Cases	E. & Y.... ...	1204—1825	All the Courts.
East	East	1801—1812	King's Bench.

REPORTS—*continued.*

Reports.	Abbreviations.	Date.	Court.
Eden	Eden	1757—1766	Chancery.
Edgar	Edg.	1724—1725	Court of Session.
Edwards	Edw.	1808—1812	Admiralty.
Elchie	Elch.	1733—1754	Scotch Courts.
Ellis & Blackburn	Ell. & Bl. *or* E. & B.	1852—1858	Queen's Bench.
Ellis & Ellis	Ell. & E.	1858—1862	Queen's Bench.
Ellis, Blackburn & Ellis...	Ell. Bl. & Ell. *or* E. B. & E.	1858	Queen's Bench.
Equity Cases Abridged ...	Eq. Cas. Abr.	Publd. 1756	Chancery.
Equity Reports	Eq. R.	1853—1855	Chancery.
Espinasse	Esp.	1793—1810	Nisi Prius.
Exchequer Reports	Exch.	1847—1856	Exchequer.
Faculty Decisions	Fac. Dec.	1805—1841	Court of Session.
Falconer	Falc.	1744—1751	Court of Session.
Falconer & Fitzherbert ...	Falc. & F.	1837—1839	Election Committees.
Ferguson	Ferg.	1738—1752	Court of Session.
Ferguson's Consistorial Reports	Ferg.	1811—1817	Consistorial Court, Scotland (now abolished).
Finch	Finch	1673—1680	Chancery.
Finch's Precedents	Prec. Ch.	1689—1722	Chancery.
Finlason's Leading Cases	Finl. L. C.	Publd. 1847	Common Law.
Fitzgibbons	Fitzg.	1727—1732	King's Bench.
Flanagan & Kelly	Fl. & K.	1840—1842	Rolls Court, Ireland.
Fonblanque	Fonb.	1849—1852	Bankruptcy.
Forbes	Forb.	1705—1713	Court of Session.
Forester's Cases t. Talbot	Cas. temp.Talbot	1733—1737	Chancery.
Forrest	Forr.	1800—1801	Exchequer.
Fortescue	Fort.	1711—1731	All the Courts.
Foster (Crown Law)	Fost. C. L.	1746—1760	Criminal Courts.
Foster & Finlason	F. & F.	1856—1867	Nisi Prius and Criminal Courts.
Fountainhall	Fount.	1678—1712	Scotch Courts.
Fox & Smith	Fox & S.	1822—1824	King's Bench, Ireland.
Fox & Smith, Registration Cases	Fox & S., Reg.	1886—1895	Registration Cases.
Fraser	Fras.	1790—1791	Election Committees.
Freeman	Freem.	1660—1706	Chancery.
Freeman	Freem.	1670—1704	Common Law.
Gale	Gale	1835—1836	Exchequer.
Gale & Davison	G. & D.	1841—1843	Queen's Bench.
Gibson	Gibs.	1621—1642	Court of Session.
Giffard	Giff. *or* Gif.	1857—1865	V.-C. Stuart.
Gilbert	Gilb.	1706—1725	Chancery, etc.
Gilmour	Gilm.	1661—1666	Court of Session.
Glascock	Glasc.	1831—1832	Irish Courts.
Glyn & Jameson	G. & J.	1821—1823	Bankruptcy, etc.
Godbolt	Godb.	1574—1638	Queen's *or* King's Bench.
Gouldsborough	Gouldsb.	1586—1597	Common Law.
Gow	Gow	1818—1820	Nisi Prius.
Gwillim	Gwill.	1285—1800	All the Courts.
Haggard (Adm.)	Hagg. Adm.	1822—1838	Admiralty.
Haggard's Consistorial Reports	Hagg. Cons.	1789—1802	Ecclesiastical Courts.

REPORTS—*continued.*

Reports.	Abbreviations.	Date.	Court.
Haggard's Ecclesiastical Reports	Hagg. Eccl. ...	1827—1833	Ecclesiastical.
Hailes	Hail.	1766—1791	Scotch Courts.
Hall & Twells	Hall & Tw. *or* H. & Tw.	1849—1850	Chancery.
Hanmer's Lord Kenyon's Notes	I.d. Ken. ...	1753—1759	King's Bench, etc.
Harcarse	Harc.	1681—1691	Scotch Courts.
Hardres	Hardr.	1655—1669	Exchequer.
Hare	Hare *or* Ha. ...	1841—1853	Vice-Chancellors' Courts.
Harrison & Rutherfurd ...	Har. & Ruth. ...	1865—1866	Common Pleas.
Harrison & Wollaston ...	Har. & W. ...	1835—1836	King's Bench.
Hayes	Hayes ...	1830—1832	Exchequer, Ireland.
Hayes & Jones ...	Hayes & J. ...	1832—1834	Exchequer, Ireland.
Hemming & Miller	Hem. & Mill. *or* H. & M.	1862—1865	V.-C. Wood.
Hetley	Het.	1627—1631	Common Pleas.
Hobart	Hob.	1613—1625	Common Law.
Hodges	Hodg. ...	1835—1837	Common Pleas.
Hogan	Hog.	1816—1834	Rolls Court, Ireland.
Holt (L. C. J.) ...	Holt ...	1688—1710	King's *or* Queen's Bench.
Holt's Nisi Prius ...	Holt ...	1815—1817	Nisi Prius.
Holt, Wm.	Holt, Eq. ...	1845 ...	Vice-Chancellors' Courts.
Home	Home	1735—1744	Court of Session.
Hopwood & Coltman ...	Hop. & C. ...	1868 to the present time	Common Pleas.
Hopwood & Philbrick ...	Hop. & Ph. ...	1863—1867	Common Pleas.
Horn & Hurlstone	H. & H. ...	1838—1839	Exchequer.
House of Lords Cases ...	H. L. Cas. ...	1847—1866	House of Lords.
Hovenden's Supplement to Vesey, junr.	Hov. Suppl. ...	... ...	Chancery.
Howell's State Trials ...	How. St. Tr. ...	1163—1820	All the Courts.
Hudson & Brooke ...	H. & B. ...	1827—1831	Common Law, Ireland.
Hume	Hume ...	1781—1822	Scotch Courts.
Hunt's Annuity Cases ...	Hunt ...	1777—1794	All the Courts.
Hurlstone & Coltman ...	H. & C. ...	1862—1865	Exchequer.
Hurlstone & Gordon ...	Included in Exch. Reports	1854—1856	Exchequer.
Hurlstone & Norman ...	H. & N. ...	1856—1861	Exchequer.
Hurlstone & Walmsley ...	H. & W. ...	1840—1841	Exchequer.
Hutton	Hutt.	1616—1639	Common Pleas.
Irish Chancery	Ir. Ch.	1850—1867	Chancery.
Irish Circuit Cases ...	Ir. Cir. Ca. ...	1841—1843	Assize Courts, Ireland.
Irish Common Law Reports	Ir. C. L. R. ...	1850—1866	Common Law, Ireland.
Irish Equity Reports ...	Ir. Eq. R. ...	1838—1850	Chancery, Ireland.
Irish Jurist	Ir. Jur.	1848—1866	Irish Courts.
Irish Law Recorder ...	Ir. L. Rec. ...	1827—1838	Irish Courts.
Irish Law Reports ...	Ir. L. Rep. ...	1838—1850	Common Law Courts, Ireland.
Irish Reports, Common Law	I. R., C. L. ...	1867 to the present time	Common Law Courts, Ireland.
Irish Reports, Equity ...	I. R., Eq. ...	1867 to the present time	Chancery, Ireland.
Jacob	Jac.	1821—1822	Chancery.

REPORTS—*continued.*

Reports.	Abbreviations.	Date.	Court.
Jacob & Walker	Jac. & W. *or* J. & W. ...	1819—1821	Chancery.
Jebb	Jebb C. C. ...	1822—1840	Criminal Courts, Ireland.
Jebb & Bourke	J. & B.	1841—1842	Queen's Bench, Ireland.
Jebb & Symes	J. & S.	1838—1841	Queen's Bench, Ireland.
Jenkins' Centuries (*i.e.*, Hundreds) of Reports	Jenk. Cent. ...	1220—1623	Exchequer Chamber.
Johnson	Johns. *or* Jo. ...	1859—1860	Chancery, V.-C. Wood.
Johnson & Hemming ...	Jo.& H. *or* J.& H.	1860—1862	Chancery, V.-C. Wood.
Jones	Jon. Ex. R. ...	1834—1838	Exchequer, Ireland.
Jones & Carey ...	Jones & C. ...	1838—1839	Exchequer, Ireland.
Jones & Latouche ...	Jo. & Lat. ...	1844—1846	Chancery, Ireland.
Jones, Sir T.	Jo.	1670—1683	Common Law.
Jones, Sir W.	Jo.	1620—1651	Common Law.
Jurist Reports	Jur.	1837—1854	All the Courts.
Jurist Reports, New Series	Jur., N. S. ...	1855—1866	All the Courts.
Jurist (Scottish)	Sc. Jur. ...	1829—1873	Scotch Courts.
Justice of the Peace ...	J. P.	1837 to the present time	All the Courts.
Kay	Kay	1853—1854	Chancery, V.-C. Wood.
Kay & Johnson ...	Kay & J. ...	1854—1858	Chancery, V.-C. Wood.
Keane & Grant	... ...	1854—1862	Registration Cases in the Common Pleas.
Keble	Keb.	1661—1678	King's Bench.
Keen	Keen *or* Kee. ...	1836—1838	Rolls Court.
Keilwey	Keil.	1496—1530	Common Law.
Kelynge	Kel.	1739—1745	Chancery.
Kenyon's Notes of Cases .	Ld. Ken. ...	1753—1759	King's Bench.
Knapp	Knapp	1829—1836	Privy Council.
Knapp & Ombler ...	Knapp. & O. ...	1834—1835	Election Committees.
Lane	Lane	1605—1612	Exchequer.
Latch	Latch	1624—1627	King's Bench.
Law Journal	L. J.	1822—1831	All the Courts.
Law Journal, New Series	L. J., N. S. *or* L.J.Rep.,N.S.*	1832 to the present time	All the Courts.
Law Recorder (Ireland) ...	Ir. L. Rec. ...	1827—1838	All the Courts, Ireland.
Law Reports†	Law Rep. *or* L. R.	1866 to the present time	All the Courts.

* (1) As the Old Series of the Law Journal Reports consisted of but nine volumes, it is not necessary to append the initials " N. S." to the references to volumes of the New Series later than the ninth, and in fact they are often omitted in such references, the omission not involving any risk of confusion.

(2) As the Law Journal Reports consist of several sections, according to the jurisdiction in which any given case is heard, the abbreviations representing the section or jurisdiction should, in referring, be added to the initials " L. J." Thus, " L. J., Ch." is a reference to the Chancery section of the Reports ; " L. J., Bank." or " L. J., Bkcy." to the Bankruptcy section, etc. Cases in the House of Lords and Exchequer Chamber are arranged according to the courts from which they originally come. From the commencement of the 45th volume in January, 1876, the Queen's Bench, Common Pleas and Exchequer Reports form one section ; so do the Probate, Divorce and Admiralty Reports.

† In references to the Law Reports, the figure representing the volume is placed between " L. R." and the abbreviation representing the particular division or series ; thus, a reference to the first page of the ninth volume of the Queen's Bench series

REPORTS—*continued.*

Reports.	Abbreviations.	Date.	Court.
Law Times Reports ...	L. T.	1846—1859	All the Courts.
Law Times, New Series...	L. T., N. S. ...	1859 to the present time	All the Courts.
Leach	Leach	1730—1814	Criminal Courts.
Lee...	Lee	1752—1758	Ecclesiastical.
Lee's Cases, tempore Hardwicke	Lee	1733—1738	King's Bench.
Legal Observer	Leg. Ob. ...	1830—1856	All the Courts.
Leigh & Cave	L. & C.... ...	1861—1865	Crown Cases Reserved.
Leonard	Leon.	1553—1615	Common Law.
Levinz	Lev.	1660—1696	Common Law.
Lewin's Crown Cases ...	Lewin	1822—1838	Criminal Courts (Northern Circuit).
Ley	Ley	1608—1629	Common Law.
Lilly's "Cases in Assize"	Lil.	Publd. 1719	Common Law.
Littleton	Littleton ...	1626—1632	Common Pleas and Exch.
Lloyd & Goold, tempore Plunkett	L. & G. *or* Ll. & G. *t.* Pl.	1834—1839	Chancery, Ireland.
Lloyd & Goold, tempore Sugden	L. & G. *or* Ll. & G. *t.* Sugd.	1835 ...	Chancery, Ireland.
Lloyd & Welsby	Ll. & Wel. ...	1829—1830	Common Law.
Lofft	Lofft	1772—1774	King's Bench.
Longfield & Townsend ...	L. & T.	1841—1842	Exchequer, Ireland.
Lowndes & Maxwell ...	L. & M. ...	1852 ...	Bail Court.
Lowndes, Maxwell & Pollock	L. M. & P. ...	1850—1851	Bail Court, etc.
Luders	Luders	1784—1787	Election Committees.
Lumley's Poor Law Cases	Lumley ...	1834—1839	All the Courts.
Lushington	Lush.	1859—1862	Admiralty.
Lutwyche...	Lutw.	1682—1704	Common Pleas.
Lutwyche's Registration Cases	Lutw. Reg. Cas.	1843—1853	Common Pleas.
Macfarlane	Macf.	1838—1839	Jury Court, Scotland.
Maclaurin...	Macl.	1670—1773	Scotch Criminal Courts.
Maclean & Robinson ...	Macl. & R. ...	1839 ...	House of Lords (Sc. App.).
Macnaghten & Gordon ...	Macn. & Gor. ...	1849—1852	Chancery Appeals.
Macpherson's Court of Session Cases	Macph.... ...	1862—1863	Court of Session.
Macpherson's Indian Appeals (in connection with the Law Reports [vol. i.])	Macph. Ind. App. *or* L. R., 1 Ind. App.	1873—1874	Privy Council (see "Cowell's Indian Appeals.").
Macqueen's Scotch Appeals	Macq. Sc. App.	1851—1865	House of Lords.
Macrae & Hertslet ...	M. & H. ...	1847—1852	Insolvent Debtors Court.
Macrory's Patent Cases ...	Mac. P. C. ...	1841—1853	All the Courts.
Maddock	Madd.	1815—1822	Chancery.
Maddock & Geldart ...	Mad. & Gel. *or* 6 Mad.	1821—1822	Chancery.

should be given as "L. R., 9 Q. B. 1." Three new series of the Law Reports commenced in 1876, of which the first (Chancery, Bankruptcy and Lunacy) series was cited as "Ch. D."; the second (Common Law) series was divided into four sections, cited as "Q. B. D.," "C. P. D.," "Ex. D." and "P. D." respectively; and the third (Appellate) series was cited as App. Cas." Since 1891 they have been cited as (1891) 1 Ch., 2 Ch.; (1891) 1 Q. B., 2 Q. B. (now K. B.); (1891) P., etc.

REPORTS—*continued.*

Reports.	Abbreviations.	Date.	Court
Magistrate, The	Mag.	1848—1849	All the Courts.
Manning & Granger ...	Man. & Gr. *or* M. & G.	1840—1844	Common Pleas.
Manning & Ryland ...	M. & R.... ...	1827—1830	King's Bench.
Manning & Ryland's Magistrates' Cases	M. & R. (M. C.)	1827—1830	King's Bench.
Manning, Granger & Scott (C.B., 1st nine volumes)	C. B. (for Common Bench)	1845—1849	Common Pleas (see "Common Bench Reports ").
Manson's Reports ...	Mans.	1894 to the present time	Bankruptcy and Company Winding up.
March's New Cases ...	Mar.	1639—1643	Common Law.
Marriot	Marr.	1776—1779	Admiralty.
Marshall	Marsh.... ...	1813—1816	Common Pleas.
Maule & Selwyn	M. & S.... ...	1813—1817	King's Bench.
M'Clean & Robinson's Scotch Appeals.	M'C. & Rob. ...	1839 ...	House of Lords.
M'Cleland	M'Clel.	1823—1824	Exchequer, Equity.
M'Cleland & Younge ...	M'Clel. & Y. ...	1824—1826	Exchequer, Equity.
Meeson & Welsby ...	Mees. & Wels. *or* M. & W.	1836—1847	Exchequer.
Megone's Company Cases	Meg.	1889—1891	Company Cases.
Merivale	Mer.	1815—1817	Chancery.
Milward	Milw.	1838—1842	Ecclesiastical Courts, Ireland.
Modern Reports (Leach's)	Mod.	1669—1700	All the Courts.
Molloy	Moll.	1827—1828	Chancery, Ireland.
Montagu	Mont.	1829—1832	Bankruptcy.
Montagu & Ayrton ...	Mont. & Ayr. *or* M. & A.	1833—1838	Bankruptcy.
Montagu & Bligh... ...	Mont. & B. *or* M. & B.	1832—1833	Bankruptcy.
Montagu & Chitty ...	Mont. & Chit. *or* M. & C.	1838—1840	Bankruptcy.
Montagu & M'Arthur ...	Mont. & M'A. ...	1826—1830	Bankruptcy.
Montagu, Deacon & De Gex	Mont. D. & D...	1840—1844	Bankruptcy.
Moody	Mood.	1824—1844	Criminal Courts.
Moody & Malkin... ...	Mood. & M. *or* M. & M.	1826—1830	Nisi Prius.
Moody & Robinson ...	Mood. & Rob. *or* M. & R. ...	1830—1844	Nisi Prius.
Moore (see also the following names)	Moor.	1485—1620	Common Law.
Moore	Moore	1817—1827	Common Pleas.
Moore & Payne ...	Moore & P. *or* M. & P.	1827—1831	Common Pleas.
Moore & Scott	Moo. & S. *or* M. & Scott.	1831—1834	Common Pleas.
Moore's Indian Appeals...	Moo. Ind. ...	1836—1872	Privy Council.
Moore's Privy Council Cases	Moo. P. C. ...	1836—1862	Privy Council.
Moore's Privy Council Cases, New Series	Moo. P. C., N. S.	1862—1873	Privy Council.
Morrel, Bankruptcy Reports	Morr. B. C. ...	1884—1893	Bankruptcy.
Mosely	Mos.	1726—1730	Chancery.
Murphy & Hurlstone ...	M. & H.	1836—1837	Exchequer.
Murray's Reports ...	Murr.	1816—1830	Jury Court, Scotland.

REPORTS—*continued.*

Reports.	Abbreviations.	Date.	Court.
Mylne & Craig	My. & C. ...	1837—1841	Chancery Appeals.
Mylne & Keen	My. & K. ...	1832—1835	Chancery Appeals.
Nelson	Nels.	1625—1692	Chancery.
Neville & Macnamara's Railway and Canal Cases	Nev. & M. ...	1855—1874	All the Courts.
Neville & Manning ...	Nev. & M. ...	1832—1836	King's Bench.
Neville & Manning (Mag. Cas.)	N. & M. (M. C.)	1832—1838	King's Bench.
Neville & Perry	Nev. & P. *or* N. & P. ...	1836—1838	King's Bench.
New County Court Cases	N. C. C. Cas. ...	1848—1851	Common Law Courts.
New Magistrates' Cases ...	N. M. C. ...	1844—1848	Common Law Courts.
New Practice Cases ...	N. P. C. ...	1844—1848	Common Law Courts.
New Reports	N. R.	1862—1865	All the Courts.
New Sessions Cases ...	New Sess. Cas.	1844—1851	Common Law Courts.
Nisbet	Nisb.	1665—1677	Court of Session.
Nolan (Magistrates' Cases)	Nolan	1791—1793	King's Bench.
Notes of Cases	Notes of Cases	1841—1850	Ecc. & Adm. Courts.
Noy	Noy	1544—1631	Common Law.
O'Malley & Hardcastle ...	O'Mall. & H. ...	1869 to the present time.	Election Judges.
Owen	Owen	1558—1615	Common Law.
Palmer	Palm.	1619—1628	King's Bench.
Parker	Park.	1743—1766	Exchequer.
Paton's Scotch Appeals ...	... ...	1759—1821	House of Lords.
Peake	Peake	1790—1795	Nisi Prius.
Peake's Additional Cases	Peake, Add. Cas.	1795—1812	Nisi Prius.
Peckwell	Peckw.... ...	1771—1806	Election Committees.
Peere Williams	P. Wms. ...	1695—1735	Chancery.
Perry & Davison	P. & D. ...	1838—1841	Queen's Bench.
Perry & Knapp	P. & K. ...	1833 ...	Election Committees.
Philipps	Phil. El. ...	1782 ...	Election Committees.
Phillimore	Phil. Eccl. ...	1809—1821	Ecclesiastical.
Phillips	Phill.	1841—1849	Chancery Appeals.
Pigot & Rodwell (Reg. Cas.)	Pig. & Rod. ...	1843—1845	Common Pleas.
Pitcairn's Criminal Trials	Pitc.	1488—1624	Court of Justiciary.
Plowden	Plowd.	1550—1579	Common Law.
Pollexfen	Pollexf. ...	1610—1683	All the Courts.
Popham	Poph.	1592—1627	Common Law.
Power, Rodwell & Dew ...	P. R. & D. ...	1848—1856	Election Committees.
Precedents in Chancery ...	Prec. Ch. ...	1689—1722	Chancery.
Price	Price	1814—1824	Exchequer.
Queen's Bench Reports ...	Q. B.	1841—1852	Queen's Bench.
Railway and Canal Cases (see also "Neville and Macnamara")	Rail. Cas. *or* Rail. & Can. Cas.	1835—1854	All the Courts.
Raymond, Lord	Ld. Raym. ...	1694—1732	Common Law.
Raymond, Sir T. ...	Raym.	1660—1683	Common Law.
Rayner's Tithe Cases ...	Rayn.	1575—1753	All the Courts.
Real Property Cases ...	R. P. Cas. ...	1843—1848	All the Courts.
Reilly's Albert Arbitration	... ...	1871—1873	Lord Cairns.

REPORTS—*continued.*

Reports.	Abbreviations.	Date.	Court.
Reilly's European Arbitrn.	... ...	1872 ...	Lord Westbury.
Reports in Chancery ...	Ch. Rep. ...	1625—1710	Chancery.
Revised Reports	R. R. ...	1785 to the present time	All the Courts.
Ridgway, Lapp & Schoales	R. L. & S. ...	1793—1795	King's Courts, Ireland.
Ridgway's Cases in the time of Lord Hardwicke	Ridgw.... ...	1733—1745	King's Bench & Chancery.
Ridgway's Parliamentary Reports	Ridgw. P. C. ...	1784—1796	House of Lords, Ireland.
Robertson (Eccl. Reports)	Rob. Eccl. ...	1844—1853	Ecclesiastical.
Robertson(Scotch Appeals)	Rob. Sc. App. .	1709—1727	House of Lords.
Robinson (Chr.)	Chr. Rob. ...	1798—1808	Admiralty.
Robinson, Geo. (Scotch Appeals)	G. Rob. ...	1840—1841	House of Lords.
Robinson, W.	W. Rob. ...	1838—1850	Admiralty.
Rolle, Sir H.	Roll, or Rolle ...	1614—1625	King's Bench.
Rose	Rose	1810—1816	Bankruptcy.
Ross' Leading Cases on Commercial Law.	... ...	Publd. 1853	All the Courts.
Ross' Leading Cases on the Law of Scotland	... ...	Publd. 1849	Scotch Courts.
Russell	Russ.	1823—1828	Chancery Appeals.
Russell & Mylne	Russ. & Myl. or R. & M.	1829—1833	Chancery Appeals.
Russell & Ryan ...	Russ. & Ry. ...	1800—1823	Criminal Courts.
Ryan & Moody	Ry. & M. ...	1823—1826	Nisi Prius.
Salkeld	Salk.	1688—1709	King's Bench (principally).
Saunders	Saund.	1666—1672	King's Bench.
Saunders &Cole(Bail Court)	B. C. R. ...	1846—1848	Bail Court.
Sausse & Scully	Sau. & Sc. ...	1835—1840	Rolls Court, Ireland.
Saville	Sav.	1580—1594	Common Law.
Sayer	Say.	1751—1756	King's Bench.
Schoales & Lefroy ...	Sch. & Lef. or S. & L.	1802—1809	Chancery, Ireland.
Scott	Scott	1834—1840	Common Pleas.
Scott's New Reports ...	Scott, N. R. ...	1840—1845	Common Pleas.
Searle & Smith ...	Se. & Sm. ...	1859—1860	Probate and Divorce.
Select Cases in Chancery	Sel. Ca. Ch. ...	1724—1733	Chancery.
Sessions Cases	Sess. Ca. ...	1710—1746	King's Bench.
Shaw	Shaw	1848—1852	Court of Justiciary.
Shaw & Dunlop	S. & D. ...	1819—1831	Court of Justiciary.
Shaw, Dunlop, Napier & Bell	S., D., N. & B. .	1821—1831	Court of Teinds.
Shaw & M'Clean's Scotch Appeals	Sh. & M'C. ...	1835—1838	House of Lords.
Shaw's Scotch Appeals ...	Sh. App. ...	1821—1824	House of Lords.
Shower	Show.	1678—1694	King's Bench.
Shower's Cases in Parlt.	Show P. C. ...	1694—1699	House of Lords.
Siderfin	Sid.	1659—1670	King's Bench.
Simons	Sim.	1826—1852	Chancery.
Simons & Stuart	Sim. & Stu. or S. & S.	1822—1826	Chancery.
Simons, New Series ...	Sim., N. S. ...	1850—1852	Chancery.
Skinner	Skinn.	1681—1697	King's Bench.
Smale & Giffard	Sm. & Giff. ...	1852—1857	Chancery, V.-C. Stuart.

REPORTS—*continued.*

Reports.	Abbreviations.	Date.	Court.
Smith	Smith	1803—1806	King's Bench.
Smith & Batty	Sm. & Bat. ...	1824—1825	King's Bench, Ireland.
Smith's Leading Cases ...	Sm., L. C. ...	7th edition published 1875	Common Law Courts.
Smith's (Lacey) Registration Cases	Smith, Reg. ...	1896—1900	Registration Cases.
Smythe	Smythe ...	1839—1840	Common Pleas, Ireland.
Solicitors' Journal and Reporter	S. J., or Sol. Jour.	Jan. 1857 to the present time	All the Courts.
Spinks	Spinks	1853—1855	Ecclesiastical and Admiralty.
Spinks' Prize Cases ...	Spinks' Pr. Cas.	1854—1856	Admiralty.
Stair	Stair	1661—1681	Court of Session.
Starkie	Stark.	1815—1823	Nisi Prius.
State Trials (ed. Howell)	How. St. Tr. ...	1163—1820	All the Courts.
Strange	Stra.	1716—1747	King's Bench.
Stuart, Milne & Peddie ...	St. M. & P. ...	1851—1853	Scotch Courts.
Style	Sty.	1646—1655	King's or Upper Bench.
Swabey	Swab.	1855—1859	Admiralty.
Swabey & Tristram ...	Sw. & Tr. ...	1858—1865	Probate and Divorce.
Swanston	Swanst. ...	1818—1819	Chancery.
Swinton	Swint.	1835—1841	Court of Justiciary.
Syme	Sym.	1826—1829	Court of Justiciary.
Tamlyn	Taml.	1829—1830	Chancery.
Taunton	Taunt.	1807—1819	Common Pleas.
Temple & Mew	T. & M.... ...	1848—1851	Crown Cases Reserved.
Term Reports, by Durnford & East	Term Rep., or T. Rep.	1785—1800	King's Bench.
Thornton's Notes of Cases	Thorn.	1841—1850	Eccl. and Mar. Courts.
Times Law Reports ...	T. L. R. ...	1884 to the present time	All the Courts.
Tothill	Toth.	1559—1641	Chancery.
Tudor's Leading Cases :—			
Mercantile and Maritime Law	Tudor L. C. Merc. Law.	2nd edition, publd. 1868	All the Courts.
Real Property and Conveyancing	Tudor L. C. R. P.	Published 1863	All the Courts (see also " White & Tudor ").
Turner & Russell... ...	Turn. & Russ. or T. & R. ...	1822—1824	Chancery.
Tyrwhitt	Tyrw.	1830—1835	Exchequer.
Tyrwhitt & Granger ...	Tyr. & Gr. ...	1835—1836	Exchequer.
Vaughan	Vaugh.	1666—1673	Common Pleas.
Ventris	Vent.	1668—1692	All the Courts.
Vernon	Vern.	1680—1719	Chancery.
Vernon & Scriven ...	V. & S.	1786—1788	Common Law, Ireland.
Vesey	... ...	... ...	(See next three names.)
Vesey & Beames	V. & B.... ...	1812—1814	Chancery.
Vesey junior	Ves. jun. or, after the first two volumes, Ves. simply.	1789—1817	Chancery.
Vesey senior	Ves. sen. ...	1746—1755	Chancery.
Wallis	Wall.	1766—1791	Irish Courts.

REPORTS—*continued.*

Reports.	Abbreviations.	Date.	Court.
Webster's Patent Cases ...	Webst.	1602—1855	All the Courts.
Weekly Notes	W. N.	1866 to the present time	All the Courts.
Weekly Reporter... ...	W. R.	1852 to the present time	All the Courts.
Welsby, Hurlstone & Gordon	Exch. (for Exchequer)	1847—1854	Exchequer.
Welsh	Welsh	... ...	Registry Cases, Ireland.
West (Chancery)... ...	West (Ch.) ...	1736—1739	Chancery.
West (House of Lords) ...	West (H. L.) ...	1839—1841	House of Lords.
White & Tudor's Leading Cases	Wh. & T., *or* L. C. Eq.	4th edition, publd. 1872	Chancery.
Wightwick	Wightw. ...	1810—1811	Exchequer.
Willes	Willes	1737—1758	Common Pleas.
Williams (Peere)... ...	P. Wms. ...	1695—1735	Chancery.
Willmore, Wollaston & Davison	W. W. & D. ...	1837 ...	King's *or* Queen's Bench.
Willmore, Wollaston & Hodges	W. W. & H. ...	1838—1839	Queen's Bench.
Wilmot's Opinions ...	Wilm.	1757—1770	All the Courts.
Wilson, George	Wils. *or* G. Wils.	1742—1774	Common Law.
Wilson, John	Wils. Ch. ...	1818—1819	Chancery.
Wilson, John	Wils. Ex. Eq. ...	1817 ...	Exchequer (Equity).
Wilson & Shaw's Scotch Appeals	Wils. & S., *or* W. & S.	1825—1834	House of Lords.
Winch	Winch	1621—1625	Common Pleas.
Wolferstan & Bristow ...	Wolf. & B., *or* W. & B.	1859—1864	Election Committees.
Wolferstan & Dew ...	Wolf. & D., *or* W. & D.	1857—1858	Election Committees.
Wollaston's Practice Cases	W. P. C. ...	1840—1841	Common Law Courts.
Wood's Tithe Causes ...	Wood	1650—1707	Exchequer.
Year Books	Y. B.	1273—1535	Common Law.
Yelverton	Yelv.	1602—1613	King's Bench.
Younge	Younge ...	1830—1832	Exchequer (Equity).
Younge & Collyer (Chancery)	You. & Coll.C.C., *or* Y. & C. C. C.	1841—1844	Chancery.
Younge & Collyer (Exchequer, Equity)	You. & Coll. Ex. Eq.,*or* Y.& C.Ex.	1834—1842	Exchequer (Equity).
Younge & Jervis	Y. & J.	1826—1830	Exchequer.

REPRESENTATION. 1. For the purposes of intestate succession to anyone, the children of a deceased relative are, within certain degrees, allowed to *represent* their parent: thus, if a man die leaving a brother A., and the children of a deceased brother B., the children of B. are said to take by *representation.* 1 *Steph. Com.*

2. The character borne by an heir or devisee, or an executor or administrator. 2 *Steph. Com.* [PERSONAL REPRESENTATIVE ; REAL REPRESENTATIVE.]

3. See MISREPRESENTATION.

REPRESENTATIVE PEERS are those who sit in the House of Lords as representing the peerage of Scotland and Ireland. 2 *Steph. Com.*

REPRIEVE. The suspension of the execution of a criminal sentence. 4 *Steph. Com.*

REPRISAL. A taking in return; that is to say, taking the goods of a wrongdoer to make compensation for the wrong he has done, or as a pledge for amends being made. 2 *Steph. Com.*; 3 *Steph. Com.* [LETTERS OF MARQUE AND REPRISAL; RECAPTION.]

REPUBLICATION OF WILL. The revival of a will revoked, either by re-execution or by a codicil adapted to the purpose. [PUBLICATION, 1.]

REPUDIATION. A rejection or disclaimer; especially of a man's disclaiming a share in a transaction to which he might otherwise be bound by tacit acquiescence.

REPUGNANT. Inconsistent; generally used of a clause in a written instrument inconsistent with some other clause or with the general object of the instrument.

REPUTATION. 1. A person's good name. 1 *Steph. Com.*; 3 *Steph. Com.*

2. That which generally hath been and many men have said and thought.

REPUTED OWNER. A bankrupt, in reference to goods and chattels in his apparent possession with the consent of the true owner, is called the *reputed owner* of such goods.

The doctrine of reputed ownership, by which a bankrupt trader is deemed the reputed owner of goods in his apparent possession, was introduced into the bankrupt laws by stat. 21 Jac. 1, c. 19, s. 11, for the purpose of protecting the creditors of a trader from the consequences of the false credit which he might acquire by being suffered to have in his possession, as apparent owner, property which did not really belong to him. Such property may in general be claimed by the trustee in the bankruptcy for the benefit of the creditors. See the *Bankruptcy Act*, 1883, *s.* 44; 2 *Steph. Com.*; *Robson's Bkcy.* [ORDER AND DISPOSITION.]

REQUEST, COURTS OF. [COURT OF REQUEST.]

REQUEST, LETTERS OF. [LETTERS OF REQUEST.]

REQUISITIONS ON TITLE are written inquiries made by the solicitor of an intending purchaser of land, or of any estate or interest therein, and addressed to the vendor's solicitor, in respect of some apparent insufficiency in the abstract of title. [ABSTRACT OF TITLE.]

RES GESTÆ. The material facts of a case as opposed to mere hearsay. The phrase is generally used in reference to that which is apparently hearsay, and yet is in fact immediately relevant to the matter in question. Thus proof may be received of the language used at seditious meetings, in order to show the objects and character of such meetings. 3 *Steph. Com.*; *Powell's Ev.*

RES INTEGRA. An affair not broached or meddled with; one on which no action had been taken, or deliberation had.

RES INTER ALIOS ACTA ALTERI NOCERE NON DEBET. *A matter litigated between two parties ought not to prejudice a third party.* This is the general rule; but it must be taken with this important qualification, that though a decision, in a case between A. and B., cannot directly prejudice C., yet if there be a legal point at issue in C.'s case identical with one which was in controversy between A. and B., the court will generally regard itself as bound by the prior decision, at least if the court which pronounced it was the same, or one of equal or superior authority.

RES IPSA LOQUITUR. The matter itself speaks; thus we say, "the thing speaks for itself." A phrase used in actions for injury occasioned by negligence where no proof is required of negligence beyond the accident itself.

RES JUDICATA. A matter which has been adjudicated upon. [EXCEPTIO REI JUDICATÆ.]

RES NULLIUS. A thing which has no owner.

RES PERIT DOMINO. (The loss falls on the owner.)

RESCOUS or **RESCUE** is a resistance against lawful authority, in taking a person or thing out of the custody of the law; as if a bailiff or other officer, upon a writ, do arrest a man, and others by violence take him away, or procure his escape; this is a *rescous in fact.* 4 *Steph. Com.* So if one distrain beasts for damage feasant [DAMAGE FEASANT] in his ground, and as he drives them, they enter the owner's house, and he will not deliver them up upon demand; this is a *rescous in law.* 3 *Steph. Com.*; *Fawcett, L. & T.*

RESCUSSOR. A person committing a *rescous* or *rescue*. [RESCOUS.]

RESERVATION. A keeping back, as when a man lets his land, *reserving* a rent. Sometimes it signifies an exception ; as when a man lets a house, and *reserves* to himself one room. 1 *Steph. Com.*

RESERVING A POINT OF LAW. It was formerly the practice for a judge at the Assizes to reserve points of law for consideration of the full court at Westminster, but now such points are argued on " further consideration " before the judge himself. See the *Appellate Jurisdiction Act*, 1876, *s.* 17, and *R. S. C.* 1883, *Ord. XXXVI. r.* 39. 3 *Steph. Com.* [NEW TRIAL.]

Questions of law may also be reserved by the court in a criminal case ; in which case the point is left for the judgment of the Court for the Consideration of Crown Cases Reserved, composed of judges of the High Court. [COURT FOR CONSIDERATION OF CROWN CASES RESERVED.]

RESIANCE. A man's abode, residence, or continuance in a place.

RESIANT ROLLS. Rolls containing the *resiants* in a tithing, etc., which were called over by the steward on holding courts leet. [COURT LEET ; TITHING.]

RESIDENCE. A continuance of a spiritual person upon his benefice. 2 *Steph. Com.* Now used generally for any person's continuance in a place, and defined for various purposes by different Acts of parliament. [SETTLEMENT.]

RESIDUARY ACCOUNT. The account which every executor and administrator (in respect of any estate exceeding £1,000 in value), after paying the debts and particular legacies of the deceased, and before paying over the *residuum*, must pass before the Board of Inland Revenue, setting forth the particulars of the assets of the estate and of the payments made thereout ; the duty being calculated on the balance found. 2 *Steph. Com.*

RESIDUARY DEVISEE. A person entitled under a will to the *residue* of the testator's lands ; that is, to such as are not specifically devised by the testator's will. By the Wills Act, 1837 (7 Will. 4 & 1 Vict. c. 26), s. 25, it is provided that, unless a contrary intention shall appear by the will, such real estate or interest as shall be comprised, or intended to be comprised, in any devise in such will contained, which shall fail or be void by reason of the death of the devisee in the lifetime of the testator, or by reason of such devise being contrary to law, or otherwise incapable of taking effect, shall be included in the residuary devise (if any) contained in such will. 1 *Steph. Com.; Wms. R. P.*

RESIDUARY ESTATE is a term used variously to mean :—

1. A testator's property not specifically devised or bequeathed.

2. Such part of the personal estate as is primarily liable to the payment of debts.

3. That which remains after debts and legacies have been paid.

RESIDUARY LEGATEE is one to whom the residue, or a proportionate share in the residue, of a testator's personal property is left, after debts, funeral expenses, and specific and pecuniary legacies have been satisfied. 2 *Steph. Com.*

RESIDUUM or **RESIDUE.** The residue of the personal estate of a deceased person after payment of debts and specific and pecuniary legacies. 2 *Steph. Com.*

RESIGNATION. 1. The giving up of a benefice into the hands of the ordinary. 2 *Steph. Com.* [See next title.]

2. And, generally, the giving up of any office by letter or other instrument in writing delivered to the party lawfully authorised to receive it. See the *Municipal Corporations Act*, 1882, *s.* 36.

RESIGNATION BOND is a bond or other engagement in writing taken by a patron from the clergyman presented by him to a living, to resign the benefice at a future period. This is allowable in certain cases under stat. 9 Geo. 4, c. 94. 2 *Steph. Com.*

RESOLUTION. Any matter resolved upon, especially at a public meeting.

I. *Resolutions of Creditors.*—These are resolutions passed at meetings of the creditors of a bankrupt or one whose property is in liquidation. Resolutions thus passed are of two kinds :—

1. An *ordinary resolution*, which is decided by a majority in value of the creditors present personally or by proxy at the meeting and voting upon such resolution.

RESOLUTION—*continued.*

2. A *special resolution*, which is decided by a majority in number and three-fourths in value of the creditors present personally or by proxy at the meeting and voting upon such resolution.

Bankruptcy Act, 1883 (*stat.* 46 & 47 *Vict. c.* 52), *s.* 168 ; *Robson, Bkcy.*

II. *Resolutions of Joint-Stock Companies.*—By s. 51 of the Companies Act, 1862 (stat. 25 & 26 Vict. c. 89), a special resolution is defined to be a resolution passed by a majority of not less than three-fourths of the members of the company present in person or by proxy, and confirmed by a majority of such members as may be present at a subsequent meeting held at an interval of not less than fourteen days, nor more than one month, from the date of the first meeting ; and by s. 129 an extraordinary resolution is one which is passed in such a manner as would, if it had been confirmed by a subsequent meeting, have constituted a special resolution.

III. *Resolutions in Parliament.*—In parliament, every question, when agreed to, assumes the form of an *order*, or a *resolution* of the house. By its *orders*, the house directs its committees, its members, its officers, the order of its own proceedings and the acts of all persons whom they concern. By its *resolutions*, the house declares its own opinions and purposes. *May's Parl. Pract.*

RESORT, COURT OF LAST.—A court from which there is no appeal.

RESPECTUM, CHALLENGE PROPTER. [CHALLENGE.]

RESPITE. Delay or forbearance. Thus :—
1. *Respite of homage* was the forbearing or excusing of the homage which ought first of all to be performed by the tenant that held by homage. [HOMAGE.]
2. *Respite of a jury* signifies the adjournment of the sittings of the jury for defect of jurors.
3. *Respite of a sentence* signifies a delay, or putting off of the execution of the sentence.

RESPONDEAT OUSTER. (Let him answer over) ; that is to say, when a dilatory plea put in by the defendant has been overruled by the Court, let him put in a more substantial plea, or *answer over* in some better manner. 3 *Steph. Com.*; 4 *Steph. Com.* [DILATORY PLEA ; PLEADING OVER.]

RESPONDEAT SUPERIOR. (Let the superior be held responsible.) In pursuance of this maxim, a principal is liable in damages for the act of his agent, and a master for the act of his servant : provided that in each case the act of the inferior, whether specifically authorised or not, was within the scope of the duties imposed by the superior. See *Broom's Legal Maxims.*

RESPONDENT. A party called upon to *answer* a petition or an appeal.

RESPONDENTIA. A loan upon the security of the goods and merchandise in a vessel, or upon the mere hazard of a voyage. 2 *Steph. Com.* [BOTTOMRY]. Such a loan is insurable. *Crump, Mar. Ins.*

RESTITUTIO IN INTEGRUM. The rescinding of a contract or contracts (*e.g.*, on the ground of fraud) so as to restore parties to their original position.

RESTITUTION. The restoring of anything unlawfully taken from another. It is most frequently used in the common law for the setting him in possession of lands and tenements that hath been unlawfully disseised of them. [See also the following titles.]

RESTITUTION OF CONJUGAL RIGHTS. A suit for restitution of conjugal rights is a suit which may be brought when either husband or wife lives separately from the other without any sufficient reason, to compel the party, so living separately, to return to the other. It was formerly brought in the Ecclesiastical Court ; but since the Divorce Act of 1857, it has been brought in the Court for Divorce and Matrimonial Causes now consolidated with the High Court of Justice. Under 47 & 48 Vict. c. 68, the Court may now make a pecuniary provision for the injured party, in lieu of specifically enforcing the decree. 2 *Steph. Com.*; 3 *Steph. Com.* ; 36 & 37 *Vict. c.* 66, *ss.* 3, 16, 34. [COURT FOR DIVORCE AND MATRIMONIAL CAUSES.]

RESTITUTION, WRIT OF. 1. A writ issued in favour of a successful plaintiff in error to restore to him all that he has lost by the judgment which has been reversed on error. The technical proceeding called a writ of error was abolished by the Judicature Act, 1875. [ERROR.]

2. A writ issued on conviction of a thief, for the restitution of the stolen goods to their true owner. 24 & 25 *Vict. c.* 96, *s.* 100. See 42 & 43 *Vict.* c. 49, *s.* 27 (3). Restitution, however, may be ordered in a summary manner without writ. 2 *Steph. Com.;* 4 *Steph. Com.* As to compensating innocent purchaser for value out of moneys found upon person convicted, see 30 & 31 Vict. c. 35, s. 9.

RESTITUTIONE EXTRACTI AB EC-CLESIA. An old writ for the restoration of a man to the sanctuary of the church, from which he had been forcibly removed. [SANCTUARY.]

RESTRAINING ORDER is an order restraining the Bank of England, or some public company, from allowing any dealing with some stock or shares specified in the order. It is granted on motion or petition. See 5 *Vict. c. 5, s. 4.*

RESTRAINING STATUTES. Those which restrict previous rights or powers ; a phrase used especially of the Acts of parliament passed to restrain simoniacal practices in presentations to livings. 1 *Steph. Com.*

RESTRAINT OF MARRIAGE. Conditions attached to a gift or bequest in *general* restraint of marriage are void on grounds of public policy, but not so conditions against second marriage, or if the restraint be *partial* only.

RESTRAINT OF TRADE. Contracts in general restraint of trade, *i.e.*, unlimited as to time or area are void. Contracts in partial restraint are, however, upheld. 2 *Steph. Com.*

RESTRICTIVE INDORSEMENT is an indorsement on a bill or note which restricts the negotiability of the bill to a particular person, or a particular purpose ; as "pay to I. S. only," or "pay John Holloway for my use." It is to be distinguished from a *blank indorsement*, which consists merely of the signature of the indorser ; from a *full indorsement*, which makes the bill or note payable to a given person or his order ; and from a *qualified indorsement*, which qualifies the liability of the indorser. See *Bills of Exchange Act*, 1882, *s.* 35. [INDORSEMENT ; QUALIFIED INDORSEMENT.]

RESTS are periodical balancings of an account made for the purpose of converting interest into principal, and charging the party liable thereon with compound interest. *Smith's Man. Eq.*

RESULTING TRUST is a trust raised by implication in favour of the author of the trust himself, or his representatives. This generally happens where an intended trust fails. 1 *Steph. Com.* [TRUST.]

RESULTING USE. A use returning by way of implication to the grantor himself. 1 *Steph. Com.* [RESULTING TRUST ; USE.]

RETAINER. 1. A servant, but not menial or familiar, that is, not continually dwelling in the house of his master, but only wearing his livery, and attending sometimes upon special occasions.

2. The right which an executor (and at common law an administrator), who is a creditor of his testator, has to *retain* so much of the testator's assets as will pay his own debt. 2 *Steph. Com.*; 3 *Steph. Com.*

3. A counsel's retaining fee. Retainers in this sense are either general or special. For rules as to retainer, see *Yearly Practice.*

4. An authority given to a solicitor to proceed in an action. This may be given verbally ; but a written retainer is always preferable. A retainer of this kind is either *general* or *special*. The solicitor of a person has an implied authority from his client to accept service of process, but he cannot in general commence an action for him without a special retainer.

RETIRING A BILL. The word "retire," in its application to bills of exchange, is an ambiguous word. In its ordinary sense it is used of an indorser who takes up the bill by handing the amount to a transferee, and thereupon holds the instrument with all his remedies intact. But it is sometimes used of an acceptor who pays a bill at maturity, and thereby extinguishes all remedies upon it. *Byles on Bills.*

RETORNA BREVIUM. The return of writs. [RETURN, 1.]

RETORNO HABENDO. The writ *de retorno habendo* is the writ of execution for the distrainor in the action of replevin, for *returning* to him the chattel distrained. 3 *Steph. Com.*

RETOUR SANS PROTET or **SANS FRAIS.** A request or direction by the drawer of a bill of exchange, that, in case the bill should be dishonoured by the drawee, it be returned without protest and without expense (*sans frais*). The effect of such a request is to disable the drawer of the bill (and perhaps also the indorsers) from resisting payment of the bill on the ground that it has not been protested. *Byles on Bills.* [BILL OF EXCHANGE; PROTEST, 3.]

RETRAXIT (he has retracted). This was an open and voluntary renunciation of his suit by the plaintiff in court, by which he for ever lost his right of action upon the matter in question. A *retraxit* differed from a nonsuit in that a nonsuit was properly a neglect by the plaintiff to appear when called upon to do so. 3 *Bl.* [NONSUIT, NOLLE PROSEQUI.]

RETURN. 1. The return of a writ by a sheriff or bailiff, or other party to whom a writ is directed, is a certificate made to the court of that which he hath done, touching the execution of the writ directed to him. 3 *Steph. Com.*

2. The return of a member or members to serve in Parliament for a given constituency. This is the return of the writ which directed the sheriff or other officer to proceed to the election. [RETURNING OFFICER.]

3. A certificate or report by commissioners on a matter on which they have been directed to inquire. The word is especially so used in reference to matters of statistical detail; thus we say, " the returns of the census," etc.

4. The return of goods replevied. [REPLEVIN; RETORNO HABENDO.]

RETURNING OFFICER. The officer to whom a writ is directed, requiring him to proceed to the election of a member or members to serve in parliament or some other public body. In parliamentary elections, he is generally the sheriff in the case of a county, and the mayor in the case of a borough. 2 *Steph. Com.; May's Parl. Pract.*

REVELAND. Land of the king not granted out to any, but resting in charge of the *reve* or bailiff of the manor. It is said to have been the thane-land of Domesday.

REVENUE signifies properly the yearly rent that accrues to every man from his lands and possessions. But it is applied especially to the income which the British constitution hath vested in the royal person in order to support the regal dignity; also to the general income received by the State in taxes, etc. 2 *Steph. Com.* [See next title.]

REVENUE SIDE OF THE EXCHEQUER. That jurisdiction of the Court of Exchequer, or of the Exchequer Division of the High Court of Justice, by which it ascertains and enforces the proprietary rights of the Crown against the subjects of the realm. By Order in Council, 1881, the Exchequer Division was merged in the Queen's Bench Division (now King's Bench Division). 3 *Steph. Com.* The practice in revenue cases is not affected by the Orders and Rules under the Judicature Act, 1875. *R. S. C.* 1883, *Ord. LXVIII.*

REVERSAL OF JUDGMENT is the annulling of a judgment, on appeal therefrom, by the court to which the appeal is brought. 3 *Steph. Com.; 4 Steph. Com.*

REVERSION. 1. A reversion signifies properly the residue of an estate *left in the grantor* to commence in possession after the determination of some particular estate granted out by him. 1 *Steph. Com.; Wms. R. P.*

2. But it is frequently, though improperly, used so as to include any future estate, whether in reversion or remainder. [ESTATE, II.; REMAINDER.]

REVERSIONARY INTEREST. An interest in real or personal property in remainder or reversion. 1 *Steph. Com.* As to the powers of married women to dispose of such interests, see 20 & 21 Vict. c. 57; and 45 & 46 Vict. c. 75. 2 *Steph. Com.* [REVERSION.]

REVERSIONARY LEASE. 1. A lease to take effect *in futuro.*

2. A general lease to take effect after the expiration of a former lease.

REVERSIONER means strictly a person entitled to an estate in reversion [REVERSION, 1]; but the word is used generally to signify any person entitled to any future estate in real or personal property, as when we speak of dealings with expectant heirs, reversioners, etc. [SALE OF REVERSIONS ACT.]

REVERTER. Returning or reversion. [FORMEDON.]

REVIEW, BILL OF. A *bill of review* was a bill sometimes brought in Chancery for the purpose of reviewing a cause already heard. This bill might be brought after the decree had been signed and enrolled, (1) if error of law appeared on the face of the decree; (2) if new evidence were discovered which could not have been had or used when the decree passed; but in the latter case only by leave of the court. Proceedings in error are now abolished, and the procedure would now be by appeal to the court of appeal.

REVIEW OF TAXATION is the reconsideration by the taxing master, or by a judge in chambers, of the items allowed or disallowed in the taxation of costs, or any of them. [TAXATION OF COSTS.]

REVISING BARRISTERS are junior barristers of not less than seven years standing, appointed every year to revise the register of parliamentary electors in each district. They hold open courts for the purpose. From their decision there is an appeal to the King's Bench Division. The appointment is for a year only, but they are generally reappointed. Their appointment is by the senior judge on the circuit during the summer circuit in any year. See 49 & 50 *Vict. c.* 42; 2 *Steph. Com.*

REVIVING is a word metaphorically applied to rents, debts and rights of action, signifying a renewal of them after they be extinguished, *e.g.*, debts barred by the Statutes of Limitation are revived by acknowledgment in some cases. 2 *Steph. Com.*

REVIVOR was a proceeding to revive a suit or action which, according to the old practice, became abated by the death of one of the parties, the marriage of a female party, or some other cause. In Chancery this was formerly done by *bill of revivor*, now abolished. [ABATEMENT, 4.]

REVIVOR, WRIT OF, was a writ to revive a judgment in an action at common law, which could not be enforced directly by writ of execution, in consequence of lapse of time or change of parties. See now *R. S. C.* 1883, *Ord. XLII. r.* 23. 3 *Steph. Com.* [ABATEMENT, 4.]

REVOCATION is the reversal by any one of a thing done by himself. Thus, when it is provided in a marriage settlement or other instrument, that an appointment may be made "with or without power of revocation," it is implied that the party making the appointment may, if he think fit, reserve the power of annulling what he has done. A power granted or reserved in a deed or other instrument to revoke an appointment already made, and to make a fresh one, is called a *power of revocation and new appointment*. Any act or instrument which is capable of being annulled by its author is said to be *revocable*. Some instruments are in their nature revocable, as wills. Deeds under seal are not in general revocable, unless a power to revoke be therein expressly reserved. A will may be revoked (1) by marriage; (2) by the execution of another will or codicil, or by some writing of revocation executed as a will; (3) by the burning, tearing, or other destruction of the original will (*animo revocandi*) by the testator, or by some other person in his presence and by his direction. 7 *Will.* 4 & 1 *Vict. c.* 26, *ss.* 19, 20; 1 *Steph. Com.*

THE REVOCATION OF PROBATE is where probate of a will, having been granted. is afterwards recalled by the Court of Probate, on proof of a subsequent will, or other sufficient cause.

REX NON POTEST PECCARE (the king can do no wrong).

REX NUNQUAM MORITUR (the king never dies).

RHODIAN LAW. An ancient code of maritime law used by the people of Rhodes, some of the principles of which have been adopted in our own maritime code. 3 *Steph. Com.*

RIDER. 1. A new clause added to a bill before parliament on its third reading. This was formerly done by tacking a separate piece of parchment on the bill, which was called a "ryder." According to the present practice, if on the third reading of a bill material amendments

RIDER—*continued*.

are required to be made, it is usual to discharge the order for the third reading, to re-commit the bill, and to introduce the amendments in committee. *May's Parl. Pract.*

2. We now use the word "rider" in a general sense, to signify a clause proposed to be added to a motion before a meeting.

RIDINGS. Three divisions of the county of York, called the North, the East, and the West Riding. The word "riding" is a corruption of "trithing," a name indicating a threefold division of a county. 1 *Steph. Com.*

RIGHT. A lawful title or claim to anything. The word is frequently used to denote a claim to a thing of which one is not in possession.

RIGHT IN COURT. [RECTUS IN CURIA.]

RIGHT OF ACTION. The right to bring an action in any given case. But the phrase is frequently used in a more extended sense, as identical with *chose in action*, to mean all rights which are not rights of possession, and to include the large class of rights over things in the possession of others, which must be asserted by action in cases where the qualified or temporary possessor refuses to deliver them up. See 3 *Steph. Com.* [CHOSE.]

RIGHT OF SEARCH. The right of a belligerent to examine and inspect the papers of a neutral vessel on the high seas, and the goods therein contained, to see whether the ship is neutral or an enemy, and to ascertain whether she has contraband of war or enemies' property on board.

RIGHT OF WAY. A right enjoyed by one man (either in his specific character or as one of the public) of passing over another's land, subject to such conditions and restrictions as are specified in the grant, or sanctioned by the custom, by virtue of which the right exists. Rights of way are susceptible of almost infinite variety : they may be limited both as to the intervals at which they may be used (as a way to church) and as to the actual extent of the user authorised (as a footway, horseway or carriageway). *Gale on Easements ; 1 Steph. Com.*

RIGHT, PETITION OF. [PETITION OF RIGHT.]

RIGHT TO BEGIN. The right to commence the argument on a trial, which belongs to that side on whom the burden of proof rests. 3 *Steph. Com.* The party beginning has also the right to reply to his adversary's case. The appellant begins all civil appeals.

RIGHT, WRIT OF. [WRIT OF RIGHT.]

RIGHTS, BILL OF. [BILL OF RIGHTS.]

RINGING THE CHANGES. A trick by which a criminal, on receiving a piece of money in payment of an article, pretends that it is not good, and, changing it in such a manner as not to be seen by the buyer, returns to the latter a spurious coin. This is held to be an uttering of false money. *Frank's case*, Dec. 1794, Leach, 644. The phrase is also generally applied to fraudulent exchanges of coin, effected in the course of paying money or receiving money in payment. *Russell on Crimes.*

RIOT. A tumultuous disturbance of the peace by three or more persons assembling together of their own authority, mutually to assist one another against any who shall oppose them in the execution of some enterprise of a private nature, and afterwards actually executing the same in a violent and turbulent manner, to the terror of the people. This is held to be a riot, whether the act be of itself lawful or unlawful. [See the two following titles.]

RIOT ACT. Stat. 1 Geo. 1, st. 2, c. 5, passed in 1715. [RIOTOUS ASSEMBLY.]

RIOTOUS ASSEMBLY. The unlawful assembling of twelve persons or more to the disturbance of the peace. In such cases it is provided by the Riot Act, 1 Geo. 1, st. 2, c. 5, that if any justice of the peace, sheriff, undersheriff, or mayor of a town, shall command them by proclamation under that Act to disperse, then if they contemn his orders, and continue together for one hour afterwards, such contempt shall be felony. The Act also contains a clause indemnifying the officers and their assistants in case any of the mob should be unfortunately killed in the endeavour to disperse them. 4 *Steph. Com. ; Oke's Magist. Syn.* Parties whose property is damaged by the acts of rioters may recover compensation out of the police rate of the district.

RIOTOUS ASSEMBLY—*continued.*
See 49 *&* 50 *Vict.* c. 38 ; 4 *Steph. Com.*
By stat. 24 & 25 Vict. c. 97, in order to constitute *felony*, the riotous act must consist in demolishing, or beginning to demolish, some house or other building.

RIPARIAN PROPRIETORS. Proprietors of the banks of a river.

RIPARIAN STATES. States whose jurisdictions are bounded by the banks of a river.

RIXATRIX COMMUNIS. A common scold. [SCOLD.]

ROBBERY. The unlawful and forcible taking of goods or money from the person of another by violence or putting him in fear. But if the taking be not directly from a man's person or in his presence, it is no robbery. This violence, or putting in fear, is that which distinguishes robbery from other larcenies. 4 *Steph. Com.*

ROE, RICHARD. A fictitious personage who often appeared in actions at law prior to the passing of the Common Law Procedure Act, 1852 ; sometimes as one of the pledges for the due prosecution of an action, and sometimes as the casual ejector in an action of ejectment. [EJECTMENT.]

ROGUE. An idle wandering beggar, vagrant or vagabond. 3 *Steph. Com.* ; 4 *Steph. Com.*

ROLL. A schedule of paper or parchment, which may be turned or wound up. [See the following titles.]

ROLL OF COURT. The court-roll of a manor, wherein the business of the court, the admissions, surrenders, names, rents, and services of the tenants are copied and enrolled. [COURT ROLLS ; MANOR.]

ROLLS COURT. The office appointed for the custody of the rolls and records of the Chancery, the master whereof is called the Master of the Rolls. The phrase is especially used to signify the court-room in which the Master of the Rolls sat as judge. [MASTER OF THE ROLLS.]

ROLLS OF PARLIAMENT. The manuscript registers of the proceedings of our old parliament.

ROLLS OFFICE OF THE CHANCERY. [ROLLS COURT.]

ROUT is where three or more meet under circumstances which constitute an unlawful assembly (which see), and make some advances towards carrying out their object. [RIOT ; UNLAWFUL ASSEMBLY.]

ROYAL ASSENT (Lat. *Regius assensus*). The assent given by the sovereign to a bill passed in both houses of parliament. The royal assent to a bill is given either in person. or by commission by letters patent under the great seal, signed with the sovereign's hand, and notified to both houses assembled together in the upper house. The bill thereupon becomes an Act. 2 *Steph. Com.* ; *May's Parl. Pract.* [LE ROY LE VEULT ; LE ROY S'AVISERA.]

ROYAL FISH. [FISH ROYAL.]

ROYAL GRANTS. Grants by letters patent or letters close from the Crown. These are always matters of record. 1 *Steph. Com.*

ROYAL MINES. Mines of silver and gold. 2 *Steph. Com.*

ROYALTY. 1. The royal dignity and prerogatives.

2. A *pro ratâ* payment to a grantor or lessor, on the working of the property leased, or otherwise on the profits of the grant or lease. The word is especially used in reference to mines, patents and copyrights.

RUBRIC. The directions in the body of the Book of Common Prayer are called *rubrics*, being, in the authorised edition of 1662, printed in red letters, as they are not unfrequently in prayer books at the present day.

RULE. 1. A regulation for the government of a society agreed to by the members thereof.

2. A rule of procedure made by a lawful judicial authority for some court or courts of justice. In this sense we have the Orders and Rules under the Judicature Acts, consolidated and amended by the Rules of the Supreme Court, 1883. [R. S. C. 1883.]

3. An order made by a superior court upon motion in some matter over which it has summary jurisdiction. A rule is either granted absolutely in the first instance, or as a *rule nisi*, or a *rule to show cause*, that is, a rule that the thing applied for be granted, *unless* the opposite party show sufficient reason against it, on a day assigned for that purpose.

RULE—*continued*.

The rule is *served* upon the opposite party, and when it comes on for argument, the court, having heard counsel, *discharges* the rule or makes it *absolute*. For the present practice see *R. S. C.* 1883, *Ord. LII.* 3 *Steph. Com.* [RULE OF COURT.]

4. A rule obtained, as of course, on the application of counsel.

5. A rule obtained at chambers without counsel's signature to a motion paper, on a note of instructions from an attorney, was called a *side-bar rule.*

6. A point of law settled by authority; as when we speak of the *Rule in Shelley's case*, etc. [See next title.]

RULE IN SHELLEY'S CASE, so called from having been quoted and insisted on in *Shelley's case*, is the following rule :—That wherever a man by any gift or conveyance takes an estate of freehold, and in the same gift or conveyance an estate is limited, either mediately or immediately, to his *heirs* in fee or in tail, the word *heirs* is a word of *limitation*, and not of *purchase*. In other words, it is to be understood as expressing the quantity of estate which the party is to take, and not as conferring any distinct estate on his heirs, or the heirs of his body, as the case may be. 1 *Steph. Com.; Wms. R. P.* [SHELLEY'S CASE.]

RULE NISI. [RULE, 3.]

RULE OF COURT. 1. An order made on motion, generally in open court, or else made generally to regulate the practice of the court. [RULE, 2, 3.]

2. A submission to arbitration, or the award of an arbitrator, is said to be made a *rule of court*, when the court makes a rule that such submission or award shall be conclusive. See now the *Arbitration Act*, 1889, *ss.* 1, 12. 3 *Steph. Com.*

RUNNING DAYS. [LAY DAYS.]

RUNNING DOWN CASE. An action against the driver of one vehicle for running down another ; or of a ship or boat for damaging another by a collision.

RUNNING WITH THE LAND. A covenant is said to *run with the land*, when each successive owner of the land is entitled to the benefit of the covenant, or liable (as the case may be) to its obligation. 1 *Steph. Com.; Fawcett, L. & T.; Spencer's case*, 1 Sm. L. C. 1.

RURAL DEAN. An officer of the church, generally a parochial clergyman, appointed to act under the bishop or archdeacon ; his proper duty being to inspect the conduct of the parochial clergy, to inquire into and report dilapidations, and to examine candidates for confirmation. 2 *Steph. Com.* [See next title.]

RURAL DEANERY. The circuit of the jurisdiction of a rural dean. Every diocese is divided into archdeaconries, each archdeaconry into rural deaneries, and each rural deanery into parishes. 1 *Steph. Com.* [RURAL DEAN.]

RURAL SANITARY AUTHORITY. [URBAN SANITARY AUTHORITY.]

S. C. An abbreviation frequently used for " same case," in giving a second reference to any case which may be cited.

S. J. [SOLICITORS' JOURNAL.]

S. P. *Sine prole*, without issue.

S. S. C. [SOLICITOR OF THE SUPREME COURT.]

SAC signifies the liberty of holding pleas (*i.e.*, assuming jurisdiction) in the court of a lordship or manor, and of imposing mulcts and forfeitures upon transgressors. [LIBERTIES.]

SACCULARII. Cutpurses ; that is, those who privately steal from a man's person, as by picking his pocket. 4 *Steph. Com.*

SACRILEGE. 1. Stealing things dedicated to the offices of religion.

2. Breaking into a church, chapel, meeting house, or other place of divine worship, and committing a felony therein ; or, being in such place, committing a felony therein, and breaking out of the same. *Stat.* 24 & 25 *Vict. c.* 96, *s.* 50 ; 4 *Steph. Com.; Oke's Mag. Syn.*

SAFE CONDUCT. A security given by the sovereign, under the great seal of England, for enabling a foreigner of a nation at war with us quietly to come in and pass out of the realm. 2 *Steph. Com.*

SAFE PLEDGE. A surety given for a man's appearance at a day assigned.

SAILING INSTRUCTIONS are written or printed directions delivered by the commanding officer of a convoy to the masters of ships under his care, by which they are enabled to understand and answer his signals, and also to know the place of rendezvous in case of dispersion. Without these sailing instructions, no vessel can have the full protection and benefit of a convoy.

SALE. A transmutation of property from one man to another, in consideration of a price paid in money. 2 *Steph. Com.*

SALE BY AUCTION ACT. By 30 & 31 Vict. c. 48, the particulars or conditions of any intended sale of land by auction must state whether the sale is without reserve, or subject to a reserve price, and whether a right to bid is reserved. And if the sale is stated to be without reserve, or to that effect, the seller may not employ any person to bid at the sale, and the auctioneer may not knowingly take a bidding from any such person. The Act also abolishes the practice of opening biddings in sales under the authority of the Court of Chancery, except in cases of fraud or mismanagement of the sale. By the Sale of Goods Act, 1893, s. 58, where a right to bid is expressly reserved, but not otherwise, the seller, or any one person on his behalf, may bid at the auction. 2 *Steph. Com.* [OPENING BIDDINGS; PUFFER; WITHOUT RESERVE.]

SALE OF REVERSIONS ACT is the stat. 31 Vict. c. 4. It was a strict rule in courts of equity to set aside sales of reversions, unless the purchaser (on whom the burden of proof rested) could show that a full consideration was paid, or that the bargain was fully made known to and approved by the person to whose estate the expectant heir hoped to succeed. The object of the above Act is to prevent any sale of a reversion from being set aside merely on the ground of *undervalue*. The burden of proof is, however, still on the purchaser, to show that he has acted fairly, and has not made any improper use of personal influence. 1 *Steph. Com.* [REVERSION, 2.]

SALIC or **SALIQUE LAW.** An ancient law of Pharamund, King of the Franks, excluding women from inheritances, and from succession to the crown.

SALUS POPULI EST SUPREMA LEX. (The safety of the people is the highest law.)

SALVAGE or **SALVAGE MONEY.** A reasonable reward payable by owners of goods saved at sea from pirates, enemies, or the perils of the sea, to those who have saved them. 2 *Steph. Com.; Crump, Mar. Ins.*

Claims for salvage may be made in the Admiralty Court (now the Probate, Divorce, and Admiralty Division of the High Court of Justice), or in the county courts having admiralty jurisdiction. 3 *Steph. Com.;* 36 & 37 *Vict.* c. 66, *s.* 34; *Abbott on Shipping.*

SALVO (*Salvo jure*). Without prejudice to.

SALVOR. A person who saves goods at sea. [SALVAGE.]

SANCTION OF A LAW. The provision for enforcing it.

SANCTUARY. A place privileged for the safeguard of men's lives that are offenders. The sanctuary was allowed to shelter the party accused, if within forty days he acknowledged his fault, swore to abjure the realm, and submitted himself to banishment. [RESTITUTIONE EXTRACTI AB ECCLESIA.]

The privilege of sanctuary was abolished by 21 Jac. 1, c. 28. 4 *Steph. Com.*

SANS FRAIS. Without incurring any expense. [RETOUR SANS PROTET.]

SANS NOMBRE. Without stint. A term sometimes applied to the case of common for cattle *levant et couchant*. But a common *sans nombre* generally means a common of pasture without any limit to the number of beasts which may be turned on it to feed there; which can only happen if it be a common in gross. 1 *Steph. Com.;* 3 *Steph. Com.* [COMMON; LEVANT AND COUCHANT; SURCHARGE OF COMMON.]

SANS RECOURS. Without recourse; meaning "without recourse to me." These words are appended to an indorsement on a bill or note to qualify it, so as not to make the indorser responsible for any payment thereon. This is the proper mode of indorsing a bill where an agent indorses on behalf of his principal. *Byles on Bills.* [BILL OF EXCHANGE; QUALIFIED INDORSEMENT.]

SATISFACTION. 1. The acceptance by a party injured of a sum of money, or other thing, in bar of any action he might otherwise have had in respect of such injury. Payment of a sum of money will not operate as satisfaction of a larger sum owing; but payment in any other form, *e.g.*, even by cheque or bill of exchange, will. 3 *Steph. Com.* [ACCORD; SATISFACTION ON THE ROLL.]

2. The making of a donation with the express or implied intention that it shall be taken as an extinguishment of some claim which the donee has upon the donor. This generally happens under one of the two following states of circumstances :—(1) When a father, or person *in loco parentis*, makes a double provision for a child, or person standing towards him in a filial relation, *i.e.*, satisfaction of portions by legacies, or legacies by portions; (2) When a debtor confers, by will or otherwise, a pecuniary benefit on his creditor. In the first case the question arises whether the later provision is *in satisfaction* of the former, or intended to be added to it. In the second, the question is whether the benefit conferred is intended *in satisfaction* of the debt, or whether the creditor is to be allowed to take advantage of it, and nevertheless claim independently against other assets of the debtor.

Satisfaction differs from *performance*, in that satisfaction implies the substitution of something different from that agreed to be given, while in cases of performance the thing agreed to be done is taken to be in truth wholly or in part performed. *Ashburner's Equity.*

SATISFACTION ON THE ROLL is the entry on the roll or record of a court that a judgment is satisfied, whether by the voluntary payment of the judgment debtor, or the compulsory process of law. 3 *Steph. Com.*

SATISFIED TERMS ACT. The stat. 8 & 9 Vict. c. 112, for abolishing satisfied outstanding terms of years in land, providing that terms which thenceforth should become attendant upon the inheritance, either by express declaration or by construction of law, were to cease and determine. This, in effect, abolishes outstanding terms. 1 *Steph. Com.; Wms. R. P.* [OUTSTANDING TERM; TERM, 2.]

SAVING THE STATUTE OF LIMITATIONS signifies the keeping a right of action alive notwithstanding the Statute of Limitations. This may be done by commencing an action and getting the writ of summons from time to time renewed. See *R. S. C.* 1883, *Ord. VIII.,* and notes thereon in the *Annual Practice.* 3 *Steph. Com.*

SAVINGS BANKS are banks for the receipt of small deposits of money, the produce of which is to accumulate at compound interest, and the principal and interest to be paid out to the depositors as required. See 43 & 44 *Vict. c.* 36; 50 & 51 *Vict. c.* 40; 54 & 55 *Vict. c.* 21; 56 & 57 *Vict. c.* 69. 3 *Steph. Com.* [POST OFFICE.]

SAXON LAGE. The laws of the West Saxons. *Cowel.* [DANE LAGE; MERCEN LAGE; WEST SAXON LAGE.]

SCACCARIUM. The exchequer. 3 *Steph. Com.* [COURT OF EXCHEQUER.]

SCANDAL. 1. A report or rumour, or action whereby one is affronted in public.
2. An irrelevant and abusive statement introduced into the pleadings in an action. By R. S. C. 1883, Ord. XIX. r. 27, the court or a judge may order scandalous statements to be struck out of the pleadings; out of interrogatories by Ord. XXXI. r. 7, and out of affidavits by Ord. XXXVIII. r. 11.

SCANDALUM MAGNATUM. Words spoken in derogation of a peer, judge, or other great officer of the realm; which are subjected to peculiar punishments by stat. 3 Edw. 1, c. 34, passed in 1275, and by divers other ancient statutes. Obsolete. 2 *Steph. Com.; * 3 *Steph. Com.*

SCHEDULE. An appendix to an Act of parliament or instrument in writing, for the purpose of facilitating reference in the Act or instrument itself.

SCIENTER. Knowingly; a word applied especially to that clause in a declaration in certain classes of actions in which the plaintiff alleged that the defendant *knowingly* did or permitted that from whence arose the damage of which the plaintiff complained. In an action of deceit the *scienter* must be averred and proved. *Scienter* must also be proved in cases of injuries done by animals, except that the statute 28 & 29 Vict. c. 60, makes it unnecessary in the case of injury done by dogs to sheep, cattle, etc. 3 *Steph. Com.*

SCILICET. "That is to say"; or, as it is sometimes expressed, "to wit." [VIDELICET.]

SCINTILLA JURIS. The kind of spark or shadow of right which subsists in a feoffee or grantee to uses since the passing of the Statute of Uses (27 Hen. 8, c. 10). 1 *Steph. Com.;* and see 23 & 24 *Vict. c.* 38, *s.* 7. [USE; USES, STATUTE OF.]

SCIRE FACIAS (that you cause him to know). A *scire facias* is a judicial writ, founded upon some matter of record, and requires the person against whom it is brought to show cause why the party bringing it should not have advantage of such record, or (as in the case of a *scire facias* to repeal grants of the Crown and letters patent, except for inventions), why the record should not be annulled and vacated. A *scire facias* may be issued against a shareholder of a company on a judgment against the company, and in various other cases. 1 *Steph. Com.;* 2 *Steph. Com.;* 3 *Steph. Com.*

SCIRE FECI. The sheriff's return on a *scire facias*, that he has caused notice to be given to the party against whom the writ was issued.

SCOLD. A troublesome and angry woman, who, by brawling and wrangling amongst her neighbours, breaks the public peace, increases discord, and becomes a public nuisance to the neighbourhood. Scolds were punished by means of the castigatory or cucking stool. 4 *Steph. Com.*

SCOT AND LOT. A customary contribution laid upon all subjects according to their ability. In some boroughs, the *scot and lot inhabitants* (that is, such as paid the poor's rate as inhabitants) were allowed to vote in parliamentary elections for the borough; and these rights were reserved by the Reform Act of 1832, so far as regarded the persons who then enjoyed them, the number of whom must now have become very small. 2 *Steph. Com.* [POT-WALLOPERS.]

SCOTCH JUDGMENT. [JUDGMENTS EXTENSION ACTS.]

SCOTCH PEERS. 1. The ancient peers of Scotland.
2. The sixteen representative peers elected to represent the peerage of Scotland in the House of Lords.

1 *Steph. Com.;* 2 *Steph. Com.* [LORDS TEMPORAL; PARLIAMENT.]

SCOTS. The name given to the rates assessed by the commissioners of sewers. 3 *Steph. Com.*

SCRIP. Certificates of shares in a public company. A scrip certificate is a certificate entitling the holder to apply for shares in a public company, either absolutely or on the fulfilment of specified conditions.

SCRIPT. A testamentary document of any kind, whether a will, codicil, draft of a will or codicil, or written instructions for the same. In testamentary causes, the plaintiff and defendant must, within eight days of the entry of an appearance on the part of the defendant, file their affidavits of scripts. *Coote's Probate Practice.*

SCRIVENER. An old word, signifying—
1. One who receives money to place it out at interest, and who supplies those who want to raise money on security.
2. One who draws contracts.

SCUTAGE, or SCUTAGRUM. The payment made by tenants in chivalry, in lieu of personal service. 1 *Steph. Com.;* 2 *Steph. Com.* [ESCUAGE; KNIGHT-SERVICE.]

SE DEFENDENDO (in defending himself). A plea for one charged with the slaying of another, that he did so in his own defence. 1 *Steph. Com.;* 4 *Steph. Com.* [HOMICIDE, 2.]

SEA MARKS. Lighthouses, buoys and beacons. 2 *Steph. Com.;* 3 *Steph. Com.*

SEAL. Wax impressed with a device, and attached as a mark of authenticity to letters and other instruments in writing. 1 *Steph. Com.* A contract under seal is called a *specialty contract* or *covenant.* It needs no valuable consideration to support it, as a contract not under seal does. An instrument under seal is necessary to pass all freehold and leasehold interests in land, except in the case of leases for periods not exceeding three years, where the rent reserved amounts at least to two-thirds of the full improved value of the land. 3 *Steph. Com.* [CONSIDERATION; CONTRACT; GREAT SEAL; PRIVY SEAL.]

SEAL DAYS. Motion days in the Court of Chancery used to be so called.

SEARCH, RIGHT OF. [RIGHT OF SEARCH.]

SEARCH WARRANT is a warrant granted by a judge or magistrate to search a house, shop, or other premises, *e.g.*, a warrant may be granted by a justice under the Larceny Act, 1861 (24 & 25 Vict. c. 96) s. 103, for the purpose of searching for stolen goods or other property in respect of which any offence punishable under that Act has been committed. And see numerous other Acts. *Stone's Justices' Manual; 3 Steph. Com.; 4 Steph. Com.* [WARRANT, I. 4.]

SEARCHES. Usually made by purchasers to find out incumbrances. See 45 & 46 Vict. c. 39, s. 2, as to official searches.

SEAWORTHY. A ship is said to be seaworthy when it is in a fit condition to perform the voyage on which it is sent. By the Merchant Shipping Act, 1894, s. 457, every person who sends, or who is party to any attempt to send, any ship to sea in an unseaworthy state, so as to endanger the life of any person, is guilty of a misdemeanor, unless he can prove that he used all reasonable means to keep the ship seaworthy and was ignorant of such unseaworthiness; or that the going to sea of such ship in an unseaworthy state was, under the circumstances, reasonable and justifiable. By s. 459 the Board of Trade is empowered to detain unsafe ships. *2 Steph. Com.; 2 Steph. Com.*

SECK RENT. [RENT.]

SECOND DELIVERANCE. [RETURN IRREPLEVISABLE.]

SECONDARY. 1. An officer who is second or next to the chief officer.

2. An under-sheriff of London, so called especially in reference to his jurisdiction in the assessment of damages under writs of inquiry. *2 Steph. Com.* [INTERLOCUTORY JUDGMENT; WRIT OF INQUIRY.]

SECONDARY CONVEYANCES. The same as derivative conveyances. [DERIVATIVE CONVEYANCE.]

SECONDARY EVIDENCE is evidence not of the best and most direct character; which is admissible in certain cases where the circumstances are such as to excuse a party from giving the proper or primary proof. Thus a copy of a deed is secondary evidence of its contents. See *3 Steph. Com.* Secondary evidence is receivable whenever its substitution for primary evidence does not create a reasonable presumption of fraud. There are no degrees in secondary evidence. The testimony of a witness is as sufficient secondary evidence of the contents of a written instrument as a copy of such instrument would be, although the latter would be more satisfactory.

Secondary evidence must not be confounded with secondhand evidence. [SECONDHAND EVIDENCE.]

SECONDARY USE. The same as a shifting use. [SHIFTING USE.]

SECONDHAND EVIDENCE is the same as *hearsay evidence*, the ordinary meaning of which is the oral or written statement of a person who is not produced in court, conveyed to the court either by a witness or by the instrumentality of a document. The general rule is that hearsay or secondhand evidence is not admissible; but there are certain exceptions to this rule. Thus, in matters of public or general interest, popular reputation or opinion, or the statements of deceased witnesses made against their own interest, will be received as evidence. *Higham v. Ridgeway*, 10 East, 109. And on charges of homicide the declarations of the deceased, made in expectation of death, are admissible in evidence for or against the accused. *Powell on Evidence. 3 Steph. Com.*

SECRETARY OF STATE. There are now five principal secretaries of state; the Secretary for the Home Department, for Foreign Affairs, for the Colonies, for the War Department, and for India. There are also several under-secretaries. *2 Steph. Com.*

SECTA, or **SUIT.** By these words were anciently understood the witnesses or followers of the plaintiff, which he brought to support his case.

SECTA CURIÆ. Suit of court; that is to say, the attendance at the lord's court, to which the tenant was bound in time of peace. *Wms. R. P.*

SECURED CREDITOR. A creditor who holds some special security for his debt, as a mortgage or lien. A secured creditor in bankruptcy may either give up his security or give credit for its value and prove for his whole debt or else realise his security and prove for the balance and receive a dividend *pari passu* with the other creditors. See *Bankruptcy Act*, 1883, *s.* 6 (2), and the *2nd Schedule*, rr. 9—17. *Robson's Bkcy.*

SECURITATE PACIS. 2 *Steph. Com.* 169. [KEEPING THE PEACE.]

SECURITY FOR COSTS. In actions at common law, where the plaintiff was a person residing out of the jurisdiction of the court, or where, being himself in a state of insolvency or extreme poverty, he had sued as a nominal plaintiff for the benefit of some other person, the courts were in the habit, on the application of the defendant, of ordering proceedings to be stayed until security should be given, to the satisfaction of the master, for payment of all such costs as might in the event become due to the defendant in respect of the cause. In Chancery it was the practice to require security for costs from a plaintiff whose address as given on the bill is false, or shows that the plaintiff resides out of the kingdom, and that not in any official capacity. Under the Judicature Act, 1875, the practice as to security for costs seems not to be affected ; but since the Judgments Extension Act, 1868, a plaintiff who resides in Scotland or Ireland will not be required to give security for costs. As to the cases in which security for costs is now required see R. S. C. 1883, Ord. LXV. r. 6, and the notes thereon in the *Annual Practice.*

SECURITY FOR GOOD BEHAVIOUR. [KEEPING THE PEACE.]

SECURITY FOR KEEPING THE PEACE. [KEEPING THE PEACE.]

SECUS. Otherwise ; not so.

SEDITION consists in attempts made, by meetings or speeches, or by publications, to disturb the tranquillity of the State, which do not amount to treason. 4 *Steph. Com.*

SEDUCTION. An action of seduction for damages may be brought by a parent, master, or one *in loco parentis* for the debauching his daughter or servant ; *per quod servitium amisit.* The woman herself has no action. 3 *Steph. Com.*

SEE (Lat. *Sedes*). The circuit of a bishop's jurisdiction ; or his office or dignity as being bishop of a given diocese. 1 *Steph. Com.; 2 Steph. Com.*

SEIGNIORY. A lordship or manor. 1 *Steph. Com. ; Wms. R. P.*

SEISED. Feudally possessed of a freehold. 1 *Steph. Com.*

SEISED IN HIS DEMESNE AS OF FEE. This technical expression describes a tenant in fee simple in possession of a corporeal hereditament. The expression means that the land to which it refers is a man's *dominicum*, or property, since it belongs to him and his heirs for ever ; yet this *dominicum*, property, or demesne is strictly not absolute or allodial, but qualified or feudal ; it is his demesne, *as of fee*, that is, it is not purely and simply his own, since it is held of a superior lord, in whom the ultimate property resides. 1 *Steph. Com.* [FEE.]

SEISIN (Scotch, *Sasine ;* French, *Sasine*) is the feudal possession of a freehold estate in land. It is opposed—(1) To a merely beneficial or equitable title ; (2) To the possession of a mere leasehold estate.
Seisin is of two kinds,—*seisin in deed*, and *seisin in law.* Seisin in deed is when an actual possession is taken. Seisin in law is where lands descend, and one hath not actually entered on them ; or where one is by wrong disseised of them. 1 *Steph. Com.*

SEISIN, LIVERY OF. The delivery of feudal possession sometimes called investiture. [FEOFFMENT.]

SEISINA FACIT STIPITEM (seisin makes the stock of descent). This was the maxim of law by which, before the Inheritance Act, 1833 (3 & 4 Will. 4, c. 106), the title by descent was traced from the person who died last seised. Now, by sect. 2 of that Act, descent is traced from the last person entitled who did not inherit. 1 *Steph. Com.* [DESCENT ; SEISIN.]

SEIZING OF HERIOTS is when the lord of a manor, on the death of a tenant, seizes the beast or other chattel due by way of heriot. 3 *Steph. Com.* [HERIOT.]

SEIZURE QUOUSQUE. By the custom of most manors, if no heir to copyhold lands came to the court to be admitted in the place of a deceased tenant, the lord of the manor after proclamation at three consecutive customary courts might seize the land *quousque, i.e.*, until some person claimed to be admitted. 1 *Steph. Com.*

SELECT COMMITTEE. A parliamentary committee, composed of certain members appointed by the house, to consider or inquire into any matters, and to report their opinion for the information of the house. *May's Parl. Pract.*

SELECT VESTRY. [VESTRY.]

SEMBLE. It appears; an expression often used in reports, to indicate that such was the opinion of the court on a point not directly before them.

SEMI-NAUFRAGIUM. Half-shipwreck; a term used by Italian lawyers, by which they understood the casting merchandise into the sea to prevent shipwreck. The word is also used to signify the state of a vessel which has been so much injured by a tempest or accident, that to repair the damage would cost more than the ship is worth. [TOTAL LOSS.]

SENESCHAL. 1. A steward.
2. Also, one who hath the dispensing of justice.

SENTENCE OF A COURT. A definitive judgment pronounced in a civil or criminal proceeding.

SENTENCE OF DEATH RECORDED. This is the recording of a sentence of death not actually pronounced, on the understanding that it will not be executed. Under stat. 4 Geo. 4, c. 48, s. 1, it is competent for the judge to do this in capital felonies other than murder. By sect. 2, such a record is to have the same effect as if the judgment had been pronounced, and the offender reprieved by the court. The number of capital felonies has, however, been so much reduced by the Criminal Law Consolidation Acts of 1861, that it is seldom we hear now of a sentence of death recorded, and not actually pronounced. *Arch. Crim. Pleadings; 4 Steph. Com.*

SEPARATE ESTATE. Such estate as is enjoyed by a married woman to her *separate use*, independently of her husband, so that she may dispose of it by will, and bind it by her contracts in writing, as if she were unmarried, provided she be not, by any instrument under which she takes it, restrained from anticipating the income thereof. The common law did not allow a married woman to possess any property independently of her husband, but the Married Women's Property Act, 1882, has almost abolished the distinction between married and unmarried women in respect of property. Restrictions on anticipation are, however, still valid subject to the relaxation contained in the Conveyancing Act, 1881, s. 39. *2 Steph. Com.* [MARRIED WOMEN'S PROPERTY.]

SEPARATE MAINTENANCE. Maintenance provided by a husband for his wife on the understanding that she is to live separate from him. *2 Steph. Com.*

SEPARATE USE. [SEPARATE ESTATE.]

SEPARATION DEED signifies a deed of separation between husband and wife, whereby each covenants not to molest the other, and the husband agrees to pay so much to trustees for her separate maintenance, the trustees covenanting to indemnify him against his wife's debts.

Though the law allows provision to be made for a separation already determined on, yet it will not sanction any agreement to provide for the contingency of a future separation. *2 Steph. Com.*

SEPARATISTS. 1. A sect of dissenters, allowed by stat. 3 & 4 Will. 4, c. 82, to make affirmation in lieu of oaths. *Toml.; 2 Steph. Com.; 3 Steph. Com.; 4 Steph. Com.*

2. Dissenters generally.

SEPTENNIAL ACT. The stat. 1 Geo. 1, stat. 2, c. 38, for prolonging the period of a parliament to seven years from the day on which, by the writ of summons, it was appointed to meet, unless sooner dissolved by the pleasure of the Crown. At the time of the passing of this Act the period of a parliament was three years. *2 Steph. Com.; May's Parl. Pract.*

SEQUELA VILLANORUM. The family retinue and appurtenances to the goods and chattels of villeins, which were at the absolute disposal of the lord.

SEQUESTER. A term used in the civil law for renouncing. The word also signifies the setting apart of a man's property, or a portion thereof, for the benefit of his creditors.

SEQUESTRARI FACIAS DE BONIS ECCLESIASTICIS. A writ of execution in an action against a beneficed clergyman, commanding the bishop to enter into the rectory and parish church, and take and sequester the same, until of the rents, tithes and profits thereof, and of the other ecclesiastical goods of the defendant, he have levied the plaintiff's debt. This writ is in the nature of a *levari facias.* See *R. S. C.* 1888, Ord. *XLIII. rr.* 3–6; *Annual Practice; 3 Steph. Com.* [LEVARI FACIAS.]

SEQUESTRATION. 1. The order sent out by a bishop in execution of the writ of *sequestrari facias*, whereby the bishop directs the churchwardens to collect the profits of the defendant's benefice, and pay the same to the plaintiff, until the full sum be raised. 2 *Steph. Com.* See preceding title.

2. A writ directed by the court to commissioners, usually four in number, commanding them to enter the lands and take the rents and profits and seize the goods of the person against whom it is directed. This may be issued against a defendant who is in contempt by reason of neglect or refusal to appear or answer, or to obey a decree of the court. This writ may be issued under the Judicature Acts, in whatever division of the High Court the action may be brought. *R. S. C.* 1883, *Ord. XLIII. r.* 6 ; 3 *Steph. Com.*

SERIATIM. Individually, separately, and in order.

SERJEANT, or **SERGEANT** (Lat. *Serviens*), is a word used variously as follows :—

1. *Serjeants at arms,* whose office is to attend the person of the sovereign ; to arrest traitors and persons of quality offending, and to attend the Lord High Steward of England sitting in judgment upon any traitor. Two of them, by allowance of the sovereign, attend on the two houses of parliament. Their duties are to execute the commands of the house in arresting offenders. *May's Parl. Pract.*

2. *Serjeant at Law.* This is the highest degree in the legal profession. A serjeant at law is so made by the royal mandate or writ, commanding him to take that degree by a certain day. This privilege was abolished by stat. 9 & 10 Vict. c. 54, by which the Court of Common Pleas was thrown open to all barristers.

A serjeant, on being so created, retired from the Inn of Court by which he was called to the bar, and became a member of Serjeants' Inn. The degree of serjeant is never taken now, though it has not been formally abolished. 1 *Steph. Com.* ; 3 *Steph. Com.*

3. *The Common Serjeant,* a judicial officer in the City of London. He acts as one of the judges of the Central Criminal Court.

SERJEANTS' INN. [SERJEANT, 2.]

SERJEANTY. An ancient tenure. [GRAND SERJEANTY ; PETIT SERJEANTY.]

SERVANT. Servants are of several descriptions : — 1. Menial servants ; being persons retained by others to live within the walls of the house, and to perform the work and business of the household. 2. Persons employed by men of trades and professions under them, to assist them in their particular callings. 3. Apprentices, who are placed with a master to learn his trade. 4. Servants in husbandry, usually hired by the year. The following points may be mentioned in connection with the law of master and servant :—1st. A master may *maintain*, that is, abet and assist his servant in any action at law against a stranger : whereas in general to do this is an offence against the law. [MAINTENANCE, 1.] 2ndly. A master may bring an action against any man for beating or maiming his servant ; but in such case he must allege his own damage by the loss of his servant, and such damage must be proved at the trial. 3rdly. If a servant by his negligence does any damage to a stranger, the master is liable for his neglect, provided the damage be done while the servant is acting in his master's employment. As to the liability of a master for injuries to a servant caused by a *fellow servant,* see the Employers' Liability Act, 1880 : the Workmen's Compensation Acts, 1897, 1900. 2 *Steph. Com.* ; *Manley Smith's Law of Master and Servant.*

SERVI. Bondmen, or servile tenants.

SERVICE (*Servitium*). 1. That duty which a tenant, by reason of his fee, owes to his lord. 1 *Steph. Com.*

2. The duty which a servant owes to his master.

3. *Service of Process.*—This is the delivery of a writ, summons, or notice in any action or suit being instituted, or notice of any step or process therein, to the party to be affected thereby, or his solicitor, or other party having an interest in the subject-matter of the suit. It is now regulated by R. S. C. 1883, Ord. IX. An *address for service* is an address at which such notice may be served, so as to bind the party whom it is thereby intended to serve. See *R. S. C.* 1883, *Ord. IV., and Ord. XII. r.* 10.

As to service out of jurisdiction, see R. S. C. 1883, Ord. XI. 3 *Steph. Com.*

4. Of notices by landlord or tenant,

SERVIENT TENEMENT. A tenement subject to an easement or servitude. [DOMINANT TENEMENT ; EASEMENT ; SERVITUDE.]

SERVITIUM LIBERUM. Free service, such as to find a man and horse, or to go with the lord into the army, or to attend his court; as opposed to base services, such as ploughing the lord's land, or hedging his demesnes, which a freeman would be unwilling to perform. [FREEHOLD.]

SERVITUDES. The name in the Roman and Scotch law for *easements*. The property subject to the easement was called the *servient tenement;* and, in the case of an easement appurtenant, the property to which the enjoyment of the easement was attached was called the *dominant tenement.* [EASEMENT.]

SESS. A tax.

SESSION. 1. The sitting of parliament from its meeting to its prorogation, of which there is in general but one in each year. See 2 *Steph. Com.*
2. The sitting of justices in court upon commission. [SESSIONS.]

SESSION, COURT OF. [COURT OF SESSION.]

SESSIONS is a sitting of justices in court upon commission, as the Sessions of Oyer and Terminer, the Quarter Sessions, the Petty Sessions, Special Sessions, etc. The Sessions of Oyer and Terminer are held before the justices of assize, the Quarter Sessions are held in counties before the justices of the peace, and in boroughs before the recorder. Special and Petty Sessions are held before justices of the peace. Petty Sessions are held periodically. [BOROUGH SESSIONS ; COUNTY SESSIONS ; OYER AND TERMINER ; PETTY SESSIONS ; SPECIAL SESSIONS.]

SESSIONS OF THE PEACE. The name given to sessions held by justices of the peace, whether general, quarter, special, or petty sessions. [SESSIONS.]

SET-OFF may be defined generally to be the merging (wholly or partially) of a claim of one person against another in a counter-claim by the latter against the former. Thus, a plea of set-off is a plea whereby a defendant acknowledges the justice of the plaintiff's demand, but sets up another demand of his own, to counterbalance that of the plaintiff, either in whole or in part. This was a defence created by 2 Geo. 2, c. 22, and was unknown to the common law.

By R. S. C. 1883, Ord. XIX. r. 3, a defendant in an action may set off or set up any right or claim by way of counter-claim against the claims of the plaintiff, and such set-off or counter-claim is to have the same effect as a statement of claim in a cross-action. 3 *Steph. Com.*

SETS OF BILLS are exemplars or parts of a bill of exchange made on separate pieces of paper; each part referring to the other parts, and containing a condition that it shall continue payable only so long as the others remain unpaid: the set or parts constitute one bill. See *Bills of Exchange Act,* 1882, *s.* 71; *Byles on Bills.*

SETTLED ESTATES. [SETTLEMENT, 2; SETTLED LAND.]

SETTLED LAND. Land limited *by way of succession* to a person other than the person for the time being entitled to the beneficial enjoyment thereof. Such last-mentioned person is called a limited owner (*q.v.*). As to the powers of leasing, sale, etc., see 40 & 41 Vict. c. 18; 45 & 46 Vict. c. 18; 47 & 48 Vict. c. 18; 50 & 51 Vict. c. 30; 52 & 53 Vict. c. 36; and 53 & 54 Vict. c. 69.

SETTLEMENT. 1. Such residence of any person in a parish, or other circumstance relating thereto, as would enable him, if in need of parochial relief, to apply for it in that parish rather than in any other. See *Archbold's Poor Law.*

2. A deed whereby property is *settled,* that is, subjected to a string of limitations. In this sense we speak of *marriage settlements* and *family settlements.*

3. A deed whereby a joint stock company is associated, which is often called a *deed of settlement,* but more frequently *articles of association.*

4. The termination of a disputed matter by the adoption of terms agreeable to the parties thereto.

5. A colony or plantation.

SETTLEMENT, ACT OF. [ACT OF SETTLEMENT.]

SETTLEMENT ESTATE DUTY. Further estate duty at the rate of 1 per cent. on settled property passing on the death of one person to another not competent to dispose of it. See *ss.* 5 and 17 of *Finance Act*, 1894 (57 & 58 *Vict. c.* 30). [ESTATE DUTY.]

SETTLING DAYS, on the Stock Exchange, are the days appointed for the settlement of accounts arising from speculative purchases and sales of stock. The settling days for English and Foreign stocks and shares occur twice in every month, the middle and the end. The settling days for Consols are once in every month, generally near the commencement of the month.

SETTLING ISSUES signifies the deciding the forms of the issues to be determined in a trial. 3 *Steph. Com.* It is provided by the R. S. C. 1883, Ord. XXXIII. r. 1, that where in any action it appears to the judge that the statement of claim or defence, or reply, does not sufficiently define the issues of fact between the parties, he may direct the parties to prepare issues ; and such issues shall, if the parties differ, be settled by the judge. [ISSUE, 5.]

SETTLOR. A person who makes a settlement of his land or personal property. [SETTLEMENT, 2.]

SEVER. [SEVERANCE.]

SEVERAL COVENANTS are covenants entered into with several persons in such a manner or under such circumstances that they are construed as separate. If the interest of several parties in a deed appears to be separate, the covenants will be construed as separate, unless the language expressly and unequivocally indicates a joint covenant. *Fawcett, L. & T.*

SEVERAL FISHERY. A fishery of which the owner is also the owner of the soil, or derives his right from the owner of the soil. Generally an exclusive right. 1 *Steph. Com.* [FISHERY.]

SEVERAL TAIL. This expression is used to denote a limitation whereby land is given and entailed severally to two. For example, land is given to two men and their wives, and the heirs of their bodies begotten ; the donees have a joint estate for their two lives, and yet they have several inheritances, because the issue of the one shall have his moiety and the issue of the other his moiety. [ENTAIL ; ESTATE ; JOINT TENANCY ; LIMITATION OF ESTATES.]

SEVERALTY, or SEVERAL TENANCY, is the holding of lands by a person in his own right only, without any other person being joined or connected with him in point of interest during his estate therein. It is thus opposed to holding in joint tenancy, in coparcenary, and in common. 1 *Steph. Com.* [COMMON, TENANCY IN ; COPARCENARY ; JOINT TENANCY.]

SEVERANCE. 1. The singling or severing of two or more that are joined in one writ, action or suit. As when two persons made defendants in a suit in respect of the same interest *sever* their defences, that is, adopt independent defences.

2. The dissolution or termination of a joint tenancy, or a tenancy in coparcenary or in common. A severance of a joint tenancy may be effected by partition or by any of the tenants disposing of his share. 1 *Steph. Com.*

SEWERS. [COURT OF COMMISSIONERS OF SEWERS.]

SHACK. *Common of shack* is the right of persons, occupying lands lying together in the same common field, to turn out their cattle after harvest to feed promiscuously in that field. 1 *Steph. Com.*

SHAM PLEA. A plea manifestly frivolous and absurd, pleaded for the purpose of vexation and delay. Under R. S. C. 1883, Ord. XIX. r. 27, the court or a judge may order to be struck out or amended any matter in the pleadings which may tend to prejudice, embarrass or delay the fair trial of the action. [IMPERTINENCE.]

SHEADING. A riding, tithing or division in the Isle of Man, of which there are six in the island.

SHELLEY'S CASE. [RULE IN SHELLEY'S CASE.]

SHEPWAY, COURT OF. A court held before the Lord Warden of the Cinque Ports. [CINQUE PORTS.]

SHERIFF, or **SHIRE-REVE**, is the chief bailiff or officer of the *shire;* an officer of great antiquity in the kingdom. He is called in Latin *vice-comes,* as being the deputy of the earl, or *comes,* to whom the custody of the shire is said to have been committed at the first division of the kingdom into counties. But the earls gradually withdrew from the county administration, and now the sheriff is the chief officer of the Crown in the county, and does all the king's business therein ; the Crown committing the custody of the county to the sheriff, and to him alone.

Sheriffs were formerly chosen by the inhabitants of the several counties, in confirmation of which it was enacted in 1300, by 28 Edw. 1, c. 8, that the people should have election of sheriffs in every shire where the shrievalty is not of inheritance ; for anciently, in some counties, the sheriffs were hereditary. As to the present mode of appointing sheriffs, see the titles, POCKET SHERIFF ; PRICKING FOR SHERIFFS. The Sheriffs Act, 1887, consolidates the law relating to sheriffs. His chief duties are to superintend parliamentary elections, to execute process, and to attend on the judges at the assizes ; he is also the principal conservator of the peace in his county. 2 *Steph. Com.* [POSSE COMITATUS ; UNDER-SHERIFF.]

SHERIFFS' COURT. 1. [CITY OF LONDON COURT.]
2. The court held by the sheriff of a county, or his deputy, either in virtue of a writ of inquiry, to assess the damages which the plaintiff has sustained in an undefended action, or to try issues sent to him for that purpose by a writ of trial. This latter jurisdiction was granted by 3 & 4 Will. 4, c. 42, ss. 17, 18 and 19 ; but it was abolished by sect. 6 of the County Courts Act, 1867 (30 & 31 Vict. c. 142). 2 *Steph. Com.*; 3 *Steph. Com.*

SHERIFFS' OFFICERS. Bailiffs ; either bailiffs of hundreds, or bound-bailiffs.

SHERIFFS' POUNDAGE. [POUNDAGE, 2.]

SHERIFFS' TOURN was a court of record, appointed to be held twice in every year, within a month after Easter and Michaelmas, before the sheriff in different parts of the county ; being, indeed, only the *turn* of the sheriff to keep a court leet, in each respective hundred. This was the great court leet of the county ; and out of it, for the ease of the sheriff, was taken the court leet, or view of frank-pledge. The sheriffs' tourn was abolished by s. 18 (4) of the Sheriffs Act, 1887. 4 *Steph. Com.* [COURT LEET ; FRANK-PLEDGE.]

SHEW CAUSE. [RULE, 3.]

SHIFTING USE is a use in land, limited in derogation of a preceding estate or interest, as when land is limited to A. and his heirs to the use of B. and his heirs, with a proviso that when C. returns from Rome, the land shall be to the use of C. and his heirs, in derogation of the use previously vested in B. 1 *Steph. Com.; Wms. R. P.*

SHIP. Under the Merchant Shipping Act, 1894 (57 & 58 Vict. c. 60), the term includes "every description of vessel used in navigation not propelled by oars."

The ownership of every British ship is divided into 64 shares. Not more than 32 persons can be registered as part owners.

SHIP MONEY. An ancient imposition that was charged upon the ports, towns, cities, boroughs and counties of the realm. Having lain dormant for many years, it was revived by King Charles I. in 1635 and 1636 ; and by stat. 17 Car. 1, c. 14, passed in 1641, was declared to be contrary to the laws and statutes of the realm.

SHIPPER. A consignor of goods to be sent by sea. 2 *Steph. Com.*

SHIP'S HUSBAND is the general agent of the owners of a vessel in its use and employment. His duty is in general to exercise an impartial judgment in the employment of tradesmen and the appointment of officers ; to see that the ship is properly repaired, equipped and manned ; to procure freights and charter-parties ; to preserve the ship's papers, make the necessary entries, adjust freight and averages, disburse and receive moneys, and keep and make up the accounts as between all parties interested. *Abbott on Shipping.*

SHIP'S PAPERS. The papers or documents required for the manifestation of property in a ship or cargo.

They are of two kinds :—
1. Those required by the law of a particular country, as the certificate of

SHIP'S PAPERS—*continued.*
registry, bills of lading, etc., required by the law of England.

2. Those required by the law of nations to be on board neutral ships, to vindicate their title to that character, such as the pass-port, muster-roll, etc.

SHIRE, derived from the Saxon *scyran,* to divide, is a portion of land called a county. 1 *Steph. Com.*

SHIRE REEVE. [SHERIFF.]

SHORT BILL. [ENTERING BILLS SHORT.]

SHORT CAUSE. If a plaintiff in the Chancery Division desires to accelerate the suit, and if the hearing will probably not occupy more than ten minutes, he may have the cause heard as a *short cause,* for which purpose he must obtain from his counsel a certificate that the matter is, in his opinion, proper to be heard as a short cause. On this certificate being produced to the registrar, he will mark the cause as "short" in the cause-book. This may be done without the consent of the defendant, but notice must be given him that the cause has been so marked.

SHORT ENTRY. [ENTERING BILLS SHORT.]

SHORT NOTICE OF TRIAL is four days' notice of trial; the ordinary notice to which a defendant is entitled being ten days. See *R. S. C.* 1883, *Ord. XXXVI. r. 4* ; 3 *Steph. Com.*

SHRIEVALTY. 1. The sheriff's office.

2. As used with reference to any given person, it means the period during which he was sheriff.

SI NON OMNES (if not all). A writ, on association of justices, by which, if all in commission cannot meet at the day assigned, it is allowed that two or more of them may finish the business.

SIC UTERE TUO UT ALIENUM NON LÆDAS (so use your own rights that you do not hurt those of another).

SIGHT, BILLS PAYABLE AT, are equivalent to bills payable on demand. See *Bills of Exchange Act,* 1882, *s.* 10. 2 *Steph. Com.*

SIGN MANUAL. The signature of the sovereign. 1 *Steph. Com.*

SIGNET. One of the king's seals with which his private letters are sealed. 1 *Steph. Com.*

SIGNIFICAVIT. A name by which the writ *de excommunicato capiendo* was known, because it expressed that the bishop *signified* to the sovereign in Chancery the contempt committed by the party to whom the writ referred. 3 *Steph. Com.* [EXCOMMUNICATO CAPIENDO.]

SIGNING JUDGMENT. [ENTERING JUDGMENT.]

SILK GOWN. A phrase used especially of the silk gowns worn by King's counsel ; hence, "to take silk" means to attain the rank of King's counsel.

SIMILITER (in like manner). A phrase indicating that when a defendant puts himself upon the country, that is, upon trial by jury (by plea of not guilty or otherwise), the plaintiff or Crown prosecutor *doth the like.* All joinders of issue were formerly called the similiter. 4 *Steph. Com.*

SIMONY is the corrupt presentation of, or the corrupt agreement to present, any person to an ecclesiastical benefice for money, gift or reward, and is generally committed in one of the two following ways :—

1. By the purchase of the next presentation to a living actually vacant.

2. By a clergyman purchasing, either in his own name or another's, the next presentation to a living, and afterwards presenting, or causing himself to be presented, thereto. But the purchase by a clergyman of an entire advowson, or even of a limited interest therein, is not simony, though the purchaser afterwards present himself. 2 *Steph. Com.*

SIMPLE CONTRACT. A contract, express or implied, which is created by verbal promise, or by writing not under seal. 2 *Steph. Com.* [CONTRACT.]

SIMPLE CONTRACT DEBT. A debt arising out of a simple contract. 2 *Steph. Com.* [ASSETS.]

SIMPLE LARCENY. Larceny which is not accompanied by such circumstances of aggravation as would constitute the offence mixed or compound larceny. 4 *Steph. Com.* ; *Oke's Mag. Syn.* [LARCENY.]

SIMPLE TRUST is a trust which requires no act to be done by the trustee except conveyance or transfer to his *cestui que trust* on request by the latter. [CESTUI QUE TRUST.]

SINE DIE. Without day : that is to say, without any day appointed for the resumption of the business on hand. Thus, an adjournment *sine die* is an adjournment without appointing any day for meeting again. [EAT INDE SINE DIE.

SINE PROLE. Without issue ; frequently abbreviated into " s. p."

SINECURE. Without cure of souls ; a word used in former times of a rector who by custom was relieved from residence, and had no spiritual duties, these being performed by the vicar. By stat. 3 & 4 Vict. c. 113, provision is made for the abolition of sinecure rectories. 2 *Steph. Com.* [RECTOR ; VICAR.] And a sinecure office is generally understood to mean a nominal office, with no duties attaching to it.

SINGLE BOND (Lat. *Simplex obligatio*). A bond whereby a party obliges himself to pay to another a certain sum of money on a day specified, without any condition for making void the obligation. This hardly ever occurs in practice. 2 *Steph. Com.*

SINGLE COMBAT. A species of trial. [WAGER OF BATTEL.]

SINGLE ENTRY is a system of book-keeping according to which each entry in the day-book, invoice-book, cash-book and bill-book is posted or entered *once* to some account in the ledger ; whereas, in *double entry* each entry is posted to *two* different accounts. [DOUBLE ENTRY.]

SINKING FUND. A fund for the reduction of the National Debt, regulated by various Acts of parliament. 2 *Steph. Com.*

SITTINGS. The division of the legal year into terms was abolished by the Judicature Act, 1873, and *sittings* are substituted. There are now four sittings in each year, viz., the Michaelmas, Hilary, Easter, and Trinity sittings. See *R. S. C.* 1883, *Ord. LXIII. r.* 1 *Yearly Practice.* 3 *Steph. Com.*
By s. 30 of the Act of 1873, sittings for trial by jury are to be held continuously throughout the year in Middlesex and London so far as practicable and subject to vacations. [VACATION.]

SITTINGS AT NISI PRIUS. [NISI PRIUS.]

SITTINGS FEE. A fee of 15*s.*, or in country agency cases 1*l.* 1*s.*, in respect of each sittings in which any proceeding in a cause or matter in the Supreme Court of Judicature, after appearance entered, has taken place. This is to cover attendances, letters, etc., which cannot be specially charged in the bill.

SITTINGS IN BANC. [BANC ; BAR, 6.]

SITTINGS IN CAMERA are sittings in a judge's private room, as opposed to sittings in open court. This course is often adopted for the hearing of cases which it is not desired to bring before the public, *e.g.*, suits for nullity of marriage. 3 *Steph. Com.*

SIX CLERKS IN CHANCERY were six officers in the Court of Chancery, whose duties were to receive and file all bills, answers, replications and other records in all causes on the equity side of the Court of Chancery. Their office was abolished in 1842, by 5 & 6 Vict. c. 103, s. 1, and their functions were thenceforth discharged by the Record and Writ Clerks. [CLERK OF RECORDS AND WRITS.]

SIX DAY LICENCE. One granted under s. 49 of the Licensing Act, 1872, containing a condition that the licensed premises shall be closed during the whole of Sunday.

SKILLED WITNESS, also called an *expert* or *professional witness*, is a person called to give evidence in a matter relating to his own trade or profession, as when a medical man is called to give evidence on the effects of poison.

SLANDER. Defamatory language used of another. It is *oral*, not in writing or print. 3 *Steph. Com.* [DEFAMATION ; LIBEL, 5.]

SLIP. An unstamped memorandum of an intended marine insurance policy. Such a document, even where, under stat. 30 Vict. c. 23, s. 7, it is invalid as a legal contract, is admissible in evidence for certain collateral purposes. Thus it has been held that the non-disclosure of facts material to the risk, discovered subsequently to the execution of the "slip," does not vitiate a policy afterwards executed. *Arnould, Mar. Ins.*

SMALL DEBTS COURTS. Courts of requests or of conscience for the recovery of small debts. Superseded by the county courts, under stat. 9 & 10 Vict. c. 95. 3 *Steph. Com.* [CONSCIENCE, COURTS OF; COUNTY COURT; COURT OF REQUEST.]

SMALL TITHES are the tithes which generally vest in the *vicar* as opposed to the *rector* or *appropriator*. They include tithes mixed and personal; that is, tithes of wool, milk, pigs, of manual occupations, trades, and fisheries, and other fruits of the personal industry of the inhabitants. 2 *Steph. Com.* [TITHES.]

SMUGGLING is the offence of importing or exporting prohibited goods, or importing or exporting goods not prohibited without paying the duties imposed thereon by the laws of the customs and excise. 4 *Steph. Com.*

SOC, SOCA, SOCNA. A word signifying a power or liberty of jurisdiction. 1 *Steph. Com.*

SOCAGE in its most general signification denotes a tenure of land by a certain and determinate service, as opposed to chivalry or knight-service, where the render was precarious and uncertain. It was of two kinds: *free-socage*, where the services were not only certain but honourable; and *villein socage* or *privileged villenage*, where the services, though certain, were of a baser nature. All tenures (with a few exceptions) were by 12 Car. 2, c. 24, turned into free and common socage. 1 *Steph. Com.; Wms. R. P.* [FREEHOLD; KNIGHT-SERVICE.]

SOCAGERS, SOCMANS, SOKEMANS or **SOCMEN** (Lat. *Socmanni*). Tenants in socage.

SOIT FAIT COMME IL EST DESIRE (let it be as it is desired). [LE ROY LE VEULT.]

SOLD NOTE. [BOUGHT AND SOLD NOTES].

SOLE. Not married, single.

SOLE CORPORATION. [CORPORATION.]

SOLE TENANT (Lat. *Solus tenens*). One that holds in severalty; that is, in his own sole right, and not with another. [SEVERAL TENANCY.]

SOLEMN FORM. There are two kinds of probate, namely, probate in *common form*, and probate in *solemn form*. Probate in common form is granted in the registry, without any formal procedure in court, upon an *ex parte* application made by the executor. Probate in solemn form is in the nature of a final decree pronounced in open court, all parties interested having been duly cited. The difference between the effect of probate in common form and probate in solemn form is, that probate in common form is revocable, whereas probate in solemn form is irrevocable as against all persons who have been cited to see the proceedings, or who can be proved to have been privy to these proceedings, except in the case where a will of subsequent date is discovered, in which case probate of an earlier will, though granted in solemn form, would be revoked. 2 *Steph. Com.* [PROBATE.]

SOLICITATION. Incitement or inducement to commit an offence.

The solicitation to the commission of an offence is a misdemeanor at common law, and punishable by fine and imprisonment, even though no offence be in fact committed. *Oke's Mag. Syn.*

SOLICITOR. Solicitors were formerly regarded specially as officers of the Court of Chancery; but by the Judicature Act, 1873 (36 & 37 Vict. c. 66, s. 87), all attornies, solicitors, and proctors were to be styled solicitors of the Supreme Court. To become a solicitor a person must now be articled to a practising solicitor generally for five years, pass the necessary examinations conducted by the Law Society, and be admitted by the Master of the Rolls. A certificate to practice must be taken out annually. A solicitor may act as advocate in county courts, petty sessions, quarter sessions (where no bar), and in most other inferior courts. Also in judges' chambers, in the Supreme Court. A solicitor can sue for costs, but is liable for negligence. [ADVOCATE; ARTICLED CLERK.]

SOLICITOR-GENERAL. The second law officer of the Crown, next to the Attorney-General. 3 *Steph. Com.*

SOLIDUM. To be bound *in solidum* is to be bound for a whole debt jointly and severally with others, as opposed to being bound, *pro ratâ*, for a proportionate part only.

SOLVENDO ESSE. To be in a state of solvency; or, as we say, to be solvent.

SOLVIT AD DIEM. A plea, in answer to an action of debt or bond, that the money claimed in the action was paid on the day appointed.

SON ASSAULT DEMESNE. His own assault; a plea by a defendant, sued for an assault, that it was the plaintiff's own assault which occasioned it. 3 *Steph. Com.*

SORCERY. [WITCHCRAFT.]

SOUL-SCOT. An ecclesiastical heriot. [HERIOT.] In many parishes, on the death of a parishioner, after the lord's heriot or best chattel was taken out, the second best chattel was reserved to the church as a mortuary. This mortuary was, in the laws of Canute, called *soul-scot.* 2 *Steph. Com.* [MORTUARY, 1.]

SOUNDING IN DAMAGES. This phrase is used of an action which is brought in point of form for damages, as in the ordinary case of an action at law. 3 *Steph. Com.*

SOVEREIGN. See KING.

SPEAKERS OF THE HOUSES OF PARLIAMENT. The Speaker is the officer who is, as it were, the common mouth of the rest; and as there are two Houses, so there are two Speakers. The one the Lord Speaker of the House of Peers, who is most commonly the Lord Chancellor, or Lord Keeper of the Great Seal of England. The other, being a member of the House of Commons, is called the Speaker of the House of Commons. The Speaker of the House of Commons holds office till the dissolution of the parliament in which he was elected, and his salary is 6,000*l.* a year, with a furnished residence. It is the duty of the Speaker to preside over the debates of the house, and manage the formality of business. The Speaker of the House of Commons may not give his opinion or argue any question in the house; but the Speaker of the House of Lords, if he be a lord of parliament (which is generally but not necessarily the case), may do so. In the House of Commons the Speaker never votes, except when the votes are equal; but in the House of Lords the Speaker has a vote with the rest of the house, but no casting vote, for should the votes be equal the non-contents prevail. 2 *Steph. Com.; May's Parl. Pract.*

SPEAKING WITH PROSECUTOR. This is in the nature of an imparlance by a defendant convicted of a misdemeanor immediately affecting an individual, as a battery, imprisonment, or the like; in which case the court may permit the defendant to speak with the prosecutor, before any judgment is pronounced; and, if the prosecutor declares himself satisfied, may inflict but a trivial punishment. 4 *Steph. Com.*

SPECIAL ACCEPTANCE OF A BILL OF EXCHANGE means the acceptance of a bill as payable at some specified place, and not elsewhere. 2 *Steph. Com.* [ACCEPTANCE OF A BILL; BILL OF EXCHANGE.]

SPECIAL ADMINISTRATION is the administration of certain specific effects of a deceased person; otherwise called a *limited* administration. 2 *Steph. Com.* [ADMINISTRATION.]

SPECIAL AGENT. An agent empowered to act as such in some particular matter, and not generally. 2 *Steph. Com.* [GENERAL AGENT.]

SPECIAL BASTARD. One born of parents who afterwards intermarry.

SPECIAL BAIL. Formerly used to denote substantial sureties, as opposed to the imaginary beings John Doe and Richard Roe, who did duty as *common bail,* both for the plaintiff's prosecution of the suit, and for the defendant's attendance and obedience. 3 *Steph. Com.* [BAIL.]

SPECIAL BAILIFFS. 1. The same as bound bailiffs. 2 *Steph. Com.*

2. Persons named by a party in a civil suit for the purpose of executing some particular process therein, and appointed by the sheriff on the application of such party. For the conduct of such officers the sheriff is not responsible. 2 *Steph. Com.* [BAILIFFS.]

SPECIAL CASE. 1. A statement of facts agreed to on behalf of two or more litigant parties, and submitted for the opinion of a court of justice as to the law bearing upon the facts so stated. 3 *Steph. Com.*

By R. S. C. 1883, Ord. XXXIV., the parties to any cause or matter may concur in stating the questions of law arising therein in the form of a special case for the opinion of the court. Every such special case must be divided

SPECIAL CASE—*continued*.

into paragraphs numbered consecutively, and must concisely state such facts and documents as may be necessary to enable the court to decide the questions raised thereby.

2. By 11 & 12 Vict. c. 78, any court of oyer and terminer, gaol delivery, or quarter sessions, may reserve any question of law arising in a case and state it in the form of a special case for the Court of Crown Cases Reserved. 4 *Steph. Com.*

3. A case stated by justices or by a police magistrate for the opinion of a superior court, under 20 & 21 Vict. c. 43, and Summary Jurisdiction Act, 1879, s. 33. 4 *Steph. Com.; Oke's Mag. Syn.*

SPECIAL COMMISSION is an extraordinary commission of oyer and terminer and gaol delivery, confined to certain offences which stand in need of immediate inquiry and punishment. 4 *Steph. Com.* [ASSIZE, COURTS OF.]

SPECIAL CONSTABLES. [CONSTABLE,6.]

SPECIAL DAMAGE. Damage which in a given case may be shown to have arisen to the plaintiff from the conduct of the defendant. In some cases, as for instance in cases of assault and false imprisonment, an action will lie without showing special damage ; in others it is necessary to show special damage in order to maintain the action. 3 *Steph. Com.*

SPECIAL DEFENCE. In an action in the county court a defendant must give notice to the plaintiff when he intends to rely upon a defence of set-off, counter-claim, infancy, coverture, statute of limitations, bankruptcy tender, statutory or equitable defence. 3 *Steph. Com.*

SPECIAL DEMURRER. A demurrer showing the special grounds on which the party demurs to the pleading of his adversary. Abolished. 3 *Steph Com.* [DEMURRER.]

SPECIAL EXAMINER was some person, not one of the Examiners of the Court of Chancery, appointed to take evidence in a particular suit.

Now by R. S. C. 1883, Ord. XXXVII. r. 5, the court or a judge may, in any cause or matter where it shall appear necessary for the purposes of justice, make an order for the examination upon oath before any officer of the court, *or any other person or persons*, and at any place, of any witness or person, and may order any deposition so taken to be filed in the court.

SPECIAL INDORSEMENT. 1. A special indorsement on a writ of summons is one which may be made where a plaintiff seeks merely to recover a debt or liquidated demand in money payable by the defendant, with or without interest, arising upon a contract express or implied (as for instance a bill, promissory note, cheque, etc.), or on a bond or contract under seal for payment of a liquidated amount of money, or on a statute where the sum sought to be recovered is a fixed sum of money, or in the nature of a debt ; or on a guaranty (whether under seal or not) where the claim against the principal is in respect of a debt or liquidated demand, or in an action for recovery of land by a landlord against his tenant whose term has expired or been duly determined by notice to quit, or has become liable to forfeiture for non-payment of rent, or against persons claiming under such tenant. Thus, a special indorsement may be made in all cases where a definite sum of money is claimed, and in the one case of recovery of land above mentioned. When the writ is thus specially indorsed, and the defendant does not appear within the time appointed, the plaintiff may then sign final judgment for any sum not exceeding the sum indorsed on the writ, or for the land. See 3 *Steph. Com.* ; R. S. C. 1883, *Ord. III. r.* 6, and *Ord. XIII. rr.* 3, 4. Moreover, under Ord. XIV. r. 1, the plaintiff may in such cases, on filing an affidavit verifying the cause of action, and swearing that in his belief there is no defence to the action, call on the defendant to show cause before the court or a judge, why the plaintiff should not be at liberty to sign final judgment for the amount so indorsed, together with interest, if any, or for the land, and costs ; and the court or judge may, unless the defendant, by affidavit or otherwise, satisfy the court or judge that he has a good defence to the action on the merits, or disclose such facts as the court or judge may think sufficient to entitle him to defend the action, make an order empowering the plaintiff to sign judgment accordingly. 3 *Steph. Com.*

SPECIAL INDORSEMENT—*continued*.

2. A special indorsement on a bill of exchange or other negotiable instrument is one which specifies the person who is to have the benefit of the indorsement. This is otherwise called an indorsement *in full*, as opposed to an indorsement *in blank*. See *Bills of Exchange Act*, 1882, *s.* 34. *2 Steph. Com.* [INDORSEMENT.]

SPECIAL JURORS' LIST. A list annually made out by the sheriff of persons qualified to serve on special juries. *3 Steph. Com.* [JURY ; SPECIAL JURY.]

SPECIAL JURY is a jury consisting of persons who are of a certain station in society : namely, esquires or persons of higher degree, or bankers. or merchants, or persons who occupy a house or premises of a certain rateable value. *33 & 34 Vict. c.* 77, *s.* 6 ; *3 Steph. Com.*; *4 Steph. Com.* ; *Oke's Mag. Syn.* Either party in an action may have a special jury upon' giving notice. See *R. S. C.* 1883, *Ord. XXXVI. r.* 7.

SPECIAL LICENCE. [MARRIAGE LICENCE.]

SPECIAL OCCUPANT. [OCCUPANT.]

SPECIAL PLEA. A plea in bar, not being the plea of the general issue. A special plea is either (1) a plea by way of justification or excuse, to show that there was never any right of action ; or (2) a plea of discharge, which, admitting that the cause of action once existed, alleges that it has been barred by matter subsequent. *3 Steph. Com.* ; *4 Steph. Com.* [PLEA.]

SPECIAL PLEADER. A lawyer whose professional occupation it is to give verbal or written opinions upon statements submitted to him, and to draw pleadings, civil and criminal, and such practical proceedings as may be out of the usual course.

Special pleaders are not necessarily at the bar ; but those that are not are required to take out annual certificates under stat. 33 & 34 Vict. c. 97, ss. 60, 63, 64. The number of special pleaders is now not large.

SPECIAL PLEADING. The science of pleading, which, until the passing of the C. L. P. Act, 1852 (15 & 16 Vict. c. 76), constituted a distinct branch of the law, with treatises and professors of its own. It had the merit of developing the points in controversy with the severest precision. But its strictness and subtlety were a frequent subject of complaint ; and one object of the above Act was to relax and simplify its rules. *3 Steph. Com.*

SPECIAL PROPERTY. A limited or qualified right in any subject of property. Thus, one who hires a horse to ride has a special property in the horse. *2 Steph. Com.*

SPECIAL SESSIONS is a sessions held by justices acting for a division of a county or riding, or for a borough, for the transaction of special business, such as licensing alehouses or appointing overseers of the poor, or surveyors of highways. A special sessions is generally held by virtue of a provision of some Act of parliament. Due notice of it is usually given to all the justices resident within the division for which it is held ; and in some cases this is required by Act of parliament. A special sessions is sometimes called a *special petty session ;* and a special sessions held for the purpose of licensing alehouses is sometimes called a *Brewster Sessions.* *2 Steph. Com.* ; *Oke's Mag. Syn.* [SESSIONS.]

SPECIAL TAIL. [TAIL SPECIAL.]

SPECIAL TRAVERSE. A form of traverse formerly in use in an action by which a party sought to explain or qualify his denial of his opponent's pleading, instead of putting his denial in a direct form.

Special traverses were abolished by the C. L. P. Act, 1852.

SPECIAL TRUST. A trust imposing active duties on the trustee ; otherwise called an *active trust.* *1 Steph. Com.*

SPECIAL VERDICT is a verdict in which the jury state the facts of a case, as they find them to be proved, leaving it to the court to draw the proper legal inferences therefrom. Special verdicts in criminal cases are very rare. *3 Steph. Com.;* *4 Steph. Com.*

SPECIALTY, or **SPECIALTY DEBT,** is an obligation contracted by matter of record, or by bond or other instrument under seal. *1 Steph. Com.;* *2 Steph. Com.* [ASSETS.]

SPECIFIC DEVISE. A devise of specific land. [RESIDUARY DEVISEE.]

SPECIFIC LEGACY. A legacy of a specific fund or of a specific chattel. *2 Steph. Com.*

If the subject of such a legacy be sold or otherwise made away with in the testator's lifetime, the legacy is gone.

SPECIFIC PERFORMANCE. A suit for specific performance is one in the Chancery Division by a person with whom another has made a contract praying that the latter may be deemed specifically to perform it. The specific performance of a contract has in general been decreed in Equity, where the contract is not a positive contract of a personal nature (as to sing at a theatre), nor one for the non-performance of which damages would be a sufficient compensation (as to pay a liquidated sum of money). *1 Steph. Com.; 3 Steph. Com.*

By the Judicature Act, 1873, actions for the specific performance of contracts between vendors and purchasers of real estates, including contracts for leases, were assigned to the Chancery Division of the High Court. See also the County Courts Act, 1888, s. 67.

SPECIFICATION is the particular description of an invention in respect of which a patent is sought. See *46 & 47 Vict. c. 57. 2 Steph. Com.* [PATENT.]

SPIRITUAL CORPORATIONS (otherwise called Ecclesiastical Corporations). [CORPORATION; ECCLESIASTICAL CORPORATION.]

SPIRITUAL COURTS are the courts otherwise called the Ecclesiastical Courts. [ECCLESIASTICAL COURTS.]

SPIRITUAL LORDS. [LORDS SPIRITUAL.]

SPIRITUALITIES OF A BISHOP are those profits which he receives as a bishop, and not as a baron of parliament, as the duties of his visitation, etc. *Cowel.* By 23 & 24 Vict. c. 124, s. 2, provision is made for the payment of these duties to the Ecclesiastical Commissioners.

SPLITTING A CAUSE OF ACTION signifies the bringing of separate actions for the different parts of a claim; or otherwise bringing several actions where one would suffice. This is prohibited in the county courts by s. 81 of the County Courts Act, 1888.

SPOLIATION. 1. An injury done by one clerk or incumbent to another, in taking the fruits of his benefice without any right thereunto, but under a pretended title; which, when the right of advowson doth not come into debate, is cognizable in the spiritual court. *3 Steph. Com.*

2. Also the writ that lies in such case for the one incumbent against the other.

SPRINGING USE. A use limited to commence *in futuro*, independently of any preceding estate; as if land be conveyed to A. and his heirs, to the use of B. and his heirs on the death of C. In this case, while C. lives, the use limited to B. and his heirs is still *in futuro*. Such a use is also called an *executory use* or *executory interest*. *1 Steph. Com.; Wms. R. P.* [USE.]

STADIUM, in Domesday Book, is a furlong, or an eighth of a mile.

STAKEHOLDER. One with whom a stake is deposited pending the decision of a wager, etc. [WAGER.]

STALLAGE. Money paid for pitching stalls in fairs or markets; or the right to do so. *1 Steph. Com.*

STAMP DUTIES are taxes imposed upon all parchment and paper, whereon any legal proceedings or private instruments of almost any nature whatsoever are written; and also upon licences for retailing wines, letting horses to hire and for certain other purposes. *2 Steph. Com.*

Where a stamp is essential to the legal validity of a writing, that writing cannot be given in evidence in civil proceedings if it be unstamped, or be insufficiently stamped, except upon complying with the conditions and the payment of the penalties specified in ss. 14 and 15 of the Stamp Act, 1891. But this rule does not apply to criminal proceedings.

By this Act the various enactments relating to stamps were consolidated, and any unstamped or unsufficiently stamped instrument may now be stamped after the execution thereof on payment of the unpaid duty and a penalty of 10*l.*, and also, by way of further penalty, where the unpaid duty exceeds 10*l.*, of interest on such duty at the rate of five per cent. per annum. And the Commissioners of Inland Revenue may remit the penalty at any time within three months after the first execution of the instrument (s. 15).

STANDING MUTE. [MUTE; PEINE FORTE ET DURE.]

STANDING ORDERS are orders framed by each house of parliament for the permanent guidance and order of its proceedings. Such orders, if not vacated or repealed, endure from one parliament to another, and are of equal force in all. They occasionally fall into desuetude, but by the law and custom of parliament they are binding as bye-laws until their operation is concluded by another vote of the house upon the same matter. 2 *Steph. Com.; May's Parl. Pract.*

STANNARIES. The mines and works where tin metal is worked. [COURTS OF STANNARIES OF CORNWALL AND DEVON.]

STANNARY COURTS. [COURT OF STANNARIES OF CORNWALL AND DEVON.]

STAPLE signifies the public mart in certain towns or cities, whither the merchants of England were, by Act of parliament, to carry their *staple commodities* for the purpose of disposing of them wholesale. 1 *Steph. Com.* [STATUTE, 2.]

STAPLE INN. One of the Inns of Chancery, between Holborn Bars and Southampton Buildings, Chancery Lane. 1 *Steph. Com.* [INNS OF CHANCERY.]

STAR-BOARD. [LARBOARD.]

STAR-CHAMBER, or **CAMERA STELLATA.** A court of very ancient origin, but new-modelled by stat. 3 Hen. 7, c. 1. It consisted of divers lords spiritual and temporal, being privy councillors, together with two judges of the courts of common law, without the intervention of any jury. Their jurisdiction extended legally over riots, perjury, misbehaviour of sheriffs, and other notorious misdemeanors contrary to the laws of the land.

It wrongfully extended its jurisdiction and was abolished in 1641 by 16 Car. 1, c. 10. 2 *Steph. Com.;* 4 *Steph. Com.*

STATEMENT OF CLAIM is the statement by the plaintiff, in an action brought in the High Court of Justice, of the ground of his complaint and of the relief or remedy to which he claims to be entitled. By R.S.C. Ord. XX. r. 1, it is provided that no further statement of claim shall be delivered where the writ of summons has been specially endorsed [SPECIAL INDORSEMENT], and that in other cases none need be delivered unless the defendant give notice requiring it, in which case it must be delivered within five weeks of the receipt of such notice. The delivery of statement of claim is however now dealt with on the Summons for Directions. Consult the *Yearly Practice.* 3 *Steph. Com.*

STATEMENT OF DEFENCE is the statement delivered by a defendant in answer of the plaintiff's statement of claim. It must be delivered within ten days after the plaintiff's delivery of his statement of claim, or from the time limited for appearance, whichever is last, unless the time be extended by a court or judge, and now subject to an order made on the Summons for Directions. The defendant may, in his statement of defence, adduce any facts on which he seeks to rely as supporting a right of set-off or counter-claim ; in which case he must state specifically that he does so by way of set-off or counter-claim. *R.S.C.* 1883, *Ord. XXI.* [STATEMENT OF CLAIM.]

STATIONERS' HALL. The hall of the Stationers' Company, at which every person claiming copyright in a book must register his title in order to be able to bring actions against persons infringing it. 5 & 6 *Vict. c.* 45; 2 *Steph. Com.*

STATUS OF IRREMOVABILITY. The right acquired by a pauper, by one whole year's residence in any parish, not to be removed therefrom. 3 *Steph. Com.*

STATUS QUO. The state in which any thing is already. Thus, when it is said that, provisionally, matters are to remain *in statu quo*, it is meant that, for the present, matters are to remain as they are. Sometimes, however, the phrase is used retrospectively ; and, if so, this will generally be indicated by the context ; as when, on a treaty of peace, matters are to *return* to the *status quo*, this means the *status quo ante bellum*, their state prior to the war.

STATUTE. 1. An Act of parliament made by the king and the three estates of the realm. 1 *Steph. Com.*

A *statute*, in the ancient sense of the word, means the legislation of a session ; the various Acts of parliament passed in it being so many *chapters* of the entire statute. Thus, when we speak of the Statute of Gloucester, the Statute of Merton, etc., we mean a body of legislation comprising various chapters on different subjects. But, in reference to modern legislation, we, in general, use the word *statute* to denote a *chapter* of legislation, or what is otherwise called an *Act of parliament.* [DECLARATORY ACT ; ENABLING STATUTE.]

2. A short writing called a *statute merchant* or *statute staple*. These are in the nature of bonds of record, and are called *statutes*, because made according to the forms expressly provided by statutes, which direct both before what persons, and in what manner, they ought to be made. Obsolete. 1 *Steph. Com.*

STATUTE MERCHANT. [STATUTE, 2.]

STATUTE OF DISTRIBUTIONS. [DISTRIBUTION.]

STATUTE OF FRAUDS, LABOURERS, LIMITATIONS, USES, etc. [FRAUDS, STATUTE OF, etc.]

STATUTE STAPLE. [STATUTE, 2.]

STATUTES AT LARGE. A phrase used to denote an edition of the statutes printed *verbatim*.

STATUTORY DECLARATION. A declaration made before a magistrate or commissioner for oaths in form prescribed by stat. 5 & 6 Will. 4, c. 62, by which voluntary affidavits, in matters where no judicial inquiry is pending, are henceforth prohibited. Any person making a statutory declaration falsely is guilty of a misdemeanor. 4 *Steph. Com.*

STAY OF PROCEEDINGS is the putting an end to the proceedings in an action by a summary order of the court. It differs from an injunction and from a prohibition, as follows :—

1. Staying proceedings is effected by the court in which the action is brought, or by some other court on appeal therefrom.

2. An injunction to restrain proceedings is an order of an independent court restraining the plaintiff from proceeding in the action.

3. A prohibition is an order of a superior court, prohibiting the court in which the action is brought from taking cognizance thereof.

Under the Judicature Act, 1873, s. 24 (5), no cause or proceedings pending in the High Court of Justice or Court of Appeal shall be restrained by prohibition or injunction, but the courts have power on motion in a summary way to stay proceedings in cases where an injunction or prohibition could formerly have been obtained. 3 *Steph. Com.*

STEALING. The fraudulent taking away of another man's goods with intent to deprive the owner thereof. [FURANDI ANIMUS ; LARCENY.]

STEALING AN HEIRESS. [HEIRESS.]

STEALING CHILDREN. This offence consists in taking away a child under the age of fourteen years, with intent to deprive any parent, guardian, or other person having the lawful care or charge of such child, of its possession, or with intent to steal some article on its person. Any person guilty of this offence is liable to penal servitude for seven years, or to imprisonment for two years with or without hard labour. 24 & 25 *Vict. c.* 100, *s.* 56 ; 4 *Steph. Com. ; Oke's Mag. Syn.*

STET PROCESSUS, in an action, is an entry on the roll, in the nature of a judgment, that by consent of the parties all further proceedings be stayed. It cannot be ordered without the consent of the parties.

STEVEDORE. A person whose occupation it is to stow packages and goods in a ship's hold, and discharge cargoes.

STEWARD (Lat. *Senescallus*).

1. *The Lord High Steward of England,* etc. [HIGH STEWARD.]

2. The *Steward of a Manor* is an officer of the lord of the manor, appointed to hold his courts, to admit tenants, to accept surrenders, etc. 3 *Steph. Com.*

3. *Steward of the Barmote Courts.* [BARMOTE COURTS.]

STINT. [SANS NOMBRE.]

STIPEND. By this word we generally understand any periodical payment for services; especially the income of an ecclesiastical living or curacy. 2 *Steph. Com.*

STIPENDIARY. A feudatory to whom an estate was granted in return for services to his lord. 1 *Steph. Com.*

STIPENDIARY MAGISTRATES are paid magistrates acting for the metropolis and other populous districts. 2 *Steph. Com.* They are appointed by the Home Secretary on behalf of the Crown; in the metropolis under 2 & 3 Vict. c. 71, and in municipal boroughs on petition by the Council under the Municipal Corporations Act, 1882, s. 161. Every stipendiary magistrate has, by 21 & 22 Vict. c. 73, s. 1, full power to do alone whatever is authorised by law to be done by any one or more justice or justices of the peace; but by sect. 3 of the last-mentioned Act this provision is not to extend to acts done at quarter sessions, nor to any act or jurisdiction in relation to the grant or transfer of any licence. See *Oke's Mag. Syn.*

STIPULATION, in the Roman law, was a solemn form giving legal validity to an agreement; in the Admiralty Courts it is a recognizance of fidejussors in the nature of bail.

STIRPES, DISTRIBUTION PER. A distribution *per stirpes* is a division of property among families according to stocks, *i.e.*, taking into consideration the representatives of deceased persons who if they had survived would themselves have taken. Thus, if A., B., C. and D. be four brothers, and A. die leaving three children, and B. die leaving two; and then C. dies unmarried, D. being still alive; then C.'s property will be divided into thirds, of which A.'s three children will take one-third, B.'s two children another third, and D. the remaining third. This division is called a distribution *per stirpes*, as opposed to a distribution *per capita*, under which D. alone would have taken, as being the nearest in degree surviving. 1 *Steph. Com.*; 2 *Steph. Com.* [CAPITA, DISTRIBUTION PER.]

STOCK. 1. A race or family. [STIRPES, DISTRIBUTION PER.]

2. In reference to the investment of money, the term "stock" implies those sums of money contributed towards raising a fund whereby certain objects, as of trade or commerce, may be effected. It is also employed to denote the moneys advanced to Government, which constitute a part of the National Debt, whereupon a certain amount of interest is payable. Since the introduction of the system of borrowing upon interminable annuities, the meaning of the word "stock" has become gradually changed; and, instead of signifying the security upon which loans are advanced, it has for a long time signified the principal of the loans themselves. In this latter sense we speak of the sale, purchase, and transfer of stock. [STOCK BROKER; STOCK EXCHANGE.]

STOCK BROKER is a person who, for a commission, negotiates for other parties the buying and selling of stocks, according to the rules of the Stock Exchange. The members of the Stock Exchange are called *jobbers* and *brokers*. The jobber is the dealer, who buys and sells at the market prices, and acts as an intermediary between the broker who buys and the broker who sells. The broker, on behalf of his principal, deals with the jobber. [STOCK EXCHANGE.]

STOCK EXCHANGE. An association of stock brokers and jobbers in the city of London. [STOCK BROKER.]

The regulations of the Stock Exchange are, like other usages of trade, recognised by courts of law as evidence of the course of dealing between the parties to a contract. 1 *Steph. Com.*

STOCK JOBBER. [STOCK BROKER.]

STOP ORDER is an order to restrain dealings with any money or stock standing in the name of the Paymaster-General (formerly the Accountant-General) to the credit of any cause or matter. This is the means by which the assignee of a fund in court may give notice of the assignment, and prevent the transfer or payment of such money or stock without notice to him, although not a party to the cause or matter in which the fund is standing. See *R. S. C. 1883, Ord. XLVI.* [PAYMENT OF MONEY INTO COURT, 2.]

STOPPAGE IN TRANSITU. The right which an unpaid vendor of goods has, on hearing that the vendee is insolvent, to stop and reclaim the goods while in their transit and not yet delivered to the vendee. This right will not be affected by the mere fact that the vendor

STOPPAGE IN TRANSITU—*continued.*
has consigned the goods to the vendee under a bill of lading ; but if the vendee has indorsed the bill of lading to a third party for valuable consideration, and without notice of the facts, such party's claim, as assignee of the property under the bill of lading, is paramount to the vendor's right to stop *in transitu.* 2 *Steph. Com.* The leading case on the subject of *stoppage in transitu* is *Lickbarrow* v. *Mason.* See 1 *Smith's Leading Cases.* See now, Sale of Goods Act, 1893, s. 44.

STOWAGE. 1. A place where goods are laid.

2. The money paid for such a place.

3. The act of stowing cargo in a vessel. The stowage of the cargo is primarily a duty of the shipowner and master, and nothing absolves them from this obligation short of express agreement with the charterer, or the unambiguous usage of the port. *Maclachlan on Merchant Shipping.*

STRANDING. A ship is said to be *stranded* within the meaning of a policy of insurance when, by tempest, by bad steering, or by violence, it is forced or driven on shore. The circumstances must be accidental, and the ship must remain on shore for a certain time, *i.e.*, a mere striking against a rock or bank would not appear to be a *stranding.*

STRAY, otherwise **ESTRAY**, is a beast gone astray, of which the owner is not known. 2 *Steph. Com.* [ESTRAYS.]

STRICT SETTLEMENT. 1. This phrase was formerly used to denote a settlement whereby land was limited to a parent for life, and after his death to his first and other sons or children in tail, with trustees interposed to preserve contingent remainders. 1 *Steph. Com.*

2. Generally, a settlement in which land is tied up to the descendants of any person to the utmost extent permitted by law, and with the usual limitations for the settlement of real estate, is called a *strict settlement.*

STRIKING OFF THE ROLL. This phrase is used to denote the removal of a solicitor of the Supreme Court from the roll of solicitors of that court. It takes place either at the party's own request, or for misconduct. 3 *Steph. Com.* [SOLICITOR.]

STRIKING OUT PLEADINGS. By Ord. XIX. r. 27, R. S. C. 1883, the court or a judge may at any stage of the proceedings strike out or amend anything in the pleadings which is scandalous, or which tends to embarrass or delay the fair trial of the action. By Ord. XXXI. r. 21, the defence may be struck out as a punishment for the defendant for default in making discovery or allowing inspection after order to do so. By r. 7 of the same order interrogatories may be struck out if they are unreasonable, vexatious, or scandalous.

STUFF GOWN. The gown of a member of the junior bar. Hence the phrase is used of junior barristers, as opposed to king's counsel. [SILK GOWN.]

SUB MODO. Under condition or restriction.

SUB SILENTIO. In silence.

SUBINFEUDATION signifies a feudal subletting, under which persons, holding estates under the king or other superior lord, carved out in their turn portions of such estates to be held of them by *tenants pararail,* or inferior tenants. This practice is forbidden, as regards England, by the Statute *Quia Emptores,* passed in 1290, except as regards the king's tenants *in capite,* for whom a similar law was enacted some years afterwards. 1 *Steph. Com.* [FEE ; IN CAPITE ; PARAMOUNT ; PARAVAIL ; QUIA EMPTORES.]

SUBMISSION is a word especially used with reference to the submission of a matter in dispute to the judgment of an arbitrator or arbitrators. 3 *Steph. Com.*

SUBORNATION OF PERJURY is the offence of instructing or procuring another to commit perjury. 4 *Steph. Com.* ; *Oke's Mag. Syn.* [PERJURY.]

SUBPŒNA (Lat. *Subpœnâ,* under a penalty).
1. A writ whereby formerly all persons under the degree of peerage were called upon to appear and answer to a bill in Chancery. It was abolished in 1852 by the Chancery Procedure Act, 15 & 16 Vict. c. 86. 3 *Steph. Com.*
2. A writ directed to a person commanding him, under a penalty, to appear and give evidence. This is called a *subpœna ad testificandum.* 3 *Steph. Com.*
3. A writ directed to a person, requiring him not only to give evidence, but to bring with him such deeds or writings

SUBPŒNA—*continued.*

as the party who issues the *subpœna* may think material for his purpose. This is called a *subpœna duces tecum*, being a species of the *subpœna ad testificandum*. 3 *Steph. Com.* See *R. S. C. Ord. XXXVII. rr.* 26—34.

SUBROGATION. Substitution.

SUBSCRIBING WITNESS is a person who puts his name to an instrument as attesting witness. 1 *Steph. Com.* [ATTESTATION.]

SUBSEQUENT CONDITION. [CONDITIONS PRECEDENT AND SUBSEQUENT.]

SUBSIDY. 1. An aid, tax or tribute granted by parliament to the king for the urgent occasions of the kingdom, to be levied of every subject upon his property, at such rate as parliament may think fit. 2 *Steph. Com.*

2. A species of custom payable upon exports and imports of staple commodities. 2 *Stepn. Com.*

SUBSTANTIAL DAMAGES, given by the verdict of a jury, are damages which amount to a substantial sum, as opposed to merely nominal damages. [NOMINAL DAMAGES.]

SUBSTITUTED SERVICE is where a writ or other process is served upon some person other than the person upon whom the service ought more properly to be effected, by reason of its being impossible to effect personal service. See *R. S. C. Ord. IX. r.* 2, and *Ord. X.* 3 *Steph. Com.*

SUBTRACTION is when any person who owes any suit, duty, custom, or service to another, withdraws it or neglects to perform it ; as in the cases of (1) the neglect of a tenant to attend his lord's court, or otherwise to perform the duties of his tenancy ; (2) the neglect by a landowner to pay tithes or ecclesiastical dues ; (3) the neglect or refusal by husband or wife to live with the other ; and in various other cases. 3 *Steph. Com.*

SUCCESSION is where one comes to property previously enjoyed by another. It is either *singular* or *universal*. Singular succession is where the purchaser, donee, or legatee of a specific chattel, or other specific property, succeeds to the right of the vendor, donor, or testator. Universal succession is the succession to an indefinite series of rights, as the succession by the trustee of a bankrupt to the estate and effects of the bankrupt, or by an executor or administrator to the estate of the deceased.

By sects. 2 and 54 of the Succession Duty Act, 1853 (16 & 17 Vict. c. 51), (1) every disposition of property, by reason whereof any person has or shall become beneficially entitled to any property, or the income thereof, upon the death of any person dying after the 19th of May, 1853, and (2) every devolution by law of any beneficial interest in property, or the income thereof, upon the death of any person dying after the 19th of May, 1853, to any other person. is to be deemed to confer a " succession " on the person entitled by reason of any such disposition or devolution ; and the term " successor " is to denote the person so entitled ; and the term " predecessor " is to denote the settlor, disponer, testator, obligor, ancestor, or other person from whom the interest of the successor is derived. See next title.

SUCCESSION DUTY. A duty payable on " succession," as defined by the Succession Duty Act. [SUCCESSION.] See now the Finance Act, 1894.

SUCCESSOR. See the two preceding titles.

SUE. To take legal proceedings claiming a civil right against anyone.

SUFFERANCE. An estate at sufferance is where one comes into possession of land under a lawful title, and, after the title has come to an end, keeps it without any title at all, by the sufferance of the rightful owner. The party continuing in possession is called a *tenant at sufferance*. 1 *Steph. Com.*

SUFFERANCE WHARF. [WHARF.]

SUFFERING A RECOVERY. The tenant in tail, who procured a common recovery of his land to be effected, to the intent that a conveyance might be made of the land in fee simple, was said to *suffer a recovery*. [RECOVERY.]

SUFFRAGAN. A word signifying *deputy*. A suffragan bishop is a titular bishop appointed to aid and assist the bishop of the diocese in his spiritual function. Bishops are also called *suffragan* in respect of their relation to the archbishops of their province. 1 *Steph. Com.* ; 2 *Steph. Com.*

SUFFRAGE. Vote, elective franchise ; aid, assistance.

SUGGESTIO FALSI. A suggestion or insinuation of something false. [MISRE-PRESENTATION.]

SUI JURIS is a phrase used to denote a person who is under no disability affecting his legal power to make conveyances of his property, to bind himself by contracts, and to sue and be sued ; as opposed to persons wholly or partially under disability, as infants, lunatics, prisoners, etc.

SUICIDE. Self-murder ; or, a self-murderer. [FELO DE SE.]

SUIT. A following. The word is used as follows :—
1. *Suit of Court ;* that is, the attendance which tenants owe to the court of their lord. [SECTA CURIÆ.] 2. *Suit covenant ;* which is, when your ancestor hath covenanted with mine to sue to his court. 3. *Suit custom ;* when I and my ancestors have been entitled to your and your ancestors' suit time out of mind. 4. *Suit regal ;* when men come to the sheriff's tourn or leet. 5. The following any one in chase. 6. A petition made to the king or any great person. 7. *Suit of the king's peace ;* that is, pursuing a man for having broken the king's peace by treasons, insurrections, or trespasses. 8. The witnesses or followers of the plaintiff in an action at law. 9. The legal proceeding itself ; hence, any litigation. In legal documents and treatises it is most usual to speak of *an action at law* and *a suit in equity.* Otherwise the word suit may include action ; and we commonly use the word "lawsuit" to denote any contentious litigation. See sect. 100 of the Judicature Act, 1873 ; 1 *Steph. Com.;* 3 *Steph. Com.*

SUITOR. A party to a suit or litigation.

SUITORS' FEE FUND. A fund formed from the payment of the fees of suitors in the Court of Chancery. The suitors' fee fund was the primary fund from which were paid the salaries of some of the officers of the court and other expenses connected therewith.

SUMMARY CONVICTION is a conviction before magistrates without the intervention of a jury. To this head may, perhaps, be added the committal of an offender by a judge for contempt of court. 4 *Steph. Com.; Oke's Mag. Syn.*

SUMMARY JURISDICTION. The power of a court to give judgment or make an order forthwith. Specially, in criminal cases, the power of magistrates to hear or dispose of a case without sending it for trial at sessions or assizes.

SUMMING UP, in a civil or criminal trial before a judge and jury, is the charge of the judge to the jury, recapitulating in greater or less detail the statements of the witnesses and the contents of the documents (if any) adduced on either side, commenting upon the manner in which they severally bear upon the issue, and giving his direction upon any matter of law that may arise upon them. 3 *Steph. Com.* See next title.

SUMMING UP EVIDENCE. This may be done by the judge, of whom it is more properly said [see the previous title], or by a counsel summing up his own case at the close of the evidence which he has adduced. 3 *Steph. Com.;* 4 *Steph. Com.*

SUMMONS may be defined generally as :— A citation to appear before a judge or magistrate. The word is used variously, as follows :—
1. A citation summoning a person to appear before a police magistrate or bench of justices. 4 *Steph. Com.* [WARRANT, I. 1.]
2. An application to a judge at chambers, whether at law or in equity. In equity, see also ADJOURED SUMMONS. 3 *Steph. Com.* [SUMMONS AND ORDER.]
3. The writ of summons which is the commencement of an action. It is a writ calling on the defendant to cause an appearance to the action to be entered for him within eight days after service, in default whereof the plaintiff may proceed to judgment and execution. There are different forms of it, according as the defendant does or does not reside within the jurisdiction, and if he does not, the period of eight days may be enlarged, with reference to the distance he may be from England. In certain cases the writ may be specially indorsed with particulars of the plaintiff's claim.
By R. S. C. 1883, Ord. II. r. 1, every action in the High Court is to be commenced by writ of summons, which must be indorsed with a statement of the nature of the claim made, or of the relief or remedy required in the action, and must also specify the division of

SUMMONS—*continued.*

the High Court to which it is intended that the action shall be assigned. It will not be necessary for the plaintiff, in the indorsement, to set forth the precise relief or remedy to which he considers himself entitled. (Ord. III. r. 2.) In cases of a liquidated demand, the writ of summons may, by Ord. III. r. 6, be specially indorsed. 3 *Steph. Com.* [SPECIAL INDORSEMENT; STATEMENT OF CLAIM; ORIGINATING SUMMONS.]

SUMPTUARY LAWS are laws made to restrain excess in apparel and other luxuries; of which we formerly had many in England, but they were mostly repealed by 1 Jac. 1, c. 25.

SUPER VISUM CORPORIS (on view of the body). A phrase applied to the view had by a coroner's jury of the body of the deceased concerning whose death they are appointed to inquire. The Coroners Act, 1887, allows a view to be dispensed with on a second inquest. 2 *Steph. Com.*

SUPERCARGO. A factor or agent who goes with a ship beyond the seas by order of the owner of the wares therein, and disposes of the same to the best advantage.

SUPERINSTITUTION signifies one institution upon another; as where A. is admitted and instituted to a benefice upon one title, and B. is admitted, instituted, etc., upon the presentment of another, claiming under an adverse title. [INSTITUTION.]

SUPERINTENDENT REGISTRAR. A local officer whose business it is to supervise the registrars of births, deaths and marriages in the registration districts within his jurisdiction. 3 *Steph. Com.* [REGISTRAR, 2.]

SUPERIOR COURTS. This expression was used to denote the Court of Chancery, the Courts of Queen's Bench (now King's Bench), Common Pleas, and Exchequer. These courts, together with the Courts of Probate, Divorce, and Admiralty, are now consolidated together in the Supreme Court of Judicature. *Stat.* 36 & 37 *Vict. c.* 66, *ss.* 3, 16; 3 *Steph. Com.* [SUPREME COURT OF JUDICATURE.]

SUPERSEDEAS. A writ in divers cases, signifying in general a command to stay or forbear the doing of anything. The word is especially used with reference to the superseding of a commission of the peace, which suspends the power of the justices therein mentioned, but does not totally destroy it. 2 *Steph. Com.*

SUPERSTITIOUS USES. A superstitious use has been defined as "one which has for its object the propagation of the rites of a religion not tolerated by the law," *e.g.*, a gift of money for saying prayers for the dead. Superstitious uses are opposed to charitable uses which are recognised by law. 1 *Steph. Com.* [CHARITABLE USES; MORTMAIN ACTS.]

SUPPLEMENTAL BILL was a bill filed in equity by way of supplement to one previously filed, when new matter arose which did not exist when the first bill was filed. Such a bill set forth the whole of the original bill, together with the new matter. Amendments of the pleadings may now be allowed at any stage of the proceedings in an action. *R. S. C., Ord. XXVIII. r.* 1. [AMENDMENT.]

SUPPLETORY OATH. An oath administered to a party in the spiritual and civil law courts in order to turn the *semiplena probatio*, which consists in the testimony of but *one witness*, into the *plena probatio*, afforded by the testimony of *two witnesses.* 3 *Steph. Com.*

SUPPLIANT. The claimant in a petition of right. [PETITION OF RIGHT, 1.]

SUPPLICAVIT was a writ issuing out of Chancery or the Queen's Bench, for taking surety of the peace against a man. It was directed to the justices of the peace for the county, and to the sheriff. Now almost obsolete. 4 *Steph. Com.* [SURETY OF THE PEACE.]

SUPPORT. The right of support is the right of a person to have his buildings or other landed property supported by his neighbour's house or land.

Every man is entitled to have his land in its natural state supported by the adjoining land of his neighbour, against whom an action will lie, if, by digging on his own land, he removes that support. This right to lateral support from adjoining soil is not held to be an easement, but is a right of property passing with the soil. Thus, if the owner of two adjoining closes conveys away one of them, the alienee, without any grant for that purpose, is

SUPPORT—*continued.*

entitled to the lateral support of the other close the very instant when the conveyance is executed, as much as he would be after the expiration of twenty years or of any longer period. *Tudor, L. C. R. P.*

But, where a person builds to the utmost extremity of his own land, and thereby increases the lateral pressure on the soil of his neighbour, if the latter digs his own ground, so as to remove some part of the soil, an action will not lie for the injury occasioned to the former, unless he has, by grant or prescription, acquired a right to the support of the house by the soil of his neighbour. See *Dalton* v. *Angus*, in *Tudor, L. C. R. P.*

SUPPRESSIO VERI. The suppression of truth; that is, the suppression, in a one-sided statement, of some material fact on the other side. [MISREPRESENTATION.]

SUPRA. Above. Often used to refer a reader to a previous part of a book.

SUPRA PROTEST. [ACCEPTANCE SUPRA PROTEST.]

SUPREME COURT OF JUDICATURE is a Court established by 36 & 37 Vict. c. 66, the Judicature Act, 1873, by sect. 3 of which it was provided that the High Court of Chancery, the Courts of Queen's Bench, Common Pleas, and Exchequer, the High Court of Admiralty, the Court of Probate, the Divorce Court, [and the London Court of Bankruptcy,] should be united, and constitute one Supreme Court of Judicature in England. By sect. 4, the Supreme Court is to consist of two divisions, one to be called his Majesty's "High Court of Justice," and the other, "His Majesty's Court of Appeal." To the High Court of Justice, under sect. 16 of the Act, is transferred the jurisdiction exercised by the Courts of Chancery, Queen's Bench, Common Pleas, Exchequer, Admiralty, Probate, Divorce, [Bankruptcy], the Court of Common Pleas at Lancaster, the Court of Pleas at Durham, and the Assize Courts ; with certain exceptions mentioned in sect. 17 of the Act, of which the most conspicuous is the appellate jurisdiction exercised by the Court of Appeal in Chancery. To his Majesty's Court of Appeal is transferred the jurisdiction exercised by the Lord Chancellor and Lords Justices of the Court of Appeal in Chancery, also the jurisdiction of the Court of Exchequer Chamber, and the jurisdiction exercised by the Judicial Committee of the Privy Council on appeal from the High Court of Admiralty, or from any order in lunacy made by the Lord Chancellor, or any other person having jurisdiction in lunacy. By sect. 31, the High Court is to be divided, for the more convenient dispatch of business, into five divisions : (1) The Chancery Division ; (2) The Queen's Bench Division ; (3) The Common Pleas Division ; (4) The Exchequer Division ; (5) The Probate, Divorce, and Admiralty Division ; but subsequently Nos. (2) and (3) were merged into the Queen's Bench (now King's Bench) Division, and by the Bankruptcy Act, 1883, s. 94, the business of the London Court of Bankruptcy was transferred to the High Court. By sect. 34, various causes and matters, hitherto cognizable in the Court of Chancery, are assigned to the Chancery Division ; and matters hitherto within the exclusive jurisdiction of the Court of Queen's Bench are assigned to the Queen's Bench Division ; and similarly with reference to the other divisions. By sect. 36, any cause or matter brought in a wrong division may be transferred therefrom or retained therein.

In the 56th and following sections of the Act of 1873, provisions are made for the trial of causes before official and special referees.

SURCHARGE AND FALSIFY. If, in an account stated, there is any mistake, omission, accident, or fraud, by which the account stated is vitiated, it has been held that a court of equity would interfere ; in some cases, by directing the whole account to be opened and taken *de novo* ; in others, by allowing it to stand, with liberty to the plaintiff to surcharge and falsify. To *surcharge* is to show an omission of something for which credit ought to have been given ; and to *falsify* is to prove an item to have been wrongly inserted. [ACCOUNT.]

SURCHARGE OF COMMON is when a commoner puts more beasts in a forest, or in pasture, than he has a right to do. 3 *Steph. Com.* [ADMEASUREMENT OF PASTURE.]

SURETY is a man who contracts to be answerable for another in such a manner that the latter is primarily answerable. As, if money be advanced to A. ; and B., his friend, joins with him in giving a bond for its repayment ; then B. is a surety for A. 2 *Steph. Com.*

SURETY OF GOOD BEHAVIOUR. [GOOD BEHAVIOUR; KEEPING THE PEACE.]

SURETY OF THE PEACE. [KEEPING THE PEACE.]

SURPLICE FEES are fees payable on burials, marriages, and the like. 2 *Steph. Com.* The non-payment of these dues is among the matters cognizable in the ecclesiastical courts. 3 *Steph. Com.*

SURPLUSAGE. A superfluity, or addition of something unnecessary, in any legal document.

SURREBUTTER was the plaintiff's answer to the defendant's rebutter, and was the plaintiff's fourth pleading. By R. S. C. 1883, Ord. XXIII. r. 2, no pleading subsequent to reply, other than a joinder of issue, shall be pleaded without leave of the court or a judge, and then upon such terms as the court or judge shall think fit.

SURREJOINDER. The answer by the plaintiff to the defendant's rejoinder. [SURREBUTTER.]

SURRENDER (Lat. *Sursum redditio*) is the falling of a less estate into a greater.
1. *Surrender in deed.* This takes place by the yielding up of an estate for life or years to him that hath the immediate revision or remainder. 1 *Steph. Com.* To constitute a valid express surrender, it is essential that it should be made to, and accepted by, the owner (in his own right) of the reversion or remainder. *Fawcett, L. & T.*
2. *Surrender by operation of law.* This phrase is properly applied to cases where the tenant for life or years has been a party to some act the validity of which he is by law afterwards estopped from disputing, and which would not be valid if his particular estate continued to exist; thus, when a lessee for years accepts a new lease from his lessor, he is estopped from saying that his lessor had not the power to make the new lease, so that the acceptance of the new lease amounts in law to a surrender of the former one. The effect of a surrender by operation of law is expressly reserved in s. 2 of the Statute of Frauds. 1 *Steph. Com.; Fawcett, L. & T.* [ESTOPPEL.]
3. *Surrender of copyholds.* This is the yielding up by a copyholder of his interest to his lord, according to the custom of the manor, generally in order that the same may be granted out again to such person or persons, and for such use or uses, as are named in the surrender. The lord is compellable by *mandamus* to admit the surrenderee, that is, the person to whose use the surrender is made. 1 *Steph. Com.* [COPYHOLD.] See also the two following titles.

SURRENDER TO USES OF WILL. Formerly a copyhold interest would not pass by will unless it had been surrendered to the use of the will. [SURRENDER, 3.] But now, by the Wills Act (7 Will. 4 & 1 Vict. c. 26), s. 3, this formality is no longer necessary. 1 *Steph. Com.*

SURRENDEREE is, properly, a person to whom a surrender is made; but the word is frequently used to denote the person to whose use a copyhold is surrendered. [SURRENDER, 3.]

SURROGATE is one that is substituted or appointed in the room of another. The word is most commonly used of a person who is appointed by the bishop for granting marriage licences. 2 *Steph. Com.*

SURVIVORSHIP is a word used not merely of the *fact* of survivorship, but of the rights arising therefrom; that is to say, of the right of the survivor or survivors of joint tenants to the estate held in joint tenancy, in exclusion of the representatives of the deceased. 1 *Steph. Com.;* 2 *Steph. Com.* [JOINT TENANCY; PRESUMPTION OF SURVIVORSHIP.]

SUS. PER COLL. An abbreviation for *suspendatur per collum* (let him be hanged by the neck); the note formerly written by the judge, in the calendar of prisoners, against the name of a prisoner sentenced to death, as a warrant to the sheriff to do execution.

SUSPENSION. 1. A temporary stop or cessation of a man's right. Or, of his exercise of an office, *e.g.,* of a clergyman by an ecclesiastical court under the Clergy Discipline Act, 1892. 2 *Steph. Com.;* 3 *Steph. Com.*
2. A temporary revocation of any law by proper authority.

SUSPENSION, PLEA IN, is a species of dilatory plea in an action, showing some matter of temporary incapacity to proceed with the suit. 3 *Steph. Com.* [ABATEMENT, 6.]

SYMBOLIC DELIVERY is a delivery of any small thing in token of a transfer of something else. Thus, with our Saxon ancestors, the delivery of a turf was a necessary solemnity to establish the conveyance of lands. And, to this day, the conveyance of copyhold estates is usually made by the delivery, on the part of the vendor, of a rod or verge to the lord or his steward, and then by the redelivery of the same from the lord to the purchaser. 1 *Steph. Com.* [FEOFFMENT.]

SYNDIC. An agent or attorney who acts for a corporation or university.

SYNGRAPH. 1. The name given by the canonists to deeds of which *both parts* (that is to say, the copies corresponding to each party) were written on the same piece of parchment, with some word or letters of the alphabet written between them, through which the parchment was cut in such a manner as to leave half the word on one part and half on the other. 1 *Steph. Com.*
2. Hence, a deed or writing under the hand and seal of all the parties.

SYNOD. A meeting or assembly of ecclesiastical persons concerning religion, of which there are four kinds :—
1. General, when bishops, etc., of all nations meet together.
2. National, when those of one nation only come together.
3. Provincial, when they of one province meet, being now what is called the Convocation.
4. Diocesan, when those of but one diocese meet.
2 *Steph. Com.*

SYNODAL. A tribute in money payable by the inferior clergy to the bishop or archdeacon at his Easter visitation. The word is also used for the Synod itself. Provision is now made by stat. 23 & 24 Vict. c. 124, s. 2, for the payment of all such dues to the Ecclesiastical Commissioners.

TACK, in Scotland, signifies a lease.

TACK DUTY. The rent reserved on a lease.

TACKING MORTGAGES. This happens when a third or subsequent mortgagee of land, by getting a conveyance to himself of the legal estate of the first mortgagee, is enabled to obtain, for his own security, priority over the second mortgagee. He is then said to *tack* his mortgage to the first mortgage. This is permitted if the person who claims to *tack* has originally advanced his money without notice of the incumbrance or incumbrances over which he claims priority, notwithstanding that he might have had notice of the same before getting in the legal estate. For the person so claiming to tack is held to have an *equity* equal to that of the incumbrancer over whom he claims priority ; and having got in the *legal estate* he obtains priority on the principle that where the equities are equal, the law shall prevail ; and mere priority of time is not regarded where there is any other ground of difference. *Wms. R. P.*

Tacking was abolished by sect. 7 of the Vendor and Purchaser Act, 1874, (37 & 38 Vict. c. 78). But that section is repealed by the 129th section of the Land Transfer Act, 1875, (38 & 39 Vict. c. 87), which is again practically repealed so far as Yorkshire is concerned by the Yorkshire Registries Act, 1884. [LEGAL ESTATE ; MORTGAGE.]

TAIL. A term used to signify an *estate tail.* [ESTATE.] See also the following titles.

TAIL AFTER POSSIBILITY OF ISSUE EXTINCT is where land is given to a man and his wife, and to the heirs of their two bodies engendered, and one of them overlives the other without issue between them begotten ; he shall hold the land for term of his own life as *tenant in tail after possibility of issue extinct,* and, notwithstanding that he do waste, he shall not be impeached of it. And even if there have been issue, yet if the issue die without issue, then the surviving parent is also such a tenant. A tenant in tail after possibility of issue extinct cannot bar the entail. *Stat. 3 & 4 Will. 4, c. 74, s. 18 ; 1 Steph. Com.* [DISENTAILING DEED ; FINE, 1 ; RECOVERY.]

TAIL FEMALE is where a real estate is settled on A. B. and the heirs female of his or her body. Under such words of limitation, females alone can succeed and would inherit together ; nor could any female claim except through females. But in practice it never occurs. 1 *Steph. Com.; Wms. R. P.*

TAIL GENERAL is where an estate is limited to a man and the heirs of his body, without any restriction at all ; or, according to some authorities, with no other restriction than that in relation to sex. Thus *tail male general* is the same thing as *tail male ;* the word *general* in such case implying that there is no other restriction upon the descent of the estate than that it must go in the *male* line. So, an estate in tail female general is an estate in tail female. 1 *Steph. Com.*

TAIL MALE is where an estate is limited to a man and the heirs male of his body ; that is, so far as regards the first generation, to males ; and, so far as regards subsequent generations, to males claiming exclusively through males. 1 *Steph. Com. ; Wms. R. P.* See the two preceding titles.

TAIL SPECIAL, in its largest sense, is where the gift is restrained to certain heirs of the donor's body, and does not go to all of them in general. 1 *Steph. Com.* [TAIL GENERAL.]

TALES. A supply of jurymen to make up a deficiency. If a sufficient number of jurors do not appear, or if by means of challenges or exemptions a sufficient number of unexceptionable ones do not remain, either party may pray a *tales.* The judge who tries the cause can award a *tales de circumstantibus ;* that is, to command the sheriff to return so many other men duly qualified as shall be present, or can be found, to make up the number required, and to add their names to the former panel. They are hence called talesmen. Seldom now required. 3 *Steph. Com. ;* 4 *Steph. Com.*

TALION. Retaliation. [LEX TALIONIS.]

TALLAGERS. Tax or toll gatherers.

TALLEY, or **TALLY.** A stick cut in two parts, on each whereof is marked, with notches or otherwise, what is due between debtors and creditors. This was the ancient way of keeping accounts, one part being kept by the creditor, the other by the debtor. Hence the *tallier* of the Exchequer, also called the *teller.* [TELLERS, 1.] The use of tallies in the Exchequer was abolished in 1783 by 23 Geo. 3, c. 82. And in consequence of the changes introduced in 1834 by 4 & 5 Will. 4, c. 15, in the keeping of the public accounts, the old tallies were ordered to be destroyed. They were accordingly employed to heat the stoves in the House of Lords, and are said to have been the cause, from having been burned in too large quantities, of the fire which broke out in October, 1834, and consumed the two houses of parliament.

TALLIAGE. A tax laid upon cities and burghs. 2 *Steph. Com.*

TALTARUM'S CASE, which was decided in Michaelmas Term, 1472 (the twelfth year of Edward IV.), is known as the case in which the judges by implication laid down those principles on which "common recoveries" were sanctioned for so many centuries, as a means of converting estates tail into fees simple. See 2 *Bl. ;* 1 *Steph. Com.* [RECOVERY.]

TAM QUAM. A writ of error, from inferior courts, when the error is supposed to be in giving the judgment as well as in awarding execution upon it.

TANGIBLE PROPERTY is property which may be touched and is the object of sensation, corporeal property ; this kind of property is opposed to intangible rights, or incorporeal property, such as patents, copyrights, advowsons, rents, etc. 1 *Steph. Com.*

TANISTRY. An old Irish tenure, by which, from time immemorial, lands descended to the *eldest* and *most worthy* of the blood and name.

TAX. A tribute or impost imposed by parliament.

TAXATION OF COSTS is the settlement by the taxing master of the amount payable by a party in respect of costs in any action or suit. The allowance of particular items in the bill will in a great measure depend on the order directing the taxation. In a bill sent in by a solicitor to his client, items would be allowed which would not be allowed in the ordinary taxation of costs between parties in a suit or action. But in some cases, even between the parties to a suit or action, costs are to be taxed *as between solicitor and client* as opposed to the ordinary taxation *as between party and party.* In cases of importance or difficulty, costs may also be directed to be taxed on the "Higher Scale" as opposed to the "Lower" or ordinary scale prescribed by the Judicature Rules. See Rules of 1902. *Summerhays* and *Twogood,* and *Johnson on Taxation of Costs.* See also the following title.

TAXING MASTERS. The officers appointed to tax costs. [TAXATION OF COSTS.] In actions at common law and in Chancery the taxation of costs is done by special taxing masters ; and in the Probate, Divorce, and Admiralty Division by the registrars.

TECHNICAL INSTRUCTION. By the Technical Instruction Acts 1889 and 1891, technical instruction in the principles of science and art applicable to industries, may be provided by local authorities at the expense of the rate-payers. 3 *Steph. Com.*

TELLERS. 1. Four officers of the Exchequer, formerly appointed to receive monies due to the king and to pay monies payable by the king. Abolished in 1834 by 4 & 5 Will. 4, c. 15, s. 1.

2. Members of parliament appointed by the Speaker to count the numbers in a parliamentary division. *May's Parl. Pract.*

TEMPLES. Two of the Inns of Court. [INNS OF COURT.]
At the suppression of the order of Knights Templars their dwelling was purchased by the professors of the common law, and converted into inns of court in the year 1340. They are called the Inner and Middle Temple. Essex House, built in 1185, was formerly a part of the house of the Templars, and was called the Outer Temple because it was situated without Temple Bar. *Haydn's Dict. Dates.*

TEMPORAL LORDS. [LORDS TEMPORAL.]

TEMPORALITIES OF BISHOPS are the revenues, lands, tenements and lay-fees belonging to the bishops' sees. 2 *Steph. Com.*

TENANT. 1. One that holds or possesses lands or tenements by any kind of right, be it for life, years, at will or at sufferance, in dower, custody or otherwise ; all lands being considered as *holden* of the king or of some superior lord. 1 *Steph. Com. ; Wms. R. P.*

2. Especially, a tenant under a lease from year to year, or other fixed period.

3. We sometimes use the word in reference to interests in pure personalty, as when we speak of any one as tenant for life of a fund, etc. 2 *Steph. Com.* See also the following titles.

TENANT AT SUFFERANCE. A person who, having been in lawful possession of land, wrongfully continues in possession after his title has come to an end, without the agreement or disagreement of the person then entitled. 1 *Steph. Com. ; Fawcett, L. & T.*

TENANT AT WILL is a person in possession of lands let to him to hold at the will of the lessor. A copyhold tenant was originally a tenant at will, and he is still nominally so, being said to hold *at the will of the lord according to the custom of the manor ;* but, as the lord's will is controlled by the custom, the so-called tenancy at will is hardly less beneficial than a freehold. 1 *Steph. Com. ; Fawcett, L. & T.*

TENANT BY SUFFERANCE. [TENANT AT SUFFERANCE.]

TENANT BY THE CURTESY. [CURTESY.]

TENANT FOR LIFE. A person who holds an estate for his life. [ESTATE.]

TENANT FROM YEAR TO YEAR. A tenancy from year to year is now fixed, by general usage, to signify a tenancy determinable at half a year's notice (or, in an agricultural tenancy, one year's notice) on either side, ending with the current year of the tenancy. If the tenancy commenced on one of the quarterly feast days, the half-year may be computed from one of such feast days to another ; otherwise, the half-year must consist of 182 days. See 1 *Steph. Com. ; Fawcett, L. & T.*

TENANT IN TAIL. [ESTATE.]

TENANT IN TAIL AFTER POSSIBILITY OF ISSUE EXTINCT. [TAIL AFTER POSSIBILITY OF ISSUE EXTINCT.]

TENANT TO THE PRÆCIPE. [PRÆCIPE, TENANT TO THE.]

TENANTABLE REPAIR. Such a state of repair in houses or buildings as renders them fit for the occupation of a tenant.
A tenant from year to year of a house is bound to keep it wind and water tight, to use it in a tenant-like manner, and to make fair and tenantable repairs, such as putting in windows or doors that have been broken by him, so as to prevent waste and decay of the premises. *Fawcett, L. & T.*

TENANT-RIGHT. 1. The right of a tenant on termination of tenancy to compensation for unexhausted improvements effected on his holding. Formerly governed by custom, but now by Agricultural Holdings Act, 1883, unless reasonable provision is made in lieu of that given by the Act. Also used to indicate the money so paid.

2. Ireland. See the *Land Law (Ireland) Act*, 1881 (44 & 45 *Vict. c.* 49).

TENANTS IN COMMON. [COMMON, TENANCY IN.]

TENDER. 1. An offer of money or any other thing in satisfaction of a debt or liability. See next title.

2. Coin or paper money, which, so far as regards the nature and quality thereof, a creditor may be compelled to accept in satisfaction of his debt, is called *legal tender*. [LEGAL TENDER.]

TENDER OF AMENDS. An offer by a person, who has been guilty of any wrong or breach of contract, to pay a sum of money by way of amends. If a defendant in an action make tender of amends, and the plaintiff decline to accept it, the defendant may pay the money into court, and plead the payment into court as a satisfaction of the plaintiff's claim. 3 *Steph. Com.; R. S. C., Ord. XXII.* [PAYMENT OF MONEY INTO COURT, 1 ; PUBLIC AUTHORITIES PROTECTION ACT.]

TENDER, PLEA OF. A plea by a defendant that he has been always ready to satisfy the plaintiff's claim, and now brings the sum demanded into court. 3 *Steph. Com.* See the two preceding titles.

TENEMENT. 1. A house or home-stall.

2. Land holden of a superior lord ; and in this sense *tenement* is one of the technical words applicable to all real estates, and includes offices and dignities which concern lands and profits issuing out of lands. 1 *Steph. Com.*

3. Especially such an interest in land within a parish as will enable a party to apply to such parish for poor law relief if in need thereof.

TENENDUM. The clause in a deed which was formerly used to signify the tenure by which the estate granted was to be holden ; as by knight service, etc. But such tenures being now reduced to free and common socage, the tenure is never specified ; and the *tenendum* in a deed is of very little use, and only kept in by custom. 1 *Steph. Com.*

TENOR. 1. By the *tenor* of a deed, or other instrument in writing, is signified the matter contained therein, according to the true intent and meaning thereof.

2. The word *tenor*, in reference to writs and records, signifies a copy or transcript, whereas *effect* signifies that the substance only is set out.

TENTERDEN'S ACT is the stat. 9 Geo. 4, c. 14, passed in 1828, at the instance of Lord Tenterden, Chief Justice of the King's Bench.

The following provisions of Lord Tenterden's Act are still in operation :—

1. In actions of debt or upon the case grounded upon any simple contract, no acknowledgment or promise by words only is to be deemed a sufficient evidence of a new and continuing contract to take the case out of the Statutes of Limitations, unless such acknowledgment or promise be in writing signed by the party chargeable thereby (sect. 1).

2. No action is to be brought whereby to charge any person upon or by reason of any assurance made concerning the character, conduct, credit, ability, trade or dealings of any person, to the intent that such person may obtain credit, money, or goods, unless such representations be in writing and signed by the party to be charged therewith (sect. 6).

TENTHS. 1. The tenth part of all spiritual preferments in the kingdom, originally payable to the Pope, and, after the Reformation, to the Crown, until applied by Queen Anne for the purposes of Queen Anne's Bounty, that is, to make up the deficiencies of smaller benefices. 2 *Steph. Com.* [FIRST-FRUITS ; QUEEN ANNE'S BOUNTY.]

2. A temporary aid issuing out of personal property anciently granted from time to time by parliament. 2 *Steph. Com.*

TENURE. The manner whereby tenements are holden of their lords. To hold land by *the tenure* of any given service is to hold land on the condition of a faithful performance of that service ; so that the non-performance thereof would be a cause of forfeiture to the lord. This forfeiture might be enforced by writ of *cessavit.* 1 *Steph. Com.; Wms. R. P.* [CESSAVIT ; ESTATE : FEE ; KNIGHT SERVICE ; MILITARY TENURES ; SOCAGE ; TENENDUM.]

TERM. 1. The period of time in which alone the superior courts of common law were formerly open for the redress of injuries. [SITTINGS.]

2. *A term of years.* This phrase is often used to denote a fixed period of time extending over several years ; but in the law of real property it is especially used to signify an estate or interest in land to be enjoyed for a fixed period. This estate is a chattel interest, and goes, on the death of its owner, to his executors or administrators. 1 *Steph. Com.* ; *Wms. R. P.* [OUTSTANDING TERM ; SATISFIED TERMS ACT.]

TERM FEE. [SITTINGS FEE.]

TERM IN GROSS. A phrase used to designate an estate for years in land *not* held in trust for the party who would be entitled to the land on the expiration of the term. [OUTSTANDING TERM ; SATISFIED TERMS ACT ; TERM, 2.]

TERMINUS A QUO. The starting point.

TERMINUS AD QUEM. The terminating point.

TERMOR. He that holds lands or tenements for a term of years or life. But we generally confine the application of the word to a person entitled for a term of years. 1 *Steph. Com.*

TERMS, TO BE UNDER. A party in an action or other legal proceeding is said to be *under terms,* when an indulgence is granted to him by the court in the exercise of its discretion, on condition of his observing certain things.

TERRA TESTAMENTALIS. Gavelkind land ; so called from being formerly devisable by will, when other lands were not so devisable. [DEVISE ; GAVELKIND.]

TERRAR. The same as *Terrier.* [TERRIER.]

TERRE TENANT. He who has the actual possession or occupation of land.

TERRIER (Lat. *Terrarium*). A land roll or survey of lands, containing the quantity of acres, tenants' names, and such like ; and in the Exchequer there is a terrier of all the glebe lands in England, made about 11 Edw. 3, that is, about 1338. In general, an ecclesiastical terrier contains a detail of the temporal possessions of the Church in every parish.

TERRITORIAL WATERS. Those within a marine league of the coast of a country are by international law held to be within the jurisdiction of that country. The Territorial Jurisdiction Act, 1878, gives the Admiralty jurisdiction over offences committed in the territorial waters of his Majesty's dominions. 1 *Steph. Com., n.*

TEST AND CORPORATION ACTS. The Test Act was 25 Car. 2, c. 2, passed in 1673 (explained by 9 Geo. 2, c. 26), by which all officers, civil and military, were directed to take the oaths and make the declaration against transubstantiation, and also receive the Sacrament of the Lord's Supper according to the usage of the Church of England, on pain of forfeiture of 500*l.*, and disability to hold the said office.

By the Corporation Act, 13 Car. 2, stat. 2, c. 1, no person could be legally elected to any office relating to the government of any city or corporation unless, within a twelvemonth before, he had received the Sacrament of the Lord's Supper according to the rites of the Church of England ; and he was also enjoined to take the oaths of allegiance and supremacy at the time of taking the oath of office' ; or, in default in either of these requisites, the election should be void.

Both these enactments were repealed in 1828 by stat. 9 Geo. 4, c. 17. See also 29 Vict., c. 22. 2 *Steph. Com.*

TESTAMENT. The true declaration of a man's last will as to that which he would have to be done after his death. Strictly speaking, a testament is a disposition of *personal* property only. 2 *Steph. Com.* [WILL, 1.]

TESTAMENTARY CAUSES are causes relating to the validity and execution of wills. The phrase is generally confined to those causes which were formerly matters of ecclesiastical jurisdiction, and are now dealt with by the Probate Division. 3 *Steph. Com.*

TESTAMENTARY GUARDIAN. A guardian appointed by will. By stat. 12 Car. 2, c. 24, passed in 1660, a father may, by deed or will, appoint a guardian to his infant children. 2 *Steph. Com.* [GUARDIAN, I. 5.]

TESTAMENTUM OMNE MORTE CONSUMMATUR (every will is perfected by death).

TESTATE. Having made a will.

TESTATOR. He who makes a will. [WILL, 1.]

TESTATRIX. She who makes a will. [WILL, 1.]

TESTATUM. The witnessing part of a deed, beginning "Now this indenture witnesseth." *Wms. R. P.*

TESTE. 1. The witnessing part of a writ, warrant, etc.

By R. S. C. 1883, Ord. II. r. 8, every writ of summons and also every other writ shall bear date on the day on which the same shall be issued, and shall be tested in the name of the Lord Chancellor, or, if the office of Lord Chancellor shall be vacant, in the name of the Lord Chief Justice of England.

2. The word is also sometimes used to signify the date of a document. 3 *Steph. Com.*

TESTES PONDERANTUR, NON NUMER-ANTUR (witnesses are weighed, not counted). It is the credibility of witnesses that is taken into account rather than their number.

TESTES, PROOF OF WILL PER, is a proof of a will by witnesses, in a more solemn form than ordinary, in cases where the validity of the will is disputed. [SOLEMN FORM.]

TESTIMONIUM CLAUSE. The final clause in a deed or will, commencing "In witness, etc."

TESTIMONY. Evidence. [EVIDENCE; PERPETUATING TESTIMONY.]

THANE. A nobleman. In Anglo-Saxon times thanes were of two orders, king's thanes and ordinary thanes.

THAVIE'S INN. Once an Inn of Chancery. [INNS OF CHANCERY.]

THEATRE. A place kept for the performance of stage plays. A licence must be obtained from the County Councils for provincial and from the Lord Chamberlain for metropolitan theatres. Also a copy of every new play intended to be performed in any theatre must be previously sent to the Lord Chamberlain. See *Local Government Act*, 1888. 3 *Steph. Com.*

THEFT. [LARCENY; STEALING.]

THEFT BOTE. The receiving, by a party robbed, of his goods back again, or other amends, upon an agreement not to prosecute. Theft bote is a species of the offence called *compounding a felony*, and is punishable by fine and imprisonment. 4 *Steph. Com.; Oke's Mag. Syn.* [COMPOUNDING.]

THELLUSSON ACT. The stat. 39 & 40 Geo. 3, c. 98, passed in 1799, in consequence of Mr. Thellusson's will. Mr. Thellusson was a person of enormous wealth, and left numerous descendants living at his death, besides two in *ventre sa mère*. By his will, after providing for his immediate descendants, he left the bulk of his property to be accumulated until his descendants living or in *ventre sa mère* at the time of his death should be dead. The Act called the Thellusson Act was passed to prevent a repetition of a bequest of this kind. By this Act a grantor or testator is forbidden to direct the accumulation of his property for a period exceeding his own life or twenty-one years from his death, or during the minority of any person living or in *ventre sa mère* at the death of such grantor or testator, or during the minority of any person who under the settlement or will would, if of full age, be entitled to the income so directed to be accumulated. Accumulations for the purpose of paying debts or raising portions are excepted from the Act. As to the settlement of property for the purpose of accumulating the rents and income thereof, see the Accumulations Act, 1892. 1 *Steph. Com.; Wms. R. P.* [ACCUMULATION.]

THESAURUS INVENTUS. [TREASURE TROVE.]

THINGS. The subjects of property, which may be either *in action* or *in possession*. Things *in action* are not immediately available to the owner without the consent of some other person, whose refusal will give a right of *action*. Things *in possession* may be used immediately without the concurrence of any other person. 1 *Steph. Com.; 2 Steph. Com.* [CHOSE.]

THIRD PARTY. One who is a stranger to a proceeding between two other persons. A third party may, by leave of the court or a judge, be introduced into an action by a defendant claiming an indemnity or other remedy over against him, by means of a notice called a "third party notice" being given him. See R. S. C. 1883, Ord. XVI. r. 48.

THIS DAY SIX MONTHS. An expression used in parliament to mean "never." Thus a proposal to read a bill "this day six months" is a proposal to reject it, because parliament would not be sitting six months hence. "This day three months" has the same meaning. The term fixed in either case is one beyond the probable duration of the session. If, however, the session should last to the time so nominally specified, it seems that the bill or bills will appear amongst the orders of the day. *May's Parl. Pract.*

THREAT has been defined to be any menace of such a nature and extent as to unsettle the mind of the person on whom it operates, and to take away from his acts that free voluntary action which alone constitutes consent. *Regina* v. *Walton*, 34 *L. J., M. C.* 79 ; 7 *L. T., N. S.* 754. Threats and threatening letters, as cognizable in criminal courts, are of various kinds :—(1) Letters threatening to publish a libel with a view to extort money. This offence is punishable under stat. 6 & 7 Vict. c. 96. s. 3, with imprisonment not exceeding three years, with or without hard labour. (2) Demanding money or other property with menaces, with intent to steal the same. This offence is felony, and punishable under sect. 45 of the Larceny Act, 1861 (stat. 24 & 25 Vict. c. 96), with two years' imprisonment, with or without hard labour. (3) Letters demanding of any person with menaces and without reasonable and probable cause, any property, chattel, money, valuably security, or other valuable thing. Any person sending such a letter, or causing the same to be received, knowing its contents, is liable, under sect. 44 of the same statute, to penal servitude for life, or to imprisonment not exceeding two years, with or without hard labour. (4) Letters threatening to accuse any person of a heinous or infamous crime, as defined in sect. 46 of the same statute. Any person guilty of sending any such letter, or causing the same to be received, knowing its contents, with a view to extort money, etc., is liable to penal servitude for life, as in the former case. (5) Letters threatening to kill or murder any person. The punishment for this offence is, by stat. 24 & 25 Vict. c. 100, s. 16, penal servitude for five years, or imprisonment for two years, with or without hard labour. 4 *Steph. Com. ; Oke's Mag. Syn.* As to the law relating to the intimidation of masters or workmen by combinations or associations, see the Conspiracy and Protection of Property Act, 1875.

THREATENING LETTERS. [THREAT.]

TICKET OF LEAVE is a written licence to a convict sentenced to penal servitude, to be at large before the expiration of his sentence. Such licence is granted under the hand or seal of one of his Majesty's principal secretaries of State (generally the Home Secretary), and is revocable for misconduct at any time before the period of the holder's sentence has expired. 27 & 28 *Vict. c.* 47 ; 54 & 55 *Vict. c.* 69 ; 4 *Steph. Com. ; Oke's Mag. Syn.*

TICKET OF LEAVE MAN. A convict who has obtained a ticket of leave. See preceding title.

TIMBER. Wood fitted for building or other such like uses. Oak, ash and elm are timber in all places ; and, by the custom of some particular counties, in which other kinds of trees are generally used for building, they are also for that reason considered as timber ; and for a tenant for life to cut down timber trees, or to do any act whereby they may decay, is waste, timber being part of the inheritance. 3 *Steph. Com. ; Fawcett, L. & T.* [WASTE.]

TIME BARGAIN is a contract for the sale of a certain amount of stock at a certain price on a future day, the vendor not in general having such stock to sell at the time of the contract, but intending to purchase it before the time appointed for the execution of the contract. Time bargains were forbidden by sect. 4 of Sir John Barnard's Act (7 Geo. 2, c. 8), under a penalty of 500*l.* Such contracts could not, therefore, be enforced by the courts of law. As, however, any party failing to meet his engagement was stigmatised in the Stock Exchange as a *lame duck,* and his name exhibited as a defaulter, the disgrace attending upon a breach of such contracts secured their general observance. Sir John Barnard's Act is now repealed by stat. 23 & 24 Vict. c. 28. [BULL 2.]

TIME IMMEMORIAL. TIME OUT OF MIND. These expressions denote time beyond legal memory ; that is, the time prior to the commencement of the reign of Richard I., A.D. 1189. 1 *Steph. Com.* [LEGAL MEMORY.]

TIME POLICY is a policy of marine insurance in which the risk is limited, not to a given voyage, but to a certain fixed term or period of time. In such policies the risk insured is entirely independent of the voyage of the ship. *Arnould, Mar. Ins.* [MIXED POLICY; VOYAGE POLICY; WARRANTY.]

TIME THE ESSENCE OF THE CONTRACT. Where a contract specifies a time for its completion, or something to be done towards it, then, if time be of the essence of the contract, the nonperformance by either party of the act in question by the time so specified will entitle the opposite party to regard the contract as broken. Whether time be or be not of the essence of the contract must, in the absence of express words, be gathered from the general character of the contract and the surrounding circumstances. By the Judicature Act, 1873, s. 25, sub-s. 7, stipulations as to time or otherwise are henceforth to receive, in all courts, the same construction as they would hitherto have received in courts of equity.

TIPSTAFF. An officer who attends the courts, his duty being to take charge of prisoners committed by the court.

TITHE RENT-CHARGE is a rent-charge established in lieu of tithes under the Tithe Commutation Act, 1836 (6 & 7 Will. 4, c. 71). Under the Tithe Act of 1891 it is payable by the land owner to the tithe owner. [RENT; TITHES.]

TITHES. The tenth part of the fruits, prædial, personal and mixed, due to the ministers of the Church for their maintenance. *Cowel.* Tithes arise from the profits and stock of lands, or from the personal industry of the inhabitants of a parish. The former class are either *prædial*, among which are tithes of corn, grass, hops and wood; or *mixed*, as of wool, milk, pigs, etc.; the latter *personal*, as of occupations, trades, fisheries and the like. Of *prædial* and *mixed* tithes the tenth must be paid in gross; but of *personal* tithes only the tenth part of the clear profits is due; nor are tithes of this latter kind generally due at all, except so far as the particular custom of the place may authorise the claim. Hence it may be inferred, that whatever is of the substance of the earth, as stone, lime, chalk and the like, is not in its nature titheable; nor, except by force of special custom, is tithe demand-able in respect to animals which are *feræ naturæ*. [FERÆ NATURÆ.]

Tithes are also divided into *great* and *small* tithes. *Small* tithes include tithes mixed and personal, whereas tithes of corn, hay and wood are generally comprised under *great* tithes; but no clear line of demarcation seems to have been drawn between them.

All tithes *primâ facie* by presumption of law belong to the *rector;* but any part of the tithes may be shown, by evidence, to belong to the *vicar.* [RECTOR; VICAR.] Such evidence may consist either of a deed of endowment, vesting certain tithes in the vicar, or of such proof of long usage as is sufficient to raise a presumption that an endowment of that description, though now lost, was anciently made. Not unfrequently an endowment vests all the *small* tithes in the vicar. *T. L.; Cowel; 1 Bl.; 2 Bl.; 2 Steph. Com.* [MODUS DECIMANDI.]

Almost all the tithes of England and Wales are now commuted into rent-charges under the Tithe Commutation Act (6 & 7 Will. 4, c. 71) and the various statutes since passed for its amendment. *2 Steph. Com.* [TITHE RENT-CHARGE.]

TITHING (Lat. *Decuria*). The number or company of ten men with their families knit together in a society, all being bound to the king for the peaceable behaviour of each other. Of these companies, there was one chief or principal person called teothing-man or tithing-man, who was in fact a constable. *1 Steph. Com.* [DECENNARY.]

TITHING-MAN. A constable or head of a tithing. *2 Steph. Com.* [TITHING.]

TITLE. 1. A title of honour; which is an addition to a person's name, implying that he has some honour, office, or dignity. *1 Steph. Com.; 2 Steph. Com.; Wms. R. P.*

2. A title to orders; which is a certificate of preferment or provision required by the 33rd Canon, in order that a person may be admitted into holy orders; unless he be a fellow or chaplain in Oxford or Cambridge, or master of arts of five years' standing in either of the universities, and living there at his sole charges; or unless the bishop himself intends shortly to admit him to some benefice or curacy. *2 Steph. Com.*

3. *Title to Lands or Goods.* This signifies either (1) a party's right to

TITLE—*continued*.

the enjoyment thereof ; *or* the means whereby such right has accrued, and by which it is evidenced ; or, as it is defined by Blackstone, the means whereby an owner hath the just possession of his property.

When we speak of a man having a *good title* to his property we mean that the evidence of his right is cogent and conclusive, or nearly so ; and when we speak of a *bad title* we mean that the evidence is weak and insufficient. A forty years' title is now in general sufficient in the case of sale of lands, under the Vendor and Purchaser Act, 1874 (37 & 38 Vict. c. 78). [DOCUMENT OF TITLE OF GOODS ; DOCUMENT OF TITLE TO LANDS ; LAND TRANSFER ACTS.]

4. The title of an Act of parliament is its heading, and sometimes it has also a "short title," more condensed than the heading, mentioned in the body of the Act as the name by which it is to be known.

5. The title of an affidavit consists of two parts : (1) the style of the court (or division of the High Court of Justice) in which the affidavit is to be used, and (2) the names of the parties to the action or other proceeding.

TITLE, COVENANTS FOR. On dispositions of real estate the transferee is entitled to covenants for title. These were formerly express and varied according to the nature of the disposition, *e.g.*, a vendor gave *limited* covenants extending to all acts done by him or any one through whom he derives title otherwise than by purchase for value ; a mortgagor gave *absolute* covenants, not confined to the above acts. They are now implied by the use of the proper words, *e.g.*, beneficial owner, trustee, etc. See *s.* 7 of *Conveyancing Act*, 1881, and see *Land Transfer Acts*, 1875 *and* 1897, and rules thereunder.

TITLE DEEDS. Deeds evidencing a person's right or title to lands, otherwise called *muniments of title*.

The possession of the title deeds is of importance, as the land cannot be sold without them. Thus, what is called an "equitable mortgage" is generally effected by a deposit of title deeds. Moreover, any mortgagee who negligently allows his mortgagor to retain the title deeds, and to raise money on a

second mortgage of the land by fraudulently concealing the first mortgage, will have his security postponed to that of the second mortgagee. 2 *Steph. Com.*

TOFT. A messuage or house, or rather a place where a messuage hath stood and is not rebuilt. *T. L. ; Cowel.*

TOLL. 1. A liberty to buy and sell within the precincts of a manor.

2. A tribute or custom paid for passage.

3. A liberty to take, or to be free from such tribute. See also the following titles ; and, for the verb *to toll*, see TOLLED.

TOLL THOROUGH. Money paid for the passage of man or beast in or through highways, or over ferries, bridges, etc. 3 *Steph. Com.*

TOLL TRAVERSE. A toll paid for passing over a private person's ground. It is thus opposed to *toll thorough*, which is paid for passing over a public highway. 3 *Steph. Com.*

TOLLED. To *toll* is to take away ; thus, when a man's right of entry upon lands was barred or taken away by lapse of time, or otherwise, it was said to be *tolled*. 3 *Steph. Com.*

TONNAGE. 1. A custom or impost paid to the king for merchandise carried out or brought in in ships, at a certain rate for every ton. It was at first granted for the defence of the realm, the safeguard of the seas, and the safe passage of merchandise. 2 *Steph. Com.*

2. The number of tons burden that a ship will carry.

TONTINE is a species of loan in which the parties who invest receive life annuities, with benefit of survivorship ; so called from Lorenzo Tonti, a Neapolitan, who lived in the 17th century. The nature of the plan is this : An annuity, after a certain rate of interest, is granted to a number of people, divided into classes according to their respective ages ; so that the whole annual fund of each class is regularly divided among the survivors of that class ; and, on the death of the last survivor, reverts to the power by which the tontine was erected. This mode of raising money has been at times used in this country. See 29 *Geo.* 3, *c.* 41 ; 30 *Geo.* 3, *c.* 45.

TOOLS are those implements which are commonly used by the hand of man in some labour necessary for his subsistence. The tools of a person's trade are, by the Bankruptcy Act, 1883, excepted from the general property which on his bankruptcy passes to his creditors.

TORT. A wrong; so called because it is wrested (*tortum*), wrung, or crooked. The word "tort" is especially used to signify a civil wrong independent of contract; that is to say, an actionable wrong not consisting in a breach of contract. An action for such a wrong is called an *action of tort*. Of this class are actions of libel, assault, trespass, etc. 3 *Steph. Com.* [WRONG.]

TORT FEASOR. A wrong-doer, a trespasser.

TORTIOUS. Wrongful. [See next title.]

TORTIOUS OPERATION OF A FEOFFMENT. When a *tenant for life* made a feoffment in fee of the lands of which he was tenant for life, a freehold of inheritance passed to the feoffee, but a freehold *by wrong*, thus divesting the person in reversion or remainder of his *estate*, and leaving him a *right of entry*, of which he might avail himself *at once*.

But feoffments by *tenants in tail* (or *discontinuances*, as they were called) operated to take away not merely the *estate* of the party entitled in remainder, but also his *right of entry without action*; so that he was driven to his action to recover his estate when the time came. This effect of a discontinuance was abolished in 1833 by stat. 3 & 4 Will. 4, c. 27, s. 39; and such meaning as was left in the doctrine of the tortious operation of a feoffment was abolished in 1845 by s. 4 of the Act to amend the Law of Real Property (8 & 9 Vict. c. 106). 1 *Steph. Com.*; *Wms. R. P.* [DISCONTINUANCE OF AN ESTATE; ESTATE; FEOFFMENT.]

TORTURE. A cruel and wanton infliction of pain on any living being.

The word is used especially in our law books of the rack or question which was sometimes applied to extort confessions from criminals. 4 *Steph. Com.* [RACK.]

TOTAL LOSS is the entire loss of an insured vessel, or of goods insured, so as to render the underwriters liable to the owner. [UNDERWRITER.]

Total loss is either *actual* or *constructive*; actual, when the thing is actually destroyed, or so damaged that it cannot ever arrive in specie at the port of destination; constructive, when the injury, though short of actual loss, is yet so great as to make the subject of it useless to its owner.

When the subject of the insurance, though not wholly destroyed, is placed in such peril as to render the successful prosecution of the venture improbable, the insured may treat the case as a total loss, and demand the full sum insured. In such case, however, he must, within a reasonable time, give notice to the insurer of his intention, and of his abandonment to the insurer of all right in the thing insured. 2 *Steph. Com.*; *Arnould, Marine Ins.* [ABANDONMENT.]

TOTIDEM VERBIS (in so many words).

TOTIES QUOTIES (as often as occasion shall require).

TOURN. [SHERIFF'S TOURN.]

TOUT TEMPS PRIST. *Always ready*; a plea, by way of defence to an action, brought by a plaintiff whose claim has never been disputed, to the effect that the defendant is, and always has been, ready to satisfy the plaintiff's demand. 3 *Steph. Com.*

TOWAGE. Money paid for towing a ship.

TOWN CLERK. A person (usually a solicitor) appointed by the council of a municipal borough to manage their legal affairs. See *Municipal Corporations Act*, 1882, *s.* 17. 3 *Steph. Com.*

TOWN COUNCIL. [MUNICIPAL CORPORATION.]

TRADE FIXTURES, in a house, or other premises occupied for the purposes of business, include machinery and utensils of a chattel nature, such as salt-pans, vats, etc., for soap-boiling; engines for working collieries; also buildings of a temporary description erected by the tenant for the purpose of carrying on his business. *Fawcett, L. & T.*; 2 *Steph. Com.*; 3 *Steph. Com.*

TRADE MARK. A mark, signature or device affixed to an article to show that it is manufactured, etc., by some particular person or firm. As to registration, see 46 & 47 Vict. c. 57. See also Merchandise Marks Acts.

TRADE UNION ACT, 1871, is the stat. 34 & 35 Vict. c. 31, passed for the purpose of giving legal recognition to trades unions. By s. 2 it is provided that the members of a trade union shall not be prosecuted for conspiracy merely by reason that the rules of such union are in restraint of trade ; and by s. 3 that the agreements of trades unions shall not on that account be void or voidable. Provisions are also made with reference to the registration and registered offices of trades unions, and other purposes connected therewith, and the Trade Union Amendment Act, 1876, provides for the registration of unions by the Registrar of Friendly Societies, and unions so registered enjoy certain privileges of friendly societies. 3 *Steph. Com.* ; 4 *Steph. Com.* [CONSPIRACY.]

TRADER. One engaged in merchandise or commerce. Formerly there was a distinction between traders and non-traders under the bankruptcy laws, but the Bankruptcy Act, 1883, did away with this distinction. As to who were traders within the meaning of the Bankruptcy Act, 1869, see schedule 1 of that Act. 2 *Steph. Com.* [BANKRUPT.]

TRANSFER OF CAUSE is the removal of a cause from one court or judge to another by lawful authority. See *R. S. C.* 1883, *Ord. XLIX.*

In certain cases, also, under the County Courts Acts, and the Judicature Acts, an action may be ordered to be transferred to the county court, or from an inferior court to the High Court. 3 *Steph. Com.*

TRANSFER OF LAND ACTS. [LAND TRANSFER ACTS.]

TRANSIRE. A warrant from the custom-house to let goods pass.

TRANSITORY ACTION. An action, the venue of which could be laid in any county as opposed to local actions. Formerly, transitory actions might be tried anywhere, but in local actions, the venue must have been laid, and the trial had, in the county where the trespass or other cause of action took place. Now, by the Judicature Act, 1875, there is no local venue for the trial of any action. 3 *Steph. Com.* [VENUE.]

TRANSITU (STOPPAGE IN). [STOPPAGE IN TRANSITU.]

TRANSLATION. 1. A version of a book or publication out of one language into another. Where the laws of copyright require a *translation* to be made of a foreign work for which copyright is claimed, this requirement is not satisfied by mere *adaptation*. 2 *Steph. Com.*
2. The removal of a bishop from one diocese to another.

TRANSPORTATION is the banishing or sending away a person convicted of crime, either pursuant to the express terms of a judicial sentence, or as a condition of pardon by the Crown, to some place out of the United Kingdom, there to remain during the term for which he is ordered to be transported.

Transportation is now superseded by penal servitude, under stat. 16 & 17 Vict. c. 99, and several amending Acts. See 4 *Steph. Com.* [PENAL SERVITUDE.]

TRAVERSE is a denial, in pleading, of facts alleged on the other side. 3 *Steph. Com.* See also the following titles.

TRAVERSE OF AN INDICTMENT. 1. The denial of an indictment by plea of not guilty.
2. The postponement of the trial of an indictment after a plea of not guilty thereto. This was formerly customary in indictments for misdemeanors, but is now prohibited by stat. 14 & 15 Vict. c. 100, s. 27. 4 *Steph. Com.*

TRAVERSE OF AN OFFICE is the challenging, by a subject, of an inquest of office, as being defective and untruly made. [INQUEST ; OFFICE FOUND.]

TRAVERSE TOLL. [TOLL TRAVERSE.]

TRAVERSING NOTE. A note filed by a plaintiff in Chancery on behalf of a defendant who had refused or neglected to answer interrogatories, the effect of which was to deny the statements of the bill, and to put the plaintiff upon proof of the whole. *Dan. Ch. Pr.*

The traversing note was not expressly abolished under the Judicature Acts, but the provisions contained in R. S. C., in reference to default in pleading render it unnecessary.

TREASON. A betraying, treachery, or breach of faith, especially against the sovereign or liege lord. Treason against the sovereign has always been regarded as *high* treason, in contradistinction to certain offences against private superiors, which were formerly ranked as *petty* treason. [PETIT TREASON.]

Treason is defined by the Statute of Treasons (25 Edw. 3, stat. 5, c. 2) (passed in 1350), as consisting in one or other of the following acts:—

1. When a man doth compass or imagine the death of our lord the king, of our lady his queen, or of their eldest son and heir. These words include a queen regnant.

2. If a man do violate the king's companion, or the king's eldest daughter unmarried, or the wife of the king's eldest son and heir.

3. If a man do levy war against our lord the king in his realm.

4. If a man be adherent to the king's enemies in his realm, giving to them aid and comfort in the realm, or elsewhere.

5. If a man counterfeit the king's great or privy seal.

6. If a man counterfeit the king's money; and if a man bring false money into the realm counterfeit to the money of England, knowing the money to be false, to merchandise and make payment withal.

7. If a man slay the chancellor, treasurer, or the king's justices of the one bench or the other, justices in eyre, or justices of assize, and all other justices assigned to hear and determine, being in their places doing their offices.

Of the above branches, Nos. 5 and 6 are no longer treason; counterfeiting the great or privy seal being an ordinary felony under 24 & 25 Vict. c. 98, relating to forgery; and No. 6 being the offence of coining, which now, under 24 & 25 Vict. c. 99, is also felony. And the protection afforded by the provision relative to the slaying of the judges is extended to the Lords of Session and the Lords of Justiciary in Scotland by 7 Anne, c. 21.

It is now sufficient to speak of high treason as treason simply, seeing that petty treason, as a distinct offence, has been abolished, and many acts which are treason under the above statute are also treason-felonies under 11 & 12 Vict. c. 12, and now prosecuted thereunder.

Men convicted of high treason were formerly sentenced to be drawn on a hurdle to the place of execution, and to be there hanged and disembowelled alive, and then beheaded and quartered. Women, for all kinds of treason, were sentenced to be burned alive.

By 30 Geo. 3, c. 48, hanging was substituted for burning in the case of women convicted of high or petty treason; and by 54 Geo. 3, c. 146, men convicted of treason were to be drawn to the place of execution, and hanged till dead, and then beheaded and quartered. And now by 33 & 34 Vict. c. 23, s. 31, the punishment of treason is reduced to hanging. Forfeiture and attainder for treason was also abolished by this Act. 4 *Steph. Com.* [See next title.]

TREASON FELONY, under statute 11 & 12 Vict. c. 12, is the offence of compassing, devising, etc. to depose his Majesty from the Crown; or to levy war in order to intimidate either house of parliament, etc.; or to stir up foreigners by any printing or writing to invade the kingdom. This offence is punishable with penal servitude for life, or for any term not less than three years, or with not more than two years imprisonment with or without hard labour. 4 *Steph. Com.* By the above statute the Government is enabled to treat as felony many offences which must formerly have been treated as high treason.

TREASURE TROVE (Lat. *Thesaurus inventus*) consists of money, coin, gold, silver, plate or bullion found hidden in the earth or other private place, the owner thereof being unknown. In such case the treasure belongs to the Crown, and any person concealing the same from the Crown is liable to fine and imprisonment. 2 *Steph. Com.*; 4 *Steph. Com.*; *Oke's Mag. Syn.*

TREASURER. [LORD |TREASURER; TREASURY.]

TREASURER'S REMEMBRANCER. [REMEMBRANCERS.]

TREASURY. The Lords Commissioners of the Treasury, being the department of State under whose control the royal revenue is administered. [LORD TREASURER.]

TREATING, providing food, drink, or entertainment before, during, or after an election, for corruptly influencing votes renders the person providing it liable to penalties, and a voter corruptly receiving it incapable of voting, and renders his vote void ; it also may invalidate the election on petition. See *Corrupt Practices Acts*, 1854, 1883 *and* 1884. *2 Steph. Com.*

TREATY. 1. A negotiation.

2. A compact between nations.

TREBUCKET. The cucking-stool or ducking-stool for scolds. 4 *Steph. Com.* [SCOLD.]

TRESPASS (Lat. *Transgressio*). 1. Any transgression or offence against the law.

2. Any misfeasance or act of one man whereby another is injuriously treated or damnified.

3. The action brought for injury done to person or property with violence. This action, when brought for an unwarrantable entry upon land of the plaintiff, was called trespass *quare clausum fregit*. [CLOSE ; QUARE CLAUSUM FREGIT.]

4. *Trespass on the case.* This is a form of action for some unlawful act, negligence or omission, whereby damage has resulted to the plaintiff. 3 *Steph. Com.* [ACTION ON THE CASE.]

TRIAL. The examination of a cause civil or criminal, before a judge who has jurisdiction over it, according to the laws of the land. 3 *Steph. Com.; 4 Steph. Com.*

The rules with regard to trials in the High Court are to be found in R. S. C. 1883, Ord. XXXVI. Actions may be tried and heard in one of the following ways :—(1) Before a judge or judges ; (2) before a judge sitting with assessors ; (3) before a judge and jury ; (4) before an official or special referee, with or without assessors. Either party, however, is entitled to insist that the action be tried before a judge and jury.

In criminal informations in the Court of King's Bench, and in indictments, wherever preferred, the trial (unless the party plead guilty) must take place before a judge or judges (or other presiding magistrate), and a jury. But minor offences against the laws are in general dealt with summarily before magistrates.

TRIAL AT BAR. [BAR, 6.]

TRIAL BY CERTIFICATE. [CERTIFICATE, TRIAL BY.]

TRIAL BY RECORD. [RECORD, TRIAL BY.]

TRINA ADMONITIO. Threefold warning. [PEINE FORTE ET DURE.]

TRINITY HOUSE. A company of masters of ships incorporated in the reign of Henry VIII., and charged by many successive Acts of parliament with numerous duties relating to the marine, especially the appointment and licensing of pilots, and the superintendence of light-houses, buoys and beacons. See 2 *Steph. Com.; 3 Steph. Com.*

Trinity House is a self-elected body, and is composed of *elder brethren* and *younger brethren.* The elder brethren manage the affairs of the society, being for the most part elected from the younger brethren.

TRINITY TERM. [SITTINGS.]

TRINODA NECESSITAS was the threefold obligation to which every man's estate was by the ancient law subject, *pontium reparatio, arcium constructio, et expeditio contra hostem;* that is, repairing bridges, building castles, and repelling invasions. 1 *Steph. Com.; 2 Steph. Com.; 3 Steph. Com.*

TRIORS, TRIOURS or **TRIERS.** 1. The lords selected to try a peer, when indicted for felony, in the Court of the Lord High Steward. [HIGH STEWARD.]

2. Two indifferent persons named by the court to try the reasonableness of an objection taken by a party to a juror on the ground of some alleged probable circumstances of suspicion, as acquaintance and the like ; or to the whole panel of jurors, on account of a like objection to the sheriff. 3 *Steph. Com.* [CHALLENGE ; FAVOUR, CHALLENGE TO.]

TRIPARTITE. Divided into three parts, having three corresponding copies ; a deed to which there are three distinct parties.

TRITHING, TRIDING or **TRIHING.** In ancient times, when a county was divided into three jurisdictions, each of them was anciently called a trithing, triding or trihing. These divisions still subsist in the large county of York, where by an easy corruption they are denominated *ridings*. 1 *Steph. Com.*

TROVER (from Fr. *Trouver*, to find) was one of the forms of action at law, being originally a kind of action of trespass on the case, based on the finding by defendant of the plaintiff's goods, and converting them to his own use. But in time the suggestion of the finding became mere matter of form, and all that it became necessary to prove was that the goods were the plaintiff's, and that the defendant converted them to his own use. In this action the plaintiff cannot recover the specific chattel, but only damages for its conversion. The fictitious suggestion of the "finding" was abolished by the Common Law Procedure Act, 1852, by which a simple form of declaration was introduced for such cases. 3 *Steph. Com.* [DETINUE; CONVERSION.]

TRUCK SYSTEM. A name given to the practice of paying the wages of workmen in goods instead of money. The plan has been for the masters to establish warehouses or shops, and the workmen in their employment have either (1) got their wages accounted for to them by supplies of goods from such depôts, without receiving any money, or (2) they have got the money, with a tacit or express understanding that they were to resort to the warehouses or shops of their masters for such articles as they were furnished with.

This system of dealing being considered open to grave abuses, was abolished in 1831 by stat. 1 & 2 Will. 4, c. 37, commonly called the Truck Act. By ss. 1 and 2, contracts for the hiring of artificers in certain trades (enumerated in s. 19) are to be made in the current coin of the realm, and without any stipulations as to the manner in which the wages shall be expended; otherwise they are declared to be illegal and void; and, by s. 10, any employer entering into such a contract, or making any illegal payment, is liable to be fined as therein mentioned. See also 50 & 51 Vict. c. 46, and 59 & 60 Vict. c. 43.

TRUE BILL. [BILL, 3.]

TRUST. 1. A confidence reposed by one person in conveying or bequeathing property to another, that the latter will apply it to a purpose or purposes desired by the former. These purposes are generally indicated in the instrument, whether deed or will, by which the disposition is made.

2. Hence it signifies the beneficial interest created by such a transaction. In this sense it may be defined as a beneficial interest in, or ownership of, real or personal property, unattended with the legal or possessory ownership thereof. 1 *Steph. Com.* [USE; USES, STATUTE OF.]

For the various kinds of trusts, see under their respective titles. See also the following titles.

TRUSTEE. A person to whom an estate is conveyed, devised, or bequeathed, in trust for another, called the *cestui que trust.*

TRUSTEE ACTS. The stats. 13 & 14 Vict. c. 60, and 15 & 16 Vict. c. 55, enabled the Court of Chancery to appoint new trustees in lieu of any who, on account of death, lunacy, absence, or otherwise were unable or unwilling to act as such; and also to make vesting orders by which legal estates and rights might be transferred from the old trustee or trustees to the new trustee or trustees so appointed. Repealed and re-enacted by the Trustee Act, 1893 (56 & 57 Vict. c. 53). 1 *Steph. Com.*; *Wms. R. P.*

TRUSTEE RELIEF ACTS. The stat. 10 & 11 Vict. c. 96, and stat. 12 & 13 Vict. c. 74, by which a trustee was enabled to pay money into court [PAYMENT OF MONEY INTO COURT] in cases where a difficulty arises respecting the title to the trust fund. Repealed and re-enacted by the Trustee Act, 1893 (56 & 57 Vict. c. 53). A trustee wishing to avail himself of these Acts must file an affidavit stating shortly the circumstances under which the difficulty has arisen, and the exact sum for which he acknowledges himself to be accountable, and the Paymaster-General will then direct the payment thereof into court. See also the Judicial Trustees Act, 1896 (59 & 60 Vict. c. 35), s. 3.

TRUSTS. [TRUST; TRUSTEE.]

TUMULTUOUS PETITIONING is a misdemeanor under 13 Car. 2, st. 1, c. 5, by which it is enacted that not more than twenty names shall be signed to any petition to the Crown or either house of parliament for the alteration of matters established by law in Church or State, unless the contents thereof be previously approved, in the country, by three justices, or the majority of the grand jury at assizes or quarter sessions; and in London, by the lord mayor, aldermen, and common council; and that no petition be delivered by a

TUMULTUOUS PETITIONING—*contd.* company of more than ten persons ; on pain, in either case, of incurring a penalty not exceeding 100*l.* and three months' imprisonment. 4 *Steph. Com.*

TUNNAGE. [TONNAGE.]

TURBARY (Lat. *Turbagium*). The right to dig turf on another man's ground. And *common of turbary* is a liberty which some tenants have by prescription to dig on the lord's waste. 1 *Steph. Com.*; *Wms. R. P.* [COMMON.]

TURPIS CAUSA. An illegal or immoral consideration by which a contract is vitiated.

TYTHES. [TITHES.]

TYTHING. [TITHING.]

UBERRIMA FIDES. The most perfect frankness. This is essential to the validity of certain contracts between persons bearing a particular relationship to one another, *e.g.*, guardian and ward, solicitor and client, insurer and insured.

UBI JUS, IBI REMEDIUM (where there is a right, there is a remedy).

ULPIAN. Domitius Ulpianus was one of the five great Roman jurists, upon whose writings the compilations of Justinian are mainly founded. The greater part of his works were written in the reign of Caracalla. On the accession of Alexander Severus, in A.D. 222, he became the emperor's chief adviser.

ULTIMATUM. A final proposal in a negotiation in which it is intimated that, in case of its rejection, the negotiation must be broken off.

ULTRA VIRES. Beyond their powers ; a phrase applied especially to directors of companies exceeding their legal powers under the articles of association or the Acts of parliament by which they are governed ; though it is equally applicable to excess of authority of any kind.

UMPIRE. 1. An arbitrator. [ARBITRATION.]

2. Especially, a referee called in to decide between the judgment of two arbitrators who cannot agree. See the *Arbitration Act*, 1889. 3 *Steph. Com.* [ARBITRATION.]

UNCERTAINTY is where a deed or will is so obscure and confused that the judges can make nothing of it, which sometimes occurs in wills made by testators without legal advice. Any disposition or conveyance to which it is impossible to affix a meaning is said to be *void for uncertainty* ; but the judges will use every effort to affix a meaning to the language used where it is possible to do so.

UNCONSCIONABLE BARGAIN. A bargain so one-sided and inequitable in its terms as to raise a presumption of fraud and oppression. [USURY, 2.]

UNCORE PRIST (*Encore prêt*). Still ready. [TOUT TEMPS PRIST.]

UNDE NIHIL HABET. [DOTE UNDE NIHIL HABET.]

UNDEFENDED. 1. When a person sued in a civil cause or accused of a crime has no counsel to speak for him on his trial, and has to make his defence himself, he is sometimes said to be *undefended*, that is, undefended by counsel.

2. An undefended cause is one in which a defendant makes default (1) in not putting in an appearance to the plaintiff's action ; (2) in not putting in his statement of defence ; (3) in not appearing at the trial, either personally or by counsel, after having received due notice of trial. *R. S. C.* 1883, *Ords. XIII., XXVII., and XXXVI., rr.* 31—33.

UNDERLEASE. A lease by a lessee for years, for a period less than the residue of the term, as opposed to an *assignment* by which the entire residue is conveyed. A lessee who grants a sublease or underlease still remains liable on the covenants to the lessor, but the sub-lessee is not liable to the original lessor, whereas an *assignee* is so liable. *Fawcett, L. & T.* ; 1 *Steph. Com.*

UNDER-SHERIFF is an officer who acts directly under the sheriff, and performs all the duties of the sheriff's office ; a few only excepted where the personal presence of the high-sheriff is necessary. The sheriff is civilly responsible for the acts or omissions of his under-sheriff. 2 *Steph. Com.*

UNDERTAKING. A promise; especially one given in the course of legal proceedings, which may be enforced by attachment and otherwise. By R. S. C. 1883, Ord. IX. r. 1, a solicitor may give an undertaking to appear on behalf of a defendant, and in this case personal service of the writ on the defendant is not required. A solicitor not appearing according to his undertaking is by Ord. XII. r. 18, liable to attachment.

UNDERWRITER is a person who *underwrites* or subscribes his name to a policy of insurance, thereby undertaking to indemnify the assured against the losses referred to in the policy, to the extent therein mentioned. The word is used especially with reference to *marine insurance.* 2 *Steph. Com.; Crump's Mar. Ins.* [INSURANCE; LLOYD'S.]

UNDUE INFLUENCE. Any improper pressure put upon a person to induce him to confer a benefit upon the party pressing. A gift or will may be set aside by the courts where such pressure has been exercised. In elections undue influence to induce persons to vote or refrain from voting by violence, restraint, threats, etc., renders the person using it guilty of a misdemeanor, and, if by a candidate, disqualifies him from sitting in that parliament for that constituency. 17 & 18 *Vict. c.* 102; 46 & 47 *Vict. c.* 51, *ss.* 2, 3; 2 *Steph. Com.* [CORRUPT PRACTICES.]

UNIFORMITY, ACT OF. [ACT OF UNIFORMITY.]

UNILATERAL. One-sided; a word used especially of a bond or contract by which one party only is bound.

UNION. The consolidation of two or more parishes into one. This may be done :—
1. For the better administration of the poor laws. Under Gilbert's Act (22 Geo. 3, c. 83) and the Poor Law Amendment Act, 1834 (4 & 5 Will. 4, c. 76), the Local Government Board has power at its discretion to consolidate any two or more parishes into one union under the government of a single board of guardians, to be elected by the owners and ratepayers of the component parishes. And each of such unions is to have a common workhouse, provided and maintained at the common expense. 3 *Steph. Com.* Such workhouse is frequently called "the union workhouse," or, more briefly, the union."
2. For ecclesiastical purposes, under the Acts for the Union of Benefices.

UNITY OF POSSESSION signifies :—
1. The joint possession by one person of two rights by several titles.
2. The holding of the same estate in undivided shares by two or more. [COMMON, TENANCY IN; COPARCENARY; JOINT TENANCY.]

UNIVERSAL AGENT is defined by Story to be a person appointed to do all the acts which the principal may lawfully do, and which he may lawfully delegate to another the power to do. *Story on Agency.*

UNIVERSITY COURTS are courts established in the Universities of Oxford and Cambridge, by ancient charters, confirmed in 1571 by stat. 13 Eliz. c. 29.
The courts in each university are :—
1. The chancellor's court, having jurisdiction in personal actions affecting members of the university, and in cases of misdemeanors and minor offences committed by them.
2. The court of the lord high steward, having jurisdiction in cases of treason, felony, and mayhem, when committed by a member of the university.
3 *Steph. Com.;* 4 *Steph. Com.* [CHANCELLOR, 4; HIGH STEWARD, 3.]

UNLAWFUL ASSEMBLY. A meeting of three or more persons to do an unlawful act or under such circumstances as to cause fear among reasonable persons.

UNLIMITED COMPANY. A joint-stock company, the liability of whose members is unlimited. 3 *Steph. Com.* [LIMITED COMPANY.]

UNLIQUIDATED DAMAGES. Damages the amount of which in money is not settled, as in cases of libel, slander, assault, etc. See 3 *Steph. Com.* [LIQUIDATED DAMAGES.]

UNWRITTEN LAW. [LEX NON SCRIPTA.]

UPPER BENCH was the name, during the protectorate of Oliver Cromwell, of the Court of King's Bench. [COURT OF KING'S BENCH.]

URBAN SANITARY AUTHORITY. By the Public Health Act, 1875 (38 & 39 Vict. c. 55), the whole of England and Wales, except the metropolis, is divided into *urban sanitary districts* and *rural sanitary districts ;* such districts to be subject for the purposes of the Act to bodies called *urban sanitary authorities* and *rural sanitary authorities* respectively. The urban sanitary authorities are now the city or borough councils or urban district councils, and the rural sanitary authorities are the rural district councils. The duties of such sanitary authorities include the management of highways, control of sewers, suppression of nuisances, the paving and lighting of streets, etc. See also the Public Health (London) Act, 1891. 3 *Steph. Com.* [PUBLIC HEALTH ACTS.]

URBAN SERVITUDES are city servitudes, or servitudes of houses ; that is to say, easements appertaining to the building and construction of houses ; as, for instance, the right to light and air, or the right to build a house so as to throw the rain-water on a neighbour's house. [EASEMENT ; SERVITUDE.]

USAGE. Practice long continued. It must always be proved, thus differing from custom, which is in some cases judicially noticed. [CUSTOM.]

USANCE, in reference to foreign bills of exchange, is the common period, fixed by the usage or habit of dealing between the country where the bill is drawn, and that where it is payable, for the payment of bills.

USE. 1. A *use*, before the Statute of Uses (27 Hen. 8, c. 10), consisted in the equitable right to receive the profit or benefit of lands and tenements, which was, in cases of lands conveyed to uses, divorced from the legal ownership thereof. The object of such conveyances was principally to evade the Statutes of Mortmain, by which lands were prohibited from being given directly to religious houses. The ecclesiastics obtained grants to persons *to the use* of religious houses, which the clerical chancellors of those days declared to be binding. Another supposed advantage of uses was that they could be dealt with and disposed of without the formalities required for the transfer of the legal estates. 1 *Steph. Com.; Wms. R. P.*

2. Since the Statute of Uses, the *use* of the land involves the *legal* ownership, for by that statute it is provided, that where any person or persons shall stand seised of any lands or other hereditaments to the use, confidence or trust of any other person or persons, the persons that have any such use, confidence or trust shall be deemed in lawful seisin and possession of the same lands and hereditaments for such estates as they have in the use, trust or confidence. 1 *Steph. Com. ; Wms. R. P.* [USES, STATUTE OF.]

3. If, since the Statute of Uses, land should be conveyed to A. to the use of B. to the use of C., B. would have the legal estate, the use to C. being *a use upon a use*, which the courts of law refused to recognise. But C. would, nevertheless, be recognised in a court of equity as the party entitled. Practically, however, the relation between B. and C. would be expressed by the word *trust* and not by the word *use*.

4. We also often speak of a copyhold being surrendered *to the use* of A. B. It must not, however, be supposed that the Statute of Uses applies to copyholds, though a court of common law will compel the admission of the surrenderee in accordance with the custom of the manor. 1 *Steph. Com. ; Wms. R. P.* [COPYHOLD ; SURRENDER.]

USE AND OCCUPATION. An action for use and occupation is an action brought by a landlord against a tenant for the profits of land. This action is allowed by stat. 11 Geo. 2, c. 19, s. 14, where there has been no demise by deed. It is also maintainable against a tenant holding over after a lease by deed has expired, in respect of such holding over. The measure of damages recoverable in this action is the rent, where a rent has been agreed upon ; and where no rent has been agreed upon, then such sum as the jury may find the occupation to be worth. *Fawcett, L. & T.*

USER. The enjoyment of property.

USES, STATUTES OF, is the stat. 27 Hen. 8, c. 10, passed in 1536.
This celebrated statute may be considered in its effect upon (1) conveyances to uses ; (2) jointures ; (3) wills :—
Conveyances to Uses.—By s. 1 it is provided, that where any person or persons shall be seised of and in any honours, castles, manors, lands, etc., to the use, confidence or trust of any other person or persons, or of any body politic, by reason of any bargain, sale,

USES, STATUTES OF—*continued.*
feoffment, fine, agreement, will or otherwise ; then all such person and persons, etc., that hereafter shall have any use, confidence or trust, etc., shall henceforth stand and be seised, and be deemed and adjudged in lawful seisin, estate and possession of and in the same honours, castles, manors, lands, etc. [USE.]

Jointures.—By s. 6 a married woman, upon whom a jointure (called in the Act "jointer") is settled, is not to be entitled to dower. [DOWER, 2 ; JOINTURE.] But by s. 9 it is provided that if the jointure be settled upon her *after* marriage (otherwise than by Act of parliament), then the wife, surviving her husband, may refuse the jointure, and elect to have her dower instead.

Wills.—The power of devising lands by will was held to be indirectly abolished by the Statute of Uses, but it was shortly afterwards restored. [WILL, 1 ; WILLS ACT.]

USES, SUPERSTITIOUS. [SUPERSTITIOUS USES.]

USES TO BAR DOWER. A form of conveyance of land to a man married before the Dower Act came into operation so as to prevent the wife's right to dower attaching, he taking only a life estate and a power of appointment. Now obsolete.

USHER. A door-keeper of a court.

USQUE AD FILUM AQUÆ, or more fully, "usque ad medium filum aquæ" (up to the middle thread of the water), is a phrase used to express half the land covered by a stream ; which, in the case of a stream not navigable, belongs to the proprietor of the adjoining bank. 1 *Steph. Com.*

USUCAPION, or **USUCAPTION.** The enjoying a thing by long continuance of time or title by prescription. [PRESCRIPTION.]

USUFRUCT, in the Roman law, was a temporary right of using a thing without having the full dominion over the substance. 1 *Steph. Com.* But in practice a usufruct was generally understood to signify a right of enjoyment of anything for the life of the usufructuary, *i.e.* of the party entitled to the usufruct. And the word is so understood in the law of Scotland.

USURA MARITIMA. Maritime usury ; that is, the loan of money on the hazard of a voyage ; otherwise called *fœnus nauticum.* 2 *Steph. Com.* [BOTTOMRY ; FŒNUS NAUTICUM.]

USURPATION. The using that which is not one's own. It is a word used especially in the common law to signify the *usurpation of an advowson* ; that is, when a stranger, who is not the patron, presents a clergyman to the living, and the clergyman so presented is thereupon admitted and instituted. 3 *Steph. Com.*

So, an usurpation of a franchise is the use of a franchise by a person who has no right to it.

USURY. 1. The gain of anything in consideration of a loan beyond the principal or thing lent ; otherwise called interest. 2 *Steph. Com.*

2. Especially any such gain above-mentioned as is illegal or excessive. 2 *Steph. Com.* The laws against usury are now repealed by stat. 17 & 18 Vict. c. 90. But this repeal does not affect the jurisdiction of the Court of Chancery in granting relief to persons who have obtained loans of money on exorbitant and iniquitous terms. 2 *Steph. Com.* See also MONEYLENDER.

UTERINE BROTHER (Lat. *Uterinus frater*). A brother by the mother's side only. 1 *Steph. Com.*

UTTER BAR. The outer or junior bar, as opposed to the serjeants-at-law and King's counsel. [OUTER BAR.]

UTTER BARRISTERS. [OUTER BAR.]

UTTERING. To *utter* coins or documents (a phrase especially used in reference to false coin and forged documents) is to pass them off as genuine. Any person knowingly uttering false coin is guilty of misdemeanor and, after a prior conviction, is guilty of felony. 24 & 25 Vict. c. 99, s. 12 ; 4 *Steph. Com.*

V.-C. An abbreviation used for—1. Vice-Chancellor. 2. Victoria Cross.

V.R. An abbreviation for Victoria Regina (Victoria the Queen).

VACANT POSSESSION is where a tenant has virtually abandoned the premises which he held. Thus where the tenant of a house locked it up and quitted it, the court held that the landlord should treat it as a vacant possession. *Toml.* Where an action of ejectment is brought for the recovery of a vacant possession, the writ may be served by posting a copy of it on the door of the dwelling-house, or other conspicuous part of the property. *R. S. C. 1883, Ord. IX. r. 9; 1 Steph. Com.*

VACANT SUCCESSION is where, on the death of a sovereign or other person of title, there is no one appointed by law to succeed. Or the phrase may be applied to an *hæreditas jacens*, where there is no one to succeed the deceased. [HÆREDITAS JACENS.]

VACATION. The time betwixt the end of one term and the beginning of another. [TERM, 1.]

By R. S. C. 1883, Ord. LXIII. r. 4, the vacations to be observed in the offices of the Supreme Court are four in number :—(1) The Long Vacation, from the 13th of August to the 23rd of October ; (2) The Christmas Vacation, from the 24th of December to the 6th of January ; (3) The Easter Vacation, from Good Friday to Tuesday in Easter week ; and (4) The Whitsun Vacation, from the day before Whit Sunday to Tuesday in Whitsun week. By rule 5, the days of the commencement and termination of each vacation are included in such vacation. See the *Yearly Practice. 3 Steph. Com.*

The County Courts are, as a rule, closed during September. See *County Courts Act,* 1888, *s.* 11.

VACATION SITTINGS. Two judges of the High Court ("vacation judges") sit during the Long Vacations for the hearing of applications requiring immediate attention. *R. S. C. 1883, Ord. LXIII. r. 11 ; 3 Steph. Com.*

VACATURA. An avoidance of an ecclesiastical benefice. *Toml.*

VADIUM MORTUUM. Dead pledge. [MORTGAGE.]

VADIUM VIVUM. The same as vifgage. [MORTGAGE ; VIFGAGE.]

VAGABOND. One that wanders about and has no certain dwelling. By various statutes it is provided that certain acts shall constitute their perpetrator a rogue and vagabond ; as leaving a wife and children chargeable to the parish ; using subtle craft to deceive his Majesty's subjects, etc. *3 Steph. Com. ; 4 Steph. Com.* [VAGRANT ; WITCHCRAFT.]

VAGRANT. A person belonging to one of the following classes :—(1) Idle and disorderly persons ; (2) rogues and vagabonds ; (3) incorrigible rogues. These several classes are defined by various Acts of parliament. *4 Steph. Com.*

VALOR BENEFICIORUM (value of benefices) is the name of an assessment of the value of ecclesiastical livings, made in the reign of Elizabeth, for the purpose of regulating the payment of first fruits. It is commonly called the *King's books,* and the clergy are at present rated in accordance with it. *2 Steph. Com.* [FIRST FRUITS.]

VALOR MARITAGII. The *value of the marriage;* which wards in knight-service forfeited, in case they refused a suitable marriage, without *disparagement* or inequality, tendered by the lord. *1 Steph. Com. ; Wms. R. P.* [MARRIAGE.]

VALUABLE CONSIDERATION. A consideration for a grant, contract, or other act which the law deems an equivalent for the same, must consist of money or money's worth. A court of justice will not in general enter into the question of the *adequacy* of a consideration which is *bonâ fide* intended as an equivalent. *1 Steph. Com. ; Anson, Contracts.* [CONSIDERATION.]

VALUE OF MARRIAGE. [VALOR MARITAGII.]

VALUE RECEIVED. A phrase implying the existence of a valuable consideration. The phrase is especially used to indicate that a bill of exchange has been accepted for value, and not by way of accommodation. *2 Steph. Com. ; Byles on Bills.* [ACCOMMODATION BILL.]

VALUED POLICY. A policy in which the sum to be recovered under it is agreed upon beforehand between the parties, and expressed on the face of the policy. The value thus agreed on is binding as between the parties, assuming that the transaction is *bonâ fide. Crump, Mar. Ins.* [OPEN POLICY.]

VALVASOUR. [VAVASOUR.]

VARIANCE. A discrepancy between the statement of the cause of action in a writ, and a count in the declaration or statement of claim; or between a statement in a pleading and the evidence adduced in its support. Power is given to the court, under different statutes, for the amendment of variances. 4 *Steph. Com.* [AMENDMENT.]

VASSAL. A tenant holding lands under a lord, and bound by his tenure to feudal services. 1 *Steph. Com.*

VASTO. A writ of waste. [WASTE.]

VASTUM. A waste or common.

VAVASOUR was anciently the first dignity, next to a peer; now quite obsolete. 2 *Steph. Com.*

VEJOURS (Lat. *Visores*). Viewers; such as are sent by the court to take a view of any place in question, for the better decision of the right. [VIEW.]

VENARY. Chase, hunting. Beasts of venary are beasts of chase, and were formerly held to belong to the king, or to such as were authorised under him.

VENDEE. A buyer, to whom lands or goods are sold.

VENDITIONI EXPONAS. A writ judicial directed to a sheriff or undersheriff, who has taken goods into his hands under a writ of execution, and cannot sell them at a reasonable price, commanding him to sell them for the best price he can get, however inadequate, in order to satisfy the judgment debt. 3 *Steph. Com.*; *R. S. C.* 1883, *Ord. XLIII. r. 2.*

VENDOR. A seller. In sales of lands the party selling is almost always spoken of as "the vendor"; but in sales of goods he is quite as frequently spoken of as "the seller."

VENDOR AND PURCHASER ACT, 1874, is the stat. 37 & 38 Vict. c. 78, which substitutes forty for sixty years as the root of title, and amends in other ways the law of vendor and purchaser.

VENDOR'S COVENANTS FOR TITLE. [TITLE, COVENANTS FOR.]

VENDOR'S LIEN is the hold which an unpaid vendor of land has over the land for the payment of the purchase-money. This lien exists against the vendee and his heirs, and against persons claiming by a voluntary conveyance from the vendee; also against purchasers under him, with notice that the purchase-money due from such vendee has not been paid.

VENIA ÆTATIS is a privilege granted by a prince or sovereign, in which a minor is entitled to act as if he were of full age. *Story's Conflict of Laws.*

VENIRE DE NOVO. This was a form of motion for a new trial; the words implying that a new *venire facias* was directed to the sheriff. It was grantable as a matter of right whenever it appeared on the face of the record that there had been a mis-trial. 3 *Steph. Com.*

These formal proceedings are superseded as regards civil actions under the Judicature Acts, by the provisions relating to motions for a new trial, and appeals. See *R. S. C.* 1883, *Ord. XXXIX.* and *Ord. LVIII.* [NEW TRIAL.]

VENIRE FACIAS (that you cause to come). A writ in the nature of a summons to cause a party to appear, who is indicted for a petty misdemeanor, or on a penal statute. 4 *Steph. Com.*

VENIRE FACIAS JURATORES was a writ judicial directed to the sheriff, when issue was joined in an action, commanding him to summon a jury.

This writ was abolished by the Common Law Procedure Act, 1852.

VENIRE FACIAS TOT MATRONAS (cause so many matrons to come). A writ directing the summoning of a jury of matrons to see if a woman be with child. [JURY OF MATRONS.]

VENTRE INSPICIENDO. [AD VENTREM INSPICIENDUM.]

VENUE (Lat. *Vicinetum*). The neighbourhood from whence a jury come for the trial of an action or indictment. In former times the direction to the sheriff was to summon a jury, not from the *body of the county* but from the *immediate neighbourhood* where the facts occurred, and from among those persons who best knew the truth of the matter; the jurors being formerly regarded as witnesses, or as persons in some measure cognizant, of their own knowledge, of the matter in dispute,

VENUE—*continued.*

and of the credit to be given to the parties ; and, in order to know into what county the *venire facias* [VENIRE FACIAS JURATORES] should issue, it was necessary that the issue in the action, and the pleadings out of which it arose, should show particularly what that place or neighbourhood was. Such place was called the *visne* or *venue ;* and the statement of it, in the pleadings, obtained the same name ; to allege the place being, in the language of pleading, to *lay the venue. Stephen on Pleading.* 4 *Steph. Com.*

A venue is either *transitory* or *local.* It is transitory when the cause of action is of a sort that might have happened anywhere, which is generally the case where the locality is not the gist of the action, as in a case of assault. It is local when it could have happened in one county only, as in an action for trespass in breaking and entering the plaintiff's close. Changing the venue means changing the place of trial, which, in civil actions before the commencement of the Judicature Acts, might be done by a special order of the judge, or by consent of the parties to the action.

By R. S. C. 1883, Ord. XXXVI. r. 1, there is to be no local venue for the trial of any civil action ; but when the plaintiff proposes to have the action tried elsewhere than in Middlesex, he shall in his statement of claim name the county or place in which he proposes that the action shall be tried, and the action shall, unless a judge otherwise orders, be tried in the county or place so named. The matter is now dealt with on the summons for directions. 3 *Steph. Com.*

VERBA ACCIPIENDA SUNT SECUNDUM SUBJECTAM MATERIEM (words are to be understood with reference to the subject-matter).

VERBA ALIQUID OPERARI DEBENT (words ought to be so interpreted as to have some operation).

VERBA CHARTARUM FORTIUS ACCIPIUNTUR CONTRA PROFERENTEM (the words of a deed are construed more strongly against the grantor).

VERBA ILLATA IN ESSE VIDENTUR (words referred to are considered to be incorporated).

VERBA INTENTIONI DEBENT INSERVIRE (words ought to be made subservient to the intent).

VERBA ITA SUNT INTELLIGENDA UT RES MAGIS VALEAT QUAM PEREAT (words are to be so construed that the object may be carried out and not fail).

VERDICT is the answer given to the court by the jury, in any cause civil or criminal committed to their trial, and is either general or special : *general* when they give it in general terms, as guilty or not guilty ; *special* when they find it at large according to the evidence given, and pray the direction of the court as to what the law is upon the facts so found. 3 *Steph. Com. ;* 4 *Steph. Com.*

VERGE. 1. The compass about the king's court, which bounded the jurisdiction of the lord steward, and of the coroner of the king's house. It extended for twelve miles from the royal residence. [COURT OF MARSHALSEA.]

2. An uncertain quantity of land from fifteen to thirty acres.

3. A stick or rod by which a copyhold tenant of a manor is admitted ; and, holding it in his hand, takes the oath of fealty to the lord of the manor.

VERIFICATION was the concluding averment, "and this he is ready to verify," which was formerly necessary in every pleading which contained new affirmative matter. *Stephen on Pleading.* By s. 67 of the Common Law Procedure Act, 1852, " no formal conclusion shall be necessary to any plea, avowry, cognizance, or subsequent pleading."

VERSUS. Against. Smith *versus* Jones is the cause of Smith against Jones.

VERY LORD AND VERY TENANT are they that are *immediate* lord and tenant one to the other.

VEST (Lat. *Vestire*). 1. To deliver to a person the full possession of land, and so to clothe him with the legal estate therein. [INVESTITURE.]

2. To become a vested interest. See the following titles.

VESTED IN INTEREST. A phrase used to indicate a present fixed right of future enjoyment, as reversions, vested remainders, and other future interests which do not depend on a period or event uncertain.

VESTED IN POSSESSION. A phrase used to indicate that an estate is an estate in possession, as opposed to an estate in reversion or remainder.

VESTED REMAINDER, in the law of real property, is a remainder which is always ready, from its beginning to its end, to come into possession at once, subject only to the determination of some prior particular estate or estates. 1 *Steph. Com.; Wms. R. P.* [ESTATE, II.; REMAINDER.]

We may adduce the two following characteristics of every vested remainder, by one or other of which it may be distinguished from any given contingent remainder :—1. A vested remainder is limited to some specific person, and not to a dubious or uncertain person. 2. A vested remainder cannot be prevented from taking effect in possession by any condition extrinsic to the limitation by which it is created. But a remainder is none the less a vested remainder merely because it may fail to take effect by virtue of some condition implied in the limitation by which it exists. [LIMITATION OF ESTATES.] Thus, if land be granted to A. for life, remainder to B. for life, B.'s estate is a vested remainder, though, if B. dies before A., it will never come into possession. But if land be granted to A. for life, remainder to B. and his heirs if B. survive A., B.'s estate is then called a contingent remainder, because the condition that B. shall survive A. is extrinsic to the limitation to B. and his heirs.

VESTING ORDER is an order of the Court of Chancery, now the Chancery Division of the High Court of Justice, vesting the legal estate in property (generally land) in any person specified in the order. This is often done under the Trustee Acts, when the trustees appointed are unwilling or unable to act in the execution of the trusts [TRUSTEE ACTS]; or when, for any reason, it is desirable to appoint new trustees, and it is found impracticable or inconvenient to procure a conveyance to them in the ordinary way. 1 *Steph. Com.*

VESTRY. 1. The place in a church where the priest's vestures are deposited.

2. An assembly of the minister, churchwardens and parishioners, held in the vestry of the church. 1 *Steph. Com.*

In large and populous parishes, a custom has obtained of yearly choosing a select number of parishioners called a select vestry to represent and manage the concerns of the parish for one year.

Most of the duties and powers of the vestries have been transferred to the parish councils and parish meetings constituted under the Local Government Act, 1894 (56 & 57 Vict. c. 73). 3 *Steph. Com.* See also the London Government Act, 1899, creating borough councils in place of the metropolitan vestries.

VESTRY CLERK, a paid officer appointed to attend vestries and take account of their proceedings. See 13 *&* 14 *Vict. c.* 57. Under the Local Government Act, 1894, in the case of rural parishes, he becomes clerk to the parish council established under that Act ; and see the London Government Act, 1899. 1 *Steph. Com.* ; 2 *Steph. Com.*

VESTURE signifies—(1) a garment ; (2) the possession or seisin of land ; (3) the profit of land.

VETERA STATUTA. Old statutes. This phrase is applied to the statutes from Magna Charta to the end of the reign of Edward II. 1 *Steph. Com.*

VETITUM NAMIUM. [WITHERNAM.]

VEXATA QUÆSTIO. A question much discussed, and not settled.

VEXATIOUS INDICTMENTS ACT. Stat. 22 & 23 Vict. c. 17, passed in 1859, for the prevention of vexatious indictments for misdemeanors. By s. 1 of that Act, no bill of indictment for any of the offences following—(1) perjury, (2) subornation of perjury, (3) conspiracy, (4) obtaining money or other property by false pretences, (5) keeping a gambling house, (6) keeping a disorderly house, (7) indecent assault, is to be presented to or found by a grand jury, unless (1) the prosecutor have been bound by recognizance to prosecute or give evidence, or (2) unless the person accused has been committed to or detained in custody, or (3) has been bound by recognizance to appear and answer for such offence, or (4) unless such indictment have been preferred by the direction of a judge of the superior courts, or by his Majesty's attorney or solicitor general, or unless (5) in a case of perjury the prosecution have been directed by any court, judge or public functionary authorised by s. 19 of 14 & 15 Vict. c. 100 (the Administration of Criminal Justice Act, 1851), to direct a prosecution for perjury. The Vexatious Indictments Act has been amended

VEXATIOUS INDICTMENTS ACT—*cond.* and explained by stat. 30 & 31 Vict. c. 35. See also the Newspaper Libel Act, 1881, s. 6. *Oke's Mag. Syn.; 4 Steph. Com.*

VI ET ARMIS. With force and arms ; a phrase formerly used in declarations for trespass, and in indictments. These words are rendered unnecessary in civil cases by s. 49 of the Common Law Procedure Act, 1852, and in criminal cases by s. 24 of the Administration of Criminal Justice Act, 1851.

VIA, in the Roman law, was the servitude (or easement) of a carriage road enjoyed by one man through another's property. [EASEMENT ; SERVITUDE.]

VIA REGIA. The king's highway or common road.

VIABILITY. Capability of living ; possibility of continued existence.

VICAR, a substitute ; one who performs the functions of another. The priest of every parish is called *rector*, unless the prædial tithes be impropriated, and then he is called vicar, *quasi rice fungens rectoris* (as if vicariously discharging the duty of a rector).

A vicar was originally the substitute of the appropriator in those parishes where the fruits of the living had been appropriated either by religious houses or by laymen. He takes only the *small* tithes, and the chancel is not vested in him. 2 *Steph. Com.* [APPROPRIATION, 1 ; RECTOR.]

VICAR GENERAL was, in ancient times, an officer *occasionally* constituted, when the bishop was called out of the diocese by foreign embassies or attendances in parliament, or other affairs ; and his commission contained in it the whole administration of the diocese, except the hearing of causes in the Consistory Court, which was the province of the *official*, otherwise called the *official principal*. [OFFICIAL.] In time, the vicar general came to be a fixed and standing officer, who should be ready (without the trouble of a special commission for every occasion), to execute the episcopal power, when the bishop himself was hindered by infirmities, avocations or other impediments. The office of *vicar general* came by degrees to be united with that of *official;* and the person in whom the two offices are united is called the bishop's *chancellor.* [CHANCELLOR, 5.]

VICARAGE. The benefice, office or parsonage house of a vicar.

VICARIAL TITHES. Tithes appropriated to a vicarage. 2 *Steph. Com.* [TITHES ; VICAR.]

VICARIUS NON HABET VICARIUM (a substitute cannot have a substitute).

VICE-ADMIRALTY COURTS are courts with an admiralty jurisdiction established in his Majesty's possessions beyond the seas. 3 *Steph. Com.*

VICE-CHANCELLOR. 1. A judicial officer having jurisdiction in equity under the Lord Chancellor. The first vice-chancellorship was appointed in 1813 under stat. 52 Geo. 3, c. 24, and two new ones were appointed in 1841. 3 *Steph. Com.* 365.

By s. 5 of the Judicature Act, 1873, the vice-chancellors were transferred to the High Court of Justice, and by s. 31, sub-s. 1, they were appointed judges of the Chancery Division ; and the Act also provides that no more vice-chancellors are to be appointed under that style.

2. A principal officer in the universities of Oxford and Cambridge. He must be selected from among the heads of colleges in the university.

VICE-COMES signifies properly the sheriff of a county, being the deputy of the count or earl. 1 *Steph. Com. ; 2 Steph. Com.*

VICEROY. A person in place of the king ; hence a governor of a dependency.

VICE-WARDEN OF THE STANNARIES. The local judge of the Stannary Courts. 3 *Steph. Com.* [COURT OF STANNARIES OF CORNWALL AND DEVON.]

VICINAGE. Neighbourhood. [COMMON, I., 3.]

VICONTIEL WRIT. A writ directed to the sheriff, and triable in the sheriff's county court, in case any question should arise touching its execution.

VICOUNT or **VISCOUNT** signifies—(1) A sheriff ; (2) a degree of nobility next to an earl. 2 *Steph. Com.* [SHERIFF ; VICE-COMES.]

VIDAME (Lat. *Vice-dominus.*) The same as *ravasour.* 2 *Steph. Com.* [VAVASOUR.]

VIDELICET. Namely ; often abbreviated in " viz." or " vizt." To state a time or other matter in a pleading with the phrase " to wit," or " that is to say," is called *laying it with a videlicet.* This was necessary in certain cases, as a matter of form, prior to the Common Law Procedure Act, 1852.

VIEW. The act of viewing ; a word especially applicable in speaking of a jury viewing any person or thing in controversy. In some cases, when the cause concerns lands or messuages, of which it is thought expedient that the jury should have a *view,* the officer of the court will, on application, draw up a rule for one. Two persons will be appointed as *showers,* and six jurymen as *viewers,* and the sheriff will return their names to the associate, for the purpose of being called at the trial. By R. S. C. 1883, Ord. L. rr. 3—5, the court or a judge may make an order for the inspection of any property or thing being the subject of any cause or matter before him, or the judge may inspect it himself. 3 *Steph. Com.*

So, where a surveyor of highways is charged before justices with non-repair of the same, they may take a *view* of the highway to see if it is in repair. 3 *Steph. Com. ; Oke's Mag. Syn.*

So a coroner's inquisition into the death of a person is held *super visum corporis* (on view of the body). 2 *Steph. Com.* [SUPER VISUM CORPORIS.]

VIEW OF FRANKPLEDGE (Lat. *Visus Franci Plegii*). [FRANK-PLEDGE ; COURT LEET.]

VIEWERS. [VIEW.]

VIFGAGE (Lat. *Virum vadium,* living pledge) is where the property of a debtor is transferred to a creditor, to be retained until the latter shall have satisfied his claim out of the rents and profits thereof. The term hardly ever occurs in practice. 1 *Steph. Com.*

VIGILANTIBUS NON DORMIENTIBUS JURA SUBVENIUNT (laws aid the vigilant, not the sleepy).

VIIS ET MODIS (by ways and means). Where there is no opportunity of effecting on a defendant in an ecclesiastical court personal service of a citation or decree, proof of the fact is made by the affidavit of the officer of the court, upon which another decree issues, called a decree *viis et modis,* directing the citation to be served so as by all *ways and means* to affect the party with the knowledge of its contents. *Phillimore's Eccl. Law.*

VILL is sometimes taken for a manor ; sometimes for a parish, or part of it ; sometimes of collections of houses consisting of ten freemen or frank-pledges. 1 *Steph. Com.* [FRANK - PLEDGE ; MANOR ; PARISH.]

VILLAIN or **VILLEIN.** A person of servile degree. There were two sorts of villains in England. The one was termed a *villain in gross,* who was immediately bound to the person of the lord and his heirs, and transferable by deed from one owner to another. The other was a villain regardant to a manor, as being a member belonging and annexed to a manor, and bound to the lord thereof. 1 *Steph. Com.* [COPYHOLD.]

VILLEIN IN GROSS. [VILLAIN.]

VILLEIN REGARDANT. [REGARDANT ; VILLAIN.]

VILLEIN SOCAGE. [PRIVILEGED VILLENAGE.]

VILLENAGE. 1. The condition of a villain or villein. [VILLAIN.]

2. A base tenure. [PRIVILEGED VILLENAGE.]

VINCULO MATRIMONII (from the bond of marriage). [DIVORCE, 2, 3.]

VINDICTIVE DAMAGES, in an action, are damages given by way of punishing the defendant over and above the actual amount of injury suffered by the plaintiff.

VIOLENT PRESUMPTION, in the law of evidence, is a presumption of such a nature as almost to amount to proof. [PRESUMPTION.]

VIRGE, TENANCY BY THE. A species of copyhold tenure. [VERGE, 3.]

VIS MAJOR. Irresistible force ; such an interposition of human agency as is from its nature and power absolutely uncontrollable ; *e.g.,* the inroads of a hostile army, or forcible robberies, may relieve from liability from contract.

VISCOUNT. [VICE-COMES ; VICOUNT.]

VISITATION. 1. The office that is performed by a bishop in every diocese once every three years, or by the archdeacon once a year, in visiting the churches and their rectors, etc. 2 *Steph. Com.*

2. The office of inquiring into and correcting the irregularities of corporations. [VISITOR.]

VISITOR. 1. A person appointed to visit, inquire into, and correct irregularities arising in a society or corporation. The ordinary is the visitor of ecclesiastical corporations; that is, of corporations composed entirely of spiritual persons, as bishops, etc. In the colleges of Oxford and Cambridge, the visitor is generally either the Crown, acting by the Lord High Chancellor, or some bishop of the Church of England, or the chancellor or vice-chancellor of the university, or the head of some college *ex officio.* The errors and abuses of civil lay incorporations are inquired into and redressed by the King's Bench Division of the High Court of Justice. 3 *Steph. Com.*

2. An official visitor of lunatics and lunatic asylums appointed to see and report upon persons found lunatic by inquisition. See the Lunacy Act, 1890. 2 *Steph. Com.*

VIVA VOCE. Orally. [WITNESS.]

VIVUM VADIUM. [VIFGAGE.]

VOID AND VOIDABLE. A transaction is said to be *void* when it is a mere nullity and incapable of confirmation; whereas a *voidable* transaction is one which may be either avoided or confirmed by matter arising *ex post facto.*

Thus, prior to the Infants' Relief Act, 1874, the contract of a minor (otherwise than for necessaries) was merely voidable, as it might be confirmed by him on coming of age; but since that Act such a contract is void, and incapable of confirmation. 1 *Steph. Com.*

VOIDANCE. The state of an ecclesiastical benefice without an incumbent.

VOIR DIRE, or **VOIRE DIRE** (Lat. *Veritatem dicere*). An examination of a witness upon the *voir dire* is in the nature of an examination as to his competency to give evidence, or some other collateral matter, and generally takes place prior to his examination in chief. It was formerly used in cases where a witness was suspected of an interest in the cause, which, until stat. 6 & 7 Vict. c. 85, rendered his testimony inadmissible. 3 *Steph. Com.*

VOLENTI NON FIT INJURIA (no injury is done to one who consents).

VOLUNTARY CONFESSION. A confession of crime made by an accused person, without any promise of worldly advantage held out to him as obtainable by confession, or any harm threatened to him if he refuses to confess. Such a confession is always admissible in evidence against the party. *Powell's Ev.*

VOLUNTARY CONVEYANCE. This phrase denotes a conveyance not founded upon a valuable consideration. [VALUABLE CONSIDERATION.] Such a conveyance was, by stat. 27 Eliz. c. 4, void as against a purchaser for valuable consideration, whether with notice of the voluntary conveyance or not; but see now 56 & 57 Vict. c. 21. 2 *Steph. Com.; Robson's Bkcy.*

VOLUNTARY OATH. An oath not taken before a magistrate or other proper officer in some civil or criminal proceeding. Voluntary oaths are now prohibited by stat. 5 & 6 Will. 4, c. 62, and statutory declarations substituted for them. 4 *Steph. Com.* [STATUTORY DECLARATION.]

VOLUNTARY SETTLEMENT. A settlement made without valuable consideration. 2 *Steph. Com.* [VOLUNTARY CONVEYANCE.]

VOLUNTARY WASTE. Waste committed on lands by the voluntary act of the tenant, as opposed to waste which is merely permissive. [WASTE.]

VOLUNTAS REPUTATUR PRO FACTO (the intention is to be taken from the deed).

VOLUNTEER. 1. A person who takes property under a voluntary conveyance. [VOLUNTARY CONVEYANCE.]

2. A member of some volunteer rifle or artillery corps. The formation of these volunteer corps was first sanctioned by stat. 44 Geo. 3, c. 54, passed in 1804; and by stat. 26 & 27 Vict. c. 65, passed in 1863 (amended in 1869 by stat. 32 & 33 Vict. c. 81), the previous Acts of parliament relating to the volunteer force are consolidated, and their enactments amended. See also the Volunteer Act, 1897 (60 & 61 Vict. c. 47). 2 *Steph. Com.*

VOUCH (Lat. *Vocare*). To call or summon.

VOUCHEE (Lat. *Vocatus*). A person "vouched" or summoned. [RECOVERY; VOUCHER, 1.]

VOUCHER. 1. *Vouching to warranty.* This, in the old form of real action for the recovery of land, was the calling in of some person to answer the action, who had warranted the title of the tenant or defendant to the land in question. 1 *Steph. Com.* [RECOVERY.]

2. A book of accounts, wherein are entered the acquittances or warrants for the accountant's discharge. Also any acquittance or receipt discharging a person, as being evidence of payment.

VOUCHING TO WARRANTY. [VOUCHER, 1.]

VOYAGE POLICY. A policy of insurance on a ship against losses incurred during a voyage specified in the policy. [TIME POLICY.]

VULGARIS PURGATIO. The name applied to the ordeal, in order to distinguish it from the canonical purgation. 4 *Steph. Com.* [BENEFIT OF CLERGY; COMPURGATORS; ORDEAL.]

WAGE. The giving security for the due performance of anything. [GAGE.] See also the following titles.

WAGER. A mutual contract for the future payment of money by A. to B., or by B. to A., according as some unknown fact or event, otherwise of no interest to the parties contracting, shall turn out. Wagers are now void in law by stat. 8 & 9 Vict. c. 109, s. 18, passed in 1845. 4 *Steph. Com.* [FEIGNED ISSUE.]

WAGER OF BATTEL. A mode of trial, in the nature of an appeal to Providence, to give the victory to him who had the right. It was introduced into England by William the Conqueror, and was available only in three cases : one military, one criminal, and the third, civil.

1. In the court-martial, or court of chivalry and honour. [COURT OF CHIVALRY.]

2. In appeals of felony, and upon approvements [APPEAL; APPROVER.]

3. Upon issue joined in a writ of right. [WRIT OF RIGHT.]

In wager of battel on a writ of right, the parties fought by their champions ; but on appeals they fought in their own proper persons, the party losing in the battle losing in the cause or appeal.

Wagers of battel were abolished, together with appeals, by stat. 59 Geo. 3, c. 46 ; 4 *Steph. Com.*

WAGER OF LAW (Lat. *Vadiatio legis*). This was a proceeding which consisted in the defendant's discharging himself from the claim on his own oath, bringing with him at the same time into court eleven of his neighbours to swear that they believed his denial to be true.

Wager of law was abolished by 3 & 4 Will. 4, c. 42. 3 *Steph. Com.*

WAGERING POLICIES are policies of assurance, in the subject-matter whereof the assured has no interest ; as, for instance, an insurance on the life of a stranger. They are rendered void by 14 Geo. 3, c. 48. 2 *Steph. Com.*

WAGES. Any money or salary paid or payable to any clerk or servant, labourer or workman. An infant can recover wages up to 50*l.* in the county court without a next friend, under s. 96 of the County Courts Act, 1888. When a master becomes bankrupt, a clerk or servant is entitled to be paid any sum owing to him, not exceeding four months' wages or salary, and not exceeding 50*l.*, in priority to the general creditors ; and any labourer or workman is entitled to be paid any sum due, not exceeding two months' wages, in priority to the general creditors. [PREFERENTIAL PAYMENTS ; TRUCK SYSTEM.]

WAIFS (Lat. *Bona waviata*). Goods stolen and thrown away by the thief in his flight, for fear of being apprehended. Waifs were formerly forfeited to the king or lord of the manor, unless they belonged to a foreign merchant. Their forfeiture was intended as a punishment to the owner for not bringing the thief to justice. 2 *Steph. Com.*

WAIVE (Lat. *Habere pro derelicto*). To forsake, to forego. [WAIFS.]

Thus we speak of a party waiving a claim, or waiving an objection, meaning that he does not put it forward. So, a man is said to *waive a tort* when he foregoes his right of treating a wrongful act as such ; which he does, when he

WAIVE—*continued.*

expressly, or by implication, adopts the acts of the wrongdoer. Thus, if goods have been wrongfully taken and sold, and the owner thinks fit to receive the price, or part thereof, he adopts the transaction, and cannot afterwards treat it as a wrong. *Addison on Torts.* 1 *Steph. Com.*

WAIVER. A waiving or forsaking the assertion of a right at the proper opportunity. [WAIVE.]

WAPENTAKE. From *weapon* and *take ;* the name in the northern counties for a hundred. 1 *Steph. Com.* [HUNDRED.]

WARD (Lat. *Custodia*) signifies *care* or *guard,* and is used variously to denote :

1. A portion of a city or town. See *Municipal Corporations Acts,* 1835, 1882.

2. The heir of the king's tenant, that held by knight's service *in capite,* was called a ward during his nonage. [IN CAPITE ; WARDSHIP.]

3. A minor under the protection of the Court of Chancery, generally called a ward in Chancery, or a ward of court.

4. And, generally, a minor under the protection or tutelage of a guardian. 2 *Steph. Com.* [GUARDIAN ; WATCH AND WARD.]

WARDEN. A guardian ; he that hath the custody of any person or thing by his office ; as the Warden of the Cinque Ports ; the warden of a college, etc.

WARDMOTE. A court anciently kept in every ward in the city of London.

WARDSHIP. The custody of a ward ; a word used especially with reference to wardship in chivalry, but also applicable to any form of the relation between guardian and ward.

WAREHOUSING SYSTEM. The system of allowing goods imported to be deposited in public warehouses, at a reasonable rent, without payment of the duties on importation if they are re-exported ; or, if they are to be withdrawn for home consumption, then without payment of such duties until they are so removed. 2 *Steph. Com.*

WARNING OF A CAVEAT. A notice to a person who has entered a caveat in the Probate Division, to appear and set forth his interest. 3 *Steph. Com.*

WARRANT signifies—

I. A written document authorising and requiring a person to do some specific act.

1. *Warrants of Arrest.*—These are most usually issued for the apprehension of persons accused or suspected of serious crimes. On information being laid before a justice that any person has committed, or is suspected to have committed, any offence, the justice will, according to the circumstances of the case, issue a summons, to be served upon the defendant, citing him to appear, or will issue a warrant for his apprehension in the first instance. In most cases of serious offences a warrant will be issued at once. In minor offences, especially those punishable on summary conviction, a warrant will not in general be issued except against a party who has disobeyed a summons. But, even in these cases, a justice may, if he think fit, issue in the first instance a warrant for apprehending the defendant. Also, where an indictment has been found against a person who is at large, a warrant may be issued for his apprehension.

Every warrant must be under the hand and seal of the justice issuing the same, and must state shortly the matter of the information or complaint on which it is founded, and name, or otherwise describe, the person against whom it is issued. [BACKING A WARRANT.]

A warrant may also be issued for bringing before the court a person who has refused to attend as a witness when summoned ; or, if a justice be satisfied, by evidence upon oath or affirmation, that such person will not attend to give evidence without being compelled to do so, the justice may issue his warrant for the purpose in the first instance. See *Statutes* 11 & 12 *Vict. cc.* 42, 43 ; *Oke's Mag. Syn.*

Power is also given to courts having jurisdiction in bankruptcy to grant warrants for the apprehension of bankrupts about to abscond. *Bankruptcy Act,* 1883 ; 2 *Steph. Com. ;* 3 *Steph. Com.*

2. *Warrants of Commitment.* — A warrant of commitment (as opposed to a warrant of arrest) is a written authority committing a person to prison. This may be done (1) in pursuance of a judicial sentence ; (2) for the purpose of securing the attendance of the party to take his trial for an indictable offence ; (3) for the purpose of a remand, for securing the party's attendance at an adjourned hearing of the charge against

WARRANT—*continued*.

him ; (4) for default in payment of a sum of money ordered to be paid, whether by way of fine or otherwise ; (5) for default in finding sureties to keep the peace ; (6) in default of sufficient property being found to satisfy a warrant of distress ; (7) for contumacy, as in a witness refusing to answer questions properly put to him. *Oke's Mag. Syn.*

3. *Distress Warrants.* — A distress warrant is a warrant issued for raising a sum of money upon the goods of a party specified in the warrant ; as, for the purpose of levying the amount of the costs upon the goods of a complainant whose complaint has been dismissed with costs ; or for levying a sum payable by a defendant, by way of penalty or otherwise. *Oke's Mag. Syn.*

4. *Search Warrants.* — These may be issued by justices of the peace, under various circumstances, as to which see title SEARCH WARRANT.

5. *General Warrants.* — By this expression we understand warrants not specifying particularly any person or subject-matter, but intended to be executed upon all persons or things coming within a general description in the warrant ; also warrants for the seizure of a party guilty of a specified offence, without naming any party. All general warrants were, in the case of *Wilkes* v. *Wood*, decided in the year 1763, and the cases of *Leach* v. *Money* and *Entick* v. *Carrington*, decided in 1765, declared to be illegal. See *Broom's Constitutional Law* ; 4 *Steph. Com.*

II. [WARRANT OF ATTORNEY.]

III. Moreover, by the caprice of language, certain negotiable instruments are spoken of as *warrants*. Thus we speak of a *dividend warrant*, which is an order in the nature of a cheque by a joint-stock company upon its bankers, directing them to pay a sum of money specified therein to a shareholder entitled thereto in respect of a dividend, or to his order. Such an instrument is generally crossed, and ought therefore to be presented through a banker. As to *dock warrants*, see DOCK WARRANT.

WARRANT OF ATTORNEY is a letter sent by a debtor to some attorney named by the creditor, empowering him to confess judgment in an action of debt to be brought by the creditor against the debtor for the specific sum due.

By sect. 4 of the Debtors Act, 1869 (stat. 32 & 33 Vict. c. 62), no warrant of attorney to confess judgment is to be valid, unless there is present with the person executing it some attorney expressly named by him and attending at his request to inform him of its nature and effect, which attorney shall subscribe his name as a witness of the due execution thereof. 3 *Steph. Com.*

WARRANTOR. A person who warrants, or gives a warranty. [WARRANTY.]

WARRANTY. A promise or covenant offered by a bargainor, to warrant or secure the bargainee against all men in the enjoyment of anything agreed on between them. The word is used especially with reference to any promise (express or implied by law, according to circumstances) from a vendor to a purchaser, that the thing sold is the vendor's to sell and is good and fit for use, or at least for such use as the purchaser intends to make of it. Warranty of title to land has fallen into disuse since 3 & 4 Will. 4. cc. 27, 74. As to warranty on sale of goods see Sale of Goods Act, 1893 (56 & 57 Vict. c. 71). 1 *Steph. Com.* ; 2 *Steph. Com.* [CAVEAT EMPTOR ; VOUCHER.]

In marine insurances an *express* warranty is an agreement expressed in the policy, whereby the assured stipulates that certain facts are or shall be true, or that certain acts shall be done relative to the risk. It may relate to an existing or past fact, or be promissory and relate to the future ; and the fact or act warranted need not be material to the risk. A formal expression is not necessary to give effect to a warranty. An *implied* warranty is such as necessarily results from the nature of the contract, as that the ship is seaworthy.

WARREN (Lat. *Vicarium*). 1. A place in which birds, fishes, or wild beasts are kept. 2. A franchise or privilege, either by prescription or grant from the king, to keep beasts and fowls of warren, which are hares, coneys, partridges, pheasants, etc. 3. Also any place to which such privilege extends. 1 *Steph. Com.* [FREE WARREN.]

WASTE. Spoil and destruction done, or allowed to be done, by a tenant for life or other particular tenant, to houses, woods, lands, or other corporeal hereditaments, during the continuance of his particular estate therein. Waste is either *voluntary*, if it be a matter of commission, as by pulling down a house ; or *permissive*, as if a house be allowed to

WASTE—*continued.*

fall into ruin for want of necessary repairs. 1 *Steph. Com.*; 2 *Steph. Com.*; 3 *Steph. Com.*

As to *equitable waste*, which is now, under the Judicature Act, 1873, s. 25, sub-s. 3, cognizable in any division of the High Court of Justice, see EQUITABLE WASTE ; WITHOUT IMPEACHMENT OF WASTE. *Wms. R. P.*

WATCH AND WARD. *Watch* was the word applicable to the night duty of constables ; *ward* to their duties in the daytime, in apprehending rioters and robbers on the highways, etc. 2 *Steph. Com.* [CONSTABLE.]

WATER. Under the word " water," in a conveyance, it seems that a right of fishing will pass, but the soil will not pass. The term land includes water but the term water does not include the land upon which it stands. *Fawcett, L. & T.*

WATER BAILIFFS. 1. Officers in port towns for the searching of ships.
2. Keepers appointed under the Salmon Fishery Acts to prevent poaching.

WATER COURSE. A right which a man may have to the benefit or flow of a river or stream. This right includes that of having the course of the stream kept free from any interruption or disturbance to the prejudice of the proprietor, by the acts of persons without his own territory; whether owing to a diversion of the water, or to its obstruction, or pollution by offensive commixture. 1 *Steph. Com.*; *Gale on Easements.*

WATER ORDEAL. [ORDEAL.]

WAVESON. Such goods as after shipwreck appear swimming upon the waves. [FLOTSAM ; WRECK.]

WAY. [HIGHWAY ; RIGHT OF WAY ; WAYS.]

WAY-GOING CROP. [AWAY-GOING CROP.]

WAYS. 1. Paths. Of these there are various kinds :—(1) A foot-way (Lat. *iter*). (2) A bridle road for horse and man (Lat. *actus*). (3) A cart-way. containing also the two preceding. (4) A drift-way or a way for driving cattle. (5) A highway. [HIGHWAY.]

2. Rights of way : especially private rights of way over a man's ground. 1 *Steph. Com.*; *Wms. R. P.* [RIGHT OF WAY.]

WEAR AND TEAR. The waste of any substance by the ordinary use of it. The words " reasonable use, wear and tear excepted," are sometimes used in connection with the covenants in a lease.

WEIGHT OF EVIDENCE, in a trial, is the preponderance in the evidence adduced on one side over that adduced on the other. A new trial is frequently applied for on the ground that the verdict is *against the weight of evidence*. But the granting of a new trial under such circumstances is in the discretion of the court, and a new trial will not be granted on this ground unless the judge who tried the case has expressed himself dissatisfied with the verdict. See *R. S. C.* 1883, *Ord. XXXIX. r. 6*, and the notes thereon in the *Yearly Practice.*

WELSH MORTGAGE is a mortgage in which there is no condition or proviso for repayment at any time. The agreement is that the mortgagee, to whom the estate is conveyed, shall receive the rents till his debt is paid, and in such case the mortgagor and his representatives are at liberty to redeem at any time.

WEREGILD. The fine formerly paid for killing a man, when such crimes were punished with a pecuniary mulct, and not with death. This fine was paid partly to the king, for the loss of his subject, partly to the lord whose vassal he was, and partly to the next of kin of the slain man. 4 *Steph. Com.*

WESTMINSTER THE SECOND, STATUTE OF. The statute 13 Edw. 1, st. 1, made at Westminster in the year 1285. This statute contains fifty chapters, beginning with the celebrated enactment *De Donis.*

WESTMINSTER THE THIRD, STATUTE OF. This statute was passed in the eighteenth year of Edward I., A.D. 1290. It commences with the words *Quia Emptores Terrarum*, and is therefore known as the Statute of *Quia Emptores*. [QUIA EMPTORES.] By c. 3 of this statute, sales of land in mortmain are forbidden.

z *

WHARF. A broad plain place near a river, canal, or other water to lay wares on that are brought to or from the water.

There are two kinds of wharfs—*legal quays* and *sufferance wharfs.* The former are established by Act of parliament, or exist as such by immemorial usage. The latter are places where goods may be landed and shipped by special permission of the Crown.

WHARFAGE. Money paid for landing wares at a wharf, or for shipping or taking goods into a boat or barge from thence.

WHITE RENTS (Lat. *Reditus albi*). [ALBA FIRMA ; BLACK MAIL.]

WHOLE BLOOD. The relation between two persons descended from a pair of nearest common ancestors ; as opposed to the relation of the half blood, in which there is but one nearest common ancestor, whether male or female. [HALF BLOOD.]

WIDOW-BENCH. The share of her husband's estate which a widow is allowed besides her jointure.

WIDOW'S QUARANTINE. [QUARANTINE.]

WIFE'S EQUITY TO A SETTLEMENT. [EQUITY TO A SETTLEMENT.]

WILD BIRDS PROTECTION ACT, 1880, amended by the W. B. P. Act, 1894, for the protection of certain wild birds during the breeding season.

WILD'S CASE was a case decided in the year 1599, in which it was held *that if A. devises his lands to B. and to his children or issue, and B. have not any issue at the time of the devise, that the same is an estate tail, but if he have issue at the time, B. and his children take joint estates for life.* This resolution is called the " Rule in Wild's Case." (See *Tudor, L. C. R. P.*) It does not apply to personalty.

WILL. The legal declaration of a man's intention which he wills to be performed after his death. [WILLS ACT.] It has been said that a will and testament are, strictly, not of the same meaning ; that a will is limited to land, and a testament to personal estate. But this distinction, if it ever existed, is now quite obsolete.

WILL, ESTATE AT. The estate of a tenant holding lands at the will of the lessor. [ESTATE ; TENANT AT WILL.]

WILLS ACT. 1. The stat. 32 Hen. 8, c. 1. passed in 1540, by which persons seised in fee simple of lands holden in socage tenure were enabled to devise the same at their will and pleasure, except to bodies corporate ; and those who held estates by the tenure of chivalry were enabled to devise two third parts thereof, [USES, STATUTE OF.]

2. The stat. 7 Will. 4 & 1 Vict. c. 26. passed in 1837, and also called Lord Langdale's Act. This Act permits of the disposition by will of every kind of interest in real and personal estate, and provides that all wills, whether of real or of personal estate, shall be in writing signed at the foot or end thereof by the testator or by some person in his presence and by his direction, and shall be attested by two witnesses, and that such attestation shall be sufficient. [FRAUDS, STATUTE OF.] Other important alterations are effected by this statute in the law of wills. See 1 *Steph. Com.* ; 2 *Steph. Com.* ; *Wms. R. P.*

WINDING UP AN ESTATE is the putting it in liquidation for the purpose of distributing the assets among creditors and others who may be found entitled thereto. It is a phrase most frequently used in connection with public companies unable to satisfy their liabilities. See the *Companies Winding-up Act.* 1890 ; 3 *Steph. Com.*

WITCHCRAFT. Supposed intercourse with evil spirits ; formerly punishable with death under stat. 33 Hen. 8, c. 8, and stat. 1 Jac. 1, c. 12, which Acts were repealed in 1736 by stat. 2 Geo. 2, c. 5, which provided that no prosecution should for the future be carried on against any persons for witchcraft, sorcery, enchantment, or conjuration. By 5 Geo. 4, c. 83, s. 4, persons using any subtle craft, means, or device by palmistry, or otherwise to deceive the people, are rogues and vagabonds, to be punished with imprisonment. [VAGABOND.]

WITENAGEMOTE. [WITTENAGEMOTE.]

WITH COSTS. A phrase which, when used with reference to the result of an action, implies that the successful party is entitled to recover his costs from his opponent. [COSTS.]

WITHDRAWAL OF JUROR. A practice occasionally adopted by consent of the parties to an action, when neither party feels sufficient confidence to render him anxious to persevere until verdict, or where the case has been settled between the parties, or where the jury are unable to agree upon a verdict. If, after the withdrawal of a juror, the plaintiff should proceed with the action, the defendant may apply to stay the proceedings. 3 *Steph. Com.* [STAY OF PROCEEDINGS.]

WITHDRAWING THE RECORD was where a plaintiff revoked the entry of a cause for trial, and thus discontinued the action. Now by R. S. C. 1883, Ord. XXVI., the plaintiff may, at any time before receipt of the defendant's statement of defence, or after such receipt before taking any other proceeding in the action (save an interlocutory application), by notice in writing, wholly discontinue his action or withdraw any part or parts of his alleged cause of complaint, and the defendant may also discontinue by leave of the court or a judge. Moreover the court or a judge may, before or at or after the hearing or trial, order the action to be discontinued, or any part of the alleged cause of complaint to be struck out. 3 *Steph. Com.*

WITHERNAM (Lat. *Vetitum namium*). An unlawful distress, or forbidden taking, as the taking or driving a thing distrained out of the county, so that the sheriff cannot upon the replevin make deliverance thereof to the party distrained. Hence it signifies also the *reprisals* for such forbidden taking as above mentioned, which was enforced by a writ of *capias in withernam.* 3 *Steph. Com.* [CAPIAS IN WITHERNAM ; REPLEVIN.]

WITHOUT DAY. [EAT INDE SINE DIE.]

WITHOUT IMPEACHMENT OF WASTE. A phrase used in conveyance to tenants for life or other particular tenants, to indicate that the tenant is not to be held responsible for waste. [WASTE.] At law the tenant could not be impeached for any form of waste, but in equity he was liable if the waste was of a serious character, hence called *equitable waste ;* that is, the commission of wanton injury, as the pulling down of the family mansion house, or felling timber left standing for ornament. 1 *Steph. Com. ; Wms. R. P.* And by the Judicature Act, 1873,

s. 25, sub-s. 3, the tenant shall not even at law have the right to commit *equitable waste,* unless an intention to confer such right shall expressly appear by the instrument creating the estate.

WITHOUT PREJUDICE to any matter in question means that a decision come to, or action taken, is not to be held to affect such question, but to leave it open. Thus, when a lawyer writes on behalf of a client to offer a compromise of a question in dispute, he guards himself from being supposed to make any admission, beyond the mere fact of his willingness to compromise, by stating that what he offers is without prejudice to any question in dispute.

WITHOUT RECOURSE TO ME. [SANS RECOURS.]

WITHOUT RESERVE. A term applied to a sale by auction, indicating that no price is reserved. In such case the seller may not employ any person to bid at the sale, and the auctioneer may not knowingly take any bidding from any such person. See *Sale of Goods Act,* 1893, *s.* 58. [SALE BY AUCTION.]

WITNESS. A person who, on oath or solemn affirmation, gives evidence in any cause or matter. [EVIDENCE.] By R. S. C. 1883, Ord. XXXVII. r. 1, the witnesses at the trial of any action, or at any assessment of damages, shall be examined *vivâ voce* and in open court, but the court or a judge may, at any time for sufficient reason, order that any particular fact or facts may be proved by affidavit, or that any witness whose attendance in court ought to be dispensed with may be examined by interrogatories or otherwise before a commissioner or examiner. This rule is to take effect in the absence of agreement between the parties. Upon any motion, petition, or summons, evidence may, by Ord. XXXVIII. r. 1, be given by affidavit. 3 *Steph. Com.*

WITTENAGEMOTE, or **WITENAGEMOTE.** The great meeting of wise men, or common council of England under the Saxons, answering to our parliament. 2 *Steph. Com.*

WOOLSACK. The seat of the Lord Chancellor in the House of Lords. It is not strictly within the house, for the lords may not speak from that part of the chamber ; and, if they sit there during a division, their votes are not reckoned. *May's Parl. Pract.*

WORDS OF LIMITATION. Words following the name of an intended grantee or devisee under a deed or will, which are intended to "limit" or mark out the estate or interest taken by the party. [LIMITATION OF ESTATES; RULE IN SHELLEY'S CASE.]

WORKHOUSE. See UNION.

WORKMAN. See SERVANT.

WOUNDING. An aggravated species of assault and battery, consisting in one person giving another some dangerous hurt. To constitute a wound, the continuity of the skin must be broken. 3 *Steph. Com.*; 4 *Steph. Com.*; *Oke's Mag. Syn.*

WRECK (Lat. *Wreccum maris*), by the ancient common law, was where any ship was lost at sea, and the goods or cargo were thrown upon the land ; in which case the goods so wrecked were adjudged to belong to the king.

In order to constitute a legal wreck the goods must come to land. The law distinguishes goods lost at sea by the barbarous names of *jetsam, flotsam* and *ligan.* See under those titles. By sect. 510 of the Merchant Shipping Act, 1894, "wreck," for the purposes of that Act includes *jetsam, flotsam, ligan* and *derelict.* 2 *Steph. Com.*

By sect. 64 of the Larceny Act, 1861, the offence of plundering or stealing from a wreck is punishable by penal servitude for fourteen years. See *Oke's Mag. Syn.* 4 *Steph. Com.*

Provision is made by sects. 465, 466 of the Merchant Shipping Act, 1894, for inquiring into losses of ships by inspecting officers of coast guard, or other person appointed by the Board of Trade ; and such officer may, if he think a formal investigation expedient, or if the Board of Trade so directs, apply to two justices or a stipendiary magistrate to hear the case, and report to the Board of Trade. By sect. 566 of the Act provision is made for the appointment of receivers of wreck. See *Oke's Mag. Syn.*

WRIT. The king's precept, whereby anything is commanded to be done touching a suit or action. Writs are distinguished into original and judicial writs. Original writs are those that were sent out for the summoning of a defendant in an action, and bear in the *teste* the name of the sovereign. Judicial writs are those that are sent out by order of the court where the cause depends, and the *teste* bears the name of the chief justice of that court whence it issues. [JUDICIAL WRIT ; ORIGINAL WRIT.]

Now, by the R. S. C. 1883, Ord. II. r. 8, every writ of summons and also every other writ shall bear date on the day on which the same shall be issued. and shall be tested in the name of the Lord Chancellor, or, if the office of Lord Chancellor shall be vacant, in the name of the Lord Chief Justice of England.

See also the following titles.

WRIT OF CAPIAS. [CAPIAS.]

WRIT OF ENTRY. [ENTRY, WRIT OF.]

WRIT OF ERROR. [ERROR.]

WRIT OF INQUIRY is a process in an action at common law, by which, after judgment by default for the plaintiff, the sheriff inquires, by the oaths of twelve honest and lawful men, what amount of damages the plaintiff hath really sustained. The inquiry is undertaken by the under-sheriff before a jury ; and when their verdict is given. which must assess *some* damages, the sheriff returns the inquisition, which is entered upon the roll ; and thereupon execution issues for the amount so assessed.

By R. S. C. 1883, Ord. XIII. r. 5. and Ord. XXVII. r. 4, where the defendant fails to appear and the plaintiff's claim is for detention of goods and damages or either of them interlocutory judgment may be entered and a writ of inquiry shall issue to assess the value of the goods and the damages. or the damages only, as the case may be, or the court or a judge may order that, instead of a writ of inquiry, the value and amount of damages, or either of them, shall be ascertained in any way in which the court or judge may direct. See the *Yearly Practice.* 3 *Steph. Com.*

WRIT OF RIGHT was the old writ in the law for asserting the right to lands in fee simple unjustly withheld from the true proprietor. This writ was properly brought, in the first instance, in the court baron of the lord of whom the lands were holden, and then it was called a *writ of right patent ;* but if the lord held no court, or had waived his right, it might be brought in the king's courts in the first instance, *quia dominus remisit curiam,* and then it

WRIT OF RIGHT—*continued.*

was called a *writ of right close*, and was directed to the sheriff and not to the lord.

Also, when one of the king's immediate tenants *in capite* [IN CAPITE] was deforced (*i.e.*, unjustly deprived of his land), his writ of right was called a *writ of right close*.

The writ of right was considered the highest writ in the law. But it could not be sued out at any distance of time, for by stat. 32 Hen. 8, c. 2, it was enacted that the seisin claimed in a writ of right should be within sixty years.

There were also various writs which were said to be in the nature of a writ of right. These writs resembled the writ of right in that they were droitural and not merely possessory actions, but differed from it in some other respects. In some of these writs (as in formedon) the fee simple was not demanded ; and in others not land, but some incorporeal hereditament. In others land was claimed in fee simple, but was so claimed under peculiar circumstances, to which the writ of right proper did not apply. [ACTION ANCESTRAL, POSSESSORY, AND DROITURAL ; FORMEDON.]

The writ of right was abolished by stat. 3 & 4 Will. 4, c. 27, s. 36. 3 *Steph. Com.* ; *4 Steph. Com.*

WRIT OF RIGHT CLOSE. [WRIT OF RIGHT.]

WRIT OF RIGHT OF ADVOWSON. A writ of right framed for the purpose of trying a right to an advowson, but in other respects corresponding with other writs of right, except that the Statutes of Limitations did not apply to it. Abolished by 3 & 4 Will. 4, c. 27, s. 36. [WRIT OF RIGHT.]

WRIT OF RIGHT OF DOWER. [DOTE.]

WRIT OF RIGHT PATENT. [WRIT OF RIGHT.]

WRIT OF SUMMONS. [SUMMONS, 3 ; WRIT.]

WRITER TO THE SIGNET.. W. S. The writers to the signet are the oldest body of law practitioners in Scotland. They perform in the Supreme Courts of Scotland duties corresponding to those of solicitors and attorneys in England. See *Bell's Scotch Law Dictionary.*

WRITINGS OBLIGATORY. This phrase is sometimes used for *bonds.* 2 *Steph. Com.* [BOND.]

WRONG. That which is *wrung* or turned aside from the right or straight way to the desired end. It corresponds to the French *tort*, from the Latin *tortum*, twisted. [TORT.]

The words *wrong* and *tort* may be used in law to signify any injury ; but they are used especially to denote such civil injuries as are independent of contract. 1 *Steph. Com.* ; 3 *Steph. Com.*

YARDLAND (Lat. *Virgata terræ*). A quantity of land containing in some counties twenty acres, in others twenty-four, and in others thirty acres of land. [FERLINGATA TERRÆ.]

YEAR. [OLD STYLE.] See also the following titles.

YEAR AND DAY. 1. Where the law of Scotland requires any act to be performed within a year, a day is generally added *in majorem evidentiam*, that it may appear with greater certainty that the year is completed.

2. The same reason will probably account for the frequent mention of the year and day in the old English law ; for instance, in reference to the time within which appeals might be brought ; also in reference to the time within which death must follow upon a mortal wound, in order to constitute the crime murder ; and in various other cases. 4 *Steph. Com.* [YEAR, DAY, AND WASTE.]

YEAR BOOKS were reports of cases in a regular series from the reign of King Edward II. to the reign of King Henry VIII. inclusive. They were taken down by the protonotaries or chief scribes of the courts, at the expense of the Crown, and published annually, whence they were known under the denomination of *Year Books.* 1 *Steph. Com.*

YEAR, DAY, AND WASTE, was part of the king's prerogative, whereby he was entitled to the profits for *a year and a day* of persons attainted of petty treason or felony, together with the right of wasting the said tenements ; afterwards restoring it to the lord of the fee.

All this is now abolished by the Felony Act, 1870 (33 & 34 Vict. c. 23), s. 1. See 4 *Steph. Com.*

YEAR TO YEAR. [TENANT FROM YEAR TO YEAR.]

YEARS, ESTATE FOR. An estate demised or granted for a term of years.

YEOMAN (Sax. *Geman;* Lat. *Communis*). He that hath free land of forty shillings a year; who was anciently thereby qualified to serve on juries, vote for knights of the shire, and do any other act, where the law required one that was *probus et legalis homo.* 2 *Steph. Com.*

YEOMANRY. The small freeholders and farmers. [YEOMAN.] The name is also given to certain local forces raised by individuals with the approbation of the king, who accepts their voluntary service. See now 51 & 52 Vict. c. 31, and 1 Edw. 7, c. 14.

YIELDING AND PAYING are words used at the beginning of the *reddendum* clause in a lease, with reference to the rent intended to be payable under the lease. [REDDENDUM.]

YORKSHIRE REGISTRIES are the registries of documents and transactions relating to land provided by Acts of parliament for the ridings of the county of York. These Acts were repealed and re-enacted with certain modifications by the Yorkshire Registries Act, 1884. 1 *Steph. Com.;* Wms. R. P.

THE END.

Ex. W. E. F.
10/4/04

BRADBURY, AGNEW, & CO. LD., PRINTERS, LONDON AND TONBRIDGE.

STEPHEN'S COMMENTARIES.

Mr. Serjeant STEPHEN's Commentaries on the Laws of
England, partly founded on BLACKSTONE, by
His Honour Judge STEPHEN.

14th Edition.

UNDER THE GENERAL EDITORSHIP OF

EDWARD JENKS, Esq., M.A., B.C.L.,

Of the Middle Temple, Barrister-at-Law;
Principal and Director of Legal Studies to the Law Society;
Reader in English Law in the University of Oxford, Tutor and Lecturer of Balliol College
Formerly Senior Student and Barstow Law Scholar of the Council of Legal
Education, and Fellow of King's College, Cambridge.

With the co-operation of the following Gentlemen, who have undertaken the
Revision of portions in which they have special knowledge.

W. ASHBURNER, Esq., M.A.,
Assistant Reader in Equity to the Council of
Legal Education;
Author of "Principles of Equity."

C. A. MONTAGUE BARLOW, Esq.,
LL.D.,
Of the Middle Temple and Lincoln's Inn.

T. WILLES CHITTY, Esq.,
A Master of the Supreme Court.

HUGH FRASER, Esq., LL.D.,
Reader in Common Law to the Council of
Legal Education.

W. M. GELDART, Esq., M.A.,
Of Lincoln's Inn; Fellow and Tutor of Trinity
College, Oxford.

J. M. GOVER, Esq., LL.D.,
Examiner to the Council of Legal Education.

W. M. GRAHAM-HARRISON, Esq.,
M.A., B.C.L.,
Of Lincoln's Inn; late Fellow of All Souls
College, Oxford.

F. W. HIRST, Esq., B.A.,
Of the Inner Temple.

E. M. KONSTAM, Esq.,
Of the Inner Temple.

J. C. LEDLIE, Esq., M.A., B.C.L.,
Of H.M. Privy Council Office.

ALEXANDER MACMORRAN, Esq.,
K.C., M.A.,
One of the Editors of "Lumley's Public
Health."

H. STUART MOORE, Esq.,
One of the Editors of "Abbot's Shipping."

J. A. SIMON, Esq., M.A.,
Of the Inner Temple; Fellow of All Souls
College, Oxford.
AND
J. A. STRAHAN, Esq., LL.B.,
Assistant Reader in the Law of Real and
Personal Property and Conveyancing to the
Council of Legal Education.
BARRISTERS-AT-LAW.

GEORGE HOLDEN, Esq.,
AND
L. H. WEST, Esq., LL.D.,
Tutor to the Law Society of the United
Kingdom;
Solicitors of the Supreme Court.

BUTTERWORTH & CO., 12, BELL YARD, LONDON, W.C.

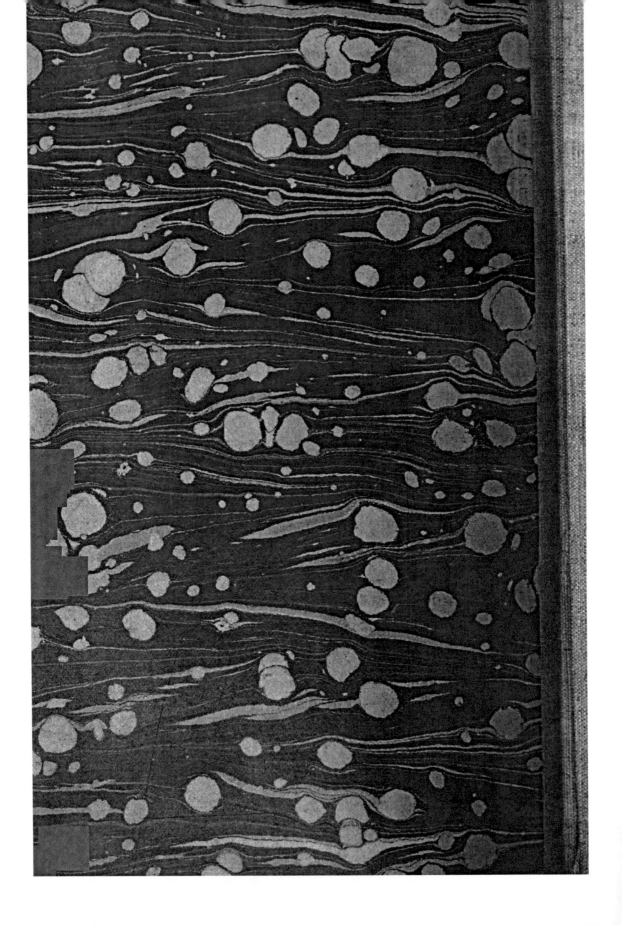